Low Fat, Low Calorie, Low Cholesterol

LIGHT COOKING

PUBLICATIONS INTERNATIONAL, LTD.

Front cover photography by New View Studios, Rosemont, IL.

Pictured on the front cover *(clockwise from top right):* Individual Strawberry Shortcakes *(page 422),* Vegetable Couscous *(page 391),* Green Bean Bundle *(page 366)* and Chicken Crimini *(page 246).*

Pictured on the back cover *(clockwise from top right):* Mexican Chicken Skewers with Spicy Yogurt Sauce *(page 237),* No-Guilt Cheesecake *(page 417),* Fruited Pork Salad *(page 335)* and Mushrooms Rockefeller *(page 19).*

ISBN: 0-7853-0683-8

Library of Congress Catalog Card Number: 93-86998

Manufactured in U.S.A.

8 7 6 5 4 3 2 1

Microwave ovens vary in wattage. The microwave cooking times given in this publication are approximate. Use the cooking times as guidelines and check for doneness before adding more time. Consult manufacturer's instructions for suitable microwave-safe cooking dishes.

CONTENTS

INTRODUCTION

The New Way to Cook Light

America has entered a new age of eating that is revolutionizing the way we think about food. Remember the once-popular high-protein diet, grapefruit diet and all-liquid diet? These dieting fads have been replaced by a healthier, more balanced approach toward food. Study after study indicates that the best way to stay trim is to develop better eating habits by following a low-fat, high-carbohydrate diet. Besides keeping hunger pangs at bay, following this approach toward eating can also help lower your blood cholesterol levels and reduce your risk of heart disease. So whether you are looking to lose a few pounds or would just like to shape up your eating habits, this marvelous recipe collection can help you achieve your goal with hundreds of recipes "fit" for any meal or occasion.

Everyone is concerned with calories, fat, cholesterol and sodium. Because of this concern, there seems to be an abundance of advice, often conflicting, pertaining to food and diets. There is no question, though, that when it comes to fat, health professionals agree—we need to decrease our fat intake. More specifically, we need to limit our total fat intake to no more than 30 percent of our daily calories, instead of our typical 40 percent. This recommendation applies to healthy adults and children over the age of two, whether or not they have a high blood cholesterol level.

Why has fat become such a villain in our diet? Why is this usually flavorless substance, which adds such richness and creaminess to so many of our favorite foods, something we should cut back on? The reason is that consuming excess saturated fat, the type found in meat and whole-milk dairy products, suppresses the body's natural mechanism for pulling cholesterol out of the bloodstream. Instead, cholesterol may be deposited on the inner walls of arteries. Over time, this buildup can constrict the blood flow to the heart. The latest research also links a high-fat diet with an increased risk for certain types of cancers. A high-fat diet also contributes to weight gain, further increasing health risks. For these reasons, experts recommend decreasing our daily fat intake.

The good news is that substituting complex carbohydrates (grains, beans, fruits and vegetables) for high-fat foods (fatty meats, cheese and butter) is an easy way to modify your diet and still enjoy nourishing meals. And, since a gram of fat contains nine calories while a gram of carbohydrate or protein contains only four, you can actually add more complex carbohydrates to your dinner plate in place of those calorie-dense fat grams. Of course, if you wish to lose weight you still have to take in fewer calories than you expend in energy. But consider that for the same number of calories, you can substitute a plain 12-ounce baked potato for a 1.5-ounce bag of potato chips and feel full and satisfied. Substituting complex carbohydrates for fats allows you to eat larger quantities of food without gaining weight. Choosing lean meats, substituting skim milk for whole and substituting low-fat or nonfat yogurt for ice cream are other ways to reduce your fat consumption.

Guidelines for Healthy Eating

We've made it easy to carry out your stay-slim and stay-healthy strategies by providing a nutritional chart with every recipe that tells you the number of calories, the grams (g) of fat, the milligrams (mg) of cholesterol and the milligrams of sodium for each serving.

Each recipe in this book contains no more than 300 calories and no more than 10 grams of fat per serving. If you do choose higher-fat items for a meal, try to choose other foods that day that are low in fat. By mixing and matching your selection of recipes and foods, your weekly diet will follow the guidelines for healthy eating. Many of the recipes are low-cholesterol and low-sodium as well. Most recipes contain less than 50 mg of cholesterol and less than 300 mg of sodium. These values were chosen after careful consideration of a number of factors.

The Food and Nutrition Board of the National Academy of Sciences proposes the Recommended Dietary Allowances (RDAs) for essential nutrients including calories, carbohydrates, fat, protein, amino acids, vitamins and minerals. The RDAs were most recently revised in 1989. The RDA for calories is broken down according to age groups and sex. For healthy men between the ages of 19 and 50, for example, the RDA for total calorie intake is 2,900 calories per day. For healthy women between the ages of 19 and 50 (who are neither pregnant nor lactating), it is 2,200 calories per day. Thus, the 300 calories or less per serving for the recipes in this book represents only about 10 percent of the RDA for most men and about 14 percent of the RDA for most women.

The American Heart Association has recommended that total fat intake should be no more than 30 percent of calories. For most men, that amounts to about 870 calories from fat (or about 97 grams of fat) per day; for most women, about 660 calories from fat (or about 73 grams of fat) per day. Thus, the 10 grams of fat or less per serving for each recipe in this book is well within recommended guidelines. The American Heart Association also recommends that cholesterol intake be less than 300 mg a day and sodium intake not exceed 3,000 mg a day.

About the Nutritional Information

The analysis for each recipe includes all the ingredients that are listed, except ingredients labeled "optional" or "for garnish." If a range is given in the yield of a recipe ("Makes 6 to 8 servings," for example), the *higher* yield was used to calculate the per serving information. If a range is offered for an ingredient (¼ to ⅛ teaspoon, for example) the *first* amount given was used to calculate the nutrition information. If an ingredient is presented with an option ("2 tablespoons margarine or butter") the *first* amount given was used to calculate the nutrition information. Foods shown in photographs on the same serving plate and offered as "serve with" suggestions at the end of a recipe are also *not* included in the recipe analysis unless it is stated in the per serving line.

The nutrition information that appears with each recipe was submitted in part by the participating companies and associations. **Every effort has been made to check the accuracy of these numbers. However, because numerous variables account for a wide range of values for certain foods, all nutritive analyses that appear in this book should be considered approximate.**

This cookbook offers you a wide variety of recipes that are, on a per serving basis, low in calories, fat and cholesterol. **The recipes in this book are NOT intended as a medically therapeutic program, nor as a substitute for medically approved diet plans for people on fat-, cholesterol- or sodium-restricted diets. You should consult your physician before beginning any diet plan.** The recipes offered here can be part of a healthy lifestyle that meets recognized dietary guidelines. A healthy lifestyle includes not only eating a balanced diet, but engaging in proper exercise as well.

Delicious recipes that follow today's nutritional guidelines, combined with easy-to-follow instructions and beautiful color photographs will inspire you to learn this healthy new approach to eating. Take that first step on the road to better living as you balance good health with pleasurable eating.

Hold off those hunger pangs with these tasty recipes perfect for guilt-free munching and crunching. Spicy salsa and guacamole, stuffed mushrooms and mini-pizzas are just a few predinner (or late-night) possibilities. Whip up a frothy milk shake, a refreshing fruit slush or a crowd-pleasing punch for powerful thirst quenching any time of day.

Shrimp Toast

Makes 2 dozen appetizers

- ½ pound raw shrimp, peeled, deveined
- 2 tablespoons chopped green onion
- 2 tablespoons finely chopped water chestnuts
- 2 tablespoons low-sodium soy sauce
- 1 teaspoon Oriental sesame oil
- 1 egg white, slightly beaten
- 6 slices white sandwich bread, crusts removed
  Red and yellow bell peppers and green onions for garnish

Finely chop shrimp. If using food processor, process with on/off pulses, about 10 times or until shrimp are finely chopped.

Combine shrimp, onion, water chestnuts, soy sauce and sesame oil in medium bowl; mix well. Stir in egg white; mix well.*

Toast bread lightly on both sides. Cut toast diagonally into quarters. Spread shrimp mixture evenly over toast to edges.

Place toast on foil-lined baking sheet or broiler pan. Broil, 6 inches from heat, 4 minutes or until lightly browned. Garnish with peppers and green onions.

The filling may be made ahead to this point; cover and refrigerate filling up to 24 hours. Proceed as directed for toasting and broiling.

Nutrients per serving (1 appetizer):

Calories	30	Cholesterol	18 mg
Fat	1 g	Sodium	102 mg

Garden Vegetable Dip

Makes 5½ cups dip

- 1 pound DOLE® Carrots
- 1 bunch DOLE® Broccoli
- 1 head DOLE® Cauliflower
- ½ cup minced onion
- 2 packages (8 ounces *each*) cream cheese, softened
- 1 teaspoon dill weed
- ½ teaspoon ground cumin
- ¼ teaspoon chili powder
- ⅛ teaspoon salt
- 10 drops hot pepper sauce
  Vegetable dippers: reserved carrot slices and broccoli and cauliflower florettes; celery and cucumber slices; bell pepper strips; mushroom slices; cherry tomatoes

Mince 1 cup of carrots; slice remaining for dippers. Break broccoli and cauliflower into florettes. Mince 1 cup of each; reserve remaining florettes for vegetable dippers. In food processor fitted with metal blade, combine minced carrots, broccoli, cauliflower, onion, cream cheese and seasonings; process until smooth. Refrigerate dip 1 hour or overnight in covered serving bowl. Serve with vegetable dippers and crackers.

Nutrients per serving (1 tablespoon dip):

Calories	19	Cholesterol	6 mg
Fat	2 g	Sodium	19 mg

Shrimp Toast

Black Bean Tortilla Pinwheels

Black Bean Tortilla Pinwheels

Makes 12 to 16 appetizer servings

1 (8-ounce) package cream cheese, softened
1 cup dairy sour cream
1 cup (4 ounces) shredded Wisconsin Monterey
   Jack cheese
¼ cup chopped, well drained pimento-stuffed
   green olives
¼ cup chopped red onion
½ teaspoon seasoned salt
⅛ teaspoon garlic powder
1 (15-ounce) can black beans, drained
5 (10-inch) flour tortillas
   Salsa

Beat cream cheese and sour cream in medium bowl
until well blended. Stir in Monterey Jack cheese,
olives, onion, salt and garlic powder. Cover;
refrigerate 2 hours. Place beans in food processor or
blender; process until smooth. Spread each tortilla
with thin layer of beans. Spread thin layer of cream
cheese mixture over beans. Roll up tortillas tightly.
Wrap in plastic wrap; refrigerate until chilled. Cut
tortillas into ¾-inch slices. Serve with salsa. Garnish
as desired.

Nutrients per serving (includes 1 teaspoon salsa):

| Calories | 159 | Cholesterol | 13 mg |
| Fat | 9 g | Sodium | 175 mg |

Favorite recipe from **Wisconsin Milk Marketing Board** © 1994

Toasted Sesame Seed Wafers

Makes 4 to 4½ dozen wafers

¼ cup sesame seeds
1½ cups all-purpose flour
¾ teaspoon salt
⅛ teaspoon paprika
   Dash garlic powder
½ cup BUTTER FLAVOR CRISCO®
3 to 4 drops hot pepper sauce
4 tablespoons cold water
1 tablespoon 2% milk

Preheat oven to 375°F. Spread sesame seeds in
8×8×2-inch baking pan. Bake for 6 to 10 minutes,
stirring occasionally, until golden brown. Transfer to
small dish; set aside.

In medium bowl, combine flour, salt, paprika and
garlic powder. Cut in Butter Flavor Crisco® until
coarse crumbs form. Stir in 3 tablespoons toasted
sesame seeds.

Combine hot pepper sauce and 4 tablespoons water.
Sprinkle over flour mixture, 1 tablespoon at a time,
mixing with fork until particles are moistened and
cling together. Form dough into ball.

Roll dough ⅛ inch thick on lightly floured board. Cut
with 2- or 2½-inch cookie cutter. Transfer cutouts to
ungreased baking sheet. Brush with milk. Sprinkle
lightly with remaining sesame seeds. Bake for 12 to
15 minutes, or until light golden brown. Cool. Store in
covered container.

Nutrients per serving (1 wafer):

| Calories | 31 | Cholesterol | trace |
| Fat | 2 g | Sodium | 30 mg |

Pickle Roll-Em-Ups

Makes 48 appetizers

1 package (6 ounces) sliced ham
1 container (8 ounces) soft cream cheese
8 medium CLAUSSEN® Whole Kosher Dill
   Pickles

Spread 1 side of each ham slice with 1 tablespoon
cream cheese. Place 1 pickle on edge of each ham
slice. Roll ham slice around pickle; press edges to
seal. Repeat with remaining ham slices. Cover and
refrigerate 1 hour. To serve, cut each pickle into
6 slices.

Nutrients per serving (1 appetizer):

| Calories | 20 | Cholesterol | 5 mg |
| Fat | 2 g | Sodium | 215 mg |

Southwest Barbecue Kabobs

Makes 6 appetizer servings

  1 cup beer
¾ cup A.1.® Steak Sauce
  2 cloves garlic, crushed
  2 teaspoons chili powder
  1 teaspoon ground cumin
1½ pounds round steak, cut into ½-inch strips
  3 small red or green bell peppers, cut into
        1-inch pieces
  1 teaspoon cornstarch

In small bowl, combine beer, steak sauce, garlic, chili powder and cumin. Pour marinade over sliced steak in nonmetal dish. Cover; refrigerate 2 hours, stirring occasionally.

Remove steak from marinade; reserve marinade. Thread steak and pepper pieces alternately onto 6 skewers. In small saucepan, heat reserved marinade and cornstarch to a boil. Grill or broil kabobs, 4 inches from heat source, for 15 minutes or until done, turning and brushing often with marinade. Heat remaining marinade to a boil; serve with kabobs.

Nutrients per serving:

Calories	198	Cholesterol	71 mg
Fat	4 g	Sodium	624 mg

Two Cheese Pesto Dip

Makes 2 cups dip

  1 cup light sour cream
½ cup light mayonnaise
½ cup finely chopped fresh parsley
¼ cup finely chopped walnuts
  1 clove garlic, minced
1½ teaspoons dried basil leaves, crushed *or*
        3 tablespoons fresh minced basil
½ cup (2 ounces) SARGENTO® Preferred Light
        Fancy Supreme Shredded Mozzarella
        Cheese
  2 tablespoons SARGENTO® Grated Parmesan
        Cheese

Combine all ingredients in medium bowl. Cover and refrigerate several hours or overnight. Garnish with whole walnuts, if desired. Serve with assorted fresh vegetables.

Nutrients per serving (1 tablespoon dip):

Calories	35	Cholesterol	5 mg
Fat	3 g	Sodium	36 mg

Tuna-Stuffed Endive

Makes about 24 appetizers

  4 ounces soft-spread herb cheese
  4 ounces reduced-calorie cream cheese,
        softened
  1 teaspoon lemon or lime juice
  2 heads Belgian endive *or* small lettuce leaves *or*
        crackers
  1 can (3¼ ounces) STARKIST® Tuna, drained
        and finely flaked
      Watercress sprigs *or* pimento strips for garnish

In blender container or food processor bowl, place cheeses and lemon juice. Cover and process until mixture is well blended. Trim ½ inch from bottom stems of endive; separate heads into leaves. Sprinkle 1 to 2 teaspoons tuna into each endive leaf; spoon or pipe 2 teaspoons cheese filling into each endive leaf. Garnish each with a sprig of watercress.

Nutrients per serving (1 appetizer):

Calories	29	Cholesterol	7 mg
Fat	2 g	Sodium	65 mg

Southwest Barbecue Kabobs

Corn and Tomatillo Salsa

Corn and Tomatillo Salsa

Makes 3 cups

4 ears fresh corn
2 jalapeño chilies
½ pound tomatillos* or tomatoes
½ red or green bell pepper,** cored, membranes removed and chopped
2 green onions, thinly sliced
2 tablespoons lime or lemon juice
2 tablespoons water
½ teaspoon ground coriander
2 tablespoons chopped fresh cilantro leaves
    Tortilla chips
    Lime slices, red chili pepper slices and fresh cilantro leaves for garnish

Shuck corn by removing husk and silk from corn; rinse under cool running water. Holding tip of one ear, stand upright on stem end in large skillet. Cut down sides of cob with paring knife, releasing kernels without cutting into cob. Press down along each cob with dull edge of utility knife to release any remaining corn and liquid.

Cut chilies*** in half lengthwise. Remove seeds, membranes and stems with small paring knife; discard. Chop chilies finely and add to corn.

Remove husks from tomatillos. Wash off sticky residue; core and chop. Add tomatillos, bell pepper, onions, lime juice, water and coriander to corn mixture; cover. Bring to a boil over high heat; reduce heat to medium-low. Simmer 5 minutes, stirring halfway through cooking. Cool; stir in cilantro. Store in refrigerator. Serve with tortilla chips. Garnish, if desired.

Despite its name and appearance, the tomatillo is not a variety of tomato. Native to Mexico, it resembles a green tomato encased in a papery husk, but its flavor is lemony.

**Use red bell pepper if using tomatillos and green bell pepper if using tomatoes for variety in color.*

***Chilies can sting and irritate skin; wear plastic disposable gloves when handling chilies and do not touch eyes. Wash hands after handling chilies.*

Nutrients per serving (½ cup salsa):

Calories	106	Cholesterol	0 mg
Fat	1 g	Sodium	157 mg

Country Herb Dip

Makes 2 cups

1 teaspoon KNOX® Unflavored Gelatine
¼ cup cold skim milk
¾ cup skim milk, heated to boiling
1 container (8 ounces) 1% milkfat cottage cheese
1 tablespoon Dijon-style mustard or horseradish
1 teaspoon fresh dill*
¼ teaspoon salt

In blender, sprinkle unflavored gelatine over cold milk; let stand 2 minutes. Add hot milk and process at low speed until gelatine is completely dissolved, about 2 minutes. Add remaining ingredients and process at high speed until blended. Pour into serving bowl; chill until set, about 2 hours. Before serving, stir until smooth. Serve with assorted crackers, bread sticks, cocktail breads or your favorite blanched vegetables.

***Substitution:** Use ¼ teaspoon dried dill weed.*

Nutrients per serving (1 tablespoon dip):

Calories	9	Cholesterol	0 mg
Fat	0 g	Sodium	64 mg

Vegetable Dip

Makes 1¼ cups

1 cup low fat (1%) Cottage cheese
2 tablespoons finely chopped green bell pepper
2 tablespoons finely chopped onion
2 tablespoons finely chopped radish
¼ teaspoon celery salt
    Assorted vegetable dippers

Drain Cottage cheese, reserving liquid. Place drained Cottage cheese in blender or food processor. (Add 1 to 2 teaspoons of reserved liquid for easier blending.) Process until smooth. Transfer mixture to small bowl; stir in green pepper, onion, radish and celery salt. Cover and chill in refrigerator at least 1 hour to allow flavors to blend. Serve with vegetable dippers.

Nutrients per serving (2 tablespoons dip):

Calories	18	Cholesterol	1 mg
Fat	trace	Sodium	119 mg

Favorite recipe from **Wisconsin Milk Marketing Board** © 1994

Crab Curry Dip

Crab Curry Dip

Makes 2 cups

½ cup *undiluted* CARNATION® Lite Evaporated
    Skimmed Milk
1 package (8 ounces) light Neufchâtel cream
    cheese, softened
4 ounces (¾ cup) imitation crabmeat, shredded
2 tablespoons finely sliced green onion
2 tablespoons finely chopped red bell pepper
½ teaspoon curry powder
¼ teaspoon garlic salt
    Assorted raw vegetables

In small mixer bowl, beat evaporated skimmed milk
and cream cheese. Stir in crab, onion, red pepper,
curry powder and garlic salt. Cover and refrigerate.
Serve with assorted raw vegetables.

Variation: *For Crab Horseradish Dip, substitute 1 to
2 teaspoons prepared horseradish for curry powder.*

Nutrients per serving (¼ cup dip):

Calories	108	Cholesterol	28 mg
Fat	7 g	Sodium	320 mg

Sweet & Spicy Salsa

Makes 8 appetizer servings

¾ cup fresh pineapple, peeled, cored and cut
    into ¼-inch cubes
½ cup (¼-inch) red bell pepper pieces
½ cup (¼-inch) yellow bell pepper pieces
½ cup finely chopped red onion
½ cup finely chopped cilantro
1 jalapeño pepper, seeded and minced
2 tablespoons fresh lime juice
1½ teaspoons firmly packed brown sugar
    Dash salt
    Dash black pepper

In medium bowl, combine pineapple, red and yellow
peppers, onion, cilantro, jalapeño pepper, lime juice,
brown sugar, salt and black pepper. Cover and
refrigerate 30 minutes before serving.

Nutrients per serving:

Calories	19	Cholesterol	0 mg
Fat	0 g	Sodium	18 mg

Favorite recipe from **National Turkey Federation**

Italian Bread Pizza

Makes 12 appetizer servings

1 large loaf Italian bread
1½ cups (6 ounces) shredded lower salt Monterey
    Jack cheese, divided
1 (16-ounce) jar prepared no salt added, no
    sugar, no fat pasta sauce
1½ tablespoons dried Italian seasoning
12 ounces ARMOUR® Lower Salt Ham, thinly
    sliced
1 (20-ounce) can pineapple rings, well drained
8 thin green bell pepper rings
8 thin red bell pepper rings

Slice bread lengthwise in half. Toast cut sides under
broiler until lightly browned. Sprinkle ¼ cup cheese
on each half; broil again about 1 to 2 minutes or until
cheese is melted. Combine pasta sauce and seasoning
in small saucepan; cook over medium heat until hot.
Spoon sauce evenly over bread halves; top evenly with
ham and pineapple rings. Place green and red pepper
rings alternately on top. Sprinkle each half with
½ cup of remaining cheese; place on baking sheet.
Broil, 4 to 5 inches from heat source, about 4 to
6 minutes or until cheese is melted. Cut each half
into 6 pieces. Garnish with parsley, if desired.

Nutrients per serving:

Calories	253	Cholesterol	29 mg
Fat	6 g	Sodium	482 mg

Tuna-Stuffed Artichokes

Makes 8 appetizer servings

4 medium artichokes
  Lemon juice
1½ cups chopped fresh mushrooms
1 cup diced yellow squash or zucchini
⅓ cup chopped green onions
1 clove garlic, minced
2 tablespoons vegetable oil
1 can (12½ ounces) STARKIST® Tuna, drained
  and flaked
½ cup (2 ounces) shredded low-fat Cheddar,
  mozzarella or Monterey Jack cheese
¼ cup seasoned bread crumbs
2 tablespoons diced drained pimento

With kitchen shears trim sharp points from artichoke leaves. Trim stems; remove loose outer leaves. Cut off 1 inch from tops. Brush cut edges with lemon juice. In a large covered saucepan or Dutch oven, bring artichokes and salted water to a boil; reduce heat to low. Simmer until a leaf pulls out easily, 20 to 30 minutes. Drain upside down.

Preheat oven to 450°F. Cut cooled artichokes lengthwise into halves. Remove fuzzy chokes and hearts. Finely chop hearts; discard chokes. In a medium skillet cook mushrooms, artichoke hearts, squash, onions and garlic in oil for 3 minutes, stirring frequently. Stir in tuna. Place artichoke halves, cut sides up, in a lightly oiled baking dish. Mound tuna mixture in centers of artichokes. In a small bowl stir together remaining ingredients; sprinkle over tuna mixture. Bake 5 to 8 minutes or until cheese is melted and topping is golden.

Nutrients per serving:			
Calories	136	Cholesterol	47 mg
Fat	10 g	Sodium	522 mg

Open-Faced Reubens

Makes about 48 appetizer servings

1 box (6 ounces) rye melba toast rounds
¼ pound thinly sliced cooked corned beef, cut
  into ½-inch squares
1 can (8 ounces) sauerkraut, rinsed, drained
  and chopped
1 cup (4 ounces) finely shredded Wisconsin
  Swiss cheese
2 teaspoons prepared mustard
  Caraway seeds

Preheat oven to 350°F. Arrange toast rounds on baking sheets. Top each with 1 beef square and 1 teaspoon sauerkraut. Combine cheese and mustard in small bowl; spoon about 1 teaspoon cheese mixture on top of sauerkraut. Sprinkle with caraway. Bake about 5 minutes or until cheese is melted.

To Microwave: Arrange 8 toast rounds around edge of microwave-safe plate lined with paper towel. Place 2 rounds in center. Top as directed. Microwave, uncovered, on MEDIUM (50% power) 1 to 2 minutes until cheese is melted, turning plate once. Repeat with remaining ingredients.

Nutrients per serving (1 toast round):			
Calories	28	Cholesterol	4 mg
Fat	1 g	Sodium	87 mg

Favorite recipe from **Wisconsin Milk Marketing Board** © 1994

Tuna-Stuffed Artichokes

Roasted Sweet Pepper Tapas

Makes 6 appetizer servings

2 red bell peppers (8 ounces *each*)
1 clove garlic, minced
1 teaspoon chopped fresh oregano leaves *or*
  ½ teaspoon dried oregano leaves, crushed
2 tablespoons olive oil
  Garlic bread (optional)
  Fresh oregano sprig for garnish

Cover broiler pan with aluminum foil. Set broiler pan about 4 inches from heat source. Preheat broiler. Place peppers on aluminum foil. Broil 15 to 20 minutes until blackened on all sides, turning peppers every 5 minutes with tongs.

To steam peppers and loosen skins, place blackened peppers in paper bag. Close bag; set aside to cool about 20 minutes. To peel peppers, cut around core, twist and remove. Cut peppers in half lengthwise; place pepper halves on cutting board. Peel off skin with paring knife; rinse under cold water to remove seeds. Lay pepper halves flat and slice lengthwise into ¼-inch strips.

Transfer pepper strips to glass jar. Add garlic, oregano and oil. Close lid; shake to blend. Marinate at least 1 hour. Serve on plates with garlic bread or refrigerate in jar up to 1 week. Garnish, if desired.

Tip: *Use this roasting technique for all types of sweet and hot peppers. Broiling time will vary depending on size of pepper. When handling hot peppers, such as Anaheim, jalapeño, poblano or serrano, wear plastic disposable gloves and use caution to prevent irritation of skin or eyes. Green bell peppers do not work as well since their skins are thinner.*

Nutrients per serving:

Calories	48	Cholesterol	0 mg
Fat	5 g	Sodium	1 mg

Corn Chips with Sweet Salsa

Makes 96 chips

6 corn tortillas
  Nonstick cooking spray (optional)
  Salt (optional)
  Sweet Salsa (recipe follows)

Preheat oven to 350°F. Cut each tortilla into 16 wedges. Place on baking sheet. Spray chips lightly with cooking spray and sprinkle with salt, if desired. Bake 20 to 25 minutes until crispy. Serve with Sweet Salsa.

Sweet Salsa

2 large ripe tomatoes, cored and sliced
3 tablespoons scallions, finely chopped
2 tablespoons sugar
2 teaspoons finely chopped green chilies
¼ teaspoon ground coriander

Place all ingredients in food processor or blender; process until blended but not smooth. Refrigerate or serve immediately. Makes 2 cups.

Nutrients per serving (10 chips with about 3 tablespoons salsa):

Calories	57	Cholesterol	0 mg
Fat	1 g	Sodium	3 mg

Favorite recipe from **The Sugar Association, Inc.**

Splendid Spinach Dip

Makes 24 servings, about 3 cups

2 cups DANNON® Plain Nonfat or Lowfat Yogurt
1 package (10 ounces) frozen chopped spinach, thawed and squeezed dry
⅓ cup finely chopped fresh onion
2 tablespoons reduced-calorie mayonnaise
1 package (1.4 ounces) instant vegetable soup mix
  Assorted fresh vegetable dippers

In a medium bowl combine yogurt, spinach, onion, mayonnaise and vegetable soup mix; mix well. Serve immediately or cover and chill up to 3 hours. Serve with vegetable dippers.

Nutrients per serving (about 2 tablespoons dip):

Calories	10	Cholesterol	trace
Fat	0 g	Sodium	32 mg

Roasted Sweet Pepper Tapas

Cheddar-Rice Patties

Cheddar-Rice Patties

Makes 4 servings, about 1 dozen

2 cups cooked rice
**1 cup (4 ounces) shredded low-fat Cheddar
   cheese**
½ cup minced onion
3 tablespoons all-purpose flour
½ teaspoon salt
¼ teaspoon ground black pepper
3 egg whites
⅛ teaspoon cream of tartar
   Nonstick cooking spray
   Apple wedges (optional)
   Low-fat sour cream (optional)

Combine rice, cheese, onion, flour, salt, and pepper in medium bowl. Beat egg whites with cream of tartar in small bowl until stiff but not dry. Fold beaten egg whites into rice mixture. Coat large skillet with nonstick cooking spray and place over medium heat until hot. Spoon 2 to 3 tablespoons batter into skillet for each patty; push batter into diamond shape using spatula. Cook patties, turning once, until golden brown on both sides. Garnish as desired. Serve warm with apple wedges and sour cream.

Nutrients per serving (3 patties):			
Calories	233	Cholesterol	18 mg
Fat	6 g	Sodium	550 mg

Favorite recipe from **USA Rice Council**

Guacamole with Tortilla Chips

Makes 12 appetizer servings

1 package (4-serving size) **JELL-O®** Brand Lemon Flavor Sugar Free Gelatin
1 cup boiling water
1 container (16 ounces) 1% low-fat cottage cheese
1 cup chopped ripe avocado
¾ cup chopped green onions, divided
¼ cup drained pickled jalapeño pepper slices
¼ cup lemon juice
2 cloves garlic
1 to 2 teaspoons chili powder
¼ cup chopped tomato
4 pitted ripe olives, sliced
Chili Tortilla Chips (recipe follows)

Completely dissolve gelatin in boiling water; pour into blender container. Add cottage cheese, avocado, ½ cup green onions, jalapeño peppers, lemon juice, garlic and chili powder; cover. Blend on low speed, scraping down sides occasionally, about 2 minutes or until mixture is smooth. Pour into shallow 5-cup serving dish; smooth top. Chill until set, about 4 hours.

When ready to serve, top guacamole with remaining ¼ cup chopped green onions, tomato and olives. Serve as a dip with fresh vegetables or Chili Tortilla Chips.

Nutrients per serving:

Calories	60	Cholesterol	0 mg
Fat	3 g	Sodium	230 mg

Chili Tortilla Chips

6 flour tortillas (7 inches diameter)
Nonstick cooking spray
Chili powder

Heat oven to 350°F. Lightly spray tortillas with nonstick cooking spray; sprinkle with chili powder. Turn tortillas over; repeat process. Cut each tortilla into 8 wedges; place on cookie sheet. Bake 8 to 10 minutes until crisp and lightly browned. Makes 12 servings, 48 chips.

Nutrients per serving (4 chips):

Calories	60	Cholesterol	0 mg
Fat	1 g	Sodium	90 mg

Antipasto Mini Pizzas

Makes 16 appetizer servings

1¾ cups (14.5-ounce can) **CONTADINA®** Pasta Ready Tomatoes
¾ cup (4-ounce can) water-packed artichoke hearts, drained and coarsely chopped
½ cup (2-ounce can) sliced ripe olives, drained
½ cup chopped green bell pepper
2 tablespoons grated Parmesan cheese
8 plain bagels, lightly toasted, each half cut crosswise into 2 pieces
1 cup (4 ounces) grated mozzarella cheese

In medium bowl, combine tomatoes, artichoke hearts, olives, bell pepper and Parmesan cheese. Place bagel pieces, cut-side up, on cookie sheets. Spoon about 4 teaspoons vegetable mixture onto each bagel piece. Sprinkle mozzarella cheese evenly over vegetable mixture. Bake in preheated 400°F oven for 6 to 8 minutes or until heated through.

Nutrients per serving:

Calories	140	Cholesterol	3 mg
Fat	3 g	Sodium	320 mg

Guacamole with Tortilla Chips

Mushrooms Rockefeller

Mushrooms Rockefeller

Makes 18 appetizers

18 large fresh button mushrooms (about 1 pound)
2 slices bacon
¼ cup chopped onion
1 package (10 ounces) frozen chopped spinach, thawed and squeezed dry
1 tablespoon lemon juice
1 teaspoon grated lemon peel
½ jar (2 ounces) chopped pimiento, drained
Lemon slices and lemon balm for garnish

Lightly oil 13×9-inch baking dish; set aside. Preheat oven to 375°F. Brush dirt from mushrooms; clean by wiping mushrooms with damp paper towel. Pull entire stem out of mushroom cap; set aside. Repeat with remaining mushrooms. Place caps in single layer in prepared baking dish; set aside.

Cut thin slice from base of each stem with paring knife; discard. Chop stems.

Cook bacon in medium skillet over medium heat until crisp. Remove bacon with tongs to paper towel; set aside. Add mushroom stems and onion to hot drippings in skillet. Cook and stir until onion is soft. Add spinach, lemon juice, lemon peel and pimiento; blend well. Stuff mushroom caps with spinach mixture using spoon. Crumble reserved bacon and sprinkle on top of mushrooms. Bake 15 minutes or until heated through. Garnish, if desired. Serve immediately.

Nutrients per serving (1 appetizer):

Calories	17	Cholesterol	trace
Fat	trace	Sodium	26 mg

Bean Dip

Makes 6 appetizer servings

2 shallots, minced
1 clove garlic, minced
2 teaspoons sugar
½ serrano chili, stemmed, seeded and chopped*
2 teaspoons water
1 (15-ounce) can pinto beans, drained
2 tablespoons water
½ teaspoon ground cumin
Dash ground red pepper (cayenne)
1 tablespoon lemon juice

To Microwave: Place shallots, garlic, sugar, chili and 2 teaspoons water in small microwave-safe bowl; microwave on HIGH (100% power) 30 to 45 seconds. Place beans, 2 tablespoons water, cumin, pepper and garlic mixture in food processor or blender; process until smooth. Transfer bean mixture to small bowl; microwave on HIGH 5 to 8 minutes until hot. Stir in lemon juice. Serve with tortilla chips and vegetable dippers.

*Chilies can sting and irritate skin; wear plastic disposable gloves when handling chilies and do not touch eyes. Wash hands after handling chilies.

Nutrients per serving:

Calories	108	Cholesterol	0 mg
Fat	trace	Sodium	2 mg

Favorite recipe from **The Sugar Association, Inc.**

Chunky Chili Dip

Makes 12 appetizer servings, about 1½ cups

⅔ cup DANNON® Plain Nonfat or Lowfat Yogurt
⅓ cup mayonnaise or salad dressing
¼ cup finely chopped green bell pepper
¼ cup chili sauce
2 tablespoons finely chopped green onion
1 tablespoon prepared horseradish
Assorted fresh vegetable dippers

In a medium bowl combine yogurt, mayonnaise, bell pepper, chili sauce, green onion and horseradish; mix well. Cover; chill before serving. Serve with vegetable dippers.

Nutrients per serving (about 2 tablespoons dip):

Calories	60	Cholesterol	trace
Fat	5 g	Sodium	121 mg

Today's Slim Line Dip

Makes about 2 cups

1 cup dry curd Cottage cheese
½ cup buttermilk
¼ teaspoon lemon juice
1 package dry onion soup mix
Assorted vegetable dippers

Place Cottage cheese, buttermilk, lemon juice and soup mix in blender or food processor. Cover and process until smooth. Refrigerate. Serve with vegetable dippers.

Nutrients per serving (2 tablespoons dip):

Calories	18	Cholesterol	1 mg
Fat	trace	Sodium	228 mg

Favorite recipe from **Wisconsin Milk Marketing Board** © 1994

Apricot and Ricotta Stuffed Celery

Makes 25 appetizers

25 celery sticks, each 1½ inches in length (about 2½ cups)
3 tablespoons coarsely chopped dried apricots
½ cup part-skim ricotta cheese
1½ teaspoons sugar
¼ teaspoon grated orange peel
⅛ teaspoon salt

Cut thin slice from bottom of each celery stick so it can lie flat; set aside. Place apricots in food processor or blender; process until finely chopped. Reserve 1 tablespoon apricots for garnish. Add ricotta cheese, sugar, orange peel and salt to food processor; process until cheese is smooth. Fill celery sticks with cheese mixture. Cover and refrigerate up to 3 hours before serving. Sprinkle with reserved chopped apricots just before serving.

Nutrients per serving (1 appetizer):

Calories	11	Cholesterol	2 mg
Fat	trace	Sodium	24 mg

Favorite recipe from **American Celery Council**

Apple Cheddar Quesadillas

Makes 24 appetizers

⅓ cup sugar
½ teaspoon ground cinnamon
Butter-flavored nonstick cooking spray
2 cups peeled and cored thin apple slices
⅓ cup raisins
½ teaspoon rum extract
8 (6-inch) flour tortillas
1½ cups shredded low fat Cheddar cheese

Combine sugar and cinnamon in small bowl. Reserve 1 tablespoon sugar-cinnamon mixture; set aside.

Spray large nonstick skillet with cooking spray. Add apples; cook over medium heat until tender, stirring occasionally. Remove from heat; stir in remaining sugar-cinnamon mixture, raisins and rum extract. Top each tortilla evenly with cheese to within ½ inch of edge. Spread apple mixture over cheese. Spray medium nonstick skillet with cooking spray; heat over medium heat until hot. Place 1 tortilla in skillet, filling side up, and heat 1 minute. Remove from skillet; quickly fold in half. Cover and keep warm while heating remaining 7 quesadillas.

To serve, cut each quesadilla into 3 wedges. Sprinkle wedges evenly with reserved sugar-cinnamon mixture. Sprinkle quesadillas lightly with powdered sugar, if desired. Serve warm.

To Microwave: Top tortillas as directed. Place 1 or 2 tortillas, filling sides up, on waxed paper. Microwave on HIGH (100% power) 30 to 60 seconds until warm. Remove from microwave; quickly fold in half. Cover and keep warm while microwaving remaining quesadillas. Serve warm.

Nutrients per serving (1 small appetizer):

Calories	75	Cholesterol	1 mg
Fat	1 g	Sodium	60 mg

Favorite recipe from **Western New York Apple Growers Association**

Roasted Red Pepper Dip

Makes 3 cups

1 envelope KNOX® Unflavored Gelatine
½ cup cold skim milk
1 cup skim milk, heated to boiling
1 container (8 ounces) 1% milkfat cottage
   cheese
¼ cup grated Parmesan cheese
½ teaspoon chopped garlic
½ teaspoon salt
⅛ teaspoon black pepper
1 jar (7 ounces) roasted red peppers, drained
   and chopped
1 cup loosely packed fresh basil leaves,
   chopped*
   Suggested Dippers**

In blender, sprinkle unflavored gelatine over cold milk; let stand 2 minutes. Add hot milk and process at low speed until gelatine is completely dissolved, about 2 minutes. Add cheeses, garlic, salt and black pepper; process at high speed until smooth, about 1 minute. Pour into 1-quart bowl; stir in red peppers and basil. Chill until set, about 3 hours. Beat with wire whisk or rotary beater until smooth. Serve with Suggested Dippers.

Substitution: Use 1 cup chopped fresh parsley plus 1 teaspoon dried basil.

**Suggested Dippers:* Use toasted French or Italian bread cubes, breadsticks or assorted cut-up vegetables.

Nutrients per serving (1 tablespoon dip):			
Calories	10	Cholesterol	1 mg
Fat	0 g	Sodium	55 mg

Cool Garden Dip

Makes 2 cups

1½ cups low fat (1%) Cottage cheese
¼ cup plain low fat yogurt
¼ teaspoon garlic salt
⅛ teaspoon black pepper
2 tablespoons finely chopped green onion or
   chives
2 tablespoons chopped parsley
2 tablespoons finely chopped red bell pepper

Place Cottage cheese, yogurt, garlic salt and black pepper in food processor or blender. Cover and process until smooth. Transfer to bowl and stir in remaining ingredients. Chill several hours. Serve with vegetable dippers, crackers or toasted pita bread wedges.

Nutrients per serving (2 tablespoons dip):			
Calories	18	Cholesterol	1 mg
Fat	trace	Sodium	121 mg

Favorite recipe from **Wisconsin Milk Marketing Board** © 1994

Savory Cheese Spread

Makes 12 appetizer servings

2 cups fresh bread crumbs
2 tablespoons finely chopped fresh parsley
1 teaspoon finely chopped garlic
2 tablespoons olive or vegetable oil
1 envelope KNOX® Unflavored Gelatine
¼ cup cold water
1 container (16 ounces) 1% milkfat cottage
   cheese
¼ cup cholesterol free egg substitute
½ cup skim milk
½ cup grated Parmesan cheese
2 tablespoons fresh basil *or* 2 teaspoons dried
   basil leaves

Preheat oven to 375°F. Line bottom of 8-inch springform pan with wax paper. Spray sides and bottom with no stick cooking spray; set aside.

In small bowl, combine bread crumbs, parsley, garlic and olive oil. Press onto bottom and sides of prepared pan. Bake 10 minutes; cool.

In small saucepan, sprinkle unflavored gelatine over cold water; let stand 1 minute. Stir over low heat until gelatine is completely dissolved, about 3 minutes.

In blender or food processor, process cottage cheese, egg substitute, milk and Parmesan cheese until smooth. While processing, through feed cap, gradually add gelatine mixture and process until blended; stir in basil. Pour into cooled crust and chill until firm, about 2 hours. Remove from pan; serve bottom side up with assorted crackers.

Nutrients per serving:			
Calories	92	Cholesterol	5 mg
Fat	4 g	Sodium	266 mg

Clockwise from top right: Colorful Corn Bread Squares, Buttermilk Herb Dip, Sour Cream Gouda Spread

Colorful Corn Bread Squares

Makes 64 squares

Corn Bread
- 1 egg
- 1 (16-ounce) carton LAND O LAKES® Light Sour Cream (2 cups), divided
- ¾ cup skim milk
- 1 cup all-purpose flour
- 1 cup yellow cornmeal
- 3 tablespoons sugar
- 2 teaspoons baking powder
- ½ teaspoon salt
- ½ teaspoon chili powder

Topping
- ½ teaspoon chili powder
- 1 cup finely chopped lettuce
- 1 cup chopped tomato
- ½ cup (2 ounces) finely shredded Cheddar cheese
- Salsa

For Corn Bread, heat oven to 400°F. In large bowl, slightly beat egg; stir in ¾ cup Light Sour Cream and milk. In medium bowl, combine remaining Corn Bread ingredients. Stir flour mixture into Light Sour Cream mixture just until moistened. Spread into greased 15×10×1-inch jelly-roll pan. Bake for 10 to 15 minutes or until wooden pick inserted in center comes out clean. Cool completely.

For Topping, just before serving spread remaining Light Sour Cream over corn bread. Sprinkle with ½ teaspoon chili powder, lettuce, tomato and cheese. Cut into 64 squares; top each square with ½ teaspoon salsa.

Nutrients per serving (1 square):			
Calories	33	Cholesterol	7 mg
Fat	1 g	Sodium	62 mg

Sour Cream Gouda Spread

Makes 2¼ cups

1 (7-ounce) Gouda cheese round
1 (8-ounce) carton LAND O LAKES® Light
    Sour Cream (1 cup)
1 tablespoon Dijon-style mustard
1 teaspoon Worcestershire sauce
¼ teaspoon garlic powder
¼ cup shredded carrot
¼ cup finely chopped celery
2 tablespoons finely chopped red bell pepper
    Crackers

Cut thin slice of wax from top of Gouda. Carefully scoop out cheese, leaving wax shell intact. Chop cheese into small (about ¼-inch) pieces; set aside. In medium bowl stir together Light Sour Cream, mustard, Worcestershire sauce and garlic powder. Stir in cheese, carrot, celery and red pepper. Cover; refrigerate until flavors are well blended (about 2 hours). To serve, fill wax shell with spread; refill as necessary. Garnish as desired. Serve with crackers.

Nutrients per serving (1 tablespoon dip):

Calories	29	Cholesterol	75 mg
Fat	2 g	Sodium	67 mg

Buttermilk Herb Dip

Makes 1¼ cups

1 (8-ounce) carton LAND O LAKES® Light
    Sour Cream (1 cup)
¼ cup buttermilk*
2 tablespoons chopped fresh parsley
½ teaspoon dill weed
¼ teaspoon salt
¼ teaspoon minced fresh garlic
⅛ teaspoon black pepper
    Fresh vegetable sticks

In medium bowl stir together all ingredients except vegetable sticks. Cover; refrigerate until flavors are well blended (about 2 hours). Garnish as desired. Serve with vegetable sticks.

¾ teaspoon vinegar plus enough milk to equal ¼ cup can be substituted for ¼ cup buttermilk.

Tip: *Dip can also be used as a salad dressing or potato topper.*

Nutrients per serving (1 tablespoon dip):

Calories	16	Cholesterol	2 mg
Fat	1 g	Sodium	42 mg

Turkey Antipasto Tray

Makes 20 appetizer servings

1 package (8 ounces) Oven-Roasted Turkey
    Breast Slices
1 can (5¾ ounces) jumbo pitted black olives,
    drained
1 package (8 ounces) Turkey Salami Slices
1 package (6 ounces) Provolone cheese slices
1 package (8 ounces) Turkey Ham Slices
1 jar (16 ounces) sweet gherkins, drained
1 pound Smoked Turkey, cut into ½-inch cubes
1 jar (6 ounces) pimiento-stuffed green olives,
    drained
1 package (8 ounces) Turkey Pastrami Slices
1 package (3½ ounces) sesame breadsticks
1 jar (7 ounces) baby corn cobs, drained
1 large green bell pepper, cut in half and seeds
    removed
1 jar (6 ounces) marinated artichoke hearts,
    drained
4 ounces jalapeño Monterey Jack cheese, cut
    into ½-inch cubes
1 large yellow bell pepper, cut in half and seeds
    removed
1 can (7½ ounces) capanato*

Cut oven-roasted turkey breast slices into 3×½-inch strips; fold strips crosswise in half and stuff into holes of black olives.

Layer 3 slices turkey salami alternately with 2 slices Provolone cheese. Cut stack into 8 wedges. Repeat with remaining slices. Spear each wedge with frilled toothpick.

Cut turkey ham slices in half; roll each half into cornucopia-style horn. Place gherkin in center of each horn. Secure turkey ham and gherkin with toothpick.

Spear smoked turkey cubes and green olives alternately onto frilled toothpicks.

Cut turkey pastrami slices into ½-inch-wide strips. Wrap strips around breadsticks. (If desired, spread breadsticks with mustard before wrapping with pastrami.)

Place corn cobs on serving tray. Fill 1 green pepper half with marinated artichokes. Fill remaining green pepper half with jalapeño Monterey Jack cheese cubes. Fill each yellow pepper half with capanato.

Capanato is an eggplant relish and can be found in the Italian section of most supermarkets or specialty food stores.

Nutrients per serving:

Calories	219	Cholesterol	44 mg
Fat	10 g	Sodium	1102 mg

Favorite recipe from **National Turkey Federation**

Sour Cream Clam Dip

Makes 1¼ cups

1 (8-ounce) carton LAND O LAKES® Light
    Sour Cream (1 cup)
1 (6¼-ounce) can minced clams, drained
2 tablespoons chopped green onions
2 teaspoons Worcestershire sauce
⅛ teaspoon black pepper
2 tablespoons cocktail sauce
    Green onion strips
    Crackers, cocktail bread or potato chips

In medium bowl stir together Light Sour Cream,
clams, 2 tablespoons chopped green onions,
Worcestershire sauce and pepper. Cover; refrigerate
until flavors are well blended (about 2 hours). Spoon
into shallow serving dish or plate; swirl cocktail sauce
over top. If desired, garnish with green onion strips.
Serve with crackers, cocktail bread or potato chips.

Nutrients per serving (1 tablespoon dip):			
Calories	30	Cholesterol	8 mg
Fat	1 g	Sodium	48 mg

Artichoke Dip

Makes 2½ cups

½ cup *each* light sour cream and processed light
    cream cheese
¼ cup FRENCH'S® Creamy Spread™ Mustard
1 package (9 ounces) frozen artichoke hearts,
    thawed and finely chopped
½ cup *each* finely chopped red and green bell
    peppers
1 teaspoon chili powder
2 tablespoons sliced green onions

To Microwave: In 1-quart microwavable bowl, combine
sour cream, cream cheese and French's® Creamy Spread™
Mustard. Stir in artichokes, peppers and chili powder.
Cover with waxed paper. Microwave at HIGH (100%
power) for 5 minutes or until hot, stirring halfway through
cooking. Garnish with green onions. Serve with vegetable
crudites or low-salt tortilla or potato chips.

Nutrients per serving (¼ cup dip):			
Calories	81	Cholesterol	16 mg
Fat	5 g	Sodium	158 mg

Pineapple Salsa

Makes 8 appetizer servings

1 can (20 ounces) DOLE® Crushed Pineapple,
    undrained
½ cup minced red bell pepper
¼ cup minced green bell pepper
1 tablespoon minced green onion
2 teaspoons *each* minced fresh cilantro leaves
    and minced jalapeño chilies*
1 teaspoon grated lime peel

Drain ½ cup juice from pineapple. (Use drained
juice for beverage.) Combine remaining undrained
pineapple and remaining ingredients in small bowl.
Serve at room temperature or refrigerate until slightly
chilled. Serve with tortilla chips.

Note: *Salsa is also tasty when heated slightly. Spoon salsa
over cooked chicken, fish, quesadillas or tacos.*

**Chilies can sting and irritate skin; wear plastic disposable
gloves when handling chilies and do not touch eyes. Wash
hands after handling chilies.*

Prep time: 15 minutes

Nutrients per serving:			
Calories	50	Cholesterol	0 mg
Fat	trace	Sodium	12 mg

Crispy Bacon Sticks

Makes 10 sticks

½ cup (1½ ounces) grated Wisconsin Parmesan
    cheese
5 slices bacon, halved lengthwise
10 bread sticks

To Microwave: Spread cheese on plate. Press one side of
bacon into cheese; wrap diagonally around bread stick with
cheese-coated side toward stick. Place on paper plate or
microwave-safe baking sheet lined with paper towels.
Repeat with remaining bacon halves. Microwave on HIGH
(100% power) 4 to 6 minutes until bacon is cooked,
checking for doneness after 4 minutes. Roll again in
Parmesan cheese. Serve warm.

Nutrients per serving (1 stick):			
Calories	150	Cholesterol	7 mg
Fat	4 g	Sodium	704 mg

Favorite recipe from **Wisconsin Milk Marketing Board © 1994**

Sour Cream Clam Dip

*Top to bottom: Spicy Zucchini and Bacon Canapé,
Party Ham Sandwich*

Party Ham Sandwiches

Makes 24 appetizer sandwiches

¾ cup plain nonfat yogurt
1 tablespoon chopped fresh chives
1 teaspoon dill mustard
1 loaf party rye or pumpernickel bread
    Leaf lettuce, washed, torn and well drained
1 ARMOUR® Lower Salt Ham Nugget (about
      1¾ pounds), shaved
1 small cucumber, thinly sliced
12 cherry tomatoes, cut in half *or* 24 slices tomato

Combine yogurt, chives and mustard in small bowl.
Arrange bread slices on serving tray; spread evenly
with yogurt mixture. Layer lettuce, ham, cucumber
slice and tomato half on top of each bread slice.
Garnish as desired.

Nutrients per serving (1 sandwich):

Calories	101	Cholesterol	16 mg
Fat	3 g	Sodium	413 mg

Spicy Zucchini and Bacon Canapés

Makes 22 to 24 canapés

1 (4-ounce) carton low-fat cottage cheese, well
    drained
2 green onions, finely chopped
½ tablespoon finely chopped jalapeño peppers
½ teaspoon MRS. DASH®, Original Blend
2 medium zucchini, cut into ¼-inch slices
8 slices ARMOUR® Lower Salt Bacon, cooked
    crisp and crumbled
2 tablespoons finely chopped red pepper *or*
    6 cherry tomatoes, quartered

Combine cottage cheese, green onions, jalapeño
peppers and seasoning in small bowl. Mound cottage
cheese mixture evenly on top of zucchini slices;
sprinkle with bacon. Top with sprinkle of red pepper
or cherry tomato quarter. Garnish with fresh chives or
small sprig of parsley, if desired.

Nutrients per serving (1 canapé):

Calories	17	Cholesterol	2 mg
Fat	1 g	Sodium	66 mg

Grilled Mushrooms with Lamb and Herbs

Makes 6 appetizer servings

¼ cup olive oil
¼ cup fresh lime juice
1 small green onion, minced
½ teaspoon grated fresh ginger
¼ teaspoon salt
¼ teaspoon black pepper
1 bunch parsley
36 medium mushroom caps
6 ounces cooked American lamb,* cut in
    ½-inch cubes or to fit mushroom caps

Combine all ingredients except mushrooms and lamb
in blender and process until finely minced. Brush
each mushroom generously with mixture and arrange
on baking sheet. Place a lamb cube in each
mushroom cap. Broil, about 4 inches from heat
source, until hot. Garnish with parsley, if desired.

**Leftover leg of lamb may be used.*

Nutrients per serving:

Calories	62	Cholesterol	20 mg
Fat	4 g	Sodium	14 mg

Favorite recipe from **American Lamb Council**

Black Bean Dip

Makes 2¼ cups

1 can (15 ounces) black beans, rinsed, drained
½ cup MIRACLE WHIP® FREE® Nonfat
   Dressing
½ cup reduced-calorie sour cream
1 can (4 ounces) chopped green chilies, drained
2 tablespoons chopped cilantro
1 teaspoon chili powder
½ teaspoon garlic powder
   Few drops hot pepper sauce

Mash beans with fork. Stir in remaining ingredients
until well blended; refrigerate. Serve with tortilla
chips.

Prep time: 10 minutes plus refrigerating

Nutrients per serving (2 tablespoons dip):			
Calories	70	Cholesterol	0 mg
Fat	1 g	Sodium	119 mg

Eggplant Caviar

Makes 1½ cups

1 large eggplant, unpeeled
¼ cup chopped onion
2 tablespoons lemon juice
1 tablespoon olive or vegetable oil
1 small clove garlic
½ teaspoon salt
¼ teaspoon TABASCO® pepper sauce
   Cooked egg white, sieved (optional)
   Lemon slice (optional)
   Toast points (optional)

Preheat oven to 350°F. Pierce eggplant with fork.
Place eggplant in shallow baking dish. Bake 1 hour or
until soft, turning once. Trim off ends; slice eggplant
in half lengthwise. Place cut sides down in colander
and let drain 10 minutes. Scoop out pulp; set aside
pulp and peel. In blender or food processor, combine
eggplant peel, onion, lemon juice, oil, garlic, salt and
TABASCO sauce. Cover; process until peel is finely
chopped. Add eggplant pulp. Cover; process just until
chopped. Place in serving dish. Garnish with egg
white and lemon slice, if desired. Serve with toast
points, if desired.

Nutrients per serving (1 tablespoon caviar):			
Calories	10	Cholesterol	0 mg
Fat	1 g	Sodium	45 mg

Ginger Shrimp

Makes about 2 dozen appetizers

1 cup (8 ounces) WISH-BONE® Lite Italian
   Dressing
½ cup sherry
4 medium shallots, peeled and halved*
3 medium green onions, cut into pieces
1 (2-inch) piece fresh ginger, peeled and cut
   into pieces**
1 teaspoon soy sauce
1 teaspoon lemon juice
1 pound uncooked large shrimp, cleaned
   (keep tails on)

Place all ingredients except shrimp in food processor
or blender; process until smooth. In large shallow
baking dish, combine dressing mixture with shrimp.
Cover and marinate in refrigerator, stirring
occasionally, at least 3 hours.

Remove shrimp and marinade to large shallow baking
pan or aluminum-foil-lined broiler rack. Broil shrimp
with marinade, turning once, 10 minutes or until
shrimp are opaque. Serve remaining marinade with
shrimp. Garnish as desired.

***Substitution:** Use ⅓ medium onion, cut into pieces.*
****Substitution:** Use 1 teaspoon ground ginger.*

Nutrients per serving (1 appetizer):			
Calories	24	Cholesterol	23 mg
Fat	0 g	Sodium	178 mg

Black Bean Dip

Shanghai Party Pleasers

Shanghai Party Pleasers

Makes 2 dozen appetizers

1 can (20 ounces) crushed pineapple in juice,
    undrained
¼ cup firmly packed brown sugar
2 tablespoons cornstarch
    Dash of ground ginger
1 cup water
2 tablespoons margarine
1 pound finely chopped, cooked, skinned
    turkey or chicken
¾ cup QUAKER® Oat Bran hot cereal, uncooked
⅓ cup plain low-fat yogurt
⅓ cup finely chopped water chestnuts, drained
⅓ cup sliced green onions
2 tablespoons lite soy sauce
1 egg white, slightly beaten
1 teaspoon ground ginger
½ teaspoon salt (optional)
    Red and green bell pepper pieces, fresh
    pineapple wedges and whole water
    chestnuts (optional)

Drain crushed pineapple, reserving juice. In medium saucepan, combine brown sugar, cornstarch and dash of ginger; mix well. Add combined pineapple juice, water, ¼ cup crushed pineapple and margarine; mix well. Bring to a boil over medium-high heat; reduce heat to low. Simmer about 1 minute, stirring frequently or until sauce is thickened and clear. Set aside.

Heat oven to 400°F. Lightly spray 13×9-inch baking pan with nonstick cooking spray, or oil lightly. Combine turkey, oat bran, yogurt, water chestnuts, onions, soy sauce, egg white, 1 teaspoon ginger, salt and remaining crushed pineapple; mix well. Shape into 1-inch balls. Place in prepared pan. Bake 20 to 25 minutes or until light golden brown. If desired, alternately thread meatballs, pepper pieces, pineapple wedges and water chestnuts onto skewers to serve. Serve with pineapple sauce.

Nutrients per serving (⅛th of recipe):			
Calories	240	Cholesterol	45 mg
Fat	6 g	Sodium	240 mg

Pineapple Shrimp Appetizers

Makes 30 appetizers

1 can (8 ounces) DOLE® Crushed Pineapple in
    Juice, drained
1 can (4¼ ounces) Pacific shrimp, drained
¼ cup reduced-calorie mayonnaise
1 tablespoon minced DOLE® Green Onion
2 teaspoons Dijon-style mustard
½ teaspoon dill weed
2 cucumbers

Combine all ingredients except cucumbers in medium bowl. Cut cucumbers in ⅛- to ¼-inch-thick slices. Spoon heaping teaspoon of pineapple mixture on top of each slice. Garnish with additional dill or minced green onion, if desired.

Nutrients per serving (1 appetizer):			
Calories	15	Cholesterol	6 mg
Fat	trace	Sodium	15 mg

Pinwheel Appetizers

Makes 36 appetizers

3 cups cooked wild rice
1 package (8 ounces) nonfat pasteurized
    process cream cheese product
⅓ cup grated Parmesan cheese
1 teaspoon dried parsley flakes
½ teaspoon Dijon-style mustard
½ teaspoon garlic powder
2 to 3 drops hot pepper sauce (optional)
3 (12-inch) flour tortillas
2½ ounces wafer-thin sliced corned beef
9 fresh spinach leaves

Combine wild rice, cream cheese, Parmesan cheese, parsley, mustard, garlic powder and hot pepper sauce in large bowl; blend well. Spread evenly over each tortilla, leaving ½-inch border around edge. Place single layer of corned beef over rice mixture. Top with layer of spinach. Moisten edges with water. Roll tortillas up tightly. Press to seal. Wrap tightly in plastic wrap and refrigerate several hours or overnight. To serve, cut into 1-inch slices.

Nutrients per serving (1 appetizer):			
Calories	34	Cholesterol	3 mg
Fat	trace	Sodium	52 mg

Favorite recipe from **Minnesota Cultivated Wild Rice Council**

Clams Diablo

Makes 6 appetizer servings

½ cup chopped onion
¼ cup chopped celery
1 crushed garlic clove
2 tablespoons olive oil
1¾ cups (14½-ounce can) CONTADINA®
    Whole Peeled Tomatoes, cut up, with juice
¼ cup red wine
½ teaspoon dried thyme leaves, crushed
¼ teaspoon salt
¼ teaspoon crushed red pepper
24 (about 4½ pounds total) scrubbed, fresh
    littleneck clams
2 tablespoons chopped fresh parsley or thyme
    leaves

Cook and stir onion, celery and garlic in oil in
medium saucepan until onion and celery are tender.
Stir in tomatoes with juice, wine, dried thyme leaves,
salt and crushed red pepper. Heat to a boil. Reduce
heat to low; simmer 10 minutes, stirring occasionally.
Add clams. Cover; boil gently just until clams open,
about 10 minutes. (Discard any clams that do not
open.) Sprinkle with parsley and serve.

Nutrients per serving:			
Calories	130	Cholesterol	55 mg
Fat	6 g	Sodium	440 mg

Twelve Carat Black-Eyed Pea Relish

Makes 2 to 3 pints

1 cup vinegar
¼ cup vegetable oil
2 cans (15 ounces each) black-eyed peas, drained
12 small carrots, steamed until crisp-tender,
    coarsely chopped
1 sweet onion, finely chopped
1 green bell pepper, finely chopped
1 cup sugar
¼ cup Worcestershire sauce
2 teaspoons black pepper
2 teaspoons salt (optional)
2 dashes ground red pepper

Combine vinegar and oil in small saucepan. Bring to
a boil over high heat. Meanwhile, combine black-
eyed peas, carrots, onion, green pepper, sugar,
Worcestershire sauce, black pepper, salt and ground
red pepper in large bowl. Pour oil mixture over
vegetable mixture. Cover and refrigerate at least
24 hours to allow flavors to blend. Store, covered, in
glass container in refrigerator. Serve cold; garnish as
desired.

Nutrients per serving (⅓ cup):			
Calories	112	Cholesterol	0 mg
Fat	3 g	Sodium	45 mg

Favorite recipe from the **Black-Eyed Pea Jamboree–Athens, Texas**

Twelve Carat Black-Eyed Pea Relish

Pan-Roasted Herbed Almonds

Makes 2 cups

1 teaspoon *each* dried thyme, oregano and basil
    leaves, crushed
½ teaspoon *each* garlic salt and onion powder
¼ teaspoon ground black pepper
2 tablespoons HOLLYWOOD® Peanut Oil
¾ pound (about 2 cups) whole blanched almonds

In small bowl, combine seasonings. In large skillet,
heat oil over low heat; add almonds and seasonings
and cook slowly, stirring, until almonds are lightly
browned, approximately 10 minutes. Place mixture
on paper towels to absorb excess oil. Can be served
immediately or at room temperature.

*Note: As almonds cool, seasonings will not adhere;
however, herb flavor will remain.*

Nutrients per serving (2 tablespoons):			
Calories	122	Cholesterol	0 mg
Fat	6 g	Sodium	135 mg

Cheese 'n' Rice Quesadillas

Makes 20 appetizers

2 cups water
1 tablespoon butter or margarine
1 package LIPTON® Rice & Sauce–Spanish
1 can (4 ounces) chopped green chilies, drained (optional)
1 package (12½ ounces) flour tortillas (10)
1¼ cups shredded Monterey Jack cheese (about 5 ounces)

In medium saucepan, bring water, butter, rice and Spanish sauce and chilies to a boil. Reduce heat and simmer, uncovered, stirring occasionally, 10 minutes or until rice is tender. Let stand 10 minutes.

Preheat broiler. Place 3 flour tortillas on 15½×10½×1-inch jelly-roll pan. Spread heaping ⅓ cup rice mixture onto 1 tortilla, leaving ½-inch border around edge; top each with ¼ cup cheese, then another tortilla. Repeat with remaining tortillas. Broil until each tortilla is lightly toasted and cheese is melted, turning once. To serve, cut each quesadilla into 4 wedges. Serve with guacamole, sour cream or chopped fresh cilantro, if desired.

Nutrients per serving (1 appetizer):

Calories	110	Cholesterol	5 mg
Fat	4 g	Sodium	270 mg

Cheese 'n' Rice Quesadillas

Savory Dijon Chicken Spread

Makes 14 appetizer servings, about 1¾ cups

1 cup finely chopped cooked chicken
4 ounces cream cheese, softened
3 tablespoons finely chopped green onion
1 tablespoon Dijon-style mustard
1½ teaspoons curry powder
½ cup DANNON® Plain Nonfat or Lowfat Yogurt
Melba rounds or rye bread

In a medium bowl combine chicken, cream cheese, green onion, mustard and curry powder; mix well. Stir in yogurt. Serve with melba rounds or rye bread.

Nutrients per serving (about 2 tablespoons spread):

Calories	60	Cholesterol	20 mg
Fat	4 g	Sodium	58 mg

Spinach Rice Balls

Makes about 3 dozen rice balls

2 cups cooked rice
1 package (10 ounces) frozen chopped spinach, thawed and squeezed dry*
⅔ cup dry Italian-style bread crumbs, divided
½ cup grated Parmesan cheese
⅓ cup minced onion
3 egg whites, beaten
¼ cup skim milk
1 tablespoon Dijon-style mustard
Nonstick cooking spray

Combine rice, spinach, ⅓ cup bread crumbs, cheese, onion, egg whites, milk, and mustard in large bowl. Shape into 1-inch balls. Roll each ball in remaining ⅓ cup bread crumbs. Place on baking sheet coated with nonstick cooking spray. Bake at 375°F for 10 to 15 minutes. Serve warm.

Substitute 1 package (10 ounces) frozen chopped broccoli, thawed and well drained, for the spinach, if desired.

Nutrients per serving (1 rice ball):

Calories	32	Cholesterol	1 mg
Fat	1 g	Sodium	102 mg

Favorite recipe from **USA Rice Council**

Scandinavian Smörgåsbord

Makes 36 appetizers

36 slices party bread, crackers or flat bread
  Reduced-calorie mayonnaise or salad dressing
  Mustard
36 small lettuce leaves *or* Belgian endive leaves
 1 can (6⅛ ounces) STARKIST® Tuna, drained
    and flaked or broken into chunks
 2 hard-cooked eggs, sliced
 ¼ pound frozen cooked bay shrimp, thawed
 ½ medium cucumber, thinly sliced
36 pieces steamed asparagus tips *or* pea pods
  Capers, plain yogurt, dill sprigs, pimento
    strips, red or black caviar, sliced green
    onion for garnish (optional)

Arrange party bread on a tray; spread each slice with
1 teaspoon mayonnaise and/or mustard. Top with a
small lettuce leaf. Top with tuna, egg slices, shrimp,
cucumber or steamed vegetables. Garnish as desired.

Nutrients per serving (1 appetizer):

Calories	47	Cholesterol	24 mg
Fat	1 g	Sodium	103 mg

Bruschetta

Makes 8 appetizer servings

 2 Italian rolls (each 5 inches long)
1¾ cups (14.5-ounce can) CONTADINA®
    Italian-Style Pear-Shaped Tomatoes
 2 tablespoons chopped fresh basil
 1 tablespoon finely chopped onion
 1 tablespoon olive oil
 1 small clove garlic, crushed
 ¼ teaspoon dried oregano leaves, crushed
 ¼ teaspoon salt
 ⅛ teaspoon black pepper

Cut rolls lengthwise in half. Cut each half crosswise
into 2 pieces. Toast cut sides. Drain tomatoes
thoroughly; chop tomatoes. Combine tomatoes with
remaining ingredients. Spoon tomato mixture onto
toasted rolls. Broil, 5 inches from heat source, until
tomato mixture is hot, about 2 minutes.

Nutrients per serving:

Calories	100	Cholesterol	17 mg
Fat	3 g	Sodium	280 mg

Steamed Mussels in White Wine

Makes 6 appetizer servings

⅓ cup WISH-BONE® Lite Italian Dressing
½ cup chopped shallots or onions
3 pounds mussels, well scrubbed
⅔ cup dry white wine
½ cup chopped fresh parsley
¼ cup water
  Generous dash crushed red pepper

In large saucepan or stockpot, heat Italian dressing
and cook shallots over medium heat, stirring
occasionally, 2 minutes or until tender. Add
remaining ingredients. Bring to a boil. Reduce heat to
low and simmer, covered, 4 minutes or until mussel
shells open. *(Discard any unopened shells.)* Serve
with Italian or French bread, if desired.

Nutrients per serving:

Calories	74	Cholesterol	18 mg
Fat	1 g	Sodium	378 mg

Artichoke Puffs

Makes 16 puffs

16 to 20 slices small party rye bread
 2 tablespoons CRISCO® Shortening, melted
 1 can (14 ounces) artichoke hearts, drained
 2 egg whites
 ⅓ teaspoon salt
 ¼ cup grated Parmesan cheese
 2 tablespoons shredded sharp Cheddar cheese
  Dash ground red pepper
  Paprika

Preheat oven to 400°F. Brush 1 side of each bread
slice with melted Crisco®. Place brushed side up on
ungreased cookie sheet.

Cut artichoke hearts in half; drain on paper towels.
Place an artichoke piece, cut side down, on each
bread slice.

Beat egg whites and salt in large bowl with electric
mixer at high speed until stiff, not dry, peaks form.
Fold in cheeses and ground red pepper.

Spoon about 1 measuring teaspoonful of egg white
mixture over each artichoke piece; sprinkle with
paprika.

Bake at 400°F for 10 to 12 minutes or until golden
brown. Serve hot. Garnish with celery leaves and
carrot curls, if desired.

Nutrients per serving (1 puff):

Calories	52	Cholesterol	2 mg
Fat	2 g	Sodium	113 mg

Scandinavian Smörgåsbord

Ground Turkey Chinese Spring Rolls

Makes 16 spring rolls

      1 pound Ground Turkey
      1 large clove garlic, minced
 1½ teaspoons minced fresh ginger
      2 cups thinly sliced bok choy
    ½ cup thinly sliced green onions
      2 tablespoons reduced-sodium soy sauce
      1 teaspoon dry sherry or rice wine
      1 teaspoon sesame oil
      8 sheets phyllo pastry
         Nonstick cooking spray

Preheat oven to 400°F. In medium nonstick skillet, over medium-high heat, cook and stir turkey, garlic and ginger 4 to 5 minutes or until turkey is no longer pink. Drain thoroughly.

In medium bowl combine turkey mixture, bok choy, onions, soy sauce, sherry and oil.

On clean, dry counter, layer phyllo sheets into a stack and cut into 2 (18×7-inch) rectangles. Work with one rectangle of phyllo at a time. (Keep remaining phyllo covered with a damp cloth following package instructions.)

Coat rectangle of phyllo with nonstick cooking spray. On counter, arrange phyllo sheet so 7-inch side is parallel to counter edge. Place ¼ cup of turkey mixture in 5-inch strip, 1 inch away from bottom and side edges of phyllo. Fold 1-inch bottom edge of phyllo over filling and fold longer edges of phyllo toward center; roll up, jelly-roll style. Phyllo may break during rolling, but will hold filling once the roll is completed.

Repeat process with remaining rectangles of phyllo and filling to make remaining spring rolls. Place rolls, seam-side-down, on 2 (10×15-inch) cookie sheets coated with nonstick cooking spray. Coat tops of rolls with nonstick cooking spray. Bake 14 to 16 minutes or until all surfaces of rolls are golden brown.

Serve immediately with Chinese mustard, hoisin sauce and additional soy sauce, if desired.

Nutrients per serving (1 spring roll):

Calories	86	Cholesterol	1 mg
Fat	3 g	Sodium	140 mg

Favorite recipe from **National Turkey Federation**

Ground Turkey Chinese Spring Rolls

Two-Tone Ricotta Loaf

Makes 8 appetizer servings

2 envelopes unflavored gelatin
1 cup cold skim milk

Pepper Layer
  1 container (15 ounces) POLLY-O FREE®
    Natural Nonfat Ricotta Cheese or
    POLLY-O LITE® Reduced-Fat Ricotta
    Cheese
  1 jar (7 ounces) roasted red peppers, undrained
  ¼ teaspoon salt
    Pinch ground black pepper

Basil Layer
  1 container (15 ounces) POLLY-O FREE®
    Natural Nonfat Ricotta Cheese or
    POLLY-O LITE® Reduced-Fat Ricotta
    Cheese
  1 cup fresh basil leaves
  ⅓ cup fresh parsley leaves
  ¾ teaspoon salt
  1 small garlic clove, crushed
    Pinch ground black pepper
  ½ cup skim milk
    Additional basil leaves for garnish (optional)

In small saucepan, sprinkle gelatin over 1 cup cold milk; let stand 5 minutes. Stir over low heat until gelatin is completely dissolved.

For Pepper Layer, in food processor combine ricotta, roasted red peppers and their juice, salt and black pepper. Process until smooth. Add ½ cup dissolved gelatin mixture and process until combined. Pour into 8×4-inch loaf pan; refrigerate until partially set, about 20 minutes.

For Basil Layer, in food processor combine ricotta, 1 cup basil, parsley, salt, garlic and black pepper. Process until herbs are finely chopped. Add remaining gelatin mixture and ½ cup skim milk. Pour into large bowl and chill, stirring occasionally, until mixture is the consistency of unbeaten egg whites. Spoon over partially set pepper layer; smooth top. Cover and refrigerate until set, at least 4 hours or overnight. To serve, unmold onto serving dish. Garnish with fresh additional basil leaves, if desired.

Nutrients per serving:

Calories	167	Cholesterol	20 mg
Fat	4 g	Sodium	382 mg

Stuffed Mushrooms

Stuffed Mushrooms

Makes 4 appetizer servings

  1 pound medium mushrooms, washed
  2 tablespoons olive oil, divided
  ½ cup finely chopped red bell pepper
  ¼ cup finely chopped onion
  ¼ cup FRENCH'S® Creamy Spread™ Mustard
  ¼ teaspoon *each* garlic powder and dried
    oregano leaves, crushed
  1 tablespoon grated Parmesan cheese
    Chopped fresh parsley for garnish (optional)

Remove and finely chop mushroom stems. Place mushroom caps right sides up on foil-lined broiler pan. Brush tops of caps with 1 tablespoon oil. Broil 5 to 10 minutes until tender; drain and set aside. Heat remaining 1 tablespoon oil in medium skillet. Over high heat, cook and stir mushroom stems, red pepper and onion for 5 minutes or until almost dry. Add French's® Creamy Spread™ Mustard and seasonings. Spoon about 1 teaspoon vegetable mixture into each mushroom cap. Sprinkle Parmesan cheese evenly over caps. Broil for 5 minutes until lightly browned. Garnish with parsley, if desired.

Nutrients per serving:

Calories	124	Cholesterol	1 mg
Fat	9 g	Sodium	229 mg

White Sangria

White Sangria

Makes 20 servings

1 carton (64 ounces) DOLE® Pine-Orange-
   Guava Juice
2 cups fruity white wine
¼ cup orange-flavored liqueur
¼ cup sugar
1 DOLE® Orange, thinly sliced
1 lime, thinly sliced
2 cups sliced DOLE® Fresh Strawberries
   Ice cubes
   Mint sprigs for garnish

Combine all ingredients except ice and mint in
2 large pitchers; cover and refrigerate for 2 hours to
blend flavors. Serve over ice. Garnish with mint sprig.

Nutrients per serving (4 ounces):			
Calories	93	Cholesterol	0 mg
Fat	trace	Sodium	7 mg

Mulled Cider

Makes about 2 quarts

2 quarts apple cider
¾ to 1 cup REALEMON® Lemon Juice from
   Concentrate
1 cup firmly packed light brown sugar
8 whole cloves
2 cinnamon sticks
¾ cup rum (optional)

In large saucepan, combine all ingredients except
rum; bring to a boil. Reduce heat; simmer, uncovered,
10 minutes to blend flavors. Remove spices; add rum
just before serving, if desired. Serve hot. Garnish with
additional cinnamon sticks, if desired.

Tip: *Can be served cold.*

Nutrients per serving (¾ cup):			
Calories	135	Cholesterol	0 mg
Fat	trace	Sodium	7 mg

Strawberry Fizz

Makes 4 servings

1 can (5 fluid ounces) PET® Evaporated Milk *or*
   PET® Light Evaporated Skimmed Milk
⅔ cup lemon-lime or orange soda, regular or
   diet
1½ cups fresh or frozen strawberries
4 teaspoons sugar *or* 1 teaspoon artificial
   sweetener

Combine all ingredients in blender until smooth.
Serve immediately.

Note: *Frozen fruit makes this beverage icy cold; if using
fresh fruit, we suggest serving over crushed ice.*

Nutrients per serving (with PET® Evaporated Milk, regular soda and sugar):			
Calories	99	Cholesterol	10 mg
Fat	3 g	Sodium	44 mg

Nutrients per serving (with PET® Light Evaporated Skimmed Milk, diet soda and artificial sweetener):			
Calories	51	Cholesterol	1 mg
Fat	trace	Sodium	46 mg

Easy Chocolate Pudding Milk Shake

Makes 5 servings

3 cups cold skim milk
1 package (4-serving size) JELL-O® Chocolate
   Flavor Sugar Free Instant Pudding and Pie
   Filling
1½ cups vanilla ice milk

Pour milk into blender container. Add remaining
ingredients; cover. Blend at high speed 15 seconds or
until smooth. Serve at once. (Mixture thickens as it
stands. Thin with additional milk, if desired.)

Note: *For double chocolate impact, use chocolate ice milk
instead of vanilla ice milk.*

Nutrients per serving:			
Calories	150	Cholesterol	10 mg
Fat	2 g	Sodium	370 mg

Strawberry Banana Yogurt Shake

Makes 6 servings

2 cups cold skim milk
1 package (4-serving size) JELL-O® Brand
   Strawberry Flavor Sugar Free Gelatin
1 container (8 ounces) plain low-fat yogurt
1 cup crushed ice
1 large banana, cut into chunks

Pour milk into blender container. Add remaining ingredients; cover. Blend at high speed 30 seconds or until smooth. Serve at once.

Nutrients per serving:

Calories	80	Cholesterol	5 mg
Fat	1 g	Sodium	115 mg

Birthday Punch

Makes 18 servings

2 quarts DOLE® Pineapple Juice
1 bottle (32 ounces) lemon-lime soda
1 can (12 ounces) frozen DOLE® Pine-Orange
   Banana Juice concentrate, thawed
   DOLE® citrus slices for garnish
   DOLE® Fresh Strawberries, halved (optional)

Combine all ingredients in large punch bowl.

Nutrients per serving (6 ounces):

Calories	89	Cholesterol	0 mg
Fat	trace	Sodium	7 mg

Birthday Punch

Skim Milk Hot Cocoa

Makes two (7-ounce) servings

3 tablespoons sugar
2 tablespoons HERSHEY⅔S Cocoa
¼ cup hot water
1½ cups skim milk
⅛ teaspoon vanilla extract

Blend sugar and cocoa in small saucepan; gradually add hot water. Cook over medium heat, stirring constantly, until mixture boils; boil and stir for 2 minutes. Add milk; heat thoroughly. Stir occasionally; *do not boil*. Remove from heat; add vanilla. Serve hot.

Nutrients per serving:

Calories	160	Cholesterol	5 mg
Fat	1 g	Sodium	100 mg

Nectarine Mocktail

Makes 8 servings

3 fresh California nectarines, diced
1 container (10 ounces) unsweetened frozen
   strawberries, partially thawed
1 bottle (28 ounces) club soda or sugar-free
   ginger ale, divided
8 mint sprigs (optional)

Place nectarines, strawberries and 1 cup club soda in blender; process until smooth. Pour into chilled glasses until each is about ⅔ full. Fill glasses with remaining club soda. Garnish each serving with mint sprig, if desired.

Nutrients per serving:

Calories	37	Cholesterol	0 mg
Fat	trace	Sodium	trace

Favorite recipe from **California Tree Fruit Agreement**

Sunlight Sipper

Makes 1 serving

¾ cup DOLE® Pine-Passion-Banana Juice,
   chilled
1 tablespoon puréed peaches
1 tablespoon orange-flavored liqueur (optional)
1 teaspoon rum extract
   Cracked ice

Combine all ingredients in glass.

Nutrients per serving:

Calories	106	Cholesterol	0 mg
Fat	trace	Sodium	9 mg

Hawaiian Tea

Makes 3 servings

3 cups DOLE® Pineapple Orange Juice
1 cinnamon stick
2 tablespoons chopped crystallized ginger
¼ teaspoon anise seeds
¼ teaspoon whole cloves
1 orange tea bag
1 peppermint tea bag
Brown sugar (optional)
Additional cinnamon sticks for garnish
(optional)

Combine juice and spices in saucepan. Bring to a boil. Reduce heat to low; simmer 1 minute. Add tea bags. Cover and steep 5 to 7 minutes. Remove tea bags and spices. Sweeten with brown sugar, if desired. Garnish with additional cinnamon sticks, if desired.

Nutrients per serving:

Calories	170	Cholesterol	0 mg
Fat	trace	Sodium	17 mg

Orange Tea Punch

Makes about 16 servings, 4 quarts

4 cups brewed tea
2 cups orange juice, chilled
1 cup REALEMON® Lemon Juice from
Concentrate
1 cup sugar
1 (1-liter) bottle ginger ale, chilled
1 quart BORDEN® or MEADOW GOLD®
Orange Sherbet

In large pitcher, combine tea, orange juice, ReaLemon® brand and sugar; stir until sugar dissolves. Chill. Just before serving, pour tea mixture into large punch bowl; add ginger ale and scoops of sherbet.

Nutrients per serving:

Calories	82	Cholesterol	0 mg
Fat	trace	Sodium	9 mg

Banana-Raspberry Smoothie

Banana-Raspberry Smoothie

Makes 2 to 3 servings

2 ripe, medium DOLE® Bananas, peeled
1½ cups DOLE® Pure & Light Country
Raspberry Juice, chilled
1 cup frozen vanilla yogurt, softened
1 cup DOLE® Fresh Raspberries

Place all ingredients in blender. Process until smooth.

Nutrients per serving:

Calories	196	Cholesterol	7 mg
Fat	2 g	Sodium	64 mg

Plum Purple Frappé

Makes 2 servings

3 fresh California plums, coarsely chopped
(1 cup)
½ cup plain low fat yogurt
2 tablespoons honey
2 tablespoons wheat germ
3 ice cubes, cracked

Place all ingredients in blender; process until smooth. Serve immediately.

Nutrients per serving (¾ cup):

Calories	167	Cholesterol	3 mg
Fat	2 g	Sodium	41 mg

Favorite recipe from **California Tree Fruit Agreement**

Peach Fizz

Makes 6 servings

3 fresh California peaches, sliced
1 can (6 ounces) pineapple juice
¼ cup frozen limeade or lemonade concentrate,
undiluted
¼ teaspoon almond extract
Finely crushed ice
3 cups club soda, chilled

Place peaches in blender or food processor. Cover and process until smooth. Measure 2 cups peach purée; pour into bowl. Stir in pineapple juice, limeade and almond extract. Fill each of six 12-ounce glasses ⅔ full with crushed ice. Add ½ cup peach mixture to each. Fill glasses with club soda. Stir gently. Serve immediately.

Nutrients per serving:

Calories	65	Cholesterol	0 mg
Fat	trace	Sodium	6 mg

Favorite recipe from **California Tree Fruit Agreement**

Luscious Pink Drink

Makes 4 servings

4 fresh California peaches, sliced (2 cups)
1 cup buttermilk
½ cup fresh strawberries, hulled *or* raspberries
1 tablespoon lemon juice
4 whole fresh strawberries *or* raspberries for
garnish (optional)

Place all ingredients except garnish in blender; process until smooth. Pour into 4 mugs. Freeze until slushy. Top each serving with 1 strawberry, if desired. Serve immediately.

Nutrients per serving (1 cup):

Calories	81	Cholesterol	2 mg
Fat	1 g	Sodium	66 mg

Favorite recipe from **California Tree Fruit Agreement**

Fruit Juicey

Makes 6 servings, 6 cups

1 cup frozen pineapple-orange-banana juice
concentrate, thawed
1 cup DANNON® Plain Nonfat or Lowfat Yogurt
¾ cup water
2 tablespoons honey
1 teaspoon vanilla
Ice cubes

In blender container combine juice concentrate, yogurt, water, honey and vanilla. Cover and blend on high speed until smooth. Add enough ice cubes to bring mixture to 6 cup level; process until smooth. Serve immediately.

Nutrients per serving (1 cup):

Calories	70	Cholesterol	trace
Fat	0 g	Sodium	78 mg

Strawberry-Banana Shake

Makes 2 servings

1 cup fresh strawberries, hulled
1 small banana, peeled and cut into chunks
1 cup nonfat plain yogurt
2 tablespoons sugar
½ teaspoon vanilla extract
6 ice cubes

Place all ingredients in blender or food processor; process until smooth. Serve immediately.

Tip: *This drink is wonderful as a quick breakfast or satisfying snack.*

Nutrients per serving (1 cup):

Calories	160	Cholesterol	2 mg
Fat	1 g	Sodium	88 mg

Favorite recipe from **The Sugar Association, Inc.**

Time-Saver Sugar Syrup

Makes about 1 cup syrup

1 cup water
1½ cups sugar
1 teaspoon grated lemon peel

Combine all ingredients in small saucepan. Heat over medium heat until sugar dissolves, stirring constantly. Cool to room temperature and strain. Refrigerate.

Lemonade: For 1 serving, combine 1½ tablespoons Time-Saver Sugar Syrup, ¼ cup fresh lemon juice and 1 cup water; stir well. For 1½ quarts, combine 1 cup Time-Saver Sugar Syrup, 1⅓ cups fresh lemon juice and 4 cups water in pitcher; stir well. Serve over ice.

Iced Tea: For 2 servings, prepare 1 cup double-strength tea with tea bags. Add 2½ tablespoons Time-Saver Sugar Syrup; stir well. Cool completely. Pour over crushed ice and serve.

Party Punch: Combine 1 cup Time-Saver Sugar Syrup, 1 cup orange juice, 1 cup pineapple juice and 4 cups seltzer in large bowl or pitcher; stir well. Serve over ice.

Nutrients per serving (Lemonade):

Calories	51	Cholesterol	0 mg
Fat	trace	Sodium	8 mg

Favorite recipe from **The Sugar Association, Inc.**

Iced French Roast

Makes 2 servings

2 cups strong brewed French Roast coffee, chilled
2 teaspoons sugar
½ teaspoon unsweetened cocoa powder
2 tablespoons low fat milk
Dash ground cinnamon

Place all ingredients in blender; process until combined. Pour over ice and serve immediately.

Nutrients per serving:

Calories	27	Cholesterol	1 mg
Fat	trace	Sodium	13 mg

Favorite recipe from **The Sugar Association, Inc.**

Fruity Spritzer

Makes 1 serving

1 teaspoon strawberry extract
2 sugar cubes
1 cup chilled seltzer water

Place strawberry extract in small bowl; add sugar cubes and let stand 5 minutes. Place flavored sugar cubes in bottom of glass and add seltzer. Let cubes dissolve; serve immediately.

Nutrients per serving:

Calories	28	Cholesterol	0 mg
Fat	0 g	Sodium	3 mg

Favorite recipe from **The Sugar Association, Inc.**

Banana-Pineapple Colada

Makes 2 servings

½ ripe banana, peeled
½ cup fresh or canned pineapple chunks
½ cup pineapple juice
½ cup ice cubes
¼ teaspoon coconut extract
1 tablespoon sugar

Place all ingredients in blender or food processor; process until blended thoroughly. Serve immediately.

Nutrients per serving:

Calories	198	Cholesterol	0 mg
Fat	trace	Sodium	5 mg

Favorite recipe from **The Sugar Association, Inc.**

Left to right: Iced French Roast, Fruity Spritzer, Banana-Pineapple Colada

Orange-Pineapple Breakfast Shake with Yogurt and Honey

Makes 2 servings

    1 cup Florida orange or tangerine juice
    ½ cup unsweetened pineapple juice
    ½ cup plain yogurt
    1 teaspoon honey
      Orange twists or fresh mint sprigs for garnish
      (optional)

Place orange juice, pineapple juice, yogurt and honey in blender; process until well combined. Pour into 2 glasses and garnish each with orange twist or fresh mint sprig.

Nutrients per serving:			
Calories	133	Cholesterol	1 mg
Fat	0 g	Sodium	46 mg

Favorite recipe from **Florida Department of Citrus**

Cantaloupe-Strawberry Shake

Makes 2 servings

    1 cup whole strawberries, hulled
    1 cup cantaloupe chunks
    2 teaspoons sugar
    ½ cup skim milk

Place all ingredients in food processor or blender; process until frothy. Serve immediately.

Nutrients per serving:			
Calories	89	Cholesterol	1 mg
Fat	1 g	Sodium	40 mg

Favorite recipe from **The Sugar Association, Inc.**

Pear-Grapefruit Drink

Makes 2 servings

    1 fresh California Bartlett pear, peeled, cored
      and diced (1½ cups)
    1 can (6 ounces) unsweetened grapefruit juice
      (¾ cup)
    1 cup ice cubes, cracked

Place all ingredients in blender; process until smooth. Serve immediately.

Nutrients per serving (1¼ cups):			
Calories	80	Cholesterol	0 mg
Fat	trace	Sodium	2 mg

Favorite recipe from **California Tree Fruit Agreement**

Red Grape Cooler

Makes 2 servings

    1 cup seedless red grapes
    2 cups club soda
    1 tablespoon sugar

Place all ingredients in blender or food processor; process until well blended. Serve over ice.

Variation: *For a bubbly drink, blend 1 cup club soda with grapes and sugar. Pour mixture into 2 glasses. Fill each glass with ½ cup club soda.*

Nutrients per serving:			
Calories	81	Cholesterol	0 mg
Fat	trace	Sodium	52 mg

Favorite recipe from **The Sugar Association, Inc.**

Creamy Plum Milk Shake

Makes 3 servings

    3 fresh California plums, coarsely chopped
    1 cup vanilla ice milk
    ½ cup low fat milk
    ½ teaspoon orange peel
    4 ice cubes, cracked

Place all ingredients in blender. Process until smooth. Serve immediately.

Nutrients per serving (⅔ cup):			
Calories	115	Cholesterol	12 mg
Fat	3 g	Sodium	55 mg

Favorite recipe from **California Tree Fruit Agreement**

Iced Nutty Coffee

Makes 2 servings

    2 cups strong brewed French Roast coffee,
      chilled
    2 teaspoons sugar
    1 teaspoon smooth peanut butter
    2 tablespoons skim milk

Place all ingredients in blender; process until smooth. Pour over ice and serve immediately.

Nutrients per serving:			
Calories	36	Cholesterol	0 mg
Fat	1 g	Sodium	21 mg

Favorite recipe from **The Sugar Association, Inc.**

Honeydew Melon Shake

Makes 2 servings

½ cup vanilla low fat yogurt
2 teaspoons sugar
1 cup honeydew melon chunks, chilled

Place all ingredients in blender or food processor; process until smooth. Serve immediately.

Variation: For strawberry-melon flavor, place yogurt, 3 teaspoons sugar, melon and 1 cup frozen strawberries in blender or food processor; process until smooth. Serve immediately.

Nutrients per serving:

Calories	94	Cholesterol	3 mg
Fat	1 g	Sodium	46 mg

Favorite recipe from **The Sugar Association, Inc.**

Breakfast Lassi

Makes 2 servings

1 cup buttermilk
2 fresh California nectarines, cubed
1 teaspoon honey
3 ice cubes, cracked

Place all ingredients except ice in blender; process until smooth. Add ice and blend until frothy. Serve immediately.

Nutrients per serving (1¼ cups):

Calories	125	Cholesterol	4 mg
Fat	2 g	Sodium	129 mg

Favorite recipe from **California Tree Fruit Agreement**

O.J. Yogurt Shake

Makes 5 servings

1 cup milk
1 carton (8 ounces) plain or vanilla yogurt
1 can (6 ounces) frozen orange juice concentrate
2 cups ice cubes

Place milk, yogurt and orange juice concentrate in blender; process until well blended. With blender running, gradually add ice cubes through feed cap; process until smooth. Serve immediately.

Nutrients per serving (1 cup):

Calories	113	Cholesterol	9 mg
Fat	2 g	Sodium	57 mg

Favorite recipe from **Wisconsin Milk Marketing Board © 1994**

Fresh Plum Breakfast Frappé

Makes 3 servings

4 fresh California plums, quartered (1½ cups)
⅔ cup strawberries, hulled and halved
2 tablespoons frozen orange juice concentrate, undiluted
8 ice cubes, cracked

Place all ingredients in blender; process until smooth. Serve immediately.

Nutrients per serving (1 cup):

Calories	73	Cholesterol	0 mg
Fat	trace	Sodium	trace

Favorite recipe from **California Tree Fruit Agreement**

Pear Shake

Makes 1 serving

½ cup canned Bartlett pear halves, undrained
½ cup vanilla yogurt
3 ice cubes

Drain pears, reserving ¼ cup liquid. Place pears, yogurt, reserved pear liquid and ice cubes in blender; process until smooth and thick. Serve immediately.

Nutrients per serving:

Calories	238	Cholesterol	6 mg
Fat	2 g	Sodium	81 mg

Favorite recipe from **Pacific Coast Canned Pear Service**

Raspberry-Watermelon Slush

Makes 2 servings

1 cup frozen raspberries
1 cup watermelon chunks, seeded
1 cup lemon-lime seltzer
1 tablespoon sugar

Place all ingredients in blender or food processor; process until well blended. Serve immediately.

Nutrients per serving:

Calories	168	Cholesterol	0 mg
Fat	1 g	Sodium	28 mg

Favorite recipe from **The Sugar Association, Inc.**

Banana Berry Blend

Makes 2 servings

1 cup DANNON® Plain Nonfat or Lowfat Yogurt
½ cup orange juice
½ cup fresh or frozen unsweetened strawberries
1 ripe banana, sliced
2 tablespoons honey
1 tablespoon wheat germ (optional)

In blender container combine all ingredients. Cover and blend on high speed until smooth. Serve immediately over ice or in frosted mugs.

Nutrients per serving:

Calories	220	Cholesterol	trace
Fat	1 g	Sodium	82 mg

Nectarine Punch Cooler

Makes 6 servings

1 pint fresh strawberries, hulled
2 medium-sized fresh California nectarines, cut into wedges
1 can (6 ounces) frozen pineapple or cranberry juice concentrate
12 ice cubes, cracked
1 to 2 cups sparkling water

Reserve 6 whole strawberries for garnish. Place remaining strawberries, nectarines and frozen juice concentrate in blender; process until smooth. Add ice and blend until smooth. Pour into punch bowl or large container. Stir in sparkling water to desired consistency. Ladle into glasses. Garnish with reserved strawberries.

Nutrients per serving (½ cup):

Calories	87	Cholesterol	0 mg
Fat	trace	Sodium	4 mg

Favorite recipe from **California Tree Fruit Agreement**

Frosty Pineapple Nog

Makes 6 servings

3 cups buttermilk
1 can (8 ounces) crushed pineapple in juice, undrained
¼ cup sugar or honey
1 teaspoon vanilla extract
¼ teaspoon salt
5 ice cubes
Fresh mint sprigs (optional)

Place buttermilk, pineapple and juice, sugar, vanilla and salt in blender. Cover; blend about 30 seconds or until combined. With blender running, add ice cubes, 1 at a time, through feed cap. Blend until mixture is smooth and frothy. Pour into 6 chilled tall glasses. Garnish each serving with mint sprig, if desired. Serve immediately.

Nutrients per serving (1 cup):

Calories	105	Cholesterol	5 mg
Fat	1 g	Sodium	218 mg

Favorite recipe from **Wisconsin Milk Marketing Board** © **1994**

Lahaina Sunset

Makes 3½ cups

2 fresh California peaches, halved
1 cup low fat milk
¼ cup pineapple juice
3 ice cubes, cracked
1 teaspoon rum extract

Place peaches, milk and pineapple juice in blender; process until smooth. Add ice and rum extract; process until smooth and frothy. Serve immediately.

Nutrients per serving (½ cup):

Calories	37	Cholesterol	3 mg
Fat	1 g	Sodium	18 mg

Favorite recipe from **California Tree Fruit Agreement**

Iced Mocha

Makes 2 servings

2 cups strong brewed coffee, chilled
½ teaspoon unsweetened cocoa powder
1 tablespoon brown sugar
¾ cup skim milk

Place all ingredients in blender; process until combined. Pour over ice and serve immediately.

Nutrients per serving:

Calories	61	Cholesterol	2 mg
Fat	trace	Sodium	56 mg

Favorite recipe from **The Sugar Association, Inc.**

Banana Berry Blend

Double Strawberry Coconut Punch

Makes 25 servings

2 cans (12 ounces each) frozen DOLE® Pine-Orange Banana Juice concentrate, thawed
4 cups DOLE® Fresh Strawberries, divided
1 can (15 ounces) real cream of coconut
4 ripe, medium DOLE® Bananas, peeled
1 pint vanilla ice cream, softened
1 cup flaked coconut (optional)

Reconstitute juice in large punch bowl according to directions. Place 2 cups strawberries, cream of coconut and bananas in blender. Process until smooth; stir into juice in punch bowl. Process remaining 2 cups strawberries in blender until smooth. Swirl into punch along with ice cream. Top with coconut, if desired.

Nutrients per serving (6 ounces):

Calories	130	Cholesterol	5 mg
Fat	5 g	Sodium	23 mg

Hot Orchard Peach Cup

Berry Power Drink

Makes 2 servings

1 cup cranberry juice
1 cup fresh or frozen strawberries
1 (8-ounce) carton vanilla low-fat yogurt
⅔ cup QUAKER® Oats (quick or old fashioned, uncooked)*
Sugar to taste (optional)
1 cup ice cubes

Place all ingredients except ice in blender container. Cover; blend on high speed about 2 minutes or until smooth. Gradually add ice; blend on high speed an additional minute or until smooth. Serve immediately.

*Or substitute ⅔ cup QUAKER® Oat Bran hot cereal, uncooked, for oats.

Nutrients per serving (about 1½ cups):

Calories	300	Cholesterol	5 mg
Fat	4 g	Sodium	80 mg

Hot Orchard Peach Cup

Makes 6 servings

1 bottle (40 ounces) DOLE® Pure & Light Orchard Peach Juice
¼ cup packed brown sugar
2 cinnamon sticks
2 tablespoons margarine
½ cup peach schnapps (optional)
Additional cinnamon sticks for garnish (optional)

Combine juice, brown sugar, 2 cinnamon sticks and margarine in Dutch oven. Heat to a boil. Remove from heat; discard cinnamon sticks. Add schnapps, if desired. Garnish with additional cinnamon sticks, if desired.

Nutrients per serving (7 ounces):

Calories	181	Cholesterol	0 mg
Fat	4 g	Sodium	70 mg

Peaches and Cream Punch

Makes 24 (4 ounce) servings

4 cups boiling water
6 LIPTON® Flo-Thru Regular or Decaffeinated
 Tea Bags
4 cans (12 ounces each) peach nectar, chilled
2 cups champagne or seltzer water, chilled
2 cups (1 pint) frozen low-fat vanilla yogurt

In teapot, pour boiling water over tea bags; cover and brew 5 minutes. Cool.

In chilled 4-quart punch bowl, blend peach nectar with tea. Add champagne. Top with scoops of yogurt and garnish, if desired, with fresh peach slices. Serve immediately.

Nutrients per serving:

Calories	77	Cholesterol	1 mg
Fat	0 g	Sodium	20 mg

Kokomo Quencher

Makes 47 servings

1 carton (64 ounces) DOLE® Pine-Orange-
 Guava Juice
2 bottles (32 ounces each) lemon-lime soda,
 chilled
1 can (46 ounces) DOLE® Pineapple Juice,
 chilled
1 package (16 ounces) frozen blackberries
1 can (15 ounces) real cream of coconut
1 lime, thinly sliced

Combine all ingredients in large punch bowl.

Nutrients per serving (4 ounces):

Calories	82	Cholesterol	0 mg
Fat	2 g	Sodium	13 mg

Lemony Light Cooler

Lemony Light Cooler

Makes 7 servings, about 7 cups

3 cups white grape juice *or* 1 bottle (750 ml)
 dry white wine, chilled
½ to ¾ cup sugar
½ cup REALEMON® Lemon Juice from
 Concentrate
1 bottle (1 liter) club soda, chilled
 Strawberries *or* plum, peach or orange slices
 ***or* other fresh fruit**
 Ice

In large pitcher, combine grape juice, sugar and ReaLemon® brand; stir until sugar dissolves. Cover; chill. Just before serving, add club soda and fruit. Serve over ice.

Tip: *Recipe may be doubled.*

Nutrients per serving (without fruit):

Calories	110	Cholesterol	0 mg
Fat	trace	Sodium	31 mg

Strawberry Watermelon Slush

Strawberry Watermelon Slush

Makes about 1 quart

1 pint (about ¾ pound) fresh strawberries,
    cleaned and hulled
2 cups seeded and cubed watermelon
⅓ cup sugar
⅓ cup vodka (optional)
¼ cup REALEMON® Lemon Juice from
    Concentrate
2 cups ice cubes

In blender container, combine all ingredients except
ice; blend well. Gradually add ice, blending until
smooth. Serve immediately. Garnish as desired.

Nutrients per serving (1 cup):			
Calories	110	Cholesterol	0 mg
Fat	1 g	Sodium	6 mg

Piña Colada Mocktail

Makes 4 servings

1½ cups DOLE® Pineapple Juice, chilled
⅓ cup canned real cream of coconut
1½ teaspoons rum extract
    Crushed ice

Place all ingredients in blender. Process until smooth.

Nutrients per serving:			
Calories	100	Cholesterol	0 mg
Fat	4 g	Sodium	13 mg

Cherry Punch

Makes 16 servings

1 can (6 ounces) frozen lemonade concentrate,
    thawed
5 cups DOLE® Pure & Light Mountain Cherry
    Juice, chilled
1 bottle (28 ounces) mineral water, chilled
    DOLE® Lemon slices for garnish
    Mint sprigs for garnish

Reconstitute lemonade according to directions in
large punch bowl. Stir in remaining ingredients. Serve
immediately.

Nutrients per serving:			
Calories	61	Cholesterol	0 mg
Fat	trace	Sodium	4 mg

Hot Spiced Lemonade

Makes 4 servings, about 4 cups

3 cups water
⅔ cup firmly packed light brown sugar
½ cup REALEMON® Lemon Juice from
    Concentrate
8 whole cloves
2 cinnamon sticks
    Additional cinnamon sticks for garnish
    (optional)

In medium saucepan, combine all ingredients except
garnish. Simmer, uncovered, 20 minutes to blend
flavors; remove spices. Serve hot in mugs with
cinnamon sticks, if desired.

To Microwave: In 1-quart glass measure, combine
ingredients as directed. Heat on HIGH (100% power) 4 to
5 minutes or until hot. Serve as directed.

Nutrients per serving:			
Calories	112	Cholesterol	0 mg
Fat	trace	Sodium	17 mg

ReaLemonade

Makes about 1 quart

½ cup sugar
½ cup REALEMON® Lemon Juice from
     Concentrate
3¼ cups cold water
     Ice

In pitcher, dissolve sugar in ReaLemon® brand; add
water. Cover; chill. Serve over ice.

Variations
Sparkling: *Substitute club soda for cold water.*

Slushy: *Reduce water to ½ cup. In blender container,
combine sugar, ReaLemon® brand and ½ cup water.
Gradually add 4 cups ice cubes, blending until smooth.
Serve immediately.*

Pink: *Stir in 1 to 2 teaspoons grenadine syrup or 1 to
2 drops red food coloring.*

Minted: *Stir in 2 to 3 drops peppermint extract.*

Low Calorie: *Omit sugar. Add 4 to 8 envelopes sugar
substitute or 1½ teaspoons liquid sugar substitute.*

Strawberry: *Increase sugar to ¾ cup. In blender or food
processor, purée 1 quart fresh strawberries, cleaned and
hulled (about 1½ pounds); add to lemonade.*

Grape: *Stir in 1 (6-ounce) can frozen grape juice
concentrate, thawed.*

Nutrients per serving (1 cup):			
Calories	97	Cholesterol	0 mg
Fat	trace	Sodium	6 mg

Frosty Fruit Shake

Makes 1 serving

1 can (6 ounces) *or* ¾ cup DOLE® Pineapple
     Juice, chilled
1 cup DOLE® Fresh Strawberries
1 ripe, medium DOLE® Banana, peeled
     Ice cubes

Place all ingredients in blender. Process until smooth.
Pour into tall glass.

Nutrients per serving:			
Calories	253	Cholesterol	0 mg
Fat	1 g	Sodium	5 mg

Orange Milk Shake

Makes 4 servings

2 cups skim milk
1 package (4-serving size) JELL-O® Brand
     Orange Flavor Sugar Free Gelatin
1 cup vanilla ice milk

Pour milk into blender container. Add remaining
ingredients; cover. Blend at high speed 30 seconds or
until smooth. Serve at once.

Note: *For a thicker shake, pour over crushed ice or add
1 cup crushed ice to ingredients in blender.*

Nutrients per serving:			
Calories	100	Cholesterol	10 mg
Fat	2 g	Sodium	150 mg

Sparkling Raspberry Mint Cooler

Makes 32 servings

1 to 2 cups fresh mint leaves
1 can (46 ounces) DOLE® Pineapple Juice,
     chilled
1 bottle (40 ounces) DOLE® Pure & Light
     Country Raspberry Juice
1 bottle (32 ounces) lemon-lime soda, chilled
1 package (12 ounces) frozen raspberries
1 DOLE® Lemon, thinly sliced

Rub mint leaves around sides of punch bowl, then
drop the bruised leaves in bottom of bowl. Combine
remaining ingredients in punch bowl.

Nutrients per serving (4 ounces):			
Calories	66	Cholesterol	0 mg
Fat	trace	Sodium	7 mg

Pear-Berry Crush

Makes 2 servings

1 package (10 ounces) unsweetened frozen raspberries or strawberries
1 fresh California Bartlett pear, cored and coarsely chopped
12 ice cubes, cracked

Place frozen berries, pear and ice in blender; process until smooth. Serve immediately.

Nutrients per serving:

Calories	97	Cholesterol	0 mg
Fat	trace	Sodium	3 mg

Favorite recipe from **California Tree Fruit Agreement**

Apple-Honey Shake

Makes 6 servings

4 cups chilled apple juice
2 cups chilled orange juice
¼ cup honey
2 teaspoons grated orange peel

Place all ingredients in blender; process until blended. Pour over ice in tall glasses. Garnish each with mint sprig, apple slices or long peel of orange, if desired. Serve immediately.

Nutrients per serving:

Calories	157	Cholesterol	0 mg
Fat	trace	Sodium	6 mg

Favorite recipe from **Western New York Apple Growers Association**

Tropical Blend

Makes 2 servings

1 cup DANNON® Plain Nonfat or Lowfat Yogurt
1 cup crushed pineapple in juice, undrained
½ cup orange juice
1 ripe kiwi fruit, peeled and sliced
2 tablespoons wheat germ

In blender container combine yogurt, pineapple, orange juice, kiwi fruit and wheat germ. Cover and blend on high speed until smooth. Serve immediately over ice or in frosted mugs.

Nutrients per serving:

Calories	210	Cholesterol	trace
Fat	1 g	Sodium	84 mg

Raspberry-Orange Brunch Smoothie

Makes 6 to 8 servings

3 cups orange juice
3 cups fresh raspberries, frozen
3 tablespoons sugar
1½ cups low fat milk

Place orange juice, raspberries and sugar in blender; process until smooth. Press mixture through sieve to remove raspberry seeds. Stir in milk and serve in chilled glasses.

Nutrients per serving:

Calories	178	Cholesterol	3 mg
Fat	1 g	Sodium	25 mg

Favorite recipe from **Wisconsin Milk Marketing Board © 1994**

Fresh Fruit Cubes

Makes 18 cubes

3 cups fresh California peaches, plums, nectarines or Bartlett pears, quartered
1 tablespoon lemon juice

Place fruit and lemon juice in blender; process until smooth. Pour into ice cube trays; freeze until firm. Serve in desired beverages.

Nutrients per serving (1 cube):

Calories	14	Cholesterol	0 mg
Fat	trace	Sodium	trace

Favorite recipe from **California Tree Fruit Agreement**

Plum Slush

Makes 8 servings

6 fresh California plums, coarsely chopped (2 cups)
1 can (6 ounces) frozen cranberry juice concentrate
20 ice cubes, cracked

Place all ingredients in blender; process until smooth. Serve immediately.

Nutrients per serving (½ cup):

Calories	48	Cholesterol	0 mg
Fat	trace	Sodium	0 mg

Favorite recipe from **California Tree Fruit Agreement**

Florida Citrus Shake

Makes 2 shakes

1 cup fresh Florida orange juice
½ cup fresh Florida grapefruit juice
1 ripe banana, peeled and cut into chunks
½ cup low fat vanilla yogurt
½ teaspoon vanilla extract

Place all ingredients in blender; process until smooth. Serve immediately.

Nutrients per serving (1 cup):			
Calories	180	Cholesterol	3 mg
Fat	1 g	Sodium	39 mg

Favorite recipe from **Florida Department of Citrus**

Sparkling Punch

Makes 4 servings

2 cups orange juice
3 tablespoons lemon juice (juice of 1 lemon), optional
¾ cup unsweetened pineapple juice (6 ounces)
1 cup unsweetened apple juice
1½ cups lemon or lime sparkling mineral water (12 ounces)

Place all ingredients in large pitcher; blend well. Pour over ice just before serving.

Nutrients per serving (1¼ cups):			
Calories	145	Cholesterol	0 mg
Fat	trace	Sodium	13 mg

Favorite recipe from **Western New York Apple Growers Association**

Peanutty Nog

Makes 2 servings

1 cup skim milk
2 teaspoons creamy peanut butter
2 teaspoons sugar
Dash pumpkin pie spice

Place all ingredients in blender or food processor; blend until well combined and frothy. Serve immediately.

Nutrients per serving:			
Calories	91	Cholesterol	2 mg
Fat	3 g	Sodium	85 mg

Favorite recipe from **The Sugar Association, Inc.**

Nectarine-Cantaloupe Smoothie

Makes 2 servings

1 fresh California nectarine, cubed
1 cup diced cantaloupe
½ cup plain low fat yogurt
1 teaspoon honey
3 ice cubes, cracked

Place nectarine and cantaloupe in blender; process until smooth. Add yogurt, honey and ice; process just until blended. Serve immediately.

Nutrients per serving (1¼ cups):			
Calories	103	Cholesterol	3 mg
Fat	1 g	Sodium	47 mg

Favorite recipe from **California Tree Fruit Agreement**

Iced Swiss Chocolate Peppermint

Makes 2 servings

2 cups strong brewed Swiss Dutch Almond coffee, chilled
1 drop peppermint extract
½ teaspoon unsweetened cocoa powder
2 teaspoons sugar
2 tablespoons low fat milk

Place all ingredients in blender; process until combined. Pour over ice and serve immediately.

Nutrients per serving:			
Calories	22	Cholesterol	trace
Fat	trace	Sodium	8 mg

Favorite recipe from **The Sugar Association, Inc.**

Fruitful Cooler

Makes 2 servings

1 fresh California Bartlett pear, cored and cubed
2 fresh California plums, chopped
½ cup plain low fat yogurt
¼ teaspoon vanilla extract
4 to 5 ice cubes, cracked

Place pear, plums, yogurt and vanilla in blender; process until smooth. Add ice and process until blended. Serve immediately.

Nutrients per serving (1 cup):			
Calories	118	Cholesterol	3 mg
Fat	2 g	Sodium	40 mg

Favorite recipe from **California Tree Fruit Agreement**

Why oversleep when a bevy of breakfast delights awaits? Quick-to-fix muffins, fluffy pancakes and hearty cereals will provide the necessary energy and stamina to meet the morning's challenges. Enjoy a leisurely brunch this weekend with slimmed-down versions of your favorite egg entrées.

Blintzes with Raspberry Sauce

Makes 10 servings

Raspberry Sauce (recipe follows)
1 (16-ounce) container low-fat cottage cheese (1% milkfat)
3 tablespoons EGG BEATERS® 99% Real Egg Product
½ teaspoon sugar
10 prepared Crêpes (recipe follows)

Prepare Raspberry Sauce. Set aside. In small bowl, combine cottage cheese, Egg Beaters® and sugar; spread about 2 tablespoonfuls mixture down center of each crêpe. Fold crêpes into thirds; fold top and bottom of each crêpe to meet in center, forming blintzes. In lightly greased nonstick skillet, over medium heat, place blintzes seam-side down; cook 4 minutes or until golden brown. Turn over; cook 4 more minutes or until golden brown. Top with Raspberry Sauce and garnish as desired.

Raspberry Sauce: In blender or food processor, purée 1 (16-ounce) package thawed frozen raspberries; strain. Stir in 2 tablespoons sugar.

Crêpes

1 cup all-purpose flour
1 cup skim milk
½ cup EGG BEATERS® 99% Real Egg Product
1 tablespoon FLEISCHMANN'S® Margarine, melted

In medium bowl, blend flour, milk, Egg Beaters® and margarine; let stand 30 minutes.

Heat lightly greased 8-inch nonstick skillet or crêpe pan over medium-high heat. Pour in scant ¼ cup batter, tilting pan to cover bottom. Cook 1 to 2 minutes; turn crêpe over and cook 30 seconds to 1 minute more. Place on waxed paper. Stir batter and repeat to make a total of 10 crêpes.

Nutrients per serving:

Calories	161	Cholesterol	2 mg
Fat	2 g	Sodium	231 mg

Latkes (Potato Pancakes)

Makes 12 pancakes

⅔ cup EGG BEATERS® 99% Real Egg Product
⅓ cup all-purpose flour
¼ cup grated onion
¼ teaspoon ground black pepper
4 large potatoes, peeled and shredded (about 4 cups)
3 tablespoons FLEISCHMANN'S® Margarine, divided
1½ cups sweetened applesauce

In medium bowl, combine Egg Beaters®, flour, onion and pepper; set aside.

Pat shredded potatoes dry with paper towel. Stir into Egg Beaters® mixture. In skillet, over medium-high heat, melt 1½ tablespoons margarine. For each pancake, spoon ⅓ cup potato mixture into skillet, spreading into 4-inch circle. Cook for 5 to 6 minutes, turning over once to brown both sides. Remove and keep warm. Repeat to make a total of 12 pancakes, using remaining margarine as needed. Garnish as desired and serve topped with applesauce.

Nutrients per serving (1 pancake plus 2 tablespoons applesauce):

Calories	115	Cholesterol	0 mg
Fat	3 g	Sodium	52 mg

Clockwise from top right: Jam French Toast Triangles (page 54),
Blintzes with Raspberry Sauce, Latkes (Potato Pancakes)

Rainbow Trout Breakfast Fillet

Rainbow Trout Breakfast Fillets

Makes 4 servings

½ cup all-purpose flour
1½ teaspoons paprika
1 teaspoon ground thyme
¼ teaspoon salt
Dash black pepper
4 CLEAR SPRINGS® Brand Idaho Rainbow
Trout fillets (4 ounces *each*)
1 egg, beaten
1 tablespoon olive oil

Combine flour, paprika, thyme, salt and pepper on waxed paper; set aside. Dip each trout fillet in egg; coat with seasoned flour mixture. Cook trout in hot oil in large skillet over medium-high heat 1 to 2 minutes per side or until fish flakes easily with fork. Serve with fruit and potatoes, if desired. Garnish as desired.

Nutrients per serving:

Calories	240	Cholesterol	115 mg
Fat	9 g	Sodium	179 mg

Jam French Toast Triangles

Makes 6 pieces

¼ cup preserves, any flavor
6 slices whole wheat bread, divided
6 tablespoons EGG BEATERS®
99% Real Egg Product
¼ cup skim milk
2 tablespoons FLEISCHMANN'S® Margarine
1 tablespoon sugar
¼ teaspoon ground cinnamon

Evenly divide and spread preserves on 3 bread slices; top with remaining bread slices to make 3 sandwiches, pressing to seal. Cut each sandwich diagonally in half. In shallow bowl, combine Egg Beaters® and skim milk. Dip each sandwich in egg mixture to coat.

In skillet or on griddle, over medium-high heat, brown sandwiches in margarine until golden brown on both sides. Combine sugar and cinnamon; sprinkle over sandwiches. Garnish as desired and serve warm.

Nutrients per serving (1 piece):

Calories	175	Cholesterol	1 mg
Fat	5 g	Sodium	224 mg

Banana Bran Loaf

Makes 1 loaf, 16 servings

1 cup mashed ripe bananas (about 2 large)
½ cup granulated sugar
⅓ cup liquid vegetable oil margarine
⅓ cup skim milk
2 egg whites, slightly beaten
1¼ cups all-purpose flour
1 cup QUAKER® Oat Bran hot cereal, uncooked
2 teaspoons baking powder
½ teaspoon baking soda

Heat oven to 350°F. Lightly spray 8×4-inch or 9×5-inch loaf pan with nonstick cooking spray, or oil lightly. Combine bananas, sugar, margarine, milk and egg whites; mix well. Add combined flour, oat bran, baking powder and baking soda, mixing just until moistened. Pour into prepared pan. Bake 55 to 60 minutes or until wooden toothpick inserted in center comes out clean. Cool 10 minutes; remove from pan. Cool completely on wire rack.

Tips: *To freeze bread slices, layer waxed paper between each slice of bread. Wrap securely in foil or place in freezer bag. Seal, label and freeze.*

To reheat bread slices, unwrap frozen bread slices and wrap in paper towels. Microwave at HIGH (100% power) about 30 seconds for each slice, or until warm.

Nutrients per serving (1 slice):

Calories	130	Cholesterol	0 mg
Fat	4 g	Sodium	110 mg

Rice Bran Granola Cereal

Makes 10 servings, 5 cups

2 cups uncooked old-fashioned rolled oats
1 cup crisp rice cereal
¾ cup rice bran
¾ cup raisins
⅓ cup slivered almonds
1 tablespoon ground cinnamon
⅓ cup honey
1 tablespoon margarine, melted
    Nonstick cooking spray

Combine oats, cereal, bran, raisins, almonds, and cinnamon in large bowl; stir in honey and margarine. Spread mixture on baking sheet coated with nonstick cooking spray. Bake in preheated 350°F oven for 8 to 10 minutes. Let cool. Serve as a topping for yogurt and/or fresh fruit. Store in a tightly covered container.

Tip: *Can be served as a cereal (with milk) or as a snack.*

Nutrients per serving (½ cup cereal only):			
Calories	199	Cholesterol	0 mg
Fat	7 g	Sodium	57 mg

Favorite recipe from **USA Rice Council**

Banana-Orange Muffins

Makes 12 muffins

2 cups all-purpose flour
1 tablespoon baking powder
¼ teaspoon salt
2 egg whites
½ cup *undiluted* CARNATION® Lite Evaporated
    Skimmed Milk
½ cup mashed very ripe banana
⅓ cup honey
¼ cup vegetable oil
1 teaspoon grated orange zest
1 tablespoon granulated sugar

In large bowl, combine flour, baking powder and salt; set aside. In small mixer bowl, slightly beat egg whites. Add evaporated skimmed milk, banana, honey, oil and orange zest; beat until blended. Add liquid ingredients to dry ingredients; stir *just* until moistened. Mixture will be lumpy. Spoon batter into 12 greased or paper-lined 2½-inch muffin cups. Sprinkle tops with sugar. Bake in preheated 400°F oven 13 to 15 minutes or until wooden pick inserted in center comes out clean. Remove from pan; cool on wire rack.

Nutrients per serving (1 muffin):			
Calories	169	Cholesterol	0 mg
Fat	5 g	Sodium	175 mg

Lemon Blueberry Poppy Seed Bread

Makes 1 loaf, 12 servings

Bread
1 package DUNCAN HINES® Bakery Style
    Blueberry Muffin Mix
2 tablespoons poppy seeds
1 egg
¾ cup water
1 tablespoon grated lemon peel

Drizzle
½ cup confectioners sugar
1 tablespoon lemon juice

1. Preheat oven to 350°F. Grease and flour 8×4-inch loaf pan.

2. Rinse blueberries with cold water and drain.

3. For Bread, combine muffin mix and poppy seeds in medium bowl. Break up any lumps. Add egg and water. Stir until moistened, about 50 strokes. Fold in blueberries and lemon peel. Pour into pan. Sprinkle with contents of topping packet from mix.

4. Bake at 350°F for 57 to 62 minutes or until wooden toothpick inserted in center comes out clean. Cool in pan 10 minutes. Loosen loaf from pan. Invert onto cooling rack. Turn right side up. Cool completely.

5. For Drizzle, combine confectioners sugar and lemon juice in small bowl. Stir until smooth. Drizzle over loaf.

Tip: *To help keep topping intact when removing loaf from pan, place aluminum foil over top.*

Nutrients per serving (1 slice):			
Calories	133	Cholesterol	18 mg
Fat	2 g	Sodium	186 mg

Lemon Blueberry Poppy Seed Bread

Streusel Bran Muffins

Makes 12 muffins

3 tablespoons all-purpose flour
2 tablespoons firmly packed brown sugar
1 tablespoon margarine, cold
1¼ cups all-purpose flour
1 tablespoon baking powder
½ teaspoon salt
½ teaspoon ground cinnamon
¼ teaspoon ground nutmeg
1½ cups KELLOGG'S® COMPLETE® Bran
   Flakes cereal
¾ cup skim milk
½ cup firmly packed brown sugar
2 egg whites
¼ cup vegetable oil
½ teaspoon vanilla
½ cup seedless raisins
   Vegetable cooking spray

1. In small bowl, combine 3 tablespoons flour and 2 tablespoons sugar. Using pastry blender, cut in margarine until mixture resembles coarse crumbs. Set aside for topping.

2. Stir together 1¼ cups flour, baking powder, salt and spices. Set aside.

3. In large mixing bowl, combine Kellogg's® Complete® Bran Flakes cereal and milk. Let stand about 3 minutes or until cereal softens. Add ½ cup sugar, egg whites, oil, vanilla and raisins. Mix well. Add flour mixture, stirring only until combined. Pour batter evenly into twelve 2½-inch muffin pan cups coated with cooking spray. Sprinkle with topping.

4. Bake at 400°F about 20 minutes or until lightly browned. Serve warm.

Nutrients per serving (1 muffin):			
Calories	190	Cholesterol	0 mg
Fat	6 g	Sodium	240 mg

Blintzes with Fresh Peach Sauce

Makes 4 servings

1 cup low fat cottage cheese
1 package (3 ounces) light cream cheese
   (Neufchâtel)
½ teaspoon vanilla extract
   Vegetable oil (optional)
4 flour tortillas (*each* 8 inches in diameter)
1 fresh California peach, sliced
   Fresh Peach Sauce (recipe follows)

Beat cheeses and vanilla in small bowl until well blended. Heat lightly oiled 10-inch nonstick skillet. Briefly heat 1 tortilla over medium heat just until soft, turning once. Remove tortilla and spoon ¼ of cheese mixture in center. Top with ¼ of peach slices. Fold 2 sides in, partially covering filling. Roll up to enclose filling and make rectangular package. Repeat with remaining filling and tortillas. Add small amount of oil, as needed, to skillet. Heat filled tortillas over medium-low heat until browned. Serve with warm Fresh Peach Sauce.

Fresh Peach Sauce

½ cup water
2 tablespoons sugar
2 tablespoons lemon juice
3 fresh California peaches, thinly sliced

Combine water, sugar and lemon juice in small saucepan. Bring to a boil. Boil, uncovered, 5 minutes. Remove from heat. Stir in peaches.

Nutrients per serving:			
Calories	272	Cholesterol	21 mg
Fat	9 g	Sodium	461 mg

Favorite recipe from **California Tree Fruit Agreement**

Banola Breakfast

Makes about 7 cups

3 cups uncooked rolled oats
1 cup wheat germ
1 cup shredded coconut
1 cup walnuts, chopped coarsely
¼ cup sesame seeds
½ cup honey
3 tablespoons molasses
1 cup raisins
   Sliced bananas (optional)
   Milk or yogurt (optional)

Preheat oven to 300°F. Combine all ingredients except raisins, bananas and milk in 14×10×2-inch roasting pan; mix well. Bake about 40 minutes or until golden brown, stirring several times. Stir in raisins. Cool completely. Store in airtight container. Serve with bananas and milk, if desired.

Nutrients per serving (¼ cup cereal mixture):			
Calories	135	Cholesterol	0 mg
Fat	5 g	Sodium	4 mg

Favorite recipe from **Wisconsin Milk Marketing Board © 1994**

Orange-Maple-Macadamia Bread

Makes 18 servings

2¼ cups all-purpose flour
1 teaspoon baking powder
1 teaspoon baking soda
⅛ teaspoon salt
1 egg, lightly beaten
¾ cup maple syrup
½ cup buttermilk
⅓ cup unsalted butter, melted and cooled
¼ cup Florida orange juice
2 tablespoons grated orange zest
½ cup coarsely chopped macadamia nuts
Orange-Maple Glaze (recipe follows)

Preheat oven to 350°F. Grease and flour 9×5×3-inch loaf pan. Combine flour, baking powder, baking soda and salt in medium bowl; set aside.

Whisk egg, syrup, buttermilk, butter, orange juice and orange zest in large bowl until blended. Stir in flour mixture just until combined; fold in macadamia nuts. Pour into prepared pan.

Bake 45 to 50 minutes until toothpick inserted in center comes out clean. Cool in pan 5 minutes. Remove from pan to wire rack. Brush top and sides with Orange-Maple Glaze. Cool completely. Cut into 18 slices.

Orange-Maple Glaze

1 tablespoon maple syrup
1 tablespoon Florida orange juice
1 tablespoon unsalted butter
½ teaspoon grated orange zest

Heat syrup, orange juice, butter and orange zest in small saucepan over low heat until well blended and warm, stirring occasionally.

Nutrients per serving (1 slice):

Calories	171	Cholesterol	23 mg
Fat	7 g	Sodium	116 mg

Favorite recipe from **Florida Department of Citrus**

Spiced Oranges

Makes 4 servings

4 oranges
¾ cup water
¼ cup lemon juice
3 tablespoons brown sugar
¼ teaspoon ground cinnamon
¼ teaspoon ground cloves
Dash ground ginger

Peel and section oranges, reserving 2-inch-long piece of peel. Cut orange sections into thirds. Combine remaining ingredients with ¼ cup orange pieces and reserved orange peel piece in noncorrosive medium saucepan. Bring to a boil over medium-high heat; reduce heat to low. Simmer 2 minutes. Place remaining orange pieces in medium bowl. Strain syrup mixture and pour over orange pieces; refrigerate 1 hour. To serve, spoon into bowls.

Nutrients per serving:

Calories	103	Cholesterol	0 mg
Fat	trace	Sodium	5 mg

Favorite recipe from **The Sugar Association, Inc.**

Breakfast Pears

Makes 4 servings

1 can (16 ounces) Bartlett pear halves
2 tablespoons maple-flavored syrup
2 teaspoons lemon juice
1½ teaspoons butter or margarine
¼ teaspoon ground nutmeg
Cooked oatmeal (optional)
1 cup low fat vanilla yogurt (optional)

To Microwave: Drain pears; place cut sides up in 8-inch square microwave-safe dish. Drizzle syrup and lemon juice over pears. Dot with butter and sprinkle with nutmeg. Cover with waxed paper and microwave on HIGH (100% power) 2 to 3 minutes. Baste with juice. Serve warm or cold over oatmeal *or* dollop with yogurt.

Nutrients per serving:

Calories	100	Cholesterol	4 mg
Fat	2 g	Sodium	20 mg

Favorite recipe from **Pacific Coast Canned Pear Service**

Blueberry-Lemon Muffins

Blueberry-Lemon Muffins

Makes 12 muffins

1¾ cups all-purpose flour
⅓ cup sugar
2½ teaspoons baking powder
¾ teaspoon salt
1 egg, beaten
1 cup DANNON® Plain or Lemon Lowfat Yogurt
⅓ cup vegetable oil
2 tablespoons milk
½ to 1 teaspoon grated lemon peel
¾ cup fresh or frozen blueberries

Preheat oven to 400°F. Grease muffin cups or line with paper baking cups. In a large bowl combine flour, sugar, baking powder and salt. In a medium bowl combine egg, yogurt, oil, milk and lemon peel; stir well. Add egg mixture all at once to flour mixture. Stir just until dry ingredients are moistened (batter should be lumpy). Gently fold blueberries into batter.

Fill prepared muffin cups ⅔ full. Bake 20 to 25 minutes or until golden and toothpick inserted into center comes out clean. Serve warm.

Nutrients per serving (1 muffin):			
Calories	170	Cholesterol	25 mg
Fat	7 g	Sodium	142 mg

Plum Good Topping

Makes 3 cups

8 fresh California plums, sliced
⅓ cup orange juice
2 to 4 tablespoons sugar to taste
1 stick cinnamon *or* ½ teaspoon ground cinnamon
½ cup currants or raisins
¼ cup almonds, coarsely chopped

Place all ingredients except almonds in large saucepan; bring to a boil over high heat. Cover and reduce heat to low; simmer 20 minutes. Stir in almonds. Serve topping over waffles, pancakes, cereal, yogurt or granola.

Nutrients per serving (¼ cup topping):			
Calories	82	Cholesterol	0 mg
Fat	2 g	Sodium	1 mg

Favorite recipe from **California Tree Fruit Agreement**

Eggs Dannon®

Makes 4 servings

4 eggs
4 thin slices Canadian bacon
1 cup DANNON® Plain Nonfat or Lowfat Yogurt
½ teaspoon dry mustard
Dash ground red pepper
2 English muffins, split and toasted

Spray a large skillet with vegetable cooking spray. Fill half full with water. Bring to a boil; reduce heat until water simmers. Break egg into a small dish and slide into water. Repeat with remaining eggs. Simmer 3 to 5 minutes or until yolks are firm.

In a large skillet over medium-high heat cook bacon 3 to 4 minutes or until heated through, turning once; set aside. In a small saucepan whisk together yogurt, mustard and red pepper. Cook and stir over low heat just until warm. *Do not boil.* Top each English muffin half with bacon slice, egg and ¼ cup sauce. Serve immediately.

Nutrients per serving:			
Calories	220	Cholesterol	230 mg
Fat	8 g	Sodium	670 mg

Breakfast in a Glass

Makes 4 servings

1 can (15 ounces) raspberries in heavy syrup, undrained*
1½ cups skim milk
1 cup vanilla frozen yogurt
¼ cup wheat bran or wheat germ (optional)
1 to 2 tablespoons honey

Place raspberries in blender or food processor; process until smooth. Strain through sieve, if desired. Return raspberry purée to blender. Add remaining ingredients; blend until smooth. To serve, pour into 4 glasses.

You may substitute any canned fruit for the raspberries.

Nutrients per serving:			
Calories	200	Cholesterol	3 mg
Fat	2 g	Sodium	78 mg

Favorite recipe from **Canned Food Information Council**

Country Breakfast Cereal

Makes 6 servings

3 cups cooked brown rice
2 cups skim milk
½ cup raisins or chopped prunes
1 tablespoon margarine (optional)
1 teaspoon ground cinnamon
⅛ teaspoon salt
    Honey or brown sugar (optional)
    Fresh fruit (optional)

Combine rice, milk, raisins, margarine, cinnamon, and salt in 2- to 3-quart saucepan. Bring to a boil; stir once or twice. Reduce heat to medium-low; cover and simmer 8 to 10 minutes or until thickened. Serve with honey and fresh fruit.

Nutrients per serving:			
Calories	174	Cholesterol	2 mg
Fat	1 g	Sodium	98 mg

Favorite recipe from **USA Rice Council**

Pineapple-Orange Sauce

Makes 8 servings, about 2 cups

1 can (20 ounces) DOLE® Pineapple Chunks in Juice, undrained
    Juice and grated peel from 1 DOLE® Orange
1 tablespoon cornstarch
1 tablespoon sugar
1 teaspoon ground ginger

Combine pineapple with juice, ½ cup orange juice and 1 teaspoon orange peel with remaining ingredients in saucepan. Cook and stir until sauce boils and thickens. Cool to room temperature.

Use sauce over frozen yogurt, pancakes or waffles.

Nutrients per serving (about ¼ cup sauce):			
Calories	64	Cholesterol	0 mg
Fat	trace	Sodium	1 mg

Pineapple-Orange Sauce

Lemon-Glazed Peach Muffins

Makes 8 muffins

1 cup all-purpose flour
3 tablespoons sugar
2 teaspoons baking powder
½ teaspoon salt
½ teaspoon pumpkin pie spice
1 can (16 ounces) sliced cling peaches in light syrup
1 cup KELLOGG'S® ALL-BRAN® Cereal
½ cup skim milk
1 egg white
2 tablespoons vegetable oil
    Lemon Sauce (recipe follows)

Stir together flour, sugar, baking powder, salt and pumpkin pie spice. Set aside. Drain peaches, reserving ⅓ cup syrup. Set aside 8 peach slices; chop remaining peach slices.

Measure Kellogg's® All-Bran® cereal, milk and ⅓ cup reserved syrup into large mixing bowl. Stir to combine. Let stand 2 minutes or until cereal is softened. Add egg white and oil. Beat well. Stir in chopped peaches.

Add flour mixture, stirring only until dry ingredients are moistened. Portion batter evenly into 8 lightly greased 2½-inch muffin pan cups. Place 1 peach slice over top of each muffin.

Bake at 400°F for 25 minutes or until golden brown. Serve warm with Lemon Sauce.

Lemon Sauce

⅓ cup sugar
2 tablespoons cornstarch
1½ cups cold water
1 teaspoon grated lemon peel
1 tablespoon lemon juice

Combine sugar and cornstarch in 2-quart saucepan. Add water, stirring until smooth. Cook over medium heat, stirring constantly, until mixture boils. Continue cooking and stirring 3 minutes longer. Remove from heat; stir in lemon peel and juice. Serve hot over warm peach muffins.

Nutrients per serving (1 muffin plus 3 tablespoons sauce):			
Calories	210	Cholesterol	1 mg
Fat	4 g	Sodium	355 mg

Bacon Morning Muffins

Makes 12 muffins

12 slices LOUIS RICH® Turkey Bacon, cut into
 ¼-inch pieces
1¼ cups all-purpose flour
1 cup quick-cooking oats, uncooked
2 teaspoons baking powder
½ cup skim milk
⅓ cup honey
¼ cup corn oil
2 large egg whites

Combine Turkey Bacon, flour, oats and baking powder in large mixing bowl. Combine remaining ingredients; add to bacon mixture. Stir just until moistened (batter will be lumpy). Spray 12 (2½-inch) muffin cups with nonstick cooking spray or line with paper bake cups. Spoon batter into muffin cups. Bake in 400°F oven 15 minutes. Refrigerate or freeze leftover muffins.

Nutrients per serving (1 muffin):

Calories	185	Cholesterol	10 mg
Fat	8 g	Sodium	260 mg

Breakfast in a Cup

Italian Baked Frittata

Makes 6 servings

1 cup broccoli flowerettes
½ cup sliced mushrooms
½ small red bell pepper, cut into rings
2 green onions, cut into 1-inch pieces
2 teaspoons FLEISCHMANN'S® Margarine
2 (8-ounce) containers EGG BEATERS®
 99% Real Egg Product
½ cup low-sodium low-fat cottage cheese
 (1% milkfat)
2 tablespoons GREY POUPON® Dijon Mustard
½ teaspoon Italian seasoning

In 10-inch nonstick ovenproof skillet, over medium-high heat, cook and stir broccoli, mushrooms, red pepper and green onions in margarine until tender-crisp, about 3 minutes. Remove from heat.

In large bowl, with electric mixer at medium speed, beat Egg Beaters®, cottage cheese, mustard and Italian seasoning until foamy, about 3 minutes. Pour into skillet over vegetables. Bake at 375°F for 20 to 25 minutes or until set. Serve immediately.

Nutrients per serving:

Calories	68	Cholesterol	1 mg
Fat	2 g	Sodium	270 mg

Breakfast in a Cup

Makes 12 servings

3 cups cooked rice
1 cup (4 ounces) shredded Cheddar cheese,
 divided
1 can (4 ounces) diced green chilies, drained
1 jar (2 ounces) diced pimientos, drained
⅓ cup skim milk
2 eggs, beaten
½ teaspoon ground cumin
½ teaspoon salt
½ teaspoon ground black pepper
 Nonstick cooking spray

Combine rice, ½ cup cheese, chilies, pimientos, milk, eggs, cumin, salt, and pepper in large bowl. Divide mixture evenly into 12 muffin cups coated with nonstick cooking spray. Sprinkle with remaining ½ cup cheese. Bake at 400°F for 15 minutes or until set.

Tip: *Breakfast in a Cup may be stored in the freezer in freezer bags or tightly sealed containers. To reheat, microwave each frozen cup on HIGH (100% power) 1 minute.*

Nutrients per serving (1 cup):

Calories	123	Cholesterol	45 mg
Fat	4 g	Sodium	368 mg

Favorite recipe from **USA Rice Council**

Plum Oatmeal Muffins

Makes 18 muffins

5 fresh California plums
2 cups all-purpose flour
1¾ cups uncooked rolled oats
¾ cup packed brown sugar
3 teaspoons baking powder
1 teaspoon salt
1 teaspoon grated orange peel
1 egg
⅓ cup vegetable oil
1 teaspoon vanilla extract

Preheat oven to 350°F. Cut up 3 plums to measure 1 cup and place in blender or food processor; process until smooth. Coarsely chop remaining 2 plums; set aside. Combine flour, oats, brown sugar, baking powder, salt and orange peel in large bowl. Combine puréed plums, egg, oil and vanilla in small bowl until blended; stir into flour mixture just until blended. Fold in reserved plums. Spoon evenly into 18 (2½-inch) nonstick muffin cups.

Bake 30 to 35 minutes or until wooden pick inserted in center comes out clean. Cool in pan 10 minutes. Remove from pan. Serve warm or cool completely on wire racks.

Nutrients per serving (1 muffin):			
Calories	165	Cholesterol	15 mg
Fat	5 g	Sodium	170 mg

Favorite recipe from **California Tree Fruit Agreement**

Spicy Pears

Makes about 2 cups

2 cups cubed U.S.A. pears, peeled if desired
¾ cup water
¼ cup sugar
3 teaspoons cornstarch
⅛ teaspoon *each* ground allspice and ground cinnamon
Dash *each* salt and ground nutmeg

Heat pears and water in large saucepan over medium heat. Bring to a boil; simmer 5 to 10 minutes until pears are fork-tender. Combine remaining ingredients in small bowl; stir into pear mixture. Cook and stir until thickened.

Serving Tip: *Spicy Pears are delicious served warm over waffles, pancakes or French toast.*

Nutrients per serving (¼ cup):			
Calories	51	Cholesterol	0 mg
Fat	trace	Sodium	16 mg

Favorite recipe from **Oregon Washington California Pear Bureau**

Florida Orange Suncakes with Blueberry-Orange Sauce

Makes 12 pancakes

2 eggs, separated
⅔ cup nonfat ricotta cheese
¼ cup low fat milk
6 tablespoons all-purpose flour
1 tablespoon grated orange zest
2 teaspoons sugar
¼ teaspoon baking powder
  Pinch salt
1 tablespoon vegetable oil
  Blueberry-Orange Sauce (recipe follows)

Add egg yolks and ricotta cheese to food processor or blender; process until smooth. Add milk, flour, orange zest, sugar, baking powder and salt; process until completely blended. Beat egg whites in large bowl with electric mixer until stiff peaks form. Fold in cheese mixture just until combined.

Heat oil in large nonstick skillet over medium heat until hot. Drop batter by ¼ cup measure onto skillet. Cook about 3 minutes or until top is bubbly and looks dry; turn and cook other side 1 to 2 minutes until golden brown. Repeat with remaining batter. Serve hot with Blueberry-Orange Sauce.

Blueberry-Orange Sauce

½ cup fresh or thawed frozen blueberries
¼ cup Florida orange juice concentrate
1 tablespoon sugar
1 teaspoon grated orange zest
½ cup fresh Florida orange sections, cut into bite-sized pieces

Combine all ingredients in medium saucepan; heat over medium heat 5 to 7 minutes until thick and syrupy, stirring frequently. Pour over Florida Orange Suncakes.

Nutrients per serving (2 pancakes with 3 tablespoons sauce):			
Calories	173	Cholesterol	71 mg
Fat	4 g	Sodium	115 mg

Favorite recipe from **Florida Department of Citrus**

Baked Banana Doughnuts

Makes about 22 doughnuts

2 ripe bananas, mashed
2 egg whites
1 tablespoon vegetable oil
1 cup packed brown sugar
1½ cups all-purpose flour
¾ cup whole wheat flour
2 teaspoons baking powder
½ teaspoon baking soda
¼ teaspoon pumpkin pie spice
1 tablespoon granulated sugar
2 tablespoons chopped walnuts (optional)

Preheat oven to 425°F. Spray baking sheet with nonstick cooking spray. Beat bananas, egg whites, oil and brown sugar in large bowl with electric mixer or process in food processor. Add flours, baking powder, baking soda and pumpkin pie spice. Mix until well blended. Let stand 5 minutes for dough to rise.

Drop 1 heaping tablespoon dough onto baking sheet. Using thin rubber spatula or butter knife, scoop out doughnut hole from center of dough (if dough sticks, spray spatula or knife with cooking spray). Using spatula, smooth outside edges of dough into round doughnut shape. Repeat with remaining dough. Sprinkle with granulated sugar and walnuts, if desired. Bake 6 to 10 minutes until tops are golden.

Baked Pumpkin Doughnuts: *Substitute 8 ounces canned pumpkin (not pumpkin pie filling) for bananas.*

Nutrients per serving (1 banana doughnut):

Calories	105	Cholesterol	0 mg
Fat	1 g	Sodium	29 mg

Favorite recipe from **The Sugar Association, Inc.**

French Toast

Makes 6 servings

1 egg
4 egg whites
¼ cup skim milk
½ teaspoon almond extract
3 tablespoons brown sugar, divided
¼ teaspoon ground cinnamon
1 teaspoon vegetable oil
6 slices bread
1 ripe banana, peeled and sliced

Beat egg and egg whites with whisk in large bowl until frothy. Whisk in milk, almond extract, 2 tablespoons brown sugar and cinnamon until well blended. Heat oil in large nonstick skillet over medium-high heat until hot. Dip 3 slices bread into egg mixture. Place bread in skillet; cook 4 to 6 minutes until browned, turning once. (If necessary, spray pan with nonstick cooking spray.) Repeat with remaining 3 slices. Top slices evenly with banana slices; sprinkle with remaining 1 tablespoon brown sugar. Serve immediately.

Nutrients per serving (1 slice):

Calories	152	Cholesterol	37 mg
Fat	3 g	Sodium	205 mg

Favorite recipe from **The Sugar Association, Inc.**

Granola-Bran Muffins

Makes 36 muffins

1 cup boiling water
2½ cups whole bran cereal
2 eggs, lightly beaten
2 cups buttermilk
½ cup vegetable oil
½ cup finely chopped apple
2 cups all-purpose flour
1 cup sugar
½ cup uncooked quick-cooking oats
½ cup wheat germ
2 teaspoons baking soda
½ teaspoon salt
1 cup raisins
½ cup shredded coconut
½ cup chopped almonds, walnuts or pecans

Pour water over bran cereal in medium bowl; cool. Preheat oven to 400°F. Grease 36 (2½-inch) muffin cups. Stir eggs, buttermilk, oil and apple into cooled bran mixture. Combine flour, sugar, oats, wheat germ, baking soda and salt in large bowl. Stir in bran mixture until blended. Stir in raisins, coconut and almonds. Spoon into prepared muffin cups, filling each ⅔ full.

Bake about 22 minutes or until wooden pick inserted in center comes out clean. Cool in pans 10 minutes. Remove from pans. Serve warm or cool completely on wire racks.

Nutrients per serving (1 muffin):

Calories	135	Cholesterol	12 mg
Fat	5 g	Sodium	131 mg

Favorite recipe from **Wisconsin Milk Marketing Board © 1994**

Fresh Strawberry Banana Omelets

Makes 2 servings

1 cup fresh strawberries, hulled and sliced
1 banana, sliced
1½ tablespoons sugar
¼ teaspoon grated lemon peel
1 tablespoon fresh lemon juice
1 cup egg substitute *or* 4 eggs, beaten
¼ teaspoon salt
2 tablespoons margarine, divided

Combine strawberries, banana, sugar, lemon peel and juice in medium bowl; mix lightly. Cover; let stand 15 minutes. Meanwhile, mix egg substitute and salt with fork in small bowl.

Heat 1 tablespoon margarine in 8-inch omelet pan or skillet over medium-high heat until just hot enough to sizzle a drop of water. Pour in half of egg mixture (about ½ cup). Mixture should set at edges at once. With back of pancake turner, carefully push cooked portions of edges toward center so that uncooked portions flow underneath. Slide pan rapidly back and forth over heat to keep mixture in motion. While top is still moist and creamy-looking, spoon ½ cup fruit mixture over half of omelet. With pancake turner, fold in half; turn onto heated platter. Keep warm. Repeat with remaining margarine, egg mixture and ½ cup fruit mixture. Top omelets with remaining fruit mixture.

Nutrients per serving:

Calories	267	Cholesterol	1 mg
Fat	10 g	Sodium	556 mg

Irish Soda Bacon Bread

Makes 12 to 15 servings

4 cups all-purpose flour
3 tablespoons sugar
1½ tablespoons low-sodium baking powder
1 teaspoon baking soda
6 tablespoons unsalted margarine or butter, cold
1 cup golden raisins
6 slices ARMOUR® Lower Salt Bacon, cooked crisp and crumbled
2 eggs
1½ cups buttermilk

Preheat oven to 375°F. Combine flour, sugar, baking powder and baking soda in large bowl; cut in cold margarine until mixture resembles coarse crumbs.

Stir in raisins and bacon. Beat eggs slightly in small bowl; reserve 1 tablespoon egg. Add buttermilk and remaining eggs to flour mixture; stir to make soft dough.

Turn out onto lightly floured surface; knead 1 to 2 minutes or until smooth. Shape dough into round loaf. Spray round 2-quart casserole dish with nonstick cooking spray; place dough in dish. With floured knife, cut a 4-inch cross about ¼ inch deep on top of loaf. Brush loaf with reserved egg.

Bake 55 to 65 minutes or until wooden toothpick inserted in center comes out clean. (Cover loaf with foil during last 30 minutes of baking to prevent overbrowning.) Cool on wire rack 10 minutes; remove from dish. Serve with light cream cheese or honey butter, if desired.

Nutrients per serving:

Calories	231	Cholesterol	40 mg
Fat	7 g	Sodium	130 mg

Fiber-Rich Muffins

Makes 12 muffins

1 inner-pack KAVLI® Rye-Bran Crispbread (½ package)
1 cup skim milk
½ cup unsweetened applesauce
1 egg, lightly beaten
2 tablespoons firmly packed brown sugar
2 tablespoons vegetable oil
1 tablespoon molasses
½ teaspoon ground cinnamon
¼ teaspoon ground cloves
¼ teaspoon ground nutmeg
¼ teaspoon salt
1¼ cups all-purpose flour
1 tablespoon baking powder

Preheat oven to 400°F. Break crispbread into chunks; process in food processor or blender until finely crushed. Place in mixing bowl. Heat milk to almost boiling. Pour over bread crumbs. Stir to mix. Let stand 5 minutes. Stir applesauce and egg into crumb mixture. Break up large lumps, if present. Add sugar, oil, molasses, spices and salt. Combine flour and baking powder. Add to crumb mixture, stirring just until flour is moistened. Fill 12 greased 2½-inch muffin cups half full. Bake 20 to 25 minutes or until browned. Remove from pans and cool slightly on wire rack before serving.

Nutrients per serving (1 muffin):

Calories	124	Cholesterol	22 mg
Fat	3 g	Sodium	152 mg

Fresh Strawberry Banana Omelet

Bran-Cherry Bread

Makes 1 loaf, 15 slices

    2 cups all-purpose flour
    ¾ cup sugar, divided
    1 tablespoon baking powder
    1 teaspoon salt
    ½ teaspoon ground nutmeg
 1½ cups KELLOGG'S® CRACKLIN' OAT BRAN®
        Cereal
 1¼ cups skim milk
    1 egg
    2 tablespoons vegetable oil
    1 jar (10 ounces) maraschino cherries, drained
        and finely chopped
    1 cup chopped walnuts, divided
    1 tablespoon margarine

Combine flour, ½ cup sugar, baking powder, salt and
nutmeg. Set aside.

Measure Kellogg's® Cracklin' Oat Bran® cereal and
milk into large mixing bowl. Let stand 10 minutes or
until cereal is softened. Add egg and oil. Beat well.
Stir in flour mixture. Set aside 2 tablespoons
chopped cherries. Fold remaining cherries and
¾ cup nuts into batter. Spread in 9×5×3-inch loaf
pan coated with nonstick cooking spray.

Melt margarine in small skillet until bubbly. Remove
from heat. Stir in remaining ¼ cup sugar, remaining
¼ cup nuts and reserved cherries. Sprinkle over
batter.

Bake at 350°F about 1 hour. Cool in pan on wire rack
10 minutes. Remove from pan.

Nutrients per serving (1 slice):

Calories	240	Cholesterol	20 mg
Fat	9 g	Sodium	260 mg

Bran-Cherry Bread

Double Bran-Lemon Muffins

Makes 12 muffins

    1 cup 100% wheat bran cereal
    ½ cup oat bran
        Grated peel of 1 SUNKIST® Lemon
    ½ cup fresh squeezed lemon juice (3 SUNKIST®
        Lemons)
    ½ cup nonfat milk
 1¼ cups all-purpose flour
    2 teaspoons baking powder
    ½ teaspoon baking soda
    ¼ cup firmly packed brown sugar
    2 egg whites
    ¼ cup honey
    ¼ cup vegetable oil

In medium bowl, combine wheat bran cereal, oat
bran, lemon peel, lemon juice and milk; let stand
10 minutes. In large bowl, sift together flour, baking
powder and baking soda; stir in brown sugar. In small
bowl, beat egg whites until foamy; add honey and oil.
Stir egg mixture into bran mixture; mix well. Add to
dry ingredients all at once; stir just until dry
ingredients are moistened. Quickly spoon into
12 paper-lined 2½-inch muffin cups; fill about
⅞ full. (Or, spray muffin pan with nonstick cooking
spray.) Bake at 400°F for 20 to 23 minutes.

Nutrients per serving (1 muffin):

Calories	153	Cholesterol	0 mg
Fat	5 g	Sodium	138 mg

Weekend Skillet Breakfast

Makes 4 servings

 12 slices LOUIS RICH® Turkey Bacon, cut into
        ½-inch pieces
    1 medium potato, peeled and cut into small
        cubes
    2 green onions with tops, thinly sliced
    ½ teaspoon chili powder
    1 carton (8 ounces) cholesterol-free egg
        substitute *or* 4 eggs, beaten

Place Turkey Bacon and potato in nonstick skillet.
Cook over medium heat about 12 minutes, stirring
frequently until potatoes are fork-tender. Stir in
onions and chili powder; pour egg substitute evenly
over mixture. Cover; reduce heat to low. Cook
5 minutes more or until mixture is set. Cut into
wedges.

Nutrients per serving:

Calories	155	Cholesterol	30 mg
Fat	7 g	Sodium	650 mg

Breakfast Burrito

Breakfast Burritos

Makes 2 burritos

4 slices LOUIS RICH® Turkey Bacon
2 flour tortillas (7 inches in diameter)
2 tablespoons shredded sharp Cheddar cheese
2 large egg whites
1 tablespoon chopped mild chilies
  Salsa or taco sauce (optional)
  Additional shredded sharp Cheddar cheese
  (optional)

Cook and stir Turkey Bacon in nonstick skillet over medium-high heat 8 to 10 minutes or until lightly browned.

Place 2 turkey bacon slices on each tortilla; sprinkle each tortilla with 1 tablespoon cheese.

Beat egg whites and chilies; add to hot skillet. Cook and stir about 2 minutes or until set.

Divide egg mixture between tortillas. Fold tortillas over filling. Top with salsa and additional cheese, if desired.

To keep burritos warm: *Wrap filled burritos in foil and place in warm oven up to 30 minutes.*

Nutrients per serving (1 burrito):

Calories	220	Cholesterol	25 mg
Fat	9 g	Sodium	470 mg

Bran Sticky Buns

Makes 9 buns

1 cup NABISCO® 100% Bran, divided
⅓ cup firmly packed light brown sugar
¼ cup FLEISCHMANN'S® Margarine, melted
1 apple, cored and sliced
2 cups buttermilk baking mix
½ cup water
¼ cup EGG BEATERS® 99% Real Egg Product
  or 2 egg whites

In small bowl, combine ¼ cup bran, brown sugar and margarine; spread in 8×8×2-inch pan. Top with apple slices; set aside. In medium bowl, combine baking mix, remaining ¾ cup bran, water and Egg Beaters® until soft dough forms. Drop dough by ¼ cupfuls over apple slices. Bake at 450°F for 13 to 15 minutes or until done. Invert onto heat-proof plate, leaving pan over buns for 2 to 3 minutes. Cool slightly; serve warm.

Nutrients per serving (1 bun):

Calories	225	Cholesterol	0 mg
Fat	6 g	Sodium	435 mg

Papaya Muffin

Papaya Muffins

Makes 12 muffins

1½ cups whole wheat flour
1 tablespoon baking powder
½ teaspoon salt
1½ cups KELLOGG'S® ALL-BRAN® Cereal
1¼ cups skim milk
¼ cup honey
¼ cup vegetable oil
1 tablespoon dark molasses
1 egg
¾ cup chopped fresh papaya
2 teaspoons finely chopped crystallized ginger

Stir together flour, baking powder and salt. Set aside. Measure Kellogg's® All-Bran® cereal and milk into large mixing bowl. Stir to combine. Let stand 2 minutes or until cereal is softened. Add honey, oil, molasses and egg. Beat well. Stir in papaya and ginger.

Add flour mixture, stirring only until combined. Portion batter evenly into 12 greased 2½-inch muffin pan cups.

Bake at 400°F about 25 minutes or until muffins are golden brown. Serve warm.

Nutrients per serving (1 muffin):			
Calories	160	Cholesterol	19 mg
Fat	6 g	Sodium	314 mg

Honey-Bran Muffins

Makes 12 servings

¾ cup 100% bran cereal
¼ cup nonfat milk
1 cup all-purpose flour
1 teaspoon baking soda
¼ teaspoon salt
2 extra-ripe, medium DOLE® Bananas, peeled
1 egg *or* 3 egg whites
¼ cup honey
¼ cup vegetable oil
¾ cup DOLE® Raisins

Combine cereal and milk in small bowl; let stand 10 minutes to soften. Stir in flour, baking soda and salt. Meanwhile, place bananas in blender. Process until puréed; use 1 cup for recipe. Combine 1 cup banana purée, egg, honey and oil in large bowl. Add cereal mixture to banana mixture, stirring until just moistened. Fold in raisins. Spoon batter into 12 greased 2½-inch muffin cups. Bake in 375°F oven 20 minutes. Cool in pan on wire rack 3 minutes. Remove from pan.

Prep time: 20 minutes
Bake time: 20 minutes

Nutrients per serving (1 muffin):			
Calories	169	Cholesterol	23 mg
Fat	5 g	Sodium	165 mg

Breakfast Sausage Bake

Makes 12 servings

2 tablespoons margarine
1 pound fresh mushrooms, finely chopped
1 cup dry fine bread crumbs
1 package (1 pound) LOUIS RICH® Turkey Breakfast Sausage, thawed
1 red or green bell pepper, chopped
3 tablespoons chopped fresh parsley *or* 1 tablespoon dried parsley flakes
¼ teaspoon ground red pepper
2 cartons (8 ounces each) cholesterol-free egg substitute *or* 8 eggs, beaten

Preheat oven to 350°F. Melt margarine in large nonstick skillet over medium-high heat. Add mushrooms. Cook and stir about 10 minutes or until mixture boils and moisture evaporates. Remove from heat; stir in bread crumbs. Spray 13×9-inch baking dish with nonstick cooking spray. Press mushroom mixture onto bottom of prepared baking dish to form crust.

In same nonstick skillet, cook sausage over medium heat about 12 minutes, breaking sausage apart into small pieces and stirring frequently until lightly browned. Remove from heat.

Stir in chopped bell pepper, parsley and ground red pepper. Spread sausage mixture over crust; pour egg substitute evenly over mixture. Bake 25 to 30 minutes or until mixture is set.

Note: *For 6 servings, use half of the ingredients; prepare and bake as above in 9-inch pie plate.*

Nutrients per serving:			
Calories	140	Cholesterol	20 mg
Fat	6 g	Sodium	370 mg

Frittata Primavera

Makes 4 servings

- 1 medium onion, chopped
- 1 medium red or green bell pepper, cut into strips
- 1 medium potato, peeled and grated (about 1 cup)
- 1 cup coarsely chopped broccoli
- 1 teaspoon dried oregano leaves, crushed
- ⅛ teaspoon ground black pepper
- 1 tablespoon FLEISCHMANN'S® Margarine
- 1 (8-ounce) container EGG BEATERS® 99% Real Egg Product

In 10-inch nonstick skillet or omelet pan, cook and stir onion, bell pepper, potato, broccoli, oregano and black pepper in margarine until vegetables are tender-crisp.

In small bowl, with electric mixer at high speed, beat Egg Beaters® for 2 minutes until light and fluffy; pour over vegetables. Cover and cook over medium heat for 5 to 7 minutes until eggs are set. Serve from pan or carefully invert onto warm serving plate. Serve immediately.

Nutrients per serving:			
Calories	97	Cholesterol	0 mg
Fat	3 g	Sodium	109 mg

Praline Pancakes

Makes 6 servings

- 1½ cups skim milk
- 2 tablespoons margarine, melted
- 2 teaspoons brandy
- 1 teaspoon vanilla extract
- 1 cup all-purpose flour
- 2 tablespoons sugar
- 1 teaspoon baking powder
- ¼ teaspoon salt
- ⅛ teaspoon ground cinnamon
- 1 cup cooked rice, cooled
- ⅓ cup pecans, coarsely chopped
- 4 egg whites, stiffly beaten
  Nonstick cooking spray
  Low-calorie syrup (optional)

Combine milk, margarine, brandy, vanilla, flour, sugar, baking powder, salt, and cinnamon in large bowl; stir until smooth. Stir in rice and pecans. Fold in beaten egg whites. Pour scant ¼ cup batter onto hot griddle coated with nonstick cooking spray. Cook over medium heat until bubbles form on top and underside is lightly browned. Turn to brown other side. Serve warm drizzled with syrup.

Nutrients per serving:			
Calories	252	Cholesterol	1 mg
Fat	9 g	Sodium	387 mg

Favorite recipe from **USA Rice Council**

Apple Cinnamon Muffins

Makes 18 muffins

- 2¼ cups oat bran cereal
- ¼ cup firmly packed brown sugar
- 1 tablespoon baking powder
- 1¼ teaspoons ground cinnamon
- ¾ cup apple juice or cider
- ½ cup skim milk
- 2 egg whites
- 2 tablespoons vegetable oil
- 1 medium apple, peeled and chopped
- ¼ cup chopped walnuts
- ¼ cup raisins

Preheat oven to 400°F. In large bowl, combine cereal, brown sugar, baking powder and cinnamon. In small bowl, combine apple juice, milk, egg whites and oil. Stir into flour mixture just until moistened. Add chopped apple, walnuts and raisins. Fill 18 greased medium muffin cups ¾ full with batter. Bake 15 to 17 minutes or until golden.

Nutrients per serving (1 muffin):			
Calories	89	Cholesterol	trace
Fat	3 g	Sodium	68 mg

Favorite recipe from **Western New York Apple Growers Association**

Apple Cinnamon Muffins

Lemon Yogurt Coffeecake

Lemon Yogurt Coffeecake

Makes 12 to 16 servings

⅓ cup canola oil
⅔ cup honey
1 egg
¾ cup cholesterol-free egg substitute
1½ teaspoons lemon extract
1¾ cups all-purpose flour
¾ cup whole wheat pastry flour or whole wheat flour
2½ teaspoons baking powder
1 cup DANNON® Lemon Lowfat Yogurt
1 tablespoon grated lemon peel
1 cup coarsely chopped cranberries

Preheat oven to 350°F. Grease and flour a 9-cup kugelhopf or 9-inch bundt pan. In a large bowl beat oil and honey until creamy. Add egg, egg substitute and lemon extract; beat until blended. In a medium bowl combine flours and baking powder; stir into honey mixture alternately with yogurt. Fold in lemon peel and cranberries. Pour into prepared pan; smooth top.

Bake 30 to 35 minutes or until toothpick inserted into center comes out clean. Cool in pan on wire rack. To serve, invert coffeecake onto platter or cake plate.

Nutrients per serving:

Calories	230	Cholesterol	20 mg
Fat	7 g	Sodium	43 mg

Turkey Bacon Breakfast Burritos

Makes 10 servings

10 slices Turkey Bacon, cut into ¼-inch pieces
½ cup chopped green bell pepper
½ cup chopped onion
5 eggs
½ cup skim milk
¼ teaspoon black pepper
1 cup grated reduced fat Cheddar cheese
10 (8-inch) flour tortillas
Salsa (optional)

Cook bacon, green pepper and onion in large nonstick skillet over medium-high heat 12 to 15 minutes until bacon is lightly browned, stirring frequently. Remove from heat.

Whisk eggs, milk and black pepper in small bowl until blended. Pour egg mixture over bacon mixture. Cook over low heat 2 minutes or until eggs are almost set, stirring frequently. Remove from heat; stir in cheese.

Place ¼ cup egg mixture on lower ⅓ of each tortilla. Roll up tortillas and place in 13×9-inch microwave-safe dish; cover with vented plastic wrap. Microwave on HIGH (100% power) 2 to 3 minutes or until burritos are hot. To serve, drizzle salsa over burritos, if desired.

Nutrients per serving:

Calories	228	Cholesterol	124 mg
Fat	7 g	Sodium	513 mg

Favorite recipe from **National Turkey Federation**

Whole Wheat French Toast with Florida Orange Slices

Makes 4 slices

1 egg
2 egg whites
1 tablespoon low fat milk
1 teaspoon grated orange zest
½ teaspoon vanilla extract
⅛ teaspoon ground cinnamon
1 tablespoon vegetable oil
4 slices whole wheat toast
Florida Orange Slices (recipe follows)

Beat egg, egg whites, milk, orange zest, vanilla and cinnamon in shallow bowl until blended.

Heat oil over medium heat in large nonstick skillet. Dip bread in egg mixture and add to skillet. Cook, turning once, until browned on both sides, 3 to 4 minutes per side. Repeat with remaining slices. Serve hot with Florida Orange Slices.

Florida Orange Slices

2 seedless Florida oranges, peeled (white pith removed), sliced into rounds (not segments)
2 teaspoons sugar
½ teaspoon vanilla extract

Combine orange slices, sugar and vanilla in small bowl, tossing to coat. Let stand 1 hour to allow flavors to blend.

Nutrients per serving (1 slice with ¼ of orange slices):

Calories	153	Cholesterol	54 mg
Fat	5 g	Sodium	204 mg

Favorite recipe from **Florida Department of Citrus**

Cheese "Danish"

Makes 20 servings

1 tablespoon sugar
1 teaspoon ground cinnamon
5 flour tortillas (6 or 7 inches in diameter)
Nonstick cooking spray
1 cup cold skim milk
1 package (4-serving size) JELL-O® Vanilla
Flavor Sugar Free Instant Pudding and Pie
Filling
1 container (8 ounces) light pasteurized process
cream cheese product
2 cups thawed COOL WHIP® LITE® Whipped
Topping
1 square BAKER'S® Semi-Sweet Chocolate

Heat oven to 350°F.

Mix sugar and cinnamon. Spray tortillas with
nonstick cooking spray. Sprinkle each tortilla with
scant ½ teaspoon sugar-cinnamon mixture. Turn
tortillas over; repeat process. Cut each tortilla into
4 wedges. Stand rounded edge of each tortilla wedge
in bottom of muffin cup by curling in sides. Bake
10 minutes or until lightly browned and crispy. Cool
in pan.

Pour milk into large mixing bowl. Add pudding mix.
Beat at low speed with electric mixer until well
blended, 1 to 2 minutes. Beat in cream cheese
product at medium speed until smooth. Gently stir in
whipped topping. Refrigerate at least 1 hour.

To serve, fill each tortilla shell with scant 3
tablespoons topping mixture using pastry bag or
spoon. Place chocolate in small plastic sandwich bag

or self-closing bag. Microwave on HIGH (100%)
about 1 minute or until chocolate is melted. Fold over
top of bag tightly; snip off one corner (about ⅛ inch).
Holding bag tightly at top, drizzle chocolate through
opening over prepared desserts. Refrigerate until
chocolate sets, about 5 minutes.

*Note: Freeze any leftover "Danish." Thaw in refrigerator as
needed.*

Nutrients per serving (1 "Danish"):

Calories	90	Cholesterol	5 mg
Fat	4 g	Sodium	180 mg

Belgian Waffle Dessert

Makes 10 waffles

2¼ cups cold 2% low-fat milk
1 package (4-serving size) JELL-O® Vanilla
Flavor Sugar Free Instant Pudding and Pie
Filling
2 tablespoons lemon juice
1 teaspoon grated lemon peel
1 cup thawed COOL WHIP® LITE® Whipped
Topping
1 pint (about 2 cups) strawberries, sliced
½ pint (about 1 cup) raspberries
½ pint (about 1 cup) blueberries or blackberries
10 small frozen Belgian or regular waffles,
toasted

Pour milk into large mixing bowl. Add pudding mix,
lemon juice and peel. Beat with wire whisk until well
blended, 1 to 2 minutes. Gently stir in whipped
topping. Refrigerate.

Mix fruit in bowl; refrigerate.

To serve, spoon about 3 tablespoons pudding mixture
on each dessert plate. Top each with waffle,
additional 2 tablespoons pudding mixture and scant
½ cup fruit. Garnish if desired. Repeat for remaining
desserts as needed. Store leftover pudding mixture
and fruit in refrigerator.

Nutrients per serving (1 waffle):

Calories	170	Cholesterol	5 mg
Fat	5 g	Sodium	310 mg

Top to bottom: Cheese "Danish",
Belgian Waffle Dessert

Honey Peanut Muffins

Makes 12 muffins

¾ cup whole wheat flour
¾ cup all-purpose flour
¼ cup sugar
1 teaspoon baking soda
¼ teaspoon salt (optional)
1¼ cups KELLOGG'S® ALL-BRAN® Cereal
1¼ cups low-fat buttermilk
¼ cup honey
2 egg whites
3 tablespoons vegetable oil
¼ cup chopped dry roasted peanuts
Nonstick cooking spray

Stir together flours, sugar, baking soda and salt. Set aside.

Measure Kellogg's® All-Bran® cereal and buttermilk into large mixing bowl. Stir to combine. Let stand 3 minutes or until cereal is softened. Add honey, egg whites, oil and peanuts. Beat well.

Add flour mixture, stirring only until combined. Portion batter evenly into 12 (2½-inch) muffin pan cups coated with nonstick cooking spray.

Bake at 400°F about 22 minutes or until golden brown. Serve warm.

Nutrients per serving (1 muffin):

Calories	180	Cholesterol	45 mg
Fat	6 g	Sodium	230 mg

Ham & Fruit Pancake Rolls

Makes 8 rolled pancakes

2 cups complete pancake mix
8 ounces ARMOUR® Lower Salt Ham, thinly sliced
8 tablespoons bottled fruit-flavored applesauce *or* canned lite cherry fruit filling

Prepare pancake mix according to package directions. Spray griddle or large skillet with nonstick cooking spray. Using ⅓ cup measure, pour batter onto hot griddle. Cook as directed on package, making eight 5-inch pancakes. Place 1 ounce of ham on each cooked pancake; top with 1 tablespoon applesauce. Roll up pancake around ham; secure with toothpicks, if needed. Repeat with remaining pancakes. Serve with additional applesauce, if desired.

Nutrients per serving (1 pancake):

Calories	145	Cholesterol	14 mg
Fat	2 g	Sodium	596 mg

Cranberry Oat Bran Muffins

Cranberry Oat Bran Muffins

Makes 12 muffins

2 cups flour
1 cup oat bran
½ cup packed brown sugar
2 teaspoons baking powder
½ teaspoon baking soda
½ teaspoon salt (optional)
½ cup MIRACLE WHIP® LIGHT Reduced Calorie Salad Dressing
3 egg whites, slightly beaten
½ cup skim milk
⅓ cup orange juice
1 teaspoon grated orange peel
1 cup coarsely chopped cranberries

Preheat oven to 375°F. Line 12 medium muffin cups with paper baking cups or spray with nonstick cooking spray. Mix together dry ingredients. Add combined dressing, egg whites, milk, juice and peel; mix just until moistened. Fold in cranberries. Fill prepared muffin cups almost full. Bake 15 to 17 minutes or until golden brown.

Nutrients per serving (1 muffin):

Calories	183	Cholesterol	4 mg
Fat	4 g	Sodium	191 mg

Banana Yogurt Muffins

Makes 12 muffins

1½ cups all-purpose flour
  3 tablespoons sugar
  2 teaspoons baking powder
  ¼ teaspoon salt
2½ cups KELLOGG'S® SPECIAL K® cereal,
    crushed to 2 cups
  1 egg white
  ¾ cup skim milk
  1 medium banana, mashed
  ⅓ cup vanilla low-fat yogurt
  3 tablespoons vegetable oil
    Vegetable cooking spray

1. Stir together flour, sugar, baking powder and salt. Set aside.

2. In large mixing bowl, combine Kellogg's® Special K® cereal, egg white, milk, banana, yogurt and oil. Let stand 1 minute or until cereal softens. Add flour mixture, stirring until combined. Pour batter evenly into twelve 2½-inch muffin-pan cups coated with cooking spray.

3. Bake at 400°F about 25 minutes or until lightly browned. Serve warm.

Nutrients per serving (1 muffin):			
Calories	150	Cholesterol	trace
Fat	4 g	Sodium	180 mg

Plum-Marmalade Coffeecake

Makes 8 servings

  ½ cup orange marmalade
    Vegetable cooking spray
  3 purple plums
  ¼ cup firmly packed brown sugar
  2 tablespoons all-purpose flour
  ½ cup all-purpose flour
  ½ cup whole wheat flour
  ¼ cup granulated sugar
  2 teaspoons baking powder
  ½ teaspoon salt
  ½ teaspoon ground nutmeg
  1 cup KELLOGG'S® ALL-BRAN® cereal
  1 cup skim milk
  1 egg
  ¼ cup margarine, softened

1. Spread marmalade evenly over bottom of 9-inch round cake pan coated with cooking spray. Remove pits from plums; discard. Cut plums into thin slices. Mix together plums, brown sugar and 2 tablespoons all-purpose flour; arrange over marmalade. Set aside.

2. Stir together ½ cup all-purpose flour, whole wheat flour, granulated sugar, baking powder, salt and nutmeg. Set aside.

3. Measure Kellogg's® All-Bran® cereal and milk into large mixing bowl. Stir to combine. Let stand 2 minutes or until cereal softens. Add egg and margarine; beat well.

4. Add flour mixture to cereal mixture, stirring only until combined. Spread evenly over plums.

5. Bake at 400°F about 25 minutes or until cake is golden brown. Remove from oven and invert immediately on serving plate. Serve warm or cool completely.

Nutrients per serving:			
Calories	260	Cholesterol	30 mg
Fat	7 g	Sodium	430 mg

Cinnamon Orange Juice Muffins

Makes 12 muffins

  2 cups Multi-Bran CHEX® brand cereal
  1 cup orange juice
  1 egg, beaten
  3 tablespoons vegetable oil
  1 cup all-purpose flour
  ⅓ cup packed brown sugar
  2 teaspoons baking powder
1½ teaspoons ground cinnamon
  ½ teaspoon baking soda

Preheat oven to 400°F. Grease or paper-line 12 (2½-inch) muffin cups. In large bowl combine cereal, orange juice, egg and oil. Let stand 5 minutes. In separate bowl combine flour, brown sugar, baking powder, cinnamon and baking soda. Add flour mixture to cereal mixture all at once, stirring just until moistened (do not over stir). Divide evenly among muffin cups. Bake 15 to 20 minutes or until toothpick inserted in center comes out clean.

Nutrients per serving (1 muffin):			
Calories	130	Cholesterol	17 mg
Fat	4 g	Sodium	128 mg

Home-Style Coffee Bread

Makes 12 servings

Bread
1 cup sugar
1 egg
2 tablespoons butter, softened
2 cups all-purpose flour
1½ teaspoons baking powder
1 teaspoon ground cinnamon
½ teaspoon baking soda
¼ teaspoon salt
¼ teaspoon ground nutmeg
1 cup buttermilk
1 cup raisins
½ cup chopped nuts

Topping
½ cup sugar
1 tablespoon all-purpose flour
1 tablespoon butter, softened
½ teaspoon ground cinnamon

Preheat oven to 350°F. Lightly grease 13×9-inch baking pan.

For Bread, combine sugar, egg and butter in large bowl. Beat with electric mixer on high speed for 30 seconds. Stir together flour, baking powder, cinnamon, baking soda, salt and nutmeg in medium bowl. Add flour mixture and buttermilk alternately to sugar mixture, beating well after each addition. Stir in raisins and nuts. Spread evenly into prepared pan.

For Topping, stir together all topping ingredients in small bowl. Sprinkle evenly over batter. Bake 25 to 30 minutes or until wooden pick inserted in center comes out clean. Cut into 12 squares. Serve warm with butter, if desired.

Nutrients per serving:

Calories	236	Cholesterol	24 mg
Fat	6 g	Sodium	168 mg

Favorite recipe from **Wisconsin Milk Marketing Board** © 1994

Multi-Bran Blueberry Muffins

Makes 12 muffins

1¾ cups Multi-Bran CHEX® brand cereal
1 egg, beaten
1 cup low-fat buttermilk*
3 tablespoons vegetable oil
1 cup all-purpose flour
½ cup packed brown sugar
2½ teaspoons baking powder
1 teaspoon ground cinnamon
1 cup fresh, frozen or canned blueberries, drained

Preheat oven to 400°F. Grease or paper-line 12 (2½-inch) muffin cups. In large bowl combine cereal, egg, buttermilk and oil. Let stand 5 minutes. Stir to break up cereal. In medium bowl combine flour, brown sugar, baking powder and cinnamon. Add flour mixture to cereal mixture all at once, stirring just until moistened. Fold in blueberries. (Batter will be thick.) Divide evenly among muffin cups. Bake 20 to 25 minutes or until toothpick inserted in center comes out clean.

**1 tablespoon lemon juice or vinegar and enough milk to equal 1 cup may be substituted for buttermilk.*

Raisin Muffins: *Use ⅓ cup raisins in place of blueberries.*

Strawberry Muffins: *Use 1 cup finely chopped fresh or frozen strawberries in place of blueberries. Use 1 teaspoon vanilla extract in place of cinnamon. Add ⅓ cup chopped pecans, if desired, to cereal mixture.*

Nutrients per serving (1 muffin):

Calories	143	Cholesterol	18 mg
Fat	5 g	Sodium	144 mg

Florida Orange Honey Butter

Makes ½ cup

½ cup unsalted butter, softened
2 tablespoons honey
1 tablespoon grated orange zest

Beat butter in small bowl with electric mixer until light and fluffy. Beat in honey and orange zest until well blended. Serve with muffins, pancakes or French toast.

Nutrients per serving (1 teaspoon spread):

Calories	39	Cholesterol	10 mg
Fat	4 g	Sodium	0 mg

Favorite recipe from **Florida Department of Citrus**

Blueberry Sour Cream Corn Muffins

Makes 12 muffins

  1 cup all-purpose flour
  ¾ cup cornmeal
  2 teaspoons baking powder
  ½ teaspoon baking soda
  ¼ teaspoon salt
  1 egg, beaten
  1 cup sour cream
  ⅓ cup thawed frozen unsweetened apple juice
     concentrate
  1½ cups fresh or frozen (not thawed) blueberries
  ⅔ cup whipped cream cheese (optional)
  2 tablespoons no sugar added blueberry fruit
     spread (optional)

Preheat oven to 400°F. Grease or paper-line 12 (2½-inch) muffin cups.

Combine dry ingredients in medium bowl. Combine egg, sour cream and apple juice concentrate in small bowl until blended; stir into flour mixture just until dry ingredients are moistened. Gently stir in blueberries. Spoon batter into prepared cups, filling each cup ¾ full.

Bake 18 to 20 minutes until golden brown. Cool in pan on wire rack 5 minutes. Remove from pan; cool slightly. Combine cream cheese and fruit spread in small bowl; serve with warm muffins, if desired.

Nutrients per serving (1 muffin):			
Calories	176	Cholesterol	35 mg
Fat	8 g	Sodium	201 mg

Fresh Pear Topping

Makes about 4 cups

  4 fresh California Bartlett pears, sliced or
     cubed (4 cups)
  1 cup low calorie maple syrup
  ⅓ cup low fat milk
  ¾ teaspoon vanilla extract

Heat pears in large nonstick skillet over medium heat until warm. Add syrup, milk and vanilla; heat until bubbly, stirring occasionally. Spoon topping over waffles, French toast, pancakes or cereal.

Nutrients per serving (2 tablespoons topping):			
Calories	32	Cholesterol	trace
Fat	trace	Sodium	2 mg

Favorite recipe from **California Tree Fruit Agreement**

Orange Fig Muffins

Makes 12 muffins

  1½ cups all-purpose flour
  1 tablespoon baking powder
  ¼ cup sugar
  3 cups KELLOGG'S® COMPLETE® Bran
     Flakes cereal
  1¼ cups orange juice
  1 egg
  ¼ cup vegetable oil
  ⅔ cup chopped dried figs
  1 teaspoon grated orange peel
     Vegetable cooking spray

1. Stir together flour, baking powder and sugar. Set aside.

2. Measure Kellogg's® Complete® Bran Flakes cereal, orange juice, egg, oil, figs and orange peel into large mixing bowl. Beat well.

3. Add dry ingredients to cereal mixture, stirring only until combined. Spoon batter evenly into twelve 2½-inch muffin-pan cups coated with cooking spray.

4. Bake at 400°F about 25 minutes or until golden brown. Serve warm.

Nutrients per serving (1 muffin):			
Calories	190	Cholesterol	25 mg
Fat	5 g	Sodium	170 mg

Citrus-Sauced Pears

Makes 6 servings

  2 tablespoons low calorie margarine
  ⅓ cup sugar
  ¾ cup freshly squeezed orange juice
  ⅓ cup freshly squeezed lemon juice
  ½ teaspoon *each* grated orange and lemon peels
  3 fresh California Bartlett pears, cored and
     sliced

Melt margarine with sugar in saucepan. Add fruit juices and peels. Bring to a boil; boil to reduce liquid slightly. Reduce heat to low; add pear slices. Heat through. Spoon over waffles, pancakes or cereal.

Nutrients per serving:			
Calories	124	Cholesterol	0 mg
Fat	2 g	Sodium	52 mg

Favorite recipe from **California Tree Fruit Agreement**

Blueberry Sour Cream Corn Muffins

Apricot Date Mini-Loaves

Apricot Date Mini-Loaves

Makes 16 servings, 4 mini-loaves

**1 package DUNCAN HINES® Bakery Style
    Cinnamon Swirl Muffin Mix**
½ teaspoon baking powder
2 egg whites
⅔ cup water
½ cup chopped dried apricots
½ cup chopped dates

1. Preheat oven to 350°F. Grease four 5⅜×2⅝×1⅞-inch pans.

2. Combine muffin mix and baking powder in large bowl. Break up any lumps. Add egg whites, water, apricots and dates. Stir until well blended, about 50 strokes.

3. Knead swirl packet for 10 seconds before opening. Cut off one end of swirl packet. Squeeze contents onto batter. Swirl into batter with knife or spatula, folding from bottom of bowl to get an even swirl. Do not completely mix into batter. Divide evenly into pans. Sprinkle with contents of topping packet from mix.

4. Bake at 350°F for 30 to 35 minutes or until wooden toothpick inserted in centers comes out clean. Cool in pans 15 minutes. Loosen loaves from pans. Lift out with knife. Place on cooling racks. Cool completely.

Tip: Recipe may also be baked in 1 greased 8½×4½×2½-inch pan at 350°F for 55 to 60 minutes or until wooden toothpick inserted in center comes out clean. Cool 10 minutes before removing from pan.

Nutrients per serving (1 slice):

Calories	167	Cholesterol	0 mg
Fat	5 g	Sodium	198 mg

Brown Rice, Mushroom, and Ham Hash

Makes 8 servings

1 tablespoon olive oil
2 cups (about 8 ounces) sliced fresh mushrooms
1 small onion, minced
1 clove garlic, minced
3 cups cooked brown rice
1 cup (6 ounces) diced turkey ham
½ cup chopped walnuts (optional)
¼ cup snipped fresh parsley
1 tablespoon white wine vinegar
1 tablespoon Dijon-style mustard
¼ teaspoon ground black pepper

Heat oil in Dutch oven or large saucepan over medium-low heat until hot. Add mushrooms, onion, and garlic; cook and stir until tender. Stir in rice, ham, walnuts, parsley, vinegar, mustard, and pepper; cook, stirring until thoroughly heated.

To Microwave: Combine oil, mushrooms, onion, and garlic in 2- to 3-quart microproof baking dish. Cook on HIGH (100% power) 3 to 4 minutes. Stir in rice, ham, walnuts, parsley, vinegar, mustard, and pepper. Cook on HIGH 3 to 4 minutes, stirring after 2 minutes, or until thoroughly heated.

Nutrients per serving:

Calories	133	Cholesterol	10 mg
Fat	4 g	Sodium	184 mg

Favorite recipe from **USA Rice Council**

Gingerbread Pancakes

Makes 12 pancakes

1½ cups all-purpose flour
½ cup SPOON SIZE® Shredded Wheat, finely rolled (about ⅓ cup crumbs)
1 tablespoon DAVIS® Baking Powder
1 teaspoon pumpkin pie spice
1¼ cups skim milk
½ cup EGG BEATERS® 99% Real Egg Product
3 tablespoons BRER RABBIT® Light Molasses
2 tablespoons FLEISCHMANN'S® Margarine, melted

In large bowl, mix flour, cereal, baking powder and pumpkin pie spice. In small bowl, blend milk, Egg Beaters®, molasses and margarine; stir into dry ingredients just until moistened.

On lightly greased preheated griddle or skillet, pour ¼ cup batter for each pancake. Cook over medium heat until surface is bubbly and bottom is lightly browned. Turn carefully and cook until done. Remove and keep warm.

Nutrients per serving (1 pancake):

Calories	110	Cholesterol	1 mg
Fat	2 g	Sodium	128 mg

Mixed Fruit Soufflé

Makes 8 servings

1 cup skim milk
¼ cup cornstarch
1½ cups chopped fresh fruit*
⅓ cup sugar
1 teaspoon vanilla extract
1 (8-ounce) container EGG BEATERS® 99% Real Egg Product

In small saucepan, gradually blend milk into cornstarch; cook over medium heat until mixture thickens and begins to boil, stirring constantly. Remove from heat; stir in fruit, sugar and vanilla. Set aside.

In medium bowl, with electric mixer at high speed, beat Egg Beaters® until foamy, about 3 minutes; fold into fruit mixture. Spoon into greased 1½-quart soufflé or casserole dish. Bake at 375°F for 45 to 50 minutes or until set. Serve immediately.

*Thawed and well-drained frozen or canned fruit may be substituted.

Nutrients per serving:

Calories	86	Cholesterol	1 mg
Fat	0 g	Sodium	54 mg

Brunch Potato Cassoulet

Makes 4 to 6 servings

2 tablespoons unsalted margarine or butter
2 cups (8 ounces) ARMOUR® Lower Salt Ham, cut into ½-inch cubes
2 cups frozen natural potato wedges
1 cup sliced mushrooms
½ cup chopped red onion
½ cup chopped green bell pepper
1 cup frozen speckled butter beans, cooked and drained according to package directions (omit salt)
Low-salt cheese (optional)

Preheat oven to 350°F. Melt margarine in large skillet over medium heat. Add ham, potatoes, mushrooms, onion and green pepper; cook and stir over medium heat 5 to 6 minutes or until onion is soft. Stir in cooked beans. Transfer to medium earthenware pot or ovenproof Dutch oven. Bake, covered, 10 to 12 minutes or until heated through. Sprinkle with low-salt cheese, if desired. Broil, 4 to 6 inches from heat source, 2 to 3 minutes or until cheese is melted and slightly browned.

Nutrients per serving:

Calories	161	Cholesterol	19 mg
Fat	7 g	Sodium	391 mg

Brunch Potato Cassoulet

Banana-Nut Bread

Makes 16 servings

½ cup granulated sugar
2 tablespoons brown sugar
5 tablespoons margarine or butter, softened
1 egg *plus* 2 egg whites
1⅓ cups mashed ripe bananas (about 3 bananas)
2½ cups sifted all-purpose flour
1 teaspoon baking soda
½ teaspoon salt
⅓ cup chopped walnuts

Preheat oven to 375°F. Spray 9×5-inch loaf pan with nonstick cooking spray.

Beat sugars and margarine in large bowl with electric mixer until creamy. Add egg, egg whites and bananas. Sift together flour, baking soda and salt in separate bowl; stir into banana mixture just until dry ingredients are moistened. Fold in walnuts. Pour into prepared pan.

Bake 1 hour. Cool in pan 10 minutes. Remove to wire rack; cool completely. To serve, cut into 16 slices.

Nutrients per serving (1 slice):			
Calories	168	Cholesterol	13 mg
Fat	6 g	Sodium	172 mg

Favorite recipe from **The Sugar Association, Inc.**

Berries Good

Makes 4 servings

1 package (10 ounces) frozen unsweetened raspberries, thawed
1 tablespoon sugar
2 teaspoons cornstarch
1 cup fresh or frozen blackberries or boysenberries, thawed
2 fresh California Bartlett pears, cored and halved
Plain low fat yogurt (optional)

Combine raspberries, sugar and cornstarch in saucepan. Cook over medium-high heat until mixture comes to a boil and thickens, stirring constantly. Cool. Spoon blackberries into pear halves. Top with raspberry mixture. Dollop with yogurt, if desired.

Nutrients per serving:			
Calories	155	Cholesterol	0 mg
Fat	trace	Sodium	trace

Favorite recipe from **California Tree Fruit Agreement**

Cinnamon Twists

Makes 20 pastries

2 packages active dry yeast
⅓ cup warm water (110° to 115°F)
1 carton (8 ounces) dairy sour cream
3 tablespoons granulated sugar
4 tablespoons butter, softened and divided
½ teaspoon salt
2¾ to 3¼ cups all-purpose flour, divided
1 egg
3 tablespoons brown sugar
1 teaspoon ground cinnamon
Powdered Sugar Glaze (recipe follows)

Soften yeast in warm water; set aside. Combine sour cream, granulated sugar, 2 tablespoons butter and salt in medium saucepan; cook over medium heat just until warm and butter is almost melted, stirring constantly. Combine 1 cup flour, sour cream mixture, yeast mixture and egg in large bowl. Beat with electric mixer on low speed for 30 seconds. Beat on high speed for 3 minutes, scraping sides of bowl frequently. Add enough remaining flour to make soft dough, stirring with wooden spoon. Turn out onto lightly floured surface. Knead in enough remaining flour to make moderately stiff dough that is smooth and elastic (6 to 8 minutes total). Let dough rest, covered, 10 minutes.

Grease baking sheet. Divide dough in half. Roll half the dough into 16×6-inch rectangle. Spread 1 tablespoon butter over rectangle. Combine brown sugar and cinnamon in small bowl; sprinkle half the mixture lengthwise down half the rectangle. Fold in half crosswise, forming 8×6-inch rectangle. Cut into ten 6×¾-inch strips. Twist each strip several times; place on prepared baking sheet. Repeat with remaining dough, 1 tablespoon butter and cinnamon-sugar mixture. Cover; let rise about 25 minutes or until doubled.

Preheat oven to 375°F. Bake 14 minutes or until golden. Remove to wire rack; drizzle with Powdered Sugar Glaze. Serve warm or cool completely.

Powdered Sugar Glaze: Combine 1 cup sifted powdered sugar and 1 to 2 tablespoons heavy cream or milk in small bowl; stir until smooth.

Nutrients per serving (1 pastry):			
Calories	153	Cholesterol	22 mg
Fat	5 g	Sodium	34 mg

Favorite recipe from **Wisconsin Milk Marketing Board © 1994**

Wisconsin Cheese Pinwheel Danish

Makes 8 pinwheels

Dough
1½ cups unbleached all-purpose flour
¾ cup whole wheat flour
3 tablespoons granulated sugar
2 teaspoons baking powder
½ teaspoon baking soda
¼ teaspoon ground cinnamon
⅛ teaspoon salt
1 cup plain low fat yogurt
2 tablespoons butter, melted

Cheese Filling
½ cup Wisconsin (part skim) Ricotta cheese
2 teaspoons granulated sugar
Grated peel of 1 lemon

Glaze
¼ cup powdered sugar
1¾ teaspoons milk
¼ teaspoon vanilla extract

Preheat oven to 400°F. For Dough, combine flours, granulated sugar, baking powder, baking soda, cinnamon and salt in large bowl. Combine yogurt and butter in small bowl. Stir yogurt mixture into flour mixture. Turn out onto floured board; knead several times to make soft dough.

Divide dough in half. Roll half the dough into 8-inch square. Cut square into four 4-inch squares. Transfer squares to baking sheet with spatula. Cut slits 1 inch from center to each corner diagonally.

For Cheese Filling, combine cheese, granulated sugar and lemon peel in small bowl; stir until smooth. Place heaping spoonful of Cheese Filling in center of each dough square. Lift and fold every other point over filling. Press center to hold points in place. Repeat with remaining dough.

Bake about 10 minutes or until golden brown. Meanwhile, for Glaze, combine all Glaze ingredients in small bowl; stir until smooth. Drizzle Glaze over pinwheels. Serve warm.

Nutrients per serving (1 pinwheel):			
Calories	224	Cholesterol	14 mg
Fat	5 g	Sodium	237 mg

Favorite recipe from **Wisconsin Milk Marketing Board** © 1994

Spiced Apple Toast

Makes 4 servings

1 tablespoon margarine
2 apples, unpeeled, cored and thinly sliced
⅓ cup orange juice
4 teaspoons brown sugar
½ teaspoon ground cinnamon
4 slices whole wheat bread, toasted
2 teaspoons granulated sugar

Preheat oven to 450°F. Melt margarine in medium nonstick skillet. Add apples, orange juice, brown sugar and cinnamon; cook over medium-high heat about 4 minutes or until apples are tender, stirring occasionally. Drain and reserve liquid. Allow apples to cool a few minutes. Place toast on lightly buttered baking sheet. Arrange apples in spiral design on top, overlapping slices. Sprinkle ½ teaspoon granulated sugar over each slice.

Bake about 4 minutes or until bread is crisp. Drizzle reserved liquid over slices. Serve immediately.

Nutrients per serving (1 slice):			
Calories	175	Cholesterol	0 mg
Fat	4 g	Sodium	134 mg

Favorite recipe from **The Sugar Association, Inc.**

Dannon® Muffins

Makes 12 muffins

1½ cups all-purpose flour
¾ cup sugar
2 teaspoons baking powder
1 teaspoon baking soda
½ teaspoon salt
⅔ cup DANNON® Plain Nonfat or Lowfat Yogurt
⅔ cup skim milk
½ cup blueberries or grated apple (optional)

Preheat oven to 400°F. Grease muffin cups or line with paper baking cups. In a large bowl combine flour, sugar, baking powder, baking soda and salt. Gently add yogurt, milk and blueberries; stir just until dry ingredients are moistened.

Fill prepared muffin cups ⅔ full. Bake 18 minutes or until lightly brown and toothpick inserted into center comes out clean. Serve warm.

Nutrients per serving (1 muffin):			
Calories	120	Cholesterol	5 mg
Fat	2 g	Sodium	177 mg

Rice Bran Buttermilk Pancakes

Rice Bran Buttermilk Pancakes

Makes about 10 (4-inch) pancakes

1 cup rice flour or all-purpose flour
¾ cup rice bran
1 tablespoon sugar
1 teaspoon baking powder
½ teaspoon baking soda
1¼ cups low-fat buttermilk
3 egg whites, beaten
   Nonstick cooking spray
   Fresh fruit or reduced-calorie syrup (optional)

Sift together flour, bran, sugar, baking powder, and baking soda into large bowl. Combine buttermilk and egg whites in small bowl; add to flour mixture. Stir until smooth. Pour ¼ cup batter onto hot griddle coated with nonstick cooking spray. Cook over medium heat until bubbles form on top and underside is lightly browned. Turn to brown other side. Serve with fresh fruit or syrup.

Variation: For Cinnamon Pancakes, add 1 teaspoon ground cinnamon to dry ingredients.

Nutrients per serving (1 pancake):

Calories	99	Cholesterol	1 mg
Fat	2 g	Sodium	119 mg

Favorite recipe from **USA Rice Council**

Alpine Fruited Oatmeal

Makes 6 servings

2 cups QUAKER® Oats (quick or old fashioned, uncooked)*
1 cup apple juice
1 cup water
¾ cup diced, dried mixed fruit or raisins
¼ teaspoon ground cinnamon
¼ teaspoon salt (optional)

Combine all ingredients; mix well. Cover; refrigerate at least 8 hours or overnight. Stir well before serving. Serve cold or hot with milk or yogurt, if desired. Store tightly covered in refrigerator for up to 1 week.

*Or, substitute 1 cup QUAKER® Oat Bran hot cereal, uncooked, for 1 cup of the oats.

Note: To heat, place ½ cup cereal in microwavable bowl. Microwave at HIGH (100% power) about 1½ minutes; stir.

Nutrients per serving (½ cup):

Calories	175	Cholesterol	0 mg
Fat	2 g	Sodium	5 mg

Aloha Muffins

Makes 12 muffins

1½ cups whole wheat flour
¾ cup sugar
¼ cup oat bran
1½ teaspoons baking powder
¾ teaspoon baking soda
1 teaspoon ground cinnamon
¼ teaspoon ground nutmeg
2 cans (8 ounces *each*) DOLE® Crushed Pineapple, drained, ¼ cup juice reserved
½ cup DOLE® Raisins
3 egg whites
¼ cup *plus* 1 tablespoon vegetable oil
½ teaspoon almond extract
¼ cup DOLE® Sliced Almonds

Preheat oven to 350°F. Combine flour, sugar, oat bran, baking powder, baking soda, cinnamon and nutmeg in small bowl. Combine drained pineapple, reserved ¼ cup juice, raisins, egg whites, oil and almond extract in large bowl. Stir dry ingredients into pineapple mixture until just moistened. Spoon into 12 greased 2½-inch muffin cups. Top with almonds. Bake 25 minutes. Remove from pan; cool on wire rack.

Nutrients per serving (1 muffin):

Calories	226	Cholesterol	0 mg
Fat	8 g	Sodium	112 mg

Apple Butter

Makes 2 cups

1 jar (23 ounces) unsweetened applesauce (2½ cups)
½ cup thawed frozen unsweetened apple juice concentrate
1 teaspoon ground cinnamon
½ teaspoon salt
½ teaspoon ground cloves
⅛ teaspoon ground allspice

Combine all ingredients in medium heavy saucepan. Cook over medium heat 50 minutes or until very thick, stirring occasionally. Store in sealed container in refrigerator up to 3 weeks. Spread on toast or muffins.

Nutrients per serving (1 tablespoon spread):

Calories	16	Cholesterol	0 mg
Fat	trace	Sodium	36 mg

Cinnamon Spiced Muffins

Makes 36 miniature or 12 regular-size muffins

1½ cups all-purpose flour
½ cup sugar
2 teaspoons baking powder
½ teaspoon salt
½ teaspoon ground nutmeg
½ teaspoon ground coriander
½ teaspoon ground allspice
½ cup low-fat milk
⅓ cup margarine, melted
1 egg
¼ cup sugar
1 teaspoon ground cinnamon
¼ cup margarine, melted

Preheat oven to 400°F. Grease 36 miniature muffin cups. In large bowl, combine flour, ½ cup sugar, baking powder, salt, nutmeg, coriander and allspice. In small bowl, combine milk, ⅓ cup margarine and egg. Stir into flour mixture just until moistened.

Spoon into muffin cups. Bake 10 to 13 minutes or until edges are lightly browned and wooden toothpick inserted in centers comes out clean. Remove from pan.

Meanwhile, combine ¼ cup sugar and cinnamon in a shallow dish. Roll warm muffin tops in ¼ cup margarine, then sugar-cinnamon mixture. Serve warm.

Cinnamon Spiced Muffins

To Microwave: Line 6 (2½-inch) microwavable muffin-pan cups with double paper liners. Prepare batter as directed. Spoon batter into each cup, filling ½ full. Microwave at HIGH (100% power) 2½ to 4½ minutes or until wooden toothpick inserted in centers comes out clean. Rotate dish ½ turn halfway through cooking. Let stand 5 minutes. Remove from pan. Repeat procedure with remaining batter.

Meanwhile, combine ¼ cup sugar and cinnamon in a shallow dish. Roll warm muffin tops in ¼ cup margarine, then sugar-cinnamon mixture. Serve warm.

Nutrients per serving (1 miniature muffin):			
Calories	64	Cholesterol	6 mg
Fat	3 g	Sodium	86 mg

Nutrients per serving (1 regular-size muffin):			
Calories	193	Cholesterol	18 mg
Fat	9 g	Sodium	257 mg

Pineapple-Almond Date Bread

Makes 28 servings

1 cup DOLE® Sliced Almonds, divided
¾ cup sugar
½ cup margarine, softened
1 egg
1 can (8¼ ounces) DOLE® Crushed Pineapple in Syrup or Juice
1 tablespoon grated orange peel
2 cups all-purpose flour
1 teaspoon baking powder
1 teaspoon baking soda
¼ teaspoon ground nutmeg
1 cup DOLE® Chopped Dates

Toast ¾ cup almonds; reserve remaining ¼ cup for topping. Beat sugar and margarine in large bowl until light and fluffy. Beat in egg until blended. Stir in undrained pineapple and orange peel. Combine flour, baking powder, baking soda and nutmeg in medium bowl. Beat into pineapple mixture until blended. Stir in ¾ cup toasted almonds and dates. Pour batter into well-greased 9×5-inch loaf pan. Sprinkle remaining ¼ cup untoasted almonds on top. Bake in 350°F oven 55 to 60 minutes or until cake tester inserted in center comes out clean. Cool in pan on wire rack 10 minutes. Remove from pan. Cool completely on wire rack before slicing. To serve, cut loaf into 14 slices, then cut each slice lengthwise in half.

Prep time: 15 minutes
Bake time: 60 minutes

Nutrients per serving:			
Calories	147	Cholesterol	10 mg
Fat	7 g	Sodium	83 mg

Brunch Quesadillas with Fruit Salsa

Brunch Quesadillas with Fruit Salsa

Makes 4 servings

1 pint fresh strawberries, hulled and diced
1 fresh ripe Anjou pear, cored and diced
1 tablespoon chopped fresh cilantro
1 tablespoon honey
1 cup (4 ounces) SARGENTO® Preferred Light Fancy Supreme Shredded Mozzarella Cheese
4 flour tortillas (8 inches in diameter)
2 teaspoons light margarine, melted
2 tablespoons light sour cream

To make Fruit Salsa, combine strawberries, pear, cilantro and honey in medium bowl; set aside.

Sprinkle 2 tablespoons cheese on one half of each tortilla. Top with ⅓ cup Fruit Salsa (drain and discard any liquid from fruit) and another 2 tablespoons cheese. Fold tortillas in half. Brush top of each folded tortilla with some of the melted margarine.

Grill folded tortillas, greased sides down, in dry preheated skillet until light golden brown and crisp, about 2 minutes. Brush tops with remaining melted margarine; turn and brown other sides. Remove to serving plate or platter. Cut each tortilla in half. Serve with remaining Fruit Salsa. Garnish with sour cream. Serve immediately.

Nutrients per serving:			
Calories	278	Cholesterol	14 mg
Fat	9 g	Sodium	264 mg

Peachy Cinnamon Coffee Cake

Brunch Sandwiches

Makes 4 servings

1 carton (8 ounces) HEALTHY CHOICE®
    Cholesterol Free Egg Product
¼ cup nonfat mayonnaise
½ teaspoon Dijon-style mustard
    Dash black pepper
4 whole wheat English muffins, toasted
4 lettuce leaves
4 slices tomato

In 8-inch skillet sprayed with nonstick cooking spray, cook egg product, covered, over very low heat 10 minutes or until just set. Cut egg product into 4 wedges.

In small bowl, combine mayonnaise, mustard and pepper. To make sandwiches, spread 4 bottom muffin halves evenly with mayonnaise mixture. Top with egg product, tomato, and lettuce. Top with remaining muffin halves.

Nutrients per serving:

Calories	190	Cholesterol	0 mg
Fat	2 g	Sodium	560 mg

Peachy Cinnamon Coffee Cake

Makes 9 servings

1 can (8¼ ounces) juice pack sliced yellow cling
    peaches
    Water
1 package DUNCAN HINES® Bakery Style
    Cinnamon Swirl with Crumb Topping
    Muffin Mix
1 egg

1. Preheat oven to 400°F. Grease 8-inch square or 9-inch round pan.

2. Drain peaches, reserving juice. Add water to reserved juice to equal ¾ cup liquid. Chop peaches.

3. Combine muffin mix, egg and ¾ cup peach liquid in medium bowl; fold in peaches. Pour batter into pan. Knead swirl packet 10 seconds before opening. Squeeze contents on top of batter and swirl with knife. Sprinkle topping over batter.

4. Bake at 400°F for 28 to 33 minutes for 8-inch pan (or for 20 to 25 minutes for 9-inch pan) or until golden. Serve warm.

Nutrients per serving:

Calories	205	Cholesterol	0 mg
Fat	7 g	Sodium	248 mg

Orange Chocolate Chip Bread

Makes 16 servings

1 cup skim milk
¼ cup orange juice
⅓ cup sugar
1 egg, slightly beaten
1 tablespoon grated fresh orange peel
3 cups all-purpose biscuit baking mix
½ cup HERSHEY₂S MINI CHIPS® Semi-Sweet
    Chocolate

Combine milk, orange juice, sugar, egg and orange peel in small bowl. Place baking mix in medium mixing bowl. Stir milk mixture into baking mix, beating until well combined, about 1 minute. Stir in Mini Chips®. Pour into greased 9×5×3-inch loaf pan. Bake at 350°F for 45 to 50 minutes or until cake tester inserted in center comes out clean. Cool in pan on wire rack 10 minutes; remove from pan. Cool completely. Slice and serve. To store leftovers, wrap in foil or plastic wrap.

Nutrients per serving (1 slice):

Calories	161	Cholesterol	17 mg
Fat	5 g	Sodium	274 mg

Banana-Cinnamon Rolls

Makes 12 servings

¼ cup granulated sugar
1 teaspoon ground cinnamon
2 cups KELLOGG'S® RAISIN BRAN® Cereal
½ cup mashed ripe banana
½ cup milk
1 egg
1 teaspoon vanilla
1¾ cups all-purpose flour
4 teaspoons baking powder
½ teaspoon salt
½ cup cold margarine

Frosting
1½ cups confectioners' sugar
2 tablespoons hot water
1 tablespoon lemon juice
¼ cup sliced almonds (optional)

Combine granulated sugar and cinnamon; set aside.

Measure Kellogg's® Raisin Bran® cereal, banana and milk into large mixing bowl. Stir to combine. Let stand 2 minutes or until cereal softens. Add egg and vanilla; beat well.

In large mixing bowl, combine flour, baking powder and salt. Using pastry blender, cut in margarine until mixture resembles coarse crumbs. Add cereal mixture, stirring only until combined.

On lightly floured surface, gently knead dough 10 times. Roll out dough to measure 12×10-inch rectangle. Sprinkle dough with sugar mixture. Starting with long side, roll up dough jelly-roll style. Cut roll into twelve 1-inch pieces. Place, cut-side-down, in greased 13×9-inch pan.

Bake in 400°F oven about 25 minutes or until lightly browned. Invert onto serving plate.

For frosting, stir together confectioners' sugar, water and lemon juice until smooth. Spread over hot rolls and sprinkle with almonds. Serve warm.

Nutrients per serving (1 roll):

Calories	260	Cholesterol	19 mg
Fat	9 g	Sodium	360 mg

Fruit & Ham Kabobs

Makes 8 to 10 kabobs

¾ cup pineapple juice
¼ cup packed brown sugar
2 tablespoons unsalted margarine or butter
1 ARMOUR® Lower Salt Ham Nugget (about 1¾ pounds), cut into 1¼-inch cubes
2 large red apples, cored and cut into sixths
2 large green apples, cored and cut into sixths
1 fresh pineapple, peeled, cored and cut into 1-inch chunks
3 kiwifruit, peeled and cut into ½-inch slices

Preheat oven to 350°F. Place pineapple juice, brown sugar and margarine in bottom of large casserole dish. Heat in oven until margarine is melted. Thread ham, apples, pineapple and kiwifruit onto 8 to 10 (10-inch) metal or wooden skewers, alternating ingredients. Place kabobs in warm sauce; turn to coat all sides with sauce. Bake 20 to 25 minutes, or until heated through. Turn kabobs twice during cooking, basting with sauce mixture. Serve over rice and garnish with red grapes, if desired.

Nutrients per serving (1 kabob):

Calories	277	Cholesterol	39 mg
Fat	7 g	Sodium	676 mg

Fruit & Ham Kabobs

Lemon Yogurt Raisin Tea Bread

Makes 12 servings

1¼ cups all-purpose flour
¾ cup whole wheat flour
4 tablespoons sugar, divided
2 teaspoons baking powder
½ teaspoon baking soda
¼ teaspoon salt
1½ cups DANNON® Lemon Lowfat Yogurt
¼ cup unsalted butter or margarine, melted
   and cooled slightly
1 egg
¾ cup raisins

Preheat oven to 350°F. Grease an 8½×4½-inch loaf pan. In a large bowl combine flours, 3 tablespoons sugar, baking powder, baking soda and salt. In a medium bowl combine yogurt, butter and egg; stir until well blended. Pour yogurt mixture into flour mixture. Add raisins; stir just until dry ingredients are moistened. Pour into prepared pan and smooth top. Sprinkle surface with remaining 1 tablespoon sugar.

Bake 40 to 45 minutes or until lightly brown and toothpick inserted just off center comes out clean. Cool in pan on wire rack 30 minutes. Remove from pan; cool completely, sugared side up.

Nutrients per serving:

Calories	190	Cholesterol	35 mg
Fat	5 g	Sodium	174 mg

Mixed Citrus Compote with Florida Orange Lime Syrup

Makes 6 servings

1 cup sugar
½ cup Florida orange juice
2 tablespoons fresh lime juice
1 tablespoon grated orange zest
2 teaspoons grated lime zest
4 seedless Florida oranges, peeled (white pith
   removed) and sectioned
2 Florida tangerines, seeded, peeled (white pith
   removed) and sectioned
2 red or pink Florida grapefruit, peeled (white
   pith removed) and sectioned
2 limes, peeled (white pith removed) and
   sectioned

Combine sugar, orange juice and lime juice in small saucepan. Bring to a boil over medium heat, stirring until sugar dissolves. Remove from heat; add orange zest and lime zest. Cool. Combine remaining ingredients in medium bowl. Add sugar syrup mixture, stirring gently to combine. Chill at least 1 hour before serving.

Nutrients per serving:

Calories	220	Cholesterol	0 mg
Fat	1 g	Sodium	1 mg

Favorite recipe from **Florida Department of Citrus**

Golden-Door Yogurt Bran Muffins

Makes 12 muffins

1½ cups wheat bran
½ cup boiling water
1⅓ cups whole wheat flour
1¼ teaspoons baking soda
½ teaspoon ground cinnamon
¼ teaspoon salt
¼ teaspoon ground cloves
¼ teaspoon ground nutmeg
1 egg
⅓ cup honey
½ cup DANNON® Plain Nonfat or Lowfat Yogurt
3 tablespoons vegetable oil
¾ cup fresh or frozen blueberries

Preheat oven to 350°F. Line muffin cups with paper baking cups. In a medium bowl combine wheat bran and boiling water; let stand 10 minutes to soften. In a large bowl combine flour, baking soda, cinnamon, salt, cloves and nutmeg. In a small bowl combine egg, honey, yogurt and oil; stir well. Add to bran mixture. Add egg mixture all at once to flour mixture; stir just until dry ingredients are moistened. Batter will be stiff. Fold in blueberries.

Fill prepared muffin cups ⅔ full. Bake 20 to 25 minutes or until toothpick inserted into center comes out clean. Serve warm.

Nutrients per serving (1 muffin):

Calories	130	Cholesterol	20 mg
Fat	5 g	Sodium	144 mg

Top to bottom: Lemon Yogurt Raisin Tea Bread, Golden-Door Yogurt Bran Muffins

Ham Breakfast Sandwich

Ham Breakfast Sandwiches

Makes 3 sandwiches

1 ounce Neufchâtel or light cream cheese, softened
2 teaspoons apricot spreadable fruit
2 teaspoons plain nonfat yogurt
6 slices raisin bread
  Lettuce leaves
1 package (6 ounces) ECKRICH® Lite Lower Salt Ham
3 Granny Smith apple rings

Combine cheese, spreadable fruit and yogurt in small bowl. Spread on bread. To make each sandwich: Place lettuce on 1 slice bread. Top with 2 slices ham, 1 apple ring and another slice of bread.

Nutrients per serving (1 sandwich):

Calories	223	Cholesterol	5 mg
Fat	5 g	Sodium	963 mg

Almond Cocoa Muffins

Makes 12 muffins

¾ cup whole wheat flour
¾ cup all-purpose flour
½ cup sugar
1 tablespoon baking powder
1 tablespoon unsweetened cocoa powder
1 teaspoon ground cinnamon
¼ teaspoon salt (optional)
1½ cups KELLOGG'S® ALL-BRAN® Cereal
1½ cups skim milk
2 egg whites
2 tablespoons vegetable oil
¼ cup chopped almonds
  Nonstick cooking spray

Stir together flours, sugar, baking powder, cocoa, cinnamon and salt. Set aside.

Measure Kellogg's® All-Bran® cereal and milk into large mixing bowl. Stir to combine. Let stand 3 minutes or until cereal is softened. Add egg whites, oil and almonds. Beat well.

Add flour mixture, stirring only until well combined. Portion batter evenly into 12 (2½-inch) muffin pan cups coated with nonstick cooking spray.

Bake at 400°F about 22 minutes or until lightly browned. Serve warm.

Nutrients per serving (1 muffin):

Calories	160	Cholesterol	45 mg
Fat	6 g	Sodium	250 mg

Five-Minute Fruit Dip

Makes 1¼ cups

½ cup MIRACLE WHIP® FREE® Nonfat Dressing
1 container (8 ounces) lemon-flavored low-fat yogurt

Mix ingredients until well blended; refrigerate. Serve with assorted fruit kabobs.

Prep time: 5 minutes plus refrigerating

Nutrients per serving (2 tablespoons):

Calories	60	Cholesterol	0 mg
Fat	1 g	Sodium	230 mg

Northern California Banana Bread

Makes 28 servings

3 extra-ripe, medium DOLE® Bananas, peeled
½ cup margarine, softened
½ cup firmly packed brown sugar
½ cup granulated sugar
1 egg
1 teaspoon vanilla extract
1¼ cups all-purpose flour
⅔ cup oat bran
½ cup whole wheat flour
2 teaspoons baking powder
1 teaspoon ground cinnamon
½ teaspoon salt
1 cup DOLE® Chopped Dates
1 cup DOLE® Chopped Almonds, toasted

Place bananas in blender. Process until puréed; use 1½ cups for recipe. Beat margarine and sugars in large bowl until light and fluffy. Beat in 1½ cups puréed bananas, egg and vanilla. Combine all-purpose flour, oat bran, whole wheat flour, baking powder, cinnamon and salt in medium bowl. Beat into banana mixture until blended. Stir in dates and almonds. Pour batter into greased 9×5-inch loaf pan. Bake in 350°F oven 65 minutes or until cake tester inserted in center comes out clean. Cool in pan on wire rack 10 minutes. Remove from pan. Cool completely on wire rack before slicing. To serve, cut loaf into 14 slices, then cut each slice lengthwise in half.

Prep time: 15 minutes
Bake time: 65 minutes

Nutrients per serving:

Calories	163	Cholesterol	10 mg
Fat	7 g	Sodium	96 mg

Brunch Rice

Makes 6 servings

1 teaspoon margarine
¾ cup shredded carrots
¾ cup diced green bell pepper
¾ cup (about 3 ounces) sliced fresh mushrooms
6 egg whites, beaten
2 eggs, beaten
½ cup skim milk
½ teaspoon salt
¼ teaspoon ground black pepper
3 cups cooked brown rice
½ cup (2 ounces) shredded Cheddar cheese
6 corn tortillas, warmed (optional)

Heat margarine in large skillet over medium-high heat until hot. Add carrots, green pepper, and mushrooms; cook and stir 2 minutes. Combine egg whites, eggs, milk, salt, and black pepper in small bowl. Reduce heat to medium and pour egg mixture over vegetables. Continue stirring 1½ to 2 minutes. Add rice and cheese; stir to gently separate grains. Heat 2 minutes. Serve immediately or spoon mixture into warmed corn tortillas.

To Microwave: Heat margarine in 2- to 3-quart microproof baking dish. Add carrots, green pepper, and mushrooms; cover and cook on HIGH (100% power) 4 minutes. Combine egg whites, eggs, milk, salt, and black pepper in small bowl; pour over vegetables. Cook on HIGH 4 minutes, stirring with fork after each minute to cut cooked eggs into small pieces. Stir in rice and cheese; cook on HIGH about 1 minute or until thoroughly heated. Serve immediately or spoon mixture into warmed corn tortillas.

Nutrients per serving:

Calories	212	Cholesterol	79 mg
Fat	7 g	Sodium	353 mg

Favorite recipe from **USA Rice Council**

Brunch Rice

Quick Nectarine Oat Muffins

Makes 20 muffins

2 cups whole wheat flour
1 cup uncooked rolled oats
½ cup unprocessed bran or wheat germ
½ cup packed light brown sugar
1½ teaspoons baking soda
3 teaspoons grated orange peel
1½ teaspoons ground cinnamon
1 teaspoon salt
2 eggs
1½ cups buttermilk
¼ cup vegetable oil
3 fresh California nectarines, chopped

Preheat oven to 400°F. Combine flour, oats, bran, brown sugar, baking soda, orange peel, cinnamon and salt in large bowl. Combine eggs, buttermilk and oil in medium bowl until blended; stir into flour mixture just until blended. Fold in nectarines. Spoon evenly into 20 (2½-inch) nonstick muffin cups.

Bake 20 minutes or until wooden pick inserted in centers comes out clean. Cool in pans 10 minutes. Remove from pans. Serve warm.

Nutrients per serving (1 muffin):

Calories	129	Cholesterol	27 mg
Fat	4 g	Sodium	199 mg

Favorite recipe from **California Tree Fruit Agreement**

Out-of-this-World Poppy Seed Bread

Makes 1 loaf

Bread
¾ cup granulated sugar
¼ cup vegetable shortening
2 eggs, beaten
1 cup orange juice
½ cup milk
¼ cup poppy seed
2 teaspoons grated orange peel
2½ cups all-purpose flour
2 cups Rice CHEX® brand cereal, crushed to 1 cup
1 tablespoon baking powder

Glaze
¾ cup sifted powdered sugar
1 tablespoon orange juice
1 teaspoon grated orange peel

For Bread, preheat oven to 350°F. Grease 9×5×3-inch loaf pan. In large bowl cream granulated sugar and shortening. Stir in eggs. In medium bowl combine orange juice, milk, poppy seed and orange peel. In separate medium bowl combine flour, cereal and baking powder. Add alternately with orange juice mixture to creamed mixture, stirring well after each addition. Spread evenly into prepared pan. Bake 55 to 60 minutes or until tester inserted in center comes out clean. Let stand 15 minutes before removing from pan. Cool completely.

For Glaze, in small bowl combine powdered sugar, orange juice and orange peel; mix well. Spread over cooled bread.

Nutrients per serving (½-inch slice):

Calories	170	Cholesterol	24 mg
Fat	5 g	Sodium	94 mg

Wild Rice Blueberry Muffins

Makes 12 muffins

1½ cups all-purpose flour
½ cup sugar
2 teaspoons baking powder
1 teaspoon ground cinnamon
½ teaspoon salt
¼ cup applesauce
4 egg whites
½ cup skim milk
1 cup fresh blueberries
1 cup well-cooked wild rice

Preheat oven to 400°F. Paper-line 12 (2½-inch) muffin cups.

Stir together flour, sugar, baking powder, cinnamon and salt in large bowl. Whisk together applesauce, egg whites and milk in small bowl. Sprinkle 1 tablespoon flour mixture over blueberries in small bowl; toss to coat. Fold applesauce mixture into flour mixture. Fold blueberries and rice into flour mixture. (Batter will be stiff.) Spoon evenly into prepared muffin cups.

Bake 15 to 20 minutes until wooden pick inserted in center comes out clean. Cool in pan 10 minutes. Remove from pan. Serve warm or cool completely on wire rack.

Nutrients per serving (1 muffin):

Calories	119	Cholesterol	trace
Fat	trace	Sodium	192 mg

Favorite recipe from **Minnesota Cultivated Wild Rice Council**

Florida Orange Date Bran Muffins

Makes 12 muffins

  2 cups shredded bran cereal
¾ cup boiling water
¼ cup vegetable oil
¾ cup buttermilk
¼ cup Florida orange juice
  2 tablespoons dark molasses
  2 tablespoons honey
  1 tablespoon grated orange zest
  1 egg
¾ cup all-purpose flour
½ cup whole wheat flour
1½ teaspoons baking soda
½ teaspoon salt
  1 cup chopped dates
¾ cup chopped walnuts (optional)

Preheat oven to 400°F. Grease 12 (2½-inch) muffin cups.

Combine bran cereal, water and oil in large bowl, stirring until bran softens. Whisk buttermilk, orange juice, molasses, honey, orange zest and egg in small bowl until blended. Combine flours, baking soda and salt in another small bowl. Add buttermilk mixture to bran mixture, stirring to combine. Add flour mixture, dates and walnuts to bran mixture, stirring just until flour mixture is moistened. Spoon evenly into muffin cups.

Bake about 18 minutes or until tops spring back when lightly pressed. Cool in pan 5 minutes before removing to wire rack. Serve warm or at room temperature.

Nutrients per serving (1 muffin):			
Calories	194	Cholesterol	18 mg
Fat	6 g	Sodium	377 mg

Favorite recipe from **Florida Department of Citrus**

Cheesy Apple Omelet

Makes 4 servings

  Nonstick cooking spray
  1 red apple, sliced
¼ cup sliced green onions
  4 eggs
  4 egg whites
¼ cup low fat milk
¼ teaspoon pepper
½ cup grated low fat Cheddar cheese

Spray nonstick skillet or omelet pan with cooking spray. Cook apple slices and green onions over medium heat until tender. Remove from pan; set aside.

Combine eggs, egg whites, milk and pepper in medium bowl; beat well with wire whisk. Coat same pan with cooking spray. Pour in ½ of egg mixture. As mixture begins to cook, gently lift edges of omelet with spatula and tilt pan to allow uncooked portion to flow underneath. When egg mixture is set, spoon ½ of apple mixture and ¼ cup grated cheese over ½ of omelet. Loosen omelet with spatula and carefully fold in half. Set omelet on warm serving platter. Cut omelet into 2 pieces. Repeat procedure with remaining ingredients. Serve immediately.

Nutrients per serving:			
Calories	188	Cholesterol	224 mg
Fat	10 g	Sodium	213 mg

Favorite recipe from **Western New York Apple Growers Association**

Apple-Walnut Muffins

Makes 12 muffins

  2 cups all-purpose flour
  2 teaspoons baking powder
1½ teaspoons ground cinnamon
¼ teaspoon ground nutmeg
¼ teaspoon salt
  2 eggs, beaten
⅔ cup thawed frozen unsweetened apple juice
      concentrate
⅓ cup butter or margarine, melted
  1 teaspoon vanilla extract
  1 cup finely chopped peeled apples (about
      2 medium apples)
½ cup chopped walnuts

Preheat oven to 350°F. Grease or paper-line 12 (2½-inch) muffin cups.

Combine dry ingredients in medium bowl. Combine eggs, apple juice concentrate, butter and vanilla in small bowl until blended; stir into flour mixture just until dry ingredients are moistened. Stir in apples and walnuts. Spoon batter into prepared cups, filling each cup ¾ full.

Bake 25 minutes or until golden brown. Cool in pan on wire rack 5 minutes. Remove from pan; cool. Serve warm or at room temperature.

Note: Cooled muffins may be wrapped tightly with aluminum foil and frozen up to 3 months.

Nutrients per serving (1 muffin):			
Calories	199	Cholesterol	49 mg
Fat	9 g	Sodium	183 mg

Rice Crêpe

Rice Crêpes

Makes 10 crêpes

1 carton (8 ounces) egg substitute*
⅔ cup evaporated skim milk
1 tablespoon margarine, melted
½ cup all-purpose flour
1 tablespoon granulated sugar
1 cup cooked rice
    Nonstick cooking spray
2½ cups fresh fruit (strawberries, raspberries,
        blueberries, or other favorite fruit)
    Low-sugar fruit spread (optional)
    Light sour cream (optional)
1 tablespoon confectioners' sugar for garnish
        (optional)

Combine egg substitute, milk, and margarine in large bowl. Stir in flour and granulated sugar until smooth and well blended. Stir in rice; let stand 5 minutes.

Heat 8-inch nonstick skillet or crêpe pan; coat with nonstick cooking spray. Spoon ¼ cup batter into pan. Lift pan off heat; quickly tilt pan in rotating motion so that bottom of pan is completely covered with batter. Place pan back on heat and continue cooking until surface is dry, about 45 seconds. Turn crêpe over and cook 15 to 20 seconds; set aside. Continue with remaining crêpe batter. Place waxed paper between crêpes. Spread each crêpe with your favorite filling: strawberries, raspberries, blueberries, fruit spread, or sour cream.

Roll up and sprinkle with confectioners' sugar for garnish.

Substitute 8 egg whites or 4 eggs for 8 ounces egg substitute, if desired.

Nutrients per serving (1 crêpe):

Calories	111	Cholesterol	1 mg
Fat	2 g	Sodium	152 mg

Favorite recipe from **USA Rice Council**

Mini Sausage Biscuit Sandwiches

Makes 20 mini-sandwiches

1 package (1 pound) LOUIS RICH®, fully
        cooked, Turkey Smoked Sausage
2 cans (10 ounces each) refrigerated buttermilk
        flaky biscuits
    Honey, barbecue sauce or ketchup (optional)

Preheat oven to 400°F. Cut sausage lengthwise into quarters; cut each quarter into 5 pieces.

Remove biscuits from can; separate. Using fingers, flatten each biscuit to about 4 inches. Place small

amount of honey, barbecue sauce or ketchup, if desired, in center of each biscuit; top each with 1 piece of sausage.

Bring up edges of biscuit and pinch together to seal over top of sausage. Place on baking sheet. Bake about 10 minutes or until lightly browned.

Nutrients per serving (1 mini-sandwich):

Calories	125	Cholesterol	15 mg
Fat	6 g	Sodium	500 mg

Blueberry Bran Muffins

Makes 12 muffins

1½ cups all-purpose flour
¼ cup sugar
1 tablespoon baking powder
¼ teaspoon salt
1½ cups KELLOGG'S® COMPLETE®
        BRAN FLAKES Cereal
1 cup skim milk
1 egg
¼ cup vegetable oil
1½ cup fresh or frozen blueberries
    Nonstick cooking spray

Stir together flour, sugar, baking powder and salt. Set aside.

Measure Kellogg's® Complete® Bran Flakes cereal and milk into large mixing bowl. Stir to combine. Let stand about 3 minutes or until cereal is softened. Add egg and oil, mixing well.

Add flour mixture, stirring only until combined. Stir in blueberries. Portion batter evenly into 12 (2½-inch) muffin pan cups coated with nonstick cooking spray.

Bake at 400°F about 20 minutes or until golden brown. Serve warm.

Nutrients per serving (1 muffin):

Calories	140	Cholesterol	25 mg
Fat	5 g	Sodium	170 mg

Double Oat Muffins

Makes 12 muffins

2 cups QUAKER® Oat Bran hot cereal,
    uncooked
⅓ cup firmly packed brown sugar
¼ cup all-purpose flour
2 teaspoons baking powder
¼ teaspoon salt (optional)
¼ teaspoon ground nutmeg (optional)
1 cup skim milk
2 egg whites, slightly beaten
3 tablespoons vegetable oil
1½ teaspoons vanilla
¼ cup QUAKER® Oats (quick or old fashioned,
    uncooked)
1 tablespoon firmly packed brown sugar

Heat oven to 400°F. Line 12 medium muffin cups
with paper baking cups or grease lightly. Combine oat
bran, ⅓ cup brown sugar, flour, baking powder, salt
and nutmeg. Add combined milk, egg whites, oil and
vanilla, mixing just until moistened. Fill muffin cups
almost full. Combine oats and 1 tablespoon brown
sugar; sprinkle evenly over muffin tops. Bake 20 to
22 minutes or until golden brown. Remove to wire
rack. Cool completely.

To Microwave: Line 6 microwavable muffin cups with
double paper baking cups. Combine oat bran, ⅓ cup
brown sugar, flour, baking powder, salt and nutmeg. Add
combined milk, egg whites, oil and vanilla, mixing just
until moistened. Fill muffin cups almost full. Combine oats
and 1 tablespoon brown sugar; sprinkle evenly over muffin
tops. Microwave at HIGH (100% power) 2½ to 3 minutes
or until wooden toothpick inserted in centers comes out

clean. Remove from pan; cool 5 minutes before serving.
Line muffin cups with additional double paper baking
cups. Repeat procedure with remaining batter.

Tips: *To freeze muffins, wrap securely in foil or place in
freezer bag. Seal, label and freeze.*

*To reheat muffins, unwrap frozen muffins. Microwave at
HIGH (100% power) about 30 seconds per muffin.*

Nutrients per serving (1 muffin):

Calories	140	Cholesterol	0 mg
Fat	5 g	Sodium	90 mg

Carrot Spice Loaf

Makes 1 loaf, 12 servings

2¼ cups all-purpose flour
1¼ cups plus 3 tablespoons QUAKER® Oats
    (quick or old fashioned, uncooked), divided
¾ cup firmly packed brown sugar
4 teaspoons baking powder
½ teaspoon baking soda
½ teaspoon ground cinnamon
¼ teaspoon salt (optional)
¼ teaspoon ground ginger (optional)
⅛ teaspoon ground cloves (optional)
½ cup frozen apple juice concentrate, thawed
⅓ cup vegetable oil
¼ cup water
4 egg whites
1 cup shredded carrots (about 2 medium)
½ cup chopped dates or raisins

Heat oven to 350°F. Lightly oil 8×4- or 9×5-inch
loaf pan. Combine dry ingredients except for
3 tablespoons oats; mix well. Add combined juice
concentrate, oil, water and egg whites, mixing just
until moistened. Fold in carrots and dates. Spread
evenly into prepared pan. Sprinkle top with remaining
3 tablespoons oats. Bake 1 hour and 10 minutes or
until wooden toothpick inserted in center comes out
clean. Cool 10 minutes; remove from pan. Cool
completely on wire rack. Store tightly covered.

Nutrients per serving (1 slice):

Calories	265	Cholesterol	0 mg
Fat	7 g	Sodium	200 mg

Double Oat Muffins

Apple Streusel Coffee Cake

Makes 9 servings

Cake
¼ cup CRISCO® Shortening
½ cup sugar
2 egg whites
1 teaspoon vanilla
¾ cup dry oat bran high fiber hot cereal
1 cup chunky applesauce
1¼ cups all-purpose flour
1½ teaspoons ground cinnamon
1 teaspoon baking powder
¾ teaspoon baking soda
¼ teaspoon salt (optional)
¼ teaspoon ground nutmeg

Filling and Topping
1 cup chunky applesauce, divided
¼ cup sugar
¼ teaspoon ground cinnamon

Heat oven to 375°F. Grease 8-inch square pan.

For Cake, combine Crisco® and ½ cup sugar in medium bowl with fork until blended and crumbly. Add egg whites and vanilla. Beat until fairly smooth. Stir in oat bran, then 1 cup applesauce. Let stand 5 minutes. Combine flour, 1½ teaspoons cinnamon, baking powder, baking soda, salt and nutmeg in small bowl. Stir into oat bran mixture. Spread half of batter in pan.

For Filling and Topping, spread ¾ cup applesauce over batter. Combine ¼ cup sugar and ¼ teaspoon cinnamon. Sprinkle half over applesauce. Add remaining batter; spread gently and evenly. Top with remaining ¼ cup applesauce; spread thinly and evenly. Sprinkle with remaining sugar-cinnamon mixture. Bake at 375°F for 30 to 35 minutes or until top is golden brown and center springs back when touched lightly. Cut into squares. Serve warm.

Nutrients per serving:			
Calories	242	Cholesterol	0 mg
Fat	6 g	Sodium	120 mg

Mexican Egg Muffin

Mexican Egg Muffin

Makes 1 serving

1 large egg
2 teaspoons water
1 teaspoon chopped green onion
1 teaspoon diet margarine
½ English muffin, toasted
4 teaspoons prepared salsa
1 slice BORDEN® Lite-line® Process Cheese Product, any flavor, cut into triangles*

In small bowl, beat egg, water and green onion. In small skillet, melt margarine; add egg mixture. Cook and stir until egg is set. Spoon egg mixture onto muffin; top with salsa, then cheese product slice. Place on baking sheet; broil until cheese product slice begins to melt. Garnish as desired.

*"½ the calories"– 8% milkfat product

Nutrients per serving:			
Calories	220	Cholesterol	226 mg
Fat	10 g	Sodium	614 mg

A steaming bowlful of hearty soup coupled with a square of tender cornbread is perfect for a lightweight lunch or supper. Create your own tempting combination, such as Beef Stew à la Italia teeming with chunky vegetables and paired with a wedge of hearty Cheesy Onion Flatbread.

Southwest Chili

Makes 4 servings

1 tablespoon olive oil
1 large onion, chopped
2 large tomatoes, chopped
1 can (4 ounces) chopped green chilies,
   undrained
1 tablespoon chili powder
1 teaspoon ground cumin
1 can (15 ounces) red kidney beans, undrained
1 can (15 ounces) great Northern beans,
   undrained
¼ cup cilantro leaves, chopped (optional)

Heat oil in large saucepan over medium heat. Add onion; cook until tender, stirring occasionally.

Stir in tomatoes, chilies with liquid, chili powder and cumin. Bring to a boil. Add beans with liquid.

Reduce heat to low; cover. Simmer 15 minutes, stirring occasionally. Sprinkle individual servings with cilantro, if desired.

Nutrients per serving:

Calories	285	Cholesterol	0 mg
Fat	5 g	Sodium	459 mg

Dijon Lamb Stew

Makes 4 servings

½ pound boneless lamb, cut into small pieces
½ medium onion, chopped
½ teaspoon dried rosemary leaves, crushed
1 tablespoon olive oil
   Salt and pepper (optional)
1 can (14½ ounces) DEL MONTE® Italian
   Recipe Stewed Tomatoes
1 carrot, julienne cut
1 tablespoon Dijon-style mustard
1 can (15 ounces) white beans or pinto beans,
   drained
   Sliced ripe olives (optional)
   Chopped fresh parsley (optional)

In large skillet, brown lamb, onion and rosemary in oil over medium-high heat, stirring occasionally. Season with salt and pepper, if desired. Add tomatoes with juice, carrot and mustard. Cover and cook over medium heat 10 minutes; add beans. Cook, uncovered, over medium heat 5 minutes, stirring occasionally until lamb is tender. Garnish with sliced ripe olives and chopped parsley, if desired.

Variation: Top sirloin steak may be substituted for lamb.

Prep time: 10 minutes
Cook time: 20 minutes

Nutrients per serving:

Calories	209	Cholesterol	29 mg
Fat	7 g	Sodium	753 mg

Top to bottom: Southwest Chili, Cheesy Corn Sticks (page 151)

Calico Chicken Soup

Navy Bean Soup

Makes 4 servings

2 tablespoons vegetable oil
1 cup chopped leeks
1½ cups (6 ounces) ARMOUR® Lower Salt Ham
cut into ½-inch cubes
1 cup uncooked navy beans, soaked overnight
and drained
1 tablespoon chopped jalapeño peppers

Heat oil in 3-quart saucepan over medium heat. Add leeks; cook and stir 3 to 5 minutes or until tender. Stir in ham, beans and peppers; add enough water to just cover beans. Bring to a boil over high heat. Reduce heat to low. Cover; simmer 1 to 1½ hours or until beans are tender.

Nutrients per serving:

Calories	282	Cholesterol	21 mg
Fat	10 g	Sodium	420 mg

Calico Chicken Soup

Makes 8 servings, 2 quarts

1 pound skinned boneless chicken breasts, cut
into chunks
1 tablespoon vegetable oil
6 cups water
2 tablespoons WYLER'S® or STEERO® Chicken-
Flavor Instant Bouillon *or* 6 Chicken-
Flavor Bouillon Cubes
2 cups broccoli flowerets
2 cups pared, sliced carrots
¾ cup chopped red bell pepper
¼ teaspoon black pepper

In large kettle or Dutch oven, brown chicken in oil. Add remaining ingredients. Bring to a boil; reduce heat. Simmer uncovered 45 minutes, stirring occasionally. Refrigerate leftovers.

Nutrients per serving (1 cup):

Calories	86	Cholesterol	23 mg
Fat	3 g	Sodium	716 mg

Vegetable Bean Soup

Makes about 6 servings, 6 cups

1 cup sliced leeks
1 clove garlic, minced
1 tablespoon vegetable or olive oil
3 cups water
1 can (16 ounces) HEINZ® Vegetarian Beans in
Tomato Sauce
1 can (8 ounces) whole kernel corn, drained
1 cup cubed (½-inch) potatoes
½ cup sliced celery
½ cup sliced carrots
2 teaspoons HEINZ® Worcestershire Sauce
1 bay leaf
¼ teaspoon dried thyme leaves, crushed
¼ teaspoon salt
⅛ teaspoon black pepper

In 3-quart saucepan, cook and stir leeks and garlic in oil until tender. Add water and remaining ingredients; bring to a boil. Reduce heat to low; cover and simmer 30 minutes or until vegetables are tender. Remove bay leaf before serving.

Nutrients per serving:

Calories	197	Cholesterol	0 mg
Fat	3 g	Sodium	542 mg

Beef Noodle Soup

Makes 10 servings

    2 tablespoons CRISCO® PURITAN® Oil
    ½ pound boneless beef sirloin, cut into thin strips
    ¼ cup chopped green onions
    1 tablespoon all-purpose flour
    3 cans (10½ ounces each) condensed chicken
        broth
    3 cups water
    2 cups cooked vermicelli or very fine egg
        noodles

Heat Crisco® Oil in 3-quart saucepan. Add beef.
Cook and stir over medium-high heat until beef is
browned.

Add onions. Cook, stirring occasionally, about
2 minutes or until onions are tender. Stir in flour. Add
chicken broth and water.

Heat to boiling, stirring occasionally. Reduce heat to
low. Simmer about 5 minutes. Stir in noodles. Simmer
until soup is heated through.

Nutrients per serving:			
Calories	144	Cholesterol	28 mg
Fat	6 g	Sodium	579 mg

Souper Surprise Barley Soup

Makes about 8 servings, 8 cups

    3 cups water
    ½ cup medium pearled barley
    3 beef bouillon cubes
    2 cups cut asparagus or broccoli pieces (fresh
        or frozen), cooked and drained
    4 cups low-fat milk
    5 slices American cheese
    ¼ teaspoon ground nutmeg
    ¼ teaspoon black pepper
    4 slices bacon (optional), cooked crisp and
        crumbled

In large saucepan, combine water, barley and
bouillon. Bring to a boil over medium-high heat.
Reduce heat to low and simmer, 50 to 60 minutes,
stirring often, until barley is tender and nearly all of
the liquid is absorbed.

Stir in asparagus, milk, cheese, nutmeg and pepper.
Add bacon, if desired. Increase heat to medium-high
and cook, stirring constantly, until cheese melts.

Nutrients per serving:			
Calories	169	Cholesterol	20 mg
Fat	6 g	Sodium	618 mg

Favorite recipe from **North Dakota Barley Council**

Zesty Tomato Turkey Soup

Makes 4 servings

    2 slices bacon
    ¼ cup chopped onion
    1 small clove garlic, minced
    2 cans (12 ounces each) cocktail vegetable juice
    1 can (8 ounces) stewed tomatoes, cut up
    1 cup (5 ounces) diced cooked BUTTERBALL®
        Turkey
    ⅓ cup chopped seeded cucumber
    ¼ cup chopped green bell pepper
    1 teaspoon chicken bouillon granules
    1 teaspoon Worcestershire sauce
    ½ teaspoon sugar

Cook bacon in large saucepan over medium-high heat
until crisp; crumble into small pieces and set aside.
In drippings, cook and stir onion and garlic until
tender. Add remaining ingredients, including reserved
bacon. Bring to a boil over high heat. Reduce heat to
low; simmer 5 minutes or until hot.

To Microwave: Cut bacon into 1-inch pieces. Cook bacon
in 2-quart microwave-safe casserole on HIGH (100%
power) 2½ to 3 minutes, stirring once. Remove bacon and
set aside. In drippings, cook onion and garlic on HIGH
2 minutes, stirring once. Add remaining ingredients,
including reserved bacon. Cook on HIGH 7 to 8 minutes
or until hot, stirring twice.

Nutrients per serving:			
Calories	127	Cholesterol	27 mg
Fat	3 g	Sodium	912 mg

Zesty Tomato Turkey Soup

Picante Onion Soup

Picante Onion Soup

Makes 6 servings

3 cups thinly sliced onions
1 clove garlic, minced
¼ cup butter or margarine
2 cups tomato juice
1 can (10½ ounces) condensed beef broth
1 soup can water
½ cup PACE® Picante Sauce
1 cup unseasoned croutons (optional)
1 cup (4 ounces) shredded Monterey Jack cheese (optional)
Additional PACE® Picante Sauce

Cook onions and garlic in butter in 3-quart saucepan over medium-low heat about 20 minutes, stirring frequently, until onions are tender and golden brown. Stir in tomato juice, broth, water and ½ cup picante sauce; bring to a boil over high heat. Reduce heat to low. Simmer, uncovered, 20 minutes. Ladle soup into bowls and sprinkle with croutons and cheese. Serve with additional Pace® picante sauce, if desired.

Nutrients per serving:

Calories	119	Cholesterol	42 mg
Fat	8 g	Sodium	1051 mg

Chilled Carrot Soup

Makes 8 servings

2 tablespoons vegetable oil
1 large onion, chopped
1½ teaspoons curry powder
3½ cups chicken broth
1 pound carrots, sliced
2 stalks celery, sliced
1 bay leaf
½ teaspoon ground cumin
½ teaspoon TABASCO® pepper sauce
1 cup low-fat milk
1 cup low-fat cottage cheese

In large saucepan heat oil; cook and stir onion and curry 3 to 5 minutes. Add broth, carrots, celery, bay leaf, cumin and TABASCO sauce; mix well. Cover; simmer 25 minutes or until vegetables are tender. Remove bay leaf. Spoon about ⅓ each carrot mixture, milk and cottage cheese into blender container or food processor. Cover; process until smooth. Pour into serving bowl. Repeat with remaining carrot mixture, milk and cottage cheese. Cover; refrigerate until chilled. Serve with additional TABASCO sauce, if desired.

Nutrients per serving:

Calories	120	Cholesterol	5 mg
Fat	5 g	Sodium	508 mg

Hearty Vegetable Stew

Makes 4 servings

1 tablespoon HOLLYWOOD® Safflower Oil
½ pound small mushrooms, sliced
½ cup chopped onion
2½ cups water
1 bay leaf
1 teaspoon dried thyme leaves, crushed
1 teaspoon low-sodium instant beef bouillon granules
¾ teaspoon garlic powder
½ teaspoon salt (optional)
¼ teaspoon ground black pepper
3 medium baking potatoes, cut into 2-inch chunks
3 large carrots, cut into 2-inch strips
2 cups coarsely chopped celery
1 pound tofu, cut into small cubes

In large saucepan, heat oil until hot. Add mushrooms and onion; cook and stir 5 minutes. Add water, bay leaf, thyme, bouillon, garlic powder, salt (if used), pepper, potatoes and carrots. Bring to a boil; reduce heat to low. Cover and simmer 20 minutes. Add celery; cover and simmer an additional 10 minutes or until vegetables are tender. Add tofu and heat through, about 5 minutes. Remove bay leaf before serving.

Nutrients per serving:

Calories	273	Cholesterol	0 mg
Fat	8 g	Sodium	88 mg

Seafood Corn Chowder

Makes 6 servings

1 tablespoon margarine
1 cup chopped onions
½ cup chopped green bell pepper
½ cup chopped red bell pepper
⅓ cup chopped celery
1 tablespoon all-purpose flour
1 can (10½ ounces) low-sodium chicken broth
2 cups skim milk
1 can (12 ounces) evaporated skim milk
8 to 12 ounces crab-flavored SURIMI Seafood chunks
2 cups fresh or frozen whole kernel corn
½ teaspoon black pepper
½ teaspoon paprika

Melt margarine in large saucepan over medium heat. Add onions, bell peppers and celery. Cook and stir, uncovered, over medium heat 4 to 5 minutes or until vegetables are tender. Add flour to vegetable mixture; cook and stir constantly 2 minutes. Gradually add chicken broth and bring to a boil. Stir in milk, evaporated milk, Surimi Seafood, corn, black pepper and paprika. Heat, stirring occasionally, 5 minutes or until chowder is hot. Serve.

Nutrients per serving:

Calories	217	Cholesterol	17 mg
Fat	3 g	Sodium	630 mg

Favorite recipe from **Surimi Seafood Education Center**

Asparagus and Surimi Seafood Soup

Makes 4 servings

3 cans (10½ ounces *each*) low-sodium chicken broth (about 4 cups)
2 thin slices fresh ginger
2 cups (about ¾ pound) diagonally sliced asparagus pieces (*each* ½ inch long)
¼ cup sliced green onions, including part of green tops
3 tablespoons rice vinegar or white wine vinegar
¼ teaspoon crushed red pepper
8 to 12 ounces crab-flavored SURIMI Seafood legs or chunks, cut diagonally

Bring chicken broth and ginger to a boil in large saucepan. Add asparagus, green onions, vinegar and crushed red pepper. Simmer 5 minutes or until asparagus is crisp-tender. Add Surimi Seafood and simmer 5 minutes longer or until seafood is hot. Remove and discard ginger. Serve hot.

Nutrients per serving:

Calories	136	Cholesterol	18 mg
Fat	3 g	Sodium	784 mg

Favorite recipe from **Surimi Seafood Education Center**

Left to right: Seafood Corn Chowder, Asparagus and Surimi Seafood Soup

Quick Deli Turkey Soup

Makes 4 servings

1 can (13¾ ounces) ready-to-serve chicken broth
1 can (14½ ounces) stewed tomatoes
1 small zucchini, cut up (about 1 cup)
¼ teaspoon dried basil leaves, crushed
½ pound BUTTERBALL® Deli Turkey Breast, cubed
½ cup cooked chili-mac pasta or macaroni

Combine broth, tomatoes with juice, zucchini and basil in large saucepan. Bring to a boil over high heat. Reduce heat to low; simmer 10 minutes or until zucchini is tender. Stir in turkey and pasta. Continue heating until turkey is hot.

Nutrients per serving:

Calories	152	Cholesterol	40 mg
Fat	3 g	Sodium	537 mg

Savory Seafood Soup

Savory Lentil Soup

Makes 6 servings

1 cup uncooked lentils
3 cups (12 ounces) small cubes ARMOUR® Lower Salt Ham
1 (14½-ounce) can no salt added stewed tomatoes
1 small onion, chopped
½ cup chopped celery
1 teaspoon hot pepper sauce
1 teaspoon MRS. DASH®, Original Blend

Wash lentils; remove any grit or broken shells. Combine all ingredients in large covered kettle; stir in 4 cups water. Bring to a boil over medium-high heat, stirring often. Reduce heat to low. Simmer, covered, for 1 hour or until lentils are tender and soup is thick. Garnish with celery leaves, if desired.

Nutrients per serving:

Calories	220	Cholesterol	28 mg
Fat	3 g	Sodium	537 mg

Savory Seafood Soup

Makes 4 servings

2½ cups water or chicken broth
1½ cups dry white wine
1 small onion, chopped
½ red bell pepper, chopped
½ green bell pepper, chopped
1 small clove garlic, minced
½ pound halibut, cut into 1-inch chunks
½ pound sea scallops, halved crosswise
1 teaspoon dried thyme leaves, crushed
Juice of ½ lime
Dash of hot pepper sauce
Salt and black pepper (optional)

Combine water, wine, onion, red and green peppers and garlic in large saucepan. Bring to a boil. Reduce heat to medium; cover. Cook 15 minutes or until vegetables are tender, stirring occasionally.

Add halibut, scallops and thyme. Continue cooking 2 minutes or until fish and scallops turn opaque. Stir in lime juice and hot pepper sauce. Season with salt and black pepper, if desired.

Nutrients per serving:

Calories	187	Cholesterol	37 mg
Fat	2 g	Sodium	178 mg

Old-Fashioned Beef Stew

Old-Fashioned Beef Stew

Makes 8 servings

1 tablespoon **CRISCO® Vegetable Oil**
1¼ **pounds boneless beef round steak, trimmed
    and cut into 1-inch cubes**
2¾ **cups water, divided**
1 **teaspoon Worcestershire sauce**
2 **bay leaves**
1 **clove garlic, minced**
½ **teaspoon paprika**
¼ **teaspoon pepper**
8 **medium carrots, quartered**
8 **small potatoes, peeled and quartered**
4 **small onions, quartered**
1 **package (9 ounces) frozen cut green beans**
1 **tablespoon cornstarch**
  Salt (optional)

1. Heat Crisco® Oil in Dutch oven on medium-high
heat. Add beef. Cook and stir until browned. Add
1½ cups water, Worcestershire sauce, bay leaves,
garlic, paprika and pepper. Bring to a boil. Reduce
heat to low. Cover. Simmer one hour 15 minutes,
stirring occasionally. Remove bay leaves.

2. Add carrots, potatoes and onions. Cover. Simmer
30 to 45 minutes or until vegetables are almost
tender. Add beans. Simmer 5 minutes or until tender.
Remove from heat. Add one cup water to Dutch oven.

3. Combine remaining ¼ cup water and cornstarch
in small bowl. Stir well. Stir into ingredients in Dutch
oven. Return to low heat. Cook and stir until
thickened. Season with salt, if desired.

Nutrients per serving:

Calories	290	Cholesterol	60 mg
Fat	8 g	Sodium	95 mg

Lobster Wild Rice Bisque

Makes 10 servings

2 **tablespoons extra light margarine**
1 **cup chopped onion**
1 **can (4 ounces) sliced mushrooms, drained**
1 **tablespoon all-purpose flour**
2 **teaspoons dried rosemary leaves, crushed**
½ **teaspoon salt**
½ **teaspoon pepper**
4 **cups low sodium chicken broth**
1 **cup skim milk**
¼ **cup cooking sherry**
2 **cups cooked wild rice**
1 **cup chopped canned tomatoes**
6 **ounces imitation lobster, cut into 1-inch
    chunks**
1 **cup shredded low fat Cheddar cheese**

Heat margarine in large saucepan until melted and
bubbly. Add onion and mushrooms; cook and stir
until onion is softened. Stir in flour, rosemary, salt
and pepper. Cook until bubbly. Gradually add
chicken broth; bring to a boil, stirring often. Stir in
milk and sherry. Add rice, tomatoes and lobster. Heat
thoroughly. Fold in Cheddar cheese just before serving.

Nutrients per serving:

Calories	138	Cholesterol	18 mg
Fat	4 g	Sodium	371 mg

Favorite recipe from **Minnesota Cultivated Wild Rice Council**

Venetian Soup or Pasta Sauce

Makes 4 servings

1 tablespoon vegetable oil
2 cups chopped onions
2 teaspoons minced garlic
2 cans (28 ounces *each*) whole tomatoes,
     drained and cut up (about 6 cups)
6 fresh California plums, cut into chunks
¾ teaspoon pepper
2 tablespoons minced fresh parsley
2 teaspoons dried basil leaves, crushed
1 teaspoon dried oregano leaves, crushed
1 bay leaf
1 teaspoon fennel seed

Heat oil in large saucepan over medium-high heat until hot; add onions. Cook and stir about 2 minutes or until onions are tender. Add garlic, tomatoes, plums and pepper; bring to a boil. Reduce heat to low; simmer gently 45 to 50 minutes. Add remaining ingredients; simmer 10 minutes more. Remove and discard bay leaf. Serve as soup or spoon over hot cooked pasta as sauce, if desired.

Nutrients per serving (1 cup):

Calories	89	Cholesterol	0 mg
Fat	2 g	Sodium	296 mg

Favorite recipe from **California Tree Fruit Agreement**

Spiced Pear-Cranberry Soup

Makes 4 servings

2 fresh California Bartlett pears, peeled and
     chopped
¼ teaspoon ground cinnamon
⅛ teaspoon ground cloves
2 thin slices fresh ginger (optional)
1½ cups low calorie cranberry juice cocktail
     Plain low fat yogurt (optional)

Combine pears, cinnamon, cloves and ginger in food processor or blender; process until smooth. With machine running, slowly add cranberry juice through feed cap, processing until soup is well blended. Garnish each serving with dollop of yogurt, if desired. Serve soup warm or cold.

Nutrients per serving (¾ cup):

Calories	66	Cholesterol	0 mg
Fat	trace	Sodium	6 mg

Favorite recipe from **California Tree Fruit Agreement**

Cream of Carrot Soup

Makes 6 servings

1 can (10¾ ounces) condensed chicken broth
6 medium carrots, peeled and sliced (1 pound)
1 cup chopped celery
1 cup chopped onion
1 cup cream-style Cottage cheese
2 cups milk
¼ teaspoon salt
⅛ teaspoon pepper
½ cup plain yogurt
     Croutons (optional)

Combine chicken broth, carrots, celery and onion in 3-quart saucepan. Bring to a boil. Reduce heat; cover and simmer for 15 to 20 minutes until vegetables are tender. Transfer mixture to blender or food processor. Add Cottage cheese; cover and blend until smooth.

Return mixture to saucepan. Stir in milk, salt and pepper; heat through (do not boil). Transfer mixture to tureen or serving bowl; dollop with yogurt. Gently swirl yogurt into soup with spoon. Sprinkle with croutons, if desired.

Nutrients per serving:

Calories	151	Cholesterol	17 mg
Fat	5 g	Sodium	501 mg

Favorite recipe from **Wisconsin Milk Marketing Board © 1994**

Cream of Carrot Soup

Golden Tomato Soup

Makes 8 servings

- 4 teaspoons reduced-calorie margarine
- 1 cup chopped onion
- 2 cloves garlic, coarsely chopped
- ½ cup chopped carrots
- ¼ cup chopped celery
- 8 medium tomatoes, blanched, peeled, seeded, chopped
- 6 cups chicken broth
- ¼ cup uncooked rice
- 2 tablespoons tomato paste
- 1 tablespoon Worcestershire sauce
- ¼ to ½ teaspoon black pepper
- ½ teaspoon dried thyme leaves, crushed
- 5 drops hot pepper sauce

Melt margarine in large Dutch oven over medium-high heat. Add onion and garlic; cook and stir 1 to 2 minutes or until onion is tender. Add carrots and celery; cook and stir 7 to 9 minutes or until tender, stirring frequently. Stir in tomatoes, broth, rice, tomato paste, Worcestershire sauce, black pepper, thyme and hot pepper sauce. Reduce heat to low; cook about 30 minutes, stirring frequently.

Remove from heat. Let cool about 10 minutes. In food processor or blender, process soup in small batches until smooth. Return soup to Dutch oven; simmer 3 to 5 minutes or until heated through. Garnish as desired.

Nutrients per serving:

Calories	91	Cholesterol	1 mg
Fat	2 g	Sodium	641 mg

Favorite recipe from **Florida Tomato Committee**

Chicken Noodle Soup

Makes 8 servings

- 1 (46-fluid ounce) can COLLEGE INN® Chicken Broth
- ½ pound boneless chicken, cut into bite-size pieces
- 1½ cups uncooked medium egg noodles
- 1 cup sliced carrots
- ½ cup chopped onion
- ⅓ cup sliced celery
- 1 teaspoon dill weed
- ¼ teaspoon ground black pepper

In large saucepan, over medium-high heat, heat chicken broth, chicken, noodles, carrots, onion, celery, dill and pepper until mixture comes to a boil. Reduce heat to low; simmer, uncovered, 20 minutes or until chicken and noodles are cooked.

Nutrients per serving:

Calories	88	Cholesterol	19 mg
Fat	2 g	Sodium	579 mg

Split Pea Soup

Makes 6 servings

- ¼ cup FILIPPO BERIO® 100% Pure Olive Oil
- 2 medium onions, chopped
- 2 cloves garlic *or* 1 shallot *or* 2 green onions, chopped
- 6 cups water
- 1 cup dried split peas, sorted and rinsed
- ½ cup sliced carrots
- 1 stalk celery, chopped
- 1 bay leaf
- ¼ teaspoon black pepper

Heat olive oil in Dutch oven over medium heat. Add 2 medium onions and garlic; cook and stir 5 minutes or until onions are tender.

Stir in water, split peas, carrots, celery, bay leaf and black pepper. Bring to a boil over medium-high heat.

Reduce heat to low and simmer for 2 hours, stirring occasionally, until peas are tender. Remove bay leaf before serving.

Nutrients per serving:

Calories	173	Cholesterol	0 mg
Fat	10 g	Sodium	21 mg

Golden Tomato Soup

Chicken Wild Rice Soup

Makes 8 servings

⅓ cup instant nonfat dry milk
2 tablespoons cornstarch
2 teaspoons low sodium instant chicken bouillon
¼ teaspoon dried onion flakes
¼ teaspoon dried basil leaves, crushed
¼ teaspoon dried thyme leaves, crushed
⅛ teaspoon pepper
4 cups low sodium chicken broth
½ cup sliced celery
½ cup sliced carrots
½ cup chopped onion
2 cups cooked wild rice
1 cup cubed cooked chicken breasts

Combine dry milk, cornstarch, bouillon, onion flakes, basil, thyme and pepper in small bowl. Stir in small amount of chicken broth until mixture dissolves; set aside. Combine remaining broth, celery, carrots and onion in large saucepan. Cook until vegetables are crisp-tender. Gradually add dry milk mixture. Stir in wild rice and chicken. Simmer 5 to 10 minutes until heated through.

Nutrients per serving:

Calories	98	Cholesterol	24 mg
Fat	3 g	Sodium	84 mg

Favorite recipe from **Minnesota Cultivated Wild Rice Council**

Nectarine-Carrot Soup

Makes 4 servings

2 tablespoons reduced calorie margarine
1 cup chopped yellow onion
1 fresh California nectarine, peeled and quartered
2 carrots, peeled and cut into chunks
2 cups low sodium chicken broth
½ cup fresh orange juice
¼ teaspoon grated orange peel
  Freshly ground black pepper
½ cup plain low fat yogurt
2 fresh California nectarines, sliced (1 cup)

Melt margarine in large saucepan over medium-high heat; add onion. Cook and stir about 3 minutes or until onion is softened. Add quartered nectarine, carrots and chicken broth. Bring to a boil; reduce heat and simmer until carrots are fork-tender. Pour into blender; process until smooth. Add orange juice and orange peel. Season with pepper. Pour into serving bowls. Garnish each serving with 2 tablespoons yogurt and nectarine slices. Serve soup hot or cold.

Nutrients per serving (1 cup):

Calories	140	Cholesterol	2 mg
Fat	4 g	Sodium	109 mg

Favorite recipe from **California Tree Fruit Agreement**

Creamless Celery-Potato Soup

Makes 4 servings, 7 cups

1 tablespoon vegetable oil
3 cups sliced celery
2 cups diced potatoes (about 1 pound)
1 cup chopped onion
1 teaspoon minced garlic
2 cans (13¾ ounces *each*) low sodium chicken broth
1 cup low fat milk
1 tablespoon Dijon-style mustard
½ cup shredded low fat Cheddar cheese

Heat oil in large saucepan over medium-high heat until hot. Add celery, potatoes, onion and garlic; cook and stir about 5 minutes or until celery is crisp-tender. Add broth; bring to a boil. Reduce heat and simmer, uncovered, about 10 minutes or until potatoes are fork-tender. Place half the soup mixture in food processor or blender; process until smooth.

Pour into remaining soup mixture. Stir in milk and mustard; heat 1 to 2 minutes until hot. Sprinkle with cheese just before serving.

Nutrients per serving:

Calories	255	Cholesterol	15 mg
Fat	9 g	Sodium	376 mg

Favorite recipe from **American Celery Council**

Gazpacho

Makes 6 servings

2 carrots, peeled
1 cucumber, unpeeled
1 medium tomato
½ red bell pepper, seeded
2 cups spicy tomato juice
½ cup water
½ cup tomato sauce
¼ cup chopped scallions
3 tablespoons vinegar
2 teaspoons sugar
1 clove garlic, minced
1 can (15 ounces) navy beans, drained and
    rinsed

Cut carrots, cucumber, tomato and pepper into large chunks. Add all ingredients except beans to food processor; process to make chunky purée. Pour into large serving bowl; stir in beans. Cover and refrigerate until chilled. Serve cold.

Nutrients per serving:			
Calories	92	Cholesterol	0 mg
Fat	trace	Sodium	310 mg

Favorite recipe from **The Sugar Association, Inc.**

Chilled Minted Cucumber Yogurt Soup

Makes 4 servings, about 3½ cups

2 cucumbers
½ small onion, cut into chunks
1 clove garlic
2 cups DANNON® Plain Nonfat or Lowfat
    Yogurt, divided
3 tablespoons thinly sliced fresh mint leaves
½ teaspoon salt
⅛ teaspoon freshly ground pepper
    Pinch ground red pepper
4 thin cucumber slices (optional)

Peel cucumbers and halve lengthwise. Scoop out seeds with spoon and discard. Cut cucumbers into chunks. Place cucumbers, onion and garlic in food processor. Process until smooth. Add 1 cup yogurt and process until smooth. Scrape into a medium bowl or soup tureen. Stir in remaining 1 cup yogurt, mint, salt, pepper and ground red pepper. Cover; chill at least 2 hours before serving. To serve, ladle into 4 soup bowls and garnish each with a cucumber slice.

Nutrients per serving:			
Calories	100	Cholesterol	10 mg
Fat	2 g	Sodium	352 mg

Calico Wild Rice Soup

Makes 4 to 6 servings

4 cups low sodium chicken broth
2 cups cooked wild rice
1 cup frozen corn
2 tablespoons chopped red bell pepper
2 tablespoons chopped green bell pepper
½ cup sliced green onions
1 tablespoon chopped fresh parsley
1 teaspoon dried tarragon leaves, crushed
2 tablespoons cornstarch
2 tablespoons water

Combine broth, rice, corn, red and green peppers, onions, parsley and tarragon in large saucepan; mix well. Cook over medium heat until mixture boils; reduce heat and simmer 5 minutes or until corn is tender. Combine cornstarch and water in small bowl. Stir into simmering soup; cook 5 minutes or until soup thickens slightly, stirring occasionally.

Nutrients per serving:			
Calories	98	Cholesterol	0 mg
Fat	1 g	Sodium	5 mg

Favorite recipe from **Minnesota Cultivated Wild Rice Council**

Celery-Chicken Gumbo

Makes 4 servings, 8 cups

1 tablespoon vegetable oil
3 cups thinly sliced celery
1 cup chopped onion
1 teaspoon minced garlic
8 ounces skinless boneless chicken breast
    halves, cut into ½-inch chunks
2 cans (13¾ ounces *each*) low sodium chicken
    broth
1 can (16 ounces) crushed tomatoes packed in
    juice, undrained
½ cup uncooked regular long-grain rice

Heat oil in large saucepan until hot. Add celery, onion and garlic; cook and stir about 5 minutes or until vegetables are crisp-tender. Add chicken; cook about 2 minutes or until chicken turns white, stirring occasionally. Stir in chicken broth, tomatoes and rice; bring to a boil. Reduce heat and simmer, covered, about 20 minutes or until rice is tender.

Nutrients per serving (2 cups):			
Calories	255	Cholesterol	33 mg
Fat	6 g	Sodium	349 mg

Favorite recipe from **American Celery Council**

Country Cream of Chicken Chowder

Makes 10 servings

¼ cup **CRISCO® Vegetable Oil**
¼ cup **finely chopped onion**
¼ cup **all-purpose flour**
4 cups **chicken broth**
2 cups **skim milk**
1 **bay leaf**
3 cups **frozen hash brown potatoes**
1 package (10 ounces) **frozen whole kernel corn**
1 package (10 ounces) **frozen cut green beans**
1 package (10 ounces) **frozen peas**
1 package (10 ounces) **frozen sliced carrots**
1½ cups **finely chopped cooked chicken**
⅛ teaspoon **pepper**
2 tablespoons **chopped fresh parsley or chives**

1. Heat Crisco® Oil in large saucepan on medium heat. Add onion. Cook and stir until tender. Stir in flour. Cook until bubbly. Stir in broth and milk gradually. Cook and stir until mixture is bubbly and slightly thickened. Add bay leaf.

2. Add potatoes, corn, beans, peas and carrots. Increase heat to medium-high. Bring mixture to a boil. Reduce heat to low. Simmer 5 minutes or until beans are tender. Stir in chicken and pepper. Heat thoroughly. Remove bay leaf. Serve sprinkled with parsley.

Nutrients per serving:

Calories	220	Cholesterol	20 mg
Fat	7 g	Sodium	685 mg

Cheesy Vegetable Soup

Makes 4 servings

2 teaspoons **CRISCO® Vegetable Oil**
¼ cup **chopped green or red bell pepper**
¼ cup **chopped onion**
2 tablespoons **all-purpose flour**
1 teaspoon **chicken flavor instant bouillon** *or* **one chicken flavor bouillon cube**
½ teaspoon **dry mustard**
⅛ teaspoon **cayenne pepper**
1 cup **water**
½ cup **skim milk**
1 package (10 ounces) **mixed vegetables (broccoli, cauliflower and carrots) in cheese flavor sauce, thawed**
1 package (9 ounces) **frozen cut green beans, thawed**
½ teaspoon **salt**

1. Heat Crisco® Oil in large saucepan on medium heat. Add green pepper and onion. Cook and stir 2 to 3 minutes or until crisp-tender. Remove from heat.

2. Stir in flour, bouillon, dry mustard and cayenne. Stir in water and milk gradually. Return to heat. Cook and stir until mixture thickens.

3. Stir in vegetables in cheese sauce, green beans and salt. Simmer 5 minutes or until vegetables are tender.

Nutrients per serving:

Calories	95	Cholesterol	0 mg
Fat	3 g	Sodium	640 mg

Meatless Italian Minestrone

Makes 16 servings

1 tablespoon **CRISCO® Vegetable Oil**
1⅓ cups **chopped celery**
½ cup **chopped onion**
2 to 3 cloves **garlic, minced**
2 cans (14½ ounces *each*) **no salt added tomatoes, undrained and chopped**
4 cups **chopped cabbage**
1⅓ cups **chopped carrots**
1 can (46 ounces) **no salt added tomato juice**
1 can (19 ounces) **white kidney beans (cannellini), drained**
1 can (15½ ounces) **red kidney beans, drained**
1 can (15 ounces) **garbanzo beans, drained**
¼ cup **chopped fresh parsley**
1 tablespoon *plus* 1 teaspoon **dried oregano leaves**
1 tablespoon *plus* 1 teaspoon **dried basil leaves**
¾ cup (4 ounces) **uncooked small elbow macaroni, cooked (without salt or fat) and well drained**
¼ cup **grated Parmesan cheese**
Salt and pepper (optional)

1. Heat Crisco® Oil in large saucepan on medium heat. Add celery, onion and garlic. Cook and stir until crisp-tender. Stir in tomatoes, cabbage and carrots. Reduce heat to low. Cover. Simmer until vegetables are tender.

2. Stir in tomato juice, beans, parsley, oregano and basil. Simmer until beans are heated. Stir in macaroni just before serving. Serve sprinkled with Parmesan cheese. Season with salt and pepper, if desired.

Nutrients per serving:

Calories	165	Cholesterol	0 mg
Fat	3 g	Sodium	265 mg

Clockwise from top left: Country Cream of Chicken Chowder,
Meatless Italian Minestrone, Cheesy Vegetable Soup

Basil-Vegetable Soup

Makes 10 to 12 servings

1 package (9 ounces) frozen cut green beans
1 can (15 ounces) cooked cannellini beans, undrained
3 medium carrots, cut into thin slices
3 medium zucchini or yellow squash, cut into thin slices
2 quarts beef broth
2 cloves garlic, minced
  Salt and pepper (optional)
2 to 3 ounces uncooked vermicelli or spaghetti
½ cup tightly packed fresh basil leaves, finely chopped
  Grated Romano cheese

Combine beans, carrots, zucchini, broth and garlic in Dutch oven. Bring to a boil over high heat. Reduce heat to low. Cover; simmer until carrots are tender. Season to taste with salt and pepper. Add vermicelli; bring to a boil over high heat. Reduce heat to low. Simmer until pasta is tender, yet firm. (If desired, pasta may be cooked separately, then added to soup just before serving.) Add basil; continue to simmer until basil is completely tender. Sprinkle with cheese.

Nutrients per serving:

Calories	110	Cholesterol	trace
Fat	1 g	Sodium	585 mg

Basil-Vegetable Soup

Italian Wedding Soup

Makes about 8 servings, 8 cups

½ pound lean ground beef
½ cup fresh bread crumbs (1 slice)
1 egg, slightly beaten
1 tablespoon finely chopped onion
5 teaspoons WYLER'S® or STEERO® Chicken-Flavor Instant Bouillon
8 cups water
½ cup uncooked CREAMETTE® Rosamarina or Acini de Pepe
1½ cups cut-up fresh spinach leaves
  Grated Parmesan cheese (optional)

In small bowl, mix meat, crumbs, egg, onion and *1 teaspoon* bouillon. Shape into 40 small meatballs. In large kettle or Dutch oven, bring water and remaining *4 teaspoons* bouillon to a boil. Add meatballs and pasta; cook 10 minutes. Add spinach; reduce heat to low and simmer 3 to 5 minutes or until tender. Serve with cheese if desired. Refrigerate leftovers.

Nutrients per serving:

Calories	109	Cholesterol	44 mg
Fat	5 g	Sodium	226 mg

Speedy Turkey Sausage Soup

Makes 10 servings

8 cups water
1 can (14½ ounces) stewed tomatoes
1 package (10 ounces) frozen chopped spinach
2 carrots, sliced
1 medium onion, chopped
2 teaspoons instant beef bouillon *or* 2 bouillon cubes
¼ teaspoon black pepper
1 package (1 pound) LOUIS RICH® Turkey Breakfast Sausage, thawed
1 cup uncooked elbow macaroni *or* other small-size pasta
  Grated Parmesan cheese (optional)

Bring water, tomatoes with juice, spinach, carrots, onion, bouillon and pepper to a full boil in large saucepan. Drop bite-size pieces of uncooked sausage into boiling soup mixture to form "dumplings," stirring occasionally. Stir in macaroni. Simmer 10 minutes or until macaroni is tender. Ladle into serving bowls and sprinkle with Parmesan cheese, if desired. Refrigerate or freeze unused portions.

Nutrients per serving:

Calories	145	Cholesterol	35 mg
Fat	3 g	Sodium	670 mg

Hearty Minestrone Gratiné

Makes 4 servings

1 cup diced zucchini
1 cup diced celery
1 can (28 ounces) tomatoes, chopped, juice
    reserved
2 cups water
2 teaspoons sugar
1 teaspoon Italian seasoning
1 can (15 ounces) garbanzo beans, drained
4 (½-inch-thick) slices French bread, toasted
1 cup (4 ounces) SARGENTO® Preferred Light
    Fancy Supreme Shredded Mozzarella
    Cheese
2 tablespoons SARGENTO® Grated Parmesan
    Cheese
    Chopped fresh parsley

Spray large saucepan or Dutch oven with nonstick cooking spray. Over medium heat, cook and stir zucchini and celery until tender. Add tomatoes with juice, water, sugar and seasoning. Simmer, uncovered, 15 to 20 minutes. Add garbanzo beans; simmer 10 minutes.

Meanwhile, heat broiler. Place toasted bread on broiler pan. Divide mozzarella evenly over bread slices. Broil until cheese melts. Ladle soup into bowls and top with cheese-topped bread slices. Sprinkle Parmesan cheese over bread slices and garnish with parsley. Serve immediately.

Nutrients per serving:

Calories	273	Cholesterol	15 mg
Fat	5 g	Sodium	999 mg

Canton Pork Stew

Makes 6 servings

1 pound lean pork shoulder or pork loin roast,
    cut into 1-inch pieces
1 teaspoon ground ginger
¼ teaspoon ground cinnamon
¼ teaspoon ground red pepper
1 tablespoon peanut or vegetable oil
1 large onion, coarsely chopped
3 cloves garlic, minced
1 can (about 14 ounces) chicken broth
¼ cup dry sherry
1 package (about 10 ounces) frozen baby
    carrots, thawed
1 large green bell pepper, cut into 1-inch pieces
3 tablespoons low-sodium soy sauce
1½ tablespoons cornstarch
    Cilantro for garnish

Canton Pork Stew

Sprinkle pork with ginger, cinnamon and ground red pepper; toss well. Heat large saucepan or Dutch oven over medium-high heat. Add oil; heat until hot.

Add pork to saucepan; brown on all sides. Add onion and garlic; cook 2 minutes, stirring frequently. Add broth and sherry. Bring to a boil over high heat. Reduce heat to medium-low. Cover and simmer 40 minutes.

Stir in carrots and green pepper; cover and simmer 10 minutes or until pork is fork tender. Blend soy sauce into cornstarch in cup until smooth. Stir into stew. Cook and stir 1 minute or until stew boils and thickens. Ladle into soup bowls. Garnish with cilantro.

Nutrients per serving:

Calories	208	Cholesterol	50 mg
Fat	10 g	Sodium	573 mg

Hearty Chicken and Rice Soup

Quick 'n' Easy Corn and Pepper Chowder

Makes 6 servings, 6 cups

- 1 tablespoon margarine
- 1 cup coarsely chopped green or red bell pepper
- 1 cup chopped onion
- 3½ cups (16-ounce package) frozen whole-kernel corn
- 1 cup chicken broth
- 4 ounces (¾ cup) cooked, lean ham (95% fat free), cubed
- ½ teaspoon ground cumin
- ¼ teaspoon ground white pepper
- 3 cups (two 12-ounce cans) *undiluted* CARNATION® Evaporated Lowfat Milk, divided
- ⅓ cup *plus* 1 tablespoon all-purpose flour

In large saucepan, melt margarine; cook and stir bell pepper and onion over medium heat for 5 minutes or until tender. Stir in corn, broth, ham, cumin and white pepper. Cook for an additional 5 minutes, stirring occasionally, until corn is cooked. Pour *½ cup* evaporated lowfat milk into medium bowl; whisk in flour until well blended. Add remaining *2½ cups* evaporated lowfat milk; mix well. Slowly pour into saucepan. Increase heat to medium-high; cook, stirring constantly, for 5 minutes until mixture comes to a boil and thickens slightly. Boil for 1 minute. (If a thinner chowder is desired, add additional chicken broth.) Garnish as desired.

Nutrients per serving:

Calories	213	Cholesterol	15 mg
Fat	6 g	Sodium	355 mg

Hearty Chicken and Rice Soup

Makes 8 servings

- 10 cups chicken broth
- 1 medium onion, chopped
- 1 cup sliced celery
- 1 cup sliced carrots
- ¼ cup snipped fresh parsley
- ½ teaspoon cracked black pepper
- ½ teaspoon dried thyme leaves, crushed
- 1 bay leaf
- 1½ cups chicken cubes (about ¾ pound)
- 2 cups cooked rice
- 2 tablespoons lime juice
    Lime slices for garnish

Combine broth, onion, celery, carrots, parsley, pepper, thyme, and bay leaf in Dutch oven. Bring to a boil over high heat. Stir once or twice. Reduce heat to low. Simmer, uncovered, 10 to 15 minutes. Add chicken; simmer, uncovered, 5 to 10 minutes or until chicken is cooked. Remove and discard bay leaf. Stir in rice and lime juice just before serving. Garnish with lime slices.

Nutrients per serving:

Calories	184	Cholesterol	23 mg
Fat	4 g	Sodium	1209 mg

Favorite recipe from **USA Rice Council**

Southern Ham and Shrimp Soup

Makes 6 servings

 2 tablespoons CRISCO® Vegetable Oil
 1 cup chopped onion
 ½ cup chopped green bell pepper
 2 tablespoons chopped fresh parsley
1½ quarts water
 3 low sodium chicken flavor bouillon cubes
 1 package (10 ounces) frozen cut okra
 ½ pound fresh shrimp, peeled and deveined
 2 cups cubed lean cooked ham
 2 cups hot cooked rice (cooked without salt
   or fat)

1. Heat Crisco® Oil in large saucepan on medium heat. Add onion and green pepper. Cook and stir 5 minutes. Stir in parsley, water and bouillon cubes. Bring to a boil.

2. Add okra. Reduce heat to low. Simmer 10 minutes, stirring after 5 minutes.

3. Add shrimp. Simmer 2 to 3 minutes or until shrimp turn pink.

4. Add ham. Heat thoroughly.

5. Ladle over rice in soup bowls.

Nutrients per serving:			
Calories	270	Cholesterol	trace
Fat	9 g	Sodium	658 mg

Creole Fish Soup

Makes 8 servings, 2 quarts

 4 slices bacon
 ½ cup chopped celery
 ½ cup chopped green bell pepper
 ½ cup chopped onion
 1 clove garlic, finely chopped
 1 (28-ounce) can whole tomatoes, undrained
   and broken up
 4 cups water
 1 tablespoon WYLER'S® or STEERO® Chicken-
   Flavor Instant Bouillon *or* 3 Chicken-
   Flavor Bouillon Cubes
 1 bay leaf
 1 teaspoon oregano leaves
 ¼ teaspoon black pepper
 1 pound fish fillets, fresh or frozen, thawed, cut
   into 1-inch pieces

In large kettle or Dutch oven, cook bacon until crisp; remove and crumble. In drippings, cook and stir celery, green pepper, onion and garlic until tender. Add tomatoes with juice, water, bouillon, bay leaf, oregano and black pepper; bring to a boil. Reduce heat; simmer uncovered 30 minutes, stirring occasionally. Add fish; simmer 5 to 8 minutes or until fish flakes with fork. Remove bay leaf. Garnish with bacon. Refrigerate leftovers.

Nutrients per serving (1 cup):			
Calories	114	Cholesterol	41 mg
Fat	3 g	Sodium	619 mg

Apple-Squash Soup

Makes 6 servings

 1 tablespoon corn oil
 1 apple, peeled and chopped
 ½ onion, chopped
 1 cup (8 ounces) low-fat ricotta cheese
 1 can (13¾ ounces) low-sodium chicken broth,
   divided
 2 packages (11 ounces each) frozen butternut
   squash, thawed
 ½ cup FRENCH'S® Creamy Spread™ Mustard
 ¼ teaspoon dried tarragon leaves, crushed

Heat oil in large saucepan. Cook and stir apple and onion in hot oil until tender; remove from heat. Place ricotta cheese in blender container; process until very smooth. Add 1 cup broth and apple mixture to blender. Cover; process until very smooth. Return to saucepan. Add remaining broth, squash, French's® Creamy Spread™ Mustard and tarragon; whisk until smooth. Cook over low heat, stirring occasionally, until heated through, 5 to 10 minutes. *(Do not boil.)* Garnish as desired.

Nutrients per serving:			
Calories	159	Cholesterol	7 mg
Fat	6 g	Sodium	446 mg

Apple-Squash Soup

Springtime Veal Soup

Springtime Veal Soup

Makes 6 servings

1½ pounds veal for stew, cut into 1-inch pieces
2 cloves garlic, minced
1 tablespoon olive oil, divided
½ teaspoon salt
3½ cups water
1 can (13¾ ounces) beef broth
1 tablespoon chopped fresh marjoram *or*
    1½ teaspoons dried marjoram leaves
¼ teaspoon freshly ground black pepper
½ pound red-skinned potatoes, cut into ½-inch
    cubes (1¾ cups)
1½ cups corn kernels, fresh or frozen
1 small zucchini (3 to 4 ounces)

Toss veal with minced garlic in medium bowl; set aside. Heat 2 teaspoons oil in Dutch oven or large, deep saucepan over medium heat. Brown veal mixture, ½ at a time, using remaining oil as needed. Pour off fat, if necessary. Season veal with salt. Return all veal mixture to saucepan. Add water, broth, marjoram and pepper. Bring to a boil. Reduce heat to low; cover and simmer 45 minutes. Add potatoes and corn. Cover and simmer 15 minutes more or until veal and potatoes are fork-tender. Meanwhile, cut zucchini in half lengthwise; cut into ¼-inch-thick slices. Add zucchini to veal mixture; cover and cook 5 minutes or until zucchini is crisp-tender.

Nutrients per serving:			
Calories	234	Cholesterol	93 mg
Fat	8 g	Sodium	477 mg

Favorite recipe from **National Live Stock and Meat Board**

Creamy Carrot Soup

Makes 6 servings

3 cups water
4 cups sliced carrots
½ cup chopped onion
2 cloves garlic, minced
2 tablespoons brown sugar
½ bouillon cube
2 teaspoons curry powder
⅛ teaspoon ground ginger
    Dash ground cinnamon
½ cup skim milk

Place water in large saucepan; bring to a boil over high heat. Add all remaining ingredients except milk. Reduce heat and simmer for 40 minutes or until carrots and onion are tender. Remove from heat; pour mixture in batches into food processor or blender. Process until smooth and return to saucepan. Stir in milk; cook over low heat until heated through (do not boil). Serve warm.

Nutrients per serving:			
Calories	81	Cholesterol	trace
Fat	trace	Sodium	149 mg

Favorite recipe from **The Sugar Association, Inc.**

Country Bean Soup

Makes 6 servings

½ pound dry navy beans or lima beans (1¼ cups)
2½ cups water
4 ounces salt pork or fully cooked ham, chopped
¼ cup chopped onion
½ teaspoon dried oregano leaves, crushed
¼ teaspoon salt
¼ teaspoon ground ginger
¼ teaspoon dried sage leaves, crushed
¼ teaspoon pepper
2 cups milk
2 tablespoons butter

Rinse beans. Place in large saucepan; add enough water to cover. Bring to a boil; reduce heat and simmer 2 minutes. Remove from heat; cover and let stand for 1 hour. (Or, cover beans with water and soak overnight.)

Drain; return beans to saucepan. Stir in 2½ cups water, salt pork, onion, oregano, salt, ginger, sage and pepper. Bring to a boil; reduce heat. Cover and simmer for 2 to 2½ hours until beans are tender. (If necessary, add more water during cooking time.) Add milk and butter, stirring until mixture is heated through and butter is melted. Season to taste with additional salt and pepper, if desired.

Nutrients per serving:			
Calories	261	Cholesterol	32 mg
Fat	9 g	Sodium	415 mg

Favorite recipe from **Wisconsin Milk Marketing Board** © 1994

Meatball & Vegetable Soup

Makes 10 servings, about 2½ quarts

1 pound lean ground beef
½ cup fresh bread crumbs (1 slice)
⅓ cup chopped onion
1 egg, slightly beaten
4 teaspoons WYLER'S® or STEERO® Beef-Flavor Instant Bouillon
⅛ teaspoon garlic powder
6 cups water
1 (28-ounce) can whole tomatoes, undrained and broken up
½ teaspoon black pepper
2 cups frozen hash brown potatoes
1 cup frozen peas and carrots

In large bowl, combine meat, crumbs, onion, egg, *1 teaspoon* bouillon and garlic powder; mix well. Shape into 1-inch meatballs. In Dutch oven, brown meatballs; pour off fat. Add water, tomatoes, pepper and remaining *3 teaspoons* bouillon. Bring to a boil; reduce heat. Simmer, uncovered, 20 minutes. Stir in vegetables; cook 15 minutes or until tender, stirring occasionally. Refrigerate leftovers.

Nutrients per serving:

Calories	201	Cholesterol	49 mg
Fat	10 g	Sodium	378 mg

Meatball & Vegetable Soup

Chicken & Rice Gumbo

Makes 10 servings

1 (46-fluid ounce) can COLLEGE INN® Chicken Broth
1 pound boneless chicken, cut into bite-size pieces
1 (17-ounce) can whole kernel sweet corn, drained
1 (14½-ounce) can stewed tomatoes, chopped
1 (10-ounce) package frozen okra, thawed and chopped
½ cup uncooked rice
1 teaspoon ground black pepper

In large saucepan, over medium-high heat, heat chicken broth, chicken, corn, tomatoes with juice, okra, rice and pepper until mixture comes to a boil. Reduce heat; simmer, uncovered, 20 minutes or until chicken and rice are cooked.

Nutrients per serving:

Calories	150	Cholesterol	19 mg
Fat	2 g	Sodium	699 mg

French Onion Soup

Makes 4 to 6 servings

1 extra-large onion (1 pound)
3 tablespoons BUTTER FLAVOR CRISCO®
1 clove garlic, minced
1 tablespoon all-purpose flour
5 cups water
¼ cup white wine (optional)
3 tablespoons instant beef bouillon granules
1 tablespoon instant chicken bouillon granules
1 teaspoon Worcestershire sauce
Seasoned croutons
Grated Parmesan cheese

Peel onion. Cut in half lengthwise, then crosswise into thin slices.

Melt Butter Flavor Crisco® in 3-quart saucepan over medium heat. Add onion and garlic; cook about 20 minutes or until onion is soft and transparent, stirring occasionally. Stir in flour. Add water, wine, beef and chicken bouillon granules and Worcestershire sauce. Heat to boiling. Reduce heat to low; cover and simmer for 15 minutes.

Ladle soup into individual serving bowls. Top with seasoned croutons and sprinkle with Parmesan cheese.

Nutrients per serving:

Calories	95	Cholesterol	trace
Fat	6 g	Sodium	602 mg

Potato-Cheese Calico Soup

Makes 6 servings, 6 cups

1 pound potatoes, peeled and thinly sliced
1 cup sliced onion
2½ cups chicken broth
½ cup low-fat milk
1 cup sliced mushrooms
½ cup diced red bell pepper
½ cup sliced green onions
1 cup (4 ounces) finely shredded Wisconsin
    Asiago Cheese
Salt and black pepper (optional)
2 tablespoons chopped fresh parsley

In 3-quart saucepan, combine potatoes, 1 cup onion and broth. Bring to a boil. Reduce heat to low. Cover; cook until potatoes are tender, about 10 minutes. Transfer to blender container; blend until smooth. Return to saucepan. Stir in milk, mushrooms, bell pepper and green onions. Bring to simmer over medium-low heat. Add cheese, a few tablespoons at a time, stirring to melt. Season with salt and black pepper. Sprinkle with parsley.

Nutrients per serving (1 cup):

Calories	151	Cholesterol	9 mg
Fat	4 g	Sodium	526 mg

Favorite recipe from **Wisconsin Milk Marketing Board** © 1994

Easy Chili Con Carne

Makes 4 servings

½ medium onion, chopped
1 stalk celery, sliced
1 teaspoon chili powder
1 can (15¼ ounces) kidney beans, drained
1 can (14½ ounces) DEL MONTE® Chili Style
    Chunky Tomatoes
1 cup cooked cubed beef

To Microwave: In 2-quart microwavable dish, combine onion, celery and chili powder. Add 1 tablespoon water. Cover and microwave on HIGH (100% power) 3 to 4 minutes. Add remaining ingredients. Cover and cook on HIGH 6 to 8 minutes or until heated through, stirring halfway through. For a spicier chili, serve with hot pepper sauce.

Prep time: 8 minutes
Microwave cook time: 12 minutes

Nutrients per serving:

Calories	193	Cholesterol	28 mg
Fat	3 g	Sodium	612 mg

Beef Stew à la Italia

Beef Stew à la Italia

Makes 8 servings, about 8 cups

1½ pounds lean beef chuck, cut into 1-inch cubes
2 teaspoons olive or vegetable oil
1 large onion, cut into thin wedges
2 garlic cloves, minced
1 can (28 ounces) plum tomatoes, undrained,
    coarsely chopped
1 large baking potato, peeled and cut into
    ¾-inch chunks (2 cups)
⅔ cup PACE® Picante Sauce
1 teaspoon dried basil leaves, crushed
½ teaspoon dried oregano leaves, crushed
½ teaspoon salt (optional)
1 large green bell pepper, cut into 1-inch pieces
1 large zucchini, sliced ½-inch thick (2 cups)
¼ cup (1 ounce) grated Parmesan cheese
    Additional Pace® Picante Sauce (optional)

Place meat on rack of broiler pan. Broil, 4 inches from heat, until lightly browned on all sides. Heat oil in large saucepan or Dutch oven over medium heat. Add onion and garlic; cook and stir 3 minutes. Add meat, tomatoes with juice, potato, ⅔ cup Pace® Picante Sauce, basil, oregano and, if desired, salt. Bring to a boil. Reduce heat to low; cover and simmer until meat is tender, about 1 hour. Stir in green pepper and zucchini; continue to simmer until vegetables are crisp-tender, about 10 minutes. Ladle into bowls; sprinkle with cheese. Serve with additional Pace® Picante Sauce, if desired.

Nutrients per serving:

Calories	222	Cholesterol	56 mg
Fat	10g	Sodium	466 mg

Summertime Gazpacho

Makes 4 to 5 servings

  6 ripe tomatoes, divided
  2 cucumbers, divided
  1 small onion, quartered
  1 clove garlic, peeled and minced
  2 cups chicken broth
  3 tablespoons red wine vinegar
  2 tablespoons olive oil
  ¼ teaspoon hot pepper sauce
  1 large green pepper, seeded and finely chopped
  1 small bunch green onions, trimmed and finely chopped

Cut 5 tomatoes into quarters; remove and discard cores. Cut 1 cucumber into quarters; remove and discard seeds. Place quartered tomatoes, quartered cucumber and small onion in food processor or blender container. Cover; process until coarsely chopped. Spoon vegetable mixture into large bowl. Stir in garlic, broth, vinegar, olive oil and hot pepper sauce; cover. Chill. Just before serving, finely chop remaining tomato and cucumber. Ladle soup into chilled bowls or cups. Top with tomato, cucumber, green pepper and green onions.

Nutrients per serving:

Calories	170	Cholesterol	1 mg
Fat	9 g	Sodium	24 mg

Country Japanese Noodle Soup

Makes 4 servings, 5 cups

  1 can (14½ ounces) DEL MONTE® Original Recipe Stewed Tomatoes
  1 can (14 ounces) low-salt chicken broth
  3 ounces uncooked linguine
  2 teaspoons low-sodium soy sauce
  1 to 1½ teaspoons minced ginger root *or*
    ¼ teaspoon ground ginger
  ¼ pound sirloin steak, cut crosswise into thin strips
  5 green onions, cut into thin 1-inch slivers
  4 ounces firm tofu, cut into small cubes
    Ground black pepper (optional)
    Additional soy sauce (optional)

In large saucepan, combine tomatoes with juice, broth, pasta, 2 teaspoons soy sauce and ginger with 1¾ cups water; bring to a boil. Cook, uncovered, over medium-high heat 5 minutes. Add meat, green onions and tofu; cook 4 minutes or until pasta is tender. Season to taste with pepper and additional soy sauce, if desired.

Prep time: 10 minutes
Cook time: 15 minutes

Nutrients per serving:

Calories	220	Cholesterol	40 mg
Fat	7 g	Sodium	535 mg

Pizza Soup

Makes 7 servings, 3½ cups

  1 medium onion, chopped
  2 ounces pepperoni or salami, cut into small pieces*
  ½ teaspoon LAWRY'S® Garlic Powder with Parsley
  ½ teaspoon dried oregano leaves, crushed
  1 envelope LIPTON® Noodle Soup Mix with Real Chicken Broth
  3 cups water
  2 tablespoons tomato paste
  ½ cup (2 ounces) shredded mozzarella cheese

In medium saucepan, cook onion, pepperoni, garlic powder and oregano over medium-high heat, stirring frequently, 3 minutes or until onion is tender. Stir in remaining ingredients except cheese. Bring to a boil. Reduce heat to low and simmer, stirring occasionally, 5 minutes. Sprinkle with cheese before serving.

To Microwave: In 2-quart microwave-safe casserole, microwave onion, pepperoni, garlic powder and oregano at HIGH (100% Power) 2 minutes. Stir in remaining ingredients except cheese. Microwave, uncovered, for 10 minutes, stirring once. Sprinkle with cheese before serving.

Variation: *Omit pepperoni or salami. Add 1 tablespoon oil.*

Nutrients per serving (½ cup):

Calories	99	Cholesterol	11 mg
Fat	6 g	Sodium	604 mg

Summertime Gazpacho

Beef Soup with Noodles

Beef Soup with Noodles

Makes 4 servings, 6 cups

  2 tablespoons low-sodium soy sauce
  1 teaspoon minced fresh ginger
  ¼ teaspoon crushed red pepper
  1 boneless beef top sirloin steak, cut 1 inch
     thick (about ¾ pound)
  1 tablespoon peanut or vegetable oil
  2 cups sliced fresh mushrooms
  2 cans (about 14 ounces each) low-sodium beef
     broth
  3 ounces (1 cup) fresh snow peas, cut diagonally
     into 1-inch pieces
1½ cups hot cooked fine egg noodles (2 ounces
     uncooked)
  1 green onion, cut diagonally into thin slices
  1 teaspoon Oriental sesame oil (optional)
     Red bell pepper strips for garnish

Combine soy sauce, ginger and crushed red pepper
in small bowl. Spread mixture evenly over both sides
of steak. Marinate at room temperature 15 minutes.

Heat deep skillet over medium-high heat. Add peanut
oil; heat until hot. Drain steak; set aside soy sauce
mixture (there will only be a small amount of
mixture). Add steak to skillet; cook 4 to 5 minutes
per side for medium-rare. (Adjust time for desired
doneness.) Remove steak from skillet; let stand on
cutting board 10 minutes.

Add mushrooms to skillet; stir-fry 2 minutes. Add
broth, snow peas and soy sauce mixture; bring to a
boil, scraping up browned meat bits. Reduce heat to
medium-low. Stir in noodles.

Cut steak across the grain into ⅛-inch slices; cut
each slice into 1-inch pieces. Stir into soup; heat
through. Stir in onion and sesame oil. Ladle into
soup bowls. Garnish with red pepper strips.

Nutrients per serving:			
Calories	245	Cholesterol	62 mg
Fat	10 g	Sodium	1004 mg

Hearty Pork Soup

Makes 12 servings

  2 tablespoons olive or vegetable oil
  1 pound pork tenderloin, trimmed and cut into
     ¾-inch cubes
  1 medium onion, chopped
  2 cloves garlic, minced
 10 cups water
  2 cups fresh broccoli flowerets
  2 cups sliced fresh mushrooms
  1 cup sliced celery
  4 medium carrots, sliced
  2 tablespoons chicken-flavor instant bouillon
  2 teaspoons dried thyme leaves, crushed
  ½ teaspoon black pepper
  ½ teaspoon salt-free herb seasoning *or*
     marjoram leaves
  ½ of a (1-pound) package CREAMETTE®
     Rotelle, uncooked

In large Dutch oven, heat oil. Add pork, onion and
garlic; cook and stir until meat is cooked through.
Add remaining ingredients except pasta. Bring to a
boil. Reduce heat to low; simmer 20 minutes.
Prepare Creamette® Rotelle according to package
directions; drain. Stir into soup. Heat through.
Refrigerate leftovers.

Note: *To reduce sodium, substitute low-sodium bouillon.*

Nutrients per serving:			
Calories	179	Cholesterol	35 mg
Fat	5 g	Sodium	480 mg

Black Bean Rice Soup

Makes 7 servings, 7 cups

½ cup chopped onion
1 clove garlic, minced
2 teaspoons vegetable oil
1½ cups water
1 can (about 14 ounces) beef broth
1 can (15 ounces) black beans or pinto beans, rinsed and drained
1 can (14½ ounces) no-salt-added stewed tomatoes
¾ cup uncooked UNCLE BEN'S® Brand Rice In An Instant
⅓ cup medium picante sauce or salsa
1 teaspoon ground cumin
¼ teaspoon dried oregano leaves, crushed
2 tablespoons chopped fresh cilantro (optional)

Cook and stir onion and garlic in hot oil in large saucepan or Dutch oven until onion is tender. Add water, broth, beans, tomatoes with juice, rice, picante sauce, cumin and oregano; bring to a boil. Cover; reduce heat to low and simmer until rice is tender, about 5 minutes. Sprinkle with cilantro before serving, if desired.

Nutrients per serving:			
Calories	113	Cholesterol	trace
Fat	2 g	Sodium	405 mg

Creole-Flavored Beef Soup

Makes 8 servings

3 to 4 pounds beef shank cross cuts
4 cups water
1 can (28 ounces) crushed tomatoes
1 cup sliced celery
1 large onion, chopped
2 cloves garlic, minced
2 beef bouillon cubes
½ teaspoon salt
¼ teaspoon *each* ground black pepper and ground red pepper
2 cups chopped cabbage
1 green bell pepper, chopped
¼ cup fresh lemon juice
2 cups cooked rice

Place beef shank cross cuts, water, tomatoes with juice, celery, onion, garlic, bouillon cubes, salt and black and red pepper in Dutch oven. Bring to a boil; reduce heat to low and simmer, covered, 2 hours, stirring occasionally. Remove shanks; cool slightly. Cut meat from bones into small pieces. Skim fat from broth. Return meat to Dutch oven; add cabbage and green pepper. Continue to simmer, covered, 30 minutes or until meat and vegetables are tender. Stir in lemon juice. To serve, spoon about ¼ cup cooked rice into each serving.

Prep time: 30 minutes
Cook time: 2 hours and 45 minutes

Nutrients per serving:			
Calories	241	Cholesterol	44 mg
Fat	5 g	Sodium	582 mg

Favorite recipe from **National Live Stock and Meat Board**

Chunky Ham Stew

Makes 4 to 6 servings

1 medium onion, chopped
2 stalks celery, sliced
2 carrots, sliced
4 cups low-sodium chicken broth
2 cups (8 ounces) ARMOUR® Lower Salt Ham cut into ½-inch cubes
1 tablespoon MRS. DASH®, Original Blend
1 cup frozen peas
2 tablespoons cornstarch

Combine onion, celery, carrots, broth, ham and seasoning in Dutch oven. Cover and cook over medium-high heat for 20 minutes or until carrots are almost tender. Stir in peas. Mix ¼ cup water and cornstarch in small bowl; add to stew. Stir constantly until stew comes to a boil and thickens. Garnish with celery leaves, if desired.

To Microwave: Combine ingredients as directed above in 10-inch microwave-safe tube pan. Cover with vented plastic wrap. Cook on HIGH (100%) power for 10 minutes. Stir; rotate pan. Continue cooking, covered, on HIGH power about 10 to 15 minutes, or until carrots are almost tender. Stir in peas. Mix ¼ cup water and cornstarch; stir into stew. Cook, covered, on HIGH power about 2 to 3 minutes or until stew comes to a boil and thickens, stirring 3 times during cooking. Garnish as above.

Nutrients per serving:			
Calories	131	Cholesterol	19 mg
Fat	3 g	Sodium	410 mg

Chunky Ham Stew

Chicken Cilantro Bisque

Makes 4 servings, about 4 cups

**6 ounces (2 medium) boneless skinless chicken
   breast halves, cut into chunks**
2½ cups low-sodium chicken broth
½ cup cilantro leaves
½ cup sliced green onions
¼ cup sliced celery
1 large clove garlic, minced
½ teaspoon ground cumin
⅓ cup all-purpose flour
**1½ cups (12-ounce can) *undiluted* CARNATION®
   Lite Evaporated Skimmed Milk**
Freshly ground black pepper, to taste

In large saucepan, combine chicken, broth, cilantro,
green onions, celery, garlic and cumin. Bring to a
boil. Reduce heat to low; cover and simmer for
15 minutes or until chicken is tender. Pour into
blender container; add flour. Cover and blend,
starting at low speed, until smooth. Pour mixture
back into saucepan. Cook over medium heat, stirring
constantly, until mixture comes to a boil and thickens.
Remove from heat. Gradually stir in evaporated
skimmed milk. Reheat just to serving temperature.
Do not boil. Season with pepper to taste. Garnish as
desired.

Nutrients per serving:			
Calories	178	Cholesterol	30 mg
Fat	2 g	Sodium	610 mg

Spicy Garden Gazpacho

Makes 7 servings, 7 cups

**1 small cucumber, peeled, seeded and coarsely
   chopped (1¼ cups)**
1 medium red bell pepper, coarsely chopped
1 stalk celery, coarsely chopped
2 medium tomatoes, coarsely chopped
¼ cup coarsely chopped onion
¼ cup cilantro leaves
1 clove garlic
3 cups chilled tomato juice, divided
½ cup PACE® Picante Sauce
½ teaspoon salt
Chopped cucumber (optional)
Additional Pace® Picante Sauce (optional)

Place 1 small cucumber, red pepper and celery in
food processor or blender container; process just until
vegetables are finely chopped. Transfer to large bowl.
Place tomatoes, onion, cilantro and garlic in food
processor or blender container; process until smooth,
about 1 minute. Add to vegetables in large bowl. Stir
in 1 cup tomato juice, ½ cup Pace® Picante Sauce
and salt. Cover and refrigerate at least 3 hours. Stir in
remaining 2 cups tomato juice. Ladle into soup bowls;
garnish with chopped cucumber, if desired. Serve
with additional Pace® Picante Sauce, if desired.

Nutrients per serving:			
Calories	45	Cholesterol	0 mg
Fat	0 g	Sodium	564 mg

Chicken Cilantro Bisque

Wild Rice Soup

Makes 4 servings, about 4 cups

⅓ cup chopped carrot
⅓ cup chopped celery
⅓ cup chopped onion
2 teaspoons margarine or butter
1⅓ cups cooked wild rice
**1 jar (12 ounces) HEINZ® HomeStyle Turkey
   Gravy**
1½ cups skim milk
2 tablespoons dry sherry

Cook and stir vegetables in margarine in 2-quart
saucepan over medium-high heat until tender. Stir in
rice, gravy and milk. Reduce heat to low. Simmer
5 minutes. Stir in sherry.

Nutrients per serving (about 1 cup):			
Calories	164	Cholesterol	7 mg
Fat	4 g	Sodium	645 mg

Southwestern Beef Stew

Southwestern Beef Stew

Makes 4 servings

  1 tablespoon vegetable oil
1¼ pounds well-trimmed beef tip roast, cut into
     1-inch pieces
  ½ cup coarsely chopped onion
  1 large clove garlic, minced
1½ teaspoons dried oregano leaves, crushed
  1 teaspoon ground cumin
  ½ teaspoon *each* crushed red pepper and salt
  4 medium tomatoes, chopped, divided (about
     4 cups)
  ½ cup water
  1 can (4 ounces) whole green chilies
  1 tablespoon cornstarch
  ¼ cup sliced green onion tops

Heat oil in Dutch oven over medium-high heat. Add beef pieces, onion and garlic; cook and stir until beef is browned. Pour off drippings. Combine oregano, cumin, red pepper and salt; sprinkle over beef. Add 3 cups tomatoes and water, stirring to combine. Reduce heat to low; cover tightly and simmer 1 hour and 55 minutes or until beef is tender, stirring occasionally. Drain green chilies; set aside liquid. Cut chilies into ½-inch pieces; add to beef mixture. Combine cornstarch and liquid; gradually stir into stew and cook, uncovered, until stew comes to a boil and thickens. Stir in remaining tomatoes; garnish with green onion tops.

Nutrients per serving:

Calories	250	Cholesterol	85 mg
Fat	8 g	Sodium	546 mg

Favorite recipe from **National Live Stock and Meat Board**

Satin Salmon Chowder

Satin Salmon Chowder

Makes 4 servings, about 5 cups

1 tablespoon margarine or butter
½ cup chopped onion
1 clove garlic, minced
2 cups water
1 cup diced peeled potatoes
1 envelope (about 3.5 grams) low-sodium
    instant chicken bouillon
1 can (8 ounces) corn kernels, drained
1 can (7½ ounces) salmon, drained and flaked
¼ cup diced green or red bell pepper
¼ teaspoon freshly ground pepper
2 cups DANNON® Plain Nonfat or Lowfat Yogurt
¼ cup all-purpose flour

In a large saucepan melt margarine over medium heat. Add onion and garlic; cook and stir 2 to 3 minutes or just until tender. Stir in water, potatoes and chicken bouillon. Bring to a boil and simmer, stirring occasionally, 4 to 5 minutes or until potatoes are tender. Reduce heat to low. Add corn, salmon, bell pepper and ground pepper. *Do not boil.*

In a medium bowl combine yogurt and flour; blend well. Gradually add to soup, stirring constantly, until smooth and slightly thickened.

Nutrients per serving:

Calories	260	Cholesterol	20 mg
Fat	7 g	Sodium	525 mg

Turkey, Corn and Sweet Potato Soup

Makes 8 servings

1 teaspoon margarine
½ cup chopped onion
1 small jalapeño chili, minced*
5 cups turkey broth or reduced sodium chicken
    bouillon
1½ pounds sweet potatoes, peeled and cut into
    1-inch cubes
2 cups ½-inch Cooked Turkey cubes
½ teaspoon salt
1½ cups frozen corn
    Fresh cilantro leaves (optional)

Heat margarine in 5-quart saucepan over medium-high heat until melted and bubbly; add onion and chili. Cook and stir 5 minutes or until onion is translucent. Add broth, potatoes, turkey and salt; bring to a boil. Reduce heat to low; cover and simmer 20 to 25 minutes or until potatoes are fork-tender. Stir in corn. Increase heat to medium and cook 5 to 6 minutes more. To serve, spoon into bowls and garnish with cilantro, if desired.

Chilies can sting and irritate the skin; wear plastic disposable gloves when handling chilies and do not touch eyes. Wash your hands after handling chilies.

Nutrients per serving (1 cup):

Calories	173	Cholesterol	27 mg
Fat	3 g	Sodium	578 mg

Favorite recipe from **National Turkey Federation**

Korean Chicken Wing Soup

Makes 4 servings

8 broiler-fryer chicken wings
1 tablespoon sesame oil
1 tablespoon peanut oil
1 carrot, peeled and thinly sliced
2 small zucchini, sliced
¼ cup chopped green onion with tops
1 clove garlic, minced
½ teaspoon freshly grated ginger root
½ teaspoon chili powder
4 cups warm chicken broth
2 tablespoons soy sauce

Brush chicken wings with sesame oil. Heat peanut oil in large Dutch oven over medium-high heat until hot. Add chicken and cook, turning, about 5 minutes to brown on all sides. Add carrot; cook and stir 3 minutes. Add zucchini, onion, garlic, ginger and chili powder. Continue to cook and stir about 3 minutes; add chicken broth and soy sauce. Bring to a boil; reduce heat to low and simmer about 10 minutes or until fork can be inserted into chicken with ease.

Note: Cooked rice may be added to soup just before serving, if desired.

Nutrients per serving:

Calories	223	Cholesterol	43 mg
Fat	9 g	Sodium	579 mg

Favorite recipe from **National Broiler Council**

Cuban Black Bean & Ham Soup

Cuban Black Bean & Ham Soup

Makes 4 servings

1 cup uncooked black beans, soaked overnight
  and drained
1 slice (2 ounces) ARMOUR® Lower Salt Ham
½ cup chopped green bell pepper
1 medium onion, finely chopped
2 teaspoons MRS. DASH®, Original Blend
1 teaspoon garlic powder
1 teaspoon ground cumin
¼ teaspoon black pepper
1½ cups (6 ounces) ARMOUR® Lower Salt Ham
  cut into ¾-inch cubes

Combine beans, ham slice, green pepper, onion and
seasonings in medium saucepan; add enough water
to just cover beans. Bring to a boil; reduce heat to low,
cover and simmer about 1½ to 2 hours or until beans
are tender and most of liquid is absorbed. Add ham
cubes. Cook 10 minutes or until ham cubes are
heated through. Remove ham slice before serving.
Serve over rice, if desired.

Nutrients per serving:			
Calories	244	Cholesterol	28 mg
Fat	4 g	Sodium	489 mg

Clam Chowder

Makes 12 servings, 3 quarts

3 tablespoons CRISCO® Shortening
6 medium potatoes (about 2 pounds), pared and
  thinly sliced
2 large yellow onions, peeled and thinly sliced
1½ cups water
2 cans (10 ounces each) shelled whole baby
  clams *or* 3 cans (6½ ounces each) minced
  clams, undrained
1 quart low-fat milk
1 teaspoon salt
¼ teaspoon ground white pepper

Melt Crisco® in large, heavy saucepan. Cook and stir
potatoes and onions for about 5 minutes until golden
brown. Add water; heat to boiling. Reduce heat to
low; simmer, covered, 10 to 15 minutes or until
potatoes are tender. Stir in clams and their liquid.
Heat 2 to 3 minutes. Remove from heat. Add milk,
salt and pepper.

Cool chowder, uncovered, 30 minutes. Place chowder,
uncovered, in refrigerator. Prior to serving, heat
chowder over medium-low heat just until steam rises
from top (about 20 minutes); *do not boil.*

Nutrients per serving (1 cup):			
Calories	180	Cholesterol	23 mg
Fat	5 g	Sodium	295 mg

Three-Bean Chili

Makes 6 servings, about 6½ cups

1 can (16 ounces) tomatoes, cut into bite-size
  pieces
1 jar (12 ounces) HEINZ® HomeStyle Brown
  Gravy
1 tablespoon chili powder
1 can (15 ounces) chili beans in chili gravy
1 can (15 ounces) garbanzo beans, drained
1 can (15 ounces) pinto or kidney beans, drained
1 can (4 ounces) chopped green chilies, drained
  Plain nonfat yogurt or light dairy sour cream,
  sliced green onions and/or shredded low-
  fat Cheddar cheese (optional)

Combine tomatoes, gravy and chili powder in 3-quart
saucepan. Bring to a boil over high heat. Stir in beans
and chilies. Reduce heat to low. Cover; simmer 15
minutes, stirring occasionally. Serve with desired
toppings.

Nutrients per serving (about 1 cup):			
Calories	281	Cholesterol	0 mg
Fat	4 g	Sodium	1135 mg

Mushroom and Rice Soup

Makes 10 servings

2 cups (about 8 ounces) sliced fresh mushrooms
1 cup (about 4 ounces) chopped fresh
    mushrooms
1 cup sliced green onions
2 tablespoons olive oil
6 cups chicken broth
2 jars (7 ounces each) whole straw mushrooms,
    undrained
1 cup water
¾ teaspoon cracked black pepper
¾ teaspoon dried thyme leaves, crushed
3 cups cooked rice
1 tablespoon dry sherry

Cook sliced and chopped mushrooms and onions in
oil in Dutch oven over medium-high heat until tender
crisp. Add broth, straw mushrooms, water, pepper,
and thyme. Reduce heat to low; simmer, uncovered,
5 to 7 minutes. Stir in rice and sherry; simmer 1 to
2 minutes.

Nutrients per serving:

| Calories | 142 | Cholesterol | 0 mg |
| Fat | 4 g | Sodium | 861 mg |

Favorite recipe from **USA Rice Council**

Carrot-Rice Soup

Makes 6 servings

1 pound carrots, peeled and chopped
1 medium onion, chopped
1 tablespoon margarine
4 cups chicken broth, divided
¼ teaspoon dried tarragon leaves, crushed
¼ teaspoon ground white pepper
2¼ cups cooked rice
¼ cup light sour cream
    Snipped fresh parsley or mint leaves for
    garnish

Cook and stir carrots and onion in margarine in large
saucepan or Dutch oven over medium-high heat 2 to
3 minutes or until onion is tender. Add 2 cups broth,
tarragon and pepper. Reduce heat to low; simmer
10 minutes. Combine vegetables and broth in food
processor or blender; process until smooth. Return
to saucepan. Add remaining 2 cups broth and rice;
thoroughly heat. Dollop sour cream on each serving
of soup. Garnish with parsley.

Nutrients per serving:

| Calories | 183 | Cholesterol | 0 mg |
| Fat | 3 g | Sodium | 860 mg |

Favorite recipe from **USA Rice Council**

West Coast Bouillabaisse

Makes 6 servings

1 cup sliced onions
2 stalks celery, cut diagonally into slices
2 cloves garlic, minced
1 tablespoon vegetable oil
4 cups chicken broth
1 can (28 ounces) tomatoes with juice, cut up
1 can (6½ ounces) minced clams with juice
½ cup dry white wine
1 teaspoon Worcestershire sauce
½ teaspoon dried thyme leaves, crushed
¼ teaspoon bottled hot pepper sauce
1 bay leaf
1 cup frozen cooked bay shrimp, thawed
1 can (6½ ounces) STARKIST® Tuna, drained
    and broken into chunks
    Salt and black pepper (optional)
6 slices lemon
6 slices French bread

In a Dutch oven, cook and stir onions, celery and
garlic in oil for 3 minutes. Stir in broth, tomatoes with
juice, clams with juice, wine, Worcestershire, thyme,
hot pepper sauce and bay leaf. Bring to a boil; reduce
heat to low. Simmer for 15 minutes. Stir in shrimp
and tuna; cook for 2 minutes to heat. Remove bay
leaf. Season with salt and pepper. Garnish with lemon
slices and serve with bread.

Nutrients per serving:

| Calories | 212 | Cholesterol | 70 mg |
| Fat | 6 g | Sodium | 1146 mg |

West Coast Bouillabaisse

Spanish Olive Cheddar Muffins

Makes 12 muffins

2 cups all-purpose flour
1 tablespoon sugar
2 teaspoons baking powder
1 teaspoon dry mustard
½ teaspoon baking soda
½ teaspoon salt
⅛ teaspoon ground red pepper
¼ cup margarine, softened
1 cup (4 ounces) shredded Cheddar cheese
½ cup chopped pimento-stuffed green olives
1 cup buttermilk
1 egg

Preheat oven to 375°F. Grease or paper-line 12 (2½-inch) muffin cups.

Combine flour, sugar, baking powder, mustard, baking soda, salt and red pepper in large bowl. Cut in margarine with pastry blender until mixture resembles fine crumbs. Stir in cheese and olives.

Combine buttermilk and egg in small bowl until blended. Stir into flour-cheese mixture just until moistened. Spoon evenly into prepared muffin cups.

Bake 25 to 30 minutes or until golden brown and wooden toothpick inserted in centers comes out clean. Immediately remove from pan. Cool on wire rack. Serve warm or cool completely.

Nutrients per serving (1 muffin):

Calories	171	Cholesterol	28 mg
Fat	8 g	Sodium	379 mg

Easy Country Biscuits

Makes about 1½ dozen biscuits

4 cups buttermilk baking mix
⅔ cup wheat germ
1½ cups (12-ounce can) *undiluted* CARNATION® Evaporated Lowfat Milk
1 to 2 tablespoons all-purpose flour

In medium bowl, combine baking mix and wheat germ. Stir in evaporated lowfat milk to make a soft dough. Turn dough out onto floured surface; knead 10 times, adding additional flour as necessary to keep dough from sticking. Roll to ½-inch thickness. Cut with floured 2½-inch round biscuit cutter; place on ungreased baking sheet. Bake in preheated 450°F oven for 8 to 10 minutes. Serve warm.

Nutrients per serving: (1 biscuit):

Calories	148	Cholesterol	2 mg
Fat	4 g	Sodium	370 mg

Common Sense® Oat Bran Bread

Makes 1 loaf, 14 slices

1¾ cups bread flour
1 cup whole wheat flour
1½ cups KELLOGG'S® COMMON SENSE® Oat Bran Cereal, any variety
½ teaspoon salt (optional)
1 package active dry yeast
2 tablespoons firmly packed brown sugar
1 cup skim milk
¼ cup margarine
3 egg whites

Stir together flours. In large electric mixer bowl, combine ½ cup flour mixture, Kellogg's® Common Sense® Oat Bran cereal, salt, yeast and sugar.

Heat milk and margarine until very warm (120° to 130°F). Gradually add to cereal mixture and beat 2 minutes on medium speed, scraping bowl occasionally. Add egg whites and 1 cup flour mixture. Beat 2 minutes on high speed.

Using dough hook on electric mixer or by hand, stir in remaining flour mixture. Knead on low speed or by hand for 5 minutes or until dough is smooth and elastic.

Place dough in lightly greased bowl, turning once to grease top. Cover and let rise in warm place (80° to 85°F) until double in volume. Punch down dough and let rest 10 minutes.

Roll dough on lightly floured surface into 14×8½-inch rectangle. Starting with short side, roll up dough lengthwise. Place, seam-side-down, in lightly greased 9×5×3-inch loaf pan. Let rise until double in volume, about 1½ hours.

Bake in 375°F oven about 30 minutes or until golden brown. Remove from pan and cool on wire rack.

Nutrients per serving (1 slice):

Calories	160	Cholesterol	0 mg
Fat	4 g	Sodium	110 mg

Spanish Olive Cheddar Muffins

Touch of Honey Bread

Touch of Honey Bread

Makes 1 loaf, 16 slices

- 2½ to 3 cups all-purpose flour, divided
- 1 cup QUAKER® Oat Bran hot cereal, uncooked
- 1 package quick-rise yeast
- ½ teaspoon salt
- 1¼ cups water
- 2 tablespoons honey
- 2 tablespoons margarine

In large mixer bowl, combine 1 cup flour, oat bran, yeast and salt. Heat water, honey and margarine until very warm (120° to 130°F). Add to dry ingredients; beat at low speed of electric mixer until moistened. Increase speed to medium; continue beating 3 minutes. Stir in enough remaining flour to form a stiff dough.

Lightly spray another large bowl with nonstick cooking spray, or oil lightly. Turn dough out onto lightly floured surface. Knead 8 to 10 minutes or until dough is smooth and elastic. Place in prepared bowl, turning once to coat surface of dough. Cover; let rise in warm place (80° to 85°F) 30 minutes or until doubled in size.

Lightly spray 8×4-inch loaf pan with nonstick cooking spray, or oil lightly. Punch down dough. Roll into 15×7-inch rectangle. Starting at narrow end, roll up dough tightly. Pinch ends and seam to seal; place, seam-side-down, in prepared pan. Cover; let rise in warm place 30 minutes or until doubled in size.

Heat oven to 375°F. Bake 35 to 40 minutes or until golden brown. Remove from pan; cool on wire rack at least 1 hour before slicing.

Nutrients per serving (1 slice):			
Calories	120	Cholesterol	0 mg
Fat	2 g	Sodium	85 mg

Cheesy Hot Pepper Bread

Makes 4 loaves, 12 slices per loaf

- 3 cups KELLOGG'S® NUTRI-GRAIN® Wheat Cereal, crushed to fine crumbs
- 5 to 6 cups all-purpose flour, divided
- 2 packages active dry yeast
- 2 teaspoons salt
- 1½ cups low-fat milk
- ¼ cup salad oil
- 2 eggs
- 1½ cups (6 ounces) shredded Monterey Jack cheese with jalapeño peppers
- ½ cup finely chopped onions
- 2 tablespoons margarine, melted (optional)

In large electric mixer bowl, stir together crushed Kellogg's® Nutri-Grain® cereal, 2 cups flour, yeast and salt. Set aside.

Heat milk and oil until very warm (120° to 130°F). Gradually add to cereal mixture and beat until well combined. Add eggs. Beat on medium speed for 2 minutes. Stir in cheese and onions.

By hand, stir in enough remaining flour to make a stiff dough. On well-floured surface, knead dough about 5 minutes or until smooth and elastic. Place dough in lightly greased bowl, turning once to grease top. Cover loosely. Let rise in warm place (80° to 85°F) until double in volume (about 1 hour).

Punch dough down. Divide into 4 pieces. On lightly floured surface, roll each into a 7×10-inch rectangle. Roll up loaves from long sides. Place, seam-side-down, on greased baking sheets. Let rise in warm place until double in volume. Make diagonal slits across top of loaves.

Bake at 400°F about 15 minutes or until golden brown. Brush baked loaves with margarine, if desired. Serve warm or cool.

Nutrients per serving (1 slice):			
Calories	100	Cholesterol	10 mg
Fat	3 g	Sodium	129 mg

Scones with Herbs and Parmesan

Makes 16 scones

2½ cups unbleached all-purpose flour
  1 tablespoon baking powder
  ¼ teaspoon salt (optional)
  ¼ teaspoon black or white pepper
  ¼ cup grated Parmesan cheese
  ½ cup low-fat buttermilk *or* plain nonfat yogurt
  ⅓ cup FILIPPO BERIO® Extra-Virgin Flavorful
    Olive Oil
  2 egg whites
  2 teaspoons lemon juice
  1 clove garlic, minced
  2 tablespoons finely minced fresh chives or
    green onions
  1 tablespoon minced fresh basil *or* 1 teaspoon
    dried basil leaves, crushed
  1 teaspoon minced fresh thyme or oregano
    leaves *or* ½ teaspoon dried thyme or
    oregano leaves, crushed

Preheat oven to 375°F. In large bowl, sift together flour, baking powder, salt and pepper. Stir in cheese until well blended.

In medium bowl, whisk together buttermilk, olive oil, egg whites, lemon juice, garlic, chives and herbs. (Mixture will look slightly curdled).

Add herb mixture to flour mixture; beat with wooden spoon until dough forms a soft ball. (Add additional flour, 1 tablespoon at a time, if necessary.)

Turn dough out onto lightly floured surface; knead 10 to 12 times. Divide dough in half; roll each half into a ball. Place each ball on ungreased baking sheet; press each ball into an 8-inch circle. Cut each circle into 8 wedges.

Bake for 15 to 20 minutes until lightly browned. Cool on wire racks 20 minutes; serve.

Nutrients per serving (1 scone):			
Calories	119	Cholesterol	1 mg
Fat	5 g	Sodium	104 mg

Crusty Oval Rolls

Makes 10 rolls

  1 package active dry yeast
1⅓ cups warm water (105° to 115°F)
  1 tablespoon honey
  1 tablespoon shortening, melted, cooled
  1 teaspoon salt
3¼ to 4 cups bread flour, divided
  ¼ cup cold water
  1 teaspoon cornstarch

In large bowl, combine yeast and warm water; stir to dissolve yeast. Stir in honey, shortening, salt and 2½ cups flour; beat until very elastic. Stir in enough of the remaining flour to make dough easy to handle.

Turn dough out onto floured surface. Knead 15 minutes or until dough is smooth and elastic, adding as much remaining flour as needed to prevent sticking. Shape dough into ball. Place in large, greased bowl; turn dough once to grease surface. Cover with towel; let rise in warm place (85°F) until doubled, about 1 hour.

Punch dough down; knead briefly on floured surface. Cover; let rest 10 minutes. Divide dough into 10 equal pieces; shape each piece into ball. Starting at center and working toward opposite ends, roll each ball on floured surface with palms of hands into tapered oval. Place, evenly spaced, on 2 greased baking sheets. Cover; let rise in warm place until almost doubled, about 25 minutes.

In small saucepan, combine cold water and cornstarch. Bring to a boil over high heat, stirring constantly. Boil until thickened and clear, about 2 minutes; cool slightly. Brush risen rolls with warm cornstarch mixture. Slash each roll lengthwise with sharp knife about ½ inch deep and to about ½ inch from each end.

Preheat oven to 375°F. Bake 30 to 35 minutes or until rolls are golden brown and sound hollow when tapped. Remove to wire racks to cool.

Nutrients per serving (1 roll):			
Calories	180	Cholesterol	0 mg
Fat	2 g	Sodium	214 mg

Crusty Oval Rolls

Dill Sour Cream Scones

Makes 1 dozen scones

> 2 cups all-purpose flour
> 2 teaspoons baking powder
> ½ teaspoon baking soda
> ½ teaspoon salt
> ¼ cup margarine, softened
> 2 eggs
> ½ cup sour cream
> 1 tablespoon chopped dill *or* 1 teaspoon dill weed

Preheat oven to 425°F. Combine flour, baking powder, baking soda and salt in large bowl. Cut in margarine with pastry blender until mixture resembles fine crumbs.

Beat eggs with fork in small bowl. Add sour cream and dill; beat until well combined. Stir into flour mixture until mixture forms soft dough that leaves sides of bowl.

Turn dough out onto well-floured surface. Knead dough 10 times. Roll dough out, using floured rolling pin, into 9×6-inch rectangle.

Cut dough, using floured knife, into 6 (3-inch) squares. Cut each square diagonally in half, making 12 triangles. Place triangles, 2 inches apart, on ungreased baking sheets.

Bake 10 to 12 minutes or until golden brown. Cool on wire racks for 10 minutes. Serve warm.

Nutrients per serving (1 scone):

Calories	137	Cholesterol	40 mg
Fat	7 g	Sodium	238 mg

Dill Sour Cream Scones

Jalapeño-Bacon Corn Bread

Makes 9 to 12 servings

> 4 slices bacon
> ¼ cup minced green onions with tops
> 2 jalapeño peppers, stemmed, seeded and minced
> 1 cup yellow cornmeal
> 1 cup all-purpose flour
> 2½ teaspoons baking powder
> ½ teaspoon baking soda
> ½ teaspoon salt
> 1 egg
> ¾ cup plain yogurt
> ¾ cup milk
> ¼ cup butter or margarine, melted
> ½ cup (2 ounces) shredded Cheddar cheese

Preheat oven to 400°F. Cook bacon in skillet until crisp; drain on paper towels. Pour 2 tablespoons bacon drippings into 9-inch cast-iron skillet or 9-inch square baking pan. Crumble bacon into small bowl; add green onions and peppers.

Combine cornmeal, flour, baking powder, baking soda and salt in large bowl. Beat egg slightly in medium bowl; add yogurt and whisk until smooth. Whisk in milk and butter. Pour liquid mixture into dry ingredients; stir just until moistened. Stir in bacon mixture. Pour into skillet; sprinkle with cheese. Bake 20 to 25 minutes or until wooden toothpick inserted in center comes out clean. Cut into wedges or squares; serve hot.

Nutrients per serving:

Calories	165	Cholesterol	27 mg
Fat	8 g	Sodium	335 mg

Garlic Mustard Loaf

Makes 10 servings

> 1 loaf (about 15 inches) Italian bread
> 2 tablespoons *each* FRENCH'S® Creamy Spread™ Mustard and olive oil
> 1¼ teaspoon *each* garlic powder and dried basil leaves, crushed

Partially cut loaf into 10 slices, cutting down to, but not through, bottom of loaf. Combine remaining ingredients in small bowl. Brush mixture evenly onto each cut bread slice. Wrap loaf in aluminum foil. Bake at 400°F for 20 minutes or until heated through.

Nutrients per serving (1 slice):

Calories	110	Cholesterol	0 mg
Fat	3 g	Sodium	214 mg

Savory French Bread

Makes 6 to 8 servings

  1 large loaf French bread
  ¼ cup butter or margarine, softened
  ½ teaspoon dried basil leaves
  ½ teaspoon dill weed
  ½ teaspoon chopped dried chives
  ¼ teaspoon garlic powder
  ¼ teaspoon paprika
  ¼ teaspoon TABASCO® pepper sauce

Preheat oven to 400°F. Slice bread diagonally, but do not cut through bottom crust of loaf. In small bowl mix remaining ingredients. Spread between bread slices; wrap bread in aluminum foil and heat in oven 15 to 20 minutes. Serve warm.

Nutrients per serving:			
Calories	216	Cholesterol	17 mg
Fat	7 g	Sodium	390 mg

Sun-Dried Tomato Muffins

Makes 12 muffins

  1 cup all-purpose flour
  ½ cup whole wheat flour
  2 teaspoons baking powder
  2 teaspoons sugar
  ½ teaspoon black pepper
  ¼ teaspoon salt
  1 cup low-fat milk
  ¼ cup vegetable oil
  1 egg
  4 to 6 tablespoons chopped green olives
  2 tablespoons chopped oil-packed sun-dried
    tomatoes, drained*

Preheat oven to 425°F. Grease or paper-line 12 (2½-inch) muffin cups. Combine dry ingredients in medium bowl. Whisk together milk, oil and egg. Add to dry ingredients, mixing just until moistened. Gently stir in olives and tomatoes.

Spoon batter into prepared muffin cups. Bake 15 minutes or until lightly browned.

If using sun-dried tomatoes not packed in oil, hydrate according to package directions before chopping.

Nutrients per serving (1 muffin):			
Calories	59	Cholesterol	10 mg
Fat	3 g	Sodium	79 mg

Pepperoni 'n' Chive Mini Muffins

Pepperoni 'n' Chive Mini Muffins

Makes 24 muffins

  1½ cups buttermilk baking mix
  1 (8-ounce) carton LAND O LAKES® Light
    Sour Cream (1 cup)
  ¼ cup chopped fresh chives *or* 4 teaspoons dried
    chives
  ¼ cup skim milk
  1 egg, slightly beaten
  ¼ teaspoon garlic powder
  ⅓ cup chopped pepperoni

Heat oven to 400°F. In medium bowl combine all ingredients except pepperoni. Stir just until moistened. Fold in pepperoni. Spoon into greased mini-muffin pans. Bake for 18 to 20 minutes or until lightly browned. Cool 5 minutes; remove from pans.

Nutrients per serving (1 muffin):			
Calories	58	Cholesterol	15 mg
Fat	3 g	Sodium	146 mg

Freezer Buttermilk Biscuits

Freezer Buttermilk Biscuits

Makes 16 biscuits

3 cups all-purpose flour
1 tablespoon baking powder
1 tablespoon sugar
1 teaspoon baking soda
½ teaspoon salt
⅔ cup shortening
1 cup buttermilk

Combine flour, baking powder, sugar, baking soda and salt in large bowl. Cut in shortening with pastry blender until mixture resembles fine crumbs.

Stir buttermilk into flour mixture until mixture forms a soft dough that leaves sides of bowl.

Turn dough out onto well-floured surface. Knead dough 10 times. (To knead dough, fold dough in half toward you; press dough away from you with heels of hands. Give dough a quarter turn and continue folding, pushing and turning.) Roll dough out into 8-inch square. Cut dough into 16 (2-inch) squares.*

Line baking sheet with plastic wrap. Place squares on lined sheet. Freeze about 3 hours or until firm. Remove frozen squares from sheet and place in freezer container. Freeze up to 1 month.

Preheat oven to 400°F. Place frozen squares, 1½ inches apart, on ungreased baking sheets.

Bake 20 to 25 minutes until golden brown. Serve warm.

*To bake biscuits immediately, preheat oven to 450°F. Prepare dough as directed, but do not freeze. Place squares, 1½ inches apart, on ungreased baking sheets. Bake 10 to 12 minutes until golden brown. Serve warm.

Note: *If desired, biscuits can be split and filled with turkey ham.*

Nutrients per serving (1 biscuit):

Calories	141	Cholesterol	2 mg
Fat	9 g	Sodium	196 mg

Whole Wheat Herb Muffins

Makes 12 muffins

1 cup all-purpose flour
1 cup whole wheat flour
⅓ cup sugar
2 teaspoons baking powder
½ teaspoon baking soda
½ teaspoon salt
½ teaspoon dried basil leaves, crushed
¼ teaspoon dried marjoram leaves, crushed
¼ teaspoon dried oregano leaves, crushed
⅛ teaspoon dried thyme leaves, crushed
¾ cup raisins
1 cup buttermilk
2 tablespoons margarine or butter, melted
1 egg, beaten
2 tablespoons wheat germ

Preheat oven to 400°F. Grease 12 (2½-inch) muffin cups. In large bowl, combine flours, sugar, baking powder, baking soda, salt, herbs and raisins. In small bowl, combine buttermilk, margarine and egg. Stir into flour mixture just until moistened. Spoon into muffin cups. Sprinkle wheat germ over tops. Bake 15 to 20 minutes or until lightly browned and wooden toothpick inserted in centers comes out clean. Remove from pan.

Nutrients per serving (1 muffin):

Calories	152	Cholesterol	19 mg
Fat	3 g	Sodium	230 mg

Spicy Onion Bread

Makes 8 servings

2 tablespoons instant minced onion
⅓ cup water
1½ cups biscuit baking mix
1 egg, slightly beaten
½ cup milk
½ teaspoon TABASCO® pepper sauce
2 tablespoons butter, melted
½ teaspoon caraway seeds (optional)

Preheat oven to 400°F. Soak instant minced onion in water 5 minutes. Combine biscuit mix, egg, milk and TABASCO sauce in large bowl and stir until blended. Stir in onion. Turn into greased 8-inch pie plate. Brush with melted butter. Sprinkle with caraway seeds. Bake 20 to 25 minutes or until golden brown.

Nutrients per serving:

Calories	139	Cholesterol	43 mg
Fat	7 g	Sodium	310 mg

Cottage Herb Rolls

Makes 1½ to 2 dozen rolls

1 package active dry yeast
¼ cup warm water (105° to 115°F)
2½ cups unsifted flour
¼ cup sugar
1 teaspoon oregano leaves
1 teaspoon salt
½ cup cold margarine or butter
1 cup BORDEN® or MEADOW GOLD®
    Cottage Cheese
1 egg, beaten
  Melted margarine or butter

Dissolve yeast in warm water. In large bowl, combine flour, sugar, oregano and salt; mix well. Cut in cold margarine until mixture resembles coarse cornmeal. Blend in cheese, egg and yeast mixture. Turn onto well-floured surface; knead. Shape into ball; place in well-greased bowl. Brush top with melted margarine. Cover; let rise until doubled. Punch down; shape as desired. Brush with melted margarine; cover. Let rise again until nearly doubled. Bake in preheated 375°F oven 12 to 15 minutes. Serve warm.

Nutrients per serving (1 roll):

Calories	102	Cholesterol	10 mg
Fat	5 g	Sodium	174 mg

Cottage Herb Rolls

Vegetable Dinner Rolls

Makes 1 dozen rolls

1½ cups all-purpose flour
1½ cups whole wheat flour
1 cup KELLOGG'S® ALL-BRAN® Cereal
2 tablespoons sugar
1 package active dry yeast
1 teaspoon dried basil leaves, crushed
½ teaspoon salt
1 cup water
2 tablespoons margarine
2 egg whites
1 cup shredded zucchini
½ cup shredded carrots
¼ cup sliced green onions
  Nonstick cooking spray
2 teaspoons sesame seeds (optional)

Stir together flours. Set aside.

In large mixing bowl, combine Kellogg's® All-Bran® cereal, 1 cup flour mixture, sugar, yeast, basil and salt. Set aside.

Heat water and margarine until very warm (115° to 120°F). Add water mixture and egg whites to cereal mixture. Beat on low speed with electric mixer 30 seconds or until thoroughly combined. Increase speed to high and beat 3 minutes longer, scraping bowl frequently. Mix in vegetables.

By hand, stir in enough remaining flour to make sticky dough. Cover loosely. Let rise in warm place (80° to 85°F) until doubled in volume. Stir down batter. Portion evenly into 12 (2½-inch) muffin pan cups coated with nonstick cooking spray. Sprinkle with sesame seeds, if desired. Let rise in warm place until doubled in volume.

Bake at 400°F about 17 minutes or until golden brown. Serve warm.

Nutrients per serving (1 roll):

Calories	160	Cholesterol	0 mg
Fat	3 g	Sodium	190 mg

Easy Poppy Seed Yeast Bread

Makes 2 loaves

2 packages (¼ ounce *each*) active dry yeast
1 cup warm water (105° to 110°F)
1½ cups (12-ounce can) *undiluted* CARNATION®
    Evaporated Lowfat Milk
3 tablespoons margarine, softened
3 tablespoons granulated sugar
2 teaspoons salt
¼ cup poppy seeds, divided
5 to 5½ cups all-purpose flour, divided
1 egg white
1 tablespoon water

In large mixer bowl, dissolve yeast in warm water.
Add evaporated lowfat milk, margarine, sugar, salt
and *3 tablespoons* poppy seeds. Gradually add *3 cups*
flour, beating on medium speed until almost smooth
(about 1 minute). Add remaining *2 to 2½ cups* flour
to form a stiff dough. Use spatula to push dough
down off beater stems. (Dough will be sticky.) Cover
bowl; let rise in warm, draft-free place (80° to 85°F)
for 30 minutes. Stir for 2 minutes. Divide dough
equally into 2 greased 8½×4½×2½-inch loaf pans.
(Flour hands for easier handling.) Push dough into
corners and pat tops until smooth. In small bowl,
combine egg white and water; brush tops of loaves.
Sprinkle with remaining *1 tablespoon* poppy seeds.
Let dough rise for 25 minutes. Bake at 375°F for
20 to 30 minutes or until loaves are brown and sound
hollow when tapped. Remove from pans; cool
completely on wire rack.

Nutrients per serving (½-inch slice):

Calories	195	Cholesterol	2 mg
Fat	3 g	Sodium	330 mg

Bran Pita Bread

Bran Pita Bread

Makes 12 servings

1 package active dry yeast
1¼ cups warm water (110° to 115°F)
1½ cups KELLOGG'S® ALL-BRAN® Cereal
1½ cups all-purpose flour, divided
½ teaspoon salt
¼ cup vegetable oil
1 cup whole wheat flour

In large bowl of electric mixer, dissolve yeast in warm
water, about 5 minutes. Add Kellogg's® All-Bran®
cereal, mixing until combined. On low speed, beat in
1 cup all-purpose flour, salt and oil. Beat on high
speed 3 minutes, scraping sides of bowl.

Using dough hook on electric mixer or by hand, stir in
whole wheat flour. Continue kneading with mixer on
low speed or by hand 5 minutes longer or until dough
is smooth and elastic. Add remaining ½ cup all-
purpose flour, if needed, to make soft dough.

Divide dough into 12 portions. Roll each portion
between floured hands into a very smooth ball. Cover
with plastic wrap or a damp cloth; let rest 10 minutes.

On a well-floured surface, lightly roll one piece of
dough at a time into 6-inch round, turning dough over
once. Do not stretch, puncture or crease dough. Keep
unrolled dough covered while rolling each dough
piece. Place 2 rounds of dough at a time on
ungreased baking sheet.

Bake in 450°F oven about 4 minutes or until dough
is puffed and slightly firm. Turn with a spatula;
continue baking about 2 minutes or until lightly
browned; cool. Repeat with remaining dough. Cut in
half and fill with a vegetable or meat filling.

Nutrients per serving (2 pita bread halves):

Calories	160	Cholesterol	0 mg
Fat	5 g	Sodium	210 mg

Old World Pumpernickel Muffins

Oat Bread Muffins

Makes 12 muffins

2 cups all-purpose flour, divided
½ cup oat bran cereal
2 tablespoons sugar
½ teaspoon salt
1 package active dry rapid-rise yeast
½ cup milk
½ cup cottage cheese
2 tablespoons butter or margarine
1 egg
¼ cup chopped fresh parsley
1 tablespoon chopped fresh dill *or* 1 teaspoon dried dill weed
2 tablespoons uncooked rolled oats (optional)

Grease or paper-line 12 (2½-inch) muffin cups.

Combine 1 cup flour, bran cereal, sugar, salt and yeast in large bowl; set aside. Place milk, cottage cheese and butter in 1-quart saucepan. Heat over low heat until very warm (120° to 130°F). Gradually beat milk mixture into flour mixture with electric mixer at low speed until well blended. Increase speed to medium; beat 2 minutes. Add ½ cup flour, egg, parsley and dill; beat 2 minutes more. Stir in remaining ½ cup flour with wooden spoon until mixture is well blended and forms thick batter. Spoon evenly into prepared muffin cups. Sprinkle oats over tops of muffins, if desired. Let rise, uncovered, 30 minutes.

Preheat oven to 400°F. Bake 20 to 25 minutes until browned and muffins sound hollow when tapped. Remove from pans. Cool on wire rack 10 minutes. Serve warm.

Nutrients per serving (1 muffin):

Calories	129	Cholesterol	24 mg
Fat	3 g	Sodium	156 mg

Old World Pumpernickel Muffins

Makes 12 muffins

1 cup all-purpose flour
½ cup rye flour
½ cup whole wheat flour
2 teaspoons caraway seed
1 teaspoon baking soda
½ teaspoon salt
1 cup buttermilk
¼ cup vegetable oil
¼ cup light molasses
1 egg
½ square (½ ounce) unsweetened chocolate, melted and cooled

Preheat oven to 400°F. Grease or paper-line 12 (2½-inch) muffin cups.

Combine flours, caraway seed, baking soda and salt in large bowl. Combine buttermilk, oil, molasses and egg in small bowl until blended; stir in melted chocolate. Stir into flour mixture just until moistened. Spoon evenly into prepared muffin cups.

Bake 20 to 25 minutes until wooden pick inserted in center comes out clean. Remove from pan. Cool on wire rack about 10 minutes. Serve warm or cool completely. Store at room temperature in tightly covered container up to 2 days.

Nutrients per serving (1 muffin):

Calories	149	Cholesterol	19 mg
Fat	6 g	Sodium	186 mg

Tomato-Cheese Bread

Makes 20 servings, 2 loaves

5½ to 6 cups all-purpose flour, divided
2 packages active dry yeast
1 cup tomato juice
¾ cup water
3 tablespoons butter
1½ teaspoons salt
1 egg
1½ cups (6 ounces) shredded Wisconsin Cheddar
   cheese

Combine 2 cups flour and yeast in large bowl. Place tomato juice, water, butter and salt in small saucepan; cook just until warm (115° to 120°F) and butter is almost melted, stirring frequently. Stir into flour mixture; add egg and cheese. Beat with electric mixer on low speed for 30 seconds. Beat on high speed for 3 minutes. Stir in as much remaining flour as possible to make soft dough. On lightly floured surface, knead in as much remaining flour as possible for 6 to 8 minutes or until moderately stiff dough forms. Shape into ball. Place in greased bowl; turn once. Cover; let rise 1 hour or until doubled. Punch down; divide in half. Cover; let rest 10 minutes. Grease two 8×4×2-inch loaf pans. Shape each dough half into 1 loaf. Place in prepared pans. Cover; let rise about 45 minutes or until nearly doubled.

Preheat oven to 375°F. Bake about 35 minutes or until loaves sound hollow when tapped. Remove from pans; cool on wire racks.

Nutrients per serving:			
Calories	182	Cholesterol	24 mg
Fat	5 g	Sodium	118 mg

Favorite recipe from **Wisconsin Milk Marketing Board** © **1994**

Wheat Germ Scones

Makes 12 scones

½ cup wheat germ, divided
1½ cups all-purpose flour
2 tablespoons packed brown sugar
1 tablespoon baking powder
½ teaspoon salt
6 tablespoons butter or margarine
⅓ cup golden raisins, coarsely chopped
2 eggs
¼ cup milk

Preheat oven to 425°F.

Reserve 1 tablespoon wheat germ. Combine remaining wheat germ, flour, brown sugar, baking powder and salt in large bowl. Cut in butter with pastry blender or 2 knives until mixture resembles coarse crumbs. Stir in raisins. Beat eggs in small bowl. Add milk; beat until well mixed. Reserve 2 tablespoons milk mixture. Add remaining milk mixture to flour mixture; stir until mixture forms soft dough that pulls away from side of bowl.

Turn out onto well-floured surface. Knead dough 10 times.* Roll dough into 9×6-inch rectangle with floured rolling pin. Cut dough into 6 (3-inch) squares. Cut each square diagonally in half, making 12 triangles. Place triangles 2 inches apart on ungreased baking sheets. Brush triangles with reserved milk mixture and sprinkle with reserved wheat germ.

Bake 10 to 12 minutes until golden brown. Cool on wire racks 10 minutes. Serve warm.

To knead dough, fold dough in half toward you and push dough away from you with heels of hands. Give dough a quarter turn and continue folding and turning.

Nutrients per serving (1 scone):			
Calories	153	Cholesterol	51 mg
Fat	7 g	Sodium	235 mg

Wheat Germ Scones

Whole Wheat Popovers

Makes 6 popovers

2 eggs
1 cup milk
2 tablespoons butter or margarine, melted
½ cup all-purpose flour
½ cup whole wheat flour
¼ teaspoon salt

Position rack in lower third of oven. Preheat oven to 450°F. Grease 6 (6-ounce) custard cups. Set custard cups in jelly-roll pan for easier handling.

Beat eggs in large bowl with electric mixer at low speed 1 minute. Beat in milk and butter until blended. Beat in flours and salt until batter is smooth. Pour batter evenly into prepared custard cups.

Bake 20 minutes. *Reduce oven temperature to 350°F.* Bake 15 minutes more; quickly make small slit in top of each popover to let out steam. Bake 5 to 10 minutes more or until browned. Remove popovers from cups. Serve warm.

Nutrients per serving (1 popover):			
Calories	140	Cholesterol	82 mg
Fat	6 g	Sodium	170 mg

Apple-Cheddar Turnovers

Makes 18 pastries

2 packages active dry yeast
¼ cup warm water (110° to 115°F)
⅓ cup butter
⅓ cup sugar
1 teaspoon salt
½ cup (2 ounces) shredded aged Wisconsin Cheddar cheese
1 carton (8 ounces) dairy sour cream
1 egg, slightly beaten
3½ to 4 cups all-purpose flour, divided
1¼ cups apple pie filling
1 cup sifted powdered sugar
½ teaspoon vanilla extract
1 to 2 teaspoons milk

Soften yeast in warm water; set aside. Heat butter, sugar and salt in large saucepan just until warm (115° to 120°F) and butter is almost melted, stirring constantly. Add cheese, stirring until melted. Pour into large bowl. Stir in sour cream and egg; mix well. Stir in 1½ cups flour; beat well. Add softened yeast; stir until smooth. Stir in as much remaining flour as possible until stiff dough forms. Turn out onto lightly floured surface; knead 2 minutes or until smooth and

elastic. Cover and let rest 10 minutes. Roll half the dough into 12-inch square. Cut into nine 4-inch squares. Place about 1 tablespoon apple pie filling in center of each square. Fold dough over to form triangle; seal edges well. Repeat with remaining dough.

Place pastries on greased baking sheets; cover and let rise in warm place about 20 minutes or until doubled. Preheat oven to 350°F. Bake 10 to 15 minutes or until lightly browned. Remove from baking sheets to wire racks.

Meanwhile, for frosting, combine powdered sugar and vanilla in small bowl. Stir in milk until frosting is of spreading consistency. Spread over warm pastries. Serve warm or cool completely.

Nutrients per serving (1 pastry):			
Calories	219	Cholesterol	30 mg
Fat	8 g	Sodium	185 mg

Favorite recipe from **Wisconsin Milk Marketing Board** © 1994

Bubbling Wisconsin Cheese Bread

Makes 16 servings

½ cup (2 ounces) shredded Wisconsin Mozzarella cheese
⅓ cup mayonnaise or salad dressing
⅛ teaspoon garlic powder
⅛ teaspoon onion powder
1 loaf French bread (16 ounces), halved lengthwise
⅓ cup (1 ounce) grated Wisconsin Parmesan cheese

Preheat oven to 350°F. Combine Mozzarella cheese, mayonnaise, garlic powder and onion powder in small bowl; stir to mix well. (Mixture will be very thick.) Spread half the mixture over each French bread half. Sprinkle half the Parmesan cheese over each half. Bake 20 to 25 minutes until bubbly and lightly browned. Cut each half into 8 slices.

Nutrients per serving (1 slice):			
Calories	132	Cholesterol	7 mg
Fat	6 g	Sodium	234 mg

Favorite recipe from **Wisconsin Milk Marketing Board** © 1994

Whole Wheat Popovers

Wild Rice Breakfast Bread

Makes 10 servings

¼ cup extra light margarine, softened
¼ cup packed brown sugar
4 egg whites
1 teaspoon vanilla extract
1½ cups well-cooked wild rice
½ cup chopped pecans
¾ cup whole wheat flour
¾ cup all-purpose flour
1 teaspoon baking powder
1 teaspoon salt
2 teaspoons ground cinnamon
¾ cup skim milk
Maple Butter (recipe follows), optional

Preheat oven to 325°F. Grease 8×4-inch loaf pan.

Beat margarine and brown sugar in large bowl until creamy. Add egg whites and beat until fluffy. Add vanilla. Stir in rice and pecans. Combine flours, baking powder, salt and cinnamon. Add flour mixture alternately with milk to rice mixture; stir just until flour mixture is moistened. Pour into prepared pan.

Bake about 55 minutes or until wooden pick inserted in center comes out clean. Serve with Maple Butter, if desired.

Maple Butter

½ cup butter, softened
¼ cup maple syrup

Beat butter in small bowl until light and fluffy. Thoroughly blend in maple syrup.

Nutrients per serving:			
Calories	143	Cholesterol	trace
Fat	3 g	Sodium	285 mg

Favorite recipe from **Minnesota Cultivated Wild Rice Council**

Double Cheese Muffins

Makes 16 muffins

1½ cups all-purpose flour
½ cup cornmeal
¼ cup sugar
1 tablespoon baking powder
1 egg, beaten
1 cup milk
½ cup (2 ounces) shredded Wisconsin Cheddar cheese
½ cup cream-style Cottage cheese
¼ cup butter, melted

Preheat oven to 400°F. Grease and flour 16 (2½-inch) muffin cups.

Combine flour, cornmeal, sugar and baking powder in large bowl. Combine egg, milk, Cheddar cheese, Cottage cheese and butter; blend well. Add egg mixture to flour mixture. Stir until moistened. Spoon evenly into prepared muffin cups, filling each ⅔ full.

Bake 20 minutes or until wooden pick inserted in center comes out clean. Serve warm.

Nutrients per serving (1 muffin):			
Calories	131	Cholesterol	28 mg
Fat	5 g	Sodium	151 mg

Favorite recipe from **Wisconsin Milk Marketing Board** © 1994

Dill Seed Bread Sticks

Makes 12 bread sticks

1 cup KELLOGG'S® ALL-BRAN® cereal
¼ cup firmly packed brown sugar
2 packages active dry yeast
½ teaspoon salt
1 cup hot skim milk (120° to 130°F)
¼ cup vegetable oil
1 cup bread flour
2 teaspoons dill seeds
1 cup whole wheat flour
1 egg white, slightly beaten
1 tablespoon minced dry onion

1. In large electric mixer bowl, combine Kellogg's® All-Bran® cereal, sugar, yeast and salt. Gradually add milk to cereal mixture. Beat on medium speed 2 minutes, scraping bowl frequently.

2. Gradually add oil, bread flour and dill seeds. Beat on high speed 2 minutes, scraping bowl frequently. Change beaters to dough hooks or by hand gradually add whole wheat flour. Knead on mixer or by hand 5 minutes until dough is smooth and elastic. Place in oiled bowl, turning once to coat surface. Cover lightly and let rise in warm place until doubled.

3. Punch dough down and divide into 12 portions. Shape each portion into a 10-inch stick. Place sticks about 1 inch apart on lightly greased baking sheet. Brush with egg white and sprinkle with onion.

4. Bake in 400°F oven about 10 minutes or until golden brown. Serve hot.

Nutrients per serving (1 bread stick):			
Calories	150	Cholesterol	trace
Fat	5 g	Sodium	188 mg

Anadama Muffins

Makes 12 muffins

2 cups all-purpose flour, divided
3 tablespoons sugar
½ teaspoon salt
1 package active dry rapid-rise yeast
¾ cup water
⅓ cup yellow cornmeal
3 tablespoons molasses
3 tablespoons butter or margarine
1 egg

Grease or paper-line 12 (2½-inch) muffin cups.

Combine 1 cup flour, sugar, salt and yeast in large bowl; set aside. Combine water, cornmeal, molasses and butter in 1-quart saucepan. Heat over low heat until very warm (120° to 130°F). Gradually beat water mixture into flour mixture with electric mixer at low speed until well blended. Increase speed to medium; beat 2 minutes. Add ½ cup flour and egg; beat 2 minutes more. Stir in remaining ½ cup flour with wooden spoon until mixture is well blended and forms thick batter. Spoon evenly into prepared muffin cups. Let rise, uncovered, 30 minutes.

Preheat oven to 400°F. Bake 20 to 25 minutes until browned and sound hollow when tapped. Remove from pans. Cool on wire rack for about 10 minutes. Serve warm.

Nutrients per serving (1 muffin):

Calories	147	Cholesterol	25 mg
Fat	4 g	Sodium	129 mg

Four-Grain Savory Muffins

Makes 12 muffins

1 cup buttermilk
½ cup high-fiber bran cereal
½ cup all-purpose flour
½ cup whole wheat flour
½ cup wheat germ
3 tablespoons sugar
1 teaspoon baking powder
1 teaspoon baking soda
½ teaspoon salt
¼ cup butter or margarine, melted
1 egg

Preheat oven to 400°F. Grease or paper-line 12 (2½-inch) muffin cups.

Pour buttermilk over bran cereal in large bowl. Let stand 5 minutes to soften. Combine flours, wheat germ, sugar, baking powder, baking soda and salt in medium bowl. Add melted butter and egg to cereal mixture; stir until blended. Stir in flour mixture just until moistened. Spoon evenly into prepared muffin cups.

Bake 20 to 25 minutes until browned and wooden pick inserted in center comes out clean. Remove from pan. Cool on wire rack about 10 minutes. Serve warm or cool completely. Store at room temperature in tightly covered container up to 2 days.

Nutrients per serving (1 muffin):

Calories	119	Cholesterol	29 mg
Fat	5 g	Sodium	267 mg

Oatmeal Green Onion Muffins

Makes 12 muffins

1¾ cups all-purpose flour
¾ cup old-fashioned oats
2 tablespoons sugar
1 tablespoon baking powder
½ teaspoon salt
¾ cup milk
½ cup cottage cheese
⅓ cup vegetable oil
¼ cup chopped green onions
1 egg

Preheat oven to 400°F. Grease or paper-line 12 (2½-inch) muffin cups.

Combine flour, oats, sugar, baking powder and salt in large bowl. Combine milk, cottage cheese, oil, green onions and egg in small bowl until blended; stir into flour mixture just until moistened. Spoon evenly into prepared muffin cups.

Bake 25 to 30 minutes until golden brown and wooden pick inserted in center comes out clean. Remove from pan. Cool on wire rack 10 minutes. Serve warm.

Nutrients per serving (1 muffin):

Calories	185	Cholesterol	19 mg
Fat	9 g	Sodium	213 mg

Caraway Cheese Muffins

Caraway Cheese Muffins

Makes 12 muffins

1¼ cups all-purpose flour
½ cup rye flour
2 tablespoons sugar
2½ teaspoons baking powder
½ teaspoon salt
1 cup (4 ounces) shredded sharp Cheddar
    or Swiss cheese
1½ teaspoons caraway seed
1 cup milk
¼ cup vegetable oil
1 egg

Preheat oven to 400°F. Paper-line 12 (2½-inch) muffin cups.

Combine flours, sugar, baking powder and salt in large bowl. Add cheese and caraway seed; toss to coat. Combine milk, oil and egg in small bowl until blended; stir into flour mixture just until moistened. Spoon evenly into prepared muffin cups.

Bake 20 to 25 minutes until golden brown and wooden pick inserted in center comes out clean. Remove from pan. Cool on wire rack about 10 minutes. Serve warm.

Nutrients per serving (1 muffin):

Calories	164	Cholesterol	28 mg
Fat	8 g	Sodium	224 mg

Wild Rice Three-Grain Bread

Makes 20 servings

1 package active dry yeast
⅓ cup warm water (105° to 115°F)
2 cups warm skim milk (105° to 115°F)
2 tablespoons shortening, melted
1½ teaspoons salt
½ cup honey
2 cups whole wheat flour
4 to 4½ cups unbleached all-purpose or
    bread flour, divided
½ cup uncooked rolled oats
½ cup rye flour
1 cup cooked wild rice
1 egg white, beaten with 1 tablespoon water
½ cup hulled sunflower seeds (optional)

Dissolve yeast in water in large bowl. Add milk, shortening, salt and honey; blend well. Stir in whole wheat flour, 2 cups all-purpose flour, oats and rye flour until soft dough forms. Stir in rice. Cover and let rest 15 minutes. Stir in additional all-purpose flour until stiff dough forms. Turn out onto lightly floured surface and knead 10 minutes. Add more all-purpose flour as necessary to keep dough from sticking. Place dough in lightly greased bowl; turn over. Cover and let rise about 2 hours or until doubled. Punch down. Knead briefly on lightly oiled surface. Divide dough into 3 pieces. Roll each piece into a rope; braid and place onto greased baking sheet, pinching ends together to make wreath. Let rise about 45 minutes or until doubled.

Preheat oven to 375°F. Brush top of wreath with egg white mixture. Sprinkle with sunflower seeds, if desired. Bake 45 minutes or until bread sounds hollow when tapped.

Nutrients per serving:

Calories	198	Cholesterol	trace
Fat	3 g	Sodium	157 mg

Favorite recipe from **Minnesota Cultivated Wild Rice Council**

Soda Bread

Makes 16 slices

1½ cups whole wheat flour
1 cup all-purpose flour
½ cup uncooked rolled oats
¼ cup sugar
1½ teaspoons baking powder
½ teaspoon baking soda
¼ teaspoon ground cinnamon
⅓ cup raisins (optional)
¼ cup walnuts (optional)
1¼ cups low fat buttermilk
1 tablespoon vegetable oil

Preheat oven to 375°F. Stir together flours, oats, sugar, baking powder, baking soda and cinnamon in large bowl. Stir in raisins and walnuts, if desired. Gradually stir in buttermilk and oil until dough forms. Knead in bowl for 30 seconds. Spray loaf pan with nonstick cooking spray; turn dough into pan. Bake 40 to 50 minutes until knife inserted in center comes out clean.

Nutrients per serving (1 slice):

Calories	126	Cholesterol	1 mg
Fat	3 g	Sodium	78 mg

Favorite recipe from **The Sugar Association, Inc.**

Cheesy Onion Flatbread

Cheesy Onion Flatbread

Makes 2 flatbreads, 8 wedges each

½ cup plus 3 tablespoons honey, divided
2⅓ cups warm water (105° to 115°F), divided
1½ packages active dry yeast
6 tablespoons olive oil, divided
3 cups whole wheat flour
⅓ cup cornmeal
1½ tablespoons coarse salt
3 to 4 cups all-purpose flour, divided
1 large red onion, thinly sliced
1 cup red wine vinegar
Additional cornmeal
1 cup grated Parmesan cheese
½ teaspoon onion salt
Freshly ground black pepper to taste

Place 3 tablespoons honey in large bowl. Pour ⅓ cup water over honey. *Do not stir.* Sprinkle yeast over water. Let stand about 15 minutes until bubbly. Add remaining 2 cups water, 3 tablespoons olive oil, whole wheat flour and cornmeal. Mix until well blended. Stir in salt and 2 cups all-purpose flour. Gradually stir in enough remaining flour until mixture clings to sides of bowl.

Turn dough out onto lightly floured surface. Knead in enough remaining flour to make a smooth and satiny dough, about 10 minutes. Divide dough in half. Place each half in large, lightly greased bowl; turn over to grease surface. Cover; let rise in warm place (80° to 85°F) until doubled.

Meanwhile, combine onion, vinegar and remaining ½ cup honey. Marinate at room temperature at least 1 hour.

Grease two 12-inch pizza pans; sprinkle each with additional cornmeal. Stretch dough and pat into pans; create valleys with fingertips. Cover; let rise in warm place until doubled, about 1 hour.

Preheat oven to 400°F. Drain onions; scatter over dough. Sprinkle with remaining 3 tablespoons olive oil, cheese and onion salt. Season with pepper.

Bake 25 to 30 minutes or until flatbread is crusty and golden. Cut each flatbread into 8 wedges. Serve warm.

Nutrients per serving (1 wedge):

Calories	296	Cholesterol	5 mg
Fat	8 g	Sodium	916 mg

Touchdown Cheese Scones

Makes 8 scones

2 cups all-purpose flour
2½ teaspoons baking powder
½ teaspoon baking soda
¼ teaspoon salt
2 tablespoons cold butter or margarine, cut into pieces
1 cup (4 ounces) shredded mild Cheddar cheese
⅔ cup buttermilk
2 large eggs, divided
¼ teaspoon TABASCO® pepper sauce

Preheat oven to 350°F. In a large bowl, sift together flour, baking powder, baking soda and salt. Cut in butter until mixture resembles cornmeal. Stir in cheese. In small bowl, blend together buttermilk, 1 egg and TABASCO sauce. Make a well in center of dry ingredients; add buttermilk mixture. Stir quickly and lightly with fork to form sticky dough. Turn dough out on lightly floured board. Knead gently 10 times. Divide dough in half; pat each half into circle about ½ inch thick. Cut each circle into 4 wedges. Combine remaining egg and 1 tablespoon water. Brush each wedge with egg mixture. Arrange on greased baking sheet. Bake 13 to 15 minutes or until golden.

Nutrients per serving (1 scone):

Calories	225	Cholesterol	92 mg
Fat	9 g	Sodium	385 mg

Cheddar-Onion Casserole Bread

Makes 1 loaf, 12 wedges

2½ cups flour
1 tablespoon baking powder
½ teaspoon salt
½ cup HELLMANN'S® or BEST FOODS®
   Light Reduced Calorie Mayonnaise
2 cups (8 ounces) shredded Cheddar cheese
½ cup minced green onions
¾ cup milk
1 egg

Preheat oven to 425°F. Grease 1½-quart casserole dish. In large bowl, combine flour, baking powder and salt. Stir in mayonnaise until mixture resembles coarse crumbs. Add cheese and green onions; toss. In small bowl, beat milk and egg. Stir into cheese mixture just until moistened. Spoon into prepared casserole dish.

Bake 35 to 45 minutes or until wooden toothpick inserted into center comes out clean. Cut into wedges; serve immediately.

Nutrients per serving (1 wedge):			
Calories	214	Cholesterol	43 mg
Fat	10 g	Sodium	301 mg

Cheesy Corn Sticks

Makes 7 to 9 corn sticks

½ cup all-purpose flour
½ cup cornmeal
2 teaspoons baking powder
¼ teaspoon salt
½ cup low-fat milk
1 egg, beaten
3 tablespoons vegetable oil
½ cup (2 ounces) shredded Cheddar cheese

Preheat oven to 425°F. Heat cast-iron corn stick pan in oven while preparing batter.

Combine flour, cornmeal, baking powder and salt in medium bowl; set aside. Combine milk, egg and oil. Add to dry ingredients, stirring just until moistened.

Carefully brush hot pan with additional oil. Spoon batter into prepared pan. Sprinkle batter with cheese. Bake 10 minutes or until lightly browned.

Nutrients per serving (1 corn stick):			
Calories	148	Cholesterol	35 mg
Fat	9 g	Sodium	211 mg

Garden Herb Muffins

Makes 12 muffins

2 cups all-purpose flour
2 tablespoons sugar
1 tablespoon baking powder
¼ teaspoon salt
1 package (3 ounces) cream cheese
¾ cup milk
½ cup finely shredded or grated carrots
¼ cup chopped green onions
¼ cup vegetable oil
1 egg

Preheat oven to 400°F. Grease or paper-line 12 (2½-inch) muffin cups.

Combine flour, sugar, baking powder and salt in large bowl. Cut in cream cheese with pastry blender until mixture resembles fine crumbs.

Combine milk, carrots, green onions, oil and egg in small bowl until blended. Stir into flour mixture just until moistened. Spoon evenly into prepared muffin cups.

Bake 25 to 30 minutes or until golden brown and wooden toothpick inserted in centers comes out clean. Immediately remove from pan. Cool on wire rack for 10 minutes. Serve warm.

Nutrients per serving (1 muffin):			
Calories	166	Cholesterol	27 mg
Fat	8 g	Sodium	163 mg

Garden Herb Muffins

For guaranteed dinnertime delights, turn low-fat cuts of beef, pork and lamb into exciting new entrées. Quick stir-fries are perfect for short-notice meals on hectic weeknights while a succulent roast or tenderloin will turn your dinner parties into memorable, yet health-minded, occasions.

Beef Kabobs over Lemon Rice

Makes 2 servings

6 ounces boneless beef sirloin steak, cut into 1-inch cubes
1 small zucchini, sliced
1 small yellow squash, sliced
1 small red bell pepper, cut into squares
1 small onion, cut into chunks
¼ cup low-calorie Italian dressing
1 cup hot cooked rice
2 teaspoons fresh lemon juice
1 tablespoon snipped fresh parsley
¼ teaspoon seasoned salt

Combine beef and vegetables in large plastic food bag with zippered closing. Add dressing and marinate 4 to 6 hours in refrigerator. Remove beef and vegetables from marinade; heat reserved marinade to a boil. Alternately thread beef and vegetables onto 4 skewers. Grill or broil kabobs, turning and basting with marinade, 5 to 7 minutes or to desired doneness. Combine rice and remaining ingredients. Serve kabobs over rice mixture. Garnish as desired.

Nutrients per serving:

Calories	273	Cholesterol	50 mg
Fat	9 g	Sodium	545 mg

Favorite recipe from **USA Rice Council**

Saucy Stuffed Peppers

Makes 12 servings

6 medium green bell peppers
1¼ cups water
2 cups low-sodium tomato juice, divided
1 can (6 ounces) tomato paste
1 teaspoon dried oregano leaves, crushed, divided
½ teaspoon dried basil leaves, crushed
½ teaspoon garlic powder, divided
1 pound lean ground beef
1½ cups QUAKER® Oats (quick or old fashioned, uncooked)
1 medium tomato, chopped
¼ cup chopped carrot
¼ cup chopped onion

Heat oven to 350°F. Cut peppers lengthwise in half. Remove membranes and seeds; set peppers aside. In large saucepan, combine water, 1 cup tomato juice, tomato paste, ½ teaspoon oregano, basil and ¼ teaspoon garlic powder. Simmer 10 to 15 minutes.

Combine beef, oats, remaining 1 cup tomato juice, ½ teaspoon oregano and ¼ teaspoon garlic powder with tomato, carrot and onion; mix well. Fill each pepper half with about ⅓ cup meat mixture. Place in 13×9-inch glass baking dish; pour sauce evenly over peppers. Bake 45 to 50 minutes.

Nutrients per serving:

Calories	174	Cholesterol	28 mg
Fat	9 g	Sodium	145 mg

Beef Kabobs over Lemon Rice

Beef 'n' Broccoli

Beef 'n' Broccoli

Makes 4 servings

½ cup A.1.® Steak Sauce
¼ cup soy sauce
2 cloves garlic, crushed
1 pound top round steak, thinly sliced
1 (16-ounce) bag frozen broccoli, red bell
    peppers, bamboo shoots and mushrooms,
    thawed*
    Hot cooked rice (optional)

In small bowl, combine steak sauce, soy sauce and garlic. Pour marinade over steak in nonmetal dish. Cover; refrigerate 1 hour, stirring occasionally.

Remove steak from marinade; reserve marinade. In large lightly oiled skillet, over medium-high heat, stir-fry steak 3 to 4 minutes or until steak is no longer pink. Remove steak with slotted spoon; keep warm.

In same skillet, heat vegetables and reserved marinade to a boil; reduce heat to low. Cover; simmer for 2 to 3 minutes. Stir in steak. Serve over rice, if desired.

*1 (16-ounce) package frozen broccoli cuts, thawed, may be substituted.

Nutrients per serving:

Calories	209	Cholesterol	65 mg
Fat	4 g	Sodium	1669 mg

Barbecued Pork Chops

Makes 6 servings

2 tablespoons CRISCO® PURITAN® Oil
6 loin pork chops, trimmed of excess fat
1 medium onion, chopped
3 cloves garlic, minced
1 can (6 ounces) no-salt-added tomato paste
½ cup cider vinegar
¼ cup plus 2 tablespoons firmly packed brown
    sugar
¼ cup water
3 tablespoons Worcestershire sauce
1 teaspoon dry mustard
1 teaspoon chili powder
¼ teaspoon black pepper
¼ teaspoon salt

Heat oven to 350°F. Heat Crisco® Puritan® Oil in large skillet over medium-high heat. Cook pork chops until lightly browned on both sides. Remove chops from skillet. Place in 11×7-inch baking dish in single layer. Set aside. Add onion and garlic to skillet. Cook and stir over medium heat until soft. Stir in remaining ingredients. Simmer 5 minutes. Pour sauce over chops. Turn to coat. Cover. Bake at 350°F for 45 to 60 minutes or until chops are tender.

To Microwave: Combine Crisco® Puritan® Oil, onion and garlic in 11×7-inch microwave-safe dish. Cover with plastic wrap. Microwave on HIGH (100% power) 3 minutes, stirring after 1½ minutes. Add remaining ingredients, except for chops. Stir well. Place uncooked chops in sauce. Turn to coat. Cover. Microwave on HIGH 16 minutes, turning dish after every 4 minutes. Rearrange chops after 8 minutes. Let stand 5 minutes, covered, before serving.

Nutrients per serving:

Calories	200	Cholesterol	70 mg
Fat	10 g	Sodium	90 mg

Oriental Beef and Broccoli Stir-Fry

Makes 4 servings

  ½ cup PACE® Picante Sauce
  2 tablespoons light or regular soy sauce
     (optional)
  1 tablespoon water
  1 tablespoon cornstarch
  ¾ pound boneless beef top sirloin steak, cut into
     2×¼-inch strips
  1 tablespoon finely shredded fresh ginger
  2 garlic cloves, minced
  1 tablespoon peanut or vegetable oil, divided
  1 teaspoon Oriental sesame oil (optional)
1½ cups quartered mushrooms
1½ cups (1-inch) broccoli florets
  1 red bell pepper, cut into 1-inch pieces
  4 green onions with tops, cut into 1-inch pieces
    Hot cooked rice (optional)
    Additional PACE® Picante Sauce (optional)

Combine ½ cup Pace® Picante Sauce, soy sauce, water and cornstarch in small bowl; mix well and set aside. Toss beef with ginger and garlic. Heat 2 teaspoons peanut oil and, if desired, sesame oil, in 10-inch skillet over medium-high heat. Add beef mixture and stir-fry 3 minutes or until no longer pink. Remove beef mixture with slotted spoon; set aside. Add remaining 1 teaspoon oil to skillet. Add mushrooms, broccoli and red pepper; stir-fry 3 minutes or until vegetables are crisp-tender. Add Pace® Picante Sauce mixture, beef mixture and green onions; cook and stir 1 minute or until sauce boils and thickens. Serve over rice, if desired. Serve with additional Pace® Picante Sauce, if desired.

Nutrients per serving:

Calories	201	Cholesterol	51 mg
Fat	8 g	Sodium	398 mg

Fiesta Meat Loaf

Makes 6 servings

  1 pound HEALTHY CHOICE® Extra Lean
    Ground Beef
  ¾ cup quick oats, uncooked
  ½ cup HEALTHY CHOICE® Cholesterol Free
    Egg Product
  ½ cup salsa, divided
  ½ cup diced green bell pepper
  ¼ cup diced onion
  1 tablespoon chili powder
  ½ teaspoon salt

In medium bowl, combine beef, oats, egg product, ¼ cup salsa, green pepper, onion, chili powder and salt. Form meat mixture into loaf shape and place in 8×4×3-inch loaf pan sprayed with nonstick cooking spray. Top with remaining ¼ cup salsa. Bake in 350°F oven for 55 minutes.

Nutrients per serving:

Calories	150	Cholesterol	35 mg
Fat	4 g	Sodium	400 mg

Pork Tenderloin Waldorf

Makes 4 to 6 servings

  2 pork tenderloins (about 1½ pounds)
  ¾ cup apple jelly
  ¼ cup REALEMON® Lemon Juice from
    Concentrate
  ¼ cup soy sauce
  ¼ cup vegetable oil
  1 tablespoon finely chopped fresh ginger root
  1 cup chopped apple
  1 cup fresh bread crumbs (2 slices bread)
  ¼ cup finely chopped celery
  ¼ cup chopped pecans

Partially slice tenderloins lengthwise, being careful not to cut all the way through; arrange in shallow dish. In small saucepan, combine jelly, ReaLemon® brand, soy sauce, oil and ginger; cook and stir until jelly melts. Reserving *3 tablespoons* jelly mixture, pour remainder over meat. Cover; refrigerate 4 hours or overnight. Place meat in shallow baking pan. Combine apple, crumbs, celery, nuts and reserved jelly mixture. Spread slits open; fill with apple mixture. Bake 30 minutes in preheated 375°F oven. Loosely cover meat; bake 10 minutes longer or until meat thermometer reaches 160°F. Refrigerate leftovers.

Nutrients per serving:

Calories	273	Cholesterol	81 mg
Fat	10 g	Sodium	448 mg

Pork Tenderloin Waldorf

Sweet and Spicy Pork Tenderloin

Sweet and Spicy Pork Tenderloin

Makes 4 servings

2 teaspoons dried tarragon leaves, crushed
½ teaspoon dried thyme leaves, crushed
⅛ to ½ teaspoon black pepper
¼ teaspoon ground red pepper
   Dash salt
1 pound pork tenderloin, trimmed and cut
   crosswise into ½-inch pieces
2 tablespoons margarine, melted
1½ tablespoons honey

In small bowl, combine tarragon, thyme, peppers and salt; blend well. Brush both sides of each pork tenderloin piece with margarine; sprinkle both sides with seasoning mixture. Arrange tenderloin pieces on broiler pan. Broil, 5 to 6 inches from heat source, for 2 minutes per side. Remove from broiler. Brush top side of each piece with honey. Broil for an additional minute. Place pork pieces on serving plate.

Nutrients per serving:

Calories	219	Cholesterol	79 mg
Fat	10 g	Sodium	158 mg

Favorite recipe from **National Pork Producers Council**

Spaghetti Pizza Deluxe

Makes 8 servings

1 package (7 ounces) CREAMETTE® Spaghetti,
   uncooked
½ cup skim milk
1 egg, beaten
   Nonstick cooking spray
½ pound lean ground beef
1 medium onion, chopped
1 medium green bell pepper, chopped
2 cloves garlic, minced
1 can (15 ounces) tomato sauce
1 teaspoon Italian seasoning
1 teaspoon salt-free herb seasoning
¼ teaspoon black pepper
2 cups sliced fresh mushrooms
2 cups shredded part-skim mozzarella cheese

Prepare Creamette® Spaghetti according to package directions. In medium bowl, blend milk and egg; add spaghetti and toss to coat. Spray 15×10-inch jelly-roll pan with nonstick cooking spray. Spread spaghetti mixture evenly in prepared pan. In large skillet, cook and stir beef, onion, green pepper and garlic until beef is no longer pink; drain. Add tomato sauce and seasonings; simmer 5 minutes. Spoon beef mixture evenly over spaghetti. Top with mushrooms and cheese. Bake in 350°F oven for 20 minutes. Let stand 5 minutes before cutting. Refrigerate leftovers.

Note: *To reduce sodium, substitute no salt added tomato sauce.*

Nutrients per serving:

Calories	267	Cholesterol	76 mg
Fat	9 g	Sodium	499 mg

Stuffed Cabbage Rolls

Makes 6 servings

¾ pound lean ground beef
½ cup chopped onion
1 cup cooked long grain white rice
¼ teaspoon ground cinnamon
1 egg white
6 large cabbage leaves
1 can (14½ ounces) DEL MONTE® Original
   Style Stewed Tomatoes (No Salt Added)
1 can (15 ounces) DEL MONTE® Tomato Sauce
   (No Salt Added)

In medium skillet, brown meat and onion over medium-high heat; drain. Add rice and cinnamon. Season with salt-free herb seasoning, if desired. Remove from heat; stir in egg white. Pre-cook cabbage leaves 3 minutes in small amount of boiling water; drain. Divide meat mixture among cabbage leaves. Roll cabbage leaves loosely around meat mixture, allowing room for rice to swell. Secure with toothpicks. In 4-quart saucepan, combine tomatoes and tomato sauce; bring to boil. Reduce heat; add cabbage rolls. Simmer, uncovered, 30 minutes.

Prep time: 15 minutes
Cook time: 30 minutes

Nutrients per serving:

Calories	238	Cholesterol	42 mg
Fat	8 g	Sodium	86 mg

Pork Loin Roulade

Makes 4 servings

    4 boneless center pork loin slices, about 1 pound
½ red bell pepper, cut into strips
½ green bell pepper, cut into strips
    1 tablespoon vegetable oil
⅔ cup orange juice
⅔ cup bottled barbecue sauce
    1 tablespoon prepared Dijon-style mustard

Place pork slices between 2 pieces of plastic wrap. Pound with a mallet to about ¼-inch thickness. Place several red and green pepper strips crosswise on each pork slice; roll up jelly-roll style. Secure rolls with wooden toothpicks.

In large heavy skillet, brown pork rolls in hot oil. Drain fat from pan. Combine remaining ingredients and add to skillet. Bring mixture to a boil; reduce heat to low. Cover and simmer 10 to 12 minutes or until pork is tender. Remove toothpicks and serve.

Nutrients per serving:

Calories	255	Cholesterol	72 mg
Fat	10 g	Sodium	530 mg

Favorite recipe from **National Pork Producers Council**

Pork Loin Roulade

Spaghetti and Bacon Toss

Makes 4 to 6 servings

    1 small zucchini, sliced
    4 green onions, chopped
    1 (8-ounce) carton plain nonfat yogurt
½ cup canned white sauce
¼ cup skim milk
    8 ounces uncooked spaghetti, cooked and drained according to package directions (omit salt)
    1 (12-ounce) package ARMOUR® Lower Salt Bacon slices, cooked crisp and crumbled
    1 large fresh tomato, seeded and chopped

Spray medium saucepan with nonstick cooking spray; place over medium heat. Add zucchini and green onions; cook and stir until tender. Combine yogurt, white sauce and milk in small bowl; add to vegetables. Cook until heated through and mixture steams. Toss warm spaghetti with bacon; top with sauce. Garnish each serving with chopped tomato.

Nutrients per serving:

Calories	289	Cholesterol	19 mg
Fat	10 g	Sodium	485 mg

Swiss and Beef Grilled Sandwiches

Makes 4 servings

    8 slices French bread (each 5 × ½-inch), divided
    4 slices (3 ounces) SARGENTO® Preferred Light Sliced Swiss Cheese, halved, divided
    1 medium tomato, cut into 8 thin slices
    4 ounces thinly sliced lean deli roast beef
    2 tablespoons light mayonnaise
    1 tablespoon Dijon-style mustard
    1 teaspoon snipped chives *or* finely chopped green onion tops

Top 4 bread slices with half the cheese and all the tomato and beef slices. Top beef with remaining cheese and bread slices. Combine mayonnaise, mustard and chives in small bowl. Spread mayonnaise mixture on outside of sandwiches. Grill over medium heat in a dry preheated skillet 2 to 3 minutes or until light golden brown. Turn and grill other side 2 to 3 minutes. Serve immediately.

Nutrients per serving:

Calories	256	Cholesterol	23 mg
Fat	9 g	Sodium	824 mg

Tabbouli Lamb Sandwiches

Makes 6 half-pocket sandwiches

1 can (14½ ounces) DEL MONTE® Original
    Style Stewed Tomatoes
½ cup bulgur wheat, uncooked
1½ cups cooked diced lamb or beef
¾ cup diced cucumber
3 tablespoons minced fresh mint or parsley
1 tablespoon fresh lemon juice
1 tablespoon olive oil
3 pita breads, cut into halves

Drain tomatoes reserving liquid; pour liquid into
measuring cup. Add water, if needed, to measure
¾ cup. In small saucepan, bring liquid to a boil; add
bulgur. Cover and simmer over low heat 20 minutes
or until tender. Cool. Chop tomatoes. In medium
bowl, combine tomatoes, meat, cucumber, mint,
lemon juice and oil. Stir in cooled bulgur. Season
with salt and pepper, if desired. Spoon about ½ cup
tabbouli into each pita bread half.

Prep & Cook time: 25 minutes
Chill time: 30 minutes

Nutrients per serving (1 half-pocket sandwich):

Calories	239	Cholesterol	35 mg
Fat	7 g	Sodium	343 mg

Pork Tenderloin Diane

Makes 5 servings

1 pound pork tenderloin, cut crosswise into
    10 pieces
2 teaspoons lemon pepper seasoning
2 tablespoons butter
2 tablespoons lemon juice
1 tablespoon Worcestershire sauce
1 teaspoon Dijon-style mustard
1 tablespoon finely chopped chives or parsley
    Whole chives for garnish

Press each tenderloin piece into 1-inch-thick
medallion; sprinkle surfaces with lemon pepper. Melt
butter in large heavy skillet over medium heat. Add
medallions; cook 3 to 4 minutes on each side.
Remove pork to serving platter; keep warm. Stir
lemon juice, Worcestershire sauce and mustard into
pan juices in skillet. Cook, stirring, until heated
through. Pour sauce over medallions; sprinkle with
chopped chives. Garnish with whole chives.

Nutrients per serving:

Calories	198	Cholesterol	84 mg
Fat	9 g	Sodium	157 mg

Favorite recipe from **National Pork Producers Council**

Beef Cubed Steak Provençale

Beef Cubed Steaks Provençale

Makes 4 servings

2 cloves garlic, minced
½ teaspoon dried basil leaves, crushed
¼ teaspoon black pepper
4 lean beef cubed steaks (about 4 ounces *each*)
1½ teaspoons olive oil
2 small zucchini, thinly sliced
6 cherry tomatoes, cut in half
1½ teaspoons grated Parmesan cheese
    Salt (optional)

Combine garlic, basil and pepper; divide mixture in
half. Press ½ of seasoning mixture evenly into both
sides of beef cubed steaks; set aside. Heat oil and
remaining seasoning mixture in large nonstick skillet
over medium heat. Add zucchini; cook and stir
3 minutes. Add tomatoes; continue cooking 1 minute,
stirring frequently. Remove zucchini mixture to
platter; sprinkle with cheese and keep warm. Increase
heat to medium-high. Add 2 steaks to same skillet;
cook to desired doneness, 3 to 4 minutes, turning
once. Repeat with remaining 2 steaks. Season steaks
with salt, if desired. Serve with zucchini mixture;
garnish as desired.

Nutrients per serving:

Calories	223	Cholesterol	81 mg
Fat	10 g	Sodium	60 mg

Favorite recipe from **National Live Stock and Meat Board**

Italian Ham Lasagna

Makes 6 servings

6 lasagna noodles (4 ounces)
1 package (10 ounces) frozen chopped spinach
1 cup milk
2 tablespoons cornstarch
1 tablespoon dried minced onion
½ cup DANNON® Plain Nonfat or Lowfat Yogurt
1 cup diced fully cooked ham
½ teaspoon Italian seasoning, crushed
¼ cup grated Parmesan cheese
1 cup lowfat cottage cheese
1 cup shredded mozzarella cheese

Cook noodles according to package directions; rinse and drain. Set aside. Cook spinach according to package directions; drain well. Set aside.

Preheat oven to 375°F. In a large saucepan combine milk, cornstarch and onion. Cook and stir until thickened and bubbly; cook and stir 2 minutes more. Remove from heat. Stir in yogurt. Spread 2 tablespoons of yogurt sauce evenly on bottom of 10×6-inch baking dish. Stir ham and Italian seasoning into remaining sauce. Place 3 lasagna noodles in dish. (Trim noodles to fit, if necessary.) Spread with ⅓ of sauce. Layer spinach on top. Sprinkle with Parmesan. Layer another ⅓ of sauce, the cottage cheese and ½ of mozzarella cheese. Place remaining noodles on top of cheese layer. Top with remaining sauce and mozzarella. Bake 30 to 35 minutes or until heated through. Let stand 10 minutes before serving.

Nutrients per serving:

Calories	270	Cholesterol	50 mg
Fat	9 g	Sodium	795 mg

Healthy Choice® Beef Chili

Makes 5 servings

2 teaspoons vegetable oil
1 large onion, chopped
1 medium green bell pepper, chopped
2 cloves garlic, minced
1 pound HEALTHY CHOICE® Ground Beef
1 can (28 ounces) tomatoes in tomato purée
1 can (15 ounces) red kidney beans
1 small bay leaf
1 tablespoon chili powder
1½ teaspoons ground cumin
1½ teaspoons dried oregano leaves, crushed
½ teaspoon salt

Heat oil in large saucepan over medium heat. Add onion, pepper and garlic; cook and stir until vegetables are tender. Crumble beef into saucepan; cook about 6 minutes or until no longer pink. Add remaining ingredients; simmer over low heat 15 to 20 minutes until heated through, stirring occasionally.

Nutrients per serving:

Calories	184	Cholesterol	44 mg
Fat	5 g	Sodium	445 mg

Wild Rice, Snow Peas and Pork Stir-Fry

Makes 6 servings

2 tablespoons canola oil
½ pound pork tenderloin, sliced ¼ inch thick
1 cup sliced celery
1 cup sliced green onions
1 cup sliced fresh mushrooms
1 can (8 ounces) sliced water chestnuts
½ pound snow peas or edible pea pods, fresh or frozen, thawed
1 tablespoon grated fresh ginger root
2 cups cooked wild rice
1 tablespoon cornstarch
3 tablespoons low sodium soy sauce
1 tablespoon dry sherry
½ teaspoon salt
Cashews, sunflower seeds or carrot cut-outs (optional)

Heat oil in large heavy skillet over medium-high heat until hot; add pork and stir-fry 2 minutes or until meat is no longer pink. Add celery, green onions, mushrooms, water chestnuts, pea pods and ginger. Stir-fry 5 minutes or until vegetables are crisp-tender. Stir in wild rice until evenly blended; move mixture up side of wok. Mix cornstarch, soy sauce, sherry and salt in small bowl. Add to juices in pan; cook about 1 minute or until thickened. Toss gently to coat with glaze. Garnish with cashews, sunflower seeds or carrot cut-outs, if desired.

Nutrients per serving:

Calories	223	Cholesterol	20 mg
Fat	7 g	Sodium	570 mg

Favorite recipe from **Minnesota Cultivated Wild Rice Council**

Italian Ham Lasagna

Sesame Pork with Broccoli

Sesame Pork with Broccoli

Makes 6 servings

1 can (14½ ounces) chicken broth
2 tablespoons cornstarch
1 tablespoon soy sauce
4 green onions with tops, finely diced
1 pound pork tenderloin, trimmed
1 tablespoon vegetable oil
1 clove garlic, minced
1½ pounds fresh broccoli, cut into bite-sized
  pieces (about 7 cups)
2 tablespoons sliced pimiento, drained
2 tablespoons sesame seed, lightly toasted
  Hot cooked rice (optional)

Combine chicken broth, cornstarch and soy sauce in small bowl; blend well. Stir in green onions; set aside. Cut pork tenderloin lengthwise into quarters; cut each quarter into bite-sized pieces. Heat oil in wok or heavy skillet over medium-high heat. Add pork and garlic; stir-fry 3 to 4 minutes or until pork is tender. Remove pork; keep warm. Add broccoli and broth mixture to wok. Cover and simmer over low heat 8 minutes. Add cooked pork and pimiento; cook just until mixture is hot, stirring frequently. Serve over rice, if desired. Sprinkle with sesame seed. Garnish as desired.

Nutrients per serving:

Calories	185	Cholesterol	79 mg
Fat	7 g	Sodium	457 mg

Favorite recipe from **National Pork Producers Council**

Mediterranean Pork Roast

Makes 6 servings

1½ cups Florida grapefruit juice
1 small red onion, finely chopped
1 clove garlic, minced
1 teaspoon sugar
1 teaspoon dried thyme leaves, crushed *or*
  1 tablespoon fresh thyme leaves
1 teaspoon dried oregano leaves, crushed *or*
  1 tablespoon minced fresh oregano leaves
2 pounds boneless pork tenderloin

For marinade, combine grapefruit juice, red onion, garlic, sugar, thyme and oregano in glass casserole dish. Add pork tenderloin; cover and marinate 1 hour, turning pork once to ensure that it marinates evenly.

Preheat oven to 425°F. Transfer pork tenderloin and onions to roasting pan, reserving marinade. Roast 20 minutes. Reduce heat to 325°F and roast about 1 to 1½ hours more until cooked through, basting occasionally with ½ cup marinade. Remove pork from roasting pan and add remaining marinade to roasting pan, stirring until pan drippings loosen. Transfer mixture to small saucepan and bring to a boil. Reduce heat and simmer, uncovered, 5 to 10 minutes until slightly thickened. Slice pork and serve with marinade mixture.

Tip: The Mediterranean Pork Roast recipe features a technique typically used in cuisine of the Middle East—marinating meat in citrus juices. In addition to enhancing the flavor of the dish, the natural acidity of citrus juice acts as a meat tenderizer.

Nutrients per serving:

Calories	248	Cholesterol	118 mg
Fat	6 g	Sodium	87 mg

Favorite recipe from **Florida Department of Citrus**

Pineapple Ham 'n' Rice

Makes 6 servings

1 can (20 ounces) DOLE® Pineapple Chunks,
  undrained
2 teaspoons vegetable oil
1 onion, minced
1 cup uncooked converted rice
1¾ cups chicken broth
1 cup baked ham cubes
½ teaspoon *each* garlic powder, dried thyme
  leaves and fines herbes
¼ teaspoon crushed red pepper flakes
1 teaspoon salt (optional)
2 cups fresh or frozen cut green beans, cooked

Drain pineapple, reserving ¼ cup juice.

Heat oil in large skillet over medium-high heat until hot. Add onion and rice; cook and stir 5 minutes. Stir in reserved juice, chicken broth, ham, garlic powder, thyme, fines herbes and red pepper. Cover; reduce heat to low and simmer 20 minutes or until liquid is absorbed. Stir in salt, if desired.

Stir in pineapple and green beans. Heat through. Serve with tossed green salad, if desired.

Prep time: 15 minutes
Cook time: 20 minutes

Nutrients per serving:

Calories	283	Cholesterol	9 mg
Fat	3 g	Sodium	524 mg

Herb-Marinated Chuck Steak

Herb-Marinated Chuck Steak

Makes 4 servings

¼ cup chopped onion
2 tablespoons *each* chopped fresh parsley and white vinegar
1 tablespoon vegetable oil
2 teaspoons Dijon-style mustard
1 clove garlic, minced
½ teaspoon dried thyme leaves, crushed
1 pound boneless beef chuck shoulder steak, cut 1 inch thick

Combine onion, parsley, vinegar, oil, mustard, garlic and thyme. Place beef chuck shoulder steak in plastic bag; add onion mixture, spreading evenly over both sides. Close bag securely; marinate in refrigerator 6 to 8 hours (or overnight, if desired), turning at least once. Pour off marinade; discard. Place steak on rack in broiler pan so surface of meat is 3 to 5 inches from heat source. Broil, about 16 minutes for rare and about 18 minutes for medium, turning once. Carve steak diagonally across the grain into thin slices. Garnish as desired.

Nutrients per serving:			
Calories	216	Cholesterol	85 mg
Fat	10 g	Sodium	94 mg

Favorite recipe from **National Live Stock and Meat Board**

Linguine Primavera

Makes 8 servings

2 tablespoons olive or vegetable oil
2 tablespoons lemon juice
1 medium red bell pepper, cut into strips
1 large onion, chopped
1 package (8 ounces) fresh mushrooms, sliced
½ pound lean fully cooked ham, cut into julienne strips
1 package (10 ounces) frozen peas, thawed
1 package (6 ounces) frozen snow peas, thawed
1 can (5 ounces) evaporated skimmed milk
½ cup shredded Provolone cheese, divided
½ of (1-pound) package CREAMETTE® Linguine
Freshly ground black pepper

In large skillet, heat olive oil and lemon juice. Add bell pepper, onion and mushrooms; cook and stir until tender-crisp. Add ham, peas, milk and ¼ cup cheese; heat through, stirring frequently. Keep warm. Prepare Creamette® Linguine according to package directions; drain. Combine hot cooked linguine and vegetable mixture in large bowl; toss to coat. Top with remaining ¼ cup cheese. Serve immediately with freshly ground black pepper. Refrigerate leftovers.

Nutrients per serving:			
Calories	273	Cholesterol	22 mg
Fat	8 g	Sodium	493 mg

Polynesian Kabobs

Makes 8 kabobs

3 cups (12 ounces) ARMOUR® Lower Salt Ham cut into 1-inch cubes
1 fresh pineapple, peeled and cut into 1-inch cubes
1 green, red and yellow bell pepper, each cut into 1-inch pieces
8 medium mushrooms
¼ cup bottled low-calorie, low-sodium red wine vinegar salad dressing

Preheat oven to 350°F. Thread ham, pineapple, peppers and mushrooms onto 8 (10-inch) metal or wooden skewers, alternating ingredients. Place in baking dish. Brush all sides with dressing. Bake for 8 minutes. Turn kabobs and baste all sides with dressing. Cook about 6 to 8 minutes or until ham is heated through. Serve over rice, if desired.

Nutrients per serving (1 kabob):			
Calories	133	Cholesterol	21 mg
Fat	2 g	Sodium	368 mg

Lasagna

Makes 12 servings

1 cup chopped onions
3 cloves garlic, minced
2 tablespoons CRISCO® PURITAN® Oil
1 pound extra lean ground beef
2 cans (14½ ounces *each*) no-salt-added stewed tomatoes
1 can (6 ounces) no-salt-added tomato paste
2 teaspoons dried basil leaves, crushed
1 teaspoon dried oregano leaves, crushed
½ teaspoon sugar
¼ teaspoon black pepper
2 cups low-fat cottage cheese
½ cup grated Parmesan cheese, divided
¼ cup chopped fresh parsley
8 ounces wide lasagna noodles
1 cup (4 ounces) shredded low-moisture part-skim mozzarella cheese, divided

Cook and stir onions and garlic in Crisco® Puritan® Oil in large skillet over medium heat until soft. Push to one side of skillet. Add ground beef. Cook, stirring well, to crumble beef. Drain, if necessary. Add tomatoes with juice. Break tomatoes into smaller pieces. Add tomato paste, basil, oregano, sugar and pepper. Stir until well blended. Simmer 30 minutes. Combine cottage cheese, ¼ cup Parmesan cheese and parsley. Set aside.

Cook lasagna noodles 7 minutes in unsalted boiling water. Drain well. Heat oven to 350°F. Place thin layer of meat sauce in 13×9×2-inch pan. Add, in layers, half the noodles, half the cottage cheese mixture, 2 tablespoons Parmesan cheese, ⅓ cup mozzarella and thin layer of sauce. Repeat noodle and cheese layers. Top with remaining sauce and remaining ⅓ cup mozzarella. Bake at 350°F for 45 minutes. Let stand 15 minutes before serving. Cut into 12 rectangles.

Nutrients per serving:

Calories	270	Cholesterol	55 mg
Fat	10 g	Sodium	300 mg

Glazed Ham with Sweet Potatoes

Makes 4 servings

1 (1¼-pound) slice ham steak
1 (16-ounce) can sliced peaches, drained
1 (16-ounce) can sweet potatoes, drained
2 tablespoons maple syrup, divided
2 tablespoons apricot jam or preserves
1 teaspoon Dijon-style mustard
Hot cooked Brussels sprouts (optional)

Preheat broiler. Position oven rack about 4 inches from heat source. Place ham in shallow pan. Surround with peaches and sweet potatoes; drizzle peaches and sweet potatoes with 1 tablespoon maple syrup. Broil 5 minutes or until lightly browned.

Meanwhile, heat combined jam and mustard in microwave or in saucepan on rangetop until jam is melted; stir until well blended. Turn ham, peaches and sweet potatoes over; brush ham with jam mixture. Drizzle peaches and sweet potatoes with remaining 1 tablespoon maple syrup. Continue broiling 5 minutes or until thoroughly heated. Serve with Brussels sprouts, if desired.

Nutrients per serving:

Calories	300	Cholesterol	60 mg
Fat	7 g	Sodium	1462 mg

Glazed Ham with Sweet Potatoes

Cajun Pork Pinwheels

Makes 6 servings

2 pork tenderloins (¾ pound *each*), trimmed
1 tablespoon vegetable oil
1 cup finely chopped red bell pepper
½ cup finely chopped onion
½ cup finely chopped celery
1 teaspoon dried thyme leaves, crushed
¼ to ½ teaspoon garlic salt
½ teaspoon ground red pepper
½ teaspoon paprika
1 tablespoon fennel seed, crushed
1 to 3 teaspoons lemon pepper seasoning

Using sharp knife, cut lengthwise slit down center of 1 pork tenderloin almost to, but not through, bottom of tenderloin. Open tenderloin so it lies flat; cover with plastic wrap. Working from center to edges, lightly pound tenderloin with flat side of meat mallet or rolling pin until about ¼ inch thick; remove plastic wrap. Repeat with remaining tenderloin.

Preheat oven to 325°F. Heat oil in large skillet over medium heat. Add red bell pepper, onion, celery, thyme, garlic salt, ground red pepper and paprika; cook about 5 minutes or until vegetables are tender, stirring frequently. Spread vegetable mixture evenly over each flattened tenderloin to within 1 inch of edges. Starting with short side, roll up jelly-roll fashion; secure edges of each roll with toothpicks or tie each roll with string. Combine fennel seed and lemon pepper in small bowl; press mixture into top and sides of each tenderloin roll. Place rolls, seam sides down, on rack in shallow pan. Roast for about 45 minutes or until meat thermometer registers 155°F. Let rolls stand 5 minutes. Remove toothpicks or strings; slice.

Nutrients per serving:

Calories	181	Cholesterol	79 mg
Fat	7 g	Sodium	327 mg

Favorite recipe from **National Pork Producers Council**

Healthy Choice® Meatloaf

Makes 5 servings

1 pound HEALTHY CHOICE® Ground Beef
½ cup uncooked rolled oats
2 egg whites *or* 1 egg, lightly beaten
½ cup ketchup
2 tablespoons finely chopped onion
⅛ teaspoon salt
⅛ teaspoon ground black pepper

Preheat oven to 350°F. Mix all ingredients together in large bowl just until combined. Press gently into lightly greased 9×5×3-inch loaf pan. Bake 45 to 50 minutes until firm and heated through. Let stand 10 minutes before slicing.

Nutrients per serving:

Calories	169	Cholesterol	44 mg
Fat	4 g	Sodium	559 mg

Mexican Barbecued Lamb Steaks

Makes 6 servings

3 American lamb sirloin steaks *or* 6 shoulder chops (about 2 pounds), cut ¾ to 1 inch thick
1 tablespoon vegetable oil
¼ cup finely chopped onion
¼ cup packed brown sugar
1 can (15 ounces) tomato sauce
1 can (4 ounces) diced green chilies
1 teaspoon Worcestershire sauce
½ teaspoon chili powder
¼ teaspoon garlic powder
¼ teaspoon black pepper
¼ teaspoon hot pepper sauce

Heat oil in large skillet over medium-high heat until hot; add onion. Cook and stir until onion is transparent. Add brown sugar; stir until dissolved. Stir in all remaining ingredients except lamb; heat thoroughly. Brush sauce mixture on lamb. Grill over moderately hot coals, basting lamb frequently with sauce mixture, until thermometer registers 150°F for medium-rare or 160°F for medium.

Serving Suggestions: *Serve with cornbread and honey, baked potatoes topped with salsa and green onions, and fresh fruit salad.*

Prep time: 10 minutes
Cook time: 15 minutes

Nutrients per serving:

Calories	230	Cholesterol	65 mg
Fat	9 g	Sodium	690 mg

Favorite recipe from **American Lamb Council**

Cajun Pork Pinwheels

Saucy Pork and Peppers

Makes 4 servings

2 fresh limes
¼ cup 62%-less-sodium soy sauce
4 cloves garlic, crushed
1 teaspoon dried oregano leaves, crushed
½ teaspoon dried thyme leaves, crushed
  Dash ground red pepper
2 to 3 fresh parsley sprigs
1 bay leaf
1 pound pork tenderloin, cut into 1-inch cubes
1 tablespoon olive oil
1 teaspoon firmly packed brown sugar
2 medium onions, each cut into 8 pieces
2 medium tomatoes, each cut into 8 pieces and
  seeded
2 large bell peppers, each cut into 8 pieces

Remove peel from limes using vegetable peeler.
Squeeze juice from limes. In small bowl, combine
lime juice and peel, soy sauce, garlic, oregano leaves,
thyme leaves, ground red pepper, parsley and bay
leaf; blend well. Place pork cubes in plastic bag or
nonmetal bowl. Pour marinade mixture over pork,
turning to coat. Seal bag or cover bowl; marinate at
least 2 hours or overnight in refrigerator, turning pork
several times.

Remove lime peel, parsley sprigs and bay leaf from
marinade; discard. Remove pork from marinade,
reserving marinade. Drain pork well. Heat oil in large
skillet over high heat. Add brown sugar; stir until
sugar is brown and bubbly. Add pork cubes; cook and
stir about 5 minutes or until pork is browned. Reduce
heat to low. Add onions, tomatoes, bell peppers and
reserved marinade; simmer 10 to 15 minutes or until
pork is tender.

Nutrients per serving:

Calories	243	Cholesterol	79 mg
Fat	8 g	Sodium	547 mg

Favorite recipe from **National Pork Producers Council**

Saucy Pork and Peppers

Pork Curry

Makes 4 servings

1 tablespoon vegetable oil
1 pound pork tenderloin, cut into ½-inch cubes
¾ cup coarsely chopped onion
⅓ cup chopped celery
1½ cups chopped apple, unpared
1 medium tomato, seeded and chopped
1 cup water
¼ cup golden raisins
1 to 3 tablespoons curry powder
1 teaspoon instant chicken bouillon granules
⅛ teaspoon garlic powder
    Hot cooked rice (optional)
    Plain yogurt (optional)
¼ cup chopped peanuts (optional)

In large frying pan, heat oil to medium hot. Add pork cubes, onion and celery. Cook, stirring occasionally, until pork is brown and vegetables are tender. Stir in apple, tomato, water, raisins, curry powder, bouillon granules and garlic powder; mix well. Reduce heat to low. Cover and cook, stirring occasionally, 10 minutes. Remove cover and continue cooking, stirring occasionally, 5 to 10 minutes, until of desired consistency. Serve on bed of hot cooked rice and top each serving with plain yogurt and chopped peanuts, if desired.

Nutrients per serving:			
Calories	243	Cholesterol	73 mg
Fat	7 g	Sodium	311 mg

Favorite recipe from **National Pork Producers Council**

Fast Beef Roast with Mushroom Sauce

Makes 6 to 8 servings

1 boneless beef rib-eye roast (about 2 pounds)
2 tablespoons vegetable oil
4 cups water
1 can (10¾ ounces) condensed beef broth
1 cup dry red wine
2 cloves garlic, minced
1 teaspoon dried marjoram leaves, crushed
4 black peppercorns
3 whole cloves
    Mushroom Sauce (recipe follows)

Tie roast with heavy string at 2-inch intervals. Heat oil in Dutch oven over medium-high heat. Cook roast until evenly browned. Pour off drippings. Add water, broth, wine, garlic, marjoram, peppercorns and cloves; bring to a boil. Reduce heat to medium-low.

Fast Beef Roast with Mushroom Sauce

Cover; simmer 15 minutes per pound. Check temperature with instant-read thermometer; temperature should be 130°F for rare. *Do not overcook.* Remove roast to serving platter; reserve cooking liquid. Cover roast tightly with plastic wrap or foil; allow to stand 10 minutes before carving (temperature will continue to rise about 10°F to 140°F for rare). Prepare Mushroom Sauce. Remove strings from roast. Carve into thin slices and top with Mushroom Sauce. Serve with assorted vegetables, if desired.

Note: A boneless beef rib-eye roast will yield 3 to 4 (3-ounce) cooked servings per pound.

Mushroom Sauce

1 tablespoon butter
1 cup sliced fresh mushrooms
1 cup reserved beef cooking liquid, strained
1½ teaspoons cornstarch
¼ teaspoon salt
2 dashes black pepper
1 tablespoon thinly sliced green onion tops

Melt butter in medium saucepan over medium-high heat. Add mushrooms; cook and stir 5 minutes. Remove and reserve. Add cooking liquid, cornstarch, salt and pepper to pan. Bring to a boil; cook and stir until thickened, 1 to 2 minutes. Remove from heat. Stir in reserved mushrooms and green onion.

Nutrients per serving (includes 3 tablespoons sauce):			
Calories	188	Cholesterol	59 mg
Fat	8 g	Sodium	327 mg

Favorite recipe from **National Live Stock and Meat Board**

Beef and Pineapple Kabobs

Beef and Pineapple Kabobs

Makes 4 servings

1 pound boneless beef top sirloin steak or beef
   top round steak, cut 1 inch thick
1 small onion, finely chopped
½ cup bottled teriyaki sauce
16 pieces (1-inch cubes) fresh pineapple
1 can (8 ounces) water chestnuts, drained

Cut steak into ¼-inch-thick strips. For marinade,
combine onion and teriyaki sauce in small bowl. Add
beef strips, stirring to coat. Alternately thread beef
strips (weaving back and forth), pineapple cubes and
water chestnuts on bamboo or thin metal skewers. (If
using bamboo skewers, soak in water for 20 to
30 minutes before using.) Place kabobs on grid over
medium coals. Grill 4 minutes, turning once, or until
meat is cooked through. Serve immediately.

Note: Recipe may also be prepared with flank steak.

*Serving suggestion: Serve with hot cooked rice, and
stir-fried broccoli, mushrooms and red bell peppers.*

Nutrients per serving (with beef top sirloin steak):			
Calories	232	Cholesterol	76 mg
Fat	6 g	Sodium	751 mg

Nutrients per serving (with beef top round steak):			
Calories	219	Cholesterol	71 mg
Fat	4 g	Sodium	747 mg

Nutrients per serving (with beef flank steak):			
Calories	242	Cholesterol	57 mg
Fat	9 g	Sodium	766 mg

Favorite recipe from **National Live Stock and Meat Board**

Sesame Pork Chops

Makes 4 servings

1 can (20 ounces) DOLE® Pineapple Chunks,
   undrained
6 thin slices ginger root
2 cloves garlic, pressed
3 tablespoons *each* light soy sauce and ketchup
2 teaspoons cornstarch
¼ teaspoon crushed red pepper flakes
4 pork chops
2 tablespoons *each* chopped green onion,
   toasted sesame seeds and slivered
   DOLE® Carrot

To microwave: Drain juice from pineapple into 8-inch
microwave-safe casserole dish. Stir in ginger root, garlic,
soy sauce, ketchup, cornstarch and pepper flakes. Add
pork chops. Cover with vented plastic wrap.

Microwave on HIGH (100% power) 6 minutes. Add
pineapple. Stir sauce. Rotate dish in oven. Microwave
on HIGH 5 minutes more. Let stand, covered, 2 minutes.
Sprinkle with green onion, sesame seeds and carrots.
Serve with steamed snow peas and yellow squash, if desired.

Prep time: 10 minutes
Cook time: 15 minutes

Nutrients per serving:			
Calories	287	Cholesterol	55 mg
Fat	9 g	Sodium	631 mg

Honey-Citrus Glazed Veal Chops

Makes 4 servings

3 tablespoons fresh lime juice
2 tablespoons honey
2 teaspoons grated fresh ginger root
½ teaspoon grated lime peel
4 veal rib chops, cut 1 inch thick (about
   8 ounces *each*)

Stir together lime juice, honey, ginger and lime peel in
small bowl. Place veal rib chops in glass dish just
large enough to hold chops. Brush lime mixture
liberally over both sides of chops. Refrigerate,
covered, 30 minutes while preparing coals.* Remove
chops from dish; brush with any remaining lime
mixture. Place chops on grid over medium coals. Grill
12 to 14 minutes for medium (160°F) or to desired
doneness, turning once. (Or, broil 4 to 5 inches from
heat source 5 to 6 minutes per side for medium or to
desired doneness, turning once.)

**To check temperature of coals, cautiously hold palm of
hand about 4 inches above coals. Count the number of
seconds you can hold it in that position before the heat
forces you to pull it away (about 4 seconds for medium coals
is normal).*

Prep time: 10 minutes
Cook time: 12 to 14 minutes

Nutrients per serving:			
Calories	186	Cholesterol	97 mg
Fat	6 g	Sodium	84 mg

Favorite recipe from **National Live Stock and Meat Board**

Creole Pepper Steak

Makes 4 servings

2 cloves garlic, crushed
1 teaspoon *each* dried thyme leaves, crushed, and paprika
½ teaspoon *each* ground white, red and black peppers
1 pound beef top round steak, cut 1 inch thick

Combine garlic, thyme, paprika and peppers in small bowl; press evenly into both sides of beef steak. Place steak on grid over medium coals. Grill steak 12 to 14 minutes for rare (140°F) to medium (160°F), turning once. Season with salt, if desired. To serve, carve steak diagonally into thin slices.

Serving suggestion: *Serve with steamed vegetable medley (asparagus, baby carrots, zucchini, yellow squash and radishes).*

Nutrients per serving:

Calories	160	Cholesterol	71 mg
Fat	4 g	Sodium	53 mg

Favorite recipe from **National Live Stock and Meat Board**

Healthy Choice® Mexican Beef and Rice

Makes 5 servings

1 teaspoon vegetable oil
½ cup chopped green bell pepper
¼ cup chopped onion
1 pound HEALTHY CHOICE® Ground Beef
1 can (16 ounces) tomatoes, undrained, cut up
1 cup whole kernel corn
1 can (15 ounces) red kidney beans, drained
½ cup uncooked long-grain rice
½ cup water
Few dashes hot pepper sauce

Heat oil in large skillet over medium heat. Add pepper and onion; cook and stir until tender. Crumble beef into skillet and cook about 6 minutes or until no longer pink. Add remaining ingredients; stir to combine. Bring to a boil. Reduce heat to low; cover and simmer 15 to 18 minutes until rice is tender.

Nutrients per serving:

Calories	257	Cholesterol	44 mg
Fat	5 g	Sodium	461 mg

Old-Fashioned Herbed Lamb Stew

Makes 6 servings

1 tablespoon oil
1 pound lean boneless American lamb leg or shoulder, cut into ½-inch cubes
2 tablespoons all-purpose flour
2 cups water
1 can (8 ounces) tomato sauce
1 cup chopped onion
1 clove garlic, minced
Salt to taste (optional)
⅛ teaspoon ground black pepper
1 cup peeled and diced potato
1 cup frozen peas
1 cup sliced carrots
1 cup sliced zucchini or yellow squash
1 cup sliced mushrooms (optional)
2 tablespoons chopped fresh parsley *or*
1 tablespoon dried parsley leaves, crushed
1 tablespoon chopped fresh oregano leaves *or*
¾ teaspoon dried oregano leaves, crushed

Heat oil in Dutch oven or heavy saucepan over medium-high heat until hot. Add lamb; cook and stir until lightly browned. Reduce heat to low. Add flour to lamb, stirring constantly. Cook until thickened. Slowly add water, tomato sauce, onion, garlic, salt and pepper, blending well.

Cover and cook 30 minutes or until lamb is tender, stirring occasionally. Add vegetables, parsley and oregano. Cook 30 minutes more or until vegetables are tender.

Prep time: 15 minutes
Cook time: 1 hour and 10 minutes

Nutrients per serving:

Calories	216	Cholesterol	51 mg
Fat	7 g	Sodium	400 mg

Favorite recipe from **American Lamb Council**

Creole Pepper Steak

Steak & Snow Peas Stir-Fry

Steak & Snow Peas Stir-Fry

Makes 6 servings

¾ pound lean, well-trimmed boneless beef top
    round steak
2 tablespoons cornstarch, divided
2 tablespoons soy sauce
1 tablespoon dry sherry
½ teaspoon sugar
½ teaspoon salt
1 cup uncooked UNCLE BEN'S®
    CONVERTED® Brand Rice
2 tablespoons thinly sliced green onions with
    tops
2 tablespoons diced red bell pepper
1 tablespoon vegetable oil
¾ cup water
1 can (8 ounces) water chestnuts, drained and
    sliced
1 package (6 ounces) frozen pea pods, thawed

Freeze meat until slightly firm. Cut meat diagonally
across grain into very thin slices; place in shallow
baking dish. Combine 1 tablespoon cornstarch, soy
sauce, sherry, sugar and salt; pour over meat.
Marinate at room temperature 30 minutes.

Prepare rice according to package directions, omitting
butter. Stir green onions and bell pepper into rice; set
aside. Drain meat, reserving marinade. Heat oil in
large nonstick skillet until hot but not smoking. Add
meat; cook and stir until lightly browned, 3 to
4 minutes. Combine remaining 1 tablespoon
cornstarch and water with meat marinade; mix well.
Add to skillet with water chestnuts and pea pods.
Cook and stir until sauce boils and is thickened and
clear. Serve meat mixture over rice mixture.

Nutrients per serving:			
Calories	255	Cholesterol	40 mg
Fat	4 g	Sodium	560 mg

Greek Lamb Sauté with Mostaccioli

Makes 8 servings

½ of (1-pound) package CREAMETTE®
    Mostaccioli, uncooked
1 tablespoon olive or vegetable oil
1 medium green bell pepper, chopped
1 medium onion, chopped
1 medium eggplant, peeled, seeded and cut into
    1-inch cubes
2 cloves garlic, minced
½ pound lean boneless lamb, cut into ¾-inch
    cubes
2 tomatoes, peeled, seeded and chopped
¼ teaspoon ground nutmeg
¼ cup grated Parmesan cheese

Prepare Creamette® Mostaccioli according to package
directions; drain. In large skillet, heat oil. Add green
pepper, onion, eggplant and garlic; cook and stir until
tender-crisp. Add lamb; cook until tender. Stir in
tomatoes and nutmeg; cook until heated through.
Toss meat mixture with hot cooked mostaccioli and
Parmesan cheese. Serve immediately. Refrigerate
leftovers.

Nutrients per serving:			
Calories	205	Cholesterol	29 mg
Fat	5 g	Sodium	82 mg

Marinated Flank Steak

Makes 4 to 6 servings

½ cup REALEMON® Lemon Juice from
    Concentrate
¼ cup vegetable oil
2 teaspoons WYLER'S® or STEERO® Beef-
    Flavor Instant Bouillon
2 cloves garlic, finely chopped
1 teaspoon ground ginger
1 (1- to 1½-pound) flank steak

In large shallow dish or plastic bag, combine
ReaLemon® brand, oil, bouillon, garlic and ginger;
add steak. Cover; marinate in refrigerator 4 to
6 hours, turning occasionally. Remove steak from
marinade; heat marinade thoroughly. Grill or broil
steak 5 to 7 minutes on each side or until steak is
cooked to desired doneness, basting frequently with
marinade. Serve immediately. Refrigerate leftovers.

Nutrients per serving:			
Calories	156	Cholesterol	48 mg
Fat	8 g	Sodium	345 mg

Sunday Supper Stuffed Shells

Makes 9 to 12 servings

   3 cloves fresh garlic
   2 tablespoons olive oil
 ¾ pound ground veal
 ¾ pound ground pork
   1 package (10 ounces) frozen chopped spinach,
       cooked, drained and squeezed dry
   1 cup finely chopped fresh parsley
   1 cup bread crumbs
   2 eggs, beaten
   3 cloves fresh garlic, minced
   3 tablespoons grated Parmesan cheese
       Salt (optional)
   1 package (12 ounces) uncooked jumbo pasta
       shells, cooked, rinsed and drained
   3 cups spaghetti sauce
       Sautéed zucchini slices (optional)

Cook and stir 3 whole garlic cloves in hot oil in large skillet over medium heat until garlic is browned. Discard garlic. Add veal and pork. Cook until lightly browned, stirring to separate meat; drain fat. Set aside.

Combine spinach, parsley, bread crumbs, eggs, minced garlic and cheese in large bowl; blend well. Season to taste with salt. Add cooled meat mixture; blend well. Fill shells with meat mixture.

Spread about 1 cup spaghetti sauce over bottom of greased 12×8-inch pan. Arrange shells in pan. Pour remaining sauce over shells. Cover with foil. Bake in preheated 375°F oven 35 to 45 minutes or until bubbly. Serve with zucchini. Garnish as desired.

Nutrients per serving:

Calories	290	Cholesterol	81 mg
Fat	10 g	Sodium	428 mg

Favorite recipe from **Christopher Ranch of Gilroy**

Sunday Supper Stuffed Shells

Cinnamon-Pineapple Pork

Cinnamon-Pineapple Pork

Makes 4 servings

1 pound pork tenderloin, trimmed and cut
   crosswise into 8 pieces
¼ teaspoon salt
2 tablespoons margarine, divided
1 medium-size red bell pepper, cut into
   julienned strips
1 can (8 ounces) pineapple chunks in juice,
   undrained
½ cup dry white wine
1 tablespoon peeled, finely chopped fresh
   ginger root
1 tablespoon finely chopped fresh jalapeño
   chili*
⅛ to ¼ teaspoon ground cinnamon
1 tablespoon chopped fresh cilantro

Sprinkle each pork tenderloin piece with salt; press
each piece into 1-inch-thick medallion. Heat
1 tablespoon margarine in large skillet over medium
heat. Add pork pieces; cook 3 to 4 minutes per side
or until pork is tender. Place pork pieces on serving
plate; keep warm.

Add remaining 1 tablespoon margarine and red bell
pepper to same skillet; cook about 3 minutes or until
crisp-tender. Reduce heat to low. Stir in pineapple
and juice, wine, ginger, jalapeño chili and cinnamon;
simmer until liquid is reduced to ¼ cup. Spoon
pineapple mixture over cooked pork pieces; sprinkle
with cilantro. Garnish as desired.

*Chilies can sting and irritate skin; wear plastic disposable
gloves when handling chilies and do not touch eyes. Wash
hands after handling chilies.*

Nutrients per serving:			
Calories	220	Cholesterol	74 mg
Fat	10 g	Sodium	260 mg

Favorite recipe from **National Pork Producers Council**

Healthy Choice® Barbecued Beef

Makes 4 servings

1 teaspoon vegetable oil
½ cup chopped onion
⅓ cup chopped green bell pepper
⅓ cup peeled and chopped carrot
1 pound HEALTHY CHOICE® Ground Beef
⅔ cup prepared barbecue sauce

Heat oil in large skillet or saucepan over medium-low
heat. Add onion, pepper and carrot; cook and stir
until tender. Crumble beef into pan; cook about
6 minutes or until no longer pink. Stir in barbecue
sauce and simmer 5 minutes or until heated through.

Nutrients per serving:			
Calories	187	Cholesterol	55 mg
Fat	6 g	Sodium	587 mg

Stuffed Green Peppers

Makes 5 servings

5 medium green bell peppers
1 tablespoon CRISCO® Vegetable Oil
½ cup chopped onion
2 tablespoons chopped celery
1 clove garlic, minced
½ pound ground beef round
1 cup cooked rice (cooked without salt or fat)
1 can (8 ounces) tomato sauce
1 jar (2½ ounces) sliced mushrooms, drained
1 tablespoon Worcestershire sauce
1½ teaspoons Italian herb seasoning
¼ teaspoon sugar
⅛ teaspoon salt
⅛ teaspoon black pepper

1. Heat oven to 350°F.

2. Remove tops and seeds from green peppers. Cook
in boiling water 5 minutes. Drain upside down.

3. Heat Crisco® Oil in large skillet on medium heat.
Add onion, celery and garlic. Cook and stir until
tender. Add meat. Cook until browned, stirring
occasionally. Remove from heat.

4. Add rice, tomato sauce, mushrooms,
Worcestershire sauce, Italian herb seasoning, sugar,
salt and black pepper. Stir until well blended. Spoon
into green peppers.

5. Place peppers upright in baking dish. Add just
enough boiling water to cover bottom of dish.

6. Bake at 350°F for 30 to 40 minutes or until
heated through.

Nutrients per serving:			
Calories	215	Cholesterol	35 mg
Fat	7 g	Sodium	470 mg

Beef Fajitas

Makes 10 fajitas

½ cup **REALEMON®** Lemon Juice from
    Concentrate
¼ cup vegetable oil
2 teaspoons **WYLER'S®** or **STEERO®** Beef-
    Flavor Instant Bouillon
2 cloves garlic, finely chopped
1 (1- to 1½-pound) top round steak
10 (6-inch) flour tortillas, warmed as package
    directs
    Garnishes: Picante sauce, shredded lettuce,
      shredded Cheddar cheese and sliced green
      onions (optional)

In large shallow dish or plastic bag, combine
ReaLemon® brand, oil, bouillon and garlic; add
steak. Cover; marinate in refrigerator 6 hours or
overnight. Remove steak from marinade; heat
marinade thoroughly. Grill or broil steak 8 to
10 minutes on each side or until steak is cooked to
desired doneness, basting frequently with marinade.
Slice steak diagonally into thin strips; place on
tortillas. Top with one or more garnishes; fold
tortillas. Serve immediately. Refrigerate leftovers.

Nutrients per serving (1 fajita):			
Calories	187	Cholesterol	29 mg
Fat	7 g	Sodium	115 mg

Beef Fajitas

Southwestern Stir-Fry

Makes 5 servings

1 pound pork tenderloin
2 tablespoons dry sherry
2 tablespoons cornstarch
1 teaspoon ground cumin
1 clove garlic, finely chopped
½ teaspoon seasoned salt
1 tablespoon vegetable oil
1 medium onion, thinly sliced
1 medium green bell pepper, cut into strips
12 cherry tomatoes, halved
    Warm flour tortillas and green chili salsa for
      serving

Cut pork tenderloin lengthwise into quarters. Cut
each quarter into ¼-inch thick slices. Combine
sherry, cornstarch, cumin, garlic and seasoned salt
in medium bowl. Add pork slices; stir to coat.

Heat oil in large, heavy skillet over medium-high
heat. Add pork mixture; stir-fry 3 to 4 minutes. Stir
in onion, bell pepper and tomatoes. Reduce heat to
low; cover and simmer 3 to 4 minutes. Serve hot with
tortillas and salsa.

Nutrients per serving:			
Calories	180	Cholesterol	41 mg
Fat	9 g	Sodium	255 mg

Favorite recipe from **National Pork Producers Council**

Eckrich® Lite Hoagie Sandwiches

Makes 8 servings

3 tablespoons low-calorie mayonnaise
1 tablespoon thinly sliced green onion
¼ teaspoon chili powder
1 loaf French bread (about 14 inches)
    Spinach leaves
1 package (6 ounces) **ECKRICH®** Lite Lower
    Salt Ham
2 ounces sliced Swiss cheese
1 package (6 ounces) **ECKRICH®** Lite Oven
    Roasted Turkey Breast
1 medium tomato, sliced

Combine mayonnaise, onion and chili powder in
small bowl. Cut bread into halves lengthwise. Spread
mayonnaise mixture on bread. Top bottom half of
bread with spinach leaves, ham, cheese, turkey and
tomato. Complete sandwich by adding top half of
bread. Cut into portions about 1½ inches wide.

Nutrients per serving:			
Calories	173	Cholesterol	28 mg
Fat	6 g	Sodium	654 mg

Oriental Stuffed Peppers

Makes 6 servings

- ½ pound extra-lean ground beef
- 2 cups frozen Oriental vegetable combination
- 1 cup cooked white rice
- 1 jar (12 ounces) HEINZ® HomeStyle Brown Gravy
- 2 tablespoons low-sodium soy sauce
- ½ teaspoon ground ginger
- ⅛ teaspoon black pepper
- 3 medium green, red or yellow bell peppers, split lengthwise and seeded

Brown beef in large skillet; drain, if necessary. Stir in vegetables and rice. Combine gravy, soy sauce, ginger and black pepper in small bowl; reserve ½ cup. Stir remaining gravy mixture into beef mixture. Place bell peppers in lightly greased 2-quart oblong baking dish. Fill bell peppers with beef mixture. Spoon reserved gravy mixture over bell peppers. Bake in 350°F oven 35 to 45 minutes or until hot.

To Microwave: Crumble beef into 2-quart microwave-safe casserole. Cover with lid or vented plastic wrap. Microwave at HIGH (100% power) 2½ to 3½ minutes or until meat is no longer pink, stirring once to break up meat. Drain. Stir in vegetables and rice. Combine gravy, soy sauce, ginger and pepper in small bowl; reserve ½ cup. Stir remaining gravy mixture into beef mixture. Place bell peppers in 2-quart microwave-safe oblong baking dish. Fill bell peppers with beef mixture. Spoon reserved gravy mixture over bell peppers. Cover with vented plastic wrap. Microwave at HIGH 10 to 11 minutes or until bell peppers are tender-crisp and beef mixture is hot.

Nutrients per serving:			
Calories	217	Cholesterol	33 mg
Fat	8 g	Sodium	575 mg

Pork with Three Onions

Makes 4 servings

- ⅓ cup teriyaki sauce
- 2 cloves garlic, minced
- ¾ pound pork tenderloin
- 2 tablespoons peanut or vegetable oil, divided
- 1 small red onion, cut into thin wedges
- 1 small yellow onion, cut into thin wedges
- 1 teaspoon sugar
- 1 teaspoon cornstarch
- 2 green onions, cut into 1-inch pieces
  Fried bean threads* (optional)

Pork with Three Onions

Combine teriyaki sauce and garlic in shallow bowl. Cut pork across the grain into ¼-inch slices; cut each slice in half. Toss pork with teriyaki mixture. Marinate at room temperature 10 minutes.

Heat large skillet over medium-high heat. Add 1 tablespoon oil; heat until hot. Drain pork; reserve marinade. Stir-fry pork 3 minutes or until no longer pink. Remove and set aside.

Heat remaining 1 tablespoon oil in skillet; add red and yellow onions. Reduce heat to medium. Cook 4 to 5 minutes until onions are softened, stirring occasionally. Sprinkle with sugar; cook 1 minute more.

Blend reserved marinade into cornstarch in cup until smooth. Stir into skillet. Stir-fry 1 minute or until sauce boils and thickens.

Return pork along with any accumulated juices to skillet; heat through. Stir in green onions. Serve over bean threads.

*To fry bean threads, follow package directions.

Nutrients per serving:			
Calories	217	Cholesterol	61 mg
Fat	10 g	Sodium	958 mg

Applesauce-Stuffed Tenderloin

Makes 8 servings

2 pork tenderloins (about 1 pound *each*), trimmed
¼ cup dry vermouth *or* apple juice
Nonstick cooking spray
⅔ cup chunky applesauce
¼ cup finely chopped dry-roasted peanuts
¼ teaspoon salt
¼ teaspoon finely crushed fennel seed
⅛ teaspoon black pepper

Using sharp knife, form a "pocket" in each pork tenderloin by cutting a lengthwise slit down center of each almost to, but not through, bottom of each tenderloin. Place in nonmetal baking dish. Pour vermouth in pockets and over tenderloins; cover dish. Marinate about 1 hour at room temperature.

Heat oven to 375°F. Spray 15×10-inch jelly-roll pan or shallow baking pan with nonstick cooking spray. In small bowl, combine applesauce, peanuts, salt, fennel seed and pepper; blend well. Spoon mixture into pocket in each tenderloin. Secure stuffed pockets with wooden toothpicks. Place stuffed tenderloins in prepared pan. Roast at 375°F for about 30 minutes or until meat thermometer registers 155°F. Let stand 5 to 10 minutes. Remove toothpicks and slice. Garnish as desired.

Nutrients per serving:			
Calories	179	Cholesterol	79 mg
Fat	6 g	Sodium	131 mg

Favorite recipe from **National Pork Producers Council**

North Beach Skillet Dinner

Makes 6 to 8 servings

½ pound bulk sausage
½ pound ground turkey
1 onion, chopped
1 clove garlic, pressed
1 teaspoon ground cumin
1 teaspoon dried oregano leaves, crumbled
⅛ to ¼ teaspoon ground red pepper
2 cups water
1 package (10 ounces) frozen chopped spinach, thawed
1 package (6.5 ounces) 5-minute long-grain and wild rice mix
1 cup DOLE® Chopped Dates

In 12-inch nonstick skillet, cook and stir sausage, turkey, onion and garlic over medium-high heat until onion is soft. Add cumin, oregano and red pepper. Stir in water, spinach and rice mix with its seasoning packet. Heat to a boil. Reduce heat to low. Cover; simmer 5 minutes. Stir in dates. Heat through.

Prep time: 5 minutes
Cook time: 10 minutes

Nutrients per serving:			
Calories	260	Cholesterol	26 mg
Fat	9 g	Sodium	587 mg

Curried Black Beans and Rice with Sausage

Makes 10 servings

1 tablespoon olive oil
1 medium onion, minced
1 tablespoon curry powder
½ pound smoked turkey sausage, thinly sliced
¾ cup chicken broth
2 cans (16 ounces *each*) black beans, drained
1 tablespoon white wine vinegar (optional)
3 cups cooked rice

Heat oil in large heavy skillet over medium heat. Cook onion and curry powder, stirring well, until onion is tender. Stir in turkey sausage and broth; simmer 5 minutes. Stir in beans; cook until hot, stirring constantly. Remove from heat and stir in vinegar. Spoon over rice.

To Microwave: Combine oil, onion and curry powder in 2- to 3-quart microproof baking dish. Cook on HIGH (100% power) 2 minutes or until onion is tender. Add turkey sausage, broth and beans; cover with vented plastic wrap and cook on HIGH 5 to 6 minutes, stirring after 3 minutes, or until thoroughly heated. Continue as directed above.

Nutrients per serving:			
Calories	267	Cholesterol	16 mg
Fat	5 g	Sodium	481 mg

Favorite recipe from **USA Rice Council**

Applesauce-Stuffed Tenderloin

Pronto Pizza

skillet 3 to 4 minutes, stirring occasionally. Add tomatoes; cook and stir 1 minute more. Place pizza shell on baking sheet or pizza pan; spread pizza sauce on shell. Top with vegetable mixture. Sprinkle with Parmesan cheese, fresh basil, if desired, reserved lamb and mozzarella cheese. Bake 8 to 10 minutes. Cool for 5 minutes. To serve, slice into wedges.

Prep time: 15 minutes
Cook time: 8 to 10 minutes

To Microwave: Prepare lamb mixture as directed, omitting oil. Place in 2-quart microwave-safe dish; microwave on HIGH (100% power) 3 minutes, stirring several times to crumble lamb. Add bell pepper and tomatoes; microwave on HIGH 2 minutes more, stirring once. Drain well. Assemble and bake pizza as directed.

Nutrients per serving:

Calories	245	Cholesterol	32 mg
Fat	9 g	Sodium	340 mg

Favorite recipe from **American Lamb Council**

Nectarine Beef Sauté

Makes 3 servings

    8 ounces sirloin steak, thinly sliced
      Black pepper
      All-purpose flour
    2 tablespoons low sodium soy sauce
    1 tablespoon honey
    1 teaspoon vegetable oil
    1 red onion, cut in half and cut into
        ¼-inch-thick slices
    1 clove garlic, finely chopped
    2 fresh California nectarines, cut into
        ¼-inch-thick slices
      Pinch ground red pepper

Season steak strips with black pepper. Lightly coat steak strips with flour; set aside. Combine soy sauce and honey in cup; set aside. Heat oil in large skillet over medium-high heat until hot. Add onion; cook and stir until onion is crisp-tender. Add garlic and steak strips; cook and stir until steak is browned. Add nectarines, reserved soy sauce mixture and red pepper. Cook about 1 minute or until nectarines are warm and liquid is reduced to glaze, stirring constantly.

Nutrients per serving:

Calories	260	Cholesterol	70 mg
Fat	8 g	Sodium	406 mg

Favorite recipe from **California Tree Fruit Agreement**

Pronto Pizza

Makes 6 to 8 servings

    6 ounces lean fresh ground American lamb
    ½ teaspoon onion salt
    ½ teaspoon fennel seed
    ¼ teaspoon dried oregano leaves, crushed
    ¼ teaspoon dried basil leaves, crushed
    ⅛ teaspoon crushed red pepper flakes
    2 teaspoons olive oil
    ½ cup chopped green bell pepper
    ½ cup chopped Italian plum tomatoes
    1 (10- to 12-inch) prebaked pizza shell
    ½ cup pizza sauce
    1 tablespoon grated Parmesan cheese
    ¼ cup thinly sliced fresh basil leaves (optional)
    ½ cup (2 ounces) grated mozzarella cheese

Preheat oven to 450°F. Combine lamb, onion salt, fennel, oregano, basil and red pepper flakes in small bowl; mix until well blended.

Heat oil in 10-inch skillet over medium-high heat until hot; add lamb mixture. Cook and stir, breaking up with spoon until lightly browned. Drain on paper towel; set aside. Cook and stir bell pepper in same

Margarita Pork Kabobs

Makes 4 servings

**1 cup margarita drink mix *or* 1 cup lime juice,
    4 teaspoons sugar and ½ teaspoon salt**
1 teaspoon ground coriander
1 clove garlic, minced
1 pound pork tenderloin, cut into 1-inch cubes
2 tablespoons butter, softened
1 tablespoon minced parsley
2 teaspoons lime juice
⅛ teaspoon sugar
2 ears corn, each cut into 8 pieces
**1 large green or red bell pepper, cut into 1-inch
    cubes**

To prepare marinade, combine margarita mix,
coriander and garlic in small bowl. Place pork cubes
in heavy plastic bag; pour marinade over to cover.
Marinate for at least 30 minutes.* Combine butter,
parsley, lime juice and sugar in small bowl; blend
well. Set aside. Thread pork cubes onto skewers,
alternating with pieces of corn and pepper. (If using
bamboo skewers, soak in water 20 to 30 minutes
before using.) Grill over hot coals 15 to 20 minutes,
basting with butter mixture and turning frequently.

Prep Time: 20 minutes
Cook Time: 20 minutes

**If marinating overnight, marinate in refrigerator.*

Nutrients per serving:			
Calories	266	Cholesterol	82 mg
Fat	10 g	Sodium	381 mg

Favorite recipe from **National Pork Producers Council**

Chili con Carne

Makes 8 servings

1 tablespoon CRISCO® Vegetable Oil
1 cup chopped onion
1 cup chopped green bell pepper
1 pound ground beef round
**1 can (28 ounces) whole tomatoes, undrained
    and chopped**
1 can (8 ounces) tomato sauce
1 tablespoon chili powder
1 teaspoon salt
¼ teaspoon black pepper
    Dash of hot pepper sauce (optional)
1 can (30 ounces) kidney beans, undrained

1. Heat Crisco® Oil in large saucepan or Dutch oven
on medium heat. Add onion and green pepper. Cook
and stir until tender. Add meat. Cook until browned,
stirring occasionally. Stir in tomatoes, tomato sauce,
chili powder, salt, black pepper and hot pepper sauce
(if used). Bring to a boil. Reduce heat to low. Simmer
45 minutes, stirring occasionally.

2. Add beans. Heat thoroughly, stirring occasionally.

Nutrients per serving:			
Calories	185	Cholesterol	35 mg
Fat	5 g	Sodium	505 mg

Orange-Pepper Steaks

Makes 4 servings

2 teaspoons coarsely ground black pepper
4 beef tenderloin steaks, cut 1 inch thick
½ cup orange marmalade
4 teaspoons cider vinegar
½ teaspoon ground ginger

Preheat broiler. Press pepper evenly into both sides of
beef steaks. Place steaks on rack in broiler pan 2 to
3 inches from heat source. Combine marmalade,
vinegar and ginger in small bowl. Brush tops of steaks
with ½ of marmalade mixture. Broil steaks 10 to
15 minutes for rare (140°F) to medium (160°F),
turning once and brushing with remaining marmalade
mixture.

Serving suggestion: *Serve with steamed new potatoes
and a medley of microwaved asparagus and baby carrots.*

Nutrients per serving:			
Calories	286	Cholesterol	71 mg
Fat	9 g	Sodium	60 mg

Favorite recipe from **National Live Stock and Meat Board**

Orange-Pepper Steak

Peppercorn Beef Kabob

Peppercorn Beef Kabobs

Makes 4 servings

1 pound boneless beef sirloin steak, cut 1 inch thick
1½ teaspoons black peppercorns, crushed
½ teaspoon *each* salt and paprika
1 clove garlic, pressed
1 medium onion, cut into 12 wedges
Cherry tomato halves (optional)

Preheat broiler. Cut beef steak into 1-inch pieces. Combine peppercorns, salt, paprika and garlic in shallow dish. Add beef; toss to coat. Thread an equal number of beef pieces onto each of four 12-inch skewers, alternating with 3 onion wedges. (If using bamboo skewers, soak in water 20 to 30 minutes before using.) Place kabobs on rack in broiler pan 3 to 4 inches from heat source.* Broil 9 to 12 minutes for rare to medium, turning occasionally. Garnish with tomatoes, if desired.

**Beef kabobs may also be grilled. Place on grid over medium coals. Grill 8 to 11 minutes.*

Serving suggestion: *Serve with microwaved medley of corn and peas.*

Nutrients per serving:

Calories	177	Cholesterol	76 mg
Fat	6 g	Sodium	331 mg

Favorite recipe from **National Live Stock and Meat Board**

Sweet and Sour Pork

Makes 6 servings

1 Florida grapefruit
1¼ pounds boneless pork tenderloin, trimmed of all fat
⅓ cup Florida grapefruit juice
2 tablespoons low sodium soy sauce
1 clove garlic, minced
2 teaspoons light brown sugar, divided
2 tablespoons cornstarch
1 tablespoon vegetable oil
2 teaspoons finely minced ginger root
8 medium scallions, cut into 2-inch pieces
1 medium red bell pepper, cut into 1-inch cubes
¼ cup ketchup
⅓ cup low sodium chicken broth

Peel grapefruit and carefully remove white pith. Carefully section grapefruit with paring knife, peeling fruit away from membrane. Set aside.

Cut pork into 1-inch cubes. Combine grapefruit juice, soy sauce, garlic and 1 teaspoon brown sugar in medium bowl until well blended. Add pork; stir to combine. Cover and marinate 30 minutes. Remove pork from marinade with slotted spoon, reserving marinade. Place cornstarch in shallow dish; add pork. Toss until lightly coated.

Heat oil in large nonstick skillet over medium-high heat until hot, but not smoking. Add pork and cook, on all sides, about 7 to 10 minutes until golden brown. Remove pork to warm plate. Add ginger, scallions and red pepper to skillet. Cook and stir 2 to 3 minutes until scallions are slightly limp. Add ketchup, chicken broth, remaining 1 teaspoon brown sugar and reserved marinade. Bring to a boil over medium-high heat. Add browned pork and grapefruit sections; cook about 1 to 2 minutes until pork is no longer pink and sauce has thickened slightly. Serve immediately.

Tip: *Sweet and Sour Pork is a hearty meal that is rich in flavor. Including 30 minutes marinating time (the acids in grapefruit juice act as natural meat tenderizers), total preparation time is still less than 45 minutes. While pork marinates, you can set the table or prepare a side dish.*

Nutrients per serving:

Calories	207	Cholesterol	75 mg
Fat	6 g	Sodium	351 mg

Favorite recipe from **Florida Department of Citrus**

Wild Rice Stuffed Peppers

Makes 8 servings

4 green bell peppers
1 pound extra lean ground beef
2 cups cooked wild rice
1 cup shredded part-skim mozzarella cheese
1 medium onion, chopped
½ cup dried fruit bits
½ to 1 teaspoon black pepper
1 teaspoon ground cinnamon
½ teaspoon salt

Preheat oven to 350°F. Cut green peppers into halves; remove stems and seeds. Combine remaining ingredients in large bowl until well blended. Lightly stuff green pepper halves with wild rice mixture. Place in baking dish and loosely cover with foil. Bake 30 minutes. Uncover; bake 10 minutes or until peppers are tender.

Nutrients per serving:

Calories	205	Cholesterol	39 mg
Fat	8 g	Sodium	202 mg

Favorite recipe from **Minnesota Cultivated Wild Rice Council**

Pork with Artichokes and Capers

Makes 4 servings

 1 pound pork tenderloin, trimmed and cut
    crosswise into 8 pieces
 2 tablespoons margarine
 1 small shallot, finely chopped
 1 tablespoon capers, drained
 ¼ cup chicken broth
 1 teaspoon Dijon-style mustard
 1 cup artichoke hearts, drained, rinsed and
    halved
    Fresh lemon slices (optional)
    Fresh chopped parsley (optional)

Press each pork tenderloin piece into 1-inch-thick medallion. Heat margarine in large skillet over medium-high heat. Add pork pieces; cook 3 to 4 minutes per side or until pork is tender. Place pork pieces on serving plate; keep warm. Reduce heat to low. Add shallot and capers to same skillet. Cook 1 to 2 minutes, stirring frequently. Stir in chicken broth, mustard and artichokes; cook just until thoroughly heated, stirring occasionally. Spoon artichoke mixture over cooked pork pieces. Garnish with lemon slices and sprinkle with parsley, if desired.

Nutrients per serving:

Calories	207	Cholesterol	94 mg
Fat	10 g	Sodium	537 mg

Favorite recipe from **National Pork Producers Council**

Stir-Fried Orange Beef

Makes 6 servings

 2 Florida oranges
 1¼ pounds top round steak, trimmed
 ½ cup Florida orange juice, divided
 2 tablespoons low sodium soy sauce
 1 tablespoon *plus* 1 teaspoon cornstarch,
    divided
 2 teaspoons brown sugar, divided
 ½ cup low sodium chicken broth
 1 tablespoon Oriental sesame oil
 1 teaspoon finely minced ginger root
 1 clove garlic, minced
 4 cups broccoli flowerets
 4 medium scallions, cut into 2-inch pieces
 1 can (8 ounces) sliced water chestnuts, rinsed
    and drained
 3 tablespoons chopped cilantro

Remove thin strips of rind from oranges with paring knife or zester; set aside. Section peeled orange; set aside. Cut steak along grain into 2-inch-wide strips. Cut steak across grain into ¼-inch-thick slices.

Combine steak, 2 tablespoons orange juice, soy sauce, 1 tablespoon cornstarch and 1 teaspoon brown sugar; stir to combine. Set aside.

Combine chicken broth, remaining 6 tablespoons orange juice, 1 teaspoon cornstarch and 1 teaspoon brown sugar in small bowl until well blended. Heat oil in large nonstick skillet over medium-high heat until hot, but not smoking. Add reserved steak; stir-fry 3 to 4 minutes until steak is browned. Remove from skillet. Add ginger, garlic, reserved orange rind, broccoli, scallions, water chestnuts and chicken broth mixture. Stir-fry 2 to 3 minutes until vegetables begin to soften. Add cilantro and reserved steak (with juices); cook and stir until sauce has thickened slightly. Stir in orange sections and serve immediately.

Tip: Stir-Fried Orange Beef is a light and tangy meal that takes only 30 minutes to prepare. This zesty dish is perfect for a festive dinner. The fresh Florida oranges add a little sunshine to the meal.

Nutrients per serving:

Calories	252	Cholesterol	66 mg
Fat	7 g	Sodium	248 mg

Favorite recipe from **Florida Department of Citrus**

Healthy Choice® Italian Meatballs in Spaghetti Sauce

Makes 6 servings

 1 pound HEALTHY CHOICE® Ground Beef
 ½ cup dry bread crumbs
 1 tablespoon finely chopped onion
 2 tablespoons grated Parmesan cheese
 ½ teaspoon Italian seasoning
 ½ teaspoon salt
 ⅛ teaspoon ground black pepper
 2 egg whites *or* 1 egg, lightly beaten
 1 jar (26 ounces) HEALTHY CHOICE®
    Spaghetti Sauce

Mix beef, bread crumbs, onion, cheese, seasoning, salt, pepper and egg whites in large bowl just until combined. Form into meatballs (each about 1½ inches in diameter). Heat spaghetti sauce in large saucepan over low heat to a simmer. Drop meatballs into sauce; cover and cook 20 minutes or until heated through.

Nutrients per serving:

Calories	144	Cholesterol	38 mg
Fat	4 g	Sodium	623 mg

Pork with Artichokes and Capers

Pork Sauced with Mustard and Grapes

Makes 2 servings

1 cup seedless or halved, seeded Chilean grapes (red, green or combination)
6 ounces boneless pork loin, cut into ½-inch-thick slices
1 tablespoon all-purpose flour
2 teaspoons olive oil, divided
¼ cup thinly sliced onion
1 cup low sodium chicken broth
1 tablespoon white wine vinegar
1 tablespoon brown sugar
1 tablespoon mustard
1 teaspoon mustard seeds
2 watercress sprigs (optional)

Rinse grapes; remove any stems and set aside. Coat pork with flour in shallow dish. Heat 1 teaspoon oil in large nonstick skillet over medium heat. Add pork; cook about 5 minutes, browning on both sides. Remove; set aside. Heat remaining 1 teaspoon oil in same skillet over medium-high heat; add onion. Cook and stir until onion is softened. Add ½ cup grapes, broth, wine vinegar, brown sugar, mustard and mustard seeds. Bring to a boil; cook until reduced by half, stirring occasionally. Return pork with juices and remaining ½ cup grapes to skillet. Heat until warm. Garnish with watercress, if desired.

Nutrients per serving:

Calories	292	Cholesterol	79 mg
Fat	8 g	Sodium	251 mg

Favorite recipe from **Chilean Fresh Fruit Association**

Pork Sauced with Mustard and Grapes

Apple-icious Lamb Kebabs

Makes 6 servings

1½ pounds fresh American lamb leg or shoulder, cut into 1¼-inch cubes
1 cup apple juice or cider
2 tablespoons Worcestershire sauce
2 cloves garlic, peeled and sliced
½ teaspoon lemon pepper
1 large apple, cut into 12 wedges
　Assorted vegetables, such as 1 large green or red bell pepper, 1 large onion and 1 small summer squash, cut into wedges
　Apple Barbecue Sauce (recipe follows)

Mix apple juice, Worcestershire sauce, garlic and lemon pepper in plastic bag or nonmetal container. Add lamb cubes; toss to coat well. To marinate, place in refrigerator for at least 2 hours and up to 24 hours.

Remove meat from marinade and thread onto skewers, alternating meat, apple wedges and vegetables; discard marinade.

To grill, place kebabs 4 inches from medium coals. Cook about 10 to 12 minutes for medium-rare, turning occasionally and brushing with Apple Barbecue Sauce. (To broil, place kebabs on broiler pan lightly oiled or sprayed with nonstick cooking spray. Broil lamb 4 inches from heat source. Cook about 10 to 12 minutes for medium-rare, turning occasionally and brushing with Apple Barbecue Sauce.)

Prep time: 20 minutes
Cook time: 15 minutes

Apple Barbecue Sauce

½ cup apple juice or cider
½ cup finely chopped onion
1 cup chili sauce
½ cup unsweetened applesauce
2 tablespoons packed brown sugar
1 tablespoon Worcestershire sauce
1 teaspoon dry mustard
5 drops hot pepper sauce

Combine apple juice and onion in 1-quart saucepan; bring to a boil. Reduce heat and simmer for 2 minutes. Stir in chili sauce, applesauce, brown sugar, Worcestershire sauce, dry mustard and hot pepper sauce. Simmer 10 minutes, stirring occasionally. Remove from heat.

Nutrients per serving:

Calories	288	Cholesterol	76 mg
Fat	7 g	Sodium	727 mg

Favorite recipe from **American Lamb Council**

Beef Steak with Peppercorn Wine Sauce

Beef Steaks with Peppercorn Wine Sauce

Makes 4 servings

4 beef eye round steaks, cut 1 inch thick
1½ teaspoons cornstarch
1 cup ready-to-serve beef broth
⅛ teaspoon dried thyme leaves, crushed
1 small bay leaf
2 tablespoons dry red wine
⅛ teaspoon black peppercorns, crushed

Heat large heavy skillet over medium heat 5 minutes. Place beef steaks in skillet and cook 8 to 10 minutes

for rare (140°F) to medium (160°F), turning once. Meanwhile, dissolve cornstarch in broth in small saucepan. Bring to a boil and cook about 1 minute or until slightly thickened. Stir in thyme and bay leaf. Reduce heat to medium and cook about 5 minutes or until mixture is reduced to ½ cup. Stir in wine and peppercorns; cook 3 minutes, stirring occasionally. Remove bay leaf. Spoon sauce over steaks.

Serving suggestion: Serve with steamed new potatoes with green onion and a red cabbage and carrot salad.

Nutrients per serving:

Calories	170	Cholesterol	64 mg
Fat	5 g	Sodium	264 mg

Favorite recipe from **National Live Stock and Meat Board**

Mushroom-Stuffed Veal Breast

Mushroom-Stuffed Veal Breast

Makes 8 to 10 servings

  4 teaspoons olive oil, divided
1½ cups chopped mushrooms
  ½ cup finely chopped red bell pepper
  2 cloves garlic, minced
  ½ teaspoon dried rosemary leaves, crushed
  1 (2½- to 3-pound) boneless veal breast
  ½ teaspoon salt
  ⅓ cup *each* marsala and water

Heat 2 teaspoons oil in 10-inch nonstick skillet over medium heat until hot. Add mushrooms, bell pepper and garlic; cook and stir about 5 minutes or just until mushrooms are tender. Stir in rosemary. Remove from heat; cool. Unroll boneless veal breast; trim excess surface fat. Sprinkle evenly with salt. Spread cooled mushroom mixture evenly over surface. Roll up veal; tie securely with string. Heat remaining 2 teaspoons oil in Dutch oven over medium heat until hot. Add veal; cook until browned on all sides. Add marsala and water. Cover and simmer over low heat 1 hour and 30 minutes to 1 hour and 45 minutes until veal is tender. Transfer veal to platter; keep warm. Skim fat from pan juices, if necessary. Cook over high heat until reduced by one third. Slice veal; discard strings. Spoon sauce over each serving.

Note: A boneless veal breast will yield 3½ (3-ounce) cooked, trimmed servings per pound.

Prep time: 20 minutes
Cook time: 1 hour and 45 minutes to 2 hours

Nutrients per serving:			
Calories	194	Cholesterol	100 mg
Fat	7 g	Sodium	188 mg

Favorite recipe from **National Live Stock and Meat Board**

Mustard Pork Chops

Makes 4 servings

  2 tablespoons Dijon-style mustard
  4 pork loin chops, cut ½ inch thick (about 1¼ pounds)
  ¼ cup fine dry bread crumbs
  2 tablespoons cornmeal
  1 tablespoon whole wheat flour
  ⅓ cup DANNON® Plain Nonfat or Lowfat Yogurt
  1 tablespoon chutney, chopped

Preheat oven to 350°F. Spread mustard on all surfaces of chops. In a medium bowl combine bread crumbs, cornmeal and flour. Coat chops with crumb mixture. Place chops in 9×9-inch baking pan.

Bake 30 to 40 minutes or until chops are no longer pink and coating is lightly browned. In a small bowl combine yogurt and chutney; spoon over chops.

Nutrients per serving:			
Calories	230	Cholesterol	50 mg
Fat	10 g	Sodium	321 mg

Spicy Pork and Vegetable Stir-Fry

Makes 4 servings, about 4 cups

  1 pound lean boneless pork loin*
  ½ cup HEINZ® Chili Sauce
  2 teaspoons light soy sauce
  ⅛ teaspoon crushed red pepper flakes
1½ teaspoons cornstarch
  1 cup julienned carrots (about 2 medium carrots)
  1 clove garlic, minced
  2 tablespoons vegetable oil, divided
  2 small zucchini, halved and cut into ½-inch slices
  8 to 10 green onions, cut into 1-inch pieces

Cut pork into thin strips; set aside. Combine chili sauce, soy sauce and red pepper; blend in cornstarch and set aside. In preheated wok or large skillet, stir-fry carrots and garlic in 1 tablespoon oil 1 minute. Add zucchini and onions. Stir-fry 1 minute longer or until vegetables are tender-crisp; remove. Stir-fry pork in 2 batches in remaining 1 tablespoon oil 1 to 2 minutes or until cooked; remove. Return vegetables and meat to wok; stir in chili sauce mixture and cook until thickened.

*1 pound skinless boneless chicken, cut into 1-inch chunks, may be substituted.

Nutrients per serving:			
Calories	258	Cholesterol	72 mg
Fat	10 g	Sodium	635 mg

New England Pork Tenderloin

New England Pork Tenderloin

Makes 4 servings

¼ cup apple jelly
2 tablespoons lemon juice
½ teaspoon pumpkin pie spice
    Vegetable cooking spray
1 pound pork tenderloin, trimmed
2 tart red cooking apples, unpeeled, cored and
    thinly sliced

Preheat oven to 375°F. Combine apple jelly, lemon juice and pumpkin pie spice in small bowl; blend well. Spray roasting rack with cooking spray; place in shallow pan. Place pork tenderloin on prepared rack; brush with half the apple jelly mixture. Roast 20 to 30 minutes until meat thermometer registers 155°F. Let stand 5 to 10 minutes.

Preheat broiler. Place apple slices on broiler pan; brush with remaining apple jelly mixture. Broil 5 to 6 inches from heat about 5 minutes or until apple slices are tender. Slice tenderloin; serve with cooked apple slices.

Nutrients per serving:

Calories	237	Cholesterol	79 mg
Fat	4 g	Sodium	57 mg

Favorite recipe from **National Pork Producers Council**

Spaghetti with Meat Sauce

Makes 8 servings

1 pound ground beef round
2 tablespoons CRISCO® Vegetable Oil
½ cup chopped carrot
½ cup chopped celery
⅓ cup chopped onion
2 cloves garlic, minced
1 can (14½ ounces) no salt added tomatoes,
    undrained
1 can (10¾ ounces) condensed reduced-sodium
    tomato soup
1 can (6 ounces) no salt added tomato paste
2 teaspoons sugar
1½ teaspoons Italian herb seasoning
1 teaspoon dried basil leaves
¼ teaspoon salt
¼ teaspoon crushed red pepper
1 bay leaf
1 pound spaghetti, cooked (without salt or fat)
    and well drained

1. Heat large skillet on medium-high heat. Add meat. Cook until browned, stirring occasionally. Remove meat from skillet. Drain. Wipe out skillet.

2. Heat Crisco® Oil in same skillet on medium heat. Add carrot, celery, onion and garlic. Cook and stir until carrot is tender.

3. Add meat, tomatoes, tomato soup, tomato paste, sugar, Italian herb seasoning, basil, salt, red pepper and bay leaf. Stir to blend. Break apart tomatoes. Bring to a boil. Reduce heat to low. Cover. Simmer 45 minutes, stirring occasionally. Remove bay leaf. Serve over hot spaghetti.

To Microwave: 1. Combine Crisco® Oil, carrot, celery, onion and garlic in large microwave-safe dish. Cover with plastic wrap. Turn back one corner of plastic wrap slightly to vent. Microwave at HIGH for 4 minutes, stirring after 2 minutes. Crumble meat into dish. Cover. Microwave at HIGH for 4 minutes, stirring after 2 minutes. Use fork to break up any large meat pieces. Drain.

2. Follow step 3 above for adding remaining ingredients. Cover. Microwave at HIGH for 8 minutes, stirring every 2 minutes.

Nutrients per serving:

Calories	285	Cholesterol	45 mg
Fat	9 g	Sodium	400 mg

Chunky Beef and Corn Chili

Makes 4 servings

4½ teaspoons Spicy Seasoning Mix, divided
    (recipe follows)
  2 teaspoons vegetable oil
  1 pound lean beef cube steaks
  1 medium onion, chopped
  1 can (28 ounces) plum tomatoes, undrained
  2 cups frozen whole kernel corn*

Prepare Spicy Seasoning Mix; set aside. Heat oil in
Dutch oven or large skillet over medium heat
5 minutes. Meanwhile, cut each beef steak lengthwise
into 1-inch-wide strips; cut crosswise into 1-inch
pieces. Sprinkle beef with 2 teaspoons Spicy
Seasoning Mix. Add beef and onion to Dutch oven;
stir-fry 2 to 3 minutes. Season with salt, if desired.
Add tomatoes (break up with back of spoon), corn
and 2½ teaspoons Spicy Seasoning Mix. Bring to a
boil; reduce heat to medium-low and simmer,
uncovered, 18 to 20 minutes until beef is tender.

**1 can (15 ounces) kidney, pinto or black beans, drained
and rinsed or 2 cups cooked cubed potatoes may be
substituted for corn.*

Spicy Seasoning Mix

  3 tablespoons chili powder
  2 teaspoons *each* ground coriander and cumin
1½ teaspoons garlic powder
  ¾ teaspoon dried oregano leaves, crushed
  ½ teaspoon ground red pepper

Combine all ingredients. Store, covered, in airtight
container. Before using, shake to blend. Makes about
⅓ cup.

Nutrients per serving:

Calories	290	Cholesterol	65 mg
Fat	8 g	Sodium	402 mg

Favorite recipe from **National Live Stock and Meat Board**

Chunky Beef and Corn Chili

Scandinavian Meatballs

Scandinavian Meatballs

Makes 6 servings

1½ cups DANNON® Plain Nonfat or Lowfat
    Yogurt, divided
½ cup soft bread crumbs
1 pound lean ground beef
1 egg
¼ cup finely chopped onion
¼ teaspoon salt (optional)
2 tablespoons all-purpose flour
1 envelope (about 3.5 grams) instant beef
    broth mix
1 teaspoon Worcestershire sauce
    Snipped fresh parsley (optional)

In a large bowl combine ½ cup yogurt and bread
crumbs; let stand 5 minutes. Add ground beef, egg,
onion and salt. Mix well and shape into 1¼-inch
meatballs. Spray a large nonstick skillet with
vegetable cooking spray. Cook meatballs over medium
heat until brown and cooked through, turning often;
drain. Wipe skillet dry.

In a small bowl combine 1 cup yogurt, flour, beef
broth mix and Worcestershire sauce until smooth.
Add to skillet. Cook over medium-low heat, stirring
constantly, until thickened. *Do not boil.* Reduce heat
to low. Add meatballs; mix with sauce and cook until
just heated through. If desired, garnish with parsley.

Nutrients per serving:

Calories	190	Cholesterol	100 mg
Fat	7 g	Sodium	230 mg

Curried Pork Tenderloin

Makes 4 servings

2 tablespoons vegetable oil
¼ cup finely chopped onion
¼ cup finely chopped celery
1 clove garlic, minced
1 tablespoon curry powder
1 tablespoon chopped fresh parsley
1 tablespoon grated lemon peel
⅓ cup lemon juice
2 tablespoons honey
2 drops hot pepper sauce
1 bay leaf
1 whole pork tenderloin (about 1 pound),
    trimmed

Heat oil in small skillet over medium-high heat. Add
onion, celery and garlic; cook and stir about 1 minute
or until vegetables are tender. Add all remaining
ingredients except pork tenderloin. Simmer,
uncovered, 3 to 4 minutes. Refrigerate until chilled.

Place pork tenderloin in plastic bag or nonmetal
baking dish. Pour chilled mixture over pork, turning
to coat. Seal bag or cover dish; marinate 4 hours or
overnight in refrigerator, turning pork several times.

Preheat oven to 375°F. Remove pork from marinade,
reserving marinade. Place in shallow pan. Roast
25 to 35 minutes or until meat thermometer registers
155°F, basting with reserved marinade occasionally.
Let stand 5 minutes; cut into thin slices.

Nutrients per serving:

Calories	236	Cholesterol	74 mg
Fat	10 g	Sodium	66 mg

Favorite recipe from **National Pork Producers Council**

Sloppy Joes on Whole Wheat Buns

Makes 8 servings

1 tablespoon CRISCO® Vegetable Oil
½ cup chopped onion
½ cup chopped celery
½ cup chopped green bell pepper
½ cup shredded carrots
1¼ pounds ground beef round
½ cup ketchup
½ cup water
1 teaspoon chili powder
½ teaspoon salt
¼ teaspoon black pepper
    Dash of hot pepper sauce
8 whole wheat light sandwich buns

1. Heat Crisco® Oil in large skillet on medium heat.
Add onion, celery, green pepper and carrots. Cook
and stir until tender.

2. Add meat. Cook until browned, stirring
occasionally. Drain. Stir in ketchup, water, chili
powder, salt, black pepper and hot pepper sauce.
Reduce heat to low.

3. Simmer 15 minutes or until thick enough to spoon
into buns.

Nutrients per serving:

Calories	270	Cholesterol	60 mg
Fat	9 g	Sodium	555 mg

Naturally lean chicken and turkey have always been popular and delicious mealtime choices, and this chapter is overflowing with healthy new twists on old favorites. Let savory Chicken Cordon Bleu or down-home Turkey Stuffed Green Peppers take center stage on your dinner plate tonight.

Chicken Olé

Makes 6 servings

- ½ cup medium-hot chunky taco sauce
- ¼ cup Dijon-style mustard
- 2 tablespoons fresh lime juice
- 3 whole chicken breasts, split, skinned and boned
- 2 tablespoons margarine
  Chopped fresh parsley for garnish
  Reduced fat sour cream (optional)

Combine taco sauce, mustard and lime juice in large bowl. Add chicken, turning to coat. Cover; marinate in refrigerator at least 30 minutes.

Melt margarine in large skillet over medium heat until foamy. Remove chicken from marinade; reserve marinade. Add chicken to skillet; cook about 10 minutes or until brown on both sides. Add marinade; cook about 5 minutes or until chicken is tender and marinade glazes chicken. Remove chicken to serving platter. Boil marinade over high heat 1 minute; pour over chicken. Garnish with parsley. Serve with sour cream.

Nutrients per serving:			
Calories	194	Cholesterol	73 mg
Fat	8 g	Sodium	329 mg

Chicken Cordon Bleu

Makes 4 servings

- 4 large chicken breast halves, boned and skinned (1 pound)
- 1 tablespoon Dijon-style mustard
- ½ teaspoon dried thyme leaves, crushed
- 4 slices (4 ounces) lean cooked ham
- 2 slices (1½ ounces) SARGENTO® Preferred Light Sliced Swiss Cheese
- ¼ cup seasoned bread crumbs
- 1 tablespoon SARGENTO® Grated Parmesan Cheese
- 4 teaspoons melted light margarine

Place chicken between 2 pieces wax paper. Pound to ¼-inch thickness. Spread mustard evenly down center of each breast. Sprinkle with thyme. Top with slice of ham and half slice cheese. Roll up, jelly-roll style, tucking in sides of ham and chicken to seal. Secure with skewers or large wooden toothpicks. Combine bread crumbs and Parmesan cheese in shallow dish. Brush each chicken breast with melted margarine and roll in crumb mixture. Place in 9×9-inch baking pan. Bake at 400°F for 10 minutes. *Reduce oven temperature to 350°F* and continue baking 20 to 25 minutes or until chicken is tender. Remove skewers. Serve immediately.

Nutrients per serving:			
Calories	262	Cholesterol	86 mg
Fat	10 g	Sodium	692 mg

Chicken Olé

margarine and oil. In same skillet, combine browned turkey slices, reserved pineapple juice, orange peel and juice, lemon peel and juice, bouillon and garlic. Bring to a boil. Add pineapple. Reduce heat to low; simmer 1 to 2 minutes. Remove turkey and pineapple to serving platter. Bring sauce to a boil; boil until reduced by half. Stir in parsley. Spoon sauce over turkey and pineapple; serve immediately.

Nutrients per serving:			
Calories	155	Cholesterol	22 mg
Fat	3 g	Sodium	403 mg

Pineapple & Citrus Sauced Turkey Slices

Pineapple & Citrus Sauced Turkey Slices

Makes 4 servings

2 cans (8 ounces each) DOLE® Pineapple Slices
    in Juice
2 tablespoons flour
¼ teaspoon ground dried sage
¼ teaspoon dried thyme leaves, crushed
¼ teaspoon salt
¼ teaspoon paprika
⅛ teaspoon black pepper
8 fresh turkey breast slices (1 pound)
1 teaspoon margarine
1 teaspoon vegetable oil
    Grated peel and juice of ½ DOLE® Orange
    Grated peel and juice of ½ DOLE® Lemon
1 chicken bouillon cube
1 large clove garlic, pressed
2 tablespoons chopped fresh parsley

Drain pineapple; reserve juice. Combine flour and seasonings in shallow dish. Coat turkey with flour mixture.

In large nonstick skillet, brown half the turkey in ½ teaspoon margarine and ½ teaspoon oil. Remove and set aside. Repeat procedure with remaining turkey,

Herb-Marinated Chicken Kabobs

Makes 4 servings

4 skinless boneless chicken breast halves
2 small zucchini, cut into ½-inch slices
1 large red bell pepper, cut into 1-inch squares
½ cup HEINZ® Gourmet Wine Vinegar
½ cup tomato juice
2 tablespoons vegetable oil
1 tablespoon chopped sweet onion
1 tablespoon firmly packed brown sugar
2 cloves garlic, minced
½ teaspoon dried oregano leaves, crushed
½ teaspoon black pepper

Lightly flatten chicken breasts; cut each breast lengthwise into 3 strips. Place chicken in bowl with zucchini and bell pepper. For marinade, combine vinegar and remaining ingredients in jar. Cover; shake vigorously. Pour marinade over chicken and vegetables. Cover; marinate in refrigerator about 1 hour.

Drain marinade into small saucepan; boil marinade. Alternately thread chicken and vegetables onto skewers; brush with marinade. Broil, 3 to 5 inches from heat source, until chicken is cooked, about 8 to 10 minutes; turn and brush occasionally with marinade. Serve with rice, if desired.

Nutrients per serving:			
Calories	224	Cholesterol	66 mg
Fat	8 g	Sodium	189 mg

Oriental Barbecued Chicken

Makes 2 servings

¾ cup DOLE® Pineapple Juice
1 tablespoon light soy sauce
1 clove garlic, pressed
¼ teaspoon Chinese five-spice powder*
2 boneless skinless chicken breast halves
    (½ pound)
¾ teaspoon cornstarch

In small bowl, combine pineapple juice, soy sauce, garlic and five-spice powder. Place chicken in plastic bag or nonmetal bowl. Add juice mixture; marinate, covered, in refrigerator 15 minutes or overnight.

Drain marinade into small saucepan. Stir in cornstarch; cook and stir until marinade boils and thickens. Place chicken on greased broiler pan. Broil, 4 inches from heat source, 10 to 15 minutes on each side or until chicken is tender and no longer pink. Baste chicken with marinade frequently during broiling.

Chinese five-spice powder is a combination of fennel, anise, ginger, cinnamon and cloves.

Prep time: 5 minutes
Cook time: 30 minutes

Nutrients per serving:			
Calories	190	Cholesterol	68 mg
Fat	2 g	Sodium	377 mg

Honey Mustard Turkey Loaf

Makes 4 to 6 servings

1½ pounds ground fresh turkey
1 cup fresh bread crumbs (2 slices)
½ cup BORDEN® or MEADOW GOLD® Milk
¼ cup chopped onion
1 egg, beaten
2 teaspoons WYLER'S® or STEERO® Chicken-Flavor Instant Bouillon
2½ teaspoons prepared mustard
1 teaspoon poultry seasoning
2 tablespoons honey
1 tablespoon firmly packed brown sugar

Preheat oven to 350°F. Combine turkey, crumbs, milk, onion, egg, bouillon, *1 teaspoon* mustard and poultry seasoning; mix well. In shallow baking dish, shape into loaf. Bake 40 minutes. Combine remaining *1½ teaspoons* mustard, honey and brown sugar. Spoon over loaf; bake 10 minutes longer. Refrigerate leftovers.

Nutrients per serving:			
Calories	235	Cholesterol	112 mg
Fat	9 g	Sodium	469 mg

Chicken Fajitas

Makes 4 servings

1 tablespoon vegetable oil
1 large green bell pepper, thinly sliced
1 large red bell pepper, thinly sliced
1 large onion, thinly sliced
1 clove garlic, minced
4 boneless skinless chicken breast halves
    (about 1 pound), cut into ½-inch strips
½ teaspoon dried oregano leaves, crushed
2 tablespoons dry white wine or water
    Salt and black pepper (optional)
12 (8-inch) flour tortillas
    Guacamole (optional)

Heat oil in large skillet over medium-high heat. Add green and red pepper, onion and garlic. Cook 3 to 4 minutes or until crisp-tender, stirring occasionally. Remove vegetables with slotted spoon; set aside.

Add chicken and oregano to skillet. Cook 4 minutes or until chicken is no longer pink in center, stirring occasionally.

Return vegetables to skillet. Add wine. Season with salt and black pepper, if desired; cover. Continue cooking 2 minutes or until thoroughly heated.

Meanwhile, warm tortillas following package directions. Fill tortillas with chicken mixture; serve with guacamole, if desired.

Nutrients per serving:			
Calories	286	Cholesterol	30 mg
Fat	7 g	Sodium	31 mg

Chicken Fajitas

Turkey and Rice Quiche

Turkey and Rice Quiche

Makes 8 servings, 16 triangles

3 cups cooked rice, cooled to room temperature
1½ cups chopped cooked turkey
1 medium tomato, seeded and finely diced
¼ cup sliced green onions
¼ cup finely diced green bell pepper
1 tablespoon chopped fresh basil *or* 1 teaspoon dried basil leaves, crushed
½ teaspoon seasoned salt
⅛ to ¼ teaspoon ground red pepper
½ cup skim milk
3 eggs, beaten
  Nonstick cooking spray
½ cup (2 ounces) shredded Cheddar cheese
½ cup (2 ounces) shredded mozzarella cheese

Combine rice, turkey, tomato, onions, green pepper, basil, salt, ground red pepper, milk, and eggs in 13×9-inch pan coated with nonstick cooking spray. Top with cheeses. Bake at 375°F for 20 minutes or until knife inserted near center comes out clean. To serve, cut quiche into 8 squares; cut each square diagonally into 2 triangles. Garnish as desired.

Nutrients per serving (2 triangles):			
Calories	231	Cholesterol	111 mg
Fat	7 g	Sodium	527 mg

Favorite recipe from **USA Rice Council**

Herb and Orange Grilled Chicken

Makes 4 servings

4 broiler-fryer chicken quarters
2 cloves garlic, minced
1 teaspoon grated orange peel
1 teaspoon salt
½ teaspoon dried thyme leaves, crushed
½ teaspoon dried rosemary leaves, crushed
½ teaspoon pepper
½ cup orange juice
2 tablespoons vinegar
1 tablespoon Worcestershire sauce

Mix together garlic, orange peel, salt, thyme, rosemary and pepper in small bowl. Slip fingers between skin and flesh of chicken, leaving skin attached. Spread ¼ of herb mixture under skin of each chicken quarter, pulling skin back over spices. Mix together orange juice, vinegar and Worcestershire sauce in another small bowl. Place chicken on prepared grill, skin sides up, about 8 inches from heat source. Cook about 40 minutes or until fork can be inserted in chicken with ease, turning and basting with orange juice mixture every 5 minutes. Serve immediately.

Nutrients per serving:			
Calories	220	Cholesterol	75 mg
Fat	9 g	Sodium	716 mg

Favorite recipe from **National Broiler Council**

Turkey Tostados

Makes 4 servings

2 cups cubed cooked Turkey
1 package (1½ ounces) taco seasoning mix
  Water
4 corn tortillas
¼ cup canned refried beans
¼ cup (1 ounce) shredded reduced-calorie Cheddar cheese
½ cup chopped tomatoes
½ cup shredded lettuce
2 tablespoons chopped onions
½ cup taco sauce
  Plain low-fat yogurt (optional)
  Guacamole (optional)

Preheat oven to 375°F. In large skillet, over medium heat, combine turkey and taco seasoning mix. Add water according to package directions. Bring mixture to a boil; reduce heat to low and simmer 5 minutes, stirring occasionally.

Place tortillas on large cookie sheet. Bake 5 to 7 minutes or until tortillas are crispy and lightly browned.

Spread each tortilla with 1 tablespoon beans. Top evenly with meat mixture and cheese. Return to oven 2 to 3 minutes or until cheese is melted.

To serve, top with tomatoes, lettuce, onions and taco sauce. Garnish with yogurt and guacamole, if desired.

Nutrients per serving:			
Calories	277	Cholesterol	59 mg
Fat	6 g	Sodium	1102 mg

Favorite recipe from **National Turkey Federation**

Turkey Burgers

Makes 4 servings

1 pound ground fresh turkey
¼ cup BENNETT'S® Chili Sauce
1 teaspoon WYLER'S® or STEERO®
Chicken-Flavor Instant Bouillon

Combine ingredients; shape into 4 patties. Grill, broil or pan-fry as desired. Refrigerate leftovers.

Nutrients per serving:

Calories	172	Cholesterol	75 mg
Fat	7 g	Sodium	510 mg

Pineapple-Mustard Glazed Turkey Breast

Makes 6 servings

1 bone-in Turkey Breast Half (2½ pounds)
⅓ cup pineapple preserves
2 teaspoons Dijon-style mustard
1 teaspoon lemon juice

Prepare grill for indirect heat cooking by pushing hot coals up sides of grill around drip pan. Place turkey, breast side up, on rack over drip pan. Cover grill; cook 1 to 1¼ hours or until meat thermometer inserted in thickest portion of breast registers 170°F.

Meanwhile, in small bowl combine preserves, mustard and lemon juice. Brush glaze on breast during last 30 minutes of cooking. Remove turkey breast from grill; let stand 15 minutes. To serve, slice breast and arrange on platter. Garnish as desired.

Nutrients per serving:

Calories	295	Cholesterol	96 mg
Fat	10 g	Sodium	134 mg

Favorite recipe from **National Turkey Federation**

Pineapple-Mustard Glazed Turkey Breast

Stuffed Chicken Breasts

Makes 4 servings

4 boneless, skinless chicken breast halves (about
1 pound), pounded to ¼-inch thickness
½ teaspoon ground black pepper, divided
¼ teaspoon salt
1 cup cooked brown rice (cooked in chicken broth)
¼ cup minced tomato
¼ cup (1 ounce) finely shredded mozzarella cheese
3 tablespoons toasted rice bran* (optional)
1 tablespoon chopped fresh basil
Nonstick cooking spray

Season insides of chicken breasts with ¼ teaspoon pepper and salt. Combine rice, tomato, cheese, bran, basil, and remaining ¼ teaspoon pepper. Spoon rice mixture on top of chicken breasts; fold over and secure sides with wooden toothpicks soaked in water. Wipe off outsides of chicken breasts with paper towel.

Coat a large skillet with nonstick cooking spray and place over medium-high heat until hot. Cook stuffed chicken breasts 1 minute on each side or just until golden brown. Transfer chicken to shallow baking pan. Bake at 350°F for 8 to 10 minutes or until chicken is tender.

*To toast rice bran, spread on baking sheet and bake at 325°F for 7 to 8 minutes.

Nutrients per serving:

Calories	223	Cholesterol	79 mg
Fat	5 g	Sodium	337 mg

Favorite recipe from **USA Rice Council**

Turkey Bacon Club Sandwiches

Makes 2 sandwiches

4 slices LOUIS RICH® Turkey Bacon, cut in half
4 teaspoons reduced-calorie mayonnaise
4 slices whole wheat bread, toasted
2 lettuce leaves
4 thin slices tomato
4 slices LOUIS RICH® Oven Roasted Deli-Thin Turkey Breast

Cook and stir Turkey Bacon in nonstick skillet over medium heat 8 to 10 minutes or until lightly browned. For each sandwich, spread 2 teaspoons mayonnaise on one toast slice; top with half the Turkey Bacon, lettuce, tomato, Turkey Breast and another toast slice. Repeat for remaining sandwich.

Nutrients per serving (1 sandwich):

Calories	255	Cholesterol	30 mg
Fat	10 g	Sodium	845 mg

Rotini Stir-Fry

Makes 8 servings

½ of a (1-pound) package CREAMETTE®
 Rotini, cooked according to package
 directions and drained
2 tablespoons olive or vegetable oil
2 whole boneless skinless chicken breasts, cut
 into strips
1 cup fresh broccoli flowerets
1 cup carrot curls
½ cup sliced red onion
¼ cup water
½ teaspoon WYLER'S® or STEERO® Chicken-
 Flavor Instant Bouillon*
½ teaspoon dried tarragon leaves, crushed
2 tablespoons grated Parmesan cheese

In large skillet, heat oil; add chicken, broccoli, carrots
and onion. Cook and stir over medium heat until
broccoli is tender-crisp. Add water, bouillon and
tarragon; cook and stir until chicken is cooked
through. Add hot cooked rotini and Parmesan cheese;
toss to coat. Serve immediately. Refrigerate leftovers.

To reduce sodium, substitute low-sodium bouillon.

Nutrients per serving:

Calories	225	Cholesterol	37 mg
Fat	6 g	Sodium	123 mg

Crunchy Ranch Chicken Fingers

Makes 4 servings

1 cup cornflake crumbs
1 tablespoon chopped fresh parsley
⅓ cup WISH-BONE® Healthy Sensation! Ranch
 Dressing
1 teaspoon water
1 pound boneless skinless chicken breasts, cut
 into thin strips

Preheat oven to 425°F. In small bowl, combine
cornflake crumbs and parsley. In separate small
bowl, combine ranch dressing and water. Dip chicken
in dressing mixture, then cornflake mixture, coating
well.

On baking pan lightly sprayed with nonstick cooking
spray, arrange chicken. Bake 8 minutes or until
chicken is tender.

Nutrients per serving:

Calories	258	Cholesterol	66 mg
Fat	2 g	Sodium	609 mg

Chicken with Pineapple Salsa

Chicken with Pineapple Salsa

Makes 4 servings

1 can (20 ounces) DOLE® Crushed Pineapple
 in Juice
4 boneless skinless chicken breast halves
 (1 pound)
1 large clove garlic, pressed
1 teaspoon ground cumin
 Salt and black pepper (optional)
1 tablespoon vegetable oil
½ cup minced DOLE® Red Bell Pepper
¼ cup minced DOLE® Green Bell Pepper
1 tablespoon minced DOLE® Green Onion
2 teaspoons minced cilantro
2 teaspoons minced fresh or drained canned
 jalapeño chilies
1 teaspoon grated lime peel

Drain pineapple; reserve juice.

Rub chicken with garlic; sprinkle with cumin, salt
and black pepper. In 12-inch skillet, cook chicken in
hot oil over medium-high heat until browned; turn
once. Add ½ cup reserved pineapple juice to
chicken. Reduce heat to low. Cover; simmer 7 to
10 minutes.

For salsa, in medium bowl, combine pineapple,
remaining reserved juice and remaining ingredients.

Cut each breast into slices. Serve chicken with salsa.
Garnish as desired.

Prep time: 5 minutes
Cook time: 15 minutes

Nutrients per serving:

Calories	262	Cholesterol	68 mg
Fat	5 g	Sodium	81 mg

French Turkey Fillets

Makes 4 servings

1 package (1 pound) PERDUE® Fit 'n Easy
    fresh skinless and boneless turkey breast
    fillets
    Salt and coarsely ground black pepper to taste
    (optional)
1 tablespoon vegetable oil
2 tablespoons light margarine, divided
3 tablespoons minced shallots or scallions
⅔ cup red wine

Pat turkey dry and season with salt and pepper. In
large nonstick skillet over medium-high heat, heat oil.
Add fillets and cook 2 minutes on each side or until
lightly browned. Reduce heat to medium-low; cook
2 to 3 minutes longer on each side until cooked
through. Remove fillets and set aside. Heat
1 tablespoon margarine in skillet until melted. Add
shallots; cook and stir 1 minute. Stir in wine. Increase
heat to medium-high; boil wine 1 to 2 minutes until
reduced to thick, syrupy sauce. Remove skillet from
heat. Stir in remaining margarine. To serve, pour
sauce over turkey fillets.

Prep time: 10 minutes
Cook time: 15 minutes

Nutrients per serving:

Calories	214	Cholesterol	70 mg
Fat	7 g	Sodium	126 mg

Healthful Chicken Casserole

Makes 6 servings

1 broiler-fryer chicken, cooked, skinned and
    chopped
1 package (10 ounces) frozen spinach
¼ cup finely chopped onion
½ teaspoon garlic powder, divided
8 ounces fresh mushrooms, sliced
2 tablespoons diet margarine, melted
1 cup low fat skim milk mozzarella cheese

Preheat oven to 350°F. Cook spinach according to
package directions, omitting salt; drain well. Mix
onion with spinach. Arrange spinach mixture in
bottom of 1½ quart baking dish; sprinkle with

¼ teaspoon garlic powder. Arrange mushrooms on
spinach; drizzle with melted margarine. Place chicken
on mushrooms; sprinkle with remaining ¼ teaspoon
garlic powder. Top with mozzarella cheese. Bake
30 minutes or until fork can be inserted in chicken
with ease. Serve immediately.

Nutrients per serving:

Calories	202	Cholesterol	74 mg
Fat	9 g	Sodium	205 mg

Favorite recipe from **National Broiler Council**

Chicken Sauté Mediterranean

Makes 5 servings

1 package (1¼ pounds) PERDUE® Fit 'n Easy
    fresh skinless and boneless chicken breasts
    Salt and ground black pepper to taste
    (optional)
1½ teaspoons dried herbs de Provence or Italian
    herb seasoning
2 teaspoons olive oil
1 to 2 cloves garlic, minced
1½ tablespoons chopped sun-dried tomatoes
1 can (8 ounces) whole tomatoes, undrained
1 can (16 ounces) great Northern or cannellini
    beans, drained and rinsed

Sprinkle breast halves lightly with salt and generously
with pepper; press herbs into chicken. In large
nonstick skillet over medium-high heat, heat oil. Add
chicken and brown 2 minutes on each side. Add
garlic and sun-dried tomatoes; cook and stir 1 minute.
Stir in canned tomatoes, including liquid, and beans.
Reduce heat to medium-low; cover partially and
simmer 15 to 20 minutes until chicken is cooked
through. Serve chicken breasts warm with tomatoes
and beans spooned over.

Nutrients per serving:

Calories	208	Cholesterol	66 mg
Fat	4 g	Sodium	301 mg

Turkey Ham and Pineapple Boats

Makes 4 servings

1 package (3 ounces) chicken-flavored instant Oriental noodle soup, cooked according to package directions
1⅓ cups 2×¼-inch Turkey Ham strips
⅓ cup thinly sliced green onions
⅓ cup chopped mango chutney
¼ cup sliced water chestnuts
¼ teaspoon ground red pepper
2 small pineapples
2 tablespoons chopped almonds, toasted

Combine noodles, turkey ham, green onions, chutney, water chestnuts and red pepper in medium bowl; toss gently. Cover and refrigerate overnight.

Just before serving, cut pineapples in half lengthwise. With grapefruit knife remove pineapple meat from each shell; set aside shells. Cut pineapple into ½-inch cubes. Add 3 cups pineapple cubes to turkey mixture; toss gently.

To serve, spoon turkey mixture into reserved shells; sprinkle with almonds.

Nutrients per serving:			
Calories	278	Cholesterol	0 mg
Fat	5 g	Sodium	814 mg

Favorite recipe from **National Turkey Federation**

Caribbean Spice Chicken

Makes 4 servings

1 can (20 ounces) DOLE® Pineapple Slices, undrained
1 teaspoon *each* ground ginger, curry powder and garlic powder
¼ teaspoon ground red pepper
1 teaspoon cornstarch
4 skinless, boneless chicken breast halves
1 teaspoon vegetable oil
¼ cup *each* shredded coconut and slivered green onions

Preheat oven to 400°F. Drain pineapple juice into large measuring cup. Combine spices in small bowl. Stir ¼ teaspoon spice mixture and cornstarch into pineapple juice; set aside.

Sprinkle remaining spice mixture over chicken. Drizzle oil over chicken. Place on rack in roasting pan. Bake 15 minutes. Arrange pineapple slices on rack with chicken. Bake 5 minutes more.

Meanwhile, stir pineapple juice mixture. Microwave, uncovered, on HIGH (100% power) 2 to 4 minutes until sauce boils and thickens.

Arrange chicken and pineapple on 4 serving plates. Spoon with pineapple sauce; sprinkle with coconut and onions. Serve with dark green vegetables, if desired.

Prep time: 10 minutes
Cook time: 20 minutes

Nutrients per serving:			
Calories	266	Cholesterol	68 mg
Fat	5 g	Sodium	95 mg

Quick Cacciatore

Makes 4 servings

1 package (1 pound) PERDUE® Fit 'n Easy fresh skinless and boneless chicken thighs
5 to 6 teaspoons olive oil
⅔ cup chopped onion
1 can (14½ ounces) Italian-style stewed tomatoes, undrained
⅔ cup dry white wine or chicken broth
Salt and ground black pepper to taste (optional)

With sharp knife, trim visible fat from chicken. In large nonstick skillet over medium-high heat, heat oil. Add chicken; brown 2 minutes on 1 side. Turn chicken and add onions to skillet. Cook 2 minutes longer or until chicken is browned and onions are golden, stirring occasionally. Stir in remaining ingredients; reduce heat to medium-low. Cover and simmer 10 to 15 minutes until chicken is tender and sauce has thickened slightly, stirring occasionally. Serve chicken with sauce.

Prep time: 10 minutes
Cook time: 15 to 20 minutes

Nutrients per serving:			
Calories	250	Cholesterol	2 mg
Fat	10 g	Sodium	460 mg

Tex-Mex Ground Turkey Potato Boat

Tex-Mex Ground Turkey Potato Boats

Makes 4 servings

   2 **potatoes, baked and cooled**
 ½ **pound Ground Turkey**
 ½ **cup chopped onion**
   1 **clove garlic, minced**
   1 **can (8 ounces) stewed tomatoes**
   1 **teaspoon chili powder**
 ¼ **teaspoon dried oregano leaves, crushed**
 ¼ **teaspoon ground cumin**
 ¼ **teaspoon crushed red pepper**
 ¼ **teaspoon salt**
 ½ **cup (2 ounces) shredded reduced-fat Cheddar cheese**

Slice potatoes lengthwise in half. Scoop out center of each potato to within ¼ inch of potato skin. Reserve potato for other use.

In medium skillet, over medium-high heat, combine turkey, onion and garlic. Cook and stir 5 minutes or until turkey is no longer pink; drain if necessary. Add tomatoes with juice, chili powder, oregano, cumin, crushed red pepper and salt. Simmer 15 minutes or until most of liquid has evaporated.

Spoon turkey mixture evenly into potato shells and sprinkle with cheese. Place shells in 13×9×2-inch pan; bake in 375°F oven 15 minutes or until cheese melts.

Nutrients per serving:

| Calories | 209 | Cholesterol | 51 mg |
| Fat | 7 g | Sodium | 446 mg |

Favorite recipe from **National Turkey Federation**

Turkey-Apple Bake

Makes 6 to 8 servings

1½ pounds ground turkey
1½ cups dry bread crumbs
　1 cup unsweetened applesauce
　2 egg whites
　¼ cup minced onion
　¼ cup finely chopped celery
　1 tablespoon prepared mustard
　1 tablespoon Worcestershire sauce
　1 teaspoon salt
　¾ teaspoon poultry seasoning
　⅛ teaspoon black pepper
　⅔ cup chili sauce

In large bowl, combine all ingredients except chili sauce; mix lightly. Press into 9×5×3-inch loaf pan. Top with chili sauce. Bake at 350°F for 1 hour or until meat is cooked through. Let stand 10 minutes before slicing.

Nutrients per serving:			
Calories	223	Cholesterol	32 mg
Fat	7 g	Sodium	768 mg

Favorite recipe from **Western New York Apple Growers Association**

Chicken & Vegetable Medley

Makes 4 servings

　4 skinned boneless chicken breast halves
　　(about 1 pound)
　1 tablespoon vegetable oil
　½ cup water
　2 teaspoons WYLER'S® or STEERO® Chicken-Flavor Instant Bouillon *or* 2 Chicken-Flavor Bouillon Cubes
　½ teaspoon thyme leaves
　¼ teaspoon onion powder
　1 cup *each* thin strips carrots, red bell pepper, summer squash and zucchini

In large skillet, brown chicken in oil. Add water, bouillon, thyme, onion powder and carrots. Cover; simmer 10 minutes. Add remaining vegetables; cover and cook 5 to 10 minutes longer or until tender. Garnish as desired. Refrigerate leftovers.

Nutrients per serving:			
Calories	216	Cholesterol	80 mg
Fat	7 g	Sodium	513 mg

Chicken Rosemary

Makes 2 servings

　2 boneless skinless chicken breast halves
　　(½ pound)
　1 teaspoon margarine
　1 teaspoon olive oil
　　Salt and black pepper (optional)
　½ small onion, sliced
　1 large clove garlic, minced
　½ teaspoon dried rosemary, crumbled
　⅛ teaspoon ground cinnamon
　½ cup DOLE® Pine-Orange-Guava Juice
　1 tablespoon orange marmalade
　2 cups sliced DOLE® Carrots

Pound chicken to ½-inch thickness. In medium skillet, over medium heat, brown chicken on both sides in margarine and oil. Sprinkle with salt and pepper.

Stir in onion, garlic, rosemary and cinnamon. Cook and stir until onion is soft.

Blend in juice and marmalade. Spoon over chicken. Cover; bring to a boil. Reduce heat to low; simmer 10 minutes. Stir in carrots. Cover; simmer 5 minutes or until carrots are tender-crisp and chicken is tender. Serve with pasta, if desired, and garnish with rosemary sprig.

Prep time: 10 minutes
Cook time: 20 minutes

Nutrients per serving:			
Calories	241	Cholesterol	46 mg
Fat	6 g	Sodium	102 mg

Chicken Rosemary

Chunky Salsa Chicken Sandwiches

Makes 6 servings

2½ cups diced cooked chicken
  1 cup DANNON® Plain Nonfat or Lowfat Yogurt
  ¼ cup chunky salsa
  ½ teaspoon ground cumin
  ½ cup finely chopped red or green bell pepper
  ⅓ cup finely chopped fresh cilantro or parsley
  ⅓ cup finely chopped green onions
  3 (6-inch) pita bread rounds, cut in half
    Toppings: shredded lettuce, sliced ripe olives, chopped tomatoes and shredded Cheddar cheese

In a large bowl combine chicken, yogurt, salsa and cumin; stir gently. Stir in bell pepper, cilantro and green onions. Line each pita half with lettuce. Spoon chicken salad mixture evenly into pockets; sprinkle remaining toppings over chicken salad mixture. Serve immediately.

Note: If using nonfat yogurt, drain excess liquid by placing yogurt in a coffee filter for 5 minutes.

Nutrients per serving:			
Calories	300	Cholesterol	90 mg
Fat	7 g	Sodium	257 mg

Turkey Zanzibar

Makes 4 servings

  1 package (1 pound) PERDUE® Fit 'n Easy fresh skinless and boneless turkey breast tenderloins
  1 tablespoon vegetable oil
  1 teaspoon curry powder
  ½ teaspoon ground cumin
    Salt and ground black pepper to taste
  ½ small lemon or lime
    Mango chutney (optional)

In shallow dish, brush tenderloins on both sides with oil and rub with seasonings. Squeeze lemon over turkey; set aside. Prepare outdoor grill for cooking or preheat broiler. Grill or broil tenderloins 5 to 6 inches from heat source 5 to 8 minutes on each side until cooked through. Serve with mango chutney, if desired.

Prep time: 10 minutes
Cook time: 10 to 15 minutes

Nutrients per serving:			
Calories	161	Cholesterol	70 mg
Fat	4 g	Sodium	57 mg

Microwave Country Chicken and Creamy Gravy

Makes 6 servings

Chicken
  ½ teaspoon paprika
  ½ teaspoon poultry seasoning
  ¼ teaspoon dried thyme leaves
  ¼ teaspoon salt
  ¼ teaspoon pepper
  6 boneless, skinless chicken breast halves (about 1½ pounds)
1½ cups corn flakes, crushed to measure ½ cup

Gravy
  1 tablespoon CRISCO® Vegetable Oil
  1 tablespoon all-purpose flour
  ½ cup skim milk
  ¼ cup condensed chicken broth, undiluted
  2 tablespoons chopped fresh chives
  ¼ teaspoon salt
  ⅛ teaspoon pepper

1. For chicken, combine paprika, poultry seasoning, thyme, salt and pepper in small bowl. Place chicken in shallow dish. Sprinkle half of seasoning mixture over chicken. Turn chicken over. Sprinkle with remaining seasoning mixture. Coat with corn flakes.

2. Place in 11¾×7½×2-inch glass microwave-safe dish with thickest portions toward outside of dish. Cover with waxed paper. Microwave at HIGH for 8 minutes or until chicken is no longer pink in center, rotating dish one half turn after 4 minutes. Remove chicken to serving platter. Keep warm.

3. For gravy, combine Crisco® Oil and flour in 4-cup glass measure. Stir until smooth. Add milk and broth slowly. Stir until smooth. Microwave at HIGH for 3 to 5 minutes or until thickened, stirring every 2 minutes. Stir in chives, salt and pepper. Spoon over chicken.

Nutrients per serving:			
Calories	185	Cholesterol	65 mg
Fat	4 g	Sodium	385 mg

Chunky Salsa Chicken Sandwiches

Turkey Medallions Piccata

Makes 4 servings

**1 pound Turkey Tenderloins, cut into ¾-inch
medallions**
Salt and black pepper (optional)
1 teaspoon olive oil
1 teaspoon margarine
1 large clove garlic, crushed
1 tablespoon lemon juice
4 teaspoons drained capers

Lightly sprinkle one side of each medallion with salt
and pepper, if desired.

In large non-stick skillet, over medium-high heat,
heat oil and margarine. Add medallions and garlic;
cook turkey for approximately 1½ minutes per side,
turning each medallion over when edges have turned
from pink to white. Stir garlic occasionally and
continue cooking until medallions are no longer pink
in centers and register 170°F on meat thermometer.

Remove skillet from heat. Pour lemon juice over
turkey medallions and sprinkle with capers; serve
immediately.

Nutrients per serving:

Calories	150	Cholesterol	70 mg
Fat	4 g	Sodium	162 mg

Favorite recipe from **National Turkey Federation**

Turkey Medallions Piccata

Chicken Curry Bombay

Makes 4 servings

1 medium onion, cut into wedges
2 cloves garlic, minced
2 teaspoons curry powder
1 tablespoon olive oil
**2 boneless chicken breast halves, skinned and
sliced ¼-inch thick (about ½ pound)**
**1 can (14½ ounces) DEL MONTE® Original
Style Stewed Tomatoes**
⅓ cup DEL MONTE® Seedless Raisins
**1 can (16 ounces) DEL MONTE® Whole New
Potatoes, drained and cut into chunks**
**1 can (16 ounces) DEL MONTE® Blue Lake Cut
Green Beans, drained**

In large skillet, cook onion, garlic and curry in oil
over medium-high heat until onion is tender, stirring
occasionally. Stir in chicken, tomatoes with juice and
raisins; bring to a boil. Reduce heat to low. Cover and
simmer over medium heat 8 minutes. Add potatoes
and green beans. Cook, uncovered, 5 minutes,
stirring occasionally. Season to taste with salt and
pepper, if desired.

Prep time: 10 minutes
Cook time: 18 minutes

Nutrients per serving:

Calories	233	Cholesterol	34 mg
Fat	5 g	Sodium	643 mg

Turkey Vegetable Medley

Makes 4 servings

**4 fresh turkey breast slices *or* 4 skinned
boneless chicken breast halves (about
1 pound)**
1 tablespoon vegetable oil
½ cup water
**2 teaspoons WYLER'S® or STEERO® Chicken-
Flavor Instant Bouillon *or* 2 Chicken-
Flavor Bouillon Cubes**
½ teaspoon thyme leaves or tarragon
¼ teaspoon onion powder
1 cup thin carrot strips
1 cup *each* thin red and green bell pepper strips

In large skillet, brown turkey in oil. Add water,
bouillon, thyme, onion powder and carrots. Cover;
simmer 10 minutes. Add peppers; cover and cook
5 minutes longer or until tender. Refrigerate leftovers.

Nutrients per serving:

Calories	145	Cholesterol	30 mg
Fat	6 g	Sodium	501 mg

Sagebrush Turkey Steaks

Makes 4 servings

1 package (about 1 pound) LOUIS RICH®
    Fresh Turkey Breast Steaks

Marinade
  ½ cup dry white wine
  ¼ cup olive oil
  1 tablespoon finely chopped onion
  1 teaspoon dried parsley flakes
  ½ teaspoon dried sage
  ½ teaspoon salt
  ⅛ teaspoon black pepper

Pierce turkey steaks well with fork. Combine marinade ingredients in glass baking dish. Add turkey to marinade; cover. Refrigerate at least 1 hour or up to 24 hours. Broil, 5 inches from heat, or cook in covered grill 8 to 10 minutes or until juices run clear, turning turkey over halfway through cooking.

Prep time: 5 minutes
Cook time: 10 minutes

Nutrients per serving:			
Calories	200	Cholesterol	60 mg
Fat	9 g	Sodium	225 mg

Ginger Spicy Chicken

Sweet Sour Chicken Sauté

Makes 4 servings

1 can (8 ounces) pineapple chunks in juice
1 tablespoon cornstarch
⅓ cup HEINZ® Apple Cider Vinegar
¼ cup firmly packed brown sugar
⅛ teaspoon black pepper
1 small red bell pepper, cut into thin strips
1 small green bell pepper, cut into thin strips
1 medium onion, thinly sliced
1 pound skinless boneless chicken breasts, cut
    into ½-inch strips

Drain pineapple; reserve juice. Combine juice, cornstarch, vinegar, sugar and black pepper in small bowl; set aside. Spray large skillet with nonstick cooking spray. Cook and stir bell peppers and onion until tender-crisp; remove. Spray skillet again; cook and stir chicken 2 to 3 minutes or until chicken browns. Stir in reserved juice mixture; cook 2 to 3 minutes or until chicken is cooked and sauce boils and thickens. Add vegetables and pineapple; heat, stirring occasionally. Serve with rice if desired.

Nutrients per serving:			
Calories	235	Cholesterol	66 mg
Fat	2 g	Sodium	80 mg

Ginger Spicy Chicken

Makes 4 servings

  Salt
2 whole chicken breasts, split, skinned and
    boned (1 pound)
2 tablespoons vegetable oil
1 medium red bell pepper, cut into 2×¼-inch
    strips
1 medium green bell pepper, cut into 2×¼-inch
    strips
1 can (8 ounces) pineapple chunks in juice,
    undrained
½ cup PACE® Picante Sauce
2 tablespoons chopped cilantro *or* fresh parsley
2 to 3 teaspoons grated fresh ginger *or* ¾ to
    1 teaspoon ground ginger

Lightly salt chicken breasts. Heat oil in large skillet over medium heat. Add chicken; cook about 5 minutes on each side or until light brown and tender. Remove chicken; keep warm. Add pepper strips, pineapple with juice, Pace® Picante Sauce, cilantro and ginger to skillet. Cook, stirring frequently, 5 to 7 minutes or until peppers are tender and sauce is thickened. Return chicken to skillet and heat through.

Nutrients per serving:			
Calories	256	Cholesterol	73 mg
Fat	10 g	Sodium	284 mg

Top to bottom: *Fiesta Turkey Pie, Black Pepper Patty*

Fiesta Turkey Pie

Makes 6 to 8 servings

**1 package (about 1 pound) LOUIS RICH®
Fresh Ground Turkey**
1 cup salsa
**1 can (8 ounces) refrigerated crescent dinner
rolls**
¼ cup (1 ounce) shredded sharp Cheddar cheese

Preheat oven to 450°F. Cook turkey in nonstick
skillet over medium heat about 10 minutes or until
turkey is no longer pink, stirring to break turkey into
small pieces. Stir in salsa.

Press crescent roll dough onto bottom, up side and on
rim of 9-inch pie plate to form crust. Spread turkey
mixture evenly over crust; sprinkle with cheese. Bake
18 to 20 minutes or until crust is browned.

Nutrients per serving:			
Calories	196	Cholesterol	35 mg
Fat	10 g	Sodium	413 mg

Black Pepper Patties

Makes 4 servings

**1 package (about 1 pound) LOUIS RICH®
Fresh Ground Turkey**
1 teaspoon instant chicken bouillon
¼ teaspoon dried thyme leaves, crushed
1 teaspoon coarsely ground black pepper

Sauce
1 large tomato, chopped
½ cup plain nonfat yogurt
1 tablespoon chopped fresh parsley

Mix turkey, bouillon and thyme in large bowl. Shape
into four 4-inch patties. Sprinkle pepper on patties
(about ⅛ teaspoon per side), lightly pressing pepper
into turkey. Cook turkey in nonstick skillet over
medium heat about 12 minutes or until no longer
pink, turning occasionally.

Meanwhile, mix sauce ingredients in small bowl.
Serve cold sauce over turkey patties.

Nutrients per serving (1 patty):			
Calories	190	Cholesterol	75 mg
Fat	8 g	Sodium	315 mg

Summer Turkey and Vegetable Bake

Makes 8 servings

**1½ pounds zucchini squash, cut into ¼-inch-thick
slices**
1 pound Ground Turkey
1 cup chopped onion
2 cloves garlic, minced
1 cup uncooked instant rice
2½ teaspoons Italian seasoning, crushed, divided
1 teaspoon salt
½ teaspoon pepper
2 cups low-fat cottage cheese
**1 cup (4 ounces) shredded low-fat mozzarella
cheese**
2 tablespoons finely chopped fresh parsley
**2½ pounds tomatoes, peeled and cut into ½-inch
slices***
1 teaspoon sugar
3 tablespoons grated Parmesan cheese

To Microwave: Arrange zucchini in 13×9-inch
microwave-safe dish; cover with vented plastic wrap.
Microwave at HIGH (100% power) 8 minutes or until
tender, rotating dish halfway through cooking. Drain
zucchini slices on paper towels; cover with additional paper
towels to absorb all liquid.

In large nonstick skillet over medium-high heat, cook and
stir turkey, onion and garlic 5 to 6 minutes or until turkey
is no longer pink. Drain if necessary. Add rice, 2
teaspoons Italian seasoning, salt and pepper. In medium
bowl combine cottage cheese, mozzarella cheese and
parsley.

In bottom of same microwave-safe dish, layer half the
zucchini slices; top with turkey mixture, half the tomato
slices, ¼ teaspoon Italian seasoning, ½ teaspoon sugar
and cheese mixture. Layer remaining zucchini and tomato
slices over cheese; sprinkle with remaining ¼ teaspoon
Italian seasoning and ½ teaspoon sugar. Cover dish with
vented plastic wrap.

Microwave at HIGH (100% power) 5 minutes. Rotate dish
one-half turn. Microwave at MEDIUM (50% power)
10 minutes. Remove plastic wrap and sprinkle with
Parmesan cheese. Cover with foil and let stand 10 minutes.
Cut into 8 portions.

Note: *To peel a tomato, cut a skin-deep "X" in the
blossom end. Drop into boiling water and blanch for
15 seconds. Lift out with slotted spoon; drop into a bowl of
ice water. Skin will slip off easily.*

Nutrients per serving:			
Calories	260	Cholesterol	53 mg
Fat	8 g	Sodium	679 mg

Favorite recipe from **National Turkey Federation**

Oven-Crisped Chicken Breasts,
Scalloped Potatoes (page 376)

Oven-Crisped Chicken Breasts

Makes 8 servings

**8 boneless, skinless chicken breast halves
 (about 2 pounds)
2 egg whites
½ cup skim milk
½ cup all-purpose flour
1 tablespoon paprika
1 teaspoon dried basil leaves
½ teaspoon salt
¼ teaspoon pepper
1 cup plain dry bread crumbs
¼ cup CRISCO® Vegetable Oil**

1. Heat oven to 425°F.

2. Rinse and dry chicken.

3. Beat egg whites in large shallow dish until frothy.
Beat in milk.

4. Combine flour, paprika, basil, salt and pepper in
large plastic food storage bag. Place bread crumbs in
another large plastic food storage bag. Shake breast
halves, one or two at a time, in flour mixture, then dip
in egg white mixture. Shake in crumbs.

5. Pour Crisco® Oil evenly into 15¼×10¼×¾-inch
jelly roll pan or other shallow pan. Place in 425°F
oven for 3 or 4 minutes or until Crisco® Oil is hot,
but not smoking. Add chicken breasts in single layer.

6. Bake at 425°F for 10 minutes. Turn chicken over.
Sprinkle with any remaining crumb mixture. Bake for
5 minutes.

Nutrients per serving:			
Calories	240	Cholesterol	66 mg
Fat	8 g	Sodium	222 mg

Italian Parmesan Chicken

Makes 4 servings

**1 cup KELLOGG'S® SPECIAL K® cereal
2 tablespoons grated Parmesan cheese
1 tablespoon all-purpose flour
2 teaspoons Italian seasoning
⅓ cup reduced calorie Italian salad dressing
4 boned, skinned chicken breasts (about
 1 pound)
Vegetable cooking spray**

1. In a food processor or electric blender container,
process Kellogg's® Special K® cereal, Parmesan
cheese, flour and Italian seasoning until cereal
resembles fine crumbs. Place mixture in shallow
bowl; set aside.

2. Pour salad dressing into another shallow bowl. Dip
chicken in salad dressing. Coat with cereal mixture.
Place in single layer in shallow baking pan coated
with cooking spray.

3. Bake at 350°F about 30 minutes or until tender.
Do not cover or turn chicken while baking.

Nutrients per serving:			
Calories	230	Cholesterol	70 mg
Fat	6 g	Sodium	485 mg

Chicken Scandia

Makes 4 servings

**1 jar (12 ounces) HEINZ® HomeStyle Chicken
 Gravy
¼ cup dairy sour cream
2 teaspoons lemon juice
1 teaspoon dried dill weed
4 skinless, boneless chicken breast halves,
 grilled or sautéed
Hot cooked noodles (optional)**

In small saucepan, combine first 4 ingredients; heat
over low heat, stirring frequently, until smooth and
bubbly. For each serving, slice chicken diagonally
across grain into 4 slices. Serve on bed of noodles;
spoon gravy mixture over chicken. Garnish with
lemon wedges, if desired.

Nutrients per serving:			
Calories	213	Cholesterol	75 mg
Fat	8 g	Sodium	607 mg

Many Peppered Fillets

Makes 4 servings

1 package (1 pound) PERDUE® Fit 'n Easy
    fresh skinless and boneless turkey breast
    fillets
1 tablespoon olive oil
    Salt and ground black pepper to taste
2 cups sliced green bell peppers
1 cup sliced onion
2 cups hot cooked couscous or brown rice
    (optional)
1 tablespoon minced fresh parsley (optional)

Prepare outdoor grill for cooking or preheat broiler.
Rub fillets with oil and lightly season with salt and
pepper. Grill or broil fillets 5 to 6 inches from heat
source 3 minutes. Turn fillets over and cover with
peppers and onion. Grill or broil 5 to 6 minutes
longer until turkey is cooked through. Serve with
couscous tossed with parsley, if desired.

Nutrients per serving:

Calories	286	Cholesterol	70 mg
Fat	6 g	Sodium	83 mg

Broiled Lemon Chicken

Makes 4 servings

4 skinless, boneless chicken breast halves
    (about 1 pound)
¼ cup HEINZ® Worcestershire Sauce
2 tablespoons lemon juice
1 teaspoon minced garlic
½ teaspoon pepper
½ teaspoon grated lemon peel
    Vegetable oil

Lightly flatten chicken breasts to uniform thickness.
For marinade, combine Worcestershire sauce and
next 4 ingredients; pour over chicken. Cover;
marinate 30 minutes, turning once. Place chicken on
broiler pan; brush with oil. Broil, 4 to 5 inches from
heat source, 3 to 4 minutes; turn. Brush with
marinade, then with oil; broil an additional 3 to
4 minutes or until chicken is tender and no
longer pink.

Nutrients per serving:

Calories	142	Cholesterol	66 mg
Fat	3 g	Sodium	239 mg

Many Peppered Fillets

Chicken ala Vineyard

Makes 4 servings

2 cups imported Chilean red grape halves
4 skinless boneless chicken breast halves
  (about 1¼ pounds)
2 tablespoons all-purpose flour
½ teaspoon salt
½ teaspoon dried basil leaves, crushed
¼ teaspoon dried tarragon leaves, crushed
¼ teaspoon paprika
⅛ teaspoon white pepper
1 tablespoon olive or vegetable oil
2 cloves garlic, minced
¾ cup chicken broth
1 tablespoon white wine vinegar
1 teaspoon lemon juice
1 tablespoon finely chopped parsley

Rinse, drain and seed grape halves. Cut each chicken breast in half lengthwise. Combine flour, salt, basil, tarragon, paprika and pepper in shallow bowl; blend well. Add chicken strips and toss to coat, reserving excess flour mixture. Heat oil in skillet over medium-high heat until hot. Add chicken and cook until golden brown; turn and brown other sides. Add garlic and sprinkle with reserved flour mixture. Add broth, vinegar and lemon juice; cover and cook 5 minutes. Add grape halves and cook, uncovered, 5 minutes more or just until chicken is fork-tender. Remove chicken and grape halves to heated serving platter. Boil pan liquid 1 minute and pour over chicken. Sprinkle with parsley.

Nutrients per serving:

Calories	276	Cholesterol	77 mg
Fat	8 g	Sodium	84 mg

Favorite recipe from **Chilean Fresh Fruit Association**

Washington Apple Turkey Gyros

Makes 8 servings

1 tablespoon vegetable oil
1 cup onion slices
1 cup thin red bell pepper slices
1 cup thin bell pepper slices
½ pound cooked turkey breast, cut into thin strips
1 medium Washington Golden Delicious or Winesap apple, cored and thinly sliced
2 tablespoons lemon juice
8 pita pockets, lightly toasted
½ cup plain yogurt

Heat oil in nonstick skillet over medium-high heat until hot. Add onion and peppers; cook and stir until onion and peppers are crisp-tender. Stir in turkey; cook until turkey is thoroughly heated. Remove from heat; stir in apple and lemon juice. Halve pita pockets and fill halves evenly with apple mixture; drizzle with yogurt. Serve warm.

Nutrients per serving (2 pita halves):

Calories	195	Cholesterol	28 mg
Fat	3 g	Sodium	244 mg

Favorite recipe from **Washington Apple Commission**

Light Chicken Cordon Bleu

Makes 6 servings

½ cup seasoned dry bread crumbs
1 tablespoon grated Parmesan cheese
1 teaspoon chopped fresh parsley
½ teaspoon paprika
1 egg white
1 package (1¼ pounds) PERDUE® Fit 'n Easy fresh skinless and boneless Oven Stuffer Roaster thin-sliced breast
1 package (6 ounces) reduced-fat Swiss cheese slices
1 package (6 ounces) turkey ham slices

To Microwave: In shallow bowl, combine bread crumbs, Parmesan cheese, parsley and paprika. In another shallow bowl, beat egg white lightly; set aside. On each chicken breast slice, place 1 slice Swiss cheese and 2 overlapping slices ham; roll up, jelly-roll style, and secure with toothpick. Dip each roll in egg white and then in bread crumb mixture, coating sides.

In microwave-safe dish, arrange chicken rolls, seam sides down, in circular pattern. Cover with waxed paper; microwave at MEDIUM-HIGH (70% power) 5 minutes. Rearrange chicken rolls; cover with a double thickness of paper towels. Microwave at MEDIUM-HIGH 8 minutes. Let stand, uncovered, 5 to 10 minutes before serving.

Nutrients per serving:

Calories	269	Cholesterol	91 mg
Fat	8 g	Sodium	676 mg

Turkey Medallions with Marsala Mustard Sauce

Makes 4 servings

¼ cup all-purpose flour
¼ teaspoon salt
¼ teaspoon pepper
1 pound Turkey Tenderloins, cut into ¾-inch medallions
½ cup marsala wine
¼ cup reduced sodium chicken bouillon
2 teaspoons Dijon-style mustard
1 tablespoon olive oil
1 clove garlic, minced

Combine flour, salt and pepper in 9-inch pie plate. Coat turkey medallions with flour mixture. Combine 2 teaspoons flour mixture, wine, bouillon and mustard in small bowl; blend well.

Heat oil in large nonstick skillet over medium heat until hot. Add medallions. Cook 4 to 5 minutes per side or until turkey is no longer pink in center. Remove medallions from pan; keep warm.

Add garlic to same skillet; cook and stir until lightly browned. Add wine mixture; cook and stir 1 minute or until mixture thickens. To serve, pour sauce over medallions.

Nutrients per serving:			
Calories	236	Cholesterol	70 mg
Fat	4 g	Sodium	309 mg

Favorite recipe from **National Turkey Federation**

Chunky Sweet 'n' Sour Sauce

Makes 12 servings

1 tablespoon vegetable oil
1 clove garlic, minced
½ cup packed light brown sugar
⅓ cup cider vinegar
4 teaspoons low sodium soy sauce
1 tablespoon paprika
1 cup water
2 tablespoons cornstarch
1 cup diced fresh pineapple
1 cup peeled, seeded and chopped tomato
½ cup diced green pepper
½ cup diced onion

Heat oil in medium saucepan over medium heat until hot. Add garlic; cook and stir 1 minute. Add brown sugar, vinegar, soy sauce, paprika and water; stir until blended. Cook over medium heat 1 minute. In measuring cup, mix cornstarch with about 3 tablespoons sauce mixture. Gradually stir cornstarch mixture into sauce mixture. Add pineapple, tomato, green pepper and onion. Cook, uncovered, 5 to 7 minutes until sauce thickens and vegetables are crisp-tender. Serve hot over grilled chicken or poached fish fillets.

Nutrients per serving (⅓ cup sauce):			
Calories	66	Cholesterol	0 mg
Fat	1 g	Sodium	38 mg

Favorite recipe from **The Sugar Association, Inc.**

Peppered Turkey Medallions with Chutney Sauce

Makes 4 servings

½ to 1 tablespoon mixed peppercorns
1 pound Turkey Tenderloins, cut into ¾-inch medallions
1 teaspoon margarine
2 teaspoons olive oil, divided
2 tablespoons minced green onion
¼ cup reduced sodium chicken bouillon
2 tablespoons brandy
¼ cup chutney

Crush peppercorns in spice grinder, food processor or in mortar with pestle. Press peppercorns onto both sides of turkey medallions. Refrigerate 30 minutes.

Heat margarine and 1 teaspoon oil in large nonstick skillet over medium heat until hot. Add medallions; cook 4 to 5 minutes per side or until turkey is no longer pink in center. Remove medallions from pan; keep warm.

Heat remaining 1 teaspoon oil in same skillet over medium-high heat until hot; add onion. Cook and stir 30 seconds. Add bouillon and cook 45 seconds to reduce liquid. Stir in brandy and cook 1 to 2 minutes. Reduce heat to low; blend in chutney. To serve, pour chutney sauce over medallions.

Nutrients per serving:			
Calories	218	Cholesterol	70 mg
Fat	4 g	Sodium	142 mg

Favorite recipe from **National Turkey Federation**

Picante Chicken Skillet

Makes 4 servings

1 pound boneless skinless chicken or turkey breasts
1 tablespoon olive or vegetable oil
1 clove garlic, minced
1 can (14½ or 16 ounces) whole tomatoes, chopped, with juice
⅓ cup PACE® Picante Sauce
1 medium yellow or green bell pepper, cut into ¾-inch chunks
1 medium onion, cut into ¼-inch wedges
¾ teaspoon ground cumin
½ teaspoon salt (optional)
1 tablespoon cornstarch
1 tablespoon water
2 cups hot cooked rice
1 to 2 tablespoons chopped cilantro
Additional PACE® Picante Sauce (optional)

Cut chicken into 1½×½×½-inch strips. Sprinkle with salt and black pepper to taste, if desired. Heat oil in 10-inch skillet. Add chicken and garlic; cook and stir until chicken is almost cooked through, about 5 minutes. Combine tomatoes with juice, ⅓ cup Pace® Picante Sauce, bell pepper, onion, cumin and salt; mix well. Stir into skillet. Simmer 5 minutes, stirring occasionally. Dissolve cornstarch in water; stir into skillet. Simmer about 1 minute or until sauce is thickened, stirring constantly. Serve over rice with cilantro and additional Pace® Picante Sauce, if desired.

Nutrients per serving:			
Calories	298	Cholesterol	65 mg
Fat	5 g	Sodium	674 mg

Picante Chicken Skillet

Turkey Stuffed Green Peppers

Makes 4 servings

1 pound Ground Turkey
½ cup instant rice, uncooked
½ cup grated carrot
¼ cup chopped onion
3 tablespoons chopped fresh parsley
1 to 2 cloves minced garlic
½ teaspoon salt
½ teaspoon black pepper
1 can (12 ounces) tomato sauce, divided
4 small green bell peppers

To Microwave: In medium bowl, combine turkey, rice, carrot, onion, parsley, garlic, salt, black pepper and 1 cup tomato sauce. Mix well. Cut tops off green peppers. Remove and discard seeds and membranes. Spoon turkey mixture evenly into peppers. Place in 8-inch square baking dish. Cover with vented plastic wrap. Microwave at HIGH (100% power) 8 to 10 minutes, rotating halfway through cooking time, until peppers and rice are tender. Spoon remaining ½ cup tomato sauce over peppers. Microwave at HIGH (100% power) 1 minute. Let stand, covered, 3 minutes.

Nutrients per serving:			
Calories	265	Cholesterol	72 mg
Fat	10 g	Sodium	885 mg

Favorite recipe from **National Turkey Federation**

Barbecue Bacon Meatloaf

Makes 10 servings

2 packages (1 pound *each*) LOUIS RICH® Ground Turkey
12 slices LOUIS RICH® Turkey Bacon, diced
1 cup quick-cooking oats, uncooked
1 medium onion, finely chopped
½ cup barbecue sauce
2 large egg whites
1 tablespoon Worcestershire sauce

Mix all ingredients in large bowl. Press mixture into ungreased 9×5-inch loaf pan. Top with additional barbecue sauce, if desired. Bake at 375°F for 1 hour 15 minutes. Allow to stand 10 minutes before slicing.

Note: *Meatloaf ingredients may be combined a day ahead and refrigerated. Bake at 375°F for 1½ hours.*

Nutrients per serving:			
Calories	215	Cholesterol	70 mg
Fat	9 g	Sodium	525 mg

Herbed Chicken and Broccoli

Makes 4 servings

**10 ounces boneless skinless chicken breasts, cut
  into ½-inch strips**
1 teaspoon Italian seasoning
**1 cup *undiluted* CARNATION® Evaporated
  Skimmed Milk**
2 tablespoons all-purpose flour
1 clove garlic, crushed
¼ teaspoon salt (optional)
⅛ teaspoon white pepper
**½ cup (2 ounces) shredded reduced-fat Swiss
  cheese**
**1 package (10 ounces) frozen broccoli spears,
  thawed, drained and cut into bite-size pieces**
Paprika

Sprinkle chicken with Italian seasoning. Pound
between sheets of waxed paper. Remove paper. Spray
nonstick skillet with nonstick cooking spray. Cook and
stir chicken strips just until no longer pink. Set aside;
keep warm. In small saucepan, whisk *small amount*
of evaporated skimmed milk into flour. Stir in
remaining milk with garlic, salt and pepper. Cook
over medium heat, stirring constantly, until mixture
just comes to a boil and thickens. Add cheese; stir
until melted.

Spray 10×6×2-inch baking dish with nonstick
cooking spray. Spread about *¼ cup* sauce on bottom
of dish. Arrange broccoli over sauce, then chicken
pieces over broccoli. Pour *remaining* sauce over top.
Sprinkle with paprika. Cover. Bake in preheated
350°F oven for 20 to 25 minutes or until heated
through.

Nutrients per serving:			
Calories	197	Cholesterol	49 mg
Fat	3 g	Sodium	315 mg

Creamy Turkey Fajitas

Creamy Turkey Fajitas

Makes 6 servings

**⅓ cup *each* FRENCH'S® Creamy Spread™
  Mustard and light sour cream**
**½ teaspoon *each* garlic powder and ground
  cumin**
½ teaspoon dried oregano leaves, crushed
1 tablespoon corn oil
2 cups sliced red or yellow bell peppers
½ cup sliced red onion
2 cups (12 ounces) thin strips cooked turkey
6 (7-inch) flour tortillas

In small bowl, combine French's® Creamy Spread™
Mustard, sour cream, garlic powder, cumin and
oregano; set aside. Heat oil in large skillet; cook and
stir peppers and onion until tender. Stir in mustard
mixture and turkey. Cook over medium-low heat,
stirring, until heated through. Spoon about ½ cup
mixture into center of each tortilla; fold sides over.
Serve hot.

Nutrients per serving:			
Calories	176	Cholesterol	4 mg
Fat	8 g	Sodium	304 mg

Yogurt-Chicken Marinade

Makes 4 servings

½ cup low-sodium chicken broth
½ cup dry white wine
¾ cup sliced leeks
2 tablespoons lemon juice
½ teaspoon grated lemon peel
¼ teaspoon ground allspice
4 boneless skinless chicken breast halves (about 1 pound), trimmed of all visible fat
1 cup DANNON® Plain Nonfat or Lowfat Yogurt
1 tablespoon Dijon-style mustard
1 tablespoon snipped fresh parsley

In a large shallow dish combine chicken broth, wine, leeks, lemon juice, lemon peel and allspice; add chicken. Cover; chill several hours or overnight. Remove chicken from marinade and place on broiler pan; reserve marinade. Broil 4 to 6 inches from heat 8 to 12 minutes or until lightly brown. *Preheat oven to 350°F.* Place chicken in shallow baking pan; set aside. In a small saucepan bring reserved marinade to a boil; reduce heat and simmer, covered, 5 minutes. Cool 10 minutes. Whisk in yogurt, mustard and parsley. Spoon over chicken. Bake 15 minutes or until chicken is no longer pink in center.

Nutrients per serving:

Calories	260	Cholesterol	100 mg
Fat	5 g	Sodium	210 mg

Mustard Glazed Turkey Loaves

Makes 4 servings

1 cup KELLOGG'S® COMMON SENSE™ Oat Bran cereal, any variety
¼ cup chopped onion
1 egg white
½ teaspoon garlic salt
⅛ teaspoon pepper
¼ cup chopped water chestnuts
2 teaspoons prepared mustard
1 tablespoon prepared horseradish
1 pound ground turkey

Glaze
2 tablespoons prepared mustard
¼ cup firmly packed brown sugar
2 teaspoons tarragon white wine vinegar

1. Combine Kellogg's® Common Sense™ Oat Bran cereal, onion, egg white, garlic salt, pepper, water chestnuts, mustard and horseradish. Mix in turkey until well blended. Shape into 4 individual loaves. Place in foil-lined 13×9×2-inch baking pan.

2. Bake in 350°F oven 20 minutes. Combine all glaze ingredients. Remove loaves from oven and spread with glaze. Return to oven and bake 10 minutes longer. Garnish with parsley, if desired.

To Microwave: Prepare as directed. Place in microwave-safe shallow baking dish. Cook on MEDIUM-HIGH (70% power) 5 minutes. Rotate dish and continue cooking 3 minutes longer. Remove from oven and spread with glaze. Cook on MEDIUM-HIGH 2 minutes longer. Let stand 2 minutes before serving. Serve garnished with parsley, if desired.

Nutrients per serving:

Calories	290	Cholesterol	70 mg
Fat	4 g	Sodium	718 mg

Peppery Maple Grill

Makes 6 servings

1 package (1½ pounds) PERDUE® Fit 'n Easy fresh skinless and boneless pick of the chick
Salt to taste (optional)
2 teaspoons coarsely ground black pepper
12 cherry tomatoes
3 ears corn, husked and cut into 2-inch pieces
6 scallions, cut into 3-inch lengths
1 tablespoon vegetable oil
¼ to ½ cup maple syrup

Prepare outdoor grill for cooking or preheat broiler. Sprinkle chicken lightly with salt and press pepper into chicken. Cut chicken into 2-inch pieces. On each of 12 skewers, alternately thread light and dark chicken, tomatoes, corn and scallions; brush with oil. Grill or broil kabobs 6 to 8 inches from heat source 10 minutes. Baste with maple syrup; continue grilling or broiling about 15 minutes until chicken is cooked through, basting occasionally with syrup. Serve warm.

Nutrients per serving:

Calories	248	Cholesterol	80 mg
Fat	6 g	Sodium	97 mg

Yogurt-Chicken Marinade

Teriyaki Kabobs

Teriyaki Kabobs

Makes 4 servings

  2 whole chicken breasts, split, boned and
     skinned (about 1 pound)
 16 (2-inch) broccoli florets, cooked crisp-tender,
     or 1 large green bell pepper, cut into 1-inch
     squares
 16 large mushrooms, stems trimmed
  ½ cup PACE® Picante Sauce
  ¼ cup reduced-calorie Italian dressing
  2 tablespoons light soy sauce
 1½ teaspoons finely shredded fresh ginger
  ½ teaspoon sugar
  8 cherry tomatoes

Pound chicken to ½-inch thickness; cut lengthwise
into 1-inch-wide strips. Place chicken, broccoli and
mushrooms in large plastic food storage bag.
Combine Pace® Picante Sauce, Italian dressing, soy
sauce, ginger and sugar in small bowl; mix well. Add
Pace® Picante Sauce mixture to chicken mixture in
bag; press out air and fasten securely. Refrigerate
1 hour, turning bag frequently. Drain chicken and
vegetables, reserving marinade. Alternately thread
chicken accordion-style with broccoli and mushrooms
onto skewers. Heat reserved marinade to a boil. Place
kabobs on grill over hot coals or on rack of broiler
pan. Brush with marinade. Grill or broil 9 to
12 minutes or until chicken is cooked through,
turning and basting once with marinade. Add
tomatoes to skewers during last minute of cooking.

Nutrients per serving:

Calories	254	Cholesterol	67 mg
Fat	6 g	Sodium	850 mg

Chicken Breasts Florentine

Makes 6 servings

  6 boneless skinless chicken breast halves (about
     1½ pounds)
  1 package (10 ounces) frozen chopped spinach,
     thawed, squeezed dry
  1 jar (2½ ounces) sliced mushrooms, drained
  ½ cup chopped onion
  ½ cup (2 ounces) shredded low-fat mozzarella
     cheese
  ½ cup low-fat ricotta cheese
  ⅛ teaspoon black pepper
  1 jar (12 ounces) HEINZ® HomeStyle Chicken
     Gravy
  ½ teaspoon dried thyme leaves, crushed

Place chicken breasts in lightly greased 13×9-inch
baking pan. Combine spinach, mushrooms, onion,
cheeses and pepper in medium bowl. Spoon spinach
mixture on top of chicken breasts. Combine gravy and
thyme; spoon over spinach mixture and chicken.
Cover; bake in 375°F oven 40 to 45 minutes or until
chicken is no longer pink in center.

To Microwave: Place chicken breasts in 13×9-inch
microwave-safe baking dish. Combine spinach,
mushrooms, onion, cheeses and pepper in medium bowl.
Spoon spinach mixture on top of chicken breasts. Combine
gravy and thyme; spoon over spinach mixture and chicken.
Cover dish with waxed paper. Microwave at HIGH (100%)
18 to 20 minutes or until chicken is no longer pink in
center, rearranging halfway through cooking.

Nutrients per serving:

Calories	227	Cholesterol	77 mg
Fat	7 g	Sodium	573 mg

Orange Glazed Chicken

Makes 4 servings

  ¼ cup HEINZ® Chili Sauce
  ¼ cup orange marmalade
 1½ teaspoons prepared mustard
  4 boneless skinless chicken breast halves
     (about 1 pound)
  1 tablespoon margarine

For glaze, combine chili sauce, marmalade and
mustard in small bowl. Lightly flatten chicken breasts
to uniform thickness. In large skillet, melt margarine.
Add chicken; cook until brown on both sides. Pour
glaze over chicken. Simmer, uncovered, 8 minutes,
basting occasionally or until chicken is tender and no
longer pink in center.

Nutrients per serving:

Calories	219	Cholesterol	66 mg
Fat	4 g	Sodium	361 mg

Mesquite Grilled Turkey Tenderloins

Makes 8 servings

1 cup mesquite chips
2 pounds Turkey Breast Tenderloins
    Black pepper to taste
    Caribbean Salsa (recipe follows)

In small bowl cover mesquite chips with water; soak for 2 hours. Preheat charcoal grill for direct-heat cooking. Drain water from mesquite chips; add chips to hot coals. Sprinkle tenderloins with black pepper; grill 8 to 10 minutes on each side until tenderloins are no longer pink in centers and register 170°F on meat thermometer. Allow to stand 10 minutes before serving.

To serve, slice tenderloins into ½-inch medallions and arrange on serving plate. Top with Caribbean Salsa.

Caribbean Salsa

    2 cups (¼-inch) mango cubes
    ½ cup peeled, seeded (¼-inch) cucumber cubes
    ¼ cup chopped fresh cilantro or parsley
    2 tablespoons finely chopped green onion
    ½ jalapeño pepper, seeded and finely chopped
    3 tablespoons fresh lime juice
    1½ teaspoons firmly packed brown sugar
    1 teaspoon minced fresh ginger
        Dash black pepper

In medium bowl combine mango, cucumber, cilantro, green onion, jalapeño pepper, lime juice, brown sugar, ginger and black pepper. Cover and refrigerate at least 1 hour to allow flavors to blend.

Nutrients per serving:

Calories	163	Cholesterol	70 mg
Fat	2 g	Sodium	79 mg

Favorite recipe from **National Turkey Federation**

Mesquite Grilled Turkey Tenderloins

Chicken Corn Sauté

Chicken Corn Sauté

Makes 6 servings

1 tablespoon chili powder
½ teaspoon salt
4 boneless, skinless chicken breast halves, cut
    into bite-size pieces (about 1 pound)
2 tablespoons CRISCO® Vegetable Oil, divided
1 cup chopped onion
2 medium green bell peppers, cut into strips
1 medium red bell pepper, cut into strips
1 package (10 ounces) frozen whole kernel
    corn, thawed
Hot pepper sauce (optional)

1. Combine chili powder and salt in shallow dish.
Add chicken. Turn to coat.

2. Heat one tablespoon Crisco® Oil in large skillet on
medium-high heat. Add chicken. Cook and stir until
no longer pink in center. Remove to serving dish.

3. Heat remaining one tablespoon Crisco® Oil in
skillet. Add onion. Cook and stir 2 minutes or until
tender. Add bell peppers. Cook and stir 3 to
4 minutes or until crisp-tender. Add corn. Heat
thoroughly, stirring occasionally. Return chicken to
skillet to reheat. Season with hot pepper sauce (if
used).

Nutrients per serving:

Calories	190	Cholesterol	45 mg
Fat	6 g	Sodium	245 mg

Chicken Breast with Orange-Basil Pesto

Makes 6 servings

½ cup fresh basil leaves
2 tablespoons grated orange rind
2 cloves garlic, peeled
3 tablespoons Florida orange juice
1 tablespoon Dijon-style mustard
2 teaspoons olive oil
    Salt and pepper to taste (optional)
3 whole chicken breasts,* halved (about
    3 pounds)

Preheat broiler. Place basil, orange rind and garlic in
food processor and process until finely chopped. Add
orange juice, mustard, olive oil, salt and pepper;
process a few seconds or until paste is formed.

Spread an equal amount of basil mixture under skin
and on bone side of each chicken breast. Place
chicken, skin sides down, on broiler pan. Place
4 inches from heat source. Broil 10 minutes. Turn
chicken over and broil 10 to 12 minutes more until
chicken is no longer pink and juices run clear when
chicken is pierced with fork. If chicken browns too
quickly, cover with foil. Remove skin from chicken
before serving.

*Tip: To prepare ahead, make basil mixture and marinate
chicken in mixture overnight in refrigerator. Cook just before
serving.*

*Note: Leaving skin on while cooking keeps the chicken
moist. Recent research shows fat does not permeate the
meat. Simply remove the skin before eating and the pesto
coating will remain for a delicious, low fat dish. Total time
from kitchen to table is only 30 minutes.*

*Do not use skinless, boneless chicken breast halves.

Nutrients per serving:

Calories	164	Cholesterol	73 mg
Fat	5 g	Sodium	98 mg

Favorite recipe from **Florida Department of Citrus**

Chicken and Two-Pepper Stir-Fry

Makes 3 to 4 servings

1 package (1 pound) PERDUE® Fit 'n Easy
    fresh skinless and boneless chicken breast
    tenders
2 tablespoons vegetable oil
2 red or yellow bell peppers, seeded and cut
    into thin strips
4 scallions, thinly sliced
⅓ cup reduced sodium stir-fry sauce with garlic
    and ginger
2 tablespoons water
    Salt and ground red pepper to taste (optional)

With sharp knife, cut tenders in half lengthwise, then
crosswise. In wok or large nonstick skillet over
medium-high heat, heat oil. Add chicken, bell
peppers and scallions. Stir-fry 2 to 3 minutes until
chicken is cooked through and lightly browned. Stir in
sauce and water; stir-fry until well combined. Season
with salt and ground red pepper. Serve warm.

Prep time: 10 minutes
Cook time: 5 minutes

Nutrients per serving:

Calories	209	Cholesterol	66 mg
Fat	8 g	Sodium	425 mg

Chicken Parmesan

Makes 4 servings

4 half boneless chicken breasts, skinned
    (about 1 pound)
2 cans (14½ ounces each) DEL MONTE®
    Italian Style Stewed Tomatoes
2 tablespoons cornstarch
½ teaspoon dried oregano or basil leaves,
    crushed
¼ teaspoon hot pepper sauce (optional)
¼ cup grated Parmesan cheese
    Chopped fresh parsley, for garnish

Preheat oven to 425°F. Slightly flatten each chicken breast; place in 11×7-inch baking dish. Cover with foil; bake 20 minutes or until chicken is no longer pink. Remove foil; drain. Meanwhile, in large saucepan, combine tomatoes with juice, cornstarch, oregano and pepper sauce. Stir until cornstarch dissolves. Cook, stirring constantly, until mixture boils and thickens. Pour over chicken; top with cheese. Return to oven; bake, uncovered, 5 minutes or until cheese is melted. Garnish with chopped parsley. Serve with hot cooked rice or pasta, if desired.

Prep & Cook time: 30 minutes

Nutrients per serving:			
Calories	228	Cholesterol	73 mg
Fat	4 g	Sodium	716 mg

Chicken Parmesan

Turkey with Orange Sauce

Makes 4 servings

2 Turkey Thighs or Turkey Drumsticks (2 to
    3 pounds)*
½ teaspoon paprika
1 medium onion, sliced
½ cup thawed orange juice concentrate,
    undiluted
⅓ cup water
2 tablespoons firmly packed brown sugar
2 tablespoons chopped fresh parsley
2 teaspoons soy sauce
½ teaspoon ground ginger

Rinse turkey and pat dry; place on rack of broiler pan. (If using only thighs, remove skin.) Broil, 4 inches from heat source, until turkey is brown. Remove to Dutch oven or roasting pan and sprinkle with paprika. Arrange onion slices over turkey. In small bowl, combine juice concentrate, water, brown sugar, parsley, soy sauce and ginger. Pour over turkey and onions.

Cover and bake approximately 1 hour in preheated 400°F oven until turkey is tender, basting once or twice. Slice turkey; coat with sauce and garnish with orange twists. Serve with rice or pasta.

*Thighs may be boned before cooking.

Nutrients per serving:			
Calories	152	Cholesterol	56 mg
Fat	5 g	Sodium	210 mg

Favorite recipe from **National Turkey Federation**

Mini Turkey Loaves

Makes 4 servings

1 pound ground turkey
1 small apple, chopped
½ small onion, chopped
½ cup uncooked rolled oats
2 teaspoons Dijon-style mustard
1 teaspoon dried rosemary leaves, crushed
1 teaspoon salt
    Dash black pepper

Preheat oven to 425°F. Grease 12 medium muffin cups. Combine all ingredients in large bowl. Press evenly into prepared muffin cups.

Bake 20 minutes or until lightly browned and no longer pink in center. Serve with cranberry sauce and garnish, if desired.

Nutrients per serving:			
Calories	210	Cholesterol	42 mg
Fat	9 g	Sodium	619 mg

Baked Tomatoes Florentine

Makes 4 servings

1 cup sliced fresh mushrooms (optional)
1 tablespoon finely chopped onion
¼ cup water
1 cup BORDEN® Lite-line® or Viva® Protein Fortified Skim Milk
3 tablespoons flour
2 teaspoons WYLER'S® or STEERO® Chicken-Flavor Instant Bouillon
6 slices BORDEN® Lite-line® Process Cheese Product,* any flavor, cut into small pieces
2 cups cubed cooked chicken (breast meat)
1 (10-ounce) package frozen chopped spinach or broccoli, thawed and well drained
4 large tomatoes, tops cut off and insides scooped out

Preheat oven to 350°F. In small saucepan, cook mushrooms, if desired, and onion in water until tender; drain. In another small saucepan, combine milk, flour and bouillon; over low heat, cook and stir until thickened. Add cheese product pieces; cook and stir until melted. In medium bowl, combine mushroom mixture, chicken, spinach and ¾ cup sauce; stuff tomatoes. Arrange in baking dish; cover and bake 15 to 20 minutes or until hot. Over low heat, heat remaining sauce with 1 to 2 tablespoons water. Spoon over tomatoes before serving. Garnish as desired. Refrigerate leftovers.

"½ the calories"– 8% milkfat product

Nutrients per serving:			
Calories	290	Cholesterol	71 mg
Fat	6 g	Sodium	1053 mg

Dad's Favorite Turkey Kabobs

Dad's Favorite Turkey Kabobs

Makes 4 servings, 8 kabobs

3 ears corn, cut into 1-inch pieces
2 medium zucchini, cut into ¾-inch pieces
2 red bell peppers, cut into 1-inch cubes
2 Turkey Tenderloins (about 1 pound), cut into 1-inch cubes
⅓ cup reduced-calorie Italian salad dressing
Additional reduced-calorie Italian salad dressing

In medium saucepan over high heat, blanch corn in boiling water about 1 to 2 minutes. Remove corn from saucepan and plunge into cold water.

In large glass bowl, place corn, zucchini, peppers, turkey and ⅓ cup dressing; cover and refrigerate 1 to 2 hours.

Drain turkey and vegetables, discarding marinade. Alternately thread turkey cubes and vegetables on skewers, leaving ½-inch space between turkey and vegetables.

On outdoor charcoal grill, cook kabobs 18 to 20 minutes or until turkey is tender, brushing with additional dressing. Turn skewers after first 10 minutes of grilling.

Nutrients per serving (2 kabobs):			
Calories	218	Cholesterol	70 mg
Fat	4 g	Sodium	381 mg

Favorite recipe from **National Turkey Federation**

Best Bartlett Bake

Makes 4 servings

½ cup dry white wine
2 tablespoons Dijon-style mustard
  Pinch ground red pepper
2 whole chicken breasts, skinned, boned and
    cut into halves
  Black pepper
  All-purpose flour
1 tablespoon vegetable oil
½ cup finely chopped onion
2 fresh California Bartlett pears, cored and cut
    into eighths

To Microwave: Preheat microwave browning dish in microwave on HIGH (100% power) 7 minutes or according to manufacturer's directions. Meanwhile, combine wine, mustard and red pepper; set aside. Season chicken with black pepper. Lightly coat chicken with flour; set aside. Drizzle oil over preheated dish; add chicken, smooth sides down. Sprinkle onion around chicken and microwave on HIGH 4 minutes. Turn chicken and pour wine mixture over chicken and onion. Cover and microwave on MEDIUM-HIGH (70% power) 6 minutes. Add pears; cover and microwave on HIGH about 1½ minutes or until chicken and pears are tender. Serve immediately.

Nutrients per serving:

Calories	250	Cholesterol	70 mg
Fat	7 g	Sodium	165 mg

Favorite recipe from **California Tree Fruit Agreement**

White Turkey and Wild Rice Chili

Makes 8 servings

1 tablespoon canola oil
1 medium onion, chopped
1 clove garlic, minced
1¼ pounds turkey breast slices, cut in ½-inch
    pieces
2 cups cooked wild rice
1 can (15 ounces) great Northern white beans,
    drained
1 can (11 ounces) white corn (optional)
2 cans (4 ounces) diced green chilies
1 can (14½ ounces) low sodium chicken broth
1 teaspoon ground cumin
  Hot pepper sauce (optional)
4 ounces low fat Monterey Jack Cheese,
    shredded
  Parsley (optional)

Heat oil in large skillet over medium heat; add onion and garlic. Cook and stir until onion is tender. Add turkey, wild rice, beans, corn, chilies, broth and cumin. Cover and simmer over low heat 30 minutes or until turkey is tender. Stir in hot pepper sauce to taste. Serve with shredded cheese. Garnish with parsley, if desired.

Nutrients per serving:

Calories	274	Cholesterol	69 mg
Fat	6 g	Sodium	102 mg

Favorite recipe from **Minnesota Cultivated Wild Rice Council**

Peruvian Chicken with Plums

Makes 8 servings

1 teaspoon vegetable oil
1 chicken (3½ pounds), skinned and cut up
1 cup chopped onion
1 cup diced green bell pepper
2 teaspoons minced garlic
1 tomato, chopped
1 fresh jalapeño chili,* seeded and diced
¼ teaspoon powdered saffron (optional)
3½ cups low sodium chicken broth
1 bay leaf
4 fresh California plums, quartered
4 cups cooked brown rice

Heat oil in large nonstick skillet until hot; add chicken pieces. Cook about 12 minutes or until golden brown on all sides, turning often. Add onion, bell pepper and garlic; cook and stir 2 minutes more. Add tomato, chili, saffron, broth and bay leaf. Bring to a boil; cover and simmer 10 minutes. Stir in plums and rice; heat through. Remove and discard bay leaf. Serve with extra plum wedges, if desired.

**Chilies can sting and irritate the skin; wear plastic disposable gloves when handling chilies and do not touch eyes. Wash hands after handling chilies.*

Nutrients per serving:

Calories	266	Cholesterol	51 mg
Fat	6 g	Sodium	54 mg

Favorite recipe from **California Tree Fruit Agreement**

Gypsy Cutlets

Makes 4 servings

1 package (1 pound) PERDUE® Fit 'n Easy
    fresh skinless and boneless thin-sliced
    turkey breast cutlets
2 teaspoons sweet paprika
    Salt and ground black pepper to taste
    (optional)
1½ tablespoons vegetable oil
½ cup thinly sliced onion
1 can (14½ ounces) Cajun or Mexican-style
    stewed tomatoes, undrained
¼ cup sour cream substitute or light sour cream

Season cutlets on both sides with paprika, salt and pepper. In large nonstick skillet over medium-high heat, heat oil. Add cutlets and brown 1 minute on each side. Remove and set aside. To same skillet, add onion; cook and stir 1 minute or until slightly softened. Add tomatoes, including liquid; cook 5 minutes or until sauce thickens, stirring often. Stir in sour cream substitute until well mixed; reduce heat to medium-low. Return cutlets and any juices to skillet; simmer 1 to 2 minutes until turkey is just cooked through. To serve, spoon sauce over turkey.

Prep time: 10 minutes
Cook time: 10 to 15 minutes

Nutrients per serving:			
Calories	207	Cholesterol	70 mg
Fat	6 g	Sodium	479 mg

Chicken Pitas with Cucumber Relish

Makes 4 servings

¼ cup HEINZ® Apple Cider Vinegar
2 teaspoons brown sugar
½ teaspoon salt
¼ teaspoon crushed red pepper
1 small cucumber, thinly sliced
¼ cup plain yogurt
4 skinless, boneless chicken breast halves
    (about 1 pound), cut into strips
1 tablespoon vegetable oil
    Salt and black pepper (optional)
    Leaf lettuce
    Sliced tomatoes
4 (6- to 7-inch diameter) fat-free pocket pita
    breads, halved

Combine vinegar, sugar, salt and red pepper. Pour over cucumber; let stand 30 minutes. Drain well; stir cucumber into yogurt. Meanwhile, cook and stir chicken in hot oil just until cooked, about 2 to 3 minutes. Season chicken with salt and black pepper. Place lettuce and tomato in pita halves. Divide chicken among pitas; top with cucumber mixture.

Nutrients per serving (2 pita halves):			
Calories	275	Cholesterol	69 mg
Fat	5 g	Sodium	361 mg

Celeried Chicken Breasts with Mustard and Dill

Makes 4 servings

1 can (13¾ ounces) ready-to-serve chicken
    broth, divided
1½ tablespoons cornstarch
2 teaspoons dried dill weed
2 teaspoons Dijon-style mustard
⅛ teaspoon pepper
1 pound boned and skinned chicken breast
    cutlets
3 cups ½-inch celery slices
1 cup sliced onion

Measure ¼ cup chicken broth; set aside. Combine remaining chicken broth, cornstarch, dill, mustard and pepper in small bowl; set aside. Heat large nonstick skillet over medium-high heat until hot. Add chicken; cook each side 2 to 3 minutes until browned. Reduce heat to medium; add reserved chicken broth. Cover and simmer about 8 minutes or until chicken is no longer pink, turning occasionally. Remove to serving platter; cover with foil to keep warm. Add celery and onion to same skillet; cook and stir about 6 minutes or until crisp-tender. Stir in reserved cornstarch mixture; cook and stir until mixture comes to a boil and thickens. Cook and stir 1 minute more. Spoon over chicken; serve immediately.

Nutrients per serving:			
Calories	182	Cholesterol	66 mg
Fat	3 g	Sodium	661 mg

Favorite recipe from **American Celery Council**

Herb Marinated Chicken Breasts

Herb Marinated Chicken Breasts

Makes 6 servings

¾ cup **MIRACLE WHIP®** Salad Dressing
¼ cup dry white wine
2 garlic cloves, minced
2 tablespoons finely chopped green onion
2 teaspoons dried basil leaves, crushed
1 teaspoon dried thyme leaves, crushed
6 boneless skinless chicken breast halves (about 1¾ pounds)

Stir together salad dressing, wine and seasonings. Pour dressing mixture over chicken. Cover; refrigerate several hours or overnight. Drain, reserving dressing mixture. Place chicken on greased rack of broiler pan. Broil 4 to 6 minutes on each side or until tender, brushing frequently with dressing mixture.

Prep time: 15 minutes plus refrigerating
Cook time: 12 minutes

Nutrients per serving:

Calories	170	Cholesterol	55 mg
Fat	7 g	Sodium	110 mg

Chicken with Cherries

Makes 6 servings

1 package (1½ pounds) **PERDUE®** Fit 'n Easy fresh skinless and boneless Oven Stuffer Roaster breasts
  Salt and ground black pepper to taste (optional)
2 teaspoons vegetable oil
2 cups canned pitted tart cherries, undrained, divided
2 teaspoons cornstarch
1 tablespoon Worcestershire sauce
1 tablespoon dry sherry
1 teaspoon firmly packed brown sugar
1 small clove garlic, peeled
½ cup finely chopped onion
¼ cup raisins
1 tablespoon minced fresh parsley
2 cups hot cooked wild rice

Preheat oven to 350°F. Sprinkle chicken lightly with salt and generously with pepper. In nonstick skillet over medium-high heat, heat oil. Add chicken and cook 6 to 8 minutes until lightly browned on both sides. Remove chicken to baking dish; set aside. Drain cherries, reserving ¼ cup juice. Add cherry juice to skillet; stir in cornstarch.

In food processor or blender container, combine 1 cup cherries, Worcestershire sauce, sherry, sugar and garlic. Process or blend until smooth; add to skillet. Stir in remaining cherries, onion and raisins; cook over medium-high heat 2 to 3 minutes until sauce boils and thickens, stirring constantly. Spoon sauce over chicken; bake 25 to 35 minutes until chicken is cooked through. To serve, sprinkle chicken with parsley. Serve with rice.

Nutrients per serving:

Calories	290	Cholesterol	66 mg
Fat	3 g	Sodium	111 mg

Chicken Paprikash

Makes 4 servings

1 package (1¼ pounds) PERDUE® Fit 'n Easy
  fresh Oven Stuffer Roaster skinless and
  boneless thighs
Salt and ground black pepper to taste
1½ tablespoons light margarine (stick form)
1 cup chopped onion
1 tablespoon all-purpose flour
1 tablespoon paprika
1 tablespoon chopped fresh dill *or* 1 teaspoon
  dried dill weed
1 can (13¾ ounces) reduced sodium chicken
  broth
3 tablespoons sour cream alternative
Hot cooked noodles (optional)

Season chicken lightly with salt and pepper. In large
nonstick skillet over medium-high heat, melt
margarine. Add chicken; cook about 5 minutes on
each side or until browned, turning once. Remove
chicken and set aside.

Stir onion into skillet; sprinkle flour, paprika and dill
evenly on top. Cook and stir 2 to 3 minutes; stir in
broth. Return chicken to skillet; reduce heat to
medium. Cook, uncovered, 15 to 20 minutes until
chicken is cooked through and juices are slightly
reduced. Remove from heat and stir in sour cream
alternative until well blended. Season with salt and
pepper to taste. Serve over noodles.

Tip: *Sour cream alternative reduces the calories and fat in
this world-famous Hungarian dish.*

Nutrients per serving:			
Calories	245	Cholesterol	118 mg
Fat	10 g	Sodium	490 mg

Brown Rice Chicken Bake

Makes 6 servings

3 cups cooked brown rice
1 package (10 ounces) frozen green peas
2 cups cooked chicken breast cubes
½ cup cholesterol-free, reduced-calorie
  mayonnaise
⅓ cup slivered almonds, toasted (optional)
2 teaspoons soy sauce
¼ teaspoon ground black pepper
¼ teaspoon garlic powder
¼ teaspoon dried tarragon leaves, crushed
Nonstick cooking spray

Combine rice, peas, chicken, mayonnaise, almonds,
soy sauce, and seasonings in large bowl. Transfer to
3-quart baking dish coated with nonstick cooking
spray. Cover and bake at 350°F for 15 to 20 minutes.

Nutrients per serving:			
Calories	270	Cholesterol	44 mg
Fat	7 g	Sodium	272 mg

Favorite recipe from **USA Rice Council**

Turkey Sloppy Joes

Makes 8 servings

1 pound Ground Turkey
1 cup thinly sliced onion
½ cup chopped green bell pepper
1 cup low-calorie, low-sodium ketchup
¼ cup sweet pickle relish
1½ teaspoons chili powder
1 teaspoon Worcestershire sauce
½ teaspoon seasoned salt
½ teaspoon garlic powder
¼ teaspoon celery seed
8 hard rolls (about 1 pound)

In large skillet over medium-high heat, cook and stir
turkey, onion and bell pepper 5 minutes or until
turkey is no longer pink. Drain if necessary. Add
ketchup, relish, chili powder, Worcestershire sauce,
seasoned salt, garlic powder and celery seed. Bring to
a boil. Reduce heat to low; cover and simmer
30 minutes.

Slice rolls in half and toast under broiler 1 to 2
minutes or until lightly browned.

To serve, spoon turkey mixture onto bottom halves of
rolls. Place top halves of rolls over turkey mixture.

Nutrients per serving:			
Calories	294	Cholesterol	40 mg
Fat	8 g	Sodium	745 mg

Favorite recipe from **National Turkey Federation**

Turkey Sloppy Joe

Citrus Chicken

Makes 4 servings

1 tablespoon vegetable oil
4 boneless skinless chicken breast halves
    (about 1 pound)
1 cup orange juice
4 teaspoons sugar
1 clove garlic, minced
1 teaspoon dried rosemary leaves, crushed
2 teaspoons cornstarch
¼ cup dry white wine
    Salt and black pepper (optional)
2 pink grapefruits, sectioned and peeled

Heat oil in large skillet over medium heat. Add chicken; cook 8 minutes or until browned on both sides and no longer pink in center, turning after 4 minutes. Remove chicken from skillet; keep warm.

Add orange juice, sugar, garlic and rosemary to skillet; bring to a boil.

Combine cornstarch and wine. Add to skillet; cook, stirring constantly, until sauce boils and thickens. Season with salt and pepper, if desired.

Add grapefruit; heat thoroughly, stirring occasionally. Serve over chicken.

Nutrients per serving:

Calories	216	Cholesterol	46 mg
Fat	6 g	Sodium	49 mg

Savory Apple Topped Turkey Medallions

Makes 4 servings

1 pound Turkey Tenderloins, cut into ¾-inch
    medallions
    Salt and pepper (optional)
1 teaspoon olive oil
1 teaspoon margarine
1 large clove garlic, crushed
⅔ cup peeled, diced apples
⅓ cup orange juice
3 tablespoons jellied cranberry sauce
4 teaspoons orange marmalade

Lightly sprinkle one side of each medallion with salt and pepper, if desired.

In large nonstick skillet over medium-high heat, heat oil and margarine. Add medallions and garlic; cook turkey approximately 1½ minutes per side, turning each medallion over when edges have turned from pink to white. Stir garlic occasionally and continue cooking until medallions are no longer pink in centers and register 170°F on meat thermometer. Remove from skillet.

In same skillet over medium heat, combine apples, orange juice, cranberry sauce and marmalade. Cook and stir until sauce is hot and apples are tender but hold their shape. Spoon sauce over medallions.

Nutrients per serving:

Calories	206	Cholesterol	70 mg
Fat	4 g	Sodium	92 mg

Favorite recipe from **National Turkey Federation**

Chicken Curry

Makes 4 servings

½ cup all-purpose flour
¼ teaspoon black pepper
2 whole chicken breasts, split, skinned and
    boned
3 tablespoons FILIPPO BERIO® Extra-Virgin
    Olive Oil
1 cup chopped onion
½ cup chopped green bell pepper
1 clove garlic, chopped
1½ teaspoons curry powder
½ teaspoon dried thyme leaves, crushed
2 cups diced fresh or canned tomatoes
    Hot cooked rice (optional)

Preheat oven to 350°F. Combine flour and pepper; sprinkle over both sides of chicken breasts.

Heat olive oil in large skillet over medium heat. Cook chicken 15 minutes or until lightly browned on both sides. Remove from skillet; place in large ovenproof casserole.

In same skillet, cook and stir onion, green pepper, garlic, curry powder and thyme 5 minutes or until onions are lightly browned. Add tomatoes. Stir until heated through.

Pour tomato mixture over chicken in casserole. Bake, uncovered, for 30 minutes or until chicken is tender. Serve over hot cooked rice, if desired.

Nutrients per serving:

Calories	294	Cholesterol	94 mg
Fat	7 g	Sodium	47 mg

Left to right: Poppy Seed Noodles (page 349), Citrus Chicken

Chicken Biscuit Bake

Makes 8 servings

Base

 1 tablespoon CRISCO® Vegetable Oil
 1 cup chopped onion
 ¼ cup all-purpose flour
 ½ teaspoon salt
 ¼ teaspoon pepper
 ¼ teaspoon dried basil leaves
 ¼ teaspoon dried thyme leaves
2½ cups skim milk
 1 tablespoon Worcestershire sauce
 1 chicken flavor bouillon cube *or* 1 teaspoon
     chicken flavor bouillon granules
 2 cups chopped cooked chicken
 1 bag (16 ounces) frozen mixed vegetables
 2 tablespoons grated Parmesan cheese

Biscuits

 1 cup all-purpose flour
 1 tablespoon sugar
1½ teaspoons baking powder
 1 tablespoon chopped fresh parsley
 ⅛ teaspoon salt
 ⅓ cup skim milk
 3 tablespoons CRISCO® Vegetable Oil

1. Heat oven to 375°F.

2. For base, heat Crisco® Oil in large saucepan on medium-high heat. Add onion. Cook and stir until tender. Remove from heat. Stir in flour, salt, pepper, basil and thyme. Add milk, Worcestershire sauce and bouillon cube. Return to medium-high heat. Cook and stir until mixture comes to a boil and is thickened. Stir in chicken, vegetables and cheese. Heat thoroughly, stirring occasionally. Pour into 2-quart casserole.

Chicken Biscuit Bake

3. For biscuits, combine flour, sugar, baking powder, parsley and salt in medium bowl. Add milk and Crisco® Oil. Stir with fork until dry ingredients are just moistened. Drop dough by well-rounded measuring tablespoonfuls onto hot chicken mixture to form 8 biscuits.

4. Bake at 375°F for 35 to 45 minutes or until chicken mixture is bubbly and biscuits are golden brown.

Nutrients per serving:

Calories	280	Cholesterol	30 mg
Fat	9 g	Sodium	485 mg

Crunchy Apple Salsa with Grilled Chicken

Makes 4 servings, 3 cups salsa

 2 cups Washington Gala apples, halved, cored
     and chopped
 ¾ cup (1 large) Anaheim chili pepper, seeded
     and chopped
 ½ cup chopped onion
 ¼ cup lime juice
     Salt and pepper to taste (optional)
     Grilled Chicken (recipe follows)

Combine all ingredients except Grilled Chicken and mix well; allow flavors to blend about 30 minutes. Serve with Grilled Chicken.

Grilled Chicken: Combine ¼ cup *each* dry white wine and apple juice, ½ teaspoon grated lime peel, ½ teaspoon salt and dash pepper in large plastic storage bag; mix well. Add 4 whole boneless, skinless chicken breast halves; marinate 20 to 30 minutes. Drain and grill over medium-hot coals until chicken is no longer pink, turning once.

Note: *Fish or lean pork chops may be substituted for chicken.*

Nutrients per serving:

Calories	214	Cholesterol	66 mg
Fat	4 g	Sodium	334 mg

Favorite recipe from **Washington Apple Commission**

Turkey Pistachio Sandwich

Makes 4 servings

 ½ cup plain yogurt
 ¼ cup salted pistachio nuts, chopped
 1 teaspoon dried dill weed
 4 lettuce leaves
 8 slices whole wheat bread
 8 ounces Cooked Turkey Breast, sliced

Combine yogurt, nuts and dill in small bowl. Cover and refrigerate at least 1 hour or overnight to allow flavors to blend.

To serve, place 1 lettuce leaf on 1 bread slice; top lettuce with 2 ounces turkey. Spoon 2 tablespoons yogurt mixture over turkey and top with another bread slice. Repeat with remaining ingredients. (Leftover yogurt mixture will keep up to 4 days in refrigerator.)

Nutrients per serving (1 sandwich):

Calories	265	Cholesterol	42 mg
Fat	7 g	Sodium	303 mg

Favorite recipe from **National Turkey Federation**

Italian Turkey Cutlets

Makes 4 servings

 1 can (8 ounces) tomato sauce
 1 tablespoon CRISCO® Vegetable Oil
 1½ teaspoons dried oregano leaves
 1 tablespoon dried parsley flakes
 1 teaspoon dried thyme leaves
 ½ teaspoon salt
 1 clove garlic, minced *or* ½ teaspoon garlic powder
 ¼ teaspoon crushed red pepper
 1 pound turkey breast cutlets

1. Combine tomato sauce, Crisco® Oil, oregano, parsley, thyme, salt, garlic and crushed red pepper in small bowl.

2. Spread one tablespoon sauce over each cutlet. Roll up. Place, seam side down, in 8-inch square baking dish. Spoon remaining sauce over cutlets. Refrigerate at least 30 minutes.

3. Heat oven to 350°F.

4. Bake at 350°F for 25 minutes.

Nutrients per serving:

Calories	180	Cholesterol	70 mg
Fat	5 g	Sodium	680 mg

Greek Lemon Chicken

Greek Lemon Chicken

Makes 4 servings

 1 PERDUE® fresh young chicken (2 to 4 pounds), quartered
 ½ cup lemon juice (about 2 lemons)
 2 tablespoons cold-pressed (extra-virgin) olive oil
 1 medium onion, sliced into thin rings
 2 tablespoons chopped fresh oregano *or* 2 teaspoons dried oregano
 2 teaspoons chopped fresh thyme *or* ½ teaspoon dried thyme
 ¼ teaspoon ground black pepper
 Ground red pepper to taste (optional)
 Lemon wedges, fresh oregano sprigs and thyme sprigs for garnish (optional)

Rinse chicken; pat dry. Remove skin, if desired. In large shallow bowl, combine all remaining ingredients except garnishes. Add chicken; marinate in refrigerator at least 30 minutes. Preheat broiler. Remove chicken from marinade; place on rack in broiler pan. Broil chicken quarters, 4 inches from heat source, 30 to 35 minutes until cooked through, turning and basting with marinade 3 to 4 times during cooking. Add onion slices from marinade during last 10 minutes of broiling time. Serve chicken with onion slices. Garnish with lemon wedges, oregano and thyme, if desired.

Note: *Chicken may also be cooked on a barbecue grill. Cook 6 to 8 inches over hot ash-covered coals.*

Nutrients per serving:

Calories	269	Cholesterol	68 mg
Fat	8 g	Sodium	33 mg

Mexican Chicken Skewers with Spicy Yogurt Sauce

Mexican Chicken Skewers with Spicy Yogurt Sauce

Makes 12 servings

1 package (1.25 ounces) taco seasoning mix, divided
6 boneless skinless chicken breast halves (about 1½ pounds), cut into 1-inch cubes
1 large clove garlic
¼ teaspoon salt
2 tablespoons olive oil
1 cup DANNON® Plain Nonfat or Lowfat Yogurt
1 red bell pepper, cut into chunks
1 green bell pepper, cut into chunks
1 yellow bell pepper, cut into chunks

In a large bowl combine 3 tablespoons seasoning mix and chicken; toss to coat well. Cover; chill 2 hours.

To make Spicy Yogurt Sauce, in a mortar and pestle or with a large knife press garlic and salt together until a smooth paste forms. Place in a small bowl with olive oil; mix well. Stir in yogurt and remaining taco seasoning mix. Cover; chill 30 minutes before serving.

Thread chicken onto skewers alternately with peppers; grill over hot coals 10 to 12 minutes, turning occasionally. Serve with Spicy Yogurt Sauce.

Note: *If using wooden skewers, soak them in water 30 minutes before serving. This will prevent skewers from charring and crumbling.*

Nutrients per serving:			
Calories	140	Cholesterol	50 mg
Fat	5 g	Sodium	204 mg

Busy Day Oven-Fried Chicken Breast

Makes 8 servings

¾ cup plain dry bread crumbs
¼ cup all-purpose flour
1 teaspoon paprika
1 teaspoon poultry seasoning
1 teaspoon onion salt
½ teaspoon garlic powder
½ teaspoon dried thyme leaves
¼ teaspoon pepper
1 tablespoon *plus* 1½ teaspoons CRISCO® Vegetable Oil
4 whole chicken breasts, skinned and split (about 4 pounds)

1. Heat oven to 400°F.

2. Combine bread crumbs, flour, paprika, poultry seasoning, onion salt, garlic powder, thyme and pepper in shallow dish. Stir with fork until well blended. Add Crisco® Oil gradually. Toss with fork to blend.

3. Moisten chicken with water. Roll in coating mixture. Place in single layer in 15½×10½×¾-inch jelly roll pan or other large shallow pan. Sprinkle any remaining crumb mixture over chicken.

4. Bake at 400°F for 30 minutes or until chicken is no longer pink in center.

Nutrients per serving:			
Calories	200	Cholesterol	65 mg
Fat	5 g	Sodium	145 mg

Chicken Cacciatore

Makes 6 servings

1 to 2 tablespoons all-purpose flour
Salt and ground black pepper to taste (optional)
1 package (2⅓ pounds) PERDUE® Fresh Whole Chicken Legs, skin removed
2 tablespoons olive oil
1 large onion, cut into chunks
1 small green bell pepper, cubed (1 cup)
1 can (16 ounces) no salt added tomatoes, drained and coarsely chopped
½ cup sliced sun-dried tomatoes, soaked ½ hour in water to cover
1 cup reduced sodium chicken broth
1 cup dry white wine
1½ teaspoons dried Italian seasoning
1 package (1 pound) pasta, such as fusilli or penne, hot cooked (optional)

In shallow bowl, combine flour, salt and black pepper; coat chicken on all sides with flour mixture. In large nonstick skillet over medium-high heat, heat oil. Add chicken; cook 8 to 10 minutes until browned on all sides, turning once. Add onion and green pepper; cook 1 minute, stirring constantly. Stir in chopped tomatoes, sun-dried tomatoes, broth, wine and Italian seasoning. Reduce heat to medium; cover and cook 50 to 60 minutes until chicken is cooked through.

Place pasta on serving platter. Remove chicken from skillet; place on top of pasta. Season sauce to taste with salt and black pepper; spoon over chicken. Serve immediately.

Nutrients per serving:			
Calories	222	Cholesterol	81 mg
Fat	9 g	Sodium	229 mg

Dad's Turkey Dagwood

Makes 8 servings

1 recipe Mock Guacamole (recipe follows)
16 slices low calorie whole wheat bread
2 tomatoes, sliced
8 cups shredded iceberg lettuce
2 packages (6 ounces) Smoked Turkey Breast
    Slices
8 slices (1 ounce *each*) reduced fat Cheddar
    cheese
8 tablespoons sweet hot mustard

Spread 3 tablespoons Mock Guacamole on each of
8 slices bread. Layer 2 tomato slices, 1 cup lettuce,
2 turkey slices and 1 cheese slice over Mock
Guacamole on each bread slice.

Spread 1 tablespoon mustard over each remaining
bread slice and place on top of each to form
sandwiches. To serve, cut each sandwich in half.

Mock Guacamole

2 large cloves garlic, peeled
2 cups frozen peas, cooked according to
    package directions and drained
½ cup fresh cilantro leaves
¼ cup chopped onion
1 tablespoon lemon juice
¼ teaspoon pepper
⅛ teaspoon hot pepper sauce

Drop garlic cloves through feed tube of food processor
fitted with metal blade while motor is running;
process 10 seconds. Add peas, cilantro, onion, lemon
juice, pepper and hot pepper sauce through feed
tube; process until smooth. Chill at least 1 hour.

Nutrients per serving (1 sandwich):			
Calories	289	Cholesterol	33 mg
Fat	8 g	Sodium	921 mg

Favorite recipe from **National Turkey Federation**

Light 'n' Lean Chicken Breasts

Makes 4 servings

4 broiler-fryer chicken breast halves, skinned
    and all visible fat removed
½ teaspoon pepper, divided
2 cloves garlic, peeled and halved
1 cup low sodium chicken broth
½ cup dry white wine
2 teaspoons arrowroot or cornstarch
⅔ cup skim milk
1 teaspoon finely chopped chives

Spray nonstick skillet with reduced calorie vegetable
cooking spray. Heat over medium heat; add chicken
and sprinkle with ¼ teaspoon pepper. Cook about
20 minutes or until brown on all sides, turning once.
Reduce heat to low; add garlic halves. Cook about
10 minutes more or until fork can be inserted in
chicken with ease. Remove chicken to warm plate,
leaving garlic in skillet. Add chicken broth and wine.
Bring to a boil over high heat; boil about 5 minutes.
Reduce heat to low. Stir arrowroot into milk and
slowly add to broth mixture. Sprinkle with remaining
¼ teaspoon pepper; cook and stir about 2 minutes or
until thickened. Return chicken to skillet and sprinkle
with chives. Spoon sauce over chicken. Cook about
5 minutes more or until chicken is heated through.
Serve over rice.

Nutrients per serving:			
Calories	174	Cholesterol	77 mg
Fat	2 g	Sodium	93 mg

Favorite recipe from **National Broiler Council**

Apple & Peach Chutney

Makes 5 cups

2 medium apples, peeled and chopped
1 medium onion, chopped
1 medium red bell pepper, chopped
1 cup apple juice
¼ cup packed brown sugar
1 cinnamon stick
½ teaspoon ground ginger (optional)
1 envelope KNOX® Unflavored Gelatine
1 can (16 ounces) sliced peaches in natural juice
    or extra light syrup, drained and chopped
    (reserve juice)

In large saucepan, combine apples, onion, red
pepper, apple juice, sugar, cinnamon stick and ginger.
Bring to a boil, then simmer, stirring occasionally,
15 minutes. Remove cinnamon stick; set aside.

Meanwhile, in small saucepan, sprinkle unflavored
gelatine over reserved juice; let stand 1 minute. Stir
over low heat until gelatine is completely dissolved,
about 3 minutes.

Stir gelatine mixture and peaches into apple mixture.
Turn into 5-cup bowl or mold; chill until firm, about
2 hours. Unmold and serve with grilled poultry, meats
or fish, or with smoked turkey or ham, if desired.

Nutrients per serving (¼ cup chutney):			
Calories	37	Cholesterol	0 mg
Fat	trace	Sodium	3 mg

California Apricot Mixed Grill

California Apricot Mixed Grill

Makes 4 servings

4 boneless skinless chicken breast halves (about 3 ounces *each*)
4 cloves garlic, peeled and coarsely chopped
¼ teaspoon salt
¼ teaspoon pepper
2 tablespoons California apricot nectar
2 tablespoons balsamic vinegar
4 teaspoons olive oil, divided
2 small red onions, cut into ⅓-inch-thick slices
6 fresh California apricots, halved and pitted
4 cups mixed salad greens

Up to 12 hours before serving, combine chicken and garlic; season with salt and pepper. Refrigerate until ready to prepare. For dressing, combine nectar and vinegar in small bowl. Whisk in 3 teaspoons olive oil until well blended; season with additional salt and pepper to taste, if desired. Set aside. Heat grill to medium-high. Brush grill lightly with oil, if desired, and grill chicken about 4 minutes on each side or just until firm to the touch and no longer pink. Meanwhile, brush onions lightly with ½ teaspoon oil and grill about 2 minutes on each side or just until fork-tender. Brush apricots lightly with remaining ½ teaspoon oil and grill about 1 minute on each side or just until tender. Toss salad greens with reserved dressing. Serve with grilled chicken, onion and apricots.

Nutrients per serving:

Calories	237	Cholesterol	72 mg
Fat	8 g	Sodium	201 mg

Favorite recipe from **California Apricot Advisory Board**

Sage and Garlic Sauté

Makes 5 servings

1 package (1¼ pounds) PERDUE® Fit 'n Easy
    fresh skinless and boneless chicken thighs
Salt and ground black pepper to taste
    (optional)
2 teaspoons olive oil
5 fresh sage leaves, minced *or* ½ teaspoon dried
    sage leaves
2 cloves garlic, peeled
2 cups hot cooked quinoa or brown rice

Sprinkle chicken lightly with salt and pepper. In large
nonstick skillet over medium-high heat, heat oil; add
chicken and brown 2 minutes on each side. Sprinkle
sage and garlic over chicken. Reduce heat to
medium-low; cover and simmer 10 to 12 minutes until
chicken is cooked through. Remove garlic. Serve
chicken with quinoa.

*Note: Quinoa is a type of grain. It is available in health
food stores and some supermarkets.*

Nutrients per serving:

Calories	280	Cholesterol	94 mg
Fat	8 g	Sodium	119 mg

Chicken Latino

Makes 6 servings

1 tablespoon lime juice
1 tablespoon adobo or taco seasoning
1 teaspoon olive oil
1 package (1½ pounds) PERDUE® Fit 'n Easy
    fresh skinless and boneless pick of the chick
1 pound small potatoes, peeled
⅔ pound onions, peeled and sliced
⅓ cup low sodium chicken broth
1 bay leaf
1 package (10-ounces) frozen tiny green peas

To Microwave: In 3-quart microwave-safe dish, stir lime
juice, adobo seasoning and olive oil until blended. Coat
chicken with lime mixture and arrange in circle on bottom
of dish. Arrange potatoes and onions on top; add broth and
bay leaf. Cover with vented plastic wrap; microwave at
HIGH (100% power) 3 minutes. Reduce power to
MEDIUM-HIGH (70% power); microwave 8 minutes,
stirring twice. Add peas; cover and microwave at
MEDIUM-HIGH 8 minutes longer or until chicken is
cooked through. Remove and discard bay leaf. Let stand,
covered, 15 minutes before serving.

Nutrients per serving:

Calories	244	Cholesterol	80 mg
Fat	4 g	Sodium	235 mg

Spicy Orange Oriental Chicken Breast

Makes 6 servings

¼ cup CRISCO® Vegetable Oil
1 teaspoon grated orange peel
1 orange, juiced (about ⅓ cup)
1 tablespoon orange marmalade
1 teaspoon soy sauce
1 teaspoon minced fresh ginger *or* ½ teaspoon
    ground ginger
Dash salt and pepper
6 boneless, skinless chicken breast halves
    (about 1½ pounds)

1. Combine Crisco® Oil, orange peel, orange juice,
marmalade, soy sauce, ginger, salt and pepper in
shallow baking dish. Stir well. Add chicken. Turn to
coat. Refrigerate 30 to 45 minutes, turning after
15 minutes.

2. Prepare grill or heat broiler.

3. Remove chicken from orange juice mixture. Grill
or broil 3 to 5 minutes per side or until chicken is no
longer pink in center.

Nutrients per serving:

Calories	165	Cholesterol	65 mg
Fat	4 g	Sodium	95 mg

Chinese Plum-Glazed Chicken

Makes 2 servings

4 fresh California plums, sliced
2 tablespoons sugar
1½ teaspoons ginger root, minced *or* ½ teaspoon
    ground ginger
2 chicken breast halves, skinned and boned
½ teaspoon *each* pepper and paprika

To Microwave: Combine plums with sugar and ginger in
microwave-safe dish. Sprinkle chicken breast halves with
pepper and paprika. Arrange on top of plums. Cover dish
with plastic wrap, turning back 1 edge about ½ inch to
form steam vent. Microwave on MEDIUM (50% power)
5 minutes. Baste chicken with juices and rotate dish
¼ turn. Microwave on MEDIUM 5 to 7 minutes more. Let
stand, covered, 2 to 3 minutes. To serve, arrange chicken
on 2 plates; spoon plum sauce over.

Nutrients per serving:

Calories	261	Cholesterol	71 mg
Fat	4 g	Sodium	65 mg

Favorite recipe from **California Tree Fruit Agreement**

Tandoori-Style Chicken

Makes 6 servings

    1 cup DANNON® Plain Nonfat or Lowfat Yogurt
    3 tablespoons distilled white vinegar
    2 teaspoons minced garlic
    1¾ teaspoons garam masala*
    1¼ teaspoons ground ginger
     ¼ teaspoon ground red pepper
    6 boneless skinless chicken breast halves (about
         1¾ pounds), trimmed of all visible fat
    1¼ teaspoons salt
    3 teaspoons olive oil, divided
    2 cups sliced onions

In a large glass bowl combine yogurt, vinegar, garlic, garam masala, ginger and red pepper. Cut 4½-inch-deep diagonal slashes in top of each chicken breast. Sprinkle salt in slashes. Add chicken to yogurt mixture. Cover; chill at least 8 hours or overnight.

Preheat oven to 375°F. Brush 13×9-inch baking dish with 1 teaspoon oil. Remove chicken from marinade and arrange in a single layer, cut side up, in baking dish. Spoon some of the marinade over chicken; discard remainder. Sprinkle onions over chicken and drizzle with remaining 2 teaspoons oil. Bake 25 to 30 minutes or until chicken is no longer pink. Place chicken under broiler 3 to 5 minutes to brown onions. Serve immediately.

Garam masala is available in most Indian specialty shops or you can make your own from common kitchen spices. In a small bowl combine 1½ teaspoons ground cumin, 1 teaspoon ground coriander, 1 teaspoon ground cardamom, 1 teaspoon pepper, ¼ teaspoon ground bay leaves and a pinch of ground cloves. (If ground bay leaves are not available, grind whole leaves to a fine powder with a mortar and pestle.)

Nutrients per serving:			
Calories	250	Cholesterol	100 mg
Fat	7 g	Sodium	520 mg

Lemon-Thyme Chicken

Makes 5 servings

    2 tablespoons vegetable oil
    2 tablespoons lemon juice
    1 tablespoon grated fresh lemon peel
    1 tablespoon minced shallot or scallion
    1 tablespoon minced fresh thyme *or* 1 teaspoon
         dried thyme leaves
      Salt and ground black pepper to taste
         (optional)
    1 package (1¼ pounds) PERDUE® Fit 'n Easy
         fresh skinless and boneless chicken breasts

In wide shallow bowl, combine oil, lemon juice, lemon peel, shallot and seasonings. Add chicken and turn to coat well. Cover and marinate in refrigerator at least 30 minutes.

Prepare outdoor grill for cooking or preheat broiler. Drain marinade into small saucepan and bring to a boil over high heat; set aside. Grill or broil chicken 6 to 8 inches from heat source 10 to 20 minutes until cooked through, turning 2 to 3 times during cooking and brushing occasionally with reserved marinade. Serve warm.

Nutrients per serving:			
Calories	177	Cholesterol	66 mg
Fat	7 g	Sodium	76 mg

Chicken Mexicana

Makes 5 servings

    1 package (1¼ pounds) PERDUE® Fit 'n Easy
         skinless and boneless fresh Oven Stuffer
         Roaster thin-sliced breast
      Salt and ground black pepper to taste
         (optional)
     ⅔ cup Italian seasoned bread crumbs
    1 teaspoon chili powder
     ¼ cup liquid egg substitute *or* 1 beaten egg
    2 tablespoons vegetable oil
      Prepared salsa (optional)

Season chicken with salt and pepper. On plate, combine bread crumbs and chili powder. Dip chicken in egg substitute and dredge in crumbs, coating both sides. In large nonstick skillet over medium-high heat, heat oil. Add chicken; cook 1½ to 2½ minutes on each side until golden brown and cooked through. Serve with salsa.

Prep time: 15 to 20 minutes
Cook time: 6 to 8 minutes

Nutrients per serving:			
Calories	249	Cholesterol	67 mg
Fat	9 g	Sodium	497 mg

Turkey Shanghai

Slice turkey into thin strips; place in medium bowl. Sprinkle with ¼ cup wine, 1 tablespoon soy sauce, cornstarch and pepper; toss to coat with mixture. Marinate at room temperature 15 minutes. In small bowl, combine remaining ¼ cup wine, 2 tablespoons soy sauce, sugar and vinegar; set aside.

Over medium-high heat, heat wok or large heavy nonstick skillet. Slowly add oil; stir in garlic, ginger and turkey. Stir-fry 3 to 4 minutes until turkey is cooked through. Add carrots, beans, scallions and reserved wine mixture; cook 1 to 2 minutes longer. Serve over Chinese noodles. Garnish with carrot and scallion flowers and cilantro sprigs, if desired.

Nutrients per serving:

Calories	246	Cholesterol	70 mg
Fat	7 g	Sodium	393 mg

Turkey Shanghai

Makes 4 servings

1 package (1 pound) PERDUE® Fit 'n Easy fresh skinless and boneless turkey tenderloins
½ cup white wine, divided
3 tablespoons reduced sodium soy sauce, divided
1 tablespoon cornstarch
   Ground black pepper to taste
1 tablespoon sugar
2 teaspoons rice vinegar or white vinegar
1½ tablespoons vegetable oil
1 clove garlic, minced
1 teaspoon minced fresh ginger
2 carrots, shredded
⅓ pound green beans, split lengthwise and lightly steamed
½ cup thinly sliced scallions
2 cups hot cooked Chinese noodles (optional)
   Carrots and scallions cut into flower shapes (optional)
   Cilantro sprigs (optional)

Baked Chicken with Red Pepper Sauce

Makes 6 servings, 2⅓ cups sauce

1 cup dry bread crumbs
2 tablespoons minced fresh parsley
½ teaspoon dried summer savory leaves, crushed
¼ teaspoon garlic salt
¼ teaspoon black pepper
6 chicken breast halves, skinned
⅓ cup reduced calorie mayonnaise
1½ cups finely chopped red bell pepper
1 clove garlic, minced
1 tablespoon butter or margarine
3 medium tomatoes, peeled, seeded and chopped
¼ cup HEINZ® 57 Sauce
¼ teaspoon salt
   Dash ground red pepper

Preheat oven to 400°F. Combine bread crumbs, parsley, summer savory, garlic salt and black pepper in shallow dish; set aside. Brush chicken on both sides with mayonnaise. Coat with crumb mixture. Place chicken in lightly greased shallow baking pan. Bake 40 to 45 minutes or until chicken is tender and juices run clear when pierced with fork. Meanwhile, for sauce, cook and stir red bell pepper and garlic in hot butter in saucepan until tender. Add tomatoes and cook over medium heat 5 minutes, stirring occasionally. Stir in 57 Sauce, salt and ground red pepper. Transfer mixture to container of blender or food processor. Cover and process until smooth. Return mixture to saucepan. Cook over medium heat until slightly thickened, stirring frequently. Serve chicken with sauce.

Nutrients per serving:

Calories	287	Cholesterol	74 mg
Fat	9 g	Sodium	314 mg

Chicken Maryland

Makes 4 servings

¼ cup all-purpose flour
  Salt and ground black pepper to taste
    (optional)
½ teaspoon paprika
1 package (1¼ pounds) PERDUE® Fit 'n Easy
    fresh skinless and boneless chicken breasts
1½ tablespoons light margarine (stick form)
1 can (8½ ounces) creamed corn

In shallow dish, combine flour, salt, pepper and
paprika; coat chicken on both sides with flour
mixture. In large nonstick skillet over medium-high
heat, melt margarine. Add chicken; cook 2 to
3 minutes on each side or until browned, turning
once. Reduce heat to medium-low; cook about
10 minutes longer or until chicken is cooked through.

Remove chicken from skillet and set aside. Add corn
to drippings in skillet; stir well. Season with salt,
pepper and paprika to taste. Serve chicken with corn
sauce.

Nutrients per serving:			
Calories	278	Cholesterol	99 mg
Fat	5 g	Sodium	334 mg

Chicken Pocket Sandwiches

Makes 10 pocket bread sandwiches, 3 to 3½ cups filling

10 ounces cooked chicken, skinned, boned and
    cubed
1 container (8 ounces) plain low fat yogurt
½ cup natural almonds, chopped
¼ cup chopped California nectarine
⅓ cup chopped green onion
1 tablespoon lemon juice
⅛ teaspoon *each* pepper and dried dill weed
5 pockets pita bread, halved
  Lettuce leaves

Combine all ingredients except pita bread and lettuce
in medium bowl. Line pita bread with lettuce leaves;
spoon mixture into pockets.

Nutrients per serving (1 pita half):			
Calories	204	Cholesterol	24 mg
Fat	6 g	Sodium	251 mg

Favorite recipe from **California Tree Fruit Agreement**

Pollo Empanizado

Makes 4 servings

½ cup WISH-BONE® Olive Oil Classics Italian
    Dressing*
2 tablespoons lime juice
½ teaspoon grated lime peel
4 boneless, skinless chicken breast halves (about
    1 pound), pounded ¼ inch thick
½ cup yellow cornmeal
½ teaspoon garlic powder with parsley
¼ teaspoon salt
1 medium red onion, chopped
  Chopped fresh cilantro or parsley leaves

In large shallow baking dish, blend olive oil classics
Italian dressing, lime juice and peel. Add chicken and
turn to coat. Cover; marinate in refrigerator, turning
occasionally, at least 2 hours. Meanwhile, in medium
bowl, combine cornmeal, garlic powder and salt.

Remove chicken, reserving marinade. Dip chicken in
cornmeal mixture, coating well. On aluminum-foil-
lined broiler rack or in greased shallow baking pan,
arrange onion around chicken. Drizzle chicken and
onion with reserved marinade. Broil 7 minutes or
until chicken is tender and no longer pink. Sprinkle
with cilantro and serve with freshly ground black
pepper, if desired.

*Also terrific with WISH-BONE® Olive Oil Classics Red
Wine Vinaigrette Dressing.*

Nutrients per serving:			
Calories	261	Cholesterol	66 mg
Fat	8 g	Sodium	591 mg

Pollo Empanizado

Creamy Chicken Primavera

Makes 4 servings

2 cups water
1 cup diced carrots
1 cup broccoli flowerets
1 cup tri-color rotini pasta
½ pound cooked chicken, cut into cubes
½ cup DANNON® Plain Nonfat or Lowfat Yogurt
¼ cup finely chopped green onions (green part only)
2 tablespoons *plus* 2 teaspoons reduced-calorie mayonnaise
2 tablespoons grated Parmesan cheese
½ teaspoon dried basil, crushed
⅛ teaspoon pepper
Carrot curls (optional)

In a medium saucepan combine water, carrots and broccoli. Cook, covered, 10 to 15 minutes or until tender-crisp; drain. Cook pasta according to package directions; rinse and drain. In a large bowl combine pasta, carrots and broccoli. Toss gently.

In a small bowl combine chicken, yogurt, green onions, mayonnaise, cheese, basil and pepper; mix well. Add to pasta mixture. Toss gently to combine. Cover; chill several hours. If desired, garnish with carrot curls.

Nutrients per serving:

Calories	290	Cholesterol	60 mg
Fat	10 g	Sodium	178 mg

Turkey Waldorf Sandwiches

Makes 4 servings

6 ounces Cooked Turkey Breast, cubed
½ cup diced celery
1 small Red Delicious apple, cored and cut into small cubes
2 tablespoons chopped walnuts
1 tablespoon reduced calorie mayonnaise
1 tablespoon nonfat yogurt
⅛ teaspoon ground nutmeg
⅛ teaspoon ground cinnamon
4 lettuce leaves
8 slices reduced calorie raisin bread

Combine turkey, celery, apple, walnuts, mayonnaise, yogurt, nutmeg and cinnamon in medium bowl; blend well. Cover and refrigerate at least 1 hour or overnight to allow flavors to blend.

To serve, place 1 lettuce leaf on 1 bread slice. Spoon ¾ cup turkey mixture over lettuce and top with another bread slice. Repeat with remaining ingredients. (Leftover turkey mixture will keep up to 4 days in refrigerator.)

Nutrients per serving (1 sandwich):

Calories	240	Cholesterol	28 mg
Fat	7 g	Sodium	233 mg

Favorite recipe from **National Turkey Federation**

Shotgun Billy's Turkey Chili with Black Beans

Makes 4 servings

1 cup coarsely chopped onion
1 red bell pepper, cut into ¼-inch cubes
2 cloves garlic, minced
2 jalapeño chilies,* seeded and minced
1 can (28 ounces) tomatoes, undrained and coarsely chopped
1 tablespoon chili powder
1½ teaspoons ground cumin
1½ teaspoons ground coriander
½ teaspoon dried oregano leaves, crushed
½ teaspoon dried marjoram leaves, crushed
¼ teaspoon crushed red pepper flakes
¼ teaspoon ground cinnamon
1 can (16 ounces) black beans, drained and rinsed
2 cups ½-inch cubes Cooked Turkey
½ cup fresh cilantro, coarsely chopped
4 tablespoons grated reduced-fat Cheddar cheese

To Microwave: Combine onion, bell pepper, garlic, chilies and tomatoes, including liquid, in 3-quart microwave-safe dish. Stir in chili powder, cumin, coriander, oregano, marjoram, red pepper flakes and cinnamon; cover. Microwave on HIGH (100% power) 10 minutes, stirring after 5 minutes. Stir in beans and turkey; cover. Microwave on HIGH 4 minutes; stir in cilantro. To serve, ladle into bowls and sprinkle with cheese.

Tip: *For full blending of flavors, prepare 1 day prior to serving.*

**Chilies can sting and irritate the skin; wear plastic disposable gloves when handling chilies and do not touch eyes. Wash hands after handling chilies.*

Nutrients per serving:

Calories	278	Cholesterol	60 mg
Fat	6 g	Sodium	632 mg

Favorite recipe from **National Turkey Federation**

Creamy Chicken Primavera

Chicken Crimini

Chicken Crimini

Makes 6 servings

1 package (1½ pounds) PERDUE® Fit 'n Easy
    fresh skinless and boneless pick of the chick
½ teaspoon ground thyme leaves, crushed
    Salt and ground black pepper (optional)
1½ tablespoons olive oil
¼ pound wild mushrooms, such as crimini,
    shiitake or oyster, thinly sliced
¼ cup reduced-sodium beef broth
3 tablespoons Marsala wine
1 tablespoon grated Parmesan cheese
2 tablespoons minced fresh parsley
1 lemon, thinly sliced (optional)

Place chicken pieces between sheets of plastic wrap.
Pound chicken with meat mallet until slightly
flattened. Season with thyme, salt and pepper and set
aside. In large, nonstick skillet over medium heat,
heat oil. Add mushrooms; cook and stir 1 to 2
minutes. With slotted spoon, remove mushrooms and
set aside. Add chicken to skillet and cook about
5 minutes on each side or until lightly browned.
Remove chicken and keep warm.

With wooden spatula or spoon, stir beef broth and
wine into skillet, scraping bottom to incorporate
browned bits into pan juices. Return chicken to
skillet; top with mushrooms. Sprinkle with Parmesan
and spoon pan juices over all. Reduce heat to low;
cover skillet and simmer 5 to 10 minutes until
chicken is cooked through. To serve, sprinkle with
parsley and garnish with lemon slices, if desired.

Nutrients per serving:

Calories	181	Cholesterol	81 mg
Fat	7 g	Sodium	103 mg

Turkey Kabobs with Gingered Mustard Sauce

Makes 5 servings

½ cup FRENCH'S® Creamy Spread™ Mustard
1 can (8 ounces) pineapple chunks, drained,
    juice reserved
1 to 2 tablespoons firmly packed brown sugar
½ teaspoon ground ginger
1 pound fresh boneless turkey cutlets, cut into
    1-inch strips
1 medium green bell pepper, cut into bite-size
    pieces
10 cherry tomatoes
5 skewers
    Hot cooked rice (optional)

In small bowl, combine French's® Creamy Spread™
Mustard, reserved pineapple juice, brown sugar and
ginger. Alternately thread pineapple chunks, turkey
strips, pepper pieces and tomatoes onto skewers.
Reserve half of mustard mixture. Grill or broil
kabobs, basting with remaining mustard mixture,
15 to 20 minutes or until turkey is tender. Serve
warm over rice with reserved mustard mixture.

Nutrients per serving:

Calories	169	Cholesterol	54 mg
Fat	3 g	Sodium	357 mg

Pepper-Chicken Fettucini Toss

Makes 12 servings

1 package (1 pound) CREAMETTE® Fettucini,
    uncooked
¼ cup olive or vegetable oil
3 whole boneless skinless chicken breasts, cut
    into strips (about 18 ounces)
2 large red bell peppers, cut into strips
2 large yellow bell peppers, cut into strips
1 medium green bell pepper, cut into strips
1 medium onion, cut into chunks
2 cups sliced fresh mushrooms
1 teaspoon salt-free herb seasoning
2 tablespoons grated Parmesan cheese

Prepare Creamette® Fettucini according to package
directions; drain. In large skillet, heat oil; add
chicken, peppers, onion, mushrooms and seasoning.
Cook and stir over medium heat until chicken is
cooked through, 8 to 10 minutes. Add hot cooked
fettucini and Parmesan cheese; toss to coat. Serve
immediately. Refrigerate leftovers.

Nutrients per serving:

Calories	264	Cholesterol	36 mg
Fat	7 g	Sodium	33 mg

Rosemary Chicken Stir-Fry

Makes 4 servings

1 Family Size bag UNCLE BEN'S® Brand
    Boil-in-Bag Rice
1½ tablespoons vegetable oil
  1 cup short thin carrot strips
  ½ cup sliced celery
  ¼ teaspoon dried rosemary leaves, crushed
  ½ pound boneless skinless chicken breasts, cut
    into thin strips
  1 cup sliced mushrooms
  ¼ cup sliced green onions with tops
  1 can (10¾ ounces) condensed chicken broth
  4 teaspoons cornstarch

Cook rice according to package directions; set aside.
Meanwhile, heat oil in large skillet over medium-high
heat. Add carrots, celery and rosemary; stir-fry until
vegetables are crisp-tender. Push vegetables to one
side of skillet; add chicken. Stir-fry 3 minutes or until
chicken is tender and no longer pink. Add mushrooms
and green onions; stir-fry 3 minutes. Stir broth into
cornstarch in small bowl until smooth; add to skillet.
Cook and stir over medium heat until mixture boils
and thickens, stirring frequently. Serve chicken
mixture over rice.

Nutrients per serving:

Calories	250	Cholesterol	23 mg
Fat	7 g	Sodium	550 mg

Turkey Parmesan

Makes 1 serving

1 teaspoon diet margarine
1 (2-ounce) fresh turkey breast slice
3 tablespoons CLASSICO® Pasta Sauce, any
    flavor
1 teaspoon grated Parmesan cheese
1 slice BORDEN® Lite-line® Process Cheese
    Product,* any flavor

In small skillet, over medium heat, melt margarine.
Add turkey breast slice. Cook 2 minutes; turn.
Reduce heat to low; top turkey with remaining
ingredients. Cover; cook 2 to 3 minutes longer or
until turkey is no longer pink. Garnish as desired.
Refrigerate leftovers.

* "½ the calories" – 8% milkfat product

Nutrients per serving:

Calories	198	Cholesterol	54 mg
Fat	7 g	Sodium	646 mg

Monterey Chicken Sandwiches

Makes 4 sandwiches

  ½ tablespoon vegetable oil
  ½ tablespoon margarine
  4 boneless skinless chicken breast halves
    (about 1 pound)
  1 teaspoon dried thyme leaves, crushed
    Salt and black pepper (optional)
  1 large red onion, thinly sliced
  4 Kaiser rolls, split
    Radicchio or lettuce leaves

Heat oil and margarine in large skillet over medium
heat. Add chicken; sprinkle with thyme. Cook
8 minutes or until browned on both sides and no
longer pink in center, turning after 4 minutes. Season
with salt and pepper, if desired. Remove from skillet;
keep warm. Add onion to skillet; cook and stir until
tender.

Fill rolls with radicchio leaves, chicken and onion.
Serve with mango chutney and olives, if desired.

Nutrients per serving (1 sandwich):

Calories	283	Cholesterol	46 mg
Fat	7 g	Sodium	369 mg

Monterey Chicken Sandwich,
Corn-on-the-Cob with Chili Spread (page 363)

Broccoli Chicken Pasta Casserole

Makes 8 servings

2 teaspoons CRISCO® Vegetable Oil
⅔ cup chopped onion
2 large cloves garlic, minced
1 pound boneless, skinless chicken breast, cut into 1-inch pieces
2 cans (14½ ounces *each*) whole tomatoes, undrained and coarsely chopped
1 can (8 ounces) tomato sauce
¼ cup ketchup
1¼ teaspoons dried basil leaves
¾ teaspoon dried oregano leaves
¼ teaspoon salt
1 package (10 ounces) frozen broccoli cuts, thawed and well drained
5 ounces uncooked small macaroni, cooked (without salt or fat) and well drained
½ cup grated Parmesan cheese, divided

1. Heat oven to 350°F.

2. Heat Crisco® Oil in large skillet on medium-high heat. Add onion and garlic. Cook and stir until tender. Add chicken. Cook and stir just until chicken is no longer pink in center. Stir in tomatoes, tomato sauce, ketchup, basil, oregano and salt. Bring to a boil. Reduce heat to low. Simmer 5 minutes, stirring occasionally.

3. Combine broccoli, macaroni, chicken mixture and ¼ cup cheese in large bowl. Stir well. Spoon into 13×9×2-inch baking dish. Sprinkle with remaining ¼ cup cheese.

4. Bake at 350°F for 20 minutes.

Nutrients per serving:			
Calories	215	Cholesterol	35 mg
Fat	4 g	Sodium	485 mg

Healthy Choice® Tortilla Pizza

Makes 6 servings

1 small red bell pepper
2 teaspoons finely chopped fresh basil leaves
1 teaspoon olive oil
6 (8-inch) flour tortillas
1 package (6 ounces) HEALTHY CHOICE® Oven Roasted Turkey Breast, diced
3 tablespoons finely chopped, blanched dried tomatoes
3 tablespoons crumbled feta cheese

Roast red pepper over gas flame or under broiler until charred. Close pepper in paper bag until cool, then peel, seed and chop.

Preheat oven to 400°F. Mix basil with olive oil; brush 1 side of each tortilla with mixture. Sprinkle equal amounts of red pepper, turkey, tomatoes and feta cheese over tortillas. Bake 6 minutes or until cheese is melted.

Nutrients per serving (1 pizza):			
Calories	162	Cholesterol	15 mg
Fat	4 g	Sodium	445 mg

Hawaiian Game Hens

Makes 2 servings

1 Cornish game hen, thawed (about 1¼ pounds)
½ teaspoon garlic powder
  Salt and pepper to taste (optional)
1 can (8 ounces) DOLE® Pineapple Slices, undrained
1 tablespoon honey
½ teaspoon grated lemon peel
½ teaspoon dried tarragon leaves, crushed
1 cup DOLE® Mini Peeled Carrots or carrot chunks
½ pound DOLE® Asparagus tips or green beans

Preheat oven to 375°F. Cut hen in half lengthwise. Sprinkle with garlic powder, salt and pepper. Place on rack in roasting pan; cover. Bake 20 minutes.

Meanwhile, drain juice from pineapple into small casserole dish. Stir in honey, lemon peel and tarragon.

Arrange pineapple slices on rack with hen. Brush pineapple and hen with some of pineapple juice mixture. Bake, uncovered, 10 to 15 minutes more until tender and golden.

Meanwhile, place carrots and asparagus in casserole with remaining pineapple juice mixture. Cover with plastic wrap. Microwave on HIGH (100% power) 4 to 5 minutes.

To serve, arrange hen halves on 2 serving plates. Arrange vegetables on plates. Spoon sauce from casserole over each serving.

Prep time: 10 minutes
Cook time: 35 minutes

Nutrients per serving:			
Calories	280	Cholesterol	49 mg
Fat	8 g	Sodium	65 mg

Garlic Crockpot Turkey

Makes 5 servings

1 package (1¼ pounds) PERDUE® Fit 'n Easy
    fresh skinless and boneless turkey thighs
Salt and ground black pepper to taste
    (optional)
1 tablespoon olive oil
1 whole head garlic, separated and cloves peeled
½ cup dry white wine
½ cup reduced sodium chicken broth

Season turkey lightly with salt and generously with pepper. In large skillet over medium-high heat, heat oil. Add turkey and brown on both sides, about 10 minutes. Place turkey in crockpot or slow cooker and add remaining ingredients. Cook on medium to high setting 2½ to 3½ hours. Remove garlic cloves from pot. Crush and return to juices, if desired. Serve juices over turkey.

Nutrients per serving:

Calories	188	Cholesterol	85 mg
Fat	7 g	Sodium	165 mg

Savory Stir-Fry

Makes 4 servings, about 3 cups

1 chicken bouillon cube
⅓ cup boiling water
3 to 4 tablespoons HEINZ® Worcestershire
    Sauce
1 tablespoon cornstarch
½ cup julienned carrot strips
2 tablespoons vegetable oil, divided
½ cup julienned zucchini strips
8 green onions, cut into 1-inch lengths
4 skinless, boneless chicken breast halves (about
    1 pound), cut into 2×2½-inch strips
Hot cooked rice (optional)

Dissolve bouillon cube in water; stir in Worcestershire sauce, then cornstarch. In preheated large skillet or wok, stir-fry carrots in 1 tablespoon oil 1 minute. Add zucchini and green onions; stir-fry 1 minute. Remove vegetables. In same skillet, stir-fry half the chicken in remaining 1 tablespoon oil 1 to 2 minutes; remove. Stir-fry remaining chicken. Return vegetables and chicken to skillet; stir in Worcestershire sauce mixture. Cook until thickened, stirring to coat chicken and vegetables. Serve with rice.

Nutrients per serving:

Calories	214	Cholesterol	66 mg
Fat	9 g	Sodium	483 mg

Zesty Caribbean Chicken Breast

Makes 6 servings

¼ cup CRISCO® Vegetable Oil
1 teaspoon grated lemon peel
¼ cup lemon juice
1 tablespoon paprika
1 tablespoon honey
1 teaspoon garlic salt
1 teaspoon ginger
1 teaspoon dried oregano leaves
¼ teaspoon hot pepper sauce
6 boneless, skinless chicken breast halves
    (about 1½ pounds)

1. Combine Crisco® Oil, lemon peel, lemon juice, paprika, honey, garlic salt, ginger, oregano and hot pepper sauce in shallow baking dish. Stir well. Add chicken. Turn to coat. Refrigerate 30 minutes or up to 4 hours, turning occasionally.

2. Heat broiler or prepare grill.

3. Remove chicken from lemon juice mixture. Broil or grill 3 to 5 minutes per side or until chicken is no longer pink in center.

Nutrients per serving:

Calories	170	Cholesterol	65 mg
Fat	6 g	Sodium	230 mg

Peach Lemon Sauce for Chicken

Makes 2½ cups

2 lemons
3 fresh California peaches, quartered
3 tablespoons low sodium chicken broth
Pepper to taste

Remove strips of peel from 1 lemon (yellow part only) with vegetable peeler; set aside. Squeeze both lemons as needed to measure ¼ cup juice. Combine juice and peaches in saucepan. Cover and cook over medium heat 20 minutes or until peaches are very tender. Meanwhile, cut reserved lemon peel into fine julienned strips, then cut in half. Boil strips in water 7 to 8 minutes. Drain; set aside. Combine cooked peaches and chicken broth in blender. Blend until smooth. Stir in julienned lemon strips and pepper. Serve hot over grilled chicken.

Nutrients per serving (¼ cup sauce):

Calories	17	Cholesterol	trace
Fat	trace	Sodium	trace

Favorite recipe from **California Tree Fruit Agreement**

SEAFOOD ENTRÉES

Turn the heads of even the most die-hard meat lovers with these enticing and nutritious seafood recipes. Flavorful marinades and sauces enhance the delicate flavors of shrimp, scallops and your favorite fish fillets. Try preparing seafood on the grill for an especially tantalizing taste treat.

Poached Salmon with Basil Mayonnaise

Makes 4 servings

    Basil Mayonnaise (recipe follows)
  1 bay leaf
  4 peppercorns
  4 salmon steaks, 1 to 1½ inches thick (1 pound)

Prepare Basil Mayonnaise; cover. Set aside.

Add bay leaf, peppercorns and enough water to medium skillet to fill to 1-inch depth. Bring to a boil. Add salmon. Reduce heat to low; cover. Simmer 5 minutes or until salmon flakes easily when tested with fork.

Remove salmon from poaching liquid; serve with Basil Mayonnaise.

Basil Mayonnaise
  ¼ cup light mayonnaise
  ¼ cup plain low-fat yogurt
  1 green onion, cut into 1-inch pieces
  1 tablespoon fresh parsley sprigs
  1 tablespoon fresh basil
    Salt and black pepper (optional)

Combine mayonnaise, yogurt, onion, parsley and basil in food processor or blender container; process until well blended. Season with salt and pepper, if desired.

Nutrients per serving (includes 2 tablespoons Basil Mayonnaise):

Calories	211	Cholesterol	69 mg
Fat	10 g	Sodium	60 mg

West Coast Tuna Pitas

Makes 8 servings

  ½ cup HEALTHY CHOICE® Cholesterol Free
    Egg Product
  1 can (6⅛ ounces) tuna packed in water, drained
  ¼ cup nonfat mayonnaise
  ¼ cup reduced-calorie cream cheese spread
  ¼ cup chopped water chestnuts
  1 tablespoon sliced green onion
  1 teaspoon lemon juice
  1 teaspoon Dijon-style mustard
  ¼ teaspoon dill weed
  4 pita bread rounds, cut in half
  1 cucumber, thinly sliced
  1 tomato, thinly sliced
    Alfalfa sprouts

Lightly coat 8-inch skillet with nonstick cooking spray. Cook egg product, covered, over very low heat 5 minutes or until just set. Let egg product cool; coarsely chop. In medium bowl, combine egg product, tuna, mayonnaise, cream cheese spread, water chestnuts, onion, lemon juice, mustard and dill; refrigerate. To serve, fill pita halves with cucumber and tomato slices, sprouts and ¼ cup tuna mixture.

Nutrients per serving:

Calories	150	Cholesterol	10 mg
Fat	1 g	Sodium	395 mg

Left to right: Pea-Pod Medley (page 355), Poached Salmon with Basil Mayonnaise

Broiled Orange Roughy with
Green Peppercorn Sauce

Broiled Orange Roughy with Green Peppercorn Sauce

Makes 4 servings

Green Peppercorn Sauce (recipe follows)
4 orange roughy fillets (about 6 ounces each)

Preheat broiler. Position oven rack about 4 inches from heat source. Prepare Green Peppercorn Sauce; set aside.

Place fish in shallow baking pan; top with sauce. Broil 10 minutes or until fish flakes easily when tested with fork.

Green Peppercorn Sauce
  1 cup loosely packed cilantro leaves
  2 tablespoons country-style Dijon mustard*
  2 tablespoons dry white wine
  ½ teaspoon green peppercorns, rinsed, drained

Combine all ingredients in food processor or blender container; process until well blended.

*Substitute your favorite herbed mustard for the country-style Dijon mustard.

Nutrients per serving:

Calories	195	Cholesterol	28 mg
Fat	10 g	Sodium	203 mg

Citrus Marinated Fish Steaks

Makes 4 servings

  ¼ cup frozen orange juice concentrate, thawed
  ¼ cup REALEMON® Lemon Juice from Concentrate
  1 tablespoon vegetable oil
  ½ teaspoon dill weed
  4 (1-inch-thick) salmon, halibut or swordfish steaks (about 1½ pounds)

In large shallow dish or plastic bag, combine juices, oil and dill weed; mix well. Add fish. Cover; marinate in refrigerator 2 hours, turning occasionally. Remove fish from marinade; heat marinade thoroughly. Grill or broil until fish flakes with fork, basting frequently with marinade. Garnish as desired. Refrigerate leftovers.

Nutrients per serving:

Calories	211	Cholesterol	30 mg
Fat	9 g	Sodium	1039 mg

Sautéed Rainbow Trout with Wild Mushrooms

Makes 4 servings

  1 tablespoon olive oil
  1 cup chopped shallots
  1 cup sliced button mushrooms
  1 cup small whole oyster mushrooms
  ¼ cup light soy sauce
  ¼ cup dry sherry
  ¼ cup water
  Ground black pepper to taste
  4 CLEAR SPRINGS® Brand Idaho Rainbow Trout fillets, butterflied (4 ounces *each*)

In large nonstick skillet, combine olive oil and shallots; cook, covered, over medium heat until shallots are translucent. Add mushrooms; continue cooking, covered, until mushrooms are soft. Stir in soy sauce, sherry and water; simmer 1 minute. Remove from heat; season with pepper. Transfer mixture to medium bowl; cover to keep warm. Coat same skillet lightly with oil. Cook trout, flesh side down, over high heat 2 minutes. Gently turn trout; cook 2 minutes more or until trout flakes with fork. Serve immediately with mushroom mixture.

Nutrients per serving:

Calories	233	Cholesterol	65 mg
Fat	7 g	Sodium	592 mg

Broiled Oriental Fish

Makes 4 servings

- ¼ cup **CRISCO® PURITAN® Oil**
- ¼ cup **reduced-sodium soy sauce**
- ¼ cup **dry white wine**
- 1½ teaspoons **sesame seeds**
- 1 teaspoon **sugar**
- ½ teaspoon **ground ginger**
- 1 pound **Dover sole fillets**
- 12 **green onions**
- ½ teaspoon **black pepper (optional)**

Heat broiler. Combine Crisco® Puritan® Oil, soy sauce, wine, sesame seeds, sugar and ginger in shallow baking dish. Stir until blended.

Place fillets in marinade. Turn to coat. Marinate 20 minutes; turn fillets occasionally.

Wash green onions. Trim tops so onions are 5 to 6 inches in length. Make 3-inch lengthwise slices in onion tops to give onions feathered look.

Place onions in marinade for last 10 minutes of marinating time.

Remove fish and onions from marinade. Place on broiler pan. Sprinkle with pepper, if desired. Place pan in oven 4 to 5 inches from heat.

Broil 3 minutes. Turn fish and onions carefully using pancake turner and broil 3 minutes more or until fish flakes easily when tested with fork.

To Microwave: Prepare and marinate fish and green onions as above. Remove fish and onions from marinade. Place in 12×8-inch microwave-safe dish. Sprinkle with pepper, if desired. Cover with vented plastic wrap. Microwave on HIGH (100% power) 2 minutes. Rotate dish. Microwave on HIGH 1½ minutes or until fish flakes easily when tested with fork. Let stand, covered, 1 minute.

Nutrients per serving:

Calories	190	Cholesterol	75 mg
Fat	9 g	Sodium	180 mg

Festival Shrimp and Saffron Rice

Makes 2 servings

- ⅓ cup **diced red bell pepper**
- ¼ cup **sliced green onion with tops**
- 1 clove **garlic, minced**
- 1 teaspoon **margarine**
- ½ pound **peeled and deveined medium shrimp**
- ½ teaspoon **seafood seasoning blend**
- 1½ cups **cooked rice (cooked with 1/16 teaspoon ground saffron or turmeric)**
- 1 tablespoon **grated Parmesan cheese**

Cook and stir bell pepper, onions, and garlic in margarine in medium skillet over medium heat 1 to 2 minutes. Add shrimp and seasoning blend; cook, stirring, 3 to 4 minutes or until shrimp are opaque. Stir in rice and cheese; cook and stir until thoroughly heated, about 2 to 3 minutes. Garnish as desired.

To Microwave: Combine bell pepper, onions, garlic, and margarine in 1-quart microproof baking dish. Cover and cook on HIGH (100% power) 2 minutes. Add shrimp and seasoning blend. Reduce setting to MEDIUM-HIGH (70% power); cover and cook 3 to 4 minutes or until shrimp are opaque. Stir in rice and cheese; cover and cook on MEDIUM-HIGH 1 to 2 minutes or until thoroughly heated. Let stand 2 minutes. Garnish as desired.

Nutrients per serving:

Calories	247	Cholesterol	176 mg
Fat	4 g	Sodium	817 mg

Favorite recipe from **USA Rice Council**

Festival Shrimp and Saffron Rice

Garlic Skewered Shrimp

Garlic Skewered Shrimp

Makes 4 servings

1 pound large raw shrimp, peeled, deveined
2 tablespoons light soy sauce
1 tablespoon peanut or vegetable oil
3 cloves garlic, minced
¼ teaspoon crushed red pepper flakes (optional)
3 green onions, cut into 1-inch pieces

Soak 4 (12-inch) bamboo skewers in water 20 minutes.

Place shrimp in large plastic food bag. Combine soy sauce, oil, garlic and crushed red pepper in cup; mix well. Pour over shrimp. Close bag securely; turn to coat. Marinate at room temperature 10 to 15 minutes.

Drain shrimp; reserve marinade. Alternately thread shrimp and onions onto skewers. Place on rack of broiler pan. Brush with reserved marinade; discard remaining marinade.

Broil shrimp, 5 to 6 inches from heat, 5 minutes. Turn shrimp over; broil an additional 5 minutes or until shrimp are opaque.

Nutrients per serving:

Calories	127	Cholesterol	174 mg
Fat	4 g	Sodium	478 mg

Sole in Ratatouille

Makes 6 servings

½ cup thinly sliced onion
1 crushed garlic clove
2 tablespoons olive oil
2 cups (½ pound) peeled cubed eggplant
1¾ cups (14.5-ounce can) CONTADINA® Whole Peeled Tomatoes, cut up, with juice
1½ cups sliced fresh mushrooms
1 cup coarsely chopped green bell pepper
1 cup water
⅔ cup (6-ounce can) CONTADINA® Tomato Paste
⅓ cup finely chopped fresh parsley
1 tablespoon finely chopped fresh basil
½ teaspoon salt
¼ teaspoon black pepper
1½ pounds sole fillets
1½ cups (3 medium) sliced zucchini or yellow squash

Cook and stir onion and garlic in oil in 12-inch skillet. Add eggplant, tomatoes with juice, mushrooms, bell pepper, water, tomato paste, parsley, basil, salt and black pepper. Cover and simmer 10 minutes, stirring occasionally. Roll up sole fillets; place in skillet, pushing down into tomato mixture. Cover; simmer 20 minutes. Add zucchini to skillet. Simmer 10 to 15 minutes or until sole flakes when tested with fork and zucchini is tender. Serve with cooked pasta, if desired.

Nutrients per serving:

Calories	300	Cholesterol	0 mg
Fat	7 g	Sodium	500 mg

Tangy Baked Fish Fillets

Makes 6 to 8 servings

¼ cup CRISCO® PURITAN® Oil
2 medium onions, thinly sliced and separated into rings
1½ to 2 pounds fish fillets, ½ inch thick, cut into serving-size pieces
½ teaspoon salt
¼ teaspoon black pepper
3 medium tomatoes, seeded and chopped
2 lemons, thinly sliced
1 bay leaf
1 tablespoon white vinegar
1 tablespoon sugar

Preheat oven to 325°F. Heat Crisco® Puritan® Oil in deep skillet with ovenproof handle. Add onions. Cook and stir over moderate heat until tender. Remove from heat.

Arrange fish over onions. Sprinkle with salt and pepper. Top with tomatoes and lemons. Add bay leaf. Sprinkle with vinegar and sugar. Cover.

Bake at 325°F for 45 minutes to 1 hour or until fish flakes easily with fork. Remove and discard bay leaf.

Nutrients per serving:

Calories	190	Cholesterol	49 mg
Fat	8 g	Sodium	200 mg

Baja Fish and Rice Bake

Baja Fish and Rice Bake

Makes 6 servings

¾ cup chopped onion
½ cup chopped celery
1 clove garlic, minced
3 tablespoons vegetable oil
½ cup uncooked rice
3½ cups (two 14½-ounce cans) CONTADINA®
    Stewed Tomatoes, cut up, with juice
1 teaspoon lemon pepper seasoning
½ teaspoon salt
⅛ teaspoon ground red pepper
1 pound fish fillets (any firm white fish)
¼ cup finely chopped fresh parsley
    Lemon slices (optional)

Cook and stir onion, celery and garlic in hot oil in large skillet over medium heat until vegetables are tender. Add rice; cook and stir about 5 minutes or until rice browns slightly. Add tomatoes with juice, lemon pepper, salt and ground red pepper. Place fish fillets on bottom of 12×7½×2-inch baking dish. Spoon rice mixture over fish. Cover with foil; bake in preheated 400°F oven for 45 to 50 minutes or until rice is tender and fish flakes with fork. Allow to stand 5 minutes before serving. Sprinkle with parsley. Garnish with lemon slices, if desired.

To Microwave: Combine onion, celery and garlic in microwave-safe bowl. Microwave at HIGH (100% power) for 3 minutes. Stir in rice, tomatoes with juice, lemon pepper, salt and ground red pepper. Microwave at HIGH power for an additional 5 minutes. Place fish fillets in 12×7½×2-inch microwave-safe baking dish. Spoon rice mixture over fish. Cover tightly with plastic wrap, turning up corner to vent. Microwave at HIGH power for 20 to 25 minutes or until rice is tender and fish flakes when tested with fork. Allow to stand 5 minutes before serving. Serve as above.

Nutrients per serving (conventional method):			
Calories	241	Cholesterol	38 mg
Fat	8 g	Sodium	580 mg

Nutrients per serving (microwave method):			
Calories	181	Cholesterol	38 mg
Fat	2 g	Sodium	580 mg

Grilled Summer Fish

Makes 4 servings

1¼ pounds fish fillets (such as cod, bluefish, haddock, sole)
1 medium green bell pepper, seeded and chopped
1 medium tomato, cored and chopped
¼ cup chopped green onions
1 tablespoon chopped dill
½ teaspoon salt
2 tablespoons lemon juice
1 cup (4 ounces) shredded Jarlsberg cheese

Grease 12×18-inch piece of heavy-duty aluminum foil. Place fish fillets in center of foil. Combine vegetables and place over fish. Sprinkle with dill and salt; drizzle with lemon juice. Top with Jarlsberg cheese. Fold up sides of foil, crimping to make a tight seal on top and ends. Place foil packet on top of hot barbecue grill. Grill for 25 minutes. Carefully open packet; if fish is still translucent in the middle, reseal and grill for an additional 5 to 10 minutes.

To Microwave: Assemble ingredients as above (omitting foil) in microwave-safe baking dish. Cover; microwave at HIGH (100% power) for 7 minutes. Fish is done when it flakes easily when tested with fork near center. If necessary, continue cooking on HIGH for an additional minute. Let stand, covered, for 5 minutes.

To Bake: Assemble ingredients as above (omitting foil) in large baking dish. Bake, uncovered, in 375°F oven for 20 minutes, or until fish flakes with fork and cheese is browned.

Nutrients per serving:

Calories	230	Cholesterol	92 mg
Fat	8 g	Sodium	429 mg

Favorite recipe from **Norseland Foods, Inc.**

Vegetable-Shrimp Stir-Fry

Makes 4 servings

1 tablespoon olive oil
6 ounces snow peas, trimmed
6 green onions, cut into 1-inch pieces
1 red bell pepper, cut into ½-inch strips
1 pound peeled, deveined medium shrimp
¼ pound large mushrooms, quartered
2 tablespoons soy sauce
1 tablespoon seasoned rice vinegar
1 teaspoon sesame oil
  Hot cooked rice (optional)

Heat olive oil in large skillet or wok over medium-high heat. Add snow peas, onions and red pepper; stir-fry 2 minutes.

Add shrimp; stir-fry 2 minutes or until shrimp are opaque. Add mushrooms; stir-fry until tender and most of liquid evaporates.

Add soy sauce, vinegar and sesame oil; heat thoroughly, stirring constantly. Serve over rice, if desired.

Nutrients per serving:

Calories	198	Cholesterol	175 mg
Fat	7 g	Sodium	688 mg

Vegetable-Shrimp Stir-Fry

Paella

Makes 6 servings

1 tablespoon olive oil
½ pound chicken breast cubes
1 cup uncooked long-grain white rice*
1 medium onion, chopped
1 clove garlic, minced
1½ cups chicken broth*
1 can (8 ounces) stewed tomatoes, chopped,
   reserving liquid
½ teaspoon paprika
⅛ to ¼ teaspoon ground red pepper
⅛ teaspoon ground saffron
½ pound medium shrimp, peeled and deveined
1 small red pepper, cut into strips
1 small green pepper, cut into strips
½ cup frozen green peas

Heat oil in Dutch oven over medium-high heat until hot. Add chicken and stir until browned. Add rice, onion, and garlic. Cook, stirring, until onion is tender and rice is lightly browned. Add broth, tomatoes, tomato liquid, paprika, ground red pepper, and saffron. Bring to a boil over high heat; stir. Reduce heat to low; cover and simmer 10 minutes. Add shrimp, pepper strips, and peas. Cover and simmer 10 minutes or until rice is tender, liquid is absorbed and shrimp are opaque.

If using medium grain rice, use 1¼ cups broth; if using parboiled rice, use 1¾ cups broth.

Nutrients per serving:

Calories	253	Cholesterol	82 mg
Fat	4 g	Sodium	392 mg

Favorite recipe from **USA Rice Council**

Shrimp Linguine

Makes 8 servings

1 pound medium shrimp, shelled and deveined
½ cup dry white wine
1 tablespoon lemon juice
1 tablespoon lime juice
¼ pound fresh snow peas
6 green onions, thinly sliced
1 tablespoon chopped fresh parsley
¾ teaspoon dried basil leaves, crushed
½ teaspoon lemon pepper seasoning
2 cloves garlic, minced
1 bay leaf
½ of a (1-pound) package CREAMETTE®
   Linguine, uncooked

In large skillet, combine shrimp, wine, lemon juice and lime juice. Bring to a boil. Reduce heat to low; simmer, covered, 3 minutes. Add remaining ingredients, *except* linguine. Cook, stirring constantly, just until snow peas are tender and shrimp are opaque, about 5 minutes. Prepare Creamette® Linguine according to package directions; drain. Remove bay leaf from shrimp mixture. Combine shrimp mixture and hot cooked linguine; toss to coat. Refrigerate leftovers.

Nutrients per serving:

Calories	191	Cholesterol	86 mg
Fat	1 g	Sodium	73 mg

No-Fuss Tuna Quiche

Makes 8 servings

1 unbaked 9-inch deep-dish pastry shell
1½ cups low-fat milk
3 extra large eggs
⅓ cup chopped green onions
1 tablespoon chopped drained pimiento
1 teaspoon dried basil leaves, crushed
½ teaspoon salt
1 can (6⅛ ounces) STARKIST® Tuna, drained
   and flaked
½ cup (2 ounces) shredded low-fat Cheddar
   cheese
8 spears (4 inches *each*) broccoli

Preheat oven to 450°F. Bake pastry shell for 5 minutes; remove to rack to cool. *Reduce oven temperature to 325°F.* For filling, in large bowl whisk together milk and eggs. Stir in onions, pimiento, basil and salt. Fold in tuna and cheese. Pour into prebaked pastry shell. Bake at 325°F for 30 minutes.

Meanwhile, in a saucepan steam broccoli spears over simmering water for 5 minutes. Drain; set aside. After 30 minutes baking time, arrange broccoli spears, spoke-fashion, over quiche. Bake 25 to 35 minutes more or until a knife inserted 2 inches from center comes out clean. Let stand for 5 minutes. Cut into 8 wedges, centering a broccoli spear in each wedge.

Note: *If desired, 1 cup chopped broccoli may be added to the filling before baking.*

Nutrients per serving:

Calories	226	Cholesterol	95 mg
Fat	10 g	Sodium	461 mg

No-Fuss Tuna Quiche

Spiced Fish and Pineapple

Makes 4 servings

1 tablespoon dried basil leaves, crushed
¼ teaspoon *each* rosemary, oregano, crushed
    red pepper flakes and anise seed
1 can (20 ounces) DOLE® Pineapple Chunks,
    undrained
1 tablespoon cornstarch
2 cloves garlic, pressed
1 tablespoon olive oil
1 pound white fish steaks, such as halibut
    Red bell pepper slivers for garnish (optional)

Preheat oven to 400°F. Combine spices in small bowl; set aside.

Drain ¼ cup juice from pineapple into 3-quart shallow casserole dish. For sauce, place undrained pineapple in large glass measuring cup. Stir in ¼ teaspoon spice mixture and cornstarch. Microwave on HIGH (100% power) 4 to 5 minutes until mixture boils and thickens; set aside.

Add remaining spice mixture, garlic and olive oil to casserole dish; blend well. Add fish. Spoon juice mixture over fish.

Bake 10 minutes until fish flakes easily with fork, spooning juice over once. Transfer to warm serving platter. Spoon remaining juices from casserole dish over fish. Garnish with red pepper slivers, if desired. Serve with reserved pineapple sauce.

Prep time: 15 minutes
Cook time: 10 minutes

Nutrients per serving:			
Calories	293	Cholesterol	47 mg
Fat	7 g	Sodium	82 mg

Spiced Fish and Pineapple

Marinated Seafood Kabobs with Orange Salsa

Makes 4 servings

Marinade
¼ cup Florida orange or tangerine juice
2 tablespoons canola or vegetable oil
2 teaspoons minced garlic
2 teaspoons minced ginger root
½ teaspoon grated orange or tangerine peel
    Salt and pepper to taste (optional)

1½ pounds firm-fleshed fish steaks, such as
    swordfish, Mako shark or tuna, cut into
    1½-inch pieces *or* 1½ pounds sea scallops

Salsa
2 large Florida oranges, peeled, white pith
    removed and diced (about 1½ cups)
1 large tomato, seeded and diced (about 1 cup)
⅓ cup minced red onion
1 teaspoon grated orange peel
1 teaspoon minced garlic
1 teaspoon minced ginger root
½ jalapeño chili,* seeded and minced
    (about 2 teaspoons)
¼ teaspoon salt
1 tablespoon minced fresh cilantro leaves

Combine marinade ingredients in medium bowl; add fish and toss to coat. Cover and refrigerate 1 hour.

For salsa, combine all salsa ingredients except cilantro in medium bowl; cover and refrigerate until ready to serve. Just before serving, stir in cilantro.

Preheat broiler. Drain fish and pat dry with paper towels. Thread onto 4 skewers. Arrange kabobs on broiler pan. Broil 4 inches from heat source 2 to 3 minutes on each side or until fish flakes easily with fork. Serve kabobs with salsa.

*Chilies can sting and irritate the skin; wear plastic disposable gloves when handling chilies and do not touch eyes. Wash hands after handling chilies.

Nutrients per serving:			
Calories	237	Cholesterol	61 mg
Fat	5 g	Sodium	512 mg

Favorite recipe from **Florida Department of Citrus**

Seafood-Pear Pasta

Makes 4 servings

    ¾ cup low fat milk
    1 cup part skim ricotta cheese
    6 ounces crab meat
    2 fresh California Bartlett pears, sliced
    ⅓ cup toasted sliced almonds (optional)
    2 tablespoons sherry
      Pepper to taste
      Dash ground nutmeg
    8 ounces pasta, hot cooked and drained

Heat milk in small saucepan over medium heat until hot but not boiling. Stir ricotta cheese into hot milk; set aside. Heat crab meat, pears and almonds in large nonstick skillet over medium heat. Stir in sherry; cook 1 minute. Add ricotta cheese mixture; blend well. Season with pepper and nutmeg. Serve over pasta.

Nutrients per serving:

Calories	265	Cholesterol	48 mg
Fat	7 g	Sodium	451 mg

Favorite recipe from **California Tree Fruit Agreement**

Today's Slim Stuffed Trout Steaks

Makes 4 servings

    1 cup low fat (1%) Cottage cheese
    ½ cup chopped tomato
    ½ cup chopped celery
    1 teaspoon dried dill weed
    ½ teaspoon salt
    ¼ teaspoon dry mustard
    1 pound fresh or thawed frozen trout steaks
    1 teaspoon butter

Combine Cottage cheese, tomato, celery, dill weed, salt and mustard in small bowl; stir until well blended. Close and secure ends of each trout steak with toothpicks to form pockets. Fill pockets with Cottage cheese mixture. Melt butter in large skillet over medium heat until hot and bubbly. Add trout steaks; cook 10 to 15 minutes until fish flakes easily with fork, turning once.

Nutrients per serving:

Calories	226	Cholesterol	70 mg
Fat	9 g	Sodium	580 mg

Favorite recipe from **Wisconsin Milk Marketing Board** © 1994

Steamed Salmon with Cabbage in Parchment

Steamed Salmon with Cabbage in Parchment

Makes 4 servings

      Parchment paper
    12 napa cabbage leaves, blanched
     2 cups cooked corn kernels, drained
     4 British Columbia Fresh Farmed Salmon
        Fillets (3½ ounces *each*)
     1 tablespoon chopped chives
     1 tablespoon chopped parsley
     4 teaspoons balsamic vinegar
        Salt and pepper to taste (optional)

Preheat oven to 425°F. Cut four 12-inch squares of parchment; fold each in half. Open parchment. Stack 3 cabbage leaves near fold on each square, with insides of leaves facing up. Place ½ cup corn, 1 salmon fillet, ¼ of chives, ¼ of parsley, 1 teaspoon vinegar, salt and pepper on 1 cabbage stack. Bring top half of parchment over mixture; fold edges together to form tight seal. Repeat with remaining 3 squares. Place parchment packages on baking sheet; bake 8 to 10 minutes until fish is firm to the touch. To serve, cut slit in top of each parchment package with scissors. Carefully open packages, allowing steam to escape.

Nutrients per serving:

Calories	249	Cholesterol	65 mg
Fat	10 g	Sodium	125 mg

Favorite recipe from **British Columbia Farmed Salmon Institute**

Citrus Fish Broil

Makes 4 servings

1¼ pounds fresh fish fillets
½ cup HEINZ® Chili Sauce
2 to 3 tablespoons frozen orange juice
    concentrate, thawed
2 tablespoons lemon juice
1 tablespoon HEINZ® Worcestershire Sauce
1 tablespoon olive or vegetable oil
    Chopped fresh parsley

Cut fish into 4 pieces; place in shallow baking dish. In small bowl, combine chili sauce, orange juice concentrate, lemon juice, Worcestershire sauce and oil; pour over fish, turning to coat. Cover; refrigerate 30 minutes.

Preheat broiler. Place fish on greased broiler pan; spoon any remaining chili sauce mixture over fish. Broil 4 inches from heat source, allowing 10 minutes cooking time for each inch of fish thickness. Fish is cooked when it turns opaque and flakes easily with fork. Sprinkle parsley over fish before serving.

Nutrients per serving:

Calories	208	Cholesterol	68 mg
Fat	5 g	Sodium	606 mg

Snappy Fish Fillets

Makes 4 servings, about 2 cups sauce

1 can (14 ounces) Italian-style stewed tomatoes,
    cut into bite-sized pieces
⅓ cup HEINZ® 57 Sauce
1 tablespoon Dijon-style mustard
1¼ pounds fish fillets or steaks (such as flounder,
    catfish, orange roughy or sole)
1 teaspoon cornstarch
1 tablespoon water
    Hot cooked rice (optional)

In large skillet, combine first 3 ingredients. Place fish in sauce mixture; spoon sauce mixture over fish. Heat over medium-high heat until sauce mixture is bubbly. Reduce heat to low; simmer, uncovered, 5 to 6 minutes until fish turns opaque and flakes easily with fork, turning once. Remove fish to warm serving plate. Combine cornstarch and water in small cup; mix well. Stir into sauce mixture. Cook until sauce thickens, stirring occasionally. Serve fish and sauce with rice, if desired.

Nutrients per serving:

Calories	188	Cholesterol	68 mg
Fat	2 g	Sodium	416 mg

Snapper Fillets with Orange-Shallot Sauce

Makes 6 servings

2 Florida oranges
6 red snapper fillets* (about 2¼ pounds)
1 tablespoon olive oil
1 cup finely chopped shallots
2 cloves garlic, minced
3 tablespoons all-purpose flour
1 cup chicken broth
1 cup Florida orange juice
1 tablespoon grated orange rind
2 tablespoons sherry
1½ teaspoons dried oregano leaves, crushed
    Salt and pepper to taste (optional)
2 tablespoons chopped parsley, for garnish

Preheat broiler. Thinly slice oranges into rounds; set aside. Place snapper fillets, skin sides down, on nonstick jelly-roll pan. Broil 4 inches from heat source 5 to 8 minutes until fish flakes easily with fork. Remove from broiler; set aside. Meanwhile, heat oil in large nonstick skillet over medium-high heat until hot, but not smoking. Add shallots and garlic; cook and stir 3 to 4 minutes until shallots begin to brown. Add flour; cook about 30 seconds, stirring until well blended. Stir in broth, orange juice, orange rind, sherry, oregano, salt and pepper. Bring to a boil, stirring constantly, until slightly thickened. Add orange slices and fish fillets, skin sides up. Cook 1 to 2 minutes until fish is heated through and orange slices are slightly softened. Garnish with parsley. Serve immediately.

*You may substitute any lightly textured fish, such as tuna, flounder, grouper, swordfish or scrod, for red snapper.

Nutrients per serving:

Calories	276	Cholesterol	62 mg
Fat	5 g	Sodium	242 mg

Favorite recipe from **Florida Department of Citrus**

Grilled Tuna with Fruit Salsa

Makes 4 servings

⅓ cup pineapple juice
1 tablespoon vegetable oil
1 tablespoon reduced sodium soy sauce
    Juice of 1 lime
4 tuna steaks* (6 to 8 ounces *each*)
1 cup chopped fresh plums
1 cup chopped fresh peaches
½ cup chopped fresh pineapple
¼ cup finely chopped red bell pepper
2 tablespoons white wine vinegar
2 tablespoons minced fresh mint leaves
    (optional)

Combine first 4 ingredients. Arrange tuna steaks in glass dish; pour pineapple juice mixture over steaks. Cover and marinate in refrigerator at least 1 hour.

Meanwhile, to prepare salsa, combine remaining ingredients in medium bowl; stir gently. Cover and refrigerate until ready to serve.

Coat grill rack with vegetable cooking spray. Remove tuna from marinade and place on grill 4 to 5 inches above medium-hot coals. Grill about 8 to 10 minutes on each side or just until fish begins to flake easily with fork. Serve warm with reserved salsa.

You may substitute swordfish, shark, halibut, catfish, tilapia or salmon steaks for tuna steaks.

Nutrients per serving:

Calories	282	Cholesterol	76 mg
Fat	5 g	Sodium	206 mg

Favorite recipe from **National Fisheries Institute**

Apple-Halibut Kabobs

Makes 4 servings

½ cup dry white wine or chicken broth
2 tablespoons olive oil
2 tablespoons lime juice
2 tablespoons finely chopped onion
1 teaspoon salt
½ teaspoon dried thyme leaves, crushed
⅛ teaspoon black pepper
1 medium Washington Golden Delicious or
    Rome Beauty apple, cored and cut into
    1-inch cubes
1 medium green or red bell pepper, cut into
    1-inch squares
1 small onion, cut into 1-inch wedges
1 to 1½ pounds halibut, cut into 1- to 1½-inch
    cubes

Combine wine, oil, lime juice, chopped onion, salt, thyme and black pepper in small bowl; mix well. Place remaining ingredients in large glass dish. Pour wine mixture over top. Cover and marinate 1 to 2 hours in refrigerator, stirring once. Alternately thread apple, bell pepper, onion and halibut pieces onto long metal or bamboo skewers;* repeat 5 times on each skewer. Place 1 apple piece on end of each skewer. Broil or grill 4 to 5 inches from heat source 6 to 8 minutes until fish flakes easily with fork. Serve warm.

If using bamboo skewers, soak in water 20 to 30 minutes before using.

Nutrients per serving:

Calories	198	Cholesterol	60 mg
Fat	6 g	Sodium	365 mg

Favorite recipe from **Washington Apple Commission**

Baked Sole Pacifica

Makes 4 servings

1 can (16 ounces) California cling peach slices
    in juice or extra light syrup, undrained
4 sole fillets (about 1 pound)
½ teaspoon dried dill weed
1 tablespoon olive oil
2 onions, peeled and cut into wedges
4 cups julienned zucchini strips
2 cups red bell pepper strips
½ teaspoon herb pepper seasoning
    Lemon wedges

Preheat broiler. Drain peaches, reserving liquid. Place fish on broiler pan. Brush both sides of fillets with peach liquid and sprinkle with dill weed. Broil 4 inches from heat source 10 minutes or until fish flakes easily with fork, turning halfway through cooking. Heat oil in 10-inch skillet over medium-high heat until hot; add onions. Cook and stir until crisp-tender. Add zucchini; cook and stir 2 minutes. Add red pepper strips and peach slices. Cook until heated through. Stir in herb pepper seasoning. To serve, place vegetable-peach mixture on serving plate and top with fish. Serve with lemon wedges.

Nutrients per serving:

Calories	230	Cholesterol	54 mg
Fat	5 g	Sodium	102 mg

Favorite recipe from **California Cling Peach Advisory Board**

Orange Roughy with Cucumber Relish

Orange Roughy with Cucumber Relish

Makes 4 servings

1 can (11 ounces) mandarin oranges, drained
1 small cucumber, peeled, seeded and finely
    chopped
⅓ cup HEINZ® Distilled White Vinegar
1 green onion, minced
1 tablespoon snipped fresh dill *or* 1 teaspoon
    dill weed
   Nonstick cooking spray
4 orange roughy fillets (about 5 ounces *each*)
   Dill sprigs

Reserve 8 orange sections for garnish; coarsely chop
remaining sections and combine with cucumber,
vinegar, onion and dill in small bowl. Spray broiler
pan with nonstick cooking spray; place fish on pan.
Spoon 1 tablespoon liquid from cucumber mixture
over each fillet. Broil, 3 to 4 inches from heat source,
8 to 10 minutes or until fish flakes with fork. To
serve, spoon cucumber relish on top of fish. Garnish
with reserved orange sections and dill sprigs.

Nutrients per serving:			
Calories	229	Cholesterol	28 mg
Fat	10 g	Sodium	95 mg

Garlic Shrimp & Vegetables

Makes 4 servings

2 tablespoons margarine
1 tablespoon olive oil
1 bunch green onions, chopped
1 red bell pepper, chopped
1 pound peeled, deveined large shrimp
2 cloves garlic, minced
   Juice of 1 lime
   Salt and black pepper (optional)
1 (9-ounce) package fresh spinach fettuccine,
    cooked and drained

Heat margarine and oil in medium skillet or wok over
medium heat. Add onions and red pepper. Stir-fry
2 minutes or until vegetables are crisp-tender.

Add shrimp and garlic; stir-fry 2 minutes or until
shrimp are opaque.

Stir in lime juice. Season with salt and black pepper,
if desired. Serve over hot fettuccine. Garnish as
desired.

Nutrients per serving:			
Calories	269	Cholesterol	196 mg
Fat	9 g	Sodium	412 mg

Peppercorn-Crusted Rainbow Trout with Corn-Yogurt Sauce

Makes 4 servings

1 can (8 ounces) corn, undrained
¾ cup nonfat plain yogurt
¾ teaspoon curry powder, divided
2 tablespoons mixed whole peppercorns (pink,
    green and white), coarsely ground
½ teaspoon ground nutmeg
4 CLEAR SPRINGS® Brand Idaho Rainbow
    Trout fillets (4 ounces *each*)

Preheat broiler. In blender or food processor, blend
corn with liquid, yogurt and ¼ teaspoon curry
powder until smooth. Transfer to small saucepan;
heat over low heat. Meanwhile, in shallow dish,
combine peppercorns with remaining ½ teaspoon
curry and nutmeg. Press flesh sides of fillets into
pepper mixture; arrange, skin sides down, in shallow
baking dish. Broil, 4 inches from heat, for 3 minutes
or until trout turns opaque. To serve, spoon hot corn
sauce on each plate and top with trout. Serve
immediately.

Nutrients per serving:			
Calories	221	Cholesterol	86 mg
Fat	8 g	Sodium	75 mg

Catfish Parmesan

Makes 4 servings

- ½ cup dry bread crumbs
- ¼ cup grated Parmesan cheese
- 2 tablespoons chopped fresh parsley
- ½ teaspoon paprika
- ¼ teaspoon dried oregano leaves, crushed
- ¼ teaspoon dried basil leaves, crushed
- ¼ teaspoon black pepper
- 1 pound skinless catfish fillets
- ⅓ cup low-fat milk
- 2 teaspoons vegetable oil

In small bowl, combine bread crumbs, Parmesan cheese and seasonings. Dip fillets in milk; roll in crumb mixture. Spray baking pan with nonstick cooking spray. Arrange fish in pan; drizzle with oil. Bake at 450°F for 8 to 10 minutes or just until fish flakes easily when tested with fork.

Nutrients per serving:

Calories	231	Cholesterol	73 mg
Fat	10 g	Sodium	213 mg

Favorite recipe from **National Fisheries Institute**

Wild Rice Seafood Salad

Makes 6 servings

- ⅓ cup low fat mayonnaise
- ⅓ cup nonfat sour cream alternative
- ¼ cup low sodium chili sauce
- 1 tablespoon lemon juice
- 1 teaspoon Dijon-style mustard
- 3 cups cooked wild rice
- ½ cup thinly sliced green onions
- 1 large tomato, peeled, seeded and diced
- 1 cup thinly sliced celery
- ½ pound imitation crabmeat
  Salt and pepper (optional)
- 6 lettuce cups (optional)
  Chopped parsley (optional)

To prepare dressing, blend together mayonnaise, sour cream, chili sauce, lemon juice and mustard in small bowl. Refrigerate.

Combine wild rice, onions, tomato, celery and imitation crabmeat. Season with salt and pepper to taste, if desired. Spoon rice mixture evenly into lettuce cups and garnish with parsley, if desired. Serve with dressing.

Nutrients per serving:

Calories	179	Cholesterol	10 mg
Fat	4 g	Sodium	327 mg

Favorite recipe from **Minnesota Cultivated Wild Rice Council**

Wisconsin Tuna Cakes with Lemon-Dill Sauce

Makes 4 servings

- 1 can (12½ ounces) STARKIST® Tuna, drained and finely flaked
- ¾ cup seasoned bread crumbs
- ¼ cup minced green onions
- 2 tablespoons chopped drained pimentos
- 1 egg
- ½ cup low-fat milk
- ½ teaspoon grated lemon peel
- 2 tablespoons margarine or butter

Lemon-Dill Sauce
- ¼ cup chicken broth
- 1 tablespoon lemon juice
- ¼ teaspoon dried dill weed

  Hot steamed shredded zucchini and carrots
  Lemon slices

In large bowl, toss together tuna, bread crumbs, onions and pimentos. In small bowl, beat together egg and milk; stir in lemon peel. Stir into tuna mixture; toss until moistened. With lightly floured hands, shape into eight 4-inch patties.

In large nonstick skillet, melt margarine. Fry patties, a few at a time, until golden brown on both sides, about 3 minutes per side. Place on ovenproof platter in 300°F oven until ready to serve.

For Lemon-Dill Sauce, in small saucepan, heat broth, lemon juice and dill. Serve tuna cakes with zucchini and carrots; spoon sauce over cakes. Garnish with lemon slices.

Nutrients per serving (2 patties plus 1 tablespoon sauce):

Calories	278	Cholesterol	85 mg
Fat	10 g	Sodium	576 mg

Wisconsin Tuna Cakes with Lemon-Dill Sauce

Salmon Yakatori with Peaches

Salmon Yakatori with Peaches

Makes 4 servings

Yakatori Sauce (recipe follows)
1 pound salmon fillet, cut into 16 large cubes
2 fresh California peaches, *each* cut into
    8 wedges
2 zucchini, cut into ¼- to ½-inch diagonal slices
1 onion, cut into 1-inch wedges

Prepare Yakatori Sauce; set aside. Alternately thread salmon, peach, zucchini and onion pieces onto 8 long metal skewers. Place in shallow baking pan in single layer and pour Yakatori Sauce over kabobs. Marinate in refrigerator 2 to 3 hours. Grill 4 to 5 inches above hot coals 5 to 6 minutes on each side until fish flakes easily with fork. Brush with remaining Yakatori Sauce while grilling. Serve immediately.

Yakatori Sauce: Combine ½ cup water, ¼ cup low sodium soy sauce, ¼ cup wine vinegar, 3 tablespoons sugar, 1 tablespoon cornstarch and 1 teaspoon grated ginger root in saucepan. Cook over medium-high heat until mixture comes to a boil and is thickened, stirring constantly. Makes about 1 cup.

Nutrients per serving:

Calories	228	Cholesterol	74 mg
Fat	7 g	Sodium	588 mg

Favorite recipe from **California Tree Fruit Agreement**

Fruitful Sole and Nectarines Rémoulade

Makes 4 servings

Rémoulade Sauce (recipe follows)
4 sole fillets (1 pound)
Pepper to taste
Dried dill weed to taste
2 tablespoons water
2 fresh California nectarines or peaches, sliced
    (about 2 cups)

To Microwave: Prepare Rémoulade Sauce; set aside. Roll up sole fillets and fasten with wooden picks. (If fillets are large, cut in half lengthwise before rolling.) Stand on end, turban-fashion, in microwave-safe dish. Season with pepper and dill weed. Add water to dish. Cover and

microwave on HIGH (100% power) 3 to 4 minutes or until fish flakes easily with fork. Add nectarine slices to dish and microwave, covered, 1 minute more or until hot. Transfer fish and fruit to serving platter and remove picks. Serve with Rémoulade Sauce.

Rémoulade Sauce: Stir together 1 cup plain low fat yogurt, ¼ cup chopped dill pickles or capers, 2 tablespoons chopped green onion, 2 teaspoons Dijon-style mustard and 1 teaspoon dried tarragon leaves, crushed, in small bowl until smooth. Makes about 1¼ cups.

Nutrients per serving:

Calories	178	Cholesterol	82 mg
Fat	4 g	Sodium	414 mg

Favorite recipe from **California Tree Fruit Agreement**

Dilled Tuna Sandwiches

Makes 4 servings

1 can (12½ ounces) chunk light tuna in water,
    drained
¼ cup thinly sliced green onion with tops
¼ cup chopped seeded cucumber
3 tablespoons reduced calorie mayonnaise
1½ teaspoons drained capers
1 teaspoon Dijon-style mustard
½ to 1 teaspoon lemon juice
¾ teaspoon dried dill weed
    White pepper to taste
4 slices multigrain bread, toasted
8 slices cucumber
2 slices tomato, cut into halves

Break tuna into chunks in medium bowl; add green onion and chopped cucumber. Stir in mayonnaise, capers, mustard, lemon juice and dill weed until blended. Season with pepper. Spread tuna mixture on toasted bread slices (open-faced); garnish with cucumber and tomato slices.

Nutrients per serving:

Calories	209	Cholesterol	17 mg
Fat	5 g	Sodium	527 mg

Favorite recipe from **Canned Food Information Council**

Fish Françoise

Fish Françoise

Makes 4 servings

1 can (14½ ounces) DEL MONTE® Original
    Style Stewed Tomatoes
1 tablespoon lemon juice
2 cloves garlic, minced
½ teaspoon dried tarragon leaves, crushed
⅛ teaspoon black pepper
3 tablespoons whipping cream
    Vegetable oil
1½ pounds firm white fish (such as halibut or cod)
    Lemon wedges

Preheat broiler; position rack 4 inches from heat. In
large saucepan, combine tomatoes with liquid, lemon
juice, garlic, tarragon and pepper. Cook, uncovered,
over medium-high heat about 10 minutes or until
liquid has evaporated. Add cream. Cook over low heat
5 minutes or until very thick; set aside. Brush broiler
pan with oil. Arrange fish on pan; season with salt
and pepper, if desired. Broil fish 3 to 4 minutes per
side or until fish flakes easily with fork. Spread
tomato mixture over top of fish. Broil 1 minute. Serve
immediately with lemon wedges.

Prep time: 5 minutes
Cook time: 19 minutes

Nutrients per serving:

Calories	240	Cholesterol	78 mg
Fat	7 g	Sodium	341 mg

Oven Steamed Rainbow Trout in Parchment

Makes 4 servings

4 tablespoons chopped fresh parsley
2 teaspoons minced garlic
2 teaspoons grated orange peel
¼ teaspoon salt
⅛ teaspoon ground black pepper
    Parchment paper
4 CLEAR SPRINGS® Brand Idaho Rainbow
    Trout fillets (4 ounces *each*)
4 teaspoons olive oil

Preheat oven to 375°F. In small bowl, combine
parsley, garlic, orange peel, salt and pepper; set
aside. Cut four 15×12-inch pieces of parchment; fold
each piece in half and trim to form semicircle. Unfold
parchment; place trout fillets, skin sides down, on
parchment near fold. Sprinkle each fillet with
1 tablespoon parsley mixture and 1 teaspoon oil. Fold
top half of parchment over trout; fold and seal edges
tightly. Place parchment bundles on baking sheet;
bake 10 minutes until parchment is browned and
puffed. Serve immediately.

Nutrients per serving:

Calories	178	Cholesterol	65 mg
Fat	8 g	Sodium	166 mg

Tuna Casserole with a Twist

Makes 4 servings

1 can (5 ounces) PET® Evaporated Skimmed
    Milk
1½ teaspoons all-purpose flour
1 cup (4 ounces) shredded low-fat Cheddar
    cheese
2 cups (8 ounces) broccoli flowerets, cooked
1 can (about 6½ ounces) tuna packed in spring
    water, drained
4 ounces corkscrew noodles, cooked according
    to package directions and drained
⅓ cup chopped onion

In large saucepan, whisk together evaporated milk
and flour; cook over medium heat until thick and
bubbly, stirring occasionally. Add cheese; stir until
cheese melts.

Stir in remaining ingredients. Cook until heated
through.

Nutrients per serving:

Calories	220	Cholesterol	38 mg
Fat	6 g	Sodium	412 mg

Singing Shrimp with Pineapple

Makes 4 servings

1 medium DOLE® Fresh Pineapple

Singing Spice
  ¼ teaspoon *each* ground allspice, ground anise
    seed (optional), ground cinnamon, ground
    cloves, ground ginger and crushed red
    pepper flakes

  1 pound large shrimp, peeled and deveined
  ½ teaspoon salt
  1 onion, cut into wedges
  1 large DOLE® Red Bell Pepper, seeded and
    sliced
  1 clove garlic, pressed
  1 teaspoon vegetable oil
  ¾ cup water
  1½ teaspoons cornstarch
  2 tablespoons chopped cilantro, divided
  2 tablespoons chopped fresh mint leaves,
    divided

Twist crown from pineapple. Cut pineapple in half
lengthwise. Refrigerate half for another use, such as
salads. Cut fruit from shell with knife. Cut fruit
crosswise into thin slices.

Combine spices in cup. Sprinkle half the spice
mixture over shrimp. Sprinkle shrimp with salt.

In 10-inch nonstick skillet, cook and stir onion, bell
pepper and garlic in oil over medium-high heat until
tender.

Blend water and cornstarch in cup. Stir cornstarch
mixture and remaining spice mixture into skillet.

Arrange shrimp on top of onion mixture. Reduce heat
to low. Cover; simmer 5 to 7 minutes or until shrimp
are opaque, stirring occasionally. Remove shrimp to
serving plate with slotted spoon.

Add pineapple to onion mixture in skillet with
1 tablespoon *each* cilantro and mint. Stir until heated
through. Serve over shrimp. Sprinkle with remaining
cilantro and mint.

Nutrients per serving:			
Calories	270	Cholesterol	157 mg
Fat	3 g	Sodium	270 mg

"Grilled" Tuna with Vegetables in Herb Butter

Makes 4 servings

  4 pieces heavy-duty aluminum foil, *each*
    12×18 inches
  1 can (12½ ounces) STARKIST® Tuna, drained
    and broken into chunks
  1 cup slivered red or green bell pepper
  1 cup slivered yellow squash or zucchini
  1 cup pea pods, cut crosswise into halves
  1 cup slivered carrots
  4 green onions, cut into 2-inch slices
    Salt and black pepper to taste (optional)

Herb Butter
  3 tablespoons butter or margarine, melted
  1 tablespoon lemon or lime juice
  1 clove garlic, minced
  2 teaspoons dried tarragon leaves, crushed
  1 teaspoon dried dill weed

On each piece of foil, mound tuna, bell pepper,
squash, pea pods, carrots and onions. Sprinkle with
salt and black pepper.

For Herb Butter, in small bowl stir together butter,
lemon juice, garlic, tarragon and dill weed. Drizzle
over tuna and vegetables. Fold edges of each foil
square together to make packets.

To grill: Place foil packets about 4 inches above hot coals.
Grill for 10 to 12 minutes or until heated through, turning
packets over halfway through grill time.

To bake: Place foil packets on baking sheet. Bake in
preheated 450°F oven for 15 to 20 minutes, or until heated
through.

To serve: Cut an "X" on top of each packet; peel back
foil.

Nutrients per serving:			
Calories	235	Cholesterol	70 mg
Fat	9 g	Sodium	519 mg

"Grilled" Tuna with Vegetables in Herb Butter

Scallop Stir-Fry

Makes 4 servings

6 ounces uncooked ramen noodles or vermicelli
1 tablespoon olive oil
1 pound asparagus, cut into 1-inch pieces
1 red bell pepper, cut into thin rings
3 green onions, chopped
1 large clove garlic, minced
1 pound sea scallops, halved crosswise
2 tablespoons soy sauce
1 teaspoon hot pepper sauce
1 teaspoon sesame oil
Juice of ½ lime

Cook noodles in lightly salted boiling water according to package directions.

Meanwhile, heat olive oil in wok or large skillet over high heat. Add asparagus, red pepper, onions and garlic. Stir-fry 2 minutes.

Add scallops; stir-fry until scallops turn opaque.

Stir in soy sauce, hot pepper sauce, sesame oil and lime juice. Add noodles; heat thoroughly, stirring occasionally.

Nutrients per serving:

Calories	220	Cholesterol	37 mg
Fat	7 g	Sodium	864 mg

Sweet and Sour Prawns

Makes 6 servings

1 can (8¼ ounces) DOLE® Pineapple Chunks in Syrup*
2 tablespoons vegetable oil
¾ pound medium shrimp, peeled and deveined
1 DOLE® Carrot, cut diagonally in thin slices
1 small DOLE® Green Bell Pepper, seeded and chunked
1 can (11 ounces) lychee fruit, drained (optional)
2 tablespoons white vinegar
2 tablespoons catsup
1½ tablespoons soy sauce
1 tablespoon chopped crystallized ginger
1 tablespoon cornstarch
2 tablespoons water
3 cups hot cooked rice

Drain pineapple; reserve syrup.

Heat wok or skillet until hot. Add oil, swirling to coat sides. Add shrimp; stir-fry 1 to 2 minutes until shrimp are opaque. Add carrot, bell pepper, lychee and pineapple. Stir-fry for about 2 minutes.

Add reserved pineapple syrup, vinegar, catsup, soy sauce and ginger. Cook, stirring, for 1 minute.

Blend cornstarch with water in cup. Add to wok. Cook, stirring, until sauce boils and thickens. Serve over rice.

*Use pineapple packed in juice, if desired.

Nutrients per serving:

Calories	260	Cholesterol	78 mg
Fat	5 g	Sodium	316 mg

Easy Tuna Melt

Makes 2 servings

1 (3½-ounce) can solid white water-pack tuna, drained
2 teaspoons reduced-calorie salad dressing
1 teaspoon dill pickle relish
1 English muffin, split and toasted
2 tomato slices
2 slices BORDEN® Lite-line® Process Cheese Product,* any flavor

Combine tuna, salad dressing and relish. Top each muffin half with tomato slice, then half the tuna mixture and cheese product slice. Broil or heat in microwave oven until cheese product begins to melt. Refrigerate leftovers.

*"½ the calories"– 8% milkfat product

Nutrients per serving:

Calories	193	Cholesterol	34 mg
Fat	7 g	Sodium	833 mg

Scallop Stir-Fry

Southwest Snapper

Makes 4 servings

1 pound red snapper, scrod or halibut fillets
   Salt and black pepper (optional)
½ cup PACE® Picante Sauce
1 medium tomato, chopped
¼ cup sliced green onions with tops
¼ cup chopped cilantro or fresh parsley
¼ cup sliced ripe olives (optional)
   Additional PACE® Picante Sauce (optional)

Place fish in shallow baking dish. Sprinkle with salt and pepper to taste. Cover; bake at 400°F or until fish just flakes when tested with fork (about 10 minutes per inch of thickness). Pour off juices. Spoon ½ cup Pace® Picante Sauce evenly over fish; top with tomato and green onions. Bake, uncovered, until heated through, about 5 minutes. Sprinkle with cilantro and olives. Serve with additional Pace® Picante Sauce, if desired. Garnish as desired.

Nutrients per serving:

Calories	130	Cholesterol	56 mg
Fat	1 g	Sodium	545 mg

Southwest Snapper

Microwaved Lemon-Apple Fish Rolls

Makes 4 servings

4 sole, cod or red snapper fillets (1 pound)
   Grated peel of 1 SUNKIST® Lemon, divided
1 teaspoon dill weed, divided
¾ cup *plus* 2 tablespoons apple juice, divided
   Juice of ½ SUNKIST® Lemon
2 tablespoons finely minced onion
1 tablespoon unsalted margarine
1 tablespoon all-purpose flour
1 tablespoon chopped fresh parsley

To Microwave: Sprinkle fish with half the lemon peel and half the dill. Roll up each fillet; place seam sides down in 8-inch round microwave-safe dish. Combine ¾ cup apple juice, lemon juice, onion, remaining lemon peel and dill; pour over fish. Dot with margarine. Cover dish loosely with vented plastic wrap. Microwave at HIGH (100% power) for 3 minutes. Uncover; spoon cooking liquid over fish. Cook, covered, 3 to 4 minutes longer, until fish flakes easily with fork. Remove fish to serving dish; let stand, covered, while preparing sauce.

Pour cooking liquid from fish into small microwave-safe bowl. Gradually blend remaining 2 tablespoons apple juice into flour; stir into cooking liquid. Microwave at HIGH, uncovered, 3 to 4 minutes (stirring twice), until sauce boils and thickens slightly. Add parsley; spoon over fish.

Nutrients per serving:

Calories	164	Cholesterol	55 mg
Fat	4 g	Sodium	94 mg

Tuna Bruschetta

Makes 4 servings

1 cup (4 ounces) SARGENTO® Preferred Light
    Fancy Shredded Supreme Mozzarella
    Cheese
1 can (3½ ounces) tuna packed in water, well
    drained and flaked
4 plum tomatoes, seeded and chopped
2 tablespoons minced onion
2 teaspoons minced fresh parsley
½ teaspoon dried oregano leaves, crushed
4 slices Italian bread (*each* 6×½ inches)
2 tablespoons olive oil
2 cloves garlic, halved

In medium bowl, combine cheese, tuna, tomatoes, onion, parsley and oregano. Set aside. Brush both sides of bread slices with olive oil and rub surfaces with cut sides of garlic. In dry preheated skillet, grill bread until light golden brown. Turn and top each toasted surface with ¼ of cheese mixture. Continue to grill until cheese melts and bread is golden brown on bottom. Serve immediately.

Nutrients per serving:

Calories	249	Cholesterol	29 mg
Fat	10 g	Sodium	420 mg

Oven Camp-Out Fish with BBQ Sauce

Makes 4 servings

¼ cup minced onion
1 clove garlic, minced
1 teaspoon margarine
1 can (8 ounces) DOLE® Pineapple Tidbits in
    Juice
½ cup bottled barbecue sauce
1 tablespoon packed brown sugar *or* honey
4 cod or red snapper fillets (1 pound)
1 tablespoon vegetable oil
    Juice from 1 DOLE® Lemon

In large skillet, cook and stir onion and garlic in margarine until onion is soft. Add pineapple with juice, barbecue sauce and brown sugar. Cook over medium heat, stirring, until thickened and slightly reduced. Brush fish with oil. Sprinkle with lemon juice. Broil, 4 to 6 inches from heat, 5 minutes. Turn fish and continue cooking 5 to 7 minutes longer until fish flakes when tested with fork. Serve fish with barbecue sauce.

Nutrients per serving:

Calories	238	Cholesterol	63 mg
Fat	6 g	Sodium	356 mg

Grilled Prawns with Salsa Vera Cruz

Grilled Prawns with Salsa Vera Cruz

Makes 4 servings

1 can (14½ ounces) DEL MONTE® Mexican
    Recipe Stewed Tomatoes
1 orange, peeled and chopped
¼ cup sliced green onion
¼ cup chopped cilantro or fresh parsley
1 tablespoon olive oil
1 to 2 teaspoons minced jalapeño pepper
1 small clove garlic, crushed
1 pound medium shrimp, peeled and deveined

Drain tomatoes, reserving liquid; chop tomatoes. For salsa, in medium bowl combine tomatoes, reserved liquid, orange, green onion, cilantro, oil, jalapeño pepper and garlic. Season to taste with salt and black pepper, if desired. Thread shrimp onto skewers; season with salt and black pepper, if desired. Brush grill lightly with olive oil. Cook shrimp over hot coals about 3 minutes per side or until shrimp just turn opaque. Top with salsa. Serve over rice, if desired.

Prep time: 27 minutes
Cook time: 6 minutes

Nutrients per serving:

Calories	166	Cholesterol	166 mg
Fat	5 g	Sodium	463 mg

Baked Fish with Honey-Mustard Sauce

Makes 4 servings

1¼ pounds firm, white fish fillets (such as cod, haddock, red snapper, halibut, orange roughy, trout or catfish)
1 teaspoon vegetable oil
1 teaspoon lemon juice
⅓ teaspoon salt
⅛ teaspoon pepper
3 tablespoons coarse-grained mustard
2 tablespoons reduced calorie mayonnaise
1 tablespoon *plus* 1 teaspoon honey
1½ teaspoons yellow mustard

Preheat oven to 450°F. Cut fish into 4 pieces and place in single layer in greased shallow baking pan. Tuck under any thin edges of fish. Combine oil and lemon juice; brush on fish. Sprinkle with salt and pepper. To make Honey-Mustard Sauce, combine coarse-grained mustard, mayonnaise, honey and yellow mustard. Stir well; set aside. Bake 4 to 6 minutes for each ½ inch of thickness or until fish flakes easily with fork at thickest part. Transfer fish with slotted spatula to plates. Serve immediately with Honey-Mustard Sauce.

Nutrients per serving (includes 2 tablespoons sauce):			
Calories	184	Cholesterol	64 mg
Fat	5 g	Sodium	397 mg

Favorite recipe from **National Fisheries Institute**

Orange Roughy Italia

Makes 5 servings

1½ pounds orange roughy fillets (about 6)
2 tablespoons bottled Italian salad dressing
2 tablespoons (¼ stick) margarine or butter
¼ cup chopped onion
¼ cup sliced celery
¼ cup *each* green and red bell pepper strips
1 teaspoon minced garlic
¼ cup chopped parsley
½ teaspoon Italian herb seasoning
1 cup Rice CHEX® brand cereal, crushed to ⅔ cup
1 cup Corn CHEX® brand cereal, crushed to ⅔ cup

Preheat broiler. Arrange fillets on greased broiler pan; drizzle with dressing. Broil 4 to 5 inches from heat source for 5 to 7 minutes or until fish flakes easily with fork. In large skillet over medium heat, melt margarine; add onion, celery, green and red peppers and garlic. Cook and stir 2 minutes or until crisp-tender. Stir in parsley, herb seasoning and cereal. Spoon over fillets. Broil 1 to 2 minutes more or until topping is golden brown. Serve immediately.

To Microwave: Arrange fillets on microwave-safe roasting rack; drizzle with dressing. Cover with waxed paper. Microwave on HIGH (100% power) 4 to 6 minutes or until fish flakes easily with fork. In 1-quart microwave-safe bowl, microwave margarine, onion, celery, green and red pepper and garlic on HIGH 2 minutes, stirring after 1 minute. Stir in parsley, herb seasoning and cereal. Spoon over fillets. Broil 1 to 2 minutes or until topping is golden brown, if desired. Serve immediately.

Nutrients per serving:			
Calories	245	Cholesterol	65 mg
Fat	10 g	Sodium	304 mg

Today's Slim Tuna-Stuffed Tomatoes

Makes 6 servings

6 medium tomatoes
1 cup dry curd Cottage cheese
½ cup low fat plain yogurt
¼ cup chopped seeded cucumber
¼ cup chopped green bell pepper
¼ cup thinly sliced radishes
¼ cup chopped green onion
½ teaspoon dried basil leaves, crushed
⅛ teaspoon garlic powder
1 can (about 6½ ounces) tuna, packed in water, drained and flaked
Lettuce leaves

Cut each tomato down to stem end into 6 wedges. (Do not cut through.) Cover and chill. Combine Cottage cheese and yogurt in medium bowl; mix well. Stir in all remaining ingredients except lettuce leaves; blend well. Place tomatoes on individual lettuce-lined plates; spread wedges apart. Spoon Cottage cheese mixture into center of each tomato.

Nutrients per serving:			
Calories	104	Cholesterol	61 mg
Fat	1 g	Sodium	140 mg

Favorite recipe from **Wisconsin Milk Marketing Board** © 1994

Chinese Steamed Fish

Makes 4 servings

12 ounces firm white fish fillets (such as
    swordfish)
  Pepper to taste
2 teaspoons cornstarch
2 teaspoons low sodium soy sauce
2 teaspoons dry sherry
1 tablespoon finely chopped green onion
¼ teaspoon minced ginger root
1 clove garlic, minced
1½ fresh California peaches, sliced
    (about 1½ cups)

Cut fish lengthwise into 2-inch-wide strips. Sprinkle with pepper, if desired. Combine cornstarch, soy sauce and sherry in bowl; mix well. Add fish, turning to coat with mixture. Arrange fish strips in spirals in shallow baking dish; sprinkle with onion, ginger, garlic and peaches. To steam fish, place low rack or trivet in bottom of 10- to 12-inch skillet. Pour hot water into bottom of pan, under rack, and bring to a boil over medium-high heat. Place baking dish on rack. Cover skillet; reduce heat to medium. Steam 10 to 15 minutes until fish flakes easily with fork. Transfer fish spirals and peaches to serving dish using wide spatula. Spoon sauce over as desired.

Nutrients per serving:

Calories	125	Cholesterol	43 mg
Fat	4 g	Sodium	142 mg

Favorite recipe from **California Tree Fruit Agreement**

Catfish Southern Shores

Makes 4 servings

2½ cups KELLOGG'S® COMPLETE® Bran
    Flakes cereal, crushed to 1 cup
¼ teaspoon salt
1 teaspoon onion powder
1 teaspoon garlic powder
1 teaspoon dried lemon peel
½ teaspoon ground red pepper
½ teaspoon dried thyme
½ teaspoon dried basil
½ teaspoon dried dill weed
⅓ cup all-purpose flour
⅓ cup water
1 pound catfish fillets, cut into 1-inch strips
  Vegetable cooking spray

1. Combine crushed cereal, salt and spices in shallow dish or pan. Set aside.

2. In small bowl, combine flour and water; stir until smooth. Dip fish in flour mixture; allow excess to drip off. Coat fish with cereal mixture. Place in single layer in foil-lined shallow baking pan coated with cooking spray. Lightly spray fish with cooking spray.

3. Bake at 350°F for 20 minutes or until fish flakes easily with fork. Serve hot.

Nutrients per serving:

Calories	260	Cholesterol	65 mg
Fat	5 g	Sodium	410 mg

California Blackened Snapper

Makes 6 servings

1 can (16 ounces) California cling peach halves
    in juice or extra light syrup, undrained
1 tablespoon paprika
1 teaspoon onion powder
1 teaspoon garlic powder
¾ teaspoon white pepper
¾ teaspoon black pepper
½ teaspoon ground red pepper
½ teaspoon dried thyme leaves, crushed
½ teaspoon dried oregano leaves, crushed
6 red snapper fillets (about 1½ pounds)
2 tablespoons margarine, softened

Drain peaches, reserving liquid in shallow dish; set aside. Combine paprika, onion powder, garlic powder, white, black and red peppers, thyme and oregano in small bowl; mix well. Dip fish in peach liquid. Sprinkle both sides with paprika mixture. Heat 10-inch skillet over high heat 5 minutes. Carefully add half the fish. Cut margarine into pieces; add half to skillet. (Skillet will smoke as margarine is added.) Cook 1½ to 2 minutes on each side or until fish flakes easily with fork. Repeat with remaining fish. Fan peach halves over fish. Serve immediately.

Nutrients per serving:

Calories	172	Cholesterol	42 mg
Fat	4 g	Sodium	122 mg

Favorite recipe from **California Cling Peach Advisory Board**

Crab Meat Fettuccine

Crab Meat Fettuccine

Makes 4 servings

1 package (5.0 ounces) UNCLE BEN'S®
    COUNTRY INN RECIPES™ Broccoli &
    White Cheddar Pasta
1 cup water
1 cup milk
6 ounces fresh cooked, thawed frozen or
    imitation crab meat, shredded or coarsely
    chopped
1 package (6 ounces) frozen pea pods, thawed,
    well drained and cut in half diagonally
2 plum tomatoes or 1 large tomato, seeded and
    chopped
¼ cup thinly sliced green onions
    Lemon wedges (optional)

Cook pasta according to package directions using
water and milk. Stir in all remaining ingredients
except lemon wedges. Heat through, stirring
occasionally, about 2 to 3 minutes. Serve with lemon
wedges, if desired.

Nutrients per serving:

Calories	238	Cholesterol	36 mg
Fat	5 g	Sodium	424 mg

Fresh Shrimp Sandwich

Makes 6 servings

2 tablespoons *each* plain low fat yogurt,
    reduced calorie mayonnaise and ketchup
1 clove garlic, chopped
¼ teaspoon black pepper
2 pinches ground red pepper
1 cup tiny bay shrimp, cooked (6 ounces)
2 fresh California nectarines, diced
½ cup diced celery
½ cup sliced green onions
6 soft sandwich buns
    Lettuce leaves (optional)

Combine yogurt, mayonnaise, ketchup, garlic, black
pepper and red pepper in large bowl; blend well. Fold
in shrimp, nectarines, celery and onions until well
blended. Serve on buns with lettuce, if desired.

Fresh Shrimp Salad: *Omit buns and serve shrimp
mixture on a bed of lettuce.*

Nutrients per serving (1 sandwich):

Calories	215	Cholesterol	44 mg
Fat	4 g	Sodium	377 mg

Favorite recipe from **California Tree Fruit Agreement**

Linguine with White Clam Sauce

Makes 8 servings

2 tablespoons CRISCO® Vegetable Oil
2 cloves garlic, minced
2 cans (6½ ounces *each*) chopped clams,
    undrained
½ cup chopped fresh parsley
¼ cup dry white wine
1 teaspoon dried basil leaves
1 pound linguine, cooked (without salt or fat)
    and well drained

1. Heat Crisco® Oil and garlic in medium skillet on
medium heat.

2. Drain clams, reserving liquid. Add reserved liquid
and parsley to skillet. Reduce heat to low. Simmer
3 minutes, stirring occasionally.

3. Add clams, wine and basil. Simmer 5 minutes,
stirring occasionally. Add to hot linguine. Toss lightly
to coat.

Nutrients per serving:

Calories	185	Cholesterol	30 mg
Fat	5 g	Sodium	55 mg

Orange Roughy Apple-Veronique

Makes 4 servings

4 orange roughy fillets
2 tablespoons water
½ cup apple juice
2 tablespoons dry white wine
1½ teaspoons cornstarch
¼ teaspoon dried rosemary leaves, crushed
½ cup thinly sliced red apples
½ cup seedless green grapes
Parsley sprig for garnish (optional)

To Microwave: Place fish in 8-inch square microwave-safe dish. Sprinkle with water. Cover with clear plastic wrap; vent by leaving small corner area unsealed. Microwave on HIGH (100% power) 5 to 7 minutes or until fish flakes easily with fork, rotating dish a quarter-turn twice.

Combine apple juice, wine, cornstarch and rosemary in 2-cup microwave-safe measuring cup. Let stand 5 minutes. Microwave, uncovered, on HIGH 1 to 2 minutes or until boiling. Microwave, uncovered, on MEDIUM (50% power) 3 minutes more, stirring twice.

Spoon apple slices and grapes on top of fillets. Pour sauce over fish. Cover casserole with clear plastic wrap; vent by leaving small corner area unsealed. Microwave on HIGH 1 to 2 minutes or until sauce and fish are heated through. Garnish with parsley, if desired.

Nutrients per serving:

Calories	226	Cholesterol	71 mg
Fat	6 g	Sodium	89 mg

Favorite recipe from **Western New York Apple Growers Association**

Crispy Oven Fried Fish Fingers

Makes 4 servings

½ cup seasoned dry bread crumbs
1 tablespoon grated Parmesan cheese
2 teaspoons grated lemon peel
¾ teaspoon dried marjoram leaves
½ teaspoon paprika
¼ teaspoon dried thyme leaves
⅛ teaspoon garlic powder
4 cod fillets (about 1 pound)
3 tablespoons lemon juice
2 tablespoons dry white wine or water
1 tablespoon CRISCO® Vegetable Oil

1. Heat oven to 425°F. Oil 13×9×2-inch pan lightly.

2. Combine bread crumbs, Parmesan cheese, lemon peel, marjoram, paprika, thyme and garlic powder in shallow dish.

3. Rinse fish fillets. Pat dry.

4. Combine lemon juice and wine in separate shallow dish. Cut fish into desired size "fingers" or "sticks." Dip each fish finger into lemon mixture, then into crumb mixture, coating well. Place in pan. Drizzle with 1 tablespoon Crisco® Oil.

5. Bake at 425°F for 10 to 12 minutes or until fish flakes easily with fork. Let stand 2 to 3 minutes in pan. Remove to serving plate. Garnish, if desired.

Nutrients per serving:

Calories	175	Cholesterol	60 mg
Fat	6 g	Sodium	180 mg

Tartar Sauce

Makes 1¼ cups

1 cup nonfat sour cream alternative
½ cup sweet pickle relish, drained
¼ cup finely chopped green onions with tops
1 teaspoon CRISCO® Vegetable Oil

Combine "sour cream," pickle relish, onions and Crisco® Oil in small bowl. Stir to blend. Garnish, if desired. Cover and refrigerate leftover sauce.

Hint: *Prepare and refrigerate at least 2 hours before serving for best flavor.*

Nutrients per serving (1 tablespoon sauce):

Calories	19	Cholesterol	0 mg
Fat	trace	Sodium	50 mg

Crispy Oven Fried Fish Fingers, Tartar Sauce

Fish Steaks with Pear Jardinière

Fish Steaks with Pear Jardinière

Makes 4 servings

   2 teaspoons vegetable oil
   1 cup thin onion slices
   1 cup julienned carrot strips
   ½ teaspoon dry mustard
   ¼ teaspoon *each* dried basil leaves, crushed, and
      dried dill weed
   2 fresh California Bartlett pears, cored and
      quartered
1½ pounds firm fish fillets, such as sea bass,
      haddock or salmon
   2 tomatoes, sliced
   1 lemon, thinly sliced

Heat oil in large nonstick skillet over medium heat
until hot. Add onion and carrots; stir to mix well.
Cover and cook 5 to 10 minutes. Mix mustard, basil
and dill weed in small bowl; add pears. Toss to coat.
Add fish, pear mixture, tomatoes and lemon to skillet.
Cover; cook 10 minutes or until fish flakes easily with
fork. Serve fish topped with vegetable-pear mixture.

Nutrients per serving:			
Calories	238	Cholesterol	100 mg
Fat	3 g	Sodium	174 mg

Favorite recipe from **California Tree Fruit Agreement**

Scampi Italienne

Makes 4 servings

   ½ pound uncooked shrimp, peeled and deveined
   ¼ cup *plus* 1 tablespoon CRISCO® Vegetable
      Oil, divided
   3 tablespoons dry white wine
   ½ teaspoon grated lemon peel
   1 tablespoon lemon juice
   ½ teaspoon dried basil leaves
   ½ teaspoon dried oregano leaves
   1 clove garlic, minced
   ¼ teaspoon salt
   ⅛ teaspoon pepper
   2 drops hot pepper sauce
   ¾ cup uncooked rice
1½ cups water
   2 tomatoes, cut into ½-inch pieces
   ¼ cup chopped fresh parsley
   2 green onions with tops, sliced

1. Place shrimp in medium glass or stainless steel
bowl.

2. Combine ¼ cup Crisco® Oil, wine, lemon peel,
lemon juice, basil, oregano, garlic, salt, pepper and
hot pepper sauce in container with tight-fitting lid.
Shake well. Remove one tablespoon oil mixture.
Reserve. Pour remaining oil mixture over shrimp.
Turn to coat. Refrigerate 30 minutes, turning after
15 minutes.

3. Heat reserved one tablespoon marinade in
medium saucepan on medium-high heat. Add rice.
Stir one minute. Pour water over rice. Stir. Bring to a
boil. Reduce heat to low. Cover. Simmer 15 to
20 minutes or until tender. Remove from heat. Fluff
with fork. Stir in tomatoes. Cover.

4. Heat remaining one tablespoon Crisco® Oil in
large skillet on high heat. Drain shrimp. Add to
skillet. Stir-fry one minute or until shrimp turn pink.

5. Spoon rice mixture onto serving platter. Pour
shrimp mixture over rice. Sprinkle with parsley and
green onions. Season with additional salt and pepper,
if desired.

Nutrients per serving:			
Calories	250	Cholesterol	85 mg
Fat	6 g	Sodium	135 mg

Fish Fillets with Yogurt Sauce

Makes 4 servings

   1 pound frozen fish fillets, thawed and drained
   ⅓ cup plain yogurt
   1 tablespoon lemon juice
   1 tablespoon Dijon-style mustard

To Microwave: Place fillets in shallow glass baking dish.
Blend together yogurt, lemon juice and mustard in small
bowl. Spread mixture over fish. Cover and microwave on
HIGH (100% power) 4 minutes or until fish just turns
opaque, turning once. Let stand, covered with foil,
3 minutes or until fish flakes easily with fork.

Nutrients per serving:			
Calories	132	Cholesterol	64 mg
Fat	1 g	Sodium	111 mg

Favorite recipe from **Wisconsin Milk Marketing Board** © 1994

Scallop Kabobs

Makes 8 kabobs

¼ cup REALEMON® Lemon Juice from
    Concentrate
2 tablespoons vegetable oil
1 teaspoon oregano leaves
½ teaspoon basil leaves
1 clove garlic, finely chopped
⅛ teaspoon salt
1 pound sea scallops
8 ounces fresh mushrooms
2 small zucchini, cut into chunks
2 small onions, cut into wedges
½ red, yellow or green bell pepper, cut into bite-
    size pieces
    Additional REALEMON® Brand

In shallow dish, combine ¼ cup ReaLemon® brand,
oil and seasonings; add scallops. Cover; marinate in
refrigerator 2 hours, stirring occasionally. Remove
scallops from marinade; discard marinade. Divide
scallops and vegetables equally among 8 skewers.
Grill or broil as desired, until scallops are opaque,
basting frequently with additional ReaLemon® brand.
Refrigerate leftovers.

Nutrients per serving (2 kabobs):			
Calories	213	Cholesterol	37 mg
Fat	8 g	Sodium	255 mg

Scallop Kabobs

Fish Vera Cruz

Makes 4 servings

1¼ pounds fish fillets or fish steaks (about ½ inch
    thick)
1 tablespoon lime juice
1 medium onion, sliced
1 medium green bell pepper, cut into ¾-inch
    chunks
1 clove garlic, minced
1 tablespoon vegetable oil
2 medium tomatoes, cut into chunks
½ cup HEINZ® Chili Sauce
¼ cup sliced pimiento-stuffed olives
    Dash ground red pepper

Sprinkle fish with lime juice; set aside. In large
skillet, cook and stir onion, green pepper and garlic
in oil until tender-crisp. Add tomatoes and remaining
ingredients. Simmer, uncovered, 3 to 5 minutes or
until most of liquid evaporates. Place fish in skillet,
spooning sauce over. Cover; simmer 6 to 8 minutes
or until fish turns opaque and begins to flake when
tested with fork. Remove fish; simmer sauce to
thicken, if necessary. Serve sauce over fish.

Nutrients per serving:			
Calories	222	Cholesterol	68 mg
Fat	6 g	Sodium	754 mg

Italian-Style Microwaved Halibut Steaks

Makes 4 servings

4 (1-inch-thick) halibut steaks (about 1 pound)
⅓ cup low-calorie Italian dressing
1 tablespoon lemon juice
¼ teaspoon black pepper
¼ teaspoon paprika

To Microwave: Place fish in microwave-safe dish.
Combine remaining ingredients; pour over fish. Cover dish
with plastic wrap and refrigerate 30 minutes, turning fish
over once. Turn back one corner of plastic wrap to vent.
Cook 4 to 5 minutes on HIGH (100% power), rotating dish
¼ turn after 2 minutes. Fish is done when it flakes with
fork. Let stand 2 to 3 minutes before serving.

Nutrients per serving:			
Calories	128	Cholesterol	34 mg
Fat	5 g	Sodium	216 mg

Favorite recipe from **National Fisheries Institute**

Oriental Seafood Stir-Fry

Oriental Seafood Stir-Fry

Makes 4 servings

½ cup water
3 tablespoons REALEMON® Lemon Juice from
    Concentrate
3 tablespoons soy sauce
1 tablespoon firmly packed brown sugar
1 tablespoon cornstarch
2 ounces fresh pea pods
¾ cup sliced fresh mushrooms
¾ cup diced red bell pepper
1 medium onion, cut into wedges
1 tablespoon vegetable oil
½ pound imitation crab blend, flaked
    Shredded napa (Chinese cabbage), angel hair
    pasta or rice noodles (optional)

Combine water, ReaLemon® brand, soy sauce, sugar
and cornstarch in small bowl. In large skillet or wok,
over medium-high heat, cook and stir vegetables in oil
until tender-crisp; remove. Add soy mixture; over
medium heat, cook and stir until slightly thickened.
Add vegetables and crab blend; heat through. Serve
with napa, pasta or rice noodles. Refrigerate leftovers.

Nutrients per serving:			
Calories	151	Cholesterol	11 mg
Fat	4 g	Sodium	1266 mg

Dieter's Fish and Spinach

Makes 2 servings

2 (4-ounce) frozen sole fillets, thawed
1 tablespoon REALEMON® Lemon Juice from
    Concentrate
  Salt and pepper
1 (10-ounce) package frozen chopped spinach,
    cooked and well drained
¼ cup BORDEN® Lite-line® or Viva® Protein
    Fortified Skim Milk
2 slices BORDEN® Lite-line® Process Cheese
    Product,* any flavor, cut into small pieces
  Paprika

Preheat oven to 400°F. Brush fillets with ReaLemon®
brand; sprinkle lightly with salt and pepper. Spread
spinach over bottom of 8-inch baking dish. Pour milk
over spinach; top with cheese product pieces, then
fillets. Cover; bake 20 minutes or until fish flakes
with fork. Sprinkle with paprika. Refrigerate leftovers.

*"½ the calories"– 8% milkfat product

Nutrients per serving:			
Calories	182	Cholesterol	65 mg
Fat	4 g	Sodium	716 mg

Whether main dishes or side dishes, salads have become a way of life. Expand your horizons with these creative and taste-tempting recipes designed to wake up your salad bowl. Chicken, seafood, pasta and fruit are just a few of the light and refreshing possibilities. Which salad to choose? It's a toss-up!

Mediterranean Tuna Salad

Makes 4 servings

¼ pound fresh green beans
1 can (12 ounces) tuna, drained, separated into chunks
2 tablespoons drained capers (optional)
1 can (15 ounces) great Northern beans, drained, rinsed
1 large tomato, chopped
12 ripe Greek olives
Snipped fresh chives (optional)
¼ cup bottled low-calorie Italian salad dressing

Cook green beans in lightly salted boiling water 5 minutes or until crisp-tender; drain. Rinse with cold water; drain again.

Place tuna in center of serving platter; sprinkle with capers. Arrange canned beans, tomato and olives around tuna; surround with green beans. Sprinkle with chives, if desired. Serve with dressing.

Nutrients per serving:

Calories	300	Cholesterol	14 mg
Fat	10 g	Sodium	434 mg

Gazpacho Salad

Makes 7 servings, 3⅔ cups

1½ cups tomato juice
1 package (4-serving size) JELL-O® Brand Lemon Flavor Sugar Free Gelatin
1 cup finely chopped tomato
½ cup finely chopped peeled cucumber
¼ cup finely chopped green bell pepper
2 tablespoons finely chopped red bell pepper
2 tablespoons sliced green onions
2 tablespoons vinegar
¼ teaspoon black pepper
⅛ teaspoon garlic powder

Bring tomato juice to a boil in small saucepan. Completely dissolve gelatin in boiling tomato juice. Chill until slightly thickened.

Combine remaining ingredients in medium bowl; mix well. Stir into gelatin mixture. Pour into individual dishes or medium serving bowl. Chill until firm, about 3 hours.

Nutrients per serving:

Calories	25	Cholesterol	0 mg
Fat	0 g	Sodium	220 mg

Mediterranean Tuna Salad

Grilled Steak and Asparagus Salad

Grilled Steak and Asparagus Salad

Makes 4 servings

½ cup bottled light olive oil vinaigrette dressing
⅓ cup A.1.® Steak Sauce
1 (1-pound) beef top round steak
1 (10-ounce) package frozen asparagus spears, cooked and cooled
½ cup thinly sliced red bell pepper
8 large lettuce leaves
1 tablespoon toasted sesame seeds

In small bowl, blend vinaigrette and steak sauce. Pour marinade over steak in nonmetal dish. Cover; refrigerate 1 hour.

Remove steak from marinade. Grill or broil steak, 4 inches from heat source, for 10 minutes or to desired doneness, basting occasionally with marinade and turning 2 or 3 times. Thinly slice steak; arrange steak, asparagus and red pepper on lettuce leaves. Heat marinade to a boil; pour over salad. Sprinkle with sesame seeds; serve immediately.

Nutrients per serving:

Calories	209	Cholesterol	65 mg
Fat	5 g	Sodium	857 mg

Mostaccioli Salad Niçoise

Makes 16 servings

1 package (1 pound) CREAMETTE®
   Mostaccioli, uncooked
2 pounds fresh green beans, steamed until tender-crisp
2 medium green bell peppers, cut into chunks
2 cups cherry tomatoes, quartered
2 cups sliced celery
½ cup sliced green onions
10 pitted ripe olives, sliced
2 (7-ounce) cans water-pack white tuna, drained and flaked
½ cup olive or vegetable oil
¼ cup red wine vinegar
3 cloves garlic, minced
4 teaspoons Dijon-style mustard
1 teaspoon salt-free herb seasoning
1 teaspoon dried basil leaves, crushed
¼ teaspoon black pepper

Prepare Creamette® Mostaccioli according to package directions; drain. In large bowl, combine mostaccioli, vegetables, olives and tuna. In small bowl, whisk together olive oil, vinegar, garlic, mustard, herb seasoning, basil and pepper; toss with salad mixture. Cover; refrigerate thoroughly. Stir before serving. Refrigerate leftovers.

Nutrients per serving:

Calories	236	Cholesterol	9 mg
Fat	9 g	Sodium	185 mg

Zesty Oil-Free Salad Dressing

Makes 1¼ cups

½ cup *undiluted* CARNATION® Evaporated Lowfat Milk
½ cup tomato sauce
2 tablespoons cider vinegar
1 tablespoon lemon juice
2 teaspoons finely chopped fresh parsley
1 teaspoon finely chopped onion
1 teaspoon Dijon-style mustard
¼ teaspoon salt
¼ teaspoon black pepper

In small bowl, combine all ingredients. Refrigerate thoroughly. Serve over favorite salad ingredients.

Nutrients per serving (2 tablespoons dressing):

Calories	15	Cholesterol	0 mg
Fat	trace	Sodium	148 mg

Chunky Spinach Salad

Makes 4 servings, 3 cups

6 cups fresh spinach leaves, rinsed and drained
2 cups toasted Italian bread cubes
6 ounces mushrooms, thinly sliced (about
    2 cups)
1 can (19 ounces) chickpeas or garbanzo beans,
    rinsed and drained
4 slices turkey bacon, crisp-cooked and
    crumbled (optional)
½ cup WISH-BONE® Healthy Sensation!
    Chunky Blue Cheese Dressing

In large salad bowl, combine all ingredients except dressing. Drizzle with Blue Cheese Dressing; toss gently.

Nutrients per serving:			
Calories	209	Cholesterol	0 mg
Fat	3 g	Sodium	599 mg

Sweet 'n' Sour Vinaigrette

Makes 8 servings

1 cup white wine vinegar
¼ cup sugar
½ teaspoon dried parsley
¼ teaspoon dry mustard

Combine all ingredients in jar with tight-fitting lid. Cover and shake vigorously until combined. Refrigerate and shake again before serving. Serve over green salad.

Nutrients per serving (2 tablespoons dressing):			
Calories	28	Cholesterol	0 mg
Fat	0 g	Sodium	trace

Favorite recipe from **The Sugar Association, Inc.**

Summer Fruit Salad

Makes 6 servings

1 DOLE® Fresh Pineapple
2 DOLE® Oranges, peeled and sliced
2 DOLE® Bananas, peeled and sliced
1 cup halved DOLE® Strawberries
1 cup seedless green DOLE® Grapes
  Strawberry-Banana Yogurt Dressing (recipe
    follows)
  Orange-Banana Yogurt Dressing (recipe
    follows)

Cut pineapple in half lengthwise through the crown. Cut fruit from shells with knife, leaving shells intact. Cut fruit into chunks. In large bowl, combine pineapple, oranges, bananas, strawberries and grapes. Spoon into pineapple shells. Serve with your choice of dressing.

Strawberry-Banana Yogurt Dressing

6 DOLE® Strawberries, halved
1 ripe DOLE® Banana, peeled
1 carton (8 ounces) vanilla yogurt
1 tablespoon packed brown sugar *or* honey

In blender or food processor, combine all ingredients and blend until smooth.

Orange-Banana Yogurt Dressing

1 DOLE® Orange
1 ripe DOLE® Banana, peeled
1 carton (8 ounces) vanilla yogurt
1 tablespoon packed brown sugar *or* honey

Grate peel from ½ orange. Juice orange (⅓ cup). In blender or food processor, combine orange peel and juice with remaining ingredients. Blend until smooth.

Nutrients per serving (with 1 tablespoon Strawberry-Banana Yogurt Dressing):			
Calories	143	Cholesterol	4 mg
Fat	2 g	Sodium	15 mg

Summer Fruit Salad

Radiatore Salad with Salmon and Papaya

Radiatore Salad with Salmon and Papaya

Makes 6 to 8 servings

1 pound radiatore or other medium pasta shape, uncooked
2 tablespoons vegetable oil
Freshly ground black pepper to taste
1 pound boneless skinless fresh or frozen salmon fillets, cooked and chopped *or* 2 cans (7½ ounces *each*) salmon, drained and flaked
1 papaya or mango, peeled, seeded and chopped *or* 2 peaches or nectarines, pitted and chopped *or* 1 can (15 ounces) papaya or favorite fruit in light syrup, drained and chopped
1 cup cherry tomatoes, cut into wedges
1 bunch scallions, thinly sliced
1 yellow bell pepper, seeded, membranes removed, chopped
1 medium cucumber, quartered lengthwise and sliced
1 small jalapeño chili,* seeded, ribs removed, finely minced
2 tablespoons chopped fresh cilantro leaves *or* 2 teaspoons dried coriander
3 tablespoons rice wine vinegar
3 tablespoons white wine vinegar
3 drops hot pepper sauce

Prepare radiatore according to package directions. Transfer to medium bowl. While still warm, add oil; toss well. Season with black pepper. Set aside to cool. Add salmon, papaya, tomatoes, scallions, yellow pepper and cucumber to radiatore. Toss to combine.

Combine jalapeño, cilantro, vinegars and pepper sauce in small bowl; blend well. Add to pasta mixture; toss and serve. Refrigerate leftovers.

Chilies can sting and irritate the skin; wear plastic disposable gloves when handling chilies and do not touch eyes. Wash hands after handling chilies.

Nutrients per serving:			
Calories	276	Cholesterol	39 mg
Fat	8 g	Sodium	67 mg

Favorite recipe from **National Pasta Association**

Golden Apple Poppy Seed Salad

Makes 5 servings

1 banana, peeled, sliced in half lengthwise and cut into large chunks
Lemon juice
1½ cups cored Golden Delicious apple chunks
1 orange, peeled, sectioned and diced
½ cup chopped walnuts
½ cup plain low fat yogurt
½ teaspoon lemon juice
½ teaspoon ground cinnamon
¼ teaspoon poppy seeds
Dash ground nutmeg
Golden or Red Delicious apple slices for garnish

Toss banana with lemon juice to prevent discoloration. Combine banana, apples, orange and walnuts in large salad bowl. Combine yogurt, ½ teaspoon lemon juice, cinnamon, poppy seeds and nutmeg in small bowl; blend well. Pour yogurt mixture over fruit; toss lightly. Garnish with apple slices.

Nutrients per serving:			
Calories	163	Cholesterol	1 mg
Fat	8 g	Sodium	17 mg

Favorite recipe from **Washington Apple Commission**

Celery Salad Dressing

Makes 1½ cups

2 cups ½-inch celery pieces
¼ cup 1-inch green onion pieces
2 tablespoons sugar
½ teaspoon salt
⅛ teaspoon pepper
3 tablespoons cider vinegar
3 tablespoons water

Place celery, green onion, sugar, salt, pepper, vinegar and water in food processor or blender; process until smooth. Serve over sliced tomatoes, spinach or other salad greens, if desired. (Dressing may be prepared 24 hours before serving; cover and refrigerate. Stir before serving.)

Nutrients per serving (1 tablespoon dressing):			
Calories	6	Cholesterol	0 mg
Fat	0 g	Sodium	54 mg

Favorite recipe from **American Celery Council**

Chicken-Asparagus Salad

Makes 4 to 5 servings

1 can (14½ ounces) chicken broth
1 bay leaf
1 green onion, cut into 1-inch pieces
1 (¼-inch-thick) slice fresh ginger, peeled
4 boneless skinless chicken breast halves (about 1 pound)
  Mustard Vinaigrette (recipe follows)
½ pound asparagus spears, cut in half, cooked until crisp-tender
1 can (8¾ ounces) whole baby sweet corn, rinsed and drained
  Spinach or lettuce leaves
3 small tomatoes, chopped

Combine broth, bay leaf, onion and ginger in medium saucepan. Bring to a boil. Add chicken; reduce heat to low. Cover; simmer 8 minutes or until chicken is tender and no longer pink in center. Remove from broth; cool slightly. (Reserve broth for another use, if desired.) Meanwhile, prepare Mustard Vinaigrette.

Cut chicken diagonally into narrow strips; place in medium bowl with asparagus and corn. Add vinaigrette; toss lightly. Marinate at room temperature 15 minutes. Drain, reserving vinaigrette.

Arrange chicken, asparagus and corn on individual spinach-lined salad plates. Top with tomatoes. Serve with reserved vinaigrette.

Mustard Vinaigrette
1 tablespoon country-style Dijon mustard
¼ cup seasoned rice vinegar
2 tablespoons vegetable oil
¼ teaspoon sesame oil
  Dash of black pepper

Whisk together all ingredients in small bowl.

Nutrients per serving:

Calories	232	Cholesterol	46 mg
Fat	10 g	Sodium	257 mg

Chicken-Asparagus Salad

Shells and Shrimp Salad Alfresco

Makes 10 servings

½ of (1-pound) package CREAMETTE® Medium Shells, uncooked
2 cups cooked medium shrimp, shelled, deveined
2 medium fresh tomatoes, peeled, seeded and chopped
2 cups torn fresh spinach
1 cup sliced fresh cauliflowerets
½ cup sliced radishes
¼ cup sliced green onions
2 tablespoons vegetable oil
2 tablespoons lemon juice
1 tablespoon Dijon-style mustard
¼ teaspoon dried thyme leaves, crushed
¼ teaspoon lemon pepper seasoning

Prepare Creamette® Medium Shells according to package directions; drain. In large bowl, combine shells, shrimp, tomatoes, spinach, cauliflowerets, radishes and green onions. In small bowl, whisk together oil, lemon juice, mustard, thyme and seasoning; add to shrimp mixture and toss to coat. Cover; refrigerate thoroughly. Toss gently before serving. Refrigerate leftovers.

Nutrients per serving:

Calories	176	Cholesterol	68 mg
Fat	4 g	Sodium	89 mg

Thousand Island Dressing

Makes about 2 cups

⅔ cup PET® Light Evaporated Skimmed Milk
⅔ cup bottled chili sauce
⅔ cup safflower oil
¼ cup sweet pickle relish
1 tablespoon lemon juice
1 tablespoon sugar
1 teaspoon salt
⅛ teaspoon ground black pepper

Using a wire whisk, combine all ingredients in small bowl. Refrigerate until well chilled. Serve over tossed green salad.

Nutrients per serving (1 tablespoon dressing):

Calories	54	Cholesterol	0 mg
Fat	5 g	Sodium	129 mg

Sparkling Berry Salad

Makes 8 servings

2 cups cranberry juice
2 packages (4-serving size) or 1 package
    (8-serving size) JELL-O® Brand Sugar
    Free Gelatin, any red flavor
1½ cups cold club soda
¼ cup creme de cassis liqueur (optional)
1 teaspoon lemon juice
1 cup raspberries
1 cup blueberries
½ cup sliced strawberries
½ cup whole strawberries, cut into fans
    Mint leaves (optional)

Bring cranberry juice to a boil in medium saucepan.
Completely dissolve gelatin in boiling cranberry juice.
Stir in club soda, liqueur and lemon juice. Chill until
slightly thickened.

Reserve a few raspberries and blueberries for garnish,
if desired. Stir remaining raspberries, blueberries and
the sliced strawberries into gelatin mixture. Spoon
into 6-cup mold that has been lightly sprayed with
nonstick cooking spray. Chill until firm, about
4 hours. Unmold. Surround with reserved berries,
strawberry fans and mint leaves, if desired.

Nutrients per serving:

Calories	100	Cholesterol	0 mg
Fat	0 g	Sodium	70 mg

Light Pasta Salad

Makes 4 servings

½ cup MIRACLE WHIP® LIGHT® Reduced
    Calorie Salad Dressing
½ cup KRAFT® "Zesty" Italian Reduced Calorie
    Dressing
2 cups (6 ounces) corkscrew noodles, cooked,
    drained
1 cup broccoli florettes, partially cooked
½ cup chopped green bell pepper
½ cup chopped tomato
¼ cup green onion slices

Mix dressings in large bowl until well blended. Add
remaining ingredients; mix lightly. Refrigerate. Serve
with freshly ground black pepper, if desired.

Nutrients per serving:

Calories	260	Cholesterol	0 mg
Fat	9 g	Sodium	450 mg

Chilean Grapes and Greens

Chilean Grapes and Greens

Makes 4 servings

1 cup seedless or halved, seeded Chilean grapes
    (red, green or combination)
2 teaspoons olive oil
1 tablespoon raspberry or white wine vinegar
1 tablespoon lemon juice
2 tablespoons water
1 shallot, chopped
2 teaspoons prepared mustard
¼ teaspoon dried tarragon leaves, crushed
    Pepper to taste
4 cups lightly packed, torn mixed salad greens
2 teaspoons toasted walnut pieces
2 tablespoons freshly grated Parmesan cheese
4 slices French bread

Preheat broiler. Rinse grapes; remove stems. Set
aside. Whisk together oil, vinegar, lemon juice, water,
shallot, mustard, tarragon and pepper in small bowl
until well blended; set aside. Combine greens, grapes
and walnuts in salad bowl; set aside. To prepare
Parmesan toasts, sprinkle cheese on bread slices;
broil about 4 inches from heat source until bread is
toasted and cheese melts. Toss salad with reserved
dressing. Serve with Parmesan toasts.

Nutrients per serving:

Calories	148	Cholesterol	2 mg
Fat	4 g	Sodium	231 mg

Favorite recipe from **Chilean Fresh Fruit Association**

Sesame Pork Salad

Makes 6 servings

   3 cups cooked rice
1½ cups slivered cooked pork*
   ¼ pound fresh snow peas, trimmed and julienned
   1 medium cucumber, peeled, seeded, and julienned
   1 medium red bell pepper, julienned
   ½ cup sliced green onions
   2 tablespoons sesame seeds, toasted (optional)
   ¼ cup chicken broth
   3 tablespoons rice or white wine vinegar
   3 tablespoons soy sauce
   1 tablespoon peanut oil
   1 teaspoon sesame oil

Combine rice, pork, snow peas, cucumber, bell pepper, onions, and sesame seeds in large bowl. Combine broth, vinegar, soy sauce, and oils in small jar with lid; shake well. Pour over rice mixture; toss lightly. Serve at room temperature or slightly chilled.

Substitute 1½ cups slivered cooked chicken for pork, if desired.

Nutrients per serving:

Calories	269	Cholesterol	32 mg
Fat	8 g	Sodium	867 mg

Favorite recipe from **USA Rice Council**

Mock Blue Cheese Dressing

Makes 6 servings, ¾ cup

   ¾ cup buttermilk
   ¼ cup low-fat cottage cheese
   2 tablespoons blue cheese, crumbled
   2 teaspoons sugar
   1 teaspoon lemon juice
   ¼ teaspoon celery seed
   ⅛ teaspoon black pepper
   ⅛ teaspoon salt
   4 drops hot pepper sauce

In blender, process all ingredients. Refrigerate or serve immediately over green salad.

Nutrients per serving (2 tablespoons dressing):

Calories	33	Cholesterol	3 mg
Fat	1 g	Sodium	148 mg

Favorite recipe from **The Sugar Association, Inc.**

Mexican Surimi Salad

Makes 4 servings

12 ounces crab-flavored SURIMI Seafood flakes, chunks or salad-style, well flaked
   1 large tomato, halved, seeded and diced
   ¼ cup sliced green onions
   ¼ cup sliced black olives
   1 tablespoon chopped cilantro or fresh parsley
   ¼ cup salsa
   3 cups salad greens, washed, drained and torn into bite-sized pieces

Combine Surimi Seafood, tomato, green onions, olives and cilantro in medium bowl. Add salsa; toss gently to combine. Arrange salad greens on 4 plates and divide seafood mixture over greens.

Nutrients per serving:

Calories	122	Cholesterol	17 mg
Fat	3 g	Sodium	794 mg

Favorite recipe from **Surimi Seafood Education Center**

Lanai Pasta Salad

Makes 6 to 8 servings

   1 can (20 ounces) DOLE® Pineapple Chunks in Juice
   3 cups cooked spiral pasta
   2 cups sugar peas or snow peas
   1 cup sliced DOLE® Carrots
   1 cup sliced cucumbers
   ½ cup bottled low-calorie Italian salad dressing
   ¼ cup chopped cilantro or fresh parsley

Drain pineapple; reserve ¼ cup juice.

Combine pineapple and reserved juice with remaining ingredients in large bowl; toss to coat.

Nutrients per serving:

Calories	181	Cholesterol	0 mg
Fat	trace	Sodium	219 mg

Sesame Pork Salad

Green Bean and Mushroom Salad

Green Bean and Mushroom Salad

Makes 4 servings

¾ **pound fresh green beans, trimmed**
¼ **cup water**
¼ **cup low-calorie mayonnaise**
3 **tablespoons chopped green onions**
2 **tablespoons fresh lemon juice**
1½ **tablespoons olive oil**
1 **tablespoon Dijon-style mustard**
2 **cups fresh mushroom slices**
¼ **cup chopped red bell pepper**
1 **tablespoon minced fresh basil *or* ¾ teaspoon
    dried basil leaves, crushed**
Dash black pepper

To Microwave: Cut beans into 1½-inch pieces; place
in 1½-quart microwave-safe dish. Add water; cover.
Microwave on HIGH (100% power) 5 to 6 minutes or until
beans are crisp-tender, stirring halfway through cooking;
drain. Cover beans with ice water to stop further cooking;
set aside. Combine mayonnaise, green onions, lemon juice,
oil and mustard in large bowl; mix well. Add drained
beans, mushrooms, red pepper and basil; mix lightly.
Cover; refrigerate several hours. Season with black pepper
just before serving. Garnish as desired.

Nutrients per serving:			
Calories	125	Cholesterol	5 mg
Fat	10 g	Sodium	63 mg

Cantaloupe Dressing

Makes 6 servings

1 **cup cantaloupe cubes**
½ **cup low-fat vanilla yogurt**
4 **teaspoons sugar**

Place all ingredients in blender container or food
processor; process until blended. Refrigerate or serve
immediately over fruit salad.

For a tangier dressing: *Substitute ½ cup kiwifruit slices
for cantaloupe. Blend all ingredients as above.*

For a thicker dressing: *Substitute 1 cup pear cubes for
cantaloupe. Blend all ingredients as above.*

Nutrients per serving (2 tablespoons dressing):			
Calories	36	Cholesterol	1 mg
Fat	trace	Sodium	15 mg

Favorite recipe from **The Sugar Association, Inc.**

Caribbean Chicken Salad

Makes 2 servings

1 **can (8 ounces) DOLE® Pineapple Slices in
    Juice, undrained**
½ **pound cooked skinless boneless chicken
    breast***
DOLE® Salad Greens
1 **cup assorted sliced or cut up DOLE® Fresh
    Fruit**
¼ **pound DOLE® Asparagus or green beans,
    steamed**
½ **cup vanilla yogurt**
2 **to 3 tablespoons chopped chutney**
1 **teaspoon grated lemon peel**

Drain pineapple; reserve 3 tablespoons juice for
dressing. Slice chicken diagonally into ½-inch slices.

Arrange sliced chicken and 2 pineapple slices on
each of 2 salad plates lined with salad greens.
Arrange fresh fruit and asparagus on same plates.

For dressing, combine yogurt, chutney, reserved
pineapple juice and lemon peel in small bowl. Serve
with salad. Garnish, if desired.

**Use roasted chicken from the deli, if desired.*

Nutrients per serving:			
Calories	252	Cholesterol	17 mg
Fat	2 g	Sodium	71 mg

Poppy Seed Fruit Sauce

Makes 1⅔ cups

½ cup MIRACLE WHIP® FREE® Nonfat
    Dressing
1 container (8 ounces) lemon-flavored low-fat
    yogurt
2 tablespoons skim milk
1 tablespoon firmly packed brown sugar
1 tablespoon poppy seeds

Mix together ingredients until well blended;
refrigerate. Serve over fresh fruit.

Prep time: 5 minutes

Nutrients per serving (3 tablespoons sauce):			
Calories	70	Cholesterol	trace
Fat	1 g	Sodium	263 mg

Cucumber Salad

Makes 6 to 8 servings

3 medium cucumbers, scored lengthwise with
    tines of fork and thinly sliced
¾ teaspoon salt, divided
⅓ cup chopped onion
⅓ cup cider vinegar
3 tablespoons CRISCO® Oil or CRISCO®
    PURITAN® Oil
2 tablespoons sugar
1½ teaspoons caraway seeds
½ teaspoon paprika
⅛ teaspoon black pepper

Place cucumbers in medium bowl. Sprinkle with
¼ teaspoon salt. Let stand about 1 hour. Drain.

Whisk together remaining ingredients with remaining
½ teaspoon salt in small bowl. Pour over cucumbers.
Toss to coat. Cover and refrigerate at least 3 hours.
Stir before serving.

Nutrients per serving:			
Calories	80	Cholesterol	0 mg
Fat	5 g	Sodium	203 mg

Poppy Seed Fruit Sauce

Garden Chicken Salad

Garden Chicken Salad

Makes 6 servings

1¼ pounds skinless chicken breasts, cooked and
    cut up
½ cup chopped zucchini
¼ cup chopped carrot
2 tablespoons chopped onion
2 tablespoons chopped fresh parsley
⅓ cup nonfat mayonnaise dressing
¼ cup nonfat sour cream alternative
½ teaspoon celery salt
⅛ teaspoon pepper
1 tablespoon CRISCO® Vegetable Oil
¼ cup sliced almonds
3 tomatoes, cut into wedges

1. Combine chicken, zucchini, carrot, onion and parsley in large bowl.

2. Combine mayonnaise dressing, "sour cream," celery salt and pepper in small bowl. Add to chicken mixture. Mix well. Cover. Refrigerate at least 2 hours.

3. Heat Crisco® Oil in small skillet on medium heat. Add nuts. Cook and stir 4 minutes or until nuts are light golden brown. Drain on paper towels. Cool.

4. Serve salad on greens-covered plate, if desired. Surround with tomato wedges. Sprinkle with nuts. Garnish, if desired.

Nutrients per serving:			
Calories	225	Cholesterol	75 mg
Fat	8 g	Sodium	365 mg

Honey Banana Dressing

Makes 1½ cups

1¼ cups Basic Lemon Cream Dressing (page 341)
½ medium banana, cut into chunks
2 tablespoons honey
1 teaspoon lemon juice

Combine Basic Lemon Cream Dressing, banana, honey and lemon juice in blender container. Blend at medium speed until smooth.

Nutrients per serving (1 tablespoon dressing):			
Calories	15	Cholesterol	0 mg
Fat	trace	Sodium	35 mg

Curry-Apple-Chicken Salad

Makes 4 to 6 servings

2 cups diced cooked chicken
1 cup sliced celery
3 Empire apples, diced
½ cup raisins
½ cup reduced calorie mayonnaise
¼ cup low fat sour cream
½ teaspoon dried rosemary leaves, crushed
⅛ teaspoon curry powder
    Salad greens
    Apple slices

Combine chicken, celery, apples and raisins in large bowl. Combine mayonnaise, sour cream, rosemary and curry powder in small bowl; blend well. Stir mayonnaise mixture into chicken mixture. Refrigerate. Serve over salad greens and garnish with apple slices.

Nutrients per serving:			
Calories	232	Cholesterol	44 mg
Fat	8 g	Sodium	165 mg

Favorite recipe from **Western New York Apple Growers Association**

Fresh Basil and Pepper Potato Salad

Makes 5 servings

3 medium potatoes (about 1 pound)
1 cup DANNON® Plain Nonfat or Lowfat Yogurt
2 tablespoons snipped fresh parsley *or*
    ½ teaspoon dried parsley flakes
1 tablespoon snipped fresh basil *or* 1 teaspoon
    dried basil, crushed
1 tablespoon sliced green onion
½ teaspoon salt
    Several dashes pepper
½ cup frozen peas, thawed
½ cup chopped red or green bell pepper

In a large saucepan bring water to a boil; add potatoes. Cover and cook 25 to 30 minutes or until tender; drain. Cool. If desired, peel potatoes. Cut potatoes into cubes.

In a large bowl combine yogurt, parsley, basil, green onion, salt and pepper. Add potatoes, peas and bell pepper; stir lightly to coat. Cover; chill several hours before serving.

Nutrients per serving:			
Calories	140	Cholesterol	trace
Fat	1 g	Sodium	279 mg

Warm Pork and Spinach Salad

Makes 6 servings

Nonstick cooking spray
1 pound boneless pork loin, trimmed and cut into 2×¼-inch strips
1 pound fresh spinach leaves, coarsely shredded
3 cups watercress sprigs
1 cup thinly sliced celery
1 cup seedless green grapes
½ cup thinly sliced green onions
1 can (8 ounces) sliced water chestnuts, drained
1 large Golden Delicious apple, cored and chopped
1 cup low calorie oil-free Italian salad dressing
2 tablespoons dry white wine
2 tablespoons Dijon-style mustard
3 tablespoons light brown sugar
2 tablespoons toasted sesame seeds*

Spray nonstick skillet with cooking spray; heat over medium-high heat until hot. Add pork strips; stir-fry about 4 to 5 minutes until pork is tender and cooked through. Set aside; keep warm. Toss spinach, watercress, celery, grapes, green onions, water chestnuts and apple in large serving bowl until combined.

Combine salad dressing, white wine, mustard and brown sugar in medium saucepan; cook over medium heat just until brown sugar is dissolved, stirring constantly. Stir cooked pork into hot dressing mixture; coat well. Remove pork; pour ½ of dressing over greens mixture; toss gently to coat. Place pork strips on top of salad. Sprinkle with sesame seeds. Serve with remaining dressing.

*To toast sesame seeds, place in nonstick skillet over medium heat; stir constantly until seeds are light brown.

Nutrients per serving:			
Calories	252	Cholesterol	48 mg
Fat	8 g	Sodium	481 mg

Favorite recipe from **National Pork Producers Council**

Indonesian Chicken and Pear Salad

Makes 4 servings

1½ cups cubed cooked chicken
3 fresh California Bartlett pears, halved and cored
½ cup macadamia nuts or peanuts, coarsely chopped (optional)
½ cup cucumber slices
3 tablespoons slivered crystallized ginger (optional)
2 tablespoons thinly sliced green onion
Curry Dressing (recipe follows)
Lemon juice
4 iceberg lettuce cups
Toasted shredded coconut (optional)

Place chicken in bowl. Cube 2 pear halves; add pear cubes, nuts, cucumber, ginger and onion to chicken. Add Curry Dressing; toss gently to mix. Place each lettuce cup on individual salad plate. Dip pear halves in lemon juice and arrange each half in 1 lettuce cup. Spoon chicken mixture evenly onto pear halves. Sprinkle with coconut, if desired.

Curry Dressing: Combine ½ cup plain low fat yogurt, ½ teaspoon curry powder and ¼ teaspoon *each* dry mustard, ground allspice and garlic powder; mix well. Prepare about 20 minutes before using to allow flavors to blend. Makes about ⅔ cup.

Nutrients per serving:			
Calories	283	Cholesterol	94 mg
Fat	5 g	Sodium	108 mg

Favorite recipe from **California Tree Fruit Agreement**

Warm Pork and Spinach Salad

Cucumber Salad

Makes 4 servings

½ cup nonfat plain yogurt
½ teaspoon sugar
1 teaspoon dried mint
2 cucumbers, sliced

Combine yogurt, sugar and mint in large bowl until well blended. Add cucumber slices; toss to coat.

Nutrients per serving:

Calories	40	Cholesterol	2 mg
Fat	1 g	Sodium	23 mg

Favorite recipe from **The Sugar Association, Inc.**

Citrus Salad with Bibb Lettuce, Watercress and Balsamic Dressing

Makes 4 servings

2 large Florida oranges
1 medium Florida pink grapefruit, peeled, white pith removed, cut into sections
2 Florida tangerines, peeled and separated into sections
1 bunch watercress leaves, rinsed and patted dry

Dressing

3 tablespoons Florida orange juice
1 tablespoon balsamic vinegar
¼ teaspoon salt
1 tablespoon canola or vegetable oil
1 large head Bibb lettuce, separated into leaves, rinsed and patted dry

Remove strips of peel (orange part only) from 1 orange; finely cut into julienned strips. Set aside for garnish.

Peel and remove white pith from each orange. Cut oranges into sections. Combine oranges, grapefruit, tangerines and watercress in medium bowl.

For dressing, combine orange juice, balsamic vinegar and salt in small bowl. Add oil; whisk until well combined. Pour over fruit and watercress; toss gently to combine. Line 4 serving plates with Bibb lettuce. Divide fruit mixture among plates. Garnish with julienned orange peel.

Nutrients per serving:

Calories	126	Cholesterol	0 mg
Fat	4 g	Sodium	145 mg

Favorite recipe from **Florida Department of Citrus**

Pineapple Waldorf Pasta Salad

Pineapple Waldorf Pasta Salad

Makes 4 servings

1 can (8 ounces) DOLE® Pineapple Chunks, undrained
2 cups cooked medium shell pasta (1½ cups dry), rinsed and cooled
1 medium red apple, cored and cubed
1 cup diced celery
3 tablespoons chopped walnuts, toasted *or* whole natural almonds
2 tablespoons light mayonnaise
2 tablespoons light sour cream
¼ teaspoon salt

Drain pineapple, reserving ¼ cup juice; set aside.

Combine drained pineapple, pasta, apple, celery and walnuts in large bowl. Combine mayonnaise, sour cream, reserved juice and salt in small bowl; blend well. Add to pasta mixture. Toss until combined.

Prep time: 20 minutes

Nutrients per serving:

Calories	240	Cholesterol	3 mg
Fat	8 g	Sodium	207 mg

Gingered Fruit Salad

Makes 8 servings

- **2 oranges, peeled and sectioned**
- **2 tart apples, cored and chopped**
- **2 peaches, sliced**
- **1 cup strawberry halves**
- **1 cup DANNON® Plain Nonfat or Lowfat Yogurt**
- **2 tablespoons packed brown sugar**
- **½ teaspoon ginger**

In a large bowl toss oranges, apples, peaches and strawberries. In a small bowl combine yogurt, brown sugar and ginger. Blend well with wire whisk or fork. Toss with fruit.

Nutrients per serving:

Calories	80	Cholesterol	trace
Fat	0 g	Sodium	21 mg

Artichoke Wild Rice Salad

Makes 6 to 8 servings

Salad
- **2 cups cooked wild rice**
- **1 cup frozen peas, thawed**
- **1 can (8 ounces) sliced water chestnuts, drained**
- **1 jar (6 ounces) marinated artichoke hearts, drained (reserve marinade)**
- **4 ounces shredded mozzarella cheese (optional)**
- **1 jar (2 ounces) diced pimiento, drained (optional)**

Dressing
- **2 tablespoons canola oil**
- **2 tablespoons reserved marinade**
- **1 tablespoon balsamic vinegar**
- **½ teaspoon dried tarragon leaves, crushed**
- **½ teaspoon Dijon-style mustard**
- **2 to 3 drops hot pepper sauce**

Combine salad ingredients in large bowl. Combine dressing ingredients in small bowl; whisk until well blended. Pour over salad and toss. Refrigerate 4 hours or overnight to allow flavors to blend.

Nutrients per serving:

Calories	135	Cholesterol	0 mg
Fat	4 g	Sodium	49 mg

Favorite recipe from **Minnesota Cultivated Wild Rice Council**

Nectarine and Pear Mélange

Makes 6 servings

- **¼ cup lemon juice**
- **1 tablespoon brown sugar**
- **1½ teaspoons fresh mint leaves, finely chopped *or* ½ teaspoon dried mint**
- **1 teaspoon finely chopped garlic**
- **¼ teaspoon pepper**
- **3 fresh California Bartlett pears, halved and cored**
- **2 fresh California nectarines, halved**
- **½ cup chopped red onion**

Combine first 5 ingredients in small bowl; blend well. Cut pear and nectarines halves into ½-inch-thick slices. Arrange slices in shallow dish. Sprinkle onion over top; drizzle with dressing. Marinate in refrigerator 2 hours before serving.

Nutrients per serving:

Calories	84	Cholesterol	0 mg
Fat	trace	Sodium	2 mg

Favorite recipe from **California Tree Fruit Agreement**

Today's Slim Cottage Shrimp Salad

Makes 2 to 4 servings

- **6 to 8 ounces cooked and drained shrimp**
- **1 cup low fat (1%) Cottage cheese**
- **¼ cup minced celery**
- **¼ cup minced onion**
- **4 slices bacon, crisply cooked, drained and crumbled**
- **1 teaspoon lemon juice**
- **⅛ teaspoon pepper**
- **Salad greens**

Combine all ingredients except salad greens in medium bowl. Mix until well blended. Cover and chill at least 1 hour. Serve over salad greens.

Nutrients per serving:

Calories	125	Cholesterol	91 mg
Fat	4 g	Sodium	432 mg

Favorite recipe from **Wisconsin Milk Marketing Board © 1994**

Gingered Fruit Salad

Black and White Bean Salad

Black and White Bean Salad

Makes 4 cups

½ cup **MIRACLE WHIP® FREE® Nonfat
    Dressing**
1 can (15 ounces) *each* navy beans and black
    beans, drained and rinsed
½ cup *each* green bell pepper strips and red
    onion slices
1 cucumber, chopped
3 tablespoons chopped fresh parsley
    Dash black pepper

Mix together ingredients until well blended; refrigerate.

Prep time: 10 minutes

Nutrients per serving (½ cup):			
Calories	200	Cholesterol	0 mg
Fat	1 g	Sodium	214 mg

Fabulous Fruit Salad for a Crowd

Makes 12 to 14 servings

¼ cup seedless raspberry jam
2 tablespoons lemon juice
1 pint strawberries, stems removed, halved
1 cup plum wedges
2 cups pineapple chunks
2 cups cantaloupe chunks
2 cups honeydew chunks
2 cups nectarine chunks
½ pint raspberries
1 cup seedless green grapes
1 cup **BLUE DIAMOND® Whole Natural
    Almonds**, toasted

In large bowl, blend jam and lemon juice. Toss with
strawberries and plum wedges. Let stand, covered,
up to 2 hours. Just before serving, fold in pineapple,
cantaloupe, honeydew, nectarines, raspberries, grapes
and almonds.

Nutrients per serving:			
Calories	135	Cholesterol	0 mg
Fat	6 g	Sodium	5 mg

Gingered Pear Salad

Makes 3 cups, 3 entrée servings

1 can (8½ ounces) pear halves in juice,
    undrained
1 package (4-serving size) JELL-O® Brand
    Lemon Flavor Sugar Free Gelatin
¾ cup boiling water
2 teaspoons lemon juice
    Ice cubes
1 cup (8 ounces) 2% low-fat cottage cheese
⅛ teaspoon salt
⅛ teaspoon ground ginger

Drain pears, reserving juice; set juice aside. Finely chop pears; set aside.

Dissolve gelatin in boiling water; add lemon juice. Add enough ice cubes to reserved pear juice to measure 1 cup. Add to gelatin; stir until slightly thickened. Remove any unmelted ice; pour gelatin into blender container. Add cottage cheese, salt and ginger; cover. Blend until smooth. Stir in pears. Pour into 3 individual plastic containers or serving dishes. Chill until firm, about 2 hours.

Nutrients per serving:

Calories	120	Cholesterol	5 mg
Fat	2 g	Sodium	480 mg

Warm Turkey Salad

Makes 2 servings

1 medium DOLE® Fresh Pineapple
4 ounces green beans or broccoli, steamed
2 DOLE® Carrots, slivered or sliced
½ cup slivered jicama or radishes
½ cup slivered DOLE® Red Bell Pepper
    DOLE® Salad Greens
    Salt and black pepper (optional)
2 turkey cutlets (½ pound)
1 tablespoon vegetable oil
    Lite Honey Mustard Dressing (recipe follows)

Twist crown from pineapple. Cut pineapple in half lengthwise. Refrigerate half for another use, such as fruit salads. Cut remaining half in half lengthwise. Remove fruit from shells with knife. Cut each quarter into 4 spears. Arrange pineapple, green beans, carrots, jicama and red bell pepper on 2 dinner plates lined with salad greens, leaving space for cooked turkey. Lightly sprinkle salt and pepper over turkey. In medium skillet, brown turkey on both sides in oil. Cover; simmer 5 to 7 minutes. (Add 1 tablespoon water if needed.) Remove from skillet. Cut turkey crosswise into 4 or 5 slices. Arrange on salad plates with pineapple and vegetables. Serve with Lite Honey Mustard Dressing.

Lite Honey Mustard Dressing

¼ cup cholesterol-free reduced-calorie
    mayonnaise
1 to 2 tablespoons pineapple juice or orange
    juice
1 teaspoon honey
1 teaspoon Dijon-style mustard
¼ teaspoon dried tarragon leaves, crumbled

Combine all ingredients in small bowl.

Nutrients per serving:

Calories	267	Cholesterol	30 mg
Fat	10 g	Sodium	233 mg

Zesty Pasta Salad

Makes 6 servings

2 cups (8 ounces) ARMOUR® Lower Salt Ham,
    cut into julienne strips
2 cups pasta bow ties or shells, cooked
    according to package directions and
    drained (omit salt)
8 ounces California-blend frozen vegetables,
    thawed
5 cherry tomatoes, cut in half
¾ cup bottled low-sodium, low-calorie zesty
    Italian salad dressing
4 cups mixed greens, washed and drained

Combine ham, pasta, vegetables, tomatoes and salad dressing in large bowl; toss to coat well. Cover; refrigerate at least 1 hour before serving to allow flavors to blend. To serve, arrange pasta mixture in lettuce-lined bowl or on platter.

Nutrients per serving:

Calories	233	Cholesterol	19 mg
Fat	3 g	Sodium	344 mg

Zesty Pasta Salad

Shrimp-Pear Pasta Salad

Makes 6 servings

8 ounces dry twistee pasta noodles or rotini,
cooked and drained
2 fresh California Bartlett pears, cored and
sliced
½ cup *each* chopped red and green bell peppers
2 green onions, chopped
¼ pound bay shrimp, cooked, shelled and
deveined
Dressing (recipe follows)
Lettuce leaves

Combine pasta, pears, peppers, onions and shrimp in
large bowl. Add Dressing; toss lightly to coat. Line
salad bowl or 6 individual salad plates with lettuce;
top with pasta mixture. Serve immediately.

Dressing: Combine 1 cup plain low fat yogurt,
2 teaspoons Dijon-style mustard, ½ teaspoon dried
dill weed and hot pepper sauce to taste; blend well.

Nutrients per serving:

Calories	130	Cholesterol	30 mg
Fat	1 g	Sodium	86 mg

Favorite recipe from **California Tree Fruit Agreement**

Spinach Chickpea Salad

Makes 4 servings

2 tablespoons red wine vinegar
2 tablespoons water
1 teaspoon sesame oil
1 teaspoon light soy sauce
1 teaspoon sugar
3 cups spinach, washed, stems removed and
leaves torn into bite-sized pieces
2 carrots, peeled and sliced
1 cup canned chickpeas, drained and rinsed
1½ tablespoons sesame seeds

For dressing, combine vinegar, water, oil, soy sauce
and sugar in small bowl; whisk until well blended.
Place spinach, carrots and chickpeas in salad bowl.
Pour dressing over salad mixture; toss until well
coated. Sprinkle with sesame seeds.

Nutrients per serving:

Calories	128	Cholesterol	0 mg
Fat	4 g	Sodium	93 mg

Favorite recipe from **The Sugar Association, Inc.**

Insalata Rustica

Makes 6 servings

4 cups torn iceberg lettuce
4 cups torn romaine lettuce
1 bunch watercress, stems removed
2 tomatoes, sliced
6 radishes, sliced
2 large fresh California peaches, cut into
wedges (about 2 cups)
Mustard Dressing (recipe follows)

Make bed of lettuce and watercress in large salad
bowl. Arrange tomatoes, radishes and peaches in
attractive pattern on top. Drizzle with Mustard
Dressing.

Mustard Dressing: Combine ¼ cup vegetable oil,
3 tablespoons white wine vinegar, 4 teaspoons Dijon-
style mustard, 2 teaspoons minced garlic and
½ teaspoon sugar in jar with tight-fitting lid. Shake
until well blended. Makes about ½ cup.

Nutrients per serving:

Calories	54	Cholesterol	0 mg
Fat	2 g	Sodium	51 mg

Favorite recipe from **California Tree Fruit Agreement**

Pasta and Walnut Fruit Salad

Makes 6 servings

8 ounces medium pasta shells, uncooked
1 container (8 ounces) nonfat plain yogurt
¼ cup frozen orange juice concentrate, thawed
1 can (15 ounces) mandarin oranges in juice,
drained
1 cup seedless red grapes, halved
1 cup seedless green grapes, halved
1 apple, cored and chopped
½ cup sliced celery
½ cup walnut halves

Prepare shells according to package directions; drain.
Blend yogurt and orange juice concentrate in small
bowl. Combine shells and remaining ingredients in
large bowl. Add yogurt mixture; toss gently to coat.
Cover and refrigerate until chilled thoroughly.

Nutrients per serving:

Calories	217	Cholesterol	1 mg
Fat	6 g	Sodium	44 mg

Favorite recipe from **National Pasta Association**

Armenian Spinach-Plum Salad

Makes 4 servings

  3 cups spinach, washed, stems removed and
      leaves torn into bite-sized pieces
  2 cups peeled and halved cucumber slices
  ¼ cup thinly sliced red onion
  ¼ cup minced fresh parsley
  2 tablespoons pistachios, shelled and chopped
      (optional)
  3 fresh California plums, cut into wedges
      Armenian Dressing (recipe follows)

Combine spinach, cucumber, onion, parsley,
pistachios and plums in salad bowl. Add Armenian
Dressing and toss lightly to coat.

Armenian Dressing: Combine ⅓ cup safflower
oil, 2 to 3 tablespoons freshly squeezed lemon juice,
½ teaspoon dried oregano leaves, ½ teaspoon
minced garlic, ¼ teaspoon dry mustard and pepper
to taste; whisk until well blended. Makes ½ cup.

Nutrients per serving (includes 1 tablespoon dressing):

Calories	150	Cholesterol	0 mg
Fat	9 g	Sodium	109 mg

Favorite recipe from **California Tree Fruit Agreement**

Saucy Herb Dressing

Makes 1⅔ cups

  1 cup nonfat cottage cheese
  ¼ cup skim milk
  2 tablespoons red wine vinegar
  2 teaspoons CRISCO® Vegetable Oil
  ¼ cup chopped green onions with tops
  ¼ cup chopped fresh parsley
  1 clove garlic, minced
  ¼ teaspoon dried oregano leaves
  ¼ teaspoon dried basil leaves
  ¼ teaspoon black pepper
  ⅛ teaspoon cayenne pepper

1. Combine cottage cheese, milk, vinegar and
Crisco® Oil in blender or food processor container.
Process until smooth.

2. Add green onions, parsley, garlic, oregano, basil,
black pepper and cayenne. Process until blended.
Serve over crisp salad greens.

Nutrients per serving (1 tablespoon dressing):

Calories	10	Cholesterol	0 mg
Fat	trace	Sodium	30 mg

Vegetable Potato Salad

Makes 8 servings

  ½ cup cider vinegar
  ¼ cup CRISCO® Vegetable Oil
  ½ teaspoon prepared mustard
  ½ teaspoon salt
  ¼ teaspoon pepper
  2¾ pounds unpeeled medium red potatoes
  3 medium carrots, cut into thin 2-inch sticks
  3 ribs celery, sliced
  3 green onions with tops, chopped
  6 radishes, sliced
  4 tomatoes, quartered

1. Combine vinegar, Crisco® Oil, mustard, salt and
pepper in container with tight-fitting lid. Shake well.

2. Cook potatoes just until tender. Cool 5 minutes.
Cut into bite-size pieces. Combine in large salad bowl
with carrots, celery, onions and radishes. Shake
dressing. Pour over salad. Toss to mix well. Serve
immediately or refrigerate. Top with tomato wedges.

Nutrients per serving:

Calories	225	Cholesterol	0 mg
Fat	7 g	Sodium	175 mg

Peach-Spinach Salad

Makes 6 servings

  1½ cups spinach, washed, stems removed and
      leaves torn into bite-sized pieces
  1 cup cucumber slices
  1 fresh California peach, sliced (about 1 cup)
  2 fresh California plums, sliced (about 1 cup)
  ¼ cup sliced green onion
      Yogurt Dressing (recipe follows)

Combine spinach, cucumber, peach, plums and onion
in large bowl; toss lightly. Divide evenly among
6 individual salad plates. Serve with Yogurt Dressing.

Yogurt Dressing: Combine 1 cup plain low fat
yogurt, 1 tablespoon fresh lemon juice, 1 tablespoon
water and ¼ teaspoon dill weed in small bowl until
smooth. Makes about 1 cup.

Nutrients per serving (includes 1 tablespoon dressing):

Calories	42	Cholesterol	trace
Fat	trace	Sodium	45 mg

Favorite recipe from **California Tree Fruit Agreement**

Turkey-Pasta Salad

Makes 6 servings, 8 cups

4 cups cooked wagon wheel or spiral pasta
  (about 2 cups uncooked)
2 cups short thin turkey or chicken strips
  (about 8 ounces)
1 large zucchini, cut into ½-inch slices, each
  slice quartered
1 large tomato, cut into ½-inch chunks
1 can (8 ounces) whole kernel corn, drained, *or*
  1 cup frozen corn kernels, thawed
1 small red bell pepper, cut into ½-inch chunks
½ cup chopped cilantro or fresh parsley
¾ cup PACE® Picante Sauce
⅓ cup reduced-calorie creamy garlic salad
  dressing
¼ teaspoon salt (optional)
  Additional PACE® Picante Sauce (optional)

Combine pasta, turkey, zucchini, tomato, corn, red
pepper and cilantro in large bowl. Combine ¾ cup
Pace® Picante Sauce, dressing and salt; mix well.
Pour over pasta mixture; toss gently. Refrigerate.
Serve with additional Pace® Picante Sauce, if desired.

Nutrients per serving:

Calories	234	Cholesterol	26 mg
Fat	4 g	Sodium	570 mg

Turkey-Pasta Salad

Taco Salad

Makes 4 servings, 5 cups

2 packages (4-serving size) or 1 package
  (8-serving size) JELL-O® Brand Lemon
  Flavor Sugar Free Gelatin
2 cups boiling water
1 cup frozen corn
1 cup canned kidney beans, drained
½ cup medium salsa
¼ cup (1 ounce) grated Cheddar cheese
2 tablespoons vinegar
½ teaspoon chili powder

Completely dissolve gelatin in boiling water. Chill until
slightly thickened. Stir in remaining ingredients.
Spoon gelatin mixture into 4 individual plastic
containers or serving dishes. Chill until firm, about
2 hours.

Nutrients per serving:

Calories	140	Cholesterol	10 mg
Fat	4 g	Sodium	560 mg

Chinese Chicken Salad

Makes 6 servings

3 cups cooked rice, cooled
1 cup cooked chicken breast cubes
1 cup sliced celery
1 can (8 ounces) sliced water chestnuts, drained
1 cup fresh bean sprouts*
½ cup (about 2 ounces) sliced fresh mushrooms
¼ cup sliced green onions
¼ cup diced red bell pepper
3 tablespoons lemon juice
2 tablespoons reduced-sodium soy sauce
2 tablespoons sesame oil
2 teaspoons grated fresh ginger root
¼ to ½ teaspoon ground white pepper
  Lettuce leaves

Combine rice, chicken, celery, water chestnuts, bean
sprouts, mushrooms, onions, and red pepper in large
bowl. Combine lemon juice, soy sauce, oil, ginger
root, and white pepper in small jar with lid; shake
well. Pour over rice mixture; toss lightly. Serve on
lettuce leaves.

**Substitute canned bean sprouts, rinsed and drained, for
fresh bean sprouts, if desired.*

Nutrients per serving:

Calories	248	Cholesterol	20 mg
Fat	6 g	Sodium	593 mg

Favorite recipe from **USA Rice Council**

Curried Fruit and Rice Salad

Makes 6 servings

    2 cups cooked rice, chilled
    1 DOLE® Orange, sliced and quartered
    1 cup halved seedless red DOLE® Grapes
    ⅓ cup mayonnaise
    ⅓ cup vanilla yogurt
    ½ teaspoon curry powder, or to taste
      Grated peel and juice from 1 lime
    1 DOLE® Banana, peeled, sliced

Combine rice, orange and grapes in large bowl.
Combine mayonnaise, yogurt, curry, lime peel and
juice; stir dressing into rice mixture. Fold in banana
just before serving.

Nutrients per serving:

Calories	189	Cholesterol	9 mg
Fat	10 g	Sodium	76 mg

Spring Shrimp and Asparagus Salad

Makes 6 servings

    ¾ cup tomato juice
    ⅓ cup HEINZ® 57 Sauce
    1 tablespoon lemon juice
    1 tablespoon vegetable oil
    1 teaspoon Dijon-style mustard
    1 teaspoon granulated sugar
    ¼ teaspoon dried thyme leaves, crushed
    ¼ teaspoon salt
    ¼ teaspoon pepper
    1 pound fresh asparagus spears
      Assorted salad greens
    1 pound medium-size raw shrimp, cooked,
      shelled and deveined
    1 cup fresh enoki or button mushrooms
    2 tomatoes, cut into wedges
    2 teaspoons grated lemon peel

For dressing, in jar with tight-fitting lid, combine first
9 ingredients; shake well and set aside. Cook
asparagus in small amount of boiling water 3 to
5 minutes or until crisp-tender. Drain; cool slightly.
On individual serving plates lined with salad greens,
arrange asparagus spears, shrimp, mushrooms and
tomatoes. Drizzle salad with dressing. Sprinkle with
grated lemon peel.

Nutrients per serving:

Calories	116	Cholesterol	58 mg
Fat	4 g	Sodium	274 mg

Cucumber and Onion Salad

Cucumber and Onion Salad

Makes 12 servings, 6 cups

    ½ cup MIRACLE WHIP® FREE® Nonfat
      Dressing
    4 cucumbers, peeled, halved lengthwise,
      seeded, sliced
    2 onions, sliced, halved
    ½ cup thin red bell pepper strips

Mix together dressing, cucumbers and onions in large
bowl. Top with peppers; refrigerate.

Prep time: 10 minutes plus refrigerating

Nutrients per serving (½ cup):

Calories	30	Cholesterol	0 mg
Fat	trace	Sodium	143 mg

East Indian Peach Salad

Makes 4 servings

    ½ cup vanilla low-fat yogurt
    ½ teaspoon curry powder, or to taste
    1 (16-ounce) can sliced peaches in light syrup,
      drained and syrup reserved
    2 cups (8 ounces) ARMOUR® Lower Salt Ham
      cut into ½-inch cubes
    1 cup seedless red or green grapes, cut in half
      Leaf lettuce, washed and drained
    2 tablespoons sliced almonds, toasted

Combine yogurt, curry powder and 1 tablespoon
reserved peach syrup in small bowl; set aside.
Combine peaches, ham and grapes in medium bowl.
Add yogurt mixture; toss gently to coat well. Serve in
lettuce-lined serving bowl or platter. Sprinkle with
almonds.

Nutrients per serving:

Calories	206	Cholesterol	29 mg
Fat	5 g	Sodium	509 mg

Lemon Ginger Sauce

Lemon Ginger Sauce

Makes ½ cup

½ cup MIRACLE WHIP® FREE® Nonfat
    Dressing
2 tablespoons lemon juice
1½ tablespoons firmly packed brown sugar
1 teaspoon grated lemon peel
1 teaspoon ground ginger

Mix together ingredients until well blended;
refrigerate. Serve over fresh fruit.

Prep time: 5 minutes plus refrigerating

Nutrients per serving (2 tablespoons sauce):			
Calories	70	Cholesterol	1 mg
Fat	trace	Sodium	422 mg

Creamettes® Chicken Salad

Makes 8 servings

1 (7-ounce) package CREAMETTES® Elbow
    Macaroni (2 cups uncooked)
2 cups cubed cooked chicken or turkey (white
    meat)
2 cups fresh broccoli florettes
4 medium oranges, peeled, sectioned and
    seeded
1 cup orange juice
¼ cup cider vinegar
1 teaspoon ground ginger
½ teaspoon paprika
¼ cup toasted sliced almonds

Prepare Creamettes® Elbow Macaroni according to
package directions; drain. In large bowl, combine
macaroni, chicken, broccoli and oranges. In small
bowl, blend orange juice, vinegar, ginger and paprika;
toss with macaroni mixture. Cover; refrigerate
thoroughly. Stir before serving. Garnish with almonds.
Refrigerate leftovers.

Nutrients per serving:			
Calories	222	Cholesterol	36 mg
Fat	4 g	Sodium	38 mg

Saffron Rice Salad

Makes 4 servings

2½ cups cooked rice (cooked in chicken broth
    and ⅛ teaspoon saffron*), cooled to room
    temperature
½ cup diced red bell pepper
½ cup diced green bell pepper
¼ cup sliced green onions
¼ cup sliced ripe olives
2 tablespoons white wine vinegar
1 teaspoon olive oil
2 to 3 drops hot pepper sauce (optional)
1 clove garlic, minced
¼ teaspoon ground white pepper
    Lettuce leaves

Combine rice, red and green peppers, onions, and
olives in large bowl. Combine vinegar, oil, pepper
sauce, garlic, and white pepper in jar with lid; shake
well. Pour over rice mixture; toss lightly. Serve on
lettuce leaves.

Substitute ground turmeric for the saffron, if desired.

Nutrients per serving:			
Calories	177	Cholesterol	0 mg
Fat	3 g	Sodium	416 mg

Favorite recipe from **USA Rice Council**

Mediterranean Couscous

Makes 6 servings, 6 cups

3 cups water
1 teaspoon salt
1 box (10 ounces) couscous
1 cup canned black beans, rinsed and drained
8 ounces cherry tomatoes, chopped
1 carrot, shredded
½ cup WISH-BONE® Healthy Sensation! Italian
    Dressing

In 2-quart saucepan, bring water and salt to a boil;
stir in couscous. Cover; remove from heat and let
stand 5 minutes. Fluff with fork; set aside 10 minutes
to cool. In large bowl, toss couscous with remaining
ingredients; refrigerate.

Nutrients per serving:			
Calories	172	Cholesterol	0 mg
Fat	trace	Sodium	587 mg

Chef's Salad

Chef's Salad

Makes 3½ cups, 3 entrée servings

1 package (4-serving size) JELL-O® Brand
  Lemon Flavor Sugar Free Gelatin
¼ teaspoon salt
¾ cup boiling water
½ cup cold water
  Ice cubes
1 tablespoon vinegar
2 teaspoons low-calorie French dressing
¼ teaspoon Worcestershire sauce
⅛ teaspoon white pepper
¾ cup chopped tomato
½ cup finely shredded lettuce
½ cup slivered cooked turkey breast
½ cup slivered Swiss cheese
2 tablespoons sliced green onions
2 tablespoons quartered radish slices

Completely dissolve gelatin and salt in boiling water.
Combine cold water and enough ice cubes to measure
1¼ cups. Add to gelatin; stir until slightly thickened.
Remove any unmelted ice. Stir in vinegar, dressing,
Worcestershire sauce and pepper. Chill until slightly
thickened.

Stir remaining ingredients into gelatin mixture. Spoon
into 3 individual plastic containers or dishes. Chill
until firm, about 2 hours. Garnish if desired.

Nutrients per serving:

Calories	100	Cholesterol	30 mg
Fat	4 g	Sodium	330 mg

Wilted Spinach Bacon Salad

Makes 4 servings

6 ounces fresh spinach leaves, cleaned and torn
  into bite-sized pieces (about 6 cups)

Dressing
8 slices LOUIS RICH® Turkey Bacon, cut into
  1-inch pieces
½ large red onion, coarsely chopped
¼ cup water
3 tablespoons sugar
2 tablespoons vinegar
⅛ teaspoon black pepper

Place spinach leaves in large serving bowl; set aside.
Combine Turkey Bacon and onion in large nonstick
skillet. Cook over medium heat 8 to 10 minutes or
until bacon begins to brown, stirring occasionally. In
small bowl, combine remaining dressing ingredients;
stir into Turkey Bacon mixture. Reduce heat to low
and simmer 3 minutes. Pour over spinach leaves and
toss.

Nutrients per serving:

Calories	120	Cholesterol	20 mg
Fat	5 g	Sodium	415 mg

Italian Pasta Salad

Makes 8 to 10 servings

10 ounces uncooked rotini pasta
½ cup chopped broccoli flowerets
1 can (6 ounces) small pitted ripe olives, drained
12 cherry tomatoes, cut in half
½ medium red onion, thinly sliced
½ cup low-calorie Italian salad dressing
2 tablespoons grated Parmesan cheese
  Freshly ground black pepper to taste

Cook rotini according to package directions. Drain.
Rinse with cold water; drain again thoroughly. Cool.
Cook broccoli in boiling salted water just until bright
green and crisp-tender. Drain. Rinse with cold water;
drain again thoroughly. Combine rotini, broccoli,
olives, tomatoes, onion and salad dressing in large
bowl. Stir in cheese and season with pepper. Cover
and refrigerate until chilled.

Nutrients per serving:

Calories	184	Cholesterol	1 mg
Fat	8 g	Sodium	149 mg

Fall Harvest Fruit Salad

Makes 4 servings

¼ cup *each* FRENCH'S® Creamy Spread™
   Mustard and plain nonfat yogurt
1 tablespoon firmly packed brown sugar
¼ teaspoon curry powder
1 apple, thinly sliced
1 pear, coarsely chopped
½ cup thinly sliced celery
½ cup seedless grapes, halved
¼ cup chopped pecans

In measuring cup or small bowl, combine French's®
Creamy Spread™ Mustard, yogurt, sugar and curry
powder; set aside. Combine remaining ingredients in
large bowl. Add mustard mixture; toss well to coat
evenly. Serve on lettuce leaves, if desired.

Nutrients per serving:

Calories	165	Cholesterol	1 mg
Fat	6 g	Sodium	227 mg

Southwestern Turkey Salad

Makes 4 servings

⅓ cup FRENCH'S® Creamy Spread™ Mustard
2 tablespoons lime juice
1 tablespoon olive oil
½ teaspoon *each* ground cumin and garlic
   powder
2 cups (12 ounces) chopped ripe tomatoes
2 green onions, thinly sliced
3 cups finely shredded romaine lettuce
2 cups (12 ounces) thin strips cooked turkey

In medium bowl, combine French's® Creamy
Spread™ Mustard, lime juice, oil, cumin and garlic
powder. Stir in tomatoes and green onions. Arrange
lettuce and turkey on 4 salad plates, dividing evenly.
Serve tomato mixture alongside turkey. Top turkey, if
desired, with additional French's® Creamy Spread™
Mustard. Serve with unsalted tortilla chips, if desired.

Nutrients per serving:

Calories	219	Cholesterol	60 mg
Fat	8 g	Sodium	305 mg

Left to right: Fall Harvest Fruit Salad, Southwestern Turkey Salad

Shrimp and Snow Pea Salad

Makes 4 servings, 6 cups

¼ pound fresh snow peas, strings removed
2 cups (6 ounces) medium pasta shells
1 cup DANNON® Plain Nonfat or Lowfat Yogurt
1 tablespoon red wine vinegar
1 teaspoon minced garlic
½ teaspoon salt
¼ teaspoon pepper
¼ teaspoon dried oregano leaves, crushed
1 pound fully cooked medium shrimp, peeled and deveined
6 cherry tomatoes, halved
½ cup red bell pepper strips
¼ cup sliced green onions
Large lettuce leaves

In a large saucepan bring water to a boil. Add snow peas and boil 1 to 2 minutes or until tender-crisp. Remove from saucepan with slotted spoon; place in ice water to cool quickly. Drain. Add pasta to boiling water; stir well and return to a boil. Reduce heat to medium-high and simmer 10 to 12 minutes, stirring often; drain. Rinse in cold water and drain again.

In a large bowl combine yogurt, vinegar, garlic, salt, pepper and oregano; stir well. Add shrimp, snow peas, pasta, cherry tomatoes, bell pepper and green onions. Toss gently. To serve, line large platter with lettuce leaves; spoon salad over lettuce.

Nutrients per serving:

Calories	290	Cholesterol	130 mg
Fat	3 g	Sodium	571 mg

Western Spinach Salad

Makes 6 servings

1 can (16 ounces) California cling peach slices in juice or extra light syrup
1 large bunch spinach, washed, stems removed and leaves torn into bite-sized pieces (about 8 cups)
1 hard-cooked egg, chopped or wedged
1 tomato, chopped or wedged
1½ cups croutons
1 cup shredded part skim mozzarella cheese
1 tablespoon olive oil
1 cup chopped onion
2 tablespoons cider vinegar
1 tablespoon sugar
¾ teaspoon garlic powder
¾ teaspoon onion powder
¾ teaspoon celery seed
1½ cups plain nonfat yogurt
¼ cup chopped parsley

Drain peaches, reserving ¼ cup liquid; reserve remainder for another use. Combine peaches, spinach, egg, tomato and croutons in large bowl; toss to mix well. Top with cheese; set aside. Heat oil in medium skillet over medium-high heat until hot. Add onion; cook and stir until softened. Stir in reserved ¼ cup peach liquid, vinegar, sugar, garlic powder, onion powder and celery seed; mix well. Blend in yogurt and parsley. To serve, spoon over spinach mixture; toss lightly.

Nutrients per serving:

Calories	215	Cholesterol	47 mg
Fat	7 g	Sodium	306 mg

Favorite recipe from **California Cling Peach Advisory Board**

Apple-Bulgur Salad

Makes 4 servings

1¾ cups chicken broth
1 cup dry bulgur
4 cups fresh parsley leaves
1 large unpeeled apple, cored
2 tablespoons fresh lemon juice
2 tablespoons olive oil
2 tablespoons water
2 tablespoons red wine vinegar
2 teaspoons sugar
¼ teaspoon dried oregano leaves, crushed

Bring broth to a boil in small saucepan over high heat. Place bulgur in medium bowl; pour broth over bulgur. Stir; let stand for 30 minutes. Meanwhile, finely chop parsley and cut apple into 2-inch cubes. For dressing, combine remaining ingredients in small bowl; whisk until well blended. Stir apple, parsley and dressing into bulgur. Serve immediately or chill in refrigerator.

Nutrients per serving:

Calories	245	Cholesterol	0 mg
Fat	8 g	Sodium	229 mg

Favorite recipe from **The Sugar Association, Inc.**

Shrimp and Snow Pea Salad

Broiled Chicken Salad

Makes 4 servings

4 boneless skinless chicken breast halves (about 1 pound)
1 (15-ounce) can black beans, drained, rinsed
2 green onions, chopped
2 tablespoons low-calorie Italian salad dressing, divided
1 (10-ounce) package frozen whole kernel corn, thawed, drained
2 tablespoons chopped pimiento
2 tablespoons chopped cilantro
2 large tomatoes, cut into wedges

Preheat broiler. Position oven rack about 4 inches from heat source. Place chicken on rack of broiler pan. Broil 8 minutes or until browned on both sides and no longer pink in center, turning after 4 minutes. Set aside.

Combine beans, onions and 1 tablespoon dressing in medium bowl; mix lightly. Set aside.

Combine corn, pimiento and cilantro in separate bowl; mix lightly. Set aside.

Diagonally cut each chicken piece into thick slices; arrange on salad plates.

Arrange tomato wedges and spoonfuls of bean and corn mixtures around chicken. Drizzle remaining 1 tablespoon dressing over chicken. Garnish as desired.

Nutrients per serving:

Calories	254	Cholesterol	46 mg
Fat	3 g	Sodium	109 mg

Broiled Chicken Salad

Fiesta Corn Salad

Makes 4 to 6 servings

1 can (14½ to 15½ ounces) dark red kidney beans or black beans, drained, rinsed
1 package (10 ounces) frozen whole kernel corn, thawed (about 2 cups)
1 medium tomato, peeled, seeded, chopped
¼ cup sliced green onions
1 jalapeño pepper, minced
¼ cup HEINZ® Chili Sauce
3 tablespoons vegetable oil
2 tablespoons HEINZ® Apple Cider Vinegar
1 teaspoon chili powder
½ teaspoon ground cumin
¼ teaspoon salt
⅛ teaspoon black pepper
Lettuce leaves

In large bowl, combine beans, corn, tomato, green onions and jalapeño pepper. In small bowl, whisk together chili sauce and remaining ingredients except lettuce leaves; pour over bean mixture and stir to coat. Refrigerate. Serve on lettuce leaves.

Nutrients per serving:

Calories	190	Cholesterol	0 mg
Fat	8 g	Sodium	511 mg

Crunchy Tuna Salad in Pepper Boats

Makes 4 servings

2 large green or yellow bell peppers, halved lengthwise, seeded
½ cup MIRACLE WHIP® FREE® Dressing
2 (6½-ounce) cans tuna in water, drained, flaked
¼ cup *each:* chopped carrot, chopped celery and chopped red onion
¼ cup chopped pecans (optional)

To Microwave: Place pepper halves on plate. Microwave on HIGH (100% power) 1 minute; refrigerate.

Mix together remaining ingredients until well blended; refrigerate. Serve in pepper halves.

Prep time: 20 minutes plus refrigerating
Microwave cook time: 1 minute

Nutrients per serving:

Calories	170	Cholesterol	29 mg
Fat	2 g	Sodium	708 mg

Five Bean Salad

Makes 8 to 10 servings

¾ cup thinly sliced red onion
1 garlic clove, minced
2 tablespoons water
15 ounces canned garbanzo beans, rinsed and drained
1½ cups fresh green beans, cut into thirds
8 ounces canned great Northern beans, rinsed and drained
8 ounces canned black beans, rinsed and drained
8 ounces canned kidney beans, rinsed and drained
⅓ cup cider vinegar
1½ tablespoons sugar
1 teaspoon olive oil
¼ teaspoon dry mustard
3 carrots, thinly sliced
½ cup chopped red bell pepper

To Microwave: In large microwave-safe casserole dish, combine onion, garlic and water. Microwave at HIGH (100% power) for 1 to 2 minutes.

Stir in all remaining ingredients except carrots and red pepper. Microwave at HIGH for an additional 3 to 5 minutes or until green beans are tender-crisp.

Stir in carrots and red pepper. Serve immediately. (Salad may also be prepared ahead of time; cover, refrigerate and serve cold.)

Nutrients per serving:

Calories	190	Cholesterol	0 mg
Fat	2 g	Sodium	14 mg

Favorite recipe from **The Sugar Association, Inc.**

Lemony Low-Cal Dressing

Makes about 1 cup

⅔ cup plus 2 tablespoons water
¼ cup REALEMON® Lemon Juice from Concentrate
1 (1.3-ounce) package low-calorie Italian salad dressing mix

In 1-pint jar with tight-fitting lid or cruet, combine ingredients; shake well. Chill to blend flavors. Refrigerate leftovers.

Nutrients per serving (1 tablespoon dressing):

Calories	8	Cholesterol	0 mg
Fat	trace	Sodium	177 mg

Sweet and Smoky Pasta Salad

Sweet and Smoky Pasta Salad

Makes 4 servings

1 can (8 ounces) DOLE® Pineapple Chunks, drained
2 cups cooked rotini, rinsed and cooled
1 cup cubed cantaloupe
½ cup red or green seedless grapes
½ cup cubed baked ham
3 to 4 tablespoons prepared honey mustard dressing
1 tablespoon minced cilantro leaves

Combine all ingredients in large bowl; toss until combined.

Prep time: 20 minutes

Nutrients per serving:

Calories	221	Cholesterol	11 mg
Fat	5 g	Sodium	334 mg

Tuna and Fresh Fruit Salad

Tuna and Fresh Fruit Salad

Makes 4 servings

Lettuce leaves (optional)
1 can (12½ ounces) STARKIST® Tuna, drained
    and broken into chunks
4 cups slices or wedges fresh fruit*
¼ cup slivered almonds (optional)

Fruit Dressing
1 container (8 ounces) lemon, mandarin orange
    or vanilla low-fat yogurt
2 tablespoons orange juice
¼ teaspoon ground cinnamon

Line a large platter, 4 individual plates or 4 large
goblets with lettuce leaves, if desired. Arrange tuna
and desired fruit in a decorative design over lettuce.
Sprinkle almonds over salad, if desired.

For Fruit Dressing, in a small bowl stir together
yogurt, orange juice and cinnamon until well blended.
Serve dressing with salad.

*Suggested fresh fruit: apples, bananas, berries, citrus fruit,
kiwifruit, melon, papaya, peaches or pears.*

Nutrients per serving:

Calories	233	Cholesterol	39 mg
Fat	1 g	Sodium	434 mg

Neptune's Salad

Makes 4 servings, 5 cups

2 packages (4-serving size) or 1 package
    (8-serving size) JELL-O® Brand Lemon
    Flavor Sugar Free Gelatin
2 cups boiling water
1 cup plain low-fat yogurt
2 tablespoons chili sauce
2 tablespoons finely chopped onion
2 tablespoons lemon juice
1 cup imitation crabmeat, flaked
½ cup chopped celery
¼ cup chopped red bell pepper

Completely dissolve gelatin in boiling water. Stir in
yogurt, chili sauce, onion and lemon juice. Chill until
slightly thickened. Stir in remaining ingredients.
Spoon into 4 individual plastic containers or serving
dishes. Chill until firm, about 2 hours.

Nutrients per serving:

Calories	110	Cholesterol	15 mg
Fat	2 g	Sodium	640 mg

Parmesan Curry Dressing

Makes 6 servings

½ cup nonfat yogurt
½ cup buttermilk
1 tablespoon Parmesan cheese
1½ teaspoons sugar
1 teaspoon drained capers
¼ teaspoon black pepper
⅛ teaspoon onion powder
⅛ teaspoon curry powder

Place all ingredients in blender container or food
processor; process until blended. Refrigerate or serve
immediately.

Nutrients per serving (2 tablespoons dressing):

Calories	27	Cholesterol	2 mg
Fat	1 g	Sodium	52 mg

Favorite recipe from **The Sugar Association, Inc.**

Veggie Delight Salad

Makes 6 servings

½ of a (1-pound) package CREAMETTES®
    Elbow Macaroni, uncooked
1 cup small fresh broccoli flowerets
2 tomatoes, seeded and chopped
1 medium cucumber, peeled, seeded and
    chopped
½ cup sliced celery
2 green onions, sliced
2 tablespoons chopped fresh parsley
3 tablespoons plain low-fat yogurt
3 tablespoons bottled low-calorie Italian salad
    dressing
1½ teaspoons salt-free seasoning

Prepare Creamettes® Elbow Macaroni according
to package directions, adding broccoli during last
3 minutes of cooking time; drain. In medium bowl,
combine macaroni mixture, tomatoes, cucumber,
celery, green onions and parsley. In small bowl, blend
yogurt, dressing and seasoning. Add to salad mixture;
toss to coat. Cover; refrigerate thoroughly. Toss gently
before serving. Refrigerate leftovers.

Nutrients per serving:

Calories	157	Cholesterol	1 mg
Fat	2 g	Sodium	82 mg

Pacific Pasta Salad

Pacific Pasta Salad

Makes 4 servings

　1 can (8 ounces) DOLE® Pineapple Chunks,
　　　drained
　2 cups cooked linguine (¼ pound dry, broken
　　　in half), rinsed and cooled
　¾ cup shredded cooked chicken
　½ cup diagonally sliced celery
　½ cup red bell pepper strips
　3 tablespoons thinly sliced green onion with tops
　3 tablespoons Italian salad dressing
　2 tablespoons coarsely chopped peanuts
　¼ teaspoon salt
　⅛ teaspoon crushed red pepper flakes

Combine all ingredients in large bowl; toss until
combined.

Prep time: 20 minutes

Nutrients per serving:

Calories	264	Cholesterol	22 mg
Fat	9 g	Sodium	256 mg

Moroccan Vegetable Salad

Makes 10 servings

　½ pound small whole mushrooms
　1½ cups cooked garbanzo beans (chick peas)
　1 cup pitted large black olives
　12 cherry tomatoes, halved
　¾ cup coarsely chopped green onions
　2 green bell peppers, chopped
　2 red bell peppers, chopped
　1 cup DANNON® Plain Nonfat or Lowfat Yogurt
　½ cup reduced-calorie mayonnaise
　2 cloves garlic, crushed
　2 tablespoons olive oil
　1 tablespoon lemon juice
　1 teaspoon ground cumin
　⅛ teaspoon ground turmeric
　　Salt and pepper
　　Lettuce leaves

Steam mushrooms over boiling water 5 minutes; cool.
In a large bowl combine mushrooms, garbanzo beans,
olives, tomatoes, green onions and bell peppers.
Cover; chill 2 hours. In a small bowl combine yogurt,
mayonnaise, garlic, olive oil, lemon juice, cumin and
turmeric. Season with salt and pepper. Cover; chill
2 hours. Just before serving, lightly toss mushroom
mixture with some of dressing. Serve on lettuce
leaves. Serve with remaining dressing.

Nutrients per serving:

Calories	130	Cholesterol	10 mg
Fat	7 g	Sodium	196 mg

Fruit and Green Salad

Makes 2 servings

　2 tablespoons plain yogurt
　1 teaspoon sugar
　1 teaspoon lemon juice
　1½ cups torn lettuce
　1 orange, peeled and cubed
　1 apple, cored and cubed
　1 teaspoon chopped walnuts

Combine yogurt, sugar and lemon juice in small bowl;
blend well. Place lettuce, orange and apple in salad
bowl; toss to combine. Pour dressing over salad
mixture; sprinkle with walnuts.

Nutrients per serving:

Calories	106	Cholesterol	1 mg
Fat	2 g	Sodium	15 mg

Favorite recipe from **The Sugar Association, Inc.**

Cabbage and Apple Slaw

Makes 8 servings

½ cup nonfat sour cream alternative
2 tablespoons cider vinegar
1 tablespoon *plus* 2 teaspoons sugar
1 tablespoon CRISCO® Vegetable Oil
1 teaspoon celery seed
¾ teaspoon salt
¼ teaspoon dry mustard
4 cups shredded cabbage
1 medium red apple, chopped
¼ cup finely chopped green bell pepper
2 tablespoons finely chopped onion

1. Combine "sour cream," vinegar, sugar, Crisco®
Oil, celery seed, salt and dry mustard in small bowl.

2. Combine cabbage, apple, green pepper and onion
in large bowl. Pour "sour cream" mixture over
vegetables. Toss to mix. Cover and refrigerate until
ready to serve. Toss again just before serving.
Garnish, if desired.

Nutrients per serving:

Calories	60	Cholesterol	0 mg
Fat	2 g	Sodium	215 mg

Blueberry-Peach Salad

Makes 10 servings

1 package (6 ounces) orange-flavored gelatin
⅓ cup sugar
2¼ cups orange juice, divided
1 teaspoon finely grated orange peel
2 cups buttermilk
1 can (8 ounces) crushed pineapple, drained
2 medium peaches, peeled and chopped
   (about 1 cup)
1 cup fresh or thawed frozen unsweetened
   blueberries
1 carton (8 ounces) dairy sour cream

Combine gelatin and sugar in medium saucepan; stir
in 2 cups orange juice and orange peel. Let stand
1 minute for gelatin to soften. Cook and stir over
medium heat until gelatin is dissolved; cool. Stir in
buttermilk. Refrigerate until thickened but not set.
Fold in fruit; spoon into 10 individual molds. Chill for
6 hours or until set. Combine sour cream and
remaining ¼ cup orange juice; refrigerate. Unmold
salads; serve with sour cream mixture.

Nutrients per serving:

Calories	175	Cholesterol	12 mg
Fat	5 g	Sodium	65 mg

Favorite recipe from **Wisconsin Milk Marketing Board** © **1994**

Curried Salad Bombay

Makes 6 servings

1 package (1½ pounds) PERDUE® Fit 'n Easy
   fresh skinless and boneless turkey breast
½ cup reduced sodium chicken broth
½ cup low calorie mayonnaise
½ cup plain low fat yogurt
1 tablespoon peach or mango chutney
2 to 3 teaspoons curry powder
   Salt and ground black pepper to taste
   (optional)
1 red apple, unpeeled, cored and sliced
1 green apple, unpeeled, cored and sliced
¾ cup red and/or green seedless grapes
2 tablespoons snipped fresh chives
   Curly green or Bibb lettuce

To Microwave: In deep 2-quart microwave-safe dish,
place turkey breast and broth. Cover with plastic wrap and
microwave at HIGH (100% power) 3 minutes. Reduce
power to MEDIUM-HIGH (70% power) and microwave
7 minutes. Turn turkey breast over; cover with plastic wrap
and microwave at MEDIUM-HIGH 7 minutes longer. Cover
dish with aluminum foil and cool in broth.

In medium bowl, combine mayonnaise, yogurt, chutney,
curry, salt and pepper; blend well. Remove turkey from
broth and cut into small cubes; add to mayonnaise mixture.
Add apples, grapes and chives; toss gently to coat
ingredients with dressing. Serve salad on bed of lettuce.

Nutrients per serving:

Calories	241	Cholesterol	78 mg
Fat	8 g	Sodium	263 mg

Curried Salad Bombay

Japanese Steak Salad

Makes 4 servings

Sesame Marinade and Dressing
  (recipe follows)
1 pound well-trimmed beef top sirloin steak,
  cut 1 inch thick
3 cups *each* sliced napa cabbage and romaine
  lettuce
½ cup *each* thin diagonally sliced carrots, thinly
  sliced radishes and thinly sliced cucumber
1 cup cooked rice
24 pea pods, blanched

Prepare Sesame Marinade and Dressing. Place beef top sirloin steak in plastic bag; add ⅓ cup Sesame Marinade, turning to coat. Close bag securely and marinate in refrigerator 2 hours, turning once.

Preheat broiler. Transfer steak to rack in broiler pan; discard marinade. Broil 3 to 4 inches from heat source 14 minutes for rare to 16 minutes for medium-rare, turning once. Let stand 5 minutes. Carve steak into thin slices. Meanwhile, combine napa cabbage, romaine, carrots and radishes; place equal amounts of each on 4 individual plates. Arrange equal number of cucumber slices in circle over salad greens on each plate. Mound ¼ cup rice on top of each cucumber circle. Fan pea pods around rice. Arrange steak slices in spoke fashion on salad greens. Serve Sesame Dressing with salad.

Sesame Marinade and Dressing

3 tablespoons *each* dry sherry, light soy sauce
  and rice wine vinegar
2 tablespoons hoisin sauce
½ teaspoon grated fresh ginger
¼ cup water
2 tablespoons chopped green onion
1 tablespoon *each* sugar and Oriental dark
  roasted sesame oil

Combine dry sherry, soy sauce, vinegar, hoisin sauce and ginger in small bowl; mix well. Divide mixture in half; reserve half for steak marinade. To prepare dressing, add water, green onion, sugar and oil to remaining mixture; whisk until well blended. Makes ⅓ cup marinade and ¾ cup dressing.

Nutrients per serving (includes 1 tablespoon dressing):

Calories	293	Cholesterol	76 mg
Fat	9 g	Sodium	348 mg

Favorite recipe from **National Live Stock and Meat Board**

Tuna Pasta Salad with Herb Vinaigrette

Makes 8 servings

4 tablespoons CRISCO® Vegetable Oil, divided
3 tablespoons red wine vinegar or cider vinegar
1 clove garlic, minced
1 teaspoon dried basil leaves
¼ teaspoon dried oregano leaves
2½ cups (8 ounces) uncooked small pasta shells
  or rotini, cooked (without salt or fat) and
  well drained
½ pound fresh green beans, trimmed and cut
  into 2-inch lengths
½ teaspoon salt
1½ cups broccoli flowerets
1 red or green bell pepper, cut into strips
1 can (6½ ounces) chunk white tuna packed in
  water, drained and flaked

1. Combine 3 tablespoons Crisco® Oil, vinegar, garlic, basil and oregano in container with tight-fitting lid. Shake well.

2. Place pasta in large bowl. Add remaining one tablespoon Crisco® Oil. Toss to coat.

3. Bring 2 quarts water to a boil in large saucepan. Add beans and salt. Boil 2 minutes. Add broccoli. Bring water back to a boil. Boil 3 minutes. Drain well.

4. Add beans, broccoli, red pepper and tuna to pasta.

5. Shake dressing. Pour over salad. Toss to coat. Season with additional basil and oregano to taste, if desired. Serve in greens-lined bowl, if desired.

To Microwave: 1. Follow steps 1 and 2 above.

2. Place beans, ¼ cup water and salt in microwave-safe dish. Cover with plastic wrap. Turn back one corner of plastic wrap slightly to vent. Microwave at HIGH 4 minutes, stirring after 2 minutes. Add broccoli. Cover. Vent. Microwave at HIGH 2 minutes. Let stand several minutes. Drain.

3. Follow steps 4 and 5 above.

Nutrients per serving:

Calories	230	Cholesterol	15 mg
Fat	8 g	Sodium	225 mg

Japanese Steak Salad

Southwest Express Chicken Salad

Makes 4 servings

 1 medium onion, cut into ¼-inch wedges
 1 tablespoon olive or vegetable oil
 3 cups shredded or diced cooked chicken or turkey
 ⅔ cup PACE® Picante Sauce
 2 medium tomatoes, diced
 1 teaspoon ground cumin
 ¾ teaspoon salt (optional)
 ½ teaspoon dried oregano leaves, crushed
 5 cups shredded lettuce
 ¼ cup chopped cilantro
   Additional PACE® Picante Sauce (optional)

In large skillet, cook and stir onion in hot oil until onion is tender but not brown. Add chicken, ⅔ cup Pace® Picante Sauce, tomatoes, cumin, salt and oregano; simmer 5 minutes, stirring occasionally. Arrange lettuce on 4 dinner plates or large platter; top with hot chicken mixture. Sprinkle with cilantro. Serve with additional Pace® Picante Sauce, if desired.

Nutrients per serving:

Calories	265	Cholesterol	89 mg
Fat	9 g	Sodium	540 mg

Southwest Express Chicken Salad

Tangy Tomato Salad Dressing

Makes 1⅓ cups

 1 can (7¼ ounces) low-sodium tomato soup
 ¼ cup vegetable oil
   Grated peel of ½ SUNKIST® Lemon
 2 tablespoons fresh squeezed lemon juice
 2 tablespoons chopped green onion
 1 teaspoon prepared horseradish
   Generous dash ground cinnamon (optional)

In small jar with lid, combine all ingredients; shake well. Refrigerate. Shake well again before serving.

Nutrients per serving (1 tablespoon dressing):

Calories	35	Cholesterol	0 mg
Fat	3 g	Sodium	2 mg

Turkey Ham Salad in Pineapple Boats

Makes 4 servings

 1 package (3 ounces) chicken-flavored instant Oriental noodle soup, cooked according to package directions and cooled
 1⅓ cups Turkey Ham, cut into 2×¼-inch strips
 ⅓ cup thinly sliced green onions
 ⅓ cup chopped mango chutney
 ¼ cup sliced water chestnuts
 ¼ teaspoon ground red pepper
 2 small fresh pineapples
 2 tablespoons toasted almonds

In medium bowl, combine noodles with broth, turkey ham, green onions, chutney, water chestnuts and ground red pepper. Cover and refrigerate overnight.

Just before serving, cut pineapples in half lengthwise through the crowns. Cut fruit from shells with knife, leaving shells intact. Cut fruit into ½-inch cubes. Add 3 cups pineapple cubes to turkey mixture.

To serve, spoon turkey mixture into pineapple shells; top with almonds.

Nutrients per serving:

Calories	278	Cholesterol	28 mg
Fat	5 g	Sodium	814 mg

Favorite recipe from **National Turkey Federation**

Lemony Apple-Bran Salad

Makes 6 servings

½ cup plain low-fat yogurt
1 tablespoon chopped fresh parsley
1 teaspoon sugar
1 teaspoon lemon juice
½ teaspoon salt
2 cups chopped and cored red apples
½ cup thinly sliced celery
½ cup halved seedless green grapes *or* ¼ cup raisins
½ cup KELLOGG'S® ALL-BRAN® cereal

In medium bowl, combine yogurt, parsley, sugar, lemon juice and salt. Stir in apples, celery and grapes or raisins. Cover and refrigerate until ready to serve. Just before serving, stir in Kellogg's® All-Bran® cereal. Serve on lettuce, if desired.

Nutrients per serving:

Calories	60	Cholesterol	1 mg
Fat	1 g	Sodium	260 mg

Marinated Vegetable Salad

Makes 1 serving

½ cup fresh broccoli flowerets
½ cup fresh cauliflower flowerets
½ cup sliced carrots
½ cup sliced celery
¼ cup bottled low-calorie Italian salad dressing
Lettuce leaves
1 cup torn lettuce
2 slices BORDEN® Lite-line® American or Swiss Flavor Process Cheese Product,* cut into strips

In small bowl or plastic bag, combine broccoli, cauliflower, carrots, celery and dressing; mix well. Cover; marinate in refrigerator 4 hours or overnight, stirring occasionally. Drain; reserve salad dressing. Line plate with lettuce leaves; top with torn lettuce then vegetables. Pour 2 tablespoons reserved dressing over salad; top with cheese product strips.

*"½ the calories" – 8% milkfat product

Nutrients per serving:

Calories	204	Cholesterol	22 mg
Fat	8 g	Sodium	856 mg

Salad Veronique

Salad Veronique

Makes 3 servings, 3 cups

1 package (4-serving size) JELL-O® Brand Lemon Flavor Sugar Free Gelatin
¼ teaspoon salt
1 cup boiling water
¼ teaspoon dried tarragon leaves, crushed (optional)
¾ cup cold water
1 tablespoon lemon juice
1 cup diced cooked turkey breast (white meat)
½ cup green or red seedless grapes, halved
½ cup finely chopped celery

Completely dissolve gelatin and salt in boiling water; stir in tarragon. Add cold water and lemon juice. Chill until slightly thickened. Stir in remaining ingredients. Spoon into 3 individual plastic containers or serving dishes. Chill until firm, about 2 hours. Garnish with grapes and celery leaf, if desired.

Nutrients per serving:

Calories	100	Cholesterol	35 mg
Fat	2 g	Sodium	310 mg

Fruity Chicken Salad

Fruity Chicken Salad

Makes 4 servings

  Creamy Yogurt Dressing (recipe follows)
  2 cups cubed cooked chicken
  1 cup cantaloupe balls
  1 cup casaba melon cubes
  1 celery stalk, chopped
  ⅓ cup dry roasted cashews
  ¼ cup green onion slices
    Lettuce leaves

Prepare Creamy Yogurt Dressing; set aside. Combine chicken, melons, celery, cashews and green onions in large bowl. Add dressing; mix lightly. Cover. Refrigerate 1 hour. Serve on lettuce leaves. Garnish as desired.

Creamy Yogurt Dressing
  ¼ cup plain yogurt
  3 tablespoons low-calorie mayonnaise
  3 tablespoons fresh lemon or lime juice
  ¾ teaspoon ground coriander
  ½ teaspoon salt
    Dash black pepper

Combine ingredients in small bowl; mix well.

Nutrients per serving:

Calories	205	Cholesterol	38 mg
Fat	10 g	Sodium	326 mg

Marinated Vegetable Spinach Salad

Makes 4 servings

  Mustard-Tarragon Marinade (recipe follows)
  8 ounces fresh mushrooms, quartered
  2 slices purple onion, separated into rings
  16 cherry tomatoes, halved
  4 cups fresh spinach leaves, washed and stems removed
  3 slices (3 ounces) SARGENTO® Preferred Light Sliced Mozzarella Cheese, cut into julienne strips
    Freshly ground black pepper

Prepare Mustard-Tarragon Marinade; set aside. Place mushrooms, onion and tomatoes in bowl. Toss with marinade and let stand 15 minutes. Arrange spinach on 4 individual plates. Divide marinated vegetables among plates and top each salad with ¼ of cheese. Serve with freshly ground black pepper, if desired.

Mustard-Tarragon Marinade
  3 tablespoons red wine vinegar
  1 tablespoon Dijon-style mustard
  ½ tablespoon dried tarragon
  2 tablespoons olive oil

Combine first 3 ingredients in small bowl. Slowly whisk oil into mixture until slightly thickened.

Nutrients per serving:

Calories	186	Cholesterol	11 mg
Fat	10 g	Sodium	334 mg

Quick Bacon-Potato Salad

Makes 6 servings

  4 medium potatoes, peeled and cut into ½-inch cubes
  ¼ cup water
  12 slices LOUIS RICH® Turkey Bacon
  ¾ cup reduced-calorie salad dressing or mayonnaise
  1 teaspoon prepared mustard
  ¼ teaspoon garlic powder
  ½ small cucumber, diced
  ½ small onion, chopped

Combine potatoes and water in 2-quart microwave-safe casserole; cover. Microwave at HIGH (100% power) 9 to 11 minutes or until tender, stirring halfway through cooking.

Meanwhile, cut turkey bacon into ½-inch pieces. Cook and stir in nonstick skillet over medium heat 8 to 10 minutes or until lightly browned. Combine salad dressing, mustard and garlic powder in large bowl. Add potatoes, turkey bacon and remaining ingredients. Refrigerate before serving.

Nutrients per serving:

Calories	210	Cholesterol	25 mg
Fat	9 g	Sodium	450 mg

Citrus Cheese Salad

Citrus Cheese Salad

Makes 1 serving

½ cup BORDEN® Lite-line® or Viva® Lowfat
   Cottage Cheese
1 slice BORDEN® Lite-line® Process Cheese
   Product,* any flavor, cut into small pieces
2 tablespoons chopped cucumber
½ fresh grapefruit, pared and sectioned
   Lettuce leaf

In small bowl, combine cottage cheese, cheese
product pieces and cucumber. On salad plate,
arrange grapefruit on lettuce. Top with cheese
mixture. Refrigerate leftovers.

*"½ the calories"–8% milkfat product

Nutrients per serving:			
Calories	200	Cholesterol	15 mg
Fat	3 g	Sodium	714 mg

Fettuccini Slaw

Makes 12 servings

½ of a (1-pound) package CREAMETTE®
   Fettuccini, broken into thirds, uncooked
3 cups finely chopped cabbage
2 cups finely shredded carrots
2 cups thinly sliced celery
2 cups finely sliced cucumber
1 container (8 ounces) plain low-fat yogurt
½ cup low-calorie mayonnaise or salad dressing
2 tablespoons white vinegar
½ teaspoon dry mustard
¼ teaspoon white pepper
   Paprika

Prepare Creamette® Fettuccini according to package
directions; drain. In large bowl, combine fettuccini,
cabbage, carrots, celery and cucumber. In small
bowl, blend yogurt, mayonnaise, vinegar, mustard and
pepper; toss with fettuccini mixture. Cover; refrigerate
thoroughly. Toss gently before serving. Garnish with
paprika. Refrigerate leftovers.

Nutrients per serving:			
Calories	209	Cholesterol	4 mg
Fat	4 g	Sodium	105 mg

Chunky Cucumber Dill Dressing

Makes about 6 servings

1 cup peeled and chopped cucumber, divided
¾ cup *plus* 2 tablespoons nonfat plain yogurt
3 tablespoons chopped fresh dill
2 teaspoons sugar
2 teaspoons lemon juice
⅛ teaspoon black pepper

In blender or food processor, blend ½ cup cucumber
with remaining ingredients. Stir in remaining ½ cup
cucumber. Refrigerate or serve immediately over
green salad or chicken salad.

Nutrients per serving (2 tablespoons dressing):			
Calories	31	Cholesterol	1 mg
Fat	trace	Sodium	71 mg

Favorite recipe from **The Sugar Association, Inc.**

Creamy Fruit Mold

Makes 7 servings

1 package (0.3 ounces) sugar-free lime flavor
   gelatin
1 cup boiling water
1 cup PET® Light Evaporated Skimmed Milk
2 cups cut-up fresh fruit*

Dissolve gelatin in boiling water. Cool slightly to
prevent milk from curdling. Stir in evaporated
skimmed milk. Refrigerate until gelatin mixture is the
consistency of unbeaten egg whites. Stir in fruit. Pour
into 8-inch square pan or 5-cup mold. Refrigerate
until firm. Garnish with additional fruit.

*Suggested fresh fruit: apples, Bing cherries, oranges,
peaches or strawberries.*

Nutrients per serving:			
Calories	51	Cholesterol	1 mg
Fat	0 g	Sodium	77 mg

Chunky Chicken Salsa Salad

Makes 4 servings

- 1 clove garlic, minced
- ½ pound boneless, skinless chicken breasts
- 1 can (16 ounces) California cling peach slices in juice or extra light syrup
- ½ teaspoon chili powder
- ¼ teaspoon *each* ground cumin and seasoned salt
- 1 head iceberg lettuce, rinsed and crisped
- 1 box (10½ ounces) frozen corn, cooked, drained and cooled
- 1 cup cherry tomatoes, halved
- ½ cup *each* sliced green onions and minced cilantro
- 1 can (4 ounces) diced green chilies, drained

Bring 2 cups water to a boil; add garlic. Add chicken breasts; simmer 10 to 15 minutes until cooked through. Drain, cool and shred chicken breasts. Drain peach slices, reserving ¼ cup liquid; save remainder for other uses. Cut peach slices in half and set aside. Blend reserved peach liquid with chili powder, cumin and seasoned salt for dressing. Set aside. Cut lettuce into chunks. Toss together lettuce chunks, shredded chicken, reserved peach slices, corn, cherry tomatoes, green onions, cilantro and diced green chilies. Drizzle salad with dressing and toss well just before serving.

Nutrients per serving:

Calories	202	Cholesterol	33 mg
Fat	1 g	Sodium	196 mg

Favorite recipe from **California Cling Peach Advisory Board**

Bombay Banana Salad

Makes 6 servings

- 2 DOLE® Oranges
- 2 firm DOLE® Bananas, peeled and sliced
- 1 cup seedless red DOLE® Grapes
- ¼ cup DOLE® Whole Almonds, toasted

Dressing
- 1 ripe DOLE® Banana, peeled
- 12 DOLE® Pitted Dates, halved
- ½ cup dairy sour cream
- 1 tablespoon packed brown sugar *or* honey
- 1 tablespoon chopped chutney
- ½ teaspoon curry powder

Grate peel from 1 orange; reserve peel for dressing. Peel and slice oranges. In bowl, toss salad ingredients with Dressing.

For Dressing, place all Dressing ingredients in blender container or food processor. Process until smooth. Stir in reserved grated orange peel.

Nutrients per serving:

Calories	240	Cholesterol	9 mg
Fat	9 g	Sodium	13 mg

Ziti Salmon Salad

Makes 6 to 8 servings

- ½ of a (1-pound) package CREAMETTE® Ziti, uncooked
- 1 (16-ounce) can salmon, drained, skin and bones removed
- 1 (6-ounce) package frozen snow peas, thawed
- 1 medium red bell pepper, chopped
- 1 medium yellow bell pepper, chopped
- ½ cup sliced green onions
- ½ cup bottled Italian salad dressing
- ½ teaspoon salt-free herb seasoning

Prepare Creamette® Ziti according to package directions; drain. In large bowl, combine ziti and remaining ingredients; mix well. Cover; refrigerate thoroughly. Toss gently before serving. Refrigerate leftovers.

Nutrients per serving:

Calories	173	Cholesterol	19 mg
Fat	4 g	Sodium	332 mg

Ziti Salmon Salad

California Marinated Salad

Makes 6 servings

3 fresh California nectarines
½ pound mushrooms, quartered
1 cup cherry tomatoes, halved
½ cup pitted ripe olives (optional)
⅓ cup 1-inch green onion pieces
1 can (8 ounces) artichoke hearts, undrained
¼ cup lemon juice
1 tablespoon vegetable oil
1 teaspoon sugar
1 teaspoon dried tarragon leaves, crushed
½ teaspoon dried thyme leaves, crushed
¼ teaspoon pepper

Cut nectarines into thick slices, then cut each slice in half. Combine nectarines, mushrooms, tomatoes, olives and onions in large salad bowl. Drain artichokes, reserving liquid. Add artichokes to salad. Combine reserved artichoke liquid with remaining ingredients in jar with tight-fitting lid. Shake well and pour over salad mixture. Cover and chill at least 2 hours, tossing once or twice.

Nutrients per serving:

| Calories | 83 | Cholesterol | 0 mg |
| Fat | 3 g | Sodium | 24 mg |

Favorite recipe from **California Tree Fruit Agreement**

Applesauce-Berry Salad

Makes 6 to 8 servings

1 package (3 ounces) sugar-free strawberry-flavored gelatin
1 package (10 ounces) frozen strawberries, thawed
1 cup applesauce
1 cup plain low fat yogurt or low fat sour cream

Dissolve gelatin in 1 cup boiling water. Stir in thawed strawberries and applesauce; pour into 10×6-inch dish. Chill until set; spread yogurt on top. Cover and chill 2 hours. To serve, cut into squares.

Nutrients per serving:

| Calories | 59 | Cholesterol | 2 mg |
| Fat | 1 g | Sodium | 22 mg |

Favorite recipe from **Western New York Apple Growers Association**

Chicken Salad with Horseradish-Dill Dressing

Makes 4 servings

⅓ cup whole natural California Almonds
3 tablespoons liquid smoke (optional)
4 chicken breasts, skinned
1 tablespoon chopped fresh dill *or* 1 teaspoon dried dill weed
    Salt and pepper to taste (optional)
16 butter lettuce leaves
1 cucumber, sliced
2 medium tomatoes, sliced
1 cup shredded carrots
    Horseradish-Dill Dressing (recipe follows)

Preheat oven to 350°F. Spread almonds in single layer on baking sheet. Toast in oven 8 to 10 minutes until lightly toasted, stirring occasionally. Cool.

Bring 1 quart water and liquid smoke to a boil in large saucepan over high heat. Add chicken; reduce heat and simmer 15 minutes or until chicken is tender and cooked through. Drain chicken; discard liquid. Cool chicken. Shred chicken; discard bones. Toss shredded chicken with dill, salt and pepper in medium bowl; refrigerate. Line 4 salad plates with lettuce leaves. To serve, arrange chicken, cucumber, tomatoes, carrots and almonds evenly on lettuce-lined plates. Drizzle each serving with Horseradish-Dill Dressing.

Horseradish-Dill Dressing

1 cup nonfat plain yogurt
3 tablespoons horseradish
1 tablespoon chopped fresh dill *or* 1 teaspoon dried dill weed

Combine ingredients in small bowl; mix until well blended. Refrigerate until ready to serve. Makes 1¼ cups.

Nutrients per serving (includes ⅓ cup dressing):

| Calories | 248 | Cholesterol | 69 mg |
| Fat | 8 g | Sodium | 110 mg |

Favorite recipe from **Almond Board of California**

Fruited Slaw

Makes 8 servings

1 can (8¼ ounces) pineapple chunks, undrained
1 carton (8 ounces) orange-flavored yogurt
1 tablespoon lemon juice
3 cups finely shredded cabbage
1 can (11 ounces) mandarin orange sections, drained
1 cup thinly sliced celery
½ cup chopped walnuts
¼ cup raisins
1 medium banana, peeled and sliced

Drain pineapple, reserving 2 tablespoons syrup. Combine reserved syrup, yogurt and lemon juice in small bowl. Combine pineapple, cabbage, oranges, celery, walnuts and raisins in large bowl; fold in yogurt mixture. Gently fold in banana. Cover; refrigerate until chilled.

Nutrients per serving:

Calories	150	Cholesterol	1 mg
Fat	5 g	Sodium	37 mg

Favorite recipe from **Wisconsin Milk Marketing Board** © 1994

Lite 'n' Creamy Garlic Dressing

Makes 2 cups

1 teaspoon KNOX® Unflavored Gelatine
¼ cup cold skim milk
¾ cup skim milk, heated to boiling
1 cup low fat sour cream
2 tablespoons sugar
½ teaspoon garlic powder with parsley
¼ teaspoon salt
⅛ teaspoon black pepper

In blender, sprinkle unflavored gelatine over cold milk; let stand 2 minutes. Add hot milk and process at low speed until gelatine is completely dissolved, about 2 minutes. Add remaining ingredients and process at high speed until blended. Pour into serving bowl and chill until slightly thickened. Before serving, stir until smooth. Dressing may be stored covered in refrigerator up to 5 days.

Nutrients per serving (1 tablespoon dressing):

Calories	15	Cholesterol	2 mg
Fat	1 g	Sodium	27 mg

Chunky Chicken and Cucumber Salad

Makes 4 servings

1 broiler-fryer chicken, cooked, skinned, boned and cut into chunks
2 cucumbers, peeled and cubed
1 red bell pepper, seeded and chopped
1 tablespoon apple cider vinegar
½ teaspoon salt
¼ teaspoon black pepper
¼ teaspoon seasoned salt
4 ounces plain nonfat yogurt

Mix cucumbers and red pepper in medium bowl; sprinkle with vinegar, salt and black pepper. Let stand about 5 minutes. Stir in chicken, seasoned salt and yogurt, tossing gently. Cover and refrigerate until completely chilled. Serve over dark curly endive leaves, if desired.

Nutrients per serving:

Calories	206	Cholesterol	97 mg
Fat	4 g	Sodium	450 mg

Favorite recipe from **National Broiler Council**

Confetti Appleslaw

Makes 7 servings

2 tablespoons thawed orange or apple juice concentrate
1 unpeeled red apple, cored and diced
4 cups shredded cabbage
2 small red onions, finely shredded
1 red or green bell pepper, thinly sliced
3 tablespoons raisins
1 tablespoon reduced calorie mayonnaise
½ cup plain low fat yogurt
½ teaspoon dry mustard
Paprika to taste
Freshly ground black pepper to taste

Stir together juice concentrate and apple in large bowl. Add cabbage, onions, bell pepper and raisins.

Stir together mayonnaise, yogurt, mustard, paprika and black pepper in small bowl. Add to vegetable mixture; toss to coat. Cover tightly and refrigerate until ready to serve.

Nutrients per serving:

Calories	64	Cholesterol	2 mg
Fat	1 g	Sodium	30 mg

Favorite recipe from **Western New York Apple Growers Association**

Herbed Chicken Salad

Makes 4 to 6 servings

3 cups cubed cooked chicken or turkey
¼ cup REALEMON® Lemon Juice from Concentrate
¼ cup vegetable oil
2 teaspoons WYLER'S® or STEERO® Chicken-Flavor Instant Bouillon
1 teaspoon sugar
1 teaspoon tarragon leaves
1 clove garlic, finely chopped
1 cup sliced fresh mushrooms
½ pound fresh green beans, cut into 1-inch pieces, cooked until tender-crisp and chilled
1 cup cherry tomato halves
Lettuce

In small bowl, combine ReaLemon® brand, oil, bouillon, sugar, tarragon and garlic; let stand 15 minutes to dissolve bouillon, stirring occasionally. In large bowl, combine chicken and mushrooms; pour dressing over. Cover; chill 4 hours or overnight, stirring occasionally. Just before serving, add green beans and tomatoes. Serve on lettuce. Refrigerate leftovers.

Tip: 1 (9-ounce) package frozen cut green beans, cooked and chilled, can be substituted for fresh green beans.

Nutrients per serving:

Calories	158	Cholesterol	23 mg
Fat	10 g	Sodium	327 mg

Herbed Chicken Salad

Cool Cucumber Lime Mold

Makes 5 cups

1 cup cottage cheese
½ cup MIRACLE WHIP FREE® Nonfat Dressing
1¾ cups cold water, divided
1 package (3 ounces) JELL-O® Brand Lime Flavor Gelatin
1 cup peeled, seeded, finely chopped cucumber
2 tablespoons finely chopped onion
2 teaspoons chopped fresh dill *or* 1 teaspoon dill weed

Place cottage cheese and dressing in blender or food processor container; process until smooth. Bring 1 cup water to a boil. Gradually add to gelatin; stir until dissolved. Stir in ¾ cup cold water. Add to cottage cheese mixture, mixing until blended. Chill until thickened but not set; fold in cucumber, onion and dill. Pour into lightly oiled 6-cup mold; chill until firm. Unmold.

Prep time: 15 minutes plus chilling

Nutrients per serving (½ cup):

Calories	70	Cholesterol	3 mg
Fat	1 g	Sodium	261 mg

Rice Salad Milano

Makes 6 servings

3 cups hot cooked rice
2 tablespoons vegetable oil
2 tablespoons lemon juice
1 clove garlic, minced
½ teaspoon salt (optional)
½ teaspoon dried rosemary leaves, crushed
½ teaspoon dried oregano leaves, crushed
½ teaspoon ground black pepper
1 small zucchini, julienned*
1 medium tomato, seeded and chopped
2 tablespoons grated Parmesan cheese

Place rice in large bowl. Combine oil, lemon juice, garlic, salt, rosemary, oregano, and pepper in small jar with lid; shake well. Pour over rice; toss lightly. Cover; let cool. Add remaining ingredients. Serve at room temperature or chilled.

*To julienne, slice zucchini diagonally. Cut slices into matchstick-size strips.

Nutrients per serving:

Calories	189	Cholesterol	1 mg
Fat	5 g	Sodium	620 mg

Favorite recipe from **USA Rice Council**

Apple Salad

Makes 3½ cups

⅓ cup MIRACLE WHIP® FREE® Nonfat
    Dressing
1 tablespoon apple juice
2 teaspoons peanut butter
⅛ teaspoon ground cinnamon
2 small apples, chopped
1 can (8 ounces) pineapple chunks, drained
½ cup *each* KRAFT® Miniature Marshmallows
    and grapes

Mix dressing, juice, peanut butter and cinnamon until
well blended. Stir in remaining ingredients; refrigerate.

Prep time: 10 minutes plus refrigerating

Nutrients per serving (½ cup):

Calories	100	Cholesterol	0 mg
Fat	1 g	Sodium	160 mg

White Sangria Splash

Makes 12 servings, 6 cups

1½ cups dry white wine
2 packages (4-serving size) or 1 package
    (8-serving size) JELL-O® Brand Lemon
    Flavor Sugar Free Gelatin
2½ cups club soda
1 tablespoon lime juice
1 tablespoon orange liqueur (optional)
1 cup sliced strawberries
1 cup seedless red grapes
1 cup seedless green grapes

Bring wine to a boil in small saucepan. Completely
dissolve gelatin in boiling wine; pour into medium
bowl. Stir in club soda, lime juice and liqueur, if
desired. Place bowl in larger bowl of ice and water; let
stand until slightly thickened, stirring occasionally.

Gently stir in fruit. Pour into 6-cup mold that has
been lightly sprayed with nonstick cooking spray.
Chill until firm, about 4 hours. Unmold. Serve with
additional fruit, if desired.

Nutrients per serving (½ cup):

Calories	50	Cholesterol	0 mg
Fat	0 g	Sodium	55 mg

Crunchy Chicken-Vegetable Salad

Crunchy Chicken-Vegetable Salad

Makes 4 servings

1 cup (8 ounces) plain yogurt
3 tablespoons low-calorie mayonnaise
2 teaspoons Dijon-style mustard
1 garlic clove, minced
½ teaspoon salt
    Dash black pepper
2 cups shredded red cabbage
2 cups fresh bean sprouts
1½ cups chopped cooked chicken or turkey,
    chilled
¼ pound fresh snow peas, trimmed
¾ cup celery slices
½ cup sliced almonds, toasted
¼ cup chopped red onion
    Fresh spinach leaves
2 hard-cooked eggs, peeled and sliced for
    garnish

Combine yogurt, mayonnaise, mustard, garlic, salt
and pepper in large bowl. Add cabbage, sprouts,
chicken, snow peas, celery, almonds and onion; mix
lightly. Serve in spinach-lined salad bowl or on
spinach-covered salad plates. Garnish with eggs.

Nutrients per serving:

Calories	209	Cholesterol	35 mg
Fat	9 g	Sodium	380 mg

California Apricot Fruit Salad

Makes 5 servings

2 cups sliced fresh California apricots
  (about 1 pound)
1½ cups sliced fresh strawberries
1½ cups peeled and sliced kiwifruit
¼ cup California apricot nectar
¼ cup shredded coconut, lightly toasted
1 tablespoon finely chopped fresh mint leaves

Combine all ingredients in medium bowl. Refrigerate until chilled. Serve as a salad *or* arrange on wooden skewers for fresh fruit kabobs.

Nutrients per serving:

Calories	118	Cholesterol	0 mg
Fat	2 g	Sodium	6 mg

Favorite recipe from **California Apricot Advisory Board**

Linguine and Fresh Fruit Cooler

Makes 4 servings

½ pound linguine, vermicelli or angel hair
  pasta, uncooked
1 cup fresh berries, such as blueberries,
  strawberries or raspberries
1 cup 1-inch chunks honeydew melon or
  cantaloupe
1 cup kiwifruit slices or fresh plum slices
¼ cup lemon juice
1 teaspoon finely grated orange peel
2 tablespoons cornstarch
1½ cups apricot nectar
1 stick cinnamon
4 whole cloves
4 whole allspice berries
¼ cup dry white wine
½ cup fresh mint leaves (optional)

Prepare pasta according to package directions; drain. Meanwhile, mix berries, melon, kiwifruit, lemon juice and orange peel in large bowl. Place cornstarch in 2-quart saucepan over high heat and slowly stir in apricot nectar. Add cinnamon stick, cloves and allspice. Bring to a boil, stirring constantly. Reduce heat and simmer, uncovered, 15 minutes or until thick. Remove and discard spices. Stir apricot mixture into fruit mixture. Add wine and linguine; toss gently to coat. Garnish with mint leaves, if desired.

Nutrients per serving:

Calories	245	Cholesterol	0 mg
Fat	1 g	Sodium	19 mg

Favorite recipe from **National Pasta Association**

Oriental Mandarin Salad

Makes 4 servings

Salad
2 tablespoons peanut oil, divided
2 tablespoons light or regular soy sauce, divided
4 teaspoons sesame seed, divided
½ teaspoon minced garlic, divided
¼ teaspoon ground ginger, divided
2 cups Rice CHEX® brand cereal
1 pound (16 ounces) boneless, skinless chicken
  breasts, cut into strips
6 cups torn spinach leaves
1 can (11 ounces) mandarin orange segments,
  drained
1 can (8 ounces) sliced water chestnuts, drained

Dressing
¼ cup orange juice
1 tablespoon honey
1 teaspoon grated orange peel
1 teaspoon light or regular soy sauce

To make cereal croutons, in large skillet combine 1 tablespoon oil, 1 tablespoon soy sauce, 2 teaspoons sesame seed, ¼ teaspoon garlic and ⅛ teaspoon ginger. Cook just until mixture comes to a boil, stirring occasionally. Add cereal, stirring until all pieces are evenly coated. Cook 2 minutes, stirring constantly. Spread on paper towels to cool.

In same skillet over high heat combine remaining 1 tablespoon oil, 1 tablespoon soy sauce, 2 teaspoons sesame seed, ¼ teaspoon garlic and ⅛ teaspoon ginger. Add chicken, stirring until all pieces are evenly coated. Cook 3 to 4 minutes or until chicken is no longer pink, stirring constantly. Remove from heat. In large bowl combine chicken, spinach, oranges and water chestnuts. In small bowl combine orange juice, honey, orange peel and 1 teaspoon soy sauce; toss with salad mixture. Add cereal croutons and toss.

Nutrients per serving:

Calories	297	Cholesterol	64 mg
Fat	9 g	Sodium	423 mg

California Apricot Fruit Salad

Pasta Primavera Salad

Green Bean, New Potato and Ham Salad

Makes 12 cups

- **3 pounds new potatoes, quartered**
- **⅔ cup cold water**
- **1 pound green beans, halved**
- **¾ cup MIRACLE WHIP® FREE® Nonfat Dressing**
- **⅓ cup stone-ground mustard**
- **2 tablespoons red wine vinegar**
- **2 cups OSCAR MAYER® Ham cubes**
- **½ cup chopped green onions**

To Microwave: Place potatoes and water in 3-quart casserole; cover. Microwave on HIGH (100%) 13 minutes. Stir in beans. Microwave on HIGH 7 to 13 minutes or until tender; drain. Mix dressing, mustard and vinegar in large bowl until well blended. Add potatoes, beans and remaining ingredients; mix lightly. Refrigerate.

Prep time: 15 minutes plus refrigerating
Microwave cook time: 26 minutes

Nutrients per serving (¾ cup):			
Calories	100	Cholesterol	5 mg
Fat	1 g	Sodium	428 mg

Pasta Primavera Salad

Makes 6 servings

- **1 package (8 ounces) elbow macaroni, cooked, drained (2 cups)**
- **2 cups DOLE® Broccoli flowerets**
- **2 cups sliced DOLE® Celery**
- **1 cup sliced DOLE® Carrots**
- **½ cup sliced DOLE® Green Onions**
- **½ cup diced DOLE® Green Bell Pepper**
- **1 cup light sour cream**
- **½ cup reduced-calorie mayonnaise**
- **1 teaspoon dill weed**
- **1 teaspoon garlic salt**

Combine cooked macaroni, broccoli, celery, carrots, onions and green pepper in large bowl. For dressing, combine remaining ingredients in small bowl. Pour over pasta mixture; toss to coat well. Refrigerate.

Prep time: 20 minutes
Cook time: 10 minutes

Nutrients per serving:			
Calories	240	Cholesterol	24 mg
Fat	7 g	Sodium	346 mg

Fresh Fruit Shell Salad

Makes 8 to 10 servings

- **½ of a (1-pound) package CREAMETTE® Medium Shells, uncooked**
- **1 (8-ounce) container plain low-fat yogurt**
- **¼ cup frozen orange juice concentrate, thawed**
- **1 (15-ounce) can juice-pack pineapple chunks, drained**
- **1 large orange, peeled, sectioned and seeded**
- **1 cup seedless red grapes, cut into halves**
- **1 cup seedless green grapes, cut into halves**
- **1 apple, cored and chopped**
- **1 banana, sliced**

Prepare Creamette® Medium Shells according to package directions; drain. In small bowl, blend yogurt and orange juice concentrate. In large bowl, combine remaining ingredients. Add yogurt mixture; toss to coat. Cover; refrigerate thoroughly. Toss gently before serving. Refrigerate leftovers.

Nutrients per serving:			
Calories	179	Cholesterol	1 mg
Fat	1 g	Sodium	20 mg

Shrimp and Strawberry Salad

Makes 6 servings

   3 cups cooked rice
   ½ pound peeled, deveined cooked small shrimp
   ¾ cup thinly sliced celery
   ⅔ cup cholesterol-free, reduced-calorie
       mayonnaise
   ½ cup low-fat strawberry yogurt
   1 teaspoon dry mustard
   1 teaspoon lemon juice
   ½ teaspoon salt
   1½ cups sliced fresh strawberries
       Romaine lettuce

Combine rice, shrimp, and celery in large bowl.
Combine mayonnaise, yogurt, mustard, lemon juice,
and salt in medium bowl; mix well. Add yogurt
mixture to rice mixture and stir well. Fold in
strawberries. Cover and refrigerate until serving time.
Arrange lettuce on individual serving plates; top with
salad.

Nutrients per serving:

Calories	274	Cholesterol	69 mg
Fat	9 g	Sodium	833 mg

Favorite recipe from **USA Rice Council**

Confetti Rice Salad

Makes 6 servings

   2 chicken-flavored bouillon cubes
   1 cup uncooked long grain white rice
   1 can (16 ounces) California cling peach slices
       in juice or extra-light syrup
   3 tablespoons tarragon-flavored white wine
       vinegar
   1 tablespoon Dijon-style mustard
   1 tablespoon olive oil
   ¼ teaspoon dried tarragon leaves, crushed
   1 cup chopped red bell peppers
   ½ cup frozen peas, thawed
   ⅓ cup raisins
   ¼ cup sliced green onions

In medium saucepan, combine bouillon cubes and
2 cups water; bring mixture to a boil. Stir in rice.
Reduce heat to low. Cover and simmer 20 minutes,
until liquid is absorbed and rice is tender. Remove
from heat; cool 5 minutes. Drain peaches, reserving

¼ cup liquid; save remainder for other uses. Cut
peach slices in half and set aside. Whisk reserved
peach liquid with vinegar, mustard, olive oil and
tarragon. Stir into cooled rice; add remaining
ingredients *except* reserved peaches. Cool completely,
tossing occasionally. Stir in reserved peaches and
refrigerate before serving.

Nutrients per serving:

Calories	210	Cholesterol	trace
Fat	3 g	Sodium	317 mg

Favorite recipe from **California Cling Peach Advisory Board**

Berry-Cottage Cheese Salad

Makes 4 servings

   1 pint strawberries, hulled and sliced, divided
   ¼ cup fresh orange juice, divided
   1 tablespoon sugar
   2 cups (16 ounces) low-fat cottage cheese
   1 teaspoon grated fresh orange peel
   ¾ cup granola cereal, divided
       Torn assorted greens

Place 1 cup strawberries, 2 tablespoons orange juice
and sugar in blender container. Cover; process until
smooth. Set aside. Combine cottage cheese,
remaining 2 tablespoons orange juice, orange peel
and ½ cup cereal in small bowl. Arrange greens on
4 salad plates; top each with cottage cheese mixture
and remaining 1 cup strawberries. Sprinkle remaining
¼ cup cereal over cottage cheese. Serve with
strawberry sauce.

Nutrients per serving:

Calories	237	Cholesterol	10 g
Fat	6 g	Sodium	504 mg

Berry-Cottage Cheese Salad

Fruited Pork Salad

Fruited Pork Salad

Makes 4 servings

Dressing
- ¼ cup grapefruit juice
- 2 tablespoons red wine vinegar
- 1 tablespoon vegetable oil
- 1 teaspoon poppy seeds
- 2 teaspoons honey
- ½ teaspoon Dijon-style mustard

Salad
- 1 pound pork tenderloin, trimmed and cut crosswise into ⅛-inch strips
- Nonstick cooking spray
- 1 small head green leaf lettuce
- 2 small red grapefruit, peeled and sectioned
- 1½ cups green seedless grapes
- 1 cup fresh strawberries

To prepare dressing, place dressing ingredients in jar with tight-fitting lid. Shake well. Let stand 15 minutes; shake again. Set aside.

To prepare salad, spray large skillet with cooking spray; heat over medium heat until hot. Add pork strips; cook about 3 minutes or until pork is tender, stirring frequently. Cover and remove from heat. Line 4 individual salad plates with lettuce. Place cooked pork strips in center of each lettuce-lined plate. Arrange grapefruit sections, grapes and strawberries around pork. Spoon dressing evenly over salads.

Nutrients per serving:

Calories	269	Cholesterol	74 mg
Fat	8 g	Sodium	81 mg

Favorite recipe from **National Pork Producers Council**

Orange Poppy Seed Dressing

Makes 8 servings, about 1 cup

- 1 cup DANNON® Plain or Vanilla Lowfat Yogurt
- 1 tablespoon honey
- 1 tablespoon frozen orange juice concentrate, thawed
- 1 teaspoon poppy seeds
- 1 teaspoon finely shredded orange peel

In a medium bowl combine yogurt, honey, orange juice concentrate, poppy seeds and orange peel; stir well. Cover; chill 2 hours.

Nutrients per serving (2 tablespoons dressing):

Calories	30	Cholesterol	trace
Fat	1 g	Sodium	20 mg

Curry Rice Salad with Apples

Makes 6 servings

- ⅓ cup plain or vanilla yogurt
- 4½ teaspoons dry sherry or cider vinegar
- 1 to 2 teaspoons curry powder
- ⅛ teaspoon ground cloves
- Salt and pepper to taste (optional)
- ¼ to ½ cup currants or raisins
- ¾ cup finely diced celery
- 2 unpeeled apples (such as Empire, McIntosh or Cortland), cored, cubed and mixed with a little lemon juice to prevent browning
- 4 cups cooked brown rice

Combine yogurt, sherry, curry, cloves, salt and pepper in large bowl. Mix well. Add currants, celery and apples. Mix well. Add rice and mix well. Refrigerate until serving.

Tip: *This easy dish stays fresh for a few days in refrigerator and improves as the flavors blend. Serve as a side dish, lunch, or a light summer supper.*

Nutrients per serving:

Calories	200	Cholesterol	1 mg
Fat	2 g	Sodium	210 mg

Favorite recipe from **Western New York Apple Growers Association**

Sunflower-Herb Dressing

Makes 8 servings, about 1 cup

- ¼ cup unsalted sunflower nuts
- 1 clove garlic, crushed
- 1 cup DANNON® Plain Nonfat or Lowfat Yogurt
- 2 tablespoons milk
- 1 teaspoon dried basil, crushed
- ½ teaspoon dried thyme, crushed
- ⅛ teaspoon dry mustard
- ⅛ teaspoon pepper

In food processor or blender combine sunflower nuts and garlic. Cover; process to a fine powder (almost a paste). Add yogurt, milk, basil, thyme, dry mustard and pepper. Process until smooth. Cover; chill 2 hours.

Nutrients per serving (2 tablespoons dressing):

Calories	35	Cholesterol	trace
Fat	2 g	Sodium	22 mg

Blue Cheese Yogurt Dressing

Makes 14 servings, about 1¾ cups

1 cup DANNON® Plain Nonfat or Lowfat Yogurt
4 ounces crumbled blue cheese
½ cup buttermilk
¼ cup minced fresh parsley
1 tablespoon olive oil
1 teaspoon sherry
½ teaspoon pepper

In a small bowl combine all ingredients; stir well. Cover; chill overnight.

Nutrients per serving (2 tablespoons dressing):

Calories	50	Cholesterol	10 mg
Fat	4 g	Sodium	134 mg

Springtime Vegetable Slaw

Makes 10 servings

1 pound shredded DOLE® Cabbage
1 cup grated DOLE® Carrots
½ cup DOLE® Broccoli florettes, chopped
½ cup halved cherry tomatoes
½ cup sliced DOLE® Celery
½ cup peeled, seeded, diced cucumber
1 cup chopped fresh parsley
⅓ cup olive oil
2 tablespoons vinegar
1 tablespoon Dijon-style mustard
1 teaspoon garlic salt

Springtime Vegetable Slaw

Combine cabbage, carrots, broccoli, tomatoes, celery and cucumber in large salad bowl. Whisk together remaining ingredients for dressing. Pour over vegetables; toss to coat well.

Nutrients per serving:

Calories	87	Cholesterol	0 mg
Fat	7 g	Sodium	147 mg

Southwest Salsa Dressing

Makes about 5 servings

⅔ cup mild salsa*
2 tablespoons nonfat plain yogurt
4 teaspoons sugar
2 teaspoons chopped cilantro (optional)

In small bowl, stir together all ingredients. Or, for a less chunky dressing, blend ingredients in food processor. Refrigerate or serve immediately over green salad, chicken or turkey salad, taco salad or seafood salad.

For a hotter and spicier dressing, use medium or hot salsa.

Nutrients per serving (2 tablespoons dressing):

Calories	30	Cholesterol	trace
Fat	trace	Sodium	226 mg

Favorite recipe from **The Sugar Association, Inc.**

Wild Rice and Pepper Salad

Makes 6 servings

1 package (6 ounces) MINUTE® Long Grain
    & Wild Rice
½ cup MIRACLE WHIP® FREE® Nonfat
    Dressing
2 tablespoons olive oil
½ teaspoon black pepper
¼ teaspoon grated lemon peel
1 cup chopped red bell pepper
1 cup chopped yellow bell pepper
¼ cup (½-inch) green onion pieces

Prepare rice as directed on package. Cool.

Mix dressing, oil, black pepper and peel in large bowl until well blended.

Add rice and remaining ingredients; mix lightly. Serve at room temperature or refrigerate.

Prep time: 30 minutes

Nutrients per serving (½ cup):

Calories	140	Cholesterol	0 mg
Fat	5 g	Sodium	284 mg

Summer Seafood Salad

Makes 4 servings

2 cups cooked rice, cooled to room temperature
½ pound cooked crabmeat*
1 can (8 ounces) sliced water chestnuts, drained
½ cup sliced celery
¼ cup sliced green onions
¼ cup plain nonfat yogurt
¼ cup light dairy sour cream
1 tablespoon lemon juice
¼ teaspoon hot pepper sauce
¼ teaspoon salt
    Lettuce leaves
    Tomato wedges for garnish

Combine rice, crabmeat, water chestnuts, celery, and onions in large bowl. Combine yogurt, sour cream, lemon juice, pepper sauce, and salt in small bowl; blend well. Pour over rice mixture; toss lightly. Serve on lettuce leaves and garnish with tomato wedges.

Substitute crab-flavored Surimi Seafood (flake or chunk style) for the crabmeat, if desired.

Nutrients per serving:

Calories	263	Cholesterol	65 mg
Fat	5 g	Sodium	731 mg

Favorite recipe from **USA Rice Council**

Dynasty Fruit Salad

Makes 6 servings

1 DOLE® Fresh Pineapple
1 firm, medium DOLE® Banana, peeled and sliced
1 DOLE® Orange, peeled and sliced
1 DOLE® Apple, cored and sliced
1 cup seedless DOLE® Grapes

Royal Dressing
1 carton (8 ounces) vanilla yogurt
1 teaspoon grated lime peel
½ teaspoon ground ginger

Cut pineapple in half lengthwise through the crown. Cut fruit from shells with knife, leaving shells intact. Cut fruit into bite-sized chunks.

Combine pineapple with remaining fruit in large bowl. Spoon fruit into pineapple shells to serve, if desired.

For Royal Dressing: combine all dressing ingredients in small bowl. Serve with fruit salad.

Nutrients per serving:

Calories	140	Cholesterol	2 mg
Fat	1 g	Sodium	28 mg

Sunset Yogurt Salad

Sunset Yogurt Salad

Makes 5 cups, 10 servings

2 packages (4-serving size) or 1 package (8-serving size) JELL-O® Brand Orange or Lemon Flavor Sugar Free Gelatin
2 cups boiling water
1 container (8 ounces) plain low-fat yogurt
¼ cup cold water
1 can (8 ounces) crushed pineapple in unsweetened juice, undrained
1 cup shredded carrots

Completely dissolve gelatin in boiling water. Measure 1 cup gelatin into medium mixing bowl; chill until slightly thickened. Stir in yogurt. Pour into medium serving bowl. Chill until set but not firm.

Add cold water to remaining gelatin. Stir in pineapple with juice and carrots. Chill until slightly thickened. Spoon over gelatin-yogurt mixture in bowl. Chill until firm, about 4 hours. Garnish with carrot curl, celery leaf and pineapple slice, if desired.

Nutrients per serving:

Calories	40	Cholesterol	0 mg
Fat	0 g	Sodium	65 mg

Black Bean and Rice Salad

![Decorative bar]

Makes 4 servings

2 cups cooked rice, cooled to room temperature
1 cup cooked black beans*
1 medium tomato, seeded and chopped
½ cup (2 ounces) shredded Cheddar cheese
    (optional)
1 tablespoon fresh snipped parsley
¼ cup prepared light Italian dressing
1 tablespoon lime juice
    Lettuce leaves

Combine rice, beans, tomato, cheese, and parsley in
large bowl. Pour dressing and lime juice over rice
mixture; toss lightly. Serve on lettuce leaves. Garnish
as desired.

*Substitute canned black beans, drained, for the cooked
beans, if desired.*

Nutrients per serving:

Calories	210	Cholesterol	0 mg
Fat	1 g	Sodium	560 mg

Favorite recipe from **USA Rice Council**

Smoked Turkey and Potato Salad

![Decorative bar]

Makes 8 servings

1 package (32 ounces) frozen hash brown
    potato cubes, thawed
¾ pound Smoked Turkey Breast, cut into
    ½-inch cubes
½ cup chopped celery
½ cup sliced green onions
¼ cup chopped green bell pepper
1 jar (2 ounces) chopped pimientos, drained
⅓ cup low-calorie mayonnaise
⅓ cup plain nonfat yogurt
2 tablespoons Dijon-style mustard
¼ teaspoon black pepper

In large saucepan, over high heat, combine potatoes
and 2 quarts boiling water. Boil 2 to 4 minutes or
until potatoes are tender. Do not overcook. Drain
potatoes thoroughly and cool to room temperature. In
large bowl, combine potatoes, turkey, celery, onions,
green pepper and pimientos. In small bowl, blend
mayonnaise, yogurt, mustard and black pepper. Add
to turkey mixture; toss until well coated. Cover and
refrigerate at least 4 hours.

Nutrients per serving:

Calories	177	Cholesterol	17 mg
Fat	4 g	Sodium	646 mg

Favorite recipe from **National Turkey Federation**

Garden Potato Salad

![Decorative bar]

Makes 6 servings

½ cup HEALTHY CHOICE® Cholesterol Free
    Egg Product
4 medium potatoes, cooked and cubed (about
    1 to 1¼ pounds)
½ cup diced celery
¼ cup chopped radishes
2 tablespoons sliced green onions
¾ cup nonfat mayonnaise
1 tablespoon sugar
1 tablespoon lemon juice
2 teaspoons prepared mustard
¼ teaspoon salt
¼ teaspoon celery seed
¼ teaspoon black pepper

In 8-inch skillet sprayed with nonstick cooking spray,
cook egg product, covered, over very low heat
5 minutes or until just set. Cool egg product; dice. In
large bowl, combine egg product with potatoes,
celery, radishes and onions. In small bowl, mix
remaining ingredients. Add mayonnaise mixture to
potato mixture, stirring until evenly coated.

Nutrients per serving:

Calories	130	Cholesterol	0 mg
Fat	trace	Sodium	530 mg

Oriental Ginger Dressing

![Decorative bar]

Makes 4 servings

½ cup pineapple juice
2 tablespoons cider vinegar
1 tablespoon soy sauce
1 tablespoon sugar
1 teaspoon grated fresh ginger
½ teaspoon sesame oil

Combine all ingredients in jar with tight-fitting lid.
Cover and shake vigorously until combined.
Refrigerate. Shake again before serving. Serve over
green salad, chicken salad or pasta salad.

Nutrients per serving (2 tablespoons dressing):

Calories	38	Cholesterol	0 mg
Fat	1 g	Sodium	258 mg

Favorite recipe from **The Sugar Association, Inc.**

Black Bean and Rice Salad

Veal-Artichoke Salad with Garlic-Chive Dressing

Veal-Artichoke Salad with Garlic-Chive Dressing

Makes 4 servings

1 jar (6 to 6½ ounces) marinated artichoke hearts
2 tablespoons white wine vinegar
1 teaspoon minced chives
1 clove garlic, minced
1 small red bell pepper, cut into short, thin strips
1 pound veal leg cutlets
Assorted salad greens

Drain artichokes, reserving marinade. Stir together 4½ teaspoons reserved marinade, vinegar, chives and garlic in large bowl. Coarsely chop artichokes. Add to dressing mixture in bowl. Stir in red pepper.

If necessary, pound veal cutlets to ¼-inch thickness. Cut veal into 3×1-inch strips. Combine veal strips with 2 tablespoons reserved marinade; let stand 5 minutes. Heat 10-inch nonstick skillet over medium-high heat 5 minutes. Drain veal strips well. Cook half the veal strips in preheated skillet just until cooked through, 2 to 3 minutes, stirring occasionally. Remove veal strips from skillet and add to bowl with artichoke mixture. Reheat skillet, then cook remaining veal strips. Add to artichoke mixture. Toss veal-artichoke mixture to coat with dressing. Serve over salad greens immediately. If desired, veal mixture may be covered and refrigerated until serving.

Prep time: 15 minutes
Cook time: 6 minutes

Nutrients per serving:

Calories	221	Cholesterol	91 mg
Fat	8 g	Sodium	162 mg

Favorite recipe from **National Live Stock and Meat Board**

Hearty Healthy Chicken Salad

Makes 6 servings

  1 broiler-fryer chicken, cooked, skinned,
    boned and cut into chunks
  1 cup dry small macaroni pasta, cooked and
    drained
  3 tomatoes, cubed
  1 cup sliced celery
  ½ cup chopped red bell pepper
  3 tablespoons chopped green onion tops
  1 teaspoon salt
  ½ teaspoon black pepper
  ¼ teaspoon dried oregano leaves, crushed
  1 cup chicken broth
  1 clove garlic, pressed
  ¼ cup wine vinegar

Mix together warm chicken, macaroni, tomatoes,
celery, red pepper and onion in large bowl. Sprinkle
with salt, black pepper and oregano. Place chicken
broth and garlic in small saucepan; bring to a boil
over high heat. Boil 10 minutes or until broth is
reduced to ½ cup. Add wine vinegar and pour over
salad, mixing well. Refrigerate until chilled.

Nutrients per serving:			
Calories	192	Cholesterol	61 mg
Fat	6 g	Sodium	603 mg

Favorite recipe from **National Broiler Council**

Basic Lemon Cream Dressing

Makes 2½ cups

  2 cups nonfat cottage cheese
  ⅓ cup skim milk
  ¼ cup fresh lemon juice
  2 teaspoons CRISCO® Vegetable Oil

Place cottage cheese, milk, lemon juice and Crisco®
Oil in blender container. Blend at medium speed until
smooth.

*Alternate Method: Mash cottage cheese with fork or
potato masher. Place in container with tight-fitting lid. Add
milk, lemon juice and Crisco® Oil. Shake well.*

Nutrients per serving (1 tablespoon dressing):			
Calories	10	Cholesterol	0 mg
Fat	trace	Sodium	40 mg

California Brown Rice Salad

Makes 6 servings, 1½ quarts

  1 can (16 ounces) California fruit cocktail in
    juice or extra light syrup
  1 cup uncooked brown rice
  1 tomato, diced
  1 cup sliced celery
  ½ cup sliced green onions
  2 tablespoons red wine vinegar
  1 tablespoon vegetable oil
  1 tablespoon Dijon-style mustard
  ½ teaspoon dried tarragon leaves, crushed
  ⅛ teaspoon garlic powder

Drain fruit cocktail, reserving ¼ cup liquid. Cook
rice according to package directions; refrigerate until
well chilled. Toss rice, fruit cocktail, tomato, celery
and green onions in large bowl. Combine reserved
fruit cocktail liquid, vinegar, oil, mustard, tarragon
and garlic powder in small bowl; whisk until well
blended. Stir dressing mixture into rice mixture;
refrigerate several hours before serving to allow
flavors to blend.

Nutrients per serving:			
Calories	183	Cholesterol	0 mg
Fat	3 g	Sodium	59 mg

Favorite recipe from **California Cling Peach Advisory Board**

Celery and Fruit Salad with Raspberry Vinaigrette

Makes 4 servings

  ⅓ cup prepared red wine vinaigrette salad
    dressing
  2 tablespoons seedless raspberry jam
  2 cups thin diagonally sliced celery
  1 cup cored, unpeeled pear slices
  1 cup seedless red grape halves
  1 head Boston lettuce
    Chopped walnuts (optional)

Combine salad dressing and jam in glass measuring
cup; whisk until well blended. Set aside. Combine
celery, pear and grapes in medium bowl; add dressing
mixture. Toss lightly. Line 4 salad plates with lettuce
leaves; spoon celery mixture evenly over lettuce.
Sprinkle with walnuts, if desired.

Nutrients per serving:			
Calories	152	Cholesterol	0 mg
Fat	6 g	Sodium	337 mg

Favorite recipe from **American Celery Council**

Tag-Along Fruit Salad

Tag-Along Fruit Salad

Makes 10 servings

Citrus Dressing
- ¼ cup CRISCO® Vegetable Oil
- ¼ cup orange juice
- 2 tablespoons lemon juice
- 2 tablespoons sugar
- ¼ teaspoon paprika

Salad
- 1 can (20 ounces) pineapple chunks in juice, drained
- 2 cups seedless green grapes
- 1¼ cups miniature marshmallows*
- 1 cup fresh orange sections
- 1 cup sliced fresh pears**
- 1 cup sliced banana**
- 1 cup sliced apples**
- ½ cup maraschino cherries, halved

1. For dressing, combine Crisco® Oil, orange juice, lemon juice, sugar and paprika in container with tight-fitting lid. Shake well.

2. For salad, combine pineapple, grapes, marshmallows, oranges, pears, banana, apples and cherries in large bowl. Shake dressing. Pour over salad. Toss to coat. Cover. Refrigerate. Garnish, if desired.

1 cup raisins may be substituted for marshmallows.

**Add Citrus Dressing to pears, banana and apples immediately after slicing to prevent discoloration.*

Nutrients per serving:			
Calories	190	Cholesterol	0 mg
Fat	6 g	Sodium	10 mg

Indian Peach Salad

Makes 4 servings

- Lettuce leaves
- ¾ pound cooked turkey or chicken, cut into strips
- 2 fresh California peaches, cut into wedges
- 2 bananas, diagonally sliced into 1-inch chunks
- 1 cup halved cucumber slices
- ¼ cup thinly sliced red onion
- Fresh mint leaves for garnish (optional)
- Mint-Yogurt Sauce (recipe follows)

Line platter or 4 individual salad plates with lettuce. Arrange turkey, peaches, bananas, cucumber and onion on lettuce. Garnish with fresh mint, if desired. Serve with Mint-Yogurt Sauce.

Mint-Yogurt Sauce: Place 8 fresh mint leaves, 3 (⅛-inch-thick) slices peeled fresh ginger root, 1 medium peeled clove garlic, 2 tablespoons lemon juice, 1 tablespoon sugar and ⅛ teaspoon ground red pepper in blender or food processor. Blend until smooth. Stir mixture into 2 cups plain low fat yogurt. Refrigerate until well chilled. Makes about 2 cups.

Nutrients per serving (includes 1 tablespoon sauce):			
Calories	234	Cholesterol	62 mg
Fat	3 g	Sodium	70 mg

Favorite recipe from **California Tree Fruit Agreement**

Cottage Potato Salad

Makes 8 to 10 servings

- ½ cup buttermilk
- ¼ cup mayonnaise or salad dressing
- ¼ cup plain yogurt
- ½ envelope (2 tablespoons) onion flavor salad dressing mix
- 2 pounds new or small red potatoes
- 1 carton (12 ounces) cream-style Cottage cheese, drained
- 1 cup thinly sliced celery
- ½ cup (2 ounces) cubed Wisconsin Colby cheese
- ½ cup sliced radishes
- 2 tablespoons thinly sliced green onion
- ½ teaspoon salt
- ¼ teaspoon pepper
- 2 hard-cooked eggs, thinly sliced

Combine buttermilk, mayonnaise and yogurt in small bowl. Stir in salad dressing mix with whisk or fork until well blended. Refrigerate while preparing salad. Place potatoes in large saucepan; cover with water. Bring to a boil over high heat; cook until fork-tender. Drain. Let potatoes cool; cut into cubes. Combine potato cubes, Cottage cheese, celery, Colby cheese, radishes, green onion, salt and pepper in large bowl. Toss lightly to mix. Gently fold in salad dressing mixture; cover and refrigerate. Just before serving, garnish with eggs.

Nutrients per serving:			
Calories	205	Cholesterol	57 mg
Fat	9 g	Sodium	450 mg

Favorite recipe from **Wisconsin Milk Marketing Board** © 1994

Turkey, Mandarin and Poppy Seed Salad

Turkey, Mandarin and Poppy Seed Salad

Makes 4 servings

    5 **cups torn red leaf lettuce**
    2 **cups torn spinach leaves**
  ½ **pound Honey Roasted Turkey, cut into ½-inch
      julienne strips**
    1 **can (10½ ounces) mandarin oranges, drained**
  ¼ **cup orange juice**
 1½ **tablespoons red wine vinegar**
 1½ **teaspoons poppy seeds**
 1½ **teaspoons olive oil**
    1 **teaspoon Dijon-style mustard**
  ⅛ **teaspoon black pepper**

In large bowl, combine lettuce, spinach, turkey and oranges. In small bowl, whisk together orange juice, vinegar, poppy seeds, oil, mustard and pepper. Pour dressing over turkey mixture; toss to coat evenly. Garnish as desired. Serve immediately.

Nutrients per serving:			
Calories	158	Cholesterol	25 mg
Fat	4 g	Sodium	667 mg

Favorite recipe from **National Turkey Federation**

Roasted Bell Pepper Dressing

Makes 6 servings

    1 **green or red bell pepper**
  ½ **cup buttermilk**
    2 **teaspoons sugar**
    1 **teaspoon fresh parsley sprigs (optional)**
  ¾ **teaspoon lemon juice**
  ¼ **teaspoon paprika**
  ⅛ **teaspoon onion powder**
  ⅛ **teaspoon salt**
  ⅛ **teaspoon black pepper**

Place bell pepper in 375°F oven; roast for 20 to 25 minutes or until tender. Cut pepper in half; remove seeds. Pat dry with paper towel. Place bell pepper and remaining ingredients in blender container or food processor; process until well blended. Refrigerate or serve immediately over green salad.

Nutrients per serving (2 tablespoons dressing):			
Calories	21	Cholesterol	1 mg
Fat	trace	Sodium	67 mg

Favorite recipe from **The Sugar Association, Inc.**

Zesty Bean Salad

Makes 8 servings

  1 cup dry white beans or dry garbanzo beans
    (chickpeas)
  1 medium onion, chopped
  ¼ cup freshly squeezed lemon juice
  ¼ cup vegetable oil
  3 tablespoons chopped fresh mint
  1 medium clove garlic, minced
    Grated peel of ½ SUNKIST® Lemon
  2 teaspoons sugar
  1 teaspoon Dijon-style mustard
  ¼ teaspoon white pepper
  ½ cup chopped red bell pepper or tomato
  ⅓ cup chopped fresh parsley

Place beans in large stockpot. Cover with water, about 6 to 8 cups. Bring to a boil over high heat. Boil 2 minutes. Cover; remove from heat and let stand 1 hour. Drain beans and replace water. Bring to boil; cover and cook over low heat 1½ to 2 hours or until beans are tender.

Combine onion, lemon juice, oil, mint, garlic, lemon peel, sugar, mustard and white pepper in large bowl. Stir in cooked beans; refrigerate until beans are cool. To serve, stir in remaining ingredients.

Nutrients per serving (½ cup):			
Calories	162	Cholesterol	0 mg
Fat	7 g	Sodium	24 mg

Sprout-Green Bean Salad

Makes 12 servings

  3 packages (9 ounces each) frozen French-cut
    green beans
  ½ cup CRISCO® PURITAN® Oil
  ¼ cup white vinegar
  2 teaspoons sugar
  ½ teaspoon salt
  ¼ teaspoon black pepper
  1 can (16 ounces) bean sprouts, rinsed and
    drained
  1 cup thinly sliced celery
  ¾ cup chopped green onions
  1 jar (2 ounces) diced pimento, drained
    Cherry tomatoes (optional)

Cook beans in 3-quart saucepan according to package directions. Drain and cool. Blend Crisco® Puritan® Oil, vinegar, sugar, salt and pepper in small mixing bowl. Set aside.

Mix green beans, bean sprouts, celery, onions and pimento in large serving bowl. Stir dressing. Pour over bean mixture. Toss to coat. Cover and refrigerate at least 3 hours. Stir before serving. Garnish with cherry tomatoes, if desired.

Nutrients per serving:			
Calories	112	Cholesterol	0 mg
Fat	9 g	Sodium	160 mg

Ham Tortellini Salad

Makes 6 servings

  1 (7- to 8-ounce) package cheese-filled spinach
    tortellini
  3 cups (12 ounces) ARMOUR® Lower Salt Ham
    cut into ¾-inch cubes
  ½ cup sliced green onions
 10 cherry tomatoes, cut in half
  1 cup bottled low-sodium creamy buttermilk *or*
    low-calorie zesty Italian salad dressing
    Leaf lettuce or butterhead lettuce, washed
    and drained
  ¼ cup finely chopped red bell pepper

Cook tortellini according to package directions omitting salt; drain and run under cold water to cool. Combine all ingredients *except* leaf lettuce and red pepper in large bowl. Toss until well blended. Serve on lettuce-lined salad plates. Sprinkle with red pepper. Serve immediately.

Nutrients per serving:			
Calories	165	Cholesterol	39 mg
Fat	4 g	Sodium	545 mg

Ham Tortellini Salad

It's time to break out of that ho-hum vegetable routine with these vibrant creations. Give stir-fried vegetables a tantalizing foreign flavor with a dash of soy sauce and a pinch of ginger. Dress up versatile rice with zesty herbs, fresh spinach and a touch of cheese. Just watch those taste buds perk up!

Pasta & Vegetable Toss

Makes 4 servings

½ cup chopped onion
1 clove garlic, finely chopped
1 teaspoon Italian seasoning
1 tablespoon olive oil
¼ cup water
2 teaspoons WYLER'S® or STEERO® Beef-Flavor Instant Bouillon
2 cups broccoli flowerets
2 cups sliced zucchini
8 ounces fresh mushrooms, sliced (about 2 cups)
1 medium red bell pepper, cut into thin strips
½ of a (1-pound) package CREAMETTE® Fettuccini, cooked according to package directions and drained

In large skillet, cook and stir onion, garlic and Italian seasoning in oil until onion is tender. Add water, bouillon and vegetables. Cover and simmer 5 to 7 minutes until vegetables are tender-crisp. Toss with hot fettuccini. Serve immediately. Refrigerate leftovers.

Nutrients per serving:

Calories	287	Cholesterol	0 mg
Fat	5 g	Sodium	481 mg

Lemon Florentine Zucchini Boats

Makes 6 servings

3 medium zucchini (about 1 pound), cut in half lengthwise
Boiling water
1 small onion, finely chopped
1 medium clove garlic, minced
⅛ teaspoon ground nutmeg
2 tablespoons unsalted margarine
1¼ cups cooked, chopped fresh spinach, well drained (1½ pounds uncooked)*
½ cup ricotta cheese
Grated peel and juice of ½ SUNKIST® Lemon
2 tablespoons grated Parmesan cheese

Parboil zucchini in boiling water for 5 minutes; drain. In large skillet over medium-high heat, cook and stir onion, garlic and nutmeg in margarine until onion is tender. Add spinach, ricotta cheese, lemon peel and juice; stir until well combined. Arrange zucchini, cut sides up, in shallow baking dish. Top zucchini halves evenly with spinach mixture. Bake at 375°F for 20 minutes. Sprinkle with Parmesan cheese. Serve immediately.

*1 package (10 ounces) frozen chopped spinach (no salt added), thawed, may be substituted.

Nutrients per serving:

Calories	94	Cholesterol	8 mg
Fat	6 g	Sodium	85 mg

Pasta & Vegetable Toss

VEGETABLES & SIDE DISHES   347

Eggplant Italiano

Eggplant Italiano

Makes 4 servings

1 eggplant (1 pound), peeled if desired
1 can (6 ounces) low-sodium cocktail vegetable
   juice (¾ cup)
½ cup QUAKER® Oat Bran hot cereal, uncooked
2 garlic cloves, minced
1 teaspoon dried basil leaves, crushed
½ teaspoon dried oregano leaves, crushed
2 medium tomatoes, chopped
1¼ cups (5 ounces) shredded part-skim
   mozzarella cheese

Heat oven to 350°F. Line cookie sheet or 15×10-inch baking pan with foil. Lightly spray with nonstick cooking spray, or oil lightly. Cut eggplant into ½-inch-thick slices; place in single layer on prepared pan. Combine vegetable juice, oat bran, garlic, basil and oregano. Spread evenly over eggplant; top with tomatoes. Sprinkle with mozzarella cheese. Bake 35 to 40 minutes or until eggplant is tender and cheese is melted. Sprinkle with additional basil or oregano, if desired.

Nutrients per serving:			
Calories	190	Cholesterol	20 mg
Fat	7 g	Sodium	190 mg

Colorful Cauliflower Bake

Makes 6 servings

1 cup KELLOGG'S® ALL-BRAN® cereal
2 tablespoons margarine, melted
¼ teaspoon garlic salt
¼ cup flour
½ teaspoon salt
⅛ teaspoon white pepper
1⅓ cups skim milk
1 chicken bouillon cube
1 package (16 ounces) frozen, cut cauliflower,
   thawed, well drained
½ cup sliced green onions
2 tablespoons drained chopped pimento

Combine Kellogg's® All-Bran® cereal, margarine and garlic salt; set aside.

In 3-quart saucepan, combine flour, salt and pepper. Gradually add milk, mixing until smooth, using a wire whisk if necessary. Add bouillon cube. Cook, stirring constantly, over medium heat until bubbly and thickened. Remove from heat. Add cauliflower, onions and pimento, mixing until combined. Spread evenly in 1½-quart baking dish. Sprinkle with cereal mixture.

Bake at 350°F about 20 minutes or until thoroughly heated and sauce is bubbly.

Note: *3½ cups fresh cauliflower flowerets, cooked crisp-tender, may be substituted for frozen cauliflower.*

Nutrients per serving:			
Calories	120	Cholesterol	1 mg
Fat	4 g	Sodium	508 mg

Sun Valley Potato Fries

Makes 6 servings

2 large baking potatoes
¼ cup HELLMANN'S® or BEST FOODS® Light
   Reduced Calorie Mayonnaise

Preheat oven to 400°F. Cut potatoes into ¼-inch sticks. Spoon mayonnaise into large plastic food bag. Add potatoes; shake to coat well. Arrange in single layer in jelly-roll pan so potatoes do not touch. If desired, sprinkle with salt to taste. Bake 20 minutes or until golden brown and crisp, turning once with spatula.

Nutrients per serving:			
Calories	75	Cholesterol	3 mg
Fat	3 g	Sodium	3 mg

Oriental Stir-Fried Vegetables

Makes 4 servings, 4 cups

- 2 tablespoons vegetable oil
- 4 to 5 cups coarsely chopped or sliced fresh vegetables* (broccoli, carrots, cauliflower, onions, mushrooms, water chestnuts, Chinese cabbage, red or green bell peppers, snow peas and/or celery)
- 1 clove garlic, minced
- 1¾ cups (14.5-ounce can) CONTADINA® Stewed Tomatoes, drained, juice reserved
- 1½ tablespoons soy sauce
- 1 tablespoon cornstarch
- ½ teaspoon ground ginger
- ½ teaspoon salt (optional)
- 2 cups hot cooked rice or oriental noodles (optional)
- ½ tablespoon toasted sesame seeds

In 12-inch skillet, heat oil. Add vegetables and garlic; cook and stir over medium-high heat for 5 to 6 minutes or until crisp-tender. In small bowl, combine reserved tomato juice, soy sauce, cornstarch, ginger and salt. Add to skillet with tomatoes. Cook, stirring constantly, for 2 minutes or until sauce is thickened. Serve over hot cooked rice or noodles, if desired. Sprinkle with sesame seeds.

If using frozen vegetable mixture, choose a mixture with large pieces. Do not thaw.

Nutrients per serving:

Calories	145	Cholesterol	0 mg
Fat	8 g	Sodium	635 mg

Poppy Seed Noodles

Makes 4 servings

- 8 ounces uncooked noodles
- 1 tablespoon margarine
- 1 teaspoon poppy seeds

Cook noodles in lightly salted boiling water according to package directions; drain. Place in serving bowl. Add margarine and poppy seeds; toss lightly.

Nutrients per serving:

Calories	245	Cholesterol	54 mg
Fat	6 g	Sodium	45 mg

Oriental Stir-Fried Vegetables

Chilled Potatoes in Creamy Herb Sauce

Chilled Potatoes in Creamy Herb Sauce

Makes 8 servings

4 red new potatoes, unpeeled and scrubbed
1 cup frozen peas, thawed
½ cup chopped green bell pepper
1½ cups DANNON® Plain Nonfat or Lowfat Yogurt
2 tablespoons snipped fresh parsley
2 tablespoons sliced green onion
1 teaspoon dried basil leaves, crushed
¼ teaspoon salt
Dash white pepper

In a medium saucepan bring small amount of water to a boil. Add potatoes; cook, covered, 25 to 30 minutes or until tender. Drain and cool. Slice and place in a large bowl. Toss with peas and bell pepper. Add yogurt, parsley, green onion, basil, salt and white pepper. Toss gently to coat. Cover; chill until ready to serve.

Nutrients per serving:

Calories	100	Cholesterol	trace
Fat	0 g	Sodium	184 mg

Yellow Squash on Red Onions

Makes 4 side-dish servings

1 pound small yellow squash
2 tablespoons vegetable oil
1 large red onion, thinly sliced
2 teaspoons white wine vinegar
½ teaspoon sugar
½ teaspoon dried tarragon leaves, crushed
Chopped chives for garnish

Rinse squash under running water. Cut tip and stem ends off squash; discard. Slice squash in half lengthwise; cut into 1-inch chunks. Set aside.

Heat oil in large skillet over medium-high heat. Separate onion slices into rings. Cook and stir onion in hot oil until limp. Stir in vinegar, sugar and tarragon. Add squash chunks. Cover; cook 5 minutes or until squash chunks are crisp-tender. Transfer to warm serving dish. Garnish, if desired. Serve immediately.

Nutrients per serving:

Calories	96	Cholesterol	0 mg
Fat	7 g	Sodium	2 mg

Plum Ratatouille

Makes 6 servings

1 tablespoon vegetable oil
2½ cups diced eggplant
2 cups sliced zucchini
1 onion, cut into wedges
2 cups diced tomatoes
4 fresh California plums, cut into wedges (about 2 cups)
2 teaspoons minced garlic
1½ teaspoons dried basil leaves, crushed
1 teaspoon dried oregano leaves, crushed
¼ teaspoon pepper
Lemon wedges

Heat oil in large nonstick skillet over medium heat until hot. Add eggplant, zucchini and onion; cook 15 minutes or until tender, stirring occasionally. Add all remaining ingredients except lemon wedges. Reduce heat to low; cover and cook about 4 minutes or until plums are tender, stirring occasionally. Transfer to serving dish and squeeze lemon juice from wedges over top. Serve immediately.

Nutrients per serving:

Calories	93	Cholesterol	0 mg
Fat	3 g	Sodium	10 mg

Favorite recipe from **California Tree Fruit Agreement**

Mint-Glazed Carrots & Snow Peas

Makes 4 servings

1 tablespoon margarine
3 medium carrots, peeled and cut diagonally into thin slices
½ pound fresh snow peas, trimmed
2 tablespoons sugar
1 tablespoon fresh lemon juice
1 tablespoon chopped fresh mint leaves *or* 1 teaspoon dried mint

Melt margarine in large nonstick skillet over medium heat. Add carrots; cook and stir 3 to 4 minutes. Add snow peas, sugar, lemon juice and mint; cook and stir 1 to 2 minutes more until vegetables are crisp-tender and glaze thickens. Serve immediately.

Nutrients per serving:

Calories	95	Cholesterol	0 mg
Fat	3 g	Sodium	59 mg

Favorite recipe from **The Sugar Association, Inc.**

Risotto with Peas and Mushrooms

Makes 6 servings

½ cup chopped onion
2 teaspoons margarine
1 cup uncooked rice
⅓ cup dry white wine
1 cup chicken broth
4 cups water
1 cup frozen peas, thawed
1 jar (2½ ounces) sliced mushrooms, drained
¼ cup grated Parmesan cheese
¼ teaspoon ground white pepper
⅓ cup 2% low-fat milk

Cook and stir onion in margarine in skillet over medium-high heat until soft. Add rice and cook, stirring constantly, 2 to 3 minutes. Add wine; stir until absorbed. Stir in broth. Cook, uncovered, stirring constantly, until broth is absorbed. Continue stirring and adding water, 1 cup at a time, allowing each cup to be absorbed before adding another, until rice is tender and has a creamy consistency, 20 to 25 minutes. Stir in remaining ingredients. Stir until creamy, 1 to 2 minutes. Serve immediately.

Tip: *Medium grain rice will yield the best consistency for risottos, but long grain rice can be used.*

Nutrients per serving:

Calories	205	Cholesterol		4 mg
Fat	6 g	Sodium		316 mg

Favorite recipe from **USA Rice Council**

Risotto with Peas and Mushrooms

Vegetable Oat Pilaf

Makes 8 servings

½ cup chopped mushrooms
½ cup chopped green bell pepper
½ cup sliced green onions
1 tablespoon vegetable oil
1¾ cups QUAKER® Oats (quick or old fashioned, uncooked)
2 egg whites *or* ¼ cup egg substitute
¾ cup low-sodium chicken broth
1 medium tomato, seeded, chopped

In large saucepan, cook and stir mushrooms, green pepper and onions in oil over medium heat 2 to 3 minutes. In small bowl, mix oats and egg whites until oats are evenly coated. Add oats to vegetable mixture in skillet; cook and stir over medium heat until oats are dry and separated, about 5 to 6 minutes. Add broth; continue cooking and stirring 2 to 3 minutes until liquid is absorbed. Stir in tomato. Serve immediately.

Nutrients per serving:

Calories	101	Cholesterol	0 mg
Fat	3 g	Sodium	20 mg

Red, Green & Gold Squash Platter

Makes 8 servings

1 pound red bell peppers (about 3 medium)
2 tablespoons olive oil
¼ teaspoon grated lemon peel
1 tablespoon lemon juice
½ teaspoon dill weed
  Salt and black pepper to taste (optional)
3 cups *each* zucchini slices and crookneck squash slices
⅓ cup BLUE DIAMOND® Sliced Natural Almonds, toasted

To Microwave: Core and quarter red bell peppers. Place in single layer in glass baking dish. Cover; microwave at HIGH (100% power) for 10 minutes. Process peppers and remaining ingredients except squash and almonds in blender container or food processor until smooth. Place squash in 9-inch square glass baking dish. Cover; microwave on HIGH 3 to 4 minutes until tender-crisp. Spoon squash onto serving platter. Toss with almonds. Drizzle with red pepper sauce to serve.

Nutrients per serving:

Calories	84	Cholesterol	0 mg
Fat	6 g	Sodium	140 mg

Broccoli with Tangerine Ginger Sauce

Makes 6 servings

½ cup chopped onion
2 teaspoons crystallized ginger
1 teaspoon margarine
1 carton (8 ounces) low-fat lemon yogurt
  Grated peel of 1 fresh tangerine
2 California-Arizona tangerines, peeled, segmented and seeded
1½ pounds broccoli, trimmed *or* 2 packages (10 ounces *each*) frozen broccoli spears, hot cooked and drained

In small nonstick skillet over low heat, cook and stir onion and ginger in margarine until onion is very tender. Stir in yogurt, tangerine peel and segments. Cook and stir over low heat until heated through (*do not boil*). Serve sauce over hot cooked broccoli. Garnish with additional grated tangerine peel, if desired.

Nutrients per serving (includes about 3½ tablespoons sauce):

Calories	103	Cholesterol	3 mg
Fat	2 g	Sodium	57 mg

Favorite recipe from **Sunkist Growers, Inc.**

Creole Stuffed Peppers

Makes 6 servings

6 large green bell peppers
  Boiling water
½ cup chopped onion
1 tablespoon margarine
2 cups chopped fresh tomatoes
2 cups fresh okra slices
2 cups fresh corn, cut off the cob (about 4 ears)
⅛ teaspoon black pepper

Preheat oven to 350°F. Cut off tops of bell peppers; remove seeds and membranes. Add bell peppers to boiling water in large saucepan; cover. Boil 5 minutes; drain. Cool. In large saucepan over medium heat, cook and stir onion in margarine. Add tomatoes, okra, corn and black pepper; cook until mixture is thoroughly heated and slightly thickened. Fill bell peppers with corn mixture; place in greased shallow baking dish. Bake 30 minutes or until bell peppers are tender.

Nutrients per serving:

Calories	119	Cholesterol	0 mg
Fat	3 g	Sodium	39 mg

Left to right: Creole Stuffed Peppers, Grilled Vegetable Kabobs

Grilled Vegetable Kabobs

Makes 4 servings

12 large fresh mushrooms
  Boiling water
¼ cup Italian dressing
2 tablespoons fresh lemon or lime juice
1½ teaspoons Worcestershire sauce
2 medium zucchini, cut into 1-inch diagonal slices
4 cherry tomatoes

Place mushrooms in medium bowl; cover with boiling water. Let stand 1 minute; drain. Combine dressing, lemon juice and Worcestershire sauce in small bowl. Alternately thread mushrooms and zucchini on four skewers. Grill kabobs over medium coals about 10 minutes, turning and brushing frequently with dressing mixture. Remove from heat. Thread cherry tomatoes onto ends of skewers. Continue grilling 5 minutes, turning and brushing with remaining dressing mixture. Garnish as desired.

Nutrients per serving:

Calories	44	Cholesterol	1 mg
Fat	2 g	Sodium	141 mg

Onion-Roasted Potatoes

Onion-Roasted Potatoes

Makes 8 servings

> 1 envelope LIPTON® Recipe Secrets™ Onion or
>   Onion-Mushroom Recipe Soup Mix
> 2 pounds all-purpose potatoes, cut into large
>   chunks
> ⅓ cup olive or vegetable oil

Preheat oven to 450°F. In large plastic food bag or
bowl, combine all ingredients. Close bag and shake
or toss in bowl until potatoes are evenly coated.
Empty potatoes into shallow baking or roasting pan;
discard bag. Bake, stirring occasionally, 40 minutes
or until potatoes are tender and golden brown.
Garnish with chopped fresh parsley, if desired.

Note: *Also terrific with LIPTON® Recipe Secrets™ Savory
Herb with Garlic Recipe Soup Mix.*

Nutrients per serving:

Calories	174	Cholesterol	0 mg
Fat	9 g	Sodium	385 mg

"Lite" Apricot Stuffing

Makes 8 servings

> 1 cup sliced celery
> ¾ cup chopped onion
> 1½ cups turkey broth or reduced-sodium chicken
>   broth
> 16 slices reduced-calorie bread, cubed and dried
> 2 tablespoons dried parsley flakes
> 1½ teaspoons poultry seasoning
> ½ teaspoon salt
> 2 egg whites
> ¼ cup chopped dried apricots

In small saucepan, over medium-high heat, combine
celery, onion and turkey broth; bring to a boil.
Reduce heat to low; cover and simmer 5 minutes
or until vegetables are tender.

In large bowl, combine celery mixture, bread cubes,
parsley, poultry seasoning, salt, egg whites and
apricots. Spoon into lightly greased 2-quart
casserole; cover. Bake at 350°F for 30 minutes
or until heated through.

Nutrients per serving:

Calories	164	Cholesterol	trace
Fat	2 g	Sodium	566 mg

Favorite recipe from **National Turkey Federation**

Stuffed Tomatoes

Makes 6 to 8 servings

> 6 to 8 medium tomatoes
> 2 tablespoons CRISCO® PURITAN® Oil
> ⅓ cup chopped celery
> 2 tablespoons chopped onion
> 2 cups cooked brown rice
> ¼ cup grated Parmesan cheese
> 1 tablespoon snipped fresh parsley
> 1 teaspoon dried basil leaves, crushed
> ⅛ teaspoon black pepper
> ⅛ teaspoon garlic powder

Cut thin slice from top of each tomato. Set aside.
Scoop out centers of tomatoes; chop pulp and reserve.
Place shells, upside-down, on paper towels to drain.

Preheat oven to 350°F. Heat Crisco® Puritan® Oil in
medium saucepan. Add celery and onion. Cook and
stir over medium heat until celery is tender. Remove
from heat. Add reserved tomato pulp, rice, Parmesan
cheese, parsley, basil, pepper and garlic powder. Mix
well. Evenly fill each tomato shell with rice mixture.
Replace tomato tops, if desired.

Lightly oil 9-inch pie plate or round baking dish with
Crisco® Puritan® Oil. Place tomatoes in dish. Cover
with aluminum foil.

Bake at 350°F for 30 to 45 minutes or until tomatoes
are tender.

Note: *Use 1 lightly oiled custard cup for each tomato
instead of pie plate or baking dish, if desired.*

Nutrients per serving:

Calories	125	Cholesterol	2 mg
Fat	5 g	Sodium	65 mg

Vegetable Soufflé in Pepper Cups

Makes 6 servings

1 cup chopped broccoli
½ cup shredded carrot
¼ cup chopped onion
1 teaspoon dried basil leaves, crushed
½ teaspoon ground black pepper
2 teaspoons FLEISCHMANN'S® Margarine
2 tablespoons all-purpose flour
1 cup skim milk
1 container (8 ounces) EGG BEATERS®
    99% Real Egg Product
3 large red, green or yellow bell peppers,
    halved lengthwise

In nonstick skillet over medium-high heat, cook and stir broccoli, carrot, onion, basil and black pepper in margarine until vegetables are tender. Stir in flour until smooth. Gradually add milk, stirring constantly until thickened. Remove from heat; set aside.

In medium bowl, with electric mixer at high speed, beat Egg Beaters® until foamy, about 3 minutes. Gently fold into broccoli mixture; spoon into bell pepper halves. Place in 13×9-inch baking pan. Bake at 375°F for 30 to 35 minutes or until knife inserted in centers comes out clean. Garnish as desired and serve immediately.

Nutrients per serving:			
Calories	75	Cholesterol	1 mg
Fat	2 g	Sodium	91 mg

Sesame-Ginger-Carrot Rice

Makes 4 servings

1⅔ cups water
½ teaspoon salt (optional)
1½ cups uncooked UNCLE BEN'S® Brand
    Rice In An Instant
1 cup shredded carrots
1 teaspoon sesame oil
1 teaspoon shredded fresh ginger
1 green onion with tops, thinly sliced

Bring water and salt to a boil in large saucepan. Stir in rice, carrots, sesame oil and ginger. Cover and remove from heat. Let stand 5 minutes or until all water is absorbed. Sprinkle with green onion before serving.

Nutrients per serving:			
Calories	143	Cholesterol	0 mg
Fat	1 g	Sodium	20 mg

Pea-Pod Medley

Makes 4 servings

2 tablespoons vegetable oil
½ pound snow peas, trimmed
¼ pound mushrooms, sliced
1 yellow or red bell pepper, cut into strips
    Salt and black pepper (optional)

Heat oil in large skillet or wok over medium-high heat. Add vegetables. Stir-fry 4 minutes or until vegetables are crisp-tender. Season with salt and black pepper, if desired.

Nutrients per serving:			
Calories	96	Cholesterol	0 mg
Fat	7 g	Sodium	4 mg

Corn Olé

Makes 6 servings

2 tablespoons margarine
3 cups chopped fresh tomatoes
2 cups fresh corn, cut off the cob (about 4 ears)
2 cups (about ¾ pound) summer squash slices,
    halved
⅓ cup chopped onion
¼ teaspoon black pepper

Melt margarine in large skillet. Add remaining ingredients; cover. Cook 10 to 15 minutes or until squash is tender, stirring occasionally.

Nutrients per serving:			
Calories	111	Cholesterol	0 mg
Fat	5 g	Sodium	59 mg

Corn Olé

Penne with Artichokes

Makes 4 to 6 servings

1 package (10 ounces) frozen artichoke hearts
1¼ cups water
2 tablespoons lemon juice
5 cloves garlic, minced
2 tablespoons olive oil, divided
2 ounces sun-dried tomatoes in oil, drained
2 small dried hot red peppers, crushed
2 tablespoons chopped fresh parsley
¼ teaspoon salt
¼ teaspoon black pepper
¾ cup fresh bread crumbs
1 tablespoon chopped garlic
12 ounces uncooked penne, hot cooked and drained
1 tablespoon grated Romano cheese

Cook artichokes in water and lemon juice in medium saucepan over medium heat until tender. Cool artichokes, then cut into quarters. Reserve artichoke liquid. Cook and stir 5 cloves minced garlic in 1½ tablespoons oil in large skillet over medium-high heat until golden. Reduce heat to low. Add artichokes and tomatoes; simmer 1 minute. Stir in artichoke liquid, red peppers, parsley, salt and black pepper. Simmer 5 minutes.

Meanwhile, in small skillet, cook and stir bread crumbs and 1 tablespoon chopped garlic in remaining ½ tablespoon oil. In large bowl, pour artichoke sauce over penne; toss gently to coat. Sprinkle with bread crumb mixture and cheese.

Nutrients per serving:			
Calories	287	Cholesterol	1 mg
Fat	7 g	Sodium	220 mg

Favorite recipe from **National Pasta Association**

Cranberry Fruit Dressing

Makes 8 servings

3 cups herb-seasoned stuffing mix
2 cups chopped mixed dried fruit
1 cup chopped celery
1 cup whole-berry cranberry sauce
⅔ cup chopped onion
½ teaspoon ground dried sage
½ teaspoon dried thyme leaves, crushed
1½ cups turkey broth or low-sodium chicken bouillon
Nonstick cooking spray

Preheat oven to 325°F. In medium bowl, combine stuffing mix, dried fruit, celery, cranberry sauce, onion, sage, thyme and turkey broth. Coat 2-quart ovenproof dish with cooking spray. Spoon dressing into dish and bake, uncovered, 40 to 45 minutes.

Nutrients per serving:			
Calories	260	Cholesterol	0 mg
Fat	2 g	Sodium	420 mg

Favorite recipe from **National Turkey Federation**

Lemon Herb Broccoli

Makes 2 to 3 servings

1 bunch DOLE® Broccoli, cut into florets
2 tablespoons margarine
3 to 4 tablespoons lemon juice
1 tablespoon Dijon-style mustard
½ teaspoon dried marjoram leaves, crumbled

Steam broccoli over boiling water in large saucepan 3 to 4 minutes until tender-crisp.

Melt margarine in small saucepan over medium heat. Blend in lemon juice, mustard and marjoram. Spoon over broccoli. Serve with grilled chicken breasts or broiled fish steaks.

Prep time: 5 minutes
Cook time: 10 minutes

Nutrients per serving:			
Calories	118	Cholesterol	0 mg
Fat	8 g	Sodium	192 mg

Wild Rice Sauté

Makes 6 servings

½ cup sliced fresh mushrooms
¼ cup chopped green onions
1 clove garlic, minced
2 tablespoons HOLLYWOOD® Safflower Oil
3 cups cooked wild rice
¼ teaspoon salt
¼ teaspoon ground black pepper
¼ teaspoon dried rosemary sprigs, crushed
2 tablespoons peach schnapps liqueur

In a large skillet, cook and stir mushrooms, onions and garlic in hot oil for 1½ minutes. Add rice, seasonings and peach schnapps; cook 1½ minutes longer, stirring frequently.

Nutrients per serving:			
Calories	143	Cholesterol	0 mg
Fat	5 g	Sodium	97 mg

Penne with Artichokes

Crispy Vegetables with Orange Flavor

Makes 4 servings

1½ cups 1-inch pieces firm tofu (about 8 ounces)
1 tablespoon soy sauce
1 packet low sodium vegetable bouillon
    dissolved in 1½ cups water *or* 1½ cups no
    salt added tomato juice
2 tablespoons cornstarch
1 tablespoon vegetable oil
2 cups diagonally sliced celery
1 cup broccoli flowerets
¾ cup red bell pepper chunks
¼ cup sliced green onions
4 (2×½-inch) strips orange peel
1½ teaspoons ground ginger
6 ounces thin spaghetti, cooked
    Orange slices for garnish (optional)

Combine tofu and soy sauce in medium bowl; toss
to coat. Set aside. Combine bouillon mixture and
cornstarch in measuring cup; blend well. Set aside.
Heat oil in large nonstick skillet or wok over medium-
high heat until hot. Add celery, broccoli, red pepper,
green onions, orange peel and ginger; cook and stir
4 minutes or until vegetables are crisp-tender. Add
cornstarch mixture to skillet; bring to a boil. Boil
about 1 minute or until mixture is slightly thickened,
stirring constantly. Gently stir in reserved tofu; cook
about 1 minute more or until heated through. Serve
over spaghetti. Garnish with orange slices, if desired.

Nutrients per serving:			
Calories	275	Cholesterol	0 mg
Fat	7 g	Sodium	542 mg

Favorite recipe from **American Celery Council**

Crispy Vegetables with Orange Flavor

Pizza Fresca Style

Makes two 12-inch pizzas, 24 slices

Herb Sauce
1 tablespoon CRISCO® Vegetable Oil
1 cup chopped onion
2 cloves garlic, minced
2 cans (14½ ounces *each*) no salt added
    tomatoes, undrained and chopped
2 cans (8 ounces *each*) no salt added tomato
    sauce
2 tablespoons chopped fresh parsley
2 teaspoons dried basil leaves
1 teaspoon sugar
½ teaspoon dried oregano leaves
¼ teaspoon black pepper

Pizza Dough
2 cups all-purpose flour, divided
1 tablespoon sugar
½ teaspoon salt
1 package (¼ ounce) active dry yeast
1 cup warm water (110°F to 115°F)
2 tablespoons CRISCO® Vegetable Oil
1 cup whole wheat flour

Fresca Topping
1 medium zucchini, thinly sliced
1 large red, yellow or green bell pepper, cut
    into thin strips
4 ounces small mushrooms, thinly sliced
2 cups (8 ounces) shredded low moisture
    part-skim mozzarella cheese
2 tablespoons grated Parmesan cheese

1. For sauce, heat 1 tablespoon Crisco® Oil in large
saucepan on low heat. Add onion and garlic. Cook
and stir until tender. Stir in tomatoes, tomato sauce,
parsley, basil, sugar, oregano and black pepper.
Simmer one hour or until very thick. Cool to room
temperature.

2. Heat oven to 425°F. Oil two 12-inch pizza pans
(or two baking sheets) lightly.

3. For dough, combine 1¼ cups all-purpose flour,
sugar, salt and yeast in large bowl. Add water and
2 tablespoons Crisco® Oil. Blend at low speed of
electric mixer 30 seconds, scraping bowl constantly.
Beat at high speed 3 minutes. Stir in whole wheat
flour. Add enough of the remaining all-purpose flour
to make soft dough. Knead on lightly floured surface
until smooth and elastic (about 6 to 8 minutes). Press
half of dough onto bottom and ½ inch up side of pan
(or roll dough into 13-inch circle on lightly floured
surface and transfer to pan). Pinch edges to form rim.
Prick bottom and sides with fork. Repeat with
remaining dough.

4. Bake at 425°F for 10 to 12 minutes or until golden brown. (Bake at 400°F if using dark pizza pans or baking sheets.) Cool. Spread half of sauce evenly over each crust.

5. Arrange zucchini, pepper strips and mushrooms on top of sauce. Sprinkle with mozzarella cheese and Parmesan cheese.

6. Bake at 425°F for 12 to 15 minutes or until cheese is bubbly and lightly browned.

Note: Herb sauce can be prepared and refrigerated for later use. Pizza dough can be lightly oiled and refrigerated in a sealed plastic bag for 2 to 3 days. Allow dough to warm to room temperature before using. Lightly browned pizza crusts can be wrapped and frozen.

Nutrients per serving (1 slice):

Calories	120	Cholesterol	5 mg
Fat	4 g	Sodium	115 mg

Sesame Snow Peas

Hot and Spicy Cabbage Medley

Makes 8 servings

- 1 teaspoon CRISCO® Vegetable Oil
- 2 ounces smoked ham, chopped
- ½ cup chopped onion
- ½ cup chopped green bell pepper
- 1 can (10 ounces) tomatoes with green chilies, undrained and chopped
- ½ teaspoon sugar
- 4 cups sliced cabbage
- ⅛ teaspoon black pepper
- ⅛ teaspoon hot pepper sauce

1. Heat Crisco® Oil in large skillet on medium heat. Add ham, onion and green pepper. Cook and stir until vegetables are crisp-tender. Add tomatoes and sugar. Simmer 3 minutes.

2. Add cabbage, black pepper and hot pepper sauce. Simmer 15 minutes, stirring occasionally.

Nutrients per serving:

Calories	35	Cholesterol	5 mg
Fat	1 g	Sodium	165 mg

Sesame Snow Peas

Makes 4 side-dish servings

- ½ pound snow peas (Chinese pea pods)
- 2 teaspoons *each* sesame and vegetable oils
- 2 green onions, cut into ¼-inch slices
- ½ teaspoon grated fresh ginger root *or* ¼ teaspoon ground ginger
- 1 medium carrot, cut into julienned strips
- 1 teaspoon soy sauce
- 1 tablespoon sesame seeds, toasted*

To de-stem peas decoratively, pinch off stem end from each pod, pulling strings down pod to remove. Make a "V-shaped" cut at opposite end of pod.

Heat wok or large skillet over high heat. Add sesame and vegetable oils, swirling to coat sides. Heat oils about 30 seconds or until hot. Add onions, ginger root, peas and carrot; briskly toss and stir, keeping vegetables in constant motion about 4 minutes or until peas are bright green and crisp-tender. Stir in soy sauce. Transfer to warm serving dish; sprinkle with sesame seeds. Serve immediately.

**To toast sesame seeds, heat small skillet over medium heat. Add sesame seeds; cook and stir about 5 minutes or until golden.*

Nutrients per serving:

Calories	85	Cholesterol	0 mg
Fat	6 g	Sodium	116 mg

Apricot-Glazed Beets

Apricot-Glazed Beets

Makes 4 side-dish servings

1 large bunch fresh beets *or* 1 pound loose beets
1 cup apricot nectar
1 tablespoon cornstarch
2 tablespoons cider or red wine vinegar
8 dried apricot halves, cut into strips
¼ teaspoon salt
   Additional apricot halves (optional)

Cut tops off beets, leaving at least 1 inch of stems (do not trim root ends). Scrub beets under running water with soft vegetable brush, being careful not to break skins. Place beets in medium saucepan; cover with water. Cover. Bring to a boil over high heat; reduce heat to medium. Simmer beets about 20 minutes or until just barely firm when pierced with fork and skins rub off easily. (Larger beets will take longer to cook.) Transfer to plate; cool. Rinse pan.

Combine apricot nectar and cornstarch in same saucepan; stir in vinegar. Add apricot strips and salt. Cook over medium heat until mixture thickens.

Cut roots and stems from beets on plate.* Peel, halve and cut beets into ¼-inch-thick slices. Add beet slices to apricot mixture; toss gently to coat. Transfer to warm serving dish. Garnish as desired. Serve immediately with apricot halves.

Do not cut beets on cutting board; the juice will stain the board.

Nutrients per serving:

Calories	93	Cholesterol	0 mg
Fat	trace	Sodium	175 mg

Bryani

Makes 6 servings

1 package (9 ounces) frozen cut green beans
   Curry Rice (recipe follows)
1 onion, chopped
1 clove garlic, minced
2 fresh California peaches, coarsely chopped
   (about 2½ cups)
½ cup roasted cashews, chopped (optional)

Preheat oven to 375°F. Place frozen beans in colander. Run hot water over to thaw; drain well. Combine Curry Rice, onion and garlic. Place half the Curry Rice mixture in 1½-quart casserole. Cover with peaches, cashews and green beans. Top with remaining Curry Rice mixture. Cover with foil and bake 50 minutes. Serve with plain low fat yogurt, additional sliced peaches and raisins, if desired.

Curry Rice: Combine 2 cups water, 2 teaspoons curry powder, ½ teaspoon turmeric and ¼ teaspoon ground cinnamon in saucepan. Cover and bring to a boil. Add 1 cup long grain white rice; cover and return to boil. Reduce heat; simmer 20 minutes or until liquid is absorbed.

Nutrients per serving:

Calories	148	Cholesterol	0 mg
Fat	trace	Sodium	6 mg

Favorite recipe from **California Tree Fruit Agreement**

Chili-Cheese Cornbread

Makes one 9-inch pan, 8 servings

1 cup yellow cornmeal
⅔ cup all-purpose flour
2 teaspoons baking powder
½ teaspoon salt
¾ cup nonfat sour cream alternative
2 egg whites
1 egg
¼ cup CRISCO® Vegetable Oil
1½ cups finely chopped fat free process cheese
   product slices (¾ ounce *each*)
1 can (8¾ ounces) whole kernel corn, drained
1 can (4 ounces) chopped green chilies, drained

1. Heat oven to 400°F. Grease 9-inch square pan.

2. Combine cornmeal, flour, baking powder and salt in small bowl.

3. Combine "sour cream," egg whites, egg and Crisco® Oil in medium bowl. Stir well. Add cornmeal mixture, cheese, corn and chilies. Mix well. Pour into pan.

4. Bake at 400°F for 30 to 35 minutes or until toothpick inserted in center comes out clean. Cool 10 to 15 minutes. Cut into squares. Serve warm.

Nutrients per serving:

Calories	255	Cholesterol	30 mg
Fat	8 g	Sodium	860 mg

Vegetable Gratin

Vegetable Gratin

Makes 4 servings

¼ cup FRENCH'S® Creamy Spread™ Mustard
2 tablespoons olive oil
½ teaspoon *each* Italian seasoning and garlic powder
¼ cup plain dry bread crumbs
3 small (12 ounces) zucchini, thinly sliced
3 medium (12 ounces) tomatoes, thinly sliced
½ cup (2 ounces) shredded low-fat mozzarella cheese

In small bowl, combine French's® Creamy Spread™ Mustard, oil and spices. Mix 1 tablespoon mustard mixture with bread crumbs; set aside. In lightly greased 9-inch pie plate, layer half the zucchini, slightly overlapping slices. Dot zucchini with some of mustard mixture. Layer half the tomatoes over zucchini in pie plate; dot with some of mustard mixture. Sprinkle with mozzarella cheese. Repeat with remaining zucchini, tomatoes and mustard mixture. Bake, uncovered, at 400°F for 30 minutes until vegetables are tender. Sprinkle with reserved bread crumb mixture. Bake, uncovered, for 5 minutes or until crumbs are golden brown. Garnish as desired.

Nutrients per serving:			
Calories	167	Cholesterol	5 mg
Fat	10 g	Sodium	375 mg

Crispened New Potatoes

Makes 4 servings

1½ pounds new potatoes (about 12)
½ cup QUAKER® Oat Bran hot cereal, uncooked
2 tablespoons grated Parmesan cheese
1 tablespoon snipped fresh parsley *or* 1 teaspoon dried parsley flakes
½ teaspoon snipped fresh dill *or* ½ teaspoon dried dill weed
½ teaspoon paprika
1 egg white, slightly beaten
¼ cup skim milk
1 tablespoon margarine, melted

Heat oven to 400°F. Lightly spray 11×7-inch dish with nonstick cooking spray or oil lightly. Cook whole potatoes in boiling water 15 minutes. Drain; rinse in cold water.

In shallow dish, combine oat bran, cheese, parsley, dill and paprika. In another shallow dish, combine egg white and milk. Coat each potato in oat bran mixture; shake off excess. Dip into egg mixture, then coat again with oat bran mixture. Place in prepared dish; drizzle with margarine. Cover; bake 10 minutes. Uncover; bake an additional 10 minutes or until potatoes are tender.

Nutrients per serving:			
Calories	230	Cholesterol	0 mg
Fat	5 g	Sodium	110 mg

Delicious Sliced Apples

Makes 6 to 8 servings

½ cup firmly packed brown sugar
2 tablespoons all-purpose flour
Dash ground cloves
2½ pounds apples, pared, cored and sliced (about 8 cups)
¼ cup CRISCO® Shortening
¼ cup water

Combine brown sugar, flour and cloves in large bowl. Stir in apple slices and toss lightly. Melt Crisco® in large skillet. Stir in apple mixture and cook over high heat for 5 minutes, stirring occasionally. Stir in water. Bring mixture to a boil; cover and reduce heat to low. Simmer for 10 minutes or until apples are tender, stirring occasionally. Serve with roast beef or turkey, if desired.

Nutrients per serving:			
Calories	195	Cholesterol	0 mg
Fat	6 g	Sodium	7 mg

Cheddar Sesame Garden Vegetables

Makes 4 side-dish or 2 entrée servings

1 tablespoon plus 2 teaspoons all-purpose flour
½ cup *undiluted* CARNATION® Lite Evaporated
   Skimmed Milk
¼ cup water
1 teaspoon country-style Dijon mustard
½ cup (2 ounces) shredded low-fat Cheddar
   cheese
3 to 4 cups steamed fresh vegetables (carrots,
   summer squash, broccoli, cauliflower or
   asparagus)
1 tablespoon toasted sesame seeds

Place flour in small saucepan; whisk in small amount
of evaporated skimmed milk. Stir in remaining
evaporated skimmed milk with water and mustard.
Cook over medium heat, stirring constantly, until
mixture comes to a boil and thickens. Add cheese;
stir until melted. Serve over vegetables. Sprinkle with
sesame seeds.

Nutrients per serving:

Calories	148	Cholesterol	12 mg
Fat	5 g	Sodium	162 mg

Corn-on-the-Cob with Chili Spread

Makes 4 servings

4 ears of corn
3 tablespoons margarine, softened
1 tablespoon snipped fresh chives
1 teaspoon chili powder
   Salt and black pepper (optional)

Bring large pan of water to a boil. Add corn; boil
5 minutes. Meanwhile, combine margarine, chives
and chili powder in small bowl.

Remove corn from water; spread with margarine
mixture. Season with salt and pepper, if desired.

Nutrients per serving:

Calories	161	Cholesterol	0 mg
Fat	10 g	Sodium	119 mg

Shrimp Stuffing

Makes 8 servings

1 pound raw shrimp, cleaned, quartered
2 tablespoons margarine
1 package (6 ounces) KELLOGG'S®
   CROUTETTES® Stuffing Mix
½ cup chopped celery
½ cup sliced green onions
¼ cup chopped green bell pepper
1 can (10¾ ounces) condensed cream of
   mushroom soup
¾ cup water
1 teaspoon dry mustard
1 teaspoon lemon juice
½ teaspoon Cajun seasoning
¼ teaspoon salt (optional)
½ cup (2 ounces) shredded part-skim
   mozzarella cheese

In 12-inch skillet, cook and stir shrimp in margarine
over medium heat just until shrimp start to change
color.

Stir in remaining ingredients *except* cheese, tossing
gently to moisten. Reduce heat to low. Cover and cook
5 minutes. Remove from heat and stir in cheese.

To Microwave: In 4-quart microwave-safe mixing bowl,
melt margarine at HIGH (100% power) 1 minute. Stir in
shrimp and remaining ingredients *except* cheese. Cover
with plastic wrap, leaving one corner open to vent.
Microwave at HIGH 9 minutes or until stuffing is hot and
shrimp are opaque, stirring every 3 minutes. (When
stirring stuffing, carefully remove plastic from bowl to
allow steam to escape.) Stir in cheese.

Nutrients per serving:

Calories	220	Cholesterol	95 mg
Fat	7 g	Sodium	827 mg

Shrimp Stuffing

Salinas Valley Potato Topper

Makes 10 servings

 1 tablespoon margarine or butter
 ½ cup chopped fresh broccoli flowerets
 1 cup DANNON® Plain Nonfat or Lowfat Yogurt
 ¼ cup shredded part-skim mozzarella cheese
   (1 ounce)
   Paprika

In a small heavy saucepan over medium heat melt margarine. Add broccoli; cook and stir just until tender. Remove from heat. Stir in yogurt and mozzarella. To serve, spoon onto baked potato halves and sprinkle with paprika.

Nutrients per serving (1 tablespoon sauce):

Calories	10	Cholesterol	trace
Fat	0 g	Sodium	48 mg

Dakota Potato Topper

Makes 8 servings

 1 cup DANNON® Plain Nonfat or Lowfat Yogurt
 3 tablespoons bacon bits
 2 teaspoons prepared white horseradish

In a small bowl combine yogurt, bacon bits and horseradish. Cover; chill until ready to serve. To serve, spoon onto baked potato halves.

Nutrients per serving (1 tablespoon sauce):

Calories	10	Cholesterol	trace
Fat	0 g	Sodium	96 mg

Clockwise from top left: Salinas Valley Potato Topper, Dakota Potato Topper, Little Italy Potato Topper

Little Italy Potato Topper

Makes 10 servings

 1 cup DANNON® Plain Nonfat or Lowfat Yogurt
 ½ cup tomato, chopped
 2 tablespoons grated Parmesan cheese
 1 tablespoon chopped fresh basil leaves *or*
   ½ teaspoon dried basil
 1 tablespoon fresh oregano *or* ¼ teaspoon
   dried oregano
 ¼ teaspoon salt

In a small bowl combine yogurt, tomato, cheese, basil, oregano and salt. Cover; chill until ready to serve. To serve, spoon onto baked potato halves.

Nutrients per serving (1 tablespoon sauce):

Calories	10	Cholesterol	trace
Fat	0 g	Sodium	112 mg

Texas Potato Topper

Makes 10 servings

 1 cup DANNON® Plain Nonfat or Lowfat Yogurt
 ⅓ cup mild or medium chunky salsa
 ⅓ cup chopped stuffed green olives

In a small bowl combine yogurt, salsa and olives. Cover; chill until ready to serve. To serve, spoon onto baked potato halves.

Nutrients per serving (1 tablespoon sauce):

Calories	10	Cholesterol	trace
Fat	0 g	Sodium	200 mg

Wild Rice Tabbouleh

Makes 6 to 8 servings

 4 cups cooked wild rice
 1 can (8 ounces) garbanzo beans, drained
 1¼ cups minced fresh parsley
 ¾ cup minced fresh mint leaves
 ¾ cup finely chopped green onions
 3 tomatoes, chopped
 ½ cup lemon juice
 ¼ cup olive oil
 ½ teaspoon salt

Mix ingredients in large bowl until well blended. Refrigerate at least 1 hour and up to 1 week. Toss and serve over lettuce leaves.

Nutrients per serving:

Calories	200	Cholesterol	0 mg
Fat	8 g	Sodium	273 mg

Favorite recipe from **Minnesota Cultivated Wild Rice Council**

Creamy Macaroni and Cheese

Makes 6 servings

2 tablespoons CRISCO® Vegetable Oil
½ cup chopped green onions with tops
1 clove garlic, minced
2 tablespoons all-purpose flour
¼ teaspoon dried basil leaves
¼ teaspoon dry mustard
⅛ teaspoon pepper
2 cups skim milk
1 cup (4 ounces) shredded (⅓ less fat) sharp
    Cheddar cheese
½ cup nonfat sour cream alternative
1 teaspoon Worcestershire sauce
    Dash of hot pepper sauce
1½ cups uncooked small elbow macaroni, cooked
    (without salt or fat) and well drained
1 tablespoon plain dry bread crumbs

1. Heat oven to 350°F. Oil 2-quart casserole lightly. Set aside.

2. Heat 2 tablespoons Crisco® Oil in large skillet on medium heat. Add onions and garlic. Cook and stir until tender.

3. Stir in flour, basil, dry mustard and pepper. Stir until well blended. Stir in milk. Cook and stir until mixture thickens and just comes to a boil. Stir in cheese, "sour cream," Worcestershire sauce and hot pepper sauce.

4. Combine macaroni and sauce mixture in large bowl. Toss to coat. Spoon into casserole. Sprinkle with bread crumbs.

5. Bake at 350°F for 25 minutes.

To Microwave: 1. Combine Crisco® Oil, onions and garlic in large microwave-safe dish. Cover with plastic wrap. Turn back one corner of plastic wrap slightly to vent. Microwave at HIGH for 2 minutes.

2. Follow step 3, above, through addition of milk. Cover. Vent. Microwave at HIGH 4 to 6 minutes or until mixture just comes to a boil, stirring every 2 minutes. Add cheese, "sour cream," Worcestershire sauce and hot pepper sauce. Stir until cheese melts. Stir in cooked macaroni. Cover. Microwave at HIGH for 4 minutes, stirring after 2 minutes. Uncover. Microwave at HIGH for 2 minutes. Sprinkle with bread crumbs.

Nutrients per serving:			
Calories	260	Cholesterol	15 mg
Fat	9 g	Sodium	215 mg

Nutmeg & Honey Carrot Crescents

Nutmeg & Honey Carrot Crescents

Makes 4 side-dish servings

1 pound fresh carrots, peeled
⅓ cup water
2 tablespoons honey
¼ teaspoon ground nutmeg
2 tablespoons chopped walnuts
2 edible flowers, such as snapdragons, for
    garnish

To make carrot crescents, place 1 carrot on cutting board. Cut carrot in half lengthwise. Place each carrot half on cutting board, cut side down, and cut into ¼-inch-diagonal slices, beginning at large end of carrot half. Repeat with remaining carrots.

Place carrot crescents and water in large saucepan; cover. Bring to a boil over high heat; reduce heat to medium-low. Simmer carrots about 8 minutes or until fork-tender.

Transfer carrots with slotted spoon to warm serving dish. Bring remaining liquid in saucepan to a boil until liquid is almost evaporated. Add honey and nutmeg; stir. Heat briefly and pour over carrots. Toss gently to coat. Sprinkle with walnuts. Garnish, if desired. Serve immediately.

Nutrients per serving:			
Calories	103	Cholesterol	0 mg
Fat	2 g	Sodium	69 mg

Green Bean Bundles

Makes 8 side-dish servings

**8 ounces haricot vert beans or other tiny, young
green beans**
1 yellow squash, about 1½ inches in diameter
1 tablespoon olive oil
1 clove garlic, minced
¼ teaspoon dried tarragon leaves, crushed
Salt and pepper to taste (optional)
**Fresh tarragon sprig and cherry tomato slices
for garnish**

Place beans in colander; rinse well. Snap off stem
end from each bean; arrange beans in 8 stacks, about
10 to 12 beans per stack.

Cut eight ½-inch-thick slices of squash; hollow out
with spoon to within ¼ inch of rind.

To make bean bundles, thread stacks of beans
through squash pieces as if each piece were a napkin
ring. Place steamer basket in large stockpot or
saucepan; add 1 inch of water. (Water should not
touch bottom of basket.) Place bean bundles in
steamer basket. Cover. Bring to a boil over high heat;
steam 4 minutes or until beans turn bright green and
are crisp-tender.

Meanwhile, heat oil in small skillet over medium-high
heat. Cook and stir garlic and tarragon in hot oil until
garlic is soft but not brown. Transfer bean bundles to
warm serving plate and pour oil mixture over top.
Season with salt and pepper. Garnish, if desired.
Serve immediately.

Nutrients per serving:

Calories	30	Cholesterol	0 mg
Fat	2 g	Sodium	1 mg

Whole Okra and Tomato Sauté

Makes 4 side-dish servings

**1 pound small whole fresh okra (no more than
2 inches long)**
2 slices bacon
1 medium onion, sliced
**1 pound ripe tomatoes, halved, seeded and
chopped**
¼ cup water
1 bay leaf
Salt and pepper to taste (optional)

Place okra in colander and rinse under cool, running
water; drain. Cut off stems but do *not* cut into the
conical cap and seed section (this will cause okra to
"weep" and become sticky). Set aside.

Cook bacon in large skillet over medium heat until
crisp. Remove bacon to paper towel; set aside.

Add onion and okra to hot drippings in skillet; cook
and stir 7 to 10 minutes until onion is transparent.

Add tomatoes, water and bay leaf to okra mixture.
Cook and stir 8 minutes or until vegetables are
tender. Remove and discard bay leaf. Season with salt
and pepper. Transfer to warm serving dish. Crumble
reserved bacon and sprinkle over top. Serve
immediately.

Nutrients per serving:

Calories	90	Cholesterol	3 mg
Fat	2 g	Sodium	67 mg

Rice and Vegetable Zucchini Boats

Makes 6 servings

**3 small zucchini (*each* 6 to 7 inches long), cut
in half lengthwise**
1 tablespoon water
1 cup cooked rice
½ cup frozen peas, thawed
**1 jar (2½ ounces) mushroom stems and pieces,
drained**
2 tablespoons finely chopped red bell pepper
¼ cup HEINZ® 57 Sauce
½ teaspoon onion salt
¼ teaspoon dried rosemary leaves, crushed
⅛ teaspoon pepper
2 tablespoons crushed cheese-flavored croutons

To Microwave: Place zucchini and water in 2-quart
oblong baking dish; cover with vented plastic wrap.
Microwave at HIGH (100% power) 4 to 5 minutes or until
crisp-tender, rearranging after 2 minutes; drain. Scoop out
and discard seeds and pulp, leaving ¼-inch-wide shell.
Combine all remaining ingredients except croutons. Spoon
about ⅓ cup mixture into each zucchini shell. Cover with
vented plastic wrap. Microwave at HIGH 4 to 5 minutes or
until hot. Sprinkle with crushed croutons.

Nutrients per serving:

Calories	80	Cholesterol	trace
Fat	2 g	Sodium	160 mg

Green Bean Bundles

Bacon Pilaf

Bacon Pilaf

Makes 4 to 6 servings

2 tablespoons unsalted margarine or butter
2 medium tomatoes, coarsely chopped
¼ cup sliced green onions
8 slices ARMOUR® Lower Salt Bacon, cooked crisp and crumbled
1 cup uncooked rice
1 teaspoon no-salt-added chicken flavor instant-bouillon

Melt margarine in large skillet or saucepan over medium heat. Add tomatoes and green onions; cook and stir for 2 minutes. Stir in 2 cups water and remaining ingredients. Heat to a boil; reduce heat to low and cover. Simmer 20 to 25 minutes or until liquid is absorbed. Fluff rice with fork. Garnish with fresh parsley, if desired.

To Microwave: Place margarine, tomatoes and green onions in large microwave-safe casserole dish. Cook, covered, on HIGH (100% power) for 5 minutes. Add 2 cups water and remaining ingredients; cover. Cook on HIGH for 5 minutes. Reduce setting to MEDIUM-HIGH (70% power); cook 10 to 12 minutes or until liquid is absorbed. Let stand, covered, 5 minutes. Fluff rice with fork before serving. Garnish as above.

Nutrients per serving:			
Calories	197	Cholesterol	8 mg
Fat	8 g	Sodium	175 mg

Cinnamon-Apple Sweet Potatoes

Makes 4 servings

4 medium sweet potatoes
1½ cups finely chopped apples
½ cup orange juice
¼ cup sugar
1½ teaspoons cornstarch
½ teaspoon ground cinnamon
½ teaspoon grated orange peel

To Microwave: Wash sweet potatoes and prick with fork. Place on paper towels. Microwave at HIGH (100% power) 10 to 13 minutes or until tender, turning halfway through cooking. Set aside. In small bowl, combine remaining ingredients. Cover; cook at HIGH 3 minutes. Stir mixture and continue cooking, uncovered, at HIGH 1½ to 2½ minutes or until sauce is thickened. Slit sweet potatoes and spoon sauce over each.

Tip: *Sauce may be made up ahead and reheated at serving time.*

Nutrients per serving:			
Calories	216	Cholesterol	0 mg
Fat	trace	Sodium	12 mg

Favorite recipe from **The Sugar Association, Inc.**

Sautéed Zucchini and Tomato

Makes 4 servings

¼ cup WISH-BONE® Italian Dressing
2 medium zucchini, thinly sliced
1 medium onion, thinly sliced
1 can (14½ ounces) whole peeled tomatoes, undrained and chopped
1 tablespoon chopped fresh basil leaves*
Salt and black pepper (optional)

In large skillet, heat Italian dressing over medium heat. Add zucchini and onion; cook, stirring occasionally, 5 minutes or until vegetables are almost tender. Stir in tomatoes with juice, basil, salt and pepper. Bring to a boil. Reduce heat to low and simmer uncovered, stirring occasionally, 20 minutes or until zucchini is tender and sauce is slightly thickened. Serve with grated Parmesan cheese, if desired.

*Substitution: *Use ½ teaspoon dried basil leaves, crushed.*

Note: *Also terrific with WISH-BONE® Robusto Italian or Blended Italian.*

Nutrients per serving:			
Calories	112	Cholesterol	0 mg
Fat	8 g	Sodium	286 mg

Almond Ratatouille

Makes 6 servings

¾ pound small new potatoes
1 medium eggplant, cubed (about 4 cups)
2 medium zucchini, sliced (about 2 cups)
2 tomatoes, chopped
1 red bell pepper, sliced
1 onion, thinly sliced
½ cup vegetable cocktail juice
2 tablespoons *each* chopped fresh cilantro and lime juice
2 tablespoons balsamic or red wine vinegar
1 tablespoon chopped fresh basil*
2 cloves garlic, minced
1½ teaspoons chopped dill*
⅔ cup blanched slivered almonds, toasted

To Microwave: Cut potatoes into bite-sized pieces. Place in 8×12-inch microwave-safe dish. Cover; microwave at HIGH (100% power) 2 minutes. Stir in remaining ingredients except almonds. Cover; microwave at HIGH 15 minutes, stirring every 5 minutes until vegetables are tender-crisp and potatoes are cooked through. Remove from oven; stir in almonds and chill thoroughly before serving.

Or use 1 teaspoon dried basil and ½ teaspoon dill weed.

Note: *Hot Almond Ratatouille makes a wonderful topping for baked potatoes or broiled fish.*

Nutrients per serving:			
Calories	190	Cholesterol	0 mg
Fat	8 g	Sodium	86 mg

Favorite recipe from **Almond Board of California**

Tomato Caper Sauce over Pasta

Makes 8 servings

2 crushed garlic cloves
3 tablespoons olive oil
3½ cups (28-ounce can) CONTADINA®
    Whole Peeled Tomatoes, cut up, with juice
½ cup rinsed and drained capers
¼ cup chopped fresh cilantro
1 tablespoon chopped fresh basil
1 tablespoon chopped fresh thyme
1 pound rigatoni, cooked and drained
    Dash black pepper

Cook and stir garlic in hot oil in medium saucepan until lightly browned. Add tomatoes with juice and capers. Reduce heat to low and simmer, uncovered, about 20 minutes. Stir in cilantro, basil and thyme. Simmer an additional 5 minutes. Toss hot pasta with sauce and pepper.

To Microwave: Combine garlic and oil in 2-quart microwave-safe dish. Microwave on HIGH (100% power) 3 minutes. Add tomatoes and capers. Microwave on HIGH 8 minutes, stirring after 4 minutes. Stir in cilantro, basil and thyme. Microwave on HIGH 1 minute. Toss hot pasta with sauce and pepper.

Nutrients per serving:			
Calories	280	Cholesterol	0 mg
Fat	7 g	Sodium	340 mg

Fresh Corn Sauté

Makes 4 to 6 servings

4 ears fresh corn
4 ounces fresh pea pods
1 red bell pepper, cut into strips
¼ cup sliced green onions
1½ teaspoons WYLER'S® or STEERO®
    Chicken-Flavor Instant Bouillon
1 teaspoon sugar
2 tablespoons olive or vegetable oil
    Freshly ground black pepper

Remove husks and silk from corn; cut corn from cobs. In large skillet, cook and stir corn, pea pods, red pepper, green onions, bouillon and sugar in oil until vegetables are tender-crisp. Serve with black pepper. Refrigerate leftovers.

Nutrients per serving:			
Calories	111	Cholesterol	0 mg
Fat	5 g	Sodium	235 mg

Fresh Corn Sauté

Smoky Kale Chiffonade

Smoky Kale Chiffonade

Makes 4 side-dish servings

¾ **pound fresh young kale**
3 **slices bacon**
2 **tablespoons crumbled blue cheese**
  Kumquat slices for garnish

Rinse kale well in large bowl of warm water; place in colander. Drain. Discard any discolored leaves. To trim away tough stem ends, make "V-shaped" cut at stem end; discard tough stems.

To prepare a chiffonade, roll up 1 leaf jelly-roll fashion.* Slice crosswise into ½-inch-thick slices; separate into strips. Repeat with remaining leaves. Set aside.

Cook bacon in medium skillet over medium heat until crisp. Remove bacon to paper towel.

Add reserved kale to drippings in skillet. Cook and stir over medium-high heat 2 to 3 minutes until wilted and tender. Crumble bacon. Toss bacon and blue cheese with kale. Transfer to warm serving dish. Garnish, if desired. Serve immediately.

**"Chiffonade" in French literally means "made of rags." In cooking, it means "cut into thin strips."*

Nutrients per serving:

Calories	69	Cholesterol	7 mg
Fat	4 g	Sodium	154 mg

Crunchy Apple Stir-Fry

Makes 4 servings

1½ **teaspoons vegetable oil**
 ½ **cup onion slices**
 2 **medium carrots, thinly sliced (about 1 cup)**
 1 **teaspoon dried basil leaves, crushed**
 1 **cup fresh or frozen Chinese pea pods**
 1 **tablespoon water**
 1 **medium Washington Golden Delicious or Criterion apple, cored and thinly sliced**

Heat oil in nonstick skillet over medium-high heat until hot. Add onion, carrots and basil; stir-fry until carrots are tender. Stir in pea pods and water; stir-fry 2 minutes. Remove from heat; stir in apple. Serve immediately.

Nutrients per serving:

Calories	69	Cholesterol	0 mg
Fat	2 g	Sodium	13 mg

Favorite recipe from **Washington Apple Commission**

Savory Matchstick Carrots

Makes 4 side-dish servings

½ **pound carrots, peeled and cut into julienned strips**
 1 **small turnip,* peeled and cut into julienned strips**
½ **cup water**
 3 **tablespoons butter or margarine, cut into chunks**
1½ **teaspoons fresh thyme leaves *or* ½ teaspoon dried thyme leaves, crushed**
⅛ **teaspoon *each* salt and pepper**
  Green onion tops and edible flowers, such as violets, for garnish

Place carrot and turnip strips in medium saucepan. Add water; cover. Bring to a boil over high heat; reduce heat to medium. Simmer 5 to 8 minutes until crisp-tender.

Drain vegetables in colander. Melt butter over medium heat in same saucepan; stir in thyme, salt and pepper. Add carrots; toss gently to coat. Transfer carrot mixture to warm serving dish. Garnish, if desired. Serve immediately.

**Or, substitute 2 extra carrots for turnip.*

Nutrients per serving:

Calories	103	Cholesterol	23 mg
Fat	9 g	Sodium	198 mg

Pear Brown Rice

Makes 6 servings

 3 **tablespoons lemon juice**
 2 **teaspoons minced garlic**
 ¼ **teaspoon *each* ground ginger and pepper**
 2 **fresh California Bartlett pears, diced**
3½ **cups cooked brown rice**
 ½ **cup sliced green onions**
 ½ **cup grated carrot**
 ½ **cup thin celery slices**
 3 **tablespoons vegetable oil**

Combine lemon juice, garlic, ginger and pepper in small bowl. Add pears; toss well. Set aside. Combine remaining ingredients in large bowl; toss to coat. Gently fold pear mixture into rice mixture. Cover and refrigerate until chilled. Serve cold.

Nutrients per serving:

Calories	238	Cholesterol	0 mg
Fat	8 g	Sodium	21 mg

Favorite recipe from **California Tree Fruit Agreement**

Light Garden Spaghetti

Makes 6 servings

1 (10-ounce) package frozen chopped broccoli, thawed and well drained
½ pound carrots *or* zucchini, sliced, cooked and drained
¼ cup chopped onion
1 clove garlic, finely chopped
3 tablespoons diet margarine
¼ cup unsifted flour
1 teaspoon WYLER'S® or STEERO® Chicken-Flavor Instant Bouillon *or* 1 Chicken-Flavor Bouillon Cube
½ teaspoon thyme leaves
2 cups BORDEN® Lite-line® or Viva® Protein Fortified Skim Milk
6 slices BORDEN® Lite-line® American or Swiss Flavor Process Cheese Product,* cut into pieces
1 (2½-ounce) jar sliced mushrooms, drained
½ of a (1-pound) package CREAMETTE® Spaghetti, cooked according to package directions and drained

In large saucepan, cook and stir onion and garlic in margarine until tender. Stir in flour, bouillon and thyme; gradually add milk. Over medium heat, cook and stir until mixture thickens. Add cheese product pieces; stir until melted. Add broccoli, carrots and mushrooms; heat through. Serve over hot cooked Creamette® spaghetti. Refrigerate leftovers.

*"½ the calories"–8% milkfat product

Nutrients per serving:

Calories	260	Cholesterol	9 mg
Fat	7 g	Sodium	579 mg

Light Garden Spaghetti

Zucchini Bake

Makes 9 servings

⅔ cup QUAKER® Oat Bran hot cereal, uncooked
½ teaspoon Italian seasoning
¼ teaspoon black pepper
1 egg white
1 tablespoon water
2 medium zucchini, sliced ¾ inch thick, quartered (about 3 cups)
1 small onion, chopped
⅔ cup low-sodium tomato sauce
2 teaspoons olive oil
2 teaspoons grated Parmesan cheese
¼ cup (1 ounce) shredded part skim mozzarella cheese

Heat oven to 375°F. Lightly spray 8-inch square baking dish with nonstick cooking spray, or oil lightly. In large plastic food bag, combine oat bran, Italian seasoning and pepper; mix well. In shallow dish, lightly beat egg white and water. Coat zucchini with oat bran mixture; shake off excess. Dip into egg mixture, then coat again with oat bran mixture. Place zucchini in prepared dish; sprinkle with onion. Spoon combined tomato sauce and oil over vegetables. Sprinkle with Parmesan cheese. Bake 30 minutes or until zucchini is crisp-tender; top with mozzarella cheese. Serve warm.

To Microwave: In large plastic food bag, combine oat bran, Italian seasoning and pepper; mix well. In shallow dish, lightly beat egg white and water. Coat zucchini with oat bran mixture; shake off excess. Dip into egg mixture, then coat again with oat bran mixture. Place zucchini in 8-inch square microwavable dish; sprinkle with onion. Spoon combined tomato sauce and oil over vegetables. Sprinkle with Parmesan cheese. Microwave at HIGH (100% power) 5½ to 6½ minutes or until zucchini is crisp-tender, rotating dish ½ turn after 3 minutes. Sprinkle with mozzarella cheese. Let stand 3 minutes before serving. Serve warm.

Nutrients per serving:

Calories	60	Cholesterol	1 mg
Fat	2 g	Sodium	35 mg

Cheese-Crumb Baked Tomatoes

Makes 4 servings

¾ cup (3 ounces) finely shredded Wisconsin
  Part-Skim Mozzarella Cheese, divided
⅓ cup fine, dry unseasoned bread crumbs
1 to 1½ tablespoons fresh chopped herbs
  (oregano, parsley and/or rosemary) *or* 1 to
  1½ teaspoons dried herbs, crushed
1 large clove garlic, minced
4 tomatoes (about 2½ inches in diameter),
  cored and cut into 3 slices each

Preheat oven to 475°F. In small bowl, mix half the
cheese, bread crumbs, herbs and garlic until
thoroughly blended. Arrange tomato slices on oiled
baking sheet. Top tomatoes evenly with some of the
crumb mixture, then with remaining cheese. Bake
10 to 12 minutes until crumbs are lightly browned.

Nutrients per serving:

Calories	112	Cholesterol	13 mg
Fat	4 g	Sodium	171 mg

Favorite recipe from **Wisconsin Milk Marketing Board** © **1994**

Microwave Glazed Carrots, Apples and Peppers

Makes 5 servings

2 cups thin diagonal carrot slices
1 cup green bell pepper chunks (½-inch pieces)
3 tablespoons water
1½ cups thinly sliced peeled apples
¼ cup firmly packed light brown sugar
1 teaspoon cornstarch
½ teaspoon ground cinnamon
2 teaspoons margarine

To Microwave: Combine carrots and bell pepper in
1-quart microwave-safe dish; add water. Cover; cook at
HIGH (100% power) 3 minutes or until carrots are crisp-
tender. Drain; add apples and toss gently. In small mixing
bowl, combine brown sugar, cornstarch and cinnamon. Cut
in margarine with fork until mixture resembles coarse
crumbs. Sprinkle mixture over apple-vegetable mixture.
Cover; cook at HIGH 3 minutes. Stir to coat vegetables
with glaze; cook, uncovered, at HIGH 2 to 3 minutes or
until glaze thickens.

Nutrients per serving (½ cup):

Calories	124	Cholesterol	0 mg
Fat	2 g	Sodium	63 mg

Favorite recipe from **The Sugar Association, Inc.**

Chinese Sweet and Sour Vegetables

Chinese Sweet and Sour Vegetables

Makes 4 servings

3 cups broccoli florets
2 medium carrots, diagonally sliced
1 large red bell pepper, cut into short, thin strips
¼ cup water
2 teaspoons cornstarch
1 teaspoon sugar
⅓ cup unsweetened pineapple juice
1 tablespoon soy sauce
1 tablespoon rice vinegar
½ teaspoon Oriental sesame oil
¼ cup diagonally sliced green onions or
  chopped cilantro (optional)

Combine broccoli, carrots and red pepper in large
skillet with tight-fitting lid. Add water; bring to a boil
over high heat. Reduce heat to medium. Cover and
steam 4 minutes or until vegetables are crisp-tender.

Meanwhile, combine cornstarch and sugar in small
bowl. Blend in pineapple juice, soy sauce and vinegar
until smooth.

Transfer vegetables to colander; drain. Stir pineapple
mixture and add to skillet. Cook and stir 2 minutes or
until sauce boils and thickens. Return vegetables to
skillet; toss with sauce. Stir in sesame oil. Garnish
with onions, if desired.

Nutrients per serving:

Calories	68	Cholesterol	0 mg
Fat	1 g	Sodium	289 mg

Summer Squash Casserole

Summer Squash Casserole

Makes 4 servings

1 tablespoon FILIPPO BERIO®
    100% Pure Olive Oil, divided
½ pound *each* zucchini and yellow squash, cut
    into ¼-inch slices
1 teaspoon salt (optional)
    Black pepper to taste
3 tablespoons grated Parmesan cheese
3 ounces sliced fontina or mozzarella cheese

Preheat oven to 350°F. Lightly coat 13×9-inch
baking pan with small amount of olive oil. Arrange
⅓ of zucchini and squash in pan. Sprinkle with ⅓ of
salt, pepper, Parmesan cheese and remaining olive
oil. Repeat layers twice. Bake for 25 minutes. Place
cheese slices on top of zucchini; bake for an
additional 5 to 8 minutes until cheese melts. Garnish
with chopped fresh parsley, if desired. Serve
immediately.

Nutrients per serving:

Calories	165	Cholesterol	10 mg
Fat	10 g	Sodium	276 mg

Family Baked Bean Dinner

Makes 6 servings

½ DOLE® Green Bell Pepper, cut into strips
½ cup chopped onion
⅓ cup brown sugar, packed
1 teaspoon dry mustard
2 cans (16 ounces each) baked beans
1 can (20 ounces) DOLE® Pineapple Chunks,
    drained

To Microwave: Place green pepper and onion in 12×8-
inch microwave dish. Cover; microwave on HIGH (100%
power) 3 minutes. In large mixing bowl, combine brown
sugar and mustard; stir in beans and pineapple. Add to
green pepper mixture. Stir to combine. Microwave,
uncovered, on HIGH 8 to 10 minutes, stirring after
4 minutes. Serve with Polish sausage or hot dogs, if desired.

Nutrients per serving:

Calories	273	Cholesterol	0 mg
Fat	1 g	Sodium	678 mg

Spanish Rice au Gratin

Makes 4 servings

  Nonstick cooking spray
½ cup chopped onion
½ cup chopped celery
⅓ cup chopped green bell pepper
1 can (16 ounces) whole tomatoes, drained and
    chopped
1 teaspoon chili powder
½ teaspoon Worcestershire sauce
2 cups cooked brown rice
½ cup (2 ounces) shredded Cheddar cheese

Coat large skillet with nonstick cooking spray and
place over medium-high heat until hot. Add onion,
celery, and bell pepper; cook and stir until tender
crisp. Add tomatoes, chili powder, and Worcestershire
sauce. Stir in rice. Reduce heat; simmer about
5 minutes to blend flavors. Remove from heat. Top
with cheese; cover and allow cheese to melt, about
3 minutes.

*Tip: Add your favorite canned beans, cooked ground beef or
chicken for a main-dish version.*

Nutrients per serving:

Calories	204	Cholesterol	15 mg
Fat	6 g	Sodium	314 mg

Favorite recipe from **USA Rice Council**

Risotto Milanese

Makes 6 servings

1 small onion, thinly sliced
1 tablespoon margarine
1 cup uncooked Arborio or other short-grain
    rice
    Pinch saffron
½ cup dry white wine
¼ teaspoon TABASCO® pepper sauce
2 cups low-sodium chicken broth, divided
    Hot water
¼ cup grated Parmesan cheese
    Salt and freshly ground white pepper
    (optional)

In large skillet, cook and stir onion in margarine over medium-high heat until soft. Add rice and saffron; cook, stirring constantly, 2 to 3 minutes. Add wine and TABASCO sauce; stir until absorbed. Stir in 1 cup broth. Cook, uncovered, stirring frequently until broth is absorbed. Add remaining broth and hot water, ½ cup at a time, stirring constantly and scraping sides of pan frequently. (Wait until rice just begins to dry out before adding more liquid.) Continue stirring and adding water until rice is tender but firm and is the consistency of creamy rice pudding.* Stir in cheese, and salt and pepper, if desired.

The total amount of liquid used will vary. Watch rice carefully to ensure proper consistency.)

Nutrients per serving:

Calories	178	Cholesterol	3 mg
Fat	4 g	Sodium	94 mg

Marinara Sauce

Makes 5 servings, 2½ cups sauce

1 tablespoon FILIPPO BERIO®
    100% Pure Olive Oil
1 small onion, chopped
1 medium clove garlic, minced
1 can (28 ounces) crushed tomatoes,
    undrained, *or* 3 pounds fresh tomatoes,
    peeled, seeded and chopped
2 tablespoons chopped fresh parsley
1 teaspoon salt
1 teaspoon dried basil leaves, crushed
½ teaspoon sugar

In 3-quart saucepan, heat oil over medium-high heat. Add onion and garlic; cook and stir until onion is tender. Add tomatoes with juice and remaining ingredients. Simmer 20 minutes, stirring occasionally, until slightly thickened. Serve over pasta.

Nutrients per serving:

Calories	70	Cholesterol	0 mg
Fat	3 g	Sodium	686 mg

Couscous with Summer Vegetables

Makes 6 servings

1½ cups PRITIKIN® Chicken Broth or water
1 cup whole wheat couscous
1 large onion, chopped
1 medium red bell pepper, diced
1 small yellow squash or zucchini, sliced
2 cloves garlic, minced
1 medium tomato, seeded and chopped
¼ cup chopped fresh basil

Bring broth to a boil in small saucepan. Stir in couscous; reduce heat to low. Cover and simmer 5 minutes or until most of liquid is absorbed. Meanwhile, lightly spray large skillet with nonstick cooking spray. Add onion, bell pepper, squash and garlic. Cook over medium-high heat 5 minutes or until vegetables are tender, stirring frequently. Add cooked couscous, tomato and basil; heat through. Serve with freshly ground black pepper, if desired.

Nutrients per serving:

Calories	140	Cholesterol	0 mg
Fat	0 g	Sodium	55 mg

Couscous with Summer Vegetables

Carrots and Raisins Revisited

Makes 6 servings, 3 cups

2 cups DANNON® Plain Nonfat or Lowfat Yogurt
1 tablespoon packed brown sugar
¼ teaspoon grated orange peel
2 tablespoons orange juice
¼ teaspoon ground nutmeg or cardamom
   Pinch salt
6 to 7 medium carrots, peeled and coarsely
   shredded (3 cups)
¼ cup raisins
3 tablespoons chopped cashews, almonds or
   pecans

Spoon yogurt into large strainer lined with double thickness of cheesecloth or a coffee filter. Place bowl beneath, but not touching strainer to catch liquid. Chill 1½ hours. Scrape yogurt into a medium bowl. Discard liquid. Add brown sugar, orange peel and juice, nutmeg and salt; stir until smooth. Add carrots and raisins; toss to coat. Cover; chill 20 to 30 minutes before serving. Just before serving, sprinkle with cashews.

Nutrients per serving (½ cup):

Calories	140	Cholesterol	trace
Fat	4 g	Sodium	75 mg

Spicy Fresh Pear Chutney

Makes 8 servings, 4 cups

3½ cups finely diced Chilean pears, about
   3 medium (1¼ pounds)
2 tablespoons lemon juice
2 tablespoons chopped fresh cilantro leaves
1 clove fresh garlic, minced
½ cup finely chopped red onion
1½ teaspoons sugar
¼ teaspoon salt
¼ teaspoon crushed red pepper flakes

Combine all ingredients in medium bowl; toss well. Cover and refrigerate at least 2 hours.

Tip: Tangy fruit chutneys are perfect complements to grilled poultry, pork or fish.

Nutrients per serving (½ cup chutney):

Calories	51	Cholesterol	0 mg
Fat	trace	Sodium	68 mg

Favorite recipe from **Chilean Fresh Fruit Association**

Scalloped Potatoes

Makes 8 servings

3 tablespoons CRISCO® Vegetable Oil
½ cup chopped onion
¼ cup all-purpose flour
¾ teaspoon salt
¼ teaspoon pepper
⅛ teaspoon paprika
2 cups skim milk
2 pounds potatoes, peeled and thinly sliced
   (8 cups)
   Paprika
2 tablespoons chopped fresh parsley

1. Heat oven to 350°F. Oil 2-quart casserole lightly.

2. Heat 3 tablespoons Crisco® Oil in medium saucepan on medium-high heat. Add onion. Cook and stir until tender. Stir in flour, salt, pepper and ⅛ teaspoon paprika. Stir in milk. Cook and stir on medium-high heat until sauce comes to a boil and is thickened.

3. Layer one-third of the potatoes in bottom of casserole. Top with one-third of the sauce. Repeat layers twice. Cover.

4. Bake at 350°F for one hour 15 minutes. Uncover. Bake 15 minutes or until potatoes are tender. Sprinkle with paprika and parsley.

Nutrients per serving:

Calories	175	Cholesterol	0 mg
Fat	6 g	Sodium	240 mg

Sesame Snow Peas

Makes 2 servings

1 teaspoon sesame oil
2 teaspoons soy sauce, divided
1 cup fresh snow peas, strings removed
1 teaspoon sugar

Heat oil in small skillet over medium-high heat. Add 1 teaspoon soy sauce and snow peas. Cook and stir 1 to 2 minutes until snow peas are crisp-tender. Remove from heat; stir in sugar and remaining 1 teaspoon soy sauce. Serve immediately.

Nutrients per serving:

Calories	65	Cholesterol	0 mg
Fat	3 g	Sodium	350 mg

Favorite recipe from **The Sugar Association, Inc.**

Carrots and Raisins Revisited

Vegetable 'n Bean Pilaf

Makes 8 servings, 4 cups

1⅓ cups water
 ½ cup uncooked long-grain rice
 1 carrot, finely chopped
 1 can (16 ounces) black-eyed peas, rinsed and
   drained
 1 can (7 ounces) whole kernel corn, drained
⅓ cup WISH-BONE® Healthy Sensation! Honey
   Dijon Dressing
 2 tablespoons chopped fresh parsley

In 2-quart saucepan, bring water to a boil. Stir in
uncooked rice and chopped carrot. Simmer, covered,
20 minutes or until liquid is absorbed and rice is
tender. Stir in black-eyed peas, corn and Honey Dijon
Dressing; heat through. Stir in parsley; serve
immediately.

Nutrients per serving:			
Calories	126	Cholesterol	0 mg
Fat	trace	Sodium	333 mg

Light Italian Spaghetti Primavera

Makes 6 servings

½ of a (1-pound) package CREAMETTE® Thin
   Spaghetti, uncooked
 ½ cup bottled reduced-calorie Italian salad
   dressing
 1 medium green bell pepper, chopped
 1 medium red bell pepper, chopped
 1 medium yellow squash, cut into strips
 1 cup sliced fresh mushrooms
 ¼ cup chopped onion
 3 tablespoons sliced pitted ripe olives
 ¼ cup shredded part-skim mozzarella cheese
 3 tablespoons chopped fresh parsley

Light Italian Spaghetti Primavera

Prepare Creamette® Thin Spaghetti according to
package directions; drain. In large skillet, combine
Italian dressing, vegetables and olives; simmer just
until vegetables are tender-crisp. Serve over hot
cooked spaghetti; sprinkle with cheese and parsley.
Refrigerate leftovers.

Nutrients per serving:			
Calories	205	Cholesterol	8 mg
Fat	5 g	Sodium	218 mg

Oriental Fried Rice

Makes 6 servings

 3 cups cooked brown rice, cold
 ½ cup slivered cooked roast pork
 ½ cup finely chopped celery
 ½ cup fresh bean sprouts*
⅓ cup sliced green onions
 1 egg, beaten
   Nonstick cooking spray
 ¼ teaspoon black pepper
 2 tablespoons soy sauce

Combine rice, pork, celery, bean sprouts, onions, and
egg in large skillet coated with nonstick cooking
spray. Cook, stirring, 3 minutes over high heat. Add
pepper and soy sauce. Cook, stirring, 1 minute longer.

To Microwave: Combine rice, pork, celery, bean sprouts,
and onions in shallow 2-quart microproof baking dish
coated with nonstick cooking spray. Cook on HIGH (100%
power) 2 to 3 minutes. Add egg, pepper, and soy sauce.
Cook on HIGH 1 to 2 minutes or until egg is set, stirring to
separate grains.

**Substitute canned bean sprouts, rinsed and drained, for
fresh, if desired.*

Tip: *When preparing fried rice always begin with cold rice.
The grains separate better if cold and it's a great way to use
leftover rice.*

Nutrients per serving:			
Calories	156	Cholesterol	45 mg
Fat	3 g	Sodium	310 mg

Favorite recipe from **USA Rice Council**

Stuffed Acorn Squash

Makes 4 to 6 servings

1 acorn squash
3 tablespoons orange juice
1 tablespoon firmly packed brown sugar
¼ teaspoon ground cinnamon
Dash ground nutmeg

To Microwave: Cut acorn squash crosswise in half. Scoop out seeds and fibers; discard. Place two halves in microwave-safe casserole dish. Prick squash pulp several times with fork (do not pierce squash rind).

Combine remaining ingredients in small dish. Pour evenly into squash halves. Cover casserole dish. Microwave at HIGH (100% power) 15 to 20 minutes or until fork tender, rotating dish halfway through cooking. Remove from microwave; let cool slightly. Pour orange juice mixture from squash halves into medium bowl. Carefully scoop out squash pulp, leaving at least one shell intact; add to orange juice mixture. Mash with fork until mixture is well blended. Spoon squash mixture back into one shell. Serve in shell.

Nutrients per serving:

Calories	84	Cholesterol	0 mg
Fat	trace	Sodium	7 mg

Favorite recipe from **The Sugar Association, Inc.**

Scalloped Pineapple

Makes 6 servings

1 can (20 ounces) crushed pineapple in juice
2 tablespoons CRISCO® Shortening
⅛ teaspoon crushed dried mint leaves *or* wintergreen extract
4 bread slices, torn into small pieces
Milk
2 tablespoons sugar
⅛ teaspoon salt
1 egg, beaten

Preheat oven to 375°F. Drain pineapple; reserve juice. Melt Crisco® in medium saucepan; stir in mint. Remove from heat. Stir in pineapple and bread; mix. Turn into ungreased 1-quart casserole. Add enough milk to reserved juice to make 1 cup. Stir in sugar, salt and egg. Pour over pineapple mixture; stir lightly. Bake 40 minutes or until knife inserted in center comes out clean. Serve with baked ham, if desired.

Nutrients per serving:

Calories	177	Cholesterol	37 mg
Fat	6 g	Sodium	157 mg

Dilled New Potatoes and Peas

Dilled New Potatoes and Peas

Makes 8 servings, about 4 cups

1 pound (6 to 8) small new potatoes, quartered
2 cups frozen peas
1 jar (12 ounces) HEINZ® HomeStyle Turkey Gravy
½ cup light dairy sour cream
1 teaspoon dried dill weed

Cook potatoes in 2-quart saucepan in lightly salted boiling water 10 to 15 minutes or until tender. Add peas; cook 1 minute. Drain well. Combine gravy, sour cream and dill; stir into vegetable mixture. Heat (*do not boil*), stirring occasionally.

To Microwave: Place potatoes and 2 tablespoons water in 2-quart casserole. Cover with lid or vented plastic wrap. Microwave at HIGH (100% power) 6 to 7 minutes or until potatoes are just tender, stirring once. Stir in peas. Cover and microwave at HIGH 1 minute. Combine gravy, sour cream and dill; stir into vegetable mixture. Cover and microwave at HIGH 7 to 8 minutes or until heated through, stirring once.

Nutrients per serving (about ½ cup):

Calories	126	Cholesterol	6 mg
Fat	1 g	Sodium	332 mg

Spinach Feta Rice

Spinach Feta Rice

Makes 6 servings

1 cup uncooked long-grain white rice
1 cup chicken broth
1 cup water
1 medium onion, chopped
1 cup (about 4 ounces) sliced fresh mushrooms
2 cloves garlic, minced
   Nonstick cooking spray
1 tablespoon lemon juice
½ teaspoon dried oregano leaves, crushed
6 cups shredded fresh spinach leaves (about ¼ pound)
4 ounces feta cheese, crumbled
   Freshly ground black pepper
   Chopped pimiento for garnish (optional)

Combine rice, broth, and water in medium saucepan. Bring to a boil; stir once or twice. Reduce heat to low; cover and simmer 15 minutes or until rice is tender and liquid is absorbed. Cook and stir onion, mushrooms, and garlic in large skillet coated with nonstick cooking spray until onion is tender. Add mushroom mixture, lemon juice, oregano, spinach, cheese, and black pepper to hot cooked rice; toss lightly until spinach is wilted. Garnish with pimiento.

To Microwave: Combine rice, broth, and water in deep 2- to 3-quart microproof baking dish. Cover and cook on HIGH (100% power) 5 minutes. Reduce setting to MEDIUM (50% power) and cook 15 minutes or until rice is tender and liquid is absorbed. Combine onion, mushrooms, and garlic in 1-quart microproof baking dish coated with nonstick cooking spray. Cook on HIGH 2 to 3 minutes. Add mushroom mixture, lemon juice, oregano, spinach, cheese, and black pepper to hot cooked rice. Cook on HIGH 1 to 2 minutes or until spinach is wilted. Garnish with pimiento.

Nutrients per serving:			
Calories	195	Cholesterol	17 mg
Fat	5 g	Sodium	387 mg

Favorite recipe from **USA Rice Council**

Italian Vegetable Sauté

Makes 4 to 6 servings

2 tablespoons CRISCO® Oil
1 clove garlic, minced
¼ teaspoon dried oregano leaves, crushed
¼ teaspoon dried marjoram leaves, crushed
2 cups julienne-cut zucchini
1 small onion, thinly sliced and separated into rings
1 can (16 ounces) whole tomatoes, drained, cut up
2 tablespoons sliced pitted black olives (optional)
½ teaspoon salt
⅛ teaspoon black pepper
2 tablespoons grated Parmesan cheese

Heat Crisco® Oil in large skillet. Add garlic, oregano and marjoram. Cook and stir over medium heat until garlic is light brown. Add zucchini and onion; stir until coated. Cook and stir 5 to 7 minutes or until tender. Stir in tomatoes, olives, salt and pepper. Cook until heated through. Stir in Parmesan cheese.

Nutrients per serving:			
Calories	77	Cholesterol	1 mg
Fat	5 g	Sodium	334 mg

Garden Medley Spaghetti

Makes 6 servings

½ of a (1-pound) package CREAMETTE® Thin Spaghetti, uncooked
2 tablespoons margarine
2 cloves garlic, minced
2 cups finely shredded carrots
1 medium zucchini, cut into julienne strips
¾ cup chopped onion
2 tablespoons grated Parmesan cheese
1 tablespoon chopped fresh dill *or* 1 teaspoon dill weed
½ teaspoon salt-free herb seasoning

Prepare Creamette® Spaghetti according to package directions; drain. In medium skillet, heat margarine with garlic. Add carrots, zucchini and onion; cook and stir until vegetables are tender. Toss vegetables with hot cooked spaghetti, Parmesan cheese, dill and seasoning. Serve immediately. Refrigerate leftovers.

Nutrients per serving:			
Calories	213	Cholesterol	2 mg
Fat	6 g	Sodium	101 mg

Broccoli Boutonnieres and Buttons

Broccoli Boutonnieres and Buttons

Makes 6 side-dish servings

1 large bunch fresh broccoli (about 1½ pounds)
2 teaspoons lemon juice
1 tablespoon cornstarch
1 teaspoon instant chicken bouillon granules
1 cup water
  White pepper to taste

Trim leaves and tough ends from broccoli stalks. Cut broccoli into flowerets by removing each head to include a small piece of stem. Peel stems with vegetable peeler, then cut crosswise into ⅛-inch pieces to make "buttons."

To steam broccoli, rinse flowerets and "buttons." Place steamer basket in large saucepan; add 1 inch of water. (Water should not touch bottom of basket.) Place "buttons" in steamer; top with flowerets. Cover. Bring to a boil over high heat; steam 4 to 6 minutes until bright green and crisp-tender.

Meanwhile, combine lemon juice and cornstarch in small saucepan. Stir in bouillon granules and water. Cook over medium heat until mixture thickens and begins to boil, stirring constantly.

Arrange "buttons" around edge of warm serving plate. Place flowerets in center. Drizzle with lemon juice sauce; season with pepper. Garnish as desired. Serve immediately.

Nutrients per serving:

Calories	39	Cholesterol	0 mg
Fat	trace	Sodium	180 mg

Brown Rice Primavera

Makes 4 servings

1¼ cups water
½ cup uncooked brown rice
½ teaspoon salt
¼ teaspoon dried basil leaves
⅛ teaspoon black pepper
1 tablespoon CRISCO® Vegetable Oil
1 medium carrot, peeled and chopped
   (about ½ cup)
1 small zucchini, chopped (about ½ cup)
1 small yellow squash, chopped (about ½ cup)
1 small red bell pepper, chopped (about ½ cup)
2 green onions with tops, thinly sliced
   (about ¼ cup)

1. Bring water to a boil in medium saucepan on medium heat. Add rice, salt, basil and black pepper. Return to a boil. Reduce heat to low. Cover. Simmer 40 to 45 minutes or until rice is tender and water is absorbed.

2. Heat Crisco® Oil in large skillet on medium-high heat. Add carrot, zucchini, yellow squash, red pepper and green onions. Cook and stir 5 to 7 minutes or until vegetables are tender.

3. Transfer rice to serving bowl. Add vegetables. Toss to combine. Serve immediately.

Nutrients per serving:

Calories	135	Cholesterol	0 mg
Fat	4 g	Sodium	275 mg

Glazed Fruit Kabobs

Makes 4 servings

- 2 fresh California nectarines, cut into 12 wedges
- 3 fresh California plums, quartered
- ½ fresh pineapple, peeled and cut into 2-inch cubes
- ¼ cup packed brown sugar
- ¾ teaspoon rum extract
- 2 tablespoons water
- 1½ teaspoons cornstarch

Alternate fruit on skewers. Combine brown sugar, rum extract, water and cornstarch in small saucepan. Bring to a boil, stirring constantly. Cook until thick and clear. Place skewers in shallow pan. Brush with glaze mixture.* Place skewers on grid over medium coals, about 4 to 5 inches from heat source. Grill 6 to 8 minutes or until hot, turning once. Brush occasionally with glaze mixture.

Cover and refrigerate overnight, if desired.

Nutrients per serving:

Calories	167	Cholesterol	0 mg
Fat	trace	Sodium	5 mg

Favorite recipe from **California Tree Fruit Agreement**

Not Fried Asian Rice

Makes 6 servings

- 2 teaspoons sesame oil
- ¾ cup chopped green onions
- ½ cup chopped red bell pepper
- 2 cloves garlic, minced
- 2 cups water
- 1 cup uncooked converted rice
- 2 egg whites
- 1 tablespoon light soy sauce
- 2 teaspoons sugar

Heat oil in nonstick skillet over medium-high heat until hot. Add onions, bell pepper and garlic; cook and stir 1 minute. Add water and bring to a boil. Reduce heat to low; stir in rice and egg whites. Simmer 20 minutes or until rice is tender, stirring frequently. Stir in soy sauce and sugar. Cook 3 to 5 minutes more until sugar caramelizes.

Nutrients per serving:

Calories	145	Cholesterol	0 mg
Fat	2 g	Sodium	108 mg

Favorite recipe from **The Sugar Association, Inc.**

Low Fat Cajun Wedges

Makes about 1 serving per potato

- Russet potatoes
- Nonstick cooking spray
- Cajun seasoning or other seasoning, such as paprika

Preheat oven to 400°F. Scrub potatoes under running water with soft vegetable brush; rinse. Dry well. (Do not peel.) Line baking sheet with aluminum foil and spray with cooking spray.

Cut potatoes in half lengthwise, then cut each half lengthwise into 3 wedges. Place potatoes, skin sides down, in single layer on prepared baking sheet. Spray potatoes lightly with cooking spray and sprinkle with seasoning.

Bake 25 minutes or until browned and fork-tender. Garnish as desired. Serve immediately.

Low Fat Potato Chips: *Follow recipe as directed except slice potatoes crosswise as thin as possible. Place in single layer on prepared baking sheet; spray and season as directed. Bake 10 to 15 minutes until browned and crisp. Serve immediately.*

Low Fat Cottage Fries: *Follow recipe as directed except cut potatoes crosswise into ¼-inch-thick slices. Place in single layer on prepared baking sheet; spray and season as directed. Bake 15 to 20 minutes until browned and fork-tender. Serve immediately.*

Nutrients per serving:

Calories	145	Cholesterol	0 mg
Fat	trace	Sodium	8 mg

Low Fat Cajun Wedges

Cottage Spinach Un-Quiche

Makes 8 servings

4 eggs
1 (16-ounce) container BORDEN® Lite-line® or
Viva® Lowfat Cottage Cheese
1 (10-ounce) package frozen chopped spinach,
thawed and *well drained*
2 tablespoons flour
2 teaspoons Dijon-style mustard
1 teaspoon WYLER'S® or STEERO®
Chicken-Flavor Instant Bouillon

Preheat oven to 350°F. In large bowl, beat eggs; add remaining ingredients. Pour into lightly oiled 9-inch pie plate. Bake 35 to 40 minutes or until set. Let stand 10 minutes before serving. Refrigerate leftovers.

Nutrients per serving:

Calories	108	Cholesterol	111 mg
Fat	4 g	Sodium	422 mg

Sweet 'n Sour Stir-Fry

Makes 6 servings

¾ cup WISH-BONE® Lite Sweet 'n Sour Spicy
French Dressing
2 tablespoons firmly packed brown sugar
2 teaspoons soy sauce
2 tablespoons vegetable oil
1 cup thinly sliced carrots
1 cup snow peas (about 4 ounces)
1 small green bell pepper, cut into chunks
1 cup drained sliced water chestnuts
1 medium tomato, cut into wedges
½ cup sliced cucumber, halved

Sweet 'n Sour Stir-Fry

Blend salad dressing, brown sugar and soy sauce in small bowl; set aside. In medium skillet, heat oil and cook carrots, snow peas and green bell pepper over medium heat, stirring frequently, 5 minutes or until crisp-tender. Add water chestnuts, tomato, cucumber and salad dressing mixture. Simmer, covered, 5 minutes or until vegetables are tender. Top with sesame seeds, if desired.

Nutrients per serving:

Calories	137	Cholesterol	0 mg
Fat	5 g	Sodium	349 mg

Feta Pockets

Makes 4 servings

2 cups alfalfa sprouts
1 small cucumber, chopped
½ cup (2 ounces) crumbled Wisconsin Feta
cheese
¼ cup plain yogurt
1 tablespoon sesame seeds, toasted
¼ teaspoon pepper
2 pita bread rounds, halved
1 medium tomato, cut into 4 slices

Stir together sprouts, cucumber, cheese, yogurt, sesame seeds and pepper in medium bowl. Spoon mixture evenly into pita bread halves. Place tomato slice on filling in each bread half.

Nutrients per serving (1 pita half):

Calories	131	Cholesterol	14 mg
Fat	5 g	Sodium	283 mg

Favorite recipe from **Wisconsin Milk Marketing Board** © 1994

Nutty Vegetable Duo

Makes 4 servings

1 (10-ounce) package frozen green beans
8 ounces frozen small whole onions
¼ cup toasted slivered almonds
1 tablespoon margarine
Salt and black pepper (optional)

Combine beans and onions in medium saucepan; cook according to package directions. Drain.

Return vegetables to saucepan. Add almonds and margarine; stir over low heat until margarine is melted and mixture is thoroughly heated. Season with salt and black pepper, if desired.

Nutrients per serving:

Calories	103	Cholesterol	0 mg
Fat	7 g	Sodium	50 mg

Vegetable Bundles

Makes 4 to 6 servings

¼ cup fresh lemon juice
2 tablespoons sugar
2 tablespoons water
1 teaspoon margarine
¼ teaspoon garlic powder
1 large carrot, cut into thin 3-inch-long sticks
½ cup thin strips red bell pepper
½ cup whole green beans
2 to 3 green onions, white parts removed and discarded

To Microwave: In small microwave-safe dish, combine lemon juice, sugar, water, margarine and garlic powder. Microwave at HIGH (100% power) for 30 seconds; stir.

In another small microwave-safe casserole dish, place carrot sticks, pepper strips and beans. Add lemon juice mixture. Microwave at HIGH 6 to 10 minutes until vegetables are tender-crisp.

Cut green onions crosswise in half. Microwave at HIGH 5 to 10 seconds until just slightly limp. Remove vegetables from lemon juice mixture; divide evenly into 4 to 6 bundles. Gently tie green onion half around each bundle to secure. Serve warm or cold.

Nutrients per serving:			
Calories	55	Cholesterol	0 mg
Fat	1 g	Sodium	20 mg

Favorite recipe from **The Sugar Association, Inc.**

Guilt-Free Turkey Gravy

Makes 4 cups

4 tablespoons cornstarch
4 tablespoons water
4 cups Turkey Broth (recipe follows)
Salt and black pepper (optional)

In small bowl combine cornstarch and water. In large saucepan over medium heat, bring Turkey Broth and pan juices to a boil. Stir in cornstarch mixture and continue heating until gravy boils and thickens. Season to taste with salt and pepper.

Turkey Broth: In large saucepan over high heat, bring 4 cups water, Turkey Giblets, 1 sliced celery stalk, 1 sliced carrot, 1 sliced onion, 1 bay leaf, 3 parsley sprigs and 4 peppercorns to a boil. Reduce heat to low; simmer for about 1 hour. Strain and defat broth.

Nutrients per serving (3 tablespoons gravy):			
Calories	85	Cholesterol	41 mg
Fat	7 g	Sodium	22 mg

Favorite recipe from **National Turkey Federation**

Tangy Asparagus Linguini

Tangy Asparagus Linguini

Makes 4 servings

2 tablespoons light margarine
¼ cup finely chopped onion
3 cloves garlic, minced
8 ounces fresh asparagus, peeled and sliced diagonally into ½-inch pieces
2 tablespoons dry white wine
2 tablespoons fresh lemon juice
Freshly ground black pepper
5 ounces linguini, cooked and drained
¼ cup (1 ounce) SARGENTO® Grated Parmesan Cheese
¾ cup (3 ounces) SARGENTO® Preferred Light Fancy Supreme Shredded Mozzarella Cheese

Melt margarine over medium heat in large skillet. Cook and stir onion and garlic until onion is soft. Add asparagus; cook and stir for an additional 2 minutes. Add wine and lemon juice; cook an additional minute. Season with pepper to taste. Remove from heat. In large bowl, toss hot pasta, Parmesan cheese and asparagus mixture. Remove to serving platter; sprinkle with mozzarella cheese. Garnish with strips of lemon zest, if desired. Serve immediately.

Nutrients per serving:			
Calories	254	Cholesterol	13 mg
Fat	8 g	Sodium	317 mg

Ratatouille-Stuffed Pepper Halves

Makes 6 side-dish servings

**3 large bell peppers (1 red, 1 yellow and 1 green
or any combination)**
¼ cup olive oil
**1 small eggplant (¾ pound), unpeeled, cut into
½-inch cubes**
1 small onion, thinly sliced
1 clove garlic, minced
1 large tomato, seeded and coarsely chopped
1 cup sliced fresh mushrooms
**½ teaspoon *each* dried basil and oregano leaves,
crushed**
½ teaspoon salt
**Dash *each* black pepper and ground red
pepper**
**1 zucchini, quartered and cut into ½-inch
chunks**
**Plum tomato slices and fresh basil leaves for
garnish**

Cut bell peppers (including stems) in half lengthwise.
Scrape out seeds and membrane with spoon, being
careful not to cut through shell. Rinse out pepper
halves under running water; drain.

Place steamer basket in large saucepan or stockpot;
add 1 inch of water. (Water should not touch bottom of
basket.) Place pepper halves, cut sides up, in steamer
basket; cover. Bring to a boil; steam 5 minutes or
until peppers are crisp-tender. Plunge pepper halves
into ice water to stop cooking. Place pepper halves in
13×9-inch baking dish.

Heat oil in large skillet over medium heat until hot.
Cook eggplant and onion in hot oil 10 minutes or
until vegetables are soft, stirring occasionally. Add
garlic, chopped tomato, mushrooms, dried basil,
oregano, salt, black pepper and ground red pepper.
Bring to a boil over medium-high heat; reduce heat to
medium-low. Simmer about 5 minutes, stirring
occasionally. Add zucchini; simmer 5 minutes more
or until mixture thickens slightly.

Preheat oven to 350°F. Spoon mixture evenly into
pepper halves.* Bake 15 minutes or until heated
through. Garnish, if desired. Serve immediately.

**Pepper halves may be refrigerated up to 4 days at this point.*

Nutrients per serving:			
Calories	121	Cholesterol	0 mg
Fat	9 g	Sodium	184 mg

Braised Celery with Swiss Cheese and Almonds

Makes 4 servings

1½ cups water
Dash ground red pepper
**4 cups 2×¼-inch celery strips or thin celery
slices**
**3 slices (¾-ounce *each*) process Swiss cheese
slices, cut in half diagonally**
2 tablespoons sliced almonds

Preheat broiler. Combine water and red pepper in
large skillet; bring to a boil over high heat. Add
celery; reduce heat to low. Cover and simmer
5 minutes or until celery is crisp-tender; drain.
Arrange celery in shallow 2-quart casserole or
ovenproof platter. Top with cheese; sprinkle with
almonds. Broil 3 inches from heat source 1 to
2 minutes or until cheese melts and almonds are
golden. Serve immediately.

Nutrients per serving:			
Calories	90	Cholesterol	14 mg
Fat	6 g	Sodium	324 mg

Favorite recipe from **American Celery Council**

Carrot Coins

Makes 2 servings

1 cup sliced carrots
3 tablespoons water
1 teaspoon butter or margarine
1 teaspoon sugar

To Microwave: Place carrots, water and butter in
microwave-safe dish. Microwave on HIGH (100% power)
5 minutes or until carrots are crisp-tender, turning dish
halfway through cooking. Sprinkle with sugar and stir.
Serve immediately.

Nutrients per serving:			
Calories	60	Cholesterol	6 mg
Fat	2 g	Sodium	68 mg

Favorite recipe from **The Sugar Association, Inc.**

Ratatouille-Stuffed Pepper Halves

Vegetable Stew Medley

Vegetable Stew Medley

Makes 12 servings

2 tablespoons CRISCO® Vegetable Oil
4 medium onions, thinly sliced and separated
    into rings
3 medium green bell peppers, cut into strips
2 cloves garlic, minced
4 medium zucchini, cut into ½-inch pieces
1 medium eggplant, cut into ½-inch pieces
    (about 1 pound)
1 can (14½ ounces) no salt added whole
    tomatoes, drained and chopped, *or* 4 or
    5 fresh tomatoes, peeled and quartered
1 teaspoon dill weed
¾ teaspoon dried basil leaves
½ teaspoon black pepper
½ teaspoon dried oregano leaves
¼ teaspoon salt
1 package (9 ounces) frozen peas
¼ cup lemon juice
2 tablespoons chopped fresh parsley *or*
    2 teaspoons dried parsley

1. Heat Crisco® Oil in Dutch oven (non-reactive or non-cast iron) on medium heat. Add onions, green peppers and garlic. Cook and stir until tender.

2. Add zucchini and eggplant. Cook 5 minutes, stirring occasionally. Stir in tomatoes, dill weed, basil, black pepper, oregano and salt. Reduce heat to low. Cover. Simmer 20 minutes, stirring occasionally.

3. Stir in peas. Simmer 3 to 5 minutes or until peas are thawed and heated, stirring occasionally. Stir in lemon juice. Serve hot or chilled sprinkled with parsley.

Nutrients per serving:			
Calories	85	Cholesterol	0 mg
Fat	3 g	Sodium	80 mg

Scalloped Red Skin Potatoes

Makes 6 side-dish servings

2 pounds red skin potatoes
2 tablespoons all-purpose flour
4 tablespoons butter or margarine, divided
    Salt, pepper and paprika to taste
1¼ cups milk
    Fresh thyme sprig for garnish

Preheat oven to 350°F. Scrub potatoes under running water with soft vegetable brush; rinse well. Cut potatoes into ¼-inch slices. Place slices on waxed paper and sprinkle with flour, tossing gently to coat.

Grease 9-inch round baking dish with 1 tablespoon butter. Place ⅓ of potatoes in dish; sprinkle with salt, pepper and paprika. Dot with 1 tablespoon butter. Repeat layers twice. Heat milk in small saucepan over medium heat until hot *(do not boil)*. Pour over potatoes; sprinkle with salt, pepper and paprika. Cover with lid or aluminum foil.

Bake 35 minutes. Uncover; bake 20 minutes more or until potatoes are fork-tender. Garnish, if desired. Serve immediately.

Nutrients per serving:			
Calories	242	Cholesterol	24 mg
Fat	9 g	Sodium	111 mg

Fresh Grape Chutney with Ginger

Makes 7 servings, 3½ cups

> 3 cups Chilean seedless red or green grapes, coarsely chopped or quartered
> ⅓ cup finely chopped onion
> 2 tablespoons chopped fresh cilantro leaves
> 1 tablespoon lime juice
> 1 clove garlic, minced
> 1½ teaspoons sugar
> 1 teaspoon grated fresh ginger *or* ¼ teaspoon ground ginger
> ¼ teaspoon salt

Combine all ingredients in medium bowl; toss well. Cover and refrigerate at least 2 hours.

Tip: *Tangy fruit chutneys are perfect complements to grilled poultry, pork or fish.*

Nutrients per serving (½ cup chutney):			
Calories	57	Cholesterol	0 mg
Fat	trace	Sodium	79 mg

Favorite recipe from **Chilean Fresh Fruit Association**

Savory Green Bean Casserole

Makes 8 servings

> 2 teaspoons CRISCO® Vegetable Oil
> 1 medium onion, chopped
> ½ medium green bell pepper, chopped
> 1 package (10 ounces) frozen green beans, thawed
> 1 can (8 ounces) tomatoes, drained
> 2 tablespoons nonfat mayonnaise dressing
> ¼ teaspoon salt
> ⅛ teaspoon crushed red pepper
> ⅛ teaspoon garlic powder
> ¼ cup plain dry bread crumbs

1. Heat oven to 375°F. Oil 1-quart casserole lightly.

2. Heat 2 teaspoons Crisco® Oil in large skillet on medium heat. Add onion and green pepper. Cook and stir until tender.

3. Add beans, tomatoes, mayonnaise dressing, salt, red pepper and garlic powder. Heat thoroughly, stirring occasionally.

4. Spoon into casserole. Sprinkle with bread crumbs. Bake at 375°F for 30 minutes.

Nutrients per serving:			
Calories	50	Cholesterol	0 mg
Fat	1 g	Sodium	170 mg

Crisp Zucchini Ribbons

Makes 4 side-dish servings

> 3 small zucchini (about ¾ pound *total*)
> 2 tablespoons olive oil
> 1 tablespoon white wine vinegar
> 2 teaspoons chopped fresh basil leaves *or* ½ teaspoon dried basil leaves, crushed
> ½ teaspoon crushed red pepper flakes
> ¼ teaspoon ground coriander
>   Salt and freshly ground black pepper to taste
>   Green onion top and julienned carrot strips for garnish

To make zucchini ribbons, cut tip and stem ends from zucchini. Using vegetable peeler, begin at stem end and make continuous ribbons down length of each zucchini.

Place steamer basket in large saucepan; add 1 inch of water. (Water should not touch bottom of basket.) Place zucchini ribbons in steamer basket; cover. Bring to a boil over high heat. When pan begins to steam, check zucchini for doneness. (It should be crisp-tender.) Transfer zucchini to warm serving dish with slotted spatula or tongs.

Combine oil, vinegar, basil, red pepper and coriander in small bowl, whisking until oil is thoroughly blended. Pour dressing mixture over zucchini ribbons; toss gently to coat. Season with salt and pepper. Garnish, if desired. Serve immediately or refrigerate up to 2 days.

Nutrients per serving:			
Calories	72	Cholesterol	0 mg
Fat	7 g	Sodium	2 mg

Crisp Zucchini Ribbons

Cabbage Wedges with Tangy Hot Dressing

Cabbage Wedges with Tangy Hot Dressing

Makes 4 side-dish servings

½ head red or green cabbage (about 1 pound)
1 slice bacon, cut crosswise into ¼-inch strips
2 teaspoons cornstarch
⅔ cup unsweetened apple juice
¼ cup cider or red wine vinegar
1 tablespoon brown sugar
½ teaspoon caraway seeds
1 green onion, thinly sliced

Discard any wilted or bruised outer leaves from cabbage. Cut cabbage half into 4 wedges. (To help keep wedges intact, do not cut core from each wedge.)

Cook bacon in large skillet over medium heat until crisp. Remove bacon with slotted spoon to paper towel; set aside. Meanwhile, dissolve cornstarch in apple juice in glass measuring cup. Stir in vinegar, brown sugar and caraway seeds; set aside. Add onion to hot drippings. Cook and stir until onion is soft but not brown.

Place cabbage wedges, flat sides down, in drippings mixture. Pour cornstarch mixture over cabbage wedges. Cook over medium heat 4 minutes. Carefully turn cabbage wedges over with spatula. Cook 6 minutes more or until cabbage is fork-tender and dressing is thickened.

Remove cabbage wedges to cutting board with spatula; carefully cut core away with utility knife. Transfer to warm serving dish. Pour hot dressing over cabbage wedges. Sprinkle with reserved bacon pieces. Garnish as desired. Serve immediately.

Nutrients per serving:

Calories	71	Cholesterol	1 mg
Fat	1 g	Sodium	49 mg

Vegetable Couscous

Makes 6 servings

1¼ cups fresh orange juice
1 cup reduced sodium chicken broth
1 tablespoon margarine
1 teaspoon grated orange peel
½ teaspoon salt (optional)
1 box (10 ounces) couscous
Nonstick cooking spray
1 large red bell pepper, finely chopped (about 1 cup)
2 green onions with tops, sliced (about ½ cup)
2 cloves garlic, minced

Place juice, broth, margarine, orange peel and salt, if desired, in medium saucepan; bring to a boil over high heat. Stir in couscous; cover and remove from heat. Let stand 5 minutes.

Meanwhile, spray large nonstick skillet lightly with cooking spray. Heat skillet over medium-high heat until hot. Add pepper, onions and garlic. Cook and stir 2 minutes or until pepper is softened.

Fluff couscous lightly with fork. Stir in pepper mixture. Serve immediately.

Nutrients per serving:

Calories	230	Cholesterol	0 mg
Fat	4 g	Sodium	62 mg

Fruited Wild Rice Stuffing

Makes 8 servings, 6 cups

3 cups cooked wild rice
1 cup bread crumbs
½ cup raisins
½ cup chopped walnuts (optional)
½ cup fresh apple chunks
¼ cup extra light margarine, melted
¼ cup orange juice

Preheat oven to 325°F. Combine all ingredients; blend well. Turn into buttered 2-quart casserole and bake, covered, 1½ hours *or* cook stuffed in game birds, turkey, capon or chicken.

Nutrients per serving:

Calories	156	Cholesterol	0 mg
Fat	4 g	Sodium	61 mg

Favorite recipe from **Minnesota Cultivated Wild Rice Council**

Broccoli Lasagna

Makes 8 servings

- 1 tablespoon CRISCO® Vegetable Oil
- 1 cup chopped onion
- 3 cloves garlic, minced
- 1 can (14½ ounces) no salt added tomatoes, undrained and chopped
- 1 can (8 ounces) no salt added tomato sauce
- 1 can (6 ounces) no salt added tomato paste
- 1 cup thinly sliced fresh mushrooms
- ¼ cup chopped fresh parsley
- 1 tablespoon red wine vinegar
- 1 teaspoon dried oregano leaves
- 1 teaspoon dried basil leaves
- 1 bay leaf
- ½ teaspoon salt
- ¼ teaspoon crushed red pepper
- 1½ cups lowfat cottage cheese
- 1 cup (4 ounces) shredded low moisture part-skim mozzarella cheese, divided
- 6 lasagna noodles, cooked (without salt or fat) and well drained
- 3 cups chopped broccoli, cooked and well drained
- 1 tablespoon grated Parmesan cheese

1. Heat oven to 350°F. Oil 11¾×7½×2-inch baking dish lightly.

2. Heat 1 tablespoon Crisco® Oil in large saucepan on medium heat. Add onion and garlic. Cook and stir until tender. Stir in tomatoes, tomato sauce, tomato paste, mushrooms, parsley, vinegar, oregano, basil, bay leaf, salt and crushed red pepper. Bring to a boil. Reduce heat to low. Cover. Simmer 30 minutes, stirring occasionally. Remove bay leaf.

3. Combine cottage cheese and ½ cup mozzarella cheese in small bowl. Stir well.

4. Place 2 lasagna noodles in bottom of baking dish. Layer with one cup broccoli, one-third of the tomato sauce and one-third of the cottage cheese mixture. Repeat layers. Cover with foil.

5. Bake at 350°F for 25 minutes. Uncover. Sprinkle with remaining ½ cup mozzarella cheese and Parmesan cheese. Bake, uncovered, 10 minutes or until cheese melts. Let stand 10 minutes before serving.

Nutrients per serving:			
Calories	195	Cholesterol	10 mg
Fat	6 g	Sodium	440 mg

Confetti Scalloped Corn

Makes 6 servings

- 1 egg, beaten
- 1 cup skim milk
- 1 cup coarsely crushed saltine crackers (about 22 two-inch square crackers), divided
- ¼ teaspoon salt
- ⅛ teaspoon pepper
- 1 can (16½ ounces) cream-style corn
- ¼ cup finely chopped onion
- 1 jar (2 ounces) chopped pimiento, drained
- 1 tablespoon CRISCO® Vegetable Oil
- 1 tablespoon chopped fresh parsley

1. Heat oven to 350°F.

2. Combine egg, milk, ⅔ cup cracker crumbs, salt and pepper in medium bowl. Stir in corn, onion and pimiento. Pour into ungreased 1-quart casserole.

3. Combine remaining ⅓ cup cracker crumbs with Crisco® Oil in small bowl. Toss to coat. Sprinkle over corn mixture.

4. Bake at 350°F for one hour or until knife inserted in center comes out clean. Sprinkle with parsley. Let stand 5 to 10 minutes before serving. Garnish, if desired.

Nutrients per serving:			
Calories	155	Cholesterol	40 mg
Fat	5 g	Sodium	485 mg

Broccoli Lasagna

Savory Mashed Potatoes

Makes 6 to 8 servings, 5 cups

1 tablespoon olive oil
1 tablespoon minced garlic
4 cups water
4 medium russet potatoes, peeled and cut into
    quarters (2 to 2¼ pounds)
1 cup DANNON® Plain Nonfat or Lowfat Yogurt
¼ cup milk
¼ cup sliced scallions or green onions
1 teaspoon salt
¼ teaspoon freshly ground pepper

In a large heavy saucepan or Dutch oven heat oil over medium-low heat. Add garlic; cook and stir 1 minute, stirring constantly, until fragrant but not browned. Add water and potatoes. Cover and bring to a boil over high heat. Reduce heat to medium-low and simmer 15 to 20 minutes or until potatoes are very tender. Drain well. Return potatoes to saucepan and mash. Add yogurt and milk and stir until creamy. Stir in scallions, salt and pepper. Serve immediately.

Nutrients per serving:

Calories	110	Cholesterol	trace
Fat	2 g	Sodium	396 mg

Today's Slim Noodles Romanov

Makes 6 to 8 servings

8 ounces uncooked noodles
1 cup low fat yogurt
1 cup low fat (1%) Cottage cheese
¼ cup finely chopped onion
¼ cup chopped fresh parsley
2 tablespoons Worcestershire sauce
½ teaspoon salt
3 drops hot pepper sauce
2 tablespoons grated Wisconsin Parmesan
    cheese

Preheat oven to 350°F. Cook and drain noodles. Mix together all remaining ingredients except Parmesan cheese in large bowl. Fold in cooked noodles. Spoon into buttered 1½-quart casserole and sprinkle with Parmesan cheese. Bake 30 minutes or until heated through. Serve warm.

Nutrients per serving:

Calories	146	Cholesterol	29 mg
Fat	2 g	Sodium	224 mg

Favorite recipe from **Wisconsin Milk Marketing Board** © 1994

Wilted Spinach Mandarin

Wilted Spinach Mandarin

Makes 4 side-dish servings

½ pound fresh spinach
1 tablespoon oil
1 cup bean sprouts
1 can (11 ounces) mandarin oranges, drained
2 tablespoons reduced sodium soy sauce
2 tablespoons orange juice
    Quartered orange slices for garnish

Separate spinach into leaves. Swish in warm water. Repeat several times with fresh warm water to remove sand and grit. Pat dry with paper towels. To remove stems from spinach leaves, fold each leaf in half, then pull stem toward top of leaf. Discard stem. Blot any moisture from leaves with paper towels.

Heat oil in wok or large skillet over medium-high heat until hot. Add spinach, bean sprouts and mandarin oranges; cook and stir 1 to 2 minutes until spinach just wilts. Transfer to serving dish. Heat soy sauce and orange juice in wok; pour over spinach mixture and toss gently to coat. Garnish, if desired. Serve immediately.

Nutrients per serving:

Calories	90	Cholesterol	0 mg
Fat	4 g	Sodium	334 mg

Chutney'd Squash Circles

Chutney'd Squash Circles

Makes 4 side-dish servings

2 acorn squash (1 pound *each*)
2 tablespoons butter or margarine
½ cup prepared chutney
2 tablespoons water
Purple kale and scented geranium leaves for garnish*

Preheat oven to 400°F. Slice tip and stem ends from squash; cut squash crosswise into ¾-inch circles. Scoop out seeds with spoon.

Tear off 18-inch square of heavy aluminum foil. Center foil in 13×9-inch baking dish. Dot foil with butter and place squash on butter, slightly overlapping circles. Spoon chutney over slices and sprinkle with water. Bring foil on long sides of pan together in center, folding over to make tight seam. Crimp ends to form tight seal.

Bake 20 to 30 minutes until squash is fork-tender. Transfer with spatula to warm serving plate. Pour pan liquid over squash. Garnish, if desired. Serve immediately.

**Be sure to use only non-toxic leaves.*

Nutrients per serving:			
Calories	205	Cholesterol	15 mg
Fat	6 g	Sodium	73 mg

Celery and Chick Pea Curry with Apple

Makes 4 servings

1 tablespoon vegetable oil
2 cups diagonally sliced celery
1 cup peeled, cored and sliced tart apple
½ cup chopped onion
2 teaspoons curry powder
1 teaspoon minced garlic
1 can (10½ ounces) chick peas, rinsed and drained
1 can (8 ounces) stewed tomatoes, broken up
3 cups hot cooked brown rice

Heat oil in large skillet over medium-high heat until hot. Add celery, apple, onion, curry powder and garlic; cook about 8 minutes until celery is crisp-tender, stirring occasionally. Stir in chick peas and tomatoes; bring to a boil. Reduce heat and simmer, uncovered, about 5 minutes to allow flavors to blend. Serve over rice.

Nutrients per serving:			
Calories	236	Cholesterol	0 mg
Fat	5 g	Sodium	230 mg

Favorite recipe from **American Celery Council**

Sweet Potato Apple Bake

Makes 6 servings

3 cups mashed cooked sweet potatoes
2 to 3 medium apples, peeled and sliced
Ground cinnamon
½ cup apple jelly

Preheat oven to 350°F. Coat 9-inch glass pie plate or quiche dish with nonstick cooking spray. Spread sweet potatoes evenly in dish. Arrange apple slices on top. Sprinkle apples with cinnamon. Melt apple jelly in small saucepan. Brush over apples to glaze. Bake 30 minutes or until apples are tender.

Nutrients per serving:			
Calories	225	Cholesterol	0 mg
Fat	trace	Sodium	100 mg

Favorite recipe from **Western New York Apple Growers Association**

Garlic Pasta Caliente

Makes 4 servings

1 cup milk
¾ cup water
⅓ cup picante sauce or salsa
1 package (5.0 ounces) UNCLE BEN'S®
    COUNTRY INN RECIPES™ Creamy
    Garlic Pasta
¼ teaspoon ground cumin
1 can (8 ounces) kidney beans, drained *or*
    ¾ cup cooked black beans, rinsed and
    drained
¾ cup frozen whole kernel corn, thawed and
    drained *or* 1 can (about 7 ounces) whole
    kernel corn, drained
1 medium tomato, seeded and chopped
¼ cup sliced green onions
2 tablespoons chopped fresh cilantro or parsley

In large saucepan, combine milk, water, picante
sauce, contents of seasoning pouch and cumin. Stir
well and bring just to a boil. Add pasta and reduce
heat to a simmer. Stirring occasionally, simmer
uncovered for 12 minutes or until pasta is tender.

(Pasta will be saucy.) Stir in all remaining ingredients
except cilantro; heat through, stirring occasionally,
about 2 to 3 minutes. Sprinkle with cilantro to serve.

Nutrients per serving:

Calories	253	Cholesterol	14 mg
Fat	5 g	Sodium	645 mg

Cauliflower with Creamy Chive Sauce

Makes 6 servings

1 head cauliflower, washed
1 cup DANNON® Plain Nonfat or Lowfat Yogurt
1 tablespoon chopped fresh chives *or*
    ½ teaspoon dried chives
1 teaspoon dry mustard

Steam cauliflower, covered, over boiling water 15 to
20 minutes or until tender. In a small bowl combine
yogurt, chives and mustard. Blend well with wire
whisk or fork. Spoon over cooked cauliflower,
allowing steam to heat sauce.

Nutrients per serving:

Calories	40	Cholesterol	trace
Fat	1 g	Sodium	75 mg

Garlic Pasta Caliente

Vegetable Rings on Broccoli Spears

Vegetable Rings on Broccoli Spears

Makes 4 side-dish servings

1 small bunch broccoli (about 12 ounces)
1 red bell pepper
3 (¼-inch-thick) center slices mild white onion
2 tablespoons butter or margarine
½ teaspoon wine vinegar
½ teaspoon dried rosemary leaves, crushed

Trim leaves and tough ends from broccoli stalks. Cut broccoli into spears. Peel stems with vegetable peeler; set aside.

Rinse red pepper under cold running water. Make circular cut around top of pepper with paring knife. Pull stem from pepper and remove stem and seeds. Scrape out any remaining seeds and membrane with spoon. Rinse out pepper under running water; drain well. Thinly slice crosswise through pepper to make rings.

To steam broccoli, place steamer basket in large saucepan; add 1 inch of water. (Water should not touch bottom of basket.) Place spears in steamer. Separate onion slices into rings; place on broccoli. Cover. Bring to a boil over high heat; steam about 8 minutes or until broccoli is crisp-tender.

Uncover; place pepper rings on top. Cover; steam briefly until pepper rings brighten in color but still hold their shape. Remove from heat; transfer vegetables with slotted spoon to warm serving dish. Melt butter in small saucepan over medium heat; stir in vinegar and rosemary. Drizzle evenly over vegetables. Serve immediately.

Nutrients per serving:			
Calories	81	Cholesterol	15 mg
Fat	6 g	Sodium	81 mg

Garden Style Pita

Makes 4 servings

1 tablespoon CRISCO® Vegetable Oil
2 cups diagonally sliced zucchini
    (about ½ pound)
2 cups diagonally sliced yellow squash
    (about ½ pound)
⅛ teaspoon dried basil leaves
⅛ teaspoon salt
⅛ teaspoon pepper
2 tablespoons grated Parmesan cheese
2 (6-inch) whole wheat pita breads, halved
    Boston lettuce leaves

1. Heat Crisco® Oil in large skillet on medium-high heat. Add zucchini and yellow squash. Cook and stir 7 to 8 minutes or until tender. Add basil, salt and pepper. Toss to mix. Remove from heat. Sprinkle with Parmesan cheese.

2. Line pita pocket with lettuce. Spoon about ½ cup vegetable mixture into each pocket.

Nutrients per serving (1 sandwich):			
Calories	150	Cholesterol	0 mg
Fat	5 g	Sodium	290 mg

Savory Bran Rice Pilaf

Makes 6 servings

½ cup uncooked white or brown rice
1 chicken bouillon cube
2 tablespoons margarine
¼ cup chopped onion
½ cup chopped celery
½ cup sliced mushrooms
¼ cup sliced water chestnuts
1 cup KELLOGG'S® ALL-BRAN® cereal
½ teaspoon dried basil leaves
¼ teaspoon ground sage
¼ teaspoon pepper
1 cup water
¼ cup chopped pimientos

1. Cook rice according to package directions, adding bouillon cube and omitting salt and margarine in package directions.

2. While rice is cooking, melt margarine in large skillet. Stir in onion, celery, mushrooms and water chestnuts. Cook over medium heat, stirring occasionally, until celery is crisp-tender.

3. Gently stir in cooked rice, Kellogg's® All-Bran® cereal and remaining ingredients. Cover and cook over low heat about 15 minutes. Serve hot.

Nutrients per serving:			
Calories	140	Cholesterol	0 mg
Fat	4 g	Sodium	410 mg

Italian Capellini and Fresh Tomato

Makes 6 servings

- ½ of a (1-pound) package CREAMETTE® Capellini, uncooked
- 2 cups peeled, seeded and finely chopped fresh tomatoes (about 3 medium)
- 2 tablespoons olive oil
- 1 teaspoon dried basil leaves, crushed
- ½ teaspoon salt
- ½ teaspoon coarsely ground black pepper

Prepare Creamette® Capellini according to package directions; drain. Quickly toss hot cooked pasta with combined remaining ingredients. Serve immediately. Refrigerate leftovers.

Nutrients per serving:

Calories	196	Cholesterol	0 mg
Fat	5 g	Sodium	170 mg

Green Beans with Pine Nuts

Makes 4 servings

- 1 pound green beans, ends removed
- 2 tablespoons margarine
- 2 tablespoons pine nuts
  Salt and black pepper (optional)

Cook beans in 1 inch water in covered 3-quart saucepan 4 to 8 minutes or until crisp-tender; drain. Melt margarine in large skillet over medium heat. Add pine nuts; cook, stirring frequently, until golden. Add beans; stir gently to coat beans with margarine. Season with salt and pepper to taste.

Nutrients per serving:

Calories	127	Cholesterol	0 mg
Fat	10 g	Sodium	1 mg

Green Beans with Pine Nuts

Linguine Primavera

Makes 8 servings

- 2 tablespoons FLEISCHMANN'S® Margarine
- 2 cups coarsely chopped broccoli
- 1 cup julienned carrot strips
- 1 medium onion, cut into wedges
- 1 teaspoon Italian seasoning
- 2 cloves garlic, crushed
- ¼ teaspoon ground black pepper
- 1 large tomato, coarsely chopped
- 1 pound linguine, cooked in unsalted water and drained
- 1 (8-ounce) carton EGG BEATERS® 99% Real Egg Product
- ¼ cup grated Parmesan cheese

Melt margarine in large skillet over medium heat. Add broccoli, carrots, onion, Italian seasoning, garlic and pepper. Cook for 3 minutes, stirring occasionally. Add tomato; cook for 1 minute more or until vegetables are tender-crisp. Toss with hot linguine, Egg Beaters® and cheese. Garnish as desired and serve immediately.

To Microwave: In 2-quart microwavable bowl, combine margarine, broccoli, carrots, onion, Italian seasoning, garlic and pepper; cover. Microwave at HIGH (100% power) for 4 minutes, stirring after 2 minutes. Add tomato; re-cover. Microwave at HIGH for 2 to 3 minutes, stirring after 1½ minutes. Toss with hot linguine, Egg Beaters® and cheese. Garnish as desired and serve immediately.

Nutrients per serving:

Calories	281	Cholesterol	2 mg
Fat	5 g	Sodium	134 mg

Vegetable Stir-Fry

Makes 4 servings

- 1 tablespoon vegetable oil
- 3 or 4 carrots, diagonally sliced
- 2 zucchini, diagonally sliced
- 3 tablespoons orange juice
  Salt and black pepper (optional)

Heat oil in medium skillet or wok over medium heat. Add carrots; stir-fry 3 minutes.

Add zucchini and orange juice; stir-fry 4 minutes or until vegetables are crisp-tender. Season with salt and pepper, if desired.

Nutrients per serving:

Calories	68	Cholesterol	0 mg
Fat	4 g	Sodium	20 mg

Zucchini and Carrots au Gratin

Makes 4 to 6 servings

¼ cup HELLMANN'S® or BEST FOODS®
   Light Reduced Calorie Mayonnaise
¼ cup minced onion
2 tablespoons flour
1 tablespoon chopped fresh parsley
¾ teaspoon salt
¼ teaspoon dried Italian seasoning
   Dash freshly ground black pepper
1 cup low-fat milk
3 medium carrots, sliced, cooked and drained
2 medium zucchini, sliced, cooked and drained
½ cup fresh bread crumbs
¼ cup grated Parmesan cheese
1 tablespoon MAZOLA® Margarine, melted

In 1-quart saucepan combine mayonnaise, onion, flour, parsley, salt, Italian seasoning and pepper. Cook over medium heat 1 minute, stirring constantly. Gradually stir in milk until smooth; cook until thick, stirring constantly (*do not boil*). In medium bowl combine carrots and zucchini. Add sauce; toss to coat well. Spoon into shallow 1-quart broilerproof casserole dish. In small bowl combine bread crumbs, Parmesan and margarine; sprinkle over vegetables. Broil, 6 inches from heat source, for 3 minutes or until golden.

Nutrients per serving:

Calories	134	Cholesterol	12 mg
Fat	7 g	Sodium	420 mg

Antipasto Rice

Makes 8 servings

1½ cups water
 ½ cup tomato juice
 1 cup uncooked rice*
 1 teaspoon dried basil leaves, crushed
 1 teaspoon dried oregano leaves, crushed
 ½ teaspoon salt (optional)
 1 can (14 ounces) artichoke hearts, drained and
   quartered
 1 jar (7 ounces) roasted red peppers, drained
   and chopped
 1 can (2¼ ounces) sliced ripe olives, drained
 2 tablespoons snipped fresh parsley
 2 tablespoons lemon juice
 ½ teaspoon ground black pepper
 2 tablespoons grated Parmesan cheese

Antipasto Rice

Combine water, tomato juice, rice, basil, oregano, and salt in 2- to 3-quart saucepan. Bring to a boil; stir once or twice. Reduce heat to low; cover and simmer 15 minutes or until rice is tender and liquid is absorbed. Stir in artichokes, red peppers, olives, parsley, lemon juice, and black pepper. Cook 5 minutes longer or until thoroughly heated. Sprinkle with cheese. Garnish as desired.

To Microwave: Combine water, tomato juice, rice, basil, oregano, and salt in deep 2- to 3-quart microproof baking dish. Cover and cook on HIGH (100% power) 5 minutes. Reduce setting to MEDIUM (50% power) and cook 15 minutes or until rice is tender and liquid is absorbed. Add artichokes, red peppers, olives, parsley, lemon juice, and black pepper. Cook on HIGH 2 to 3 minutes or until mixture is thoroughly heated. Sprinkle with cheese. Garnish as desired.

*Recipe based on regular-milled long grain white rice. For medium grain rice, use 1¼ cups water and cook for 15 minutes. For parboiled rice, use 1¾ cups water and cook for 20 to 25 minutes. For brown rice, use 1¾ cups water and cook for 45 to 50 minutes.

Nutrients per serving:

Calories	131	Cholesterol	1 mg
Fat	2 g	Sodium	522 mg

Favorite recipe from **USA Rice Council**

Cob Corn in Barbecue Butter

Cob Corn in Barbecue Butter

Makes 4 side-dish servings

    4 ears fresh corn
    2 tablespoons butter or margarine, softened
    ½ teaspoon dry barbecue seasoning
    ¼ teaspoon salt
      Cherry tomato wedges and Italian parsley for
        garnish

To shuck corn, pull outer husks down each ear to base. Snap off husks and stem at base. Strip away silk from corn by hand. Remove any remaining silk with dry vegetable brush. Trim any blemishes from corn and rinse under cold running water.

Pour 1 inch of water into large saucepan or skillet. (Do *not* add salt, as it will make corn tough.) Bring to a boil over medium-high heat. Add ears; cover. Cook 4 to 7 minutes until kernels are slightly crisp when pierced with fork.*

Remove corn with tongs to warm serving platter. Blend butter, barbecue seasoning and salt in small bowl until smooth. Serve immediately with corn. Garnish, if desired.

Length of cooking time depends on size and age of corn.

Nutrients per serving:			
Calories	188	Cholesterol	15 mg
Fat	7 g	Sodium	213 mg

Oven French Fries

Makes 6 servings

    4 medium potatoes
    1 tablespoon CRISCO® Vegetable Oil
    ½ teaspoon celery salt
    ⅛ teaspoon garlic powder
    ⅛ teaspoon pepper
    ⅛ teaspoon paprika

1. Heat oven to 425°F.

2. Peel potatoes. Cut into long ½-inch-wide strips. Dry with paper towels. Place in large bowl. Add Crisco® Oil. Toss to coat. Place potatoes in single layer on baking sheet.

3. Combine celery salt, garlic powder, pepper and paprika in small bowl. Sprinkle potatoes with half of seasoning mixture. Turn potatoes over. Sprinkle with remaining seasoning mixture.

4. Bake at 425°F for 25 to 30 minutes or until potatoes are tender and evenly browned, turning occasionally.

Nutrients per serving:			
Calories	80	Cholesterol	0 mg
Fat	2 g	Sodium	95 mg

Chunky Vegetable Sauté

Makes 4 to 6 servings

    1 clove garlic, minced
    2 tablespoons vegetable oil
    1 small onion, cut into 8 wedges
    1 teaspoon dried basil leaves, crushed
    ⅛ teaspoon salt
    ⅛ teaspoon black pepper
    1 medium red bell pepper, cut into 1½×¼-inch
        strips
    1 medium zucchini, cut into ½-inch chunks
        (about 2 cups)
    6 small fresh mushrooms, quartered (about
        1½ cups)
    1½ tablespoons HEINZ® Worcestershire Sauce

In large skillet, cook and stir garlic in oil 30 seconds. Stir in onion, basil, salt and black pepper; heat 1 minute. Add red bell pepper, zucchini and mushrooms; cook and stir 5 minutes or until crisp-tender, stirring frequently. Add Worcestershire sauce, stirring to coat vegetables. Serve immediately.

Nutrients per serving:			
Calories	90	Cholesterol	0 mg
Fat	7 g	Sodium	130 mg

Apple & Carrot Casserole

Makes 6 servings

- 6 large carrots, peeled and sliced
- 4 large apples, peeled and sliced
- 5 tablespoons all-purpose flour
- 1 tablespoon brown sugar
- ½ teaspoon ground nutmeg
- 1 tablespoon margarine, sliced
- ½ cup orange juice
- ½ teaspoon salt (optional)

Preheat oven to 350°F. Cook carrots in boiling water 5 minutes or until tender; drain. Layer carrots and apples in large casserole. Mix flour, brown sugar and nutmeg in small bowl; sprinkle over carrots and apples. Dot with margarine; add orange juice and sprinkle with salt, if desired. Bake 30 minutes or until apples are tender.

Nutrients per serving:			
Calories	137	Cholesterol	0 mg
Fat	2 g	Sodium	49 mg

Favorite recipe from **Western New York Apple Growers Association**

Zesty Fresh Nectarine Coconut Chutney

Makes 7 servings, 3½ cups

- 3 cups diced Chilean nectarines, about 3 small (¾ pound)
- ⅓ cup thinly sliced green onions
- ¼ cup shredded coconut
- 1 clove garlic, minced
- 1 tablespoon lemon juice
- 1 tablespoon sugar
- ⅛ teaspoon ground cumin
- ⅛ teaspoon salt
  Pinch ground red pepper

Combine all ingredients in medium bowl; toss well. Cover and refrigerate at least 3 hours.

Tip: *Tangy fruit chutneys are perfect complements to grilled poultry, pork or fish.*

Nutrients per serving (½ cup chutney):			
Calories	47	Cholesterol	0 mg
Fat	1 g	Sodium	44 mg

Favorite recipe from **Chilean Fresh Fruit Association**

Frenched Beans with Celery

Makes 6 side-dish servings

- ¾ pound fresh green beans
- 2 ribs celery
- 2 tablespoons butter, melted
- 2 tablespoons toasted sunflower seeds*
  Celery leaves and carrot slices for garnish

Place beans in colander; rinse well. Snap off stem end from each bean. Slice beans lengthwise on cutting board; set aside.

To prepare celery, trim stem ends and leaves from ribs. Reserve leaves for garnish, if desired. Slice celery thinly on the diagonal.

Bring 1 inch of water in 2-quart saucepan to a boil over high heat. Add beans and celery. Cover; reduce heat to medium-low. Simmer 8 minutes or until beans are crisp-tender; drain.

Toss beans and celery with butter. Transfer to warm serving dish. Sprinkle with sunflower seeds. Garnish, if desired. Serve immediately.

*To toast sunflower seeds, *heat ½ teaspoon oil in small skillet over medium heat. Add shelled sunflower seeds; cook and stir 3 minutes or until lightly browned, shaking pan constantly. Remove with slotted spoon to paper towels.*

Nutrients per serving:			
Calories	70	Cholesterol	10 mg
Fat	5 g	Sodium	41 mg

Frenched Beans with Celery

Asparagus Wreath

Makes 4 side-dish servings

1 pound fresh asparagus
1 tablespoon butter or margarine
1 teaspoon lemon juice
6 thin slices pepperoni, finely chopped
¼ cup seasoned dry bread crumbs
   Pimiento strips for garnish

To prepare asparagus, snap off tough ends of spears where they break easily. Peel stem ends with vegetable peeler.

To steam asparagus, rinse asparagus and place in steamer basket. Place steamer basket in large saucepan; add 1 inch of water. (Water should not touch bottom of basket.) Cover. Bring to a boil over high heat; steam asparagus 5 to 8 minutes until crisp-tender.

Remove spears from basket and make wreath of spears on warm, round serving platter. Melt butter with lemon juice in small saucepan over medium heat; pour over asparagus. Combine chopped pepperoni and bread crumbs in small bowl; sprinkle over asparagus. Garnish, if desired. Serve immediately.

Nutrients per serving:

Calories	116	Cholesterol	14 mg
Fat	7 g	Sodium	247 mg

Summer Vegetable Paella

Makes 6 servings

1 teaspoon vegetable or olive oil
3 cups broccoli flowerets
2 zucchini, diagonally sliced
1 tomato, diced
2 fresh California nectarines, sliced (about 2 cups)

Heat oil in large nonstick skillet over medium-high heat. Add broccoli and zucchini; stir-fry 5 minutes or until vegetables are crisp-tender. Add tomato and nectarines; cover and cook 2 to 3 minutes until heated through. Serve immediately.

Nutrients per serving:

Calories	54	Cholesterol	0 mg
Fat	2 g	Sodium	9 mg

Favorite recipe from **California Tree Fruit Agreement**

Sweet Citrus Celery

Makes 4 servings, 4 cups

1 tablespoon vegetable oil
4 cups diagonally sliced celery
1 cup diced red bell pepper
1 cup green onion pieces (each 1 inch long)
1 tablespoon grated fresh ginger *or* ¾ teaspoon ground ginger
½ cup orange juice.
1 teaspoon cornstarch
1 tablespoon light brown sugar
½ teaspoon salt (optional)
2 cups hot cooked rice

Heat oil in large nonstick skillet over medium-high heat until hot; add celery, bell pepper, green onions and ginger. Cook and stir about 5 minutes or until celery is almost crisp-tender. Combine orange juice, cornstarch, brown sugar and salt in measuring cup. Stir into vegetable mixture. Cook and stir until mixture thickens and boils. Boil 1 minute longer, stirring constantly. Serve immediately over hot rice.

Nutrients per serving (1 cup):

Calories	230	Cholesterol	0 mg
Fat	4 g	Sodium	113 mg

Favorite recipe from **American Celery Council**

Creamed Peas

Makes 4 servings

1 cup DANNON® Plain Nonfat or Lowfat Yogurt
2 tablespoons all-purpose flour
2 tablespoons finely chopped fresh dill weed *or* 1 teaspoon dried dill weed
1 jar (2 ounces) diced pimiento, drained
½ teaspoon salt
¼ teaspoon pepper
1½ cups fresh or frozen English peas
3 tablespoons chicken broth

In a small bowl combine yogurt, flour, dill weed, pimiento, salt and pepper; stir until smooth. Set aside.

In a small saucepan combine peas and broth; cover and bring to a boil. Reduce heat and simmer 5 minutes or until peas are tender. Stir in yogurt mixture; cook over low heat until thickened, stirring constantly.

Nutrients per serving:

Calories	90	Cholesterol	trace
Fat	0 g	Sodium	377 mg

Asparagus Wreath

Light & Easy Cheese Sauce

Makes about 1¾ cups

1 (8-ounce) package BORDEN® Lite-line®
Process Cheese Product,* any flavor, each
slice cut into quarters
1 cup BORDEN® Lite-line® or Viva® Protein
Fortified Skim Milk
Ground red pepper (optional)

In medium saucepan, combine ingredients. Over medium heat, cook and stir until cheese product melts. Serve warm over fresh or steamed vegetables, pasta, baked potatoes or LaFamous® Tortilla Chips.

*"½ the calories"–8% milkfat product

Nutrients per serving (1 tablespoon sauce):

Calories	18	Cholesterol	2 mg
Fat	trace	Sodium	110 mg

Vegetables Italiano

Makes 8 servings

1 cup Italian seasoned bread crumbs
⅓ cup grated Parmesan cheese
⅔ cup HELLMANN'S® or BEST FOODS®
Light Reduced Calorie Mayonnaise
6 cups assorted vegetables: broccoli florets,
carrot slices, cauliflower florets, small
mushrooms, green and/or red bell pepper
strips, yellow squash slices and/or zucchini
strips

Vegetables Italiano

Preheat oven to 425°F. In large plastic food storage bag combine crumbs and Parmesan; shake to blend well. In another large plastic food storage bag combine mayonnaise and vegetables; shake to coat well. Add mayonnaise-coated vegetables, half at a time, to crumb mixture; shake to coat well. Arrange in single layer on ungreased cookie sheet so that pieces do not touch. Bake 10 minutes or until golden.

Nutrients per serving:

Calories	119	Cholesterol	6 mg
Fat	5 g	Sodium	258 mg

Macaroni Relleno

Makes 6 to 8 servings

1 (7-ounce) package CREAMETTES® Elbow
Macaroni
1 egg
½ cup skim milk
¼ teaspoon ground cumin
1 (4-ounce) can chopped green chilies, drained
1 (4-ounce) can diced pimentos, drained
Nonstick cooking spray
1 (15-ounce) can pinto beans, heated and
drained
1 cup (4 ounces) shredded Monterey Jack cheese
1 medium tomato, peeled, seeded and chopped
1 medium green bell pepper, chopped
¼ cup sliced green onions

Prepare Creamettes® Elbow Macaroni according to package directions; drain. In medium bowl, blend egg, milk and cumin; stir in hot cooked macaroni, chilies and pimento. Spray 9-inch nonstick skillet with nonstick cooking spray; heat skillet. Add macaroni mixture. Cover; cook over low heat until mixture is set, about 15 minutes. Loosen edge with rubber spatula and invert onto warm platter. Top with remaining ingredients. Let stand 5 minutes before serving. Refrigerate leftovers.

Note: *To reduce sodium, rinse and drain chilies, pimentos and pinto beans; reheat beans in a small amount of water.*

Nutrients per serving:

Calories	260	Cholesterol	135 mg
Fat	6 g	Sodium	96 mg

Almond Brown Rice Stuffing

Almond Brown Rice Stuffing

Makes 6 servings

⅓ cup slivered almonds
2 teaspoons margarine
2 medium tart apples, cored and diced
½ cup chopped onion
½ cup chopped celery
½ teaspoon poultry seasoning
¼ teaspoon dried thyme leaves, crushed
¼ teaspoon ground white pepper
3 cups cooked brown rice (cooked in chicken broth)

Cook and stir almonds in margarine in large skillet over medium-high heat until brown. Add apples, onion, celery, poultry seasoning, thyme, and pepper; cook and stir until vegetables are tender-crisp. Add rice; cook and stir until thoroughly heated. Serve or use as stuffing for poultry or pork roast. Stuffing may be baked in covered baking dish at 375°F for 15 to 20 minutes.

To Microwave: Combine almonds and margarine in 2- to 3-quart microproof baking dish. Cook on HIGH (100% power) 2 to 3 minutes or until browned. Add apples, onion, celery, poultry seasoning, thyme, and pepper. Cover with waxed paper and cook on HIGH 2 minutes. Stir in rice; cook on HIGH 2 to 3 minutes, stirring after 1½ minutes, or until thoroughly heated. Serve as above.

Variations: *For Mushroom Stuffing, add 2 cups (about 8 ounces) sliced mushrooms; cook with apples, onion, celery, and seasonings. For Raisin Stuffing, add ½ cup raisins; cook with apples, onion, celery, and seasonings.*

Nutrients per serving:

Calories	198	Cholesterol	0 mg
Fat	6 g	Sodium	30 mg

Favorite recipe from USA Rice Council

Pasta Delight

Pasta Delight

Makes 4 to 6 servings

1 medium zucchini, sliced
1 tablespoon olive oil
2 tablespoons chopped shallots
2 cloves garlic, chopped
1 medium tomato, diced
2 tablespoons chopped fresh basil *or*
   ½ teaspoon dried basil leaves, crushed
2 tablespoons grated Parmesan cheese
12 ounces uncooked penne pasta, hot cooked
   and drained

Cook and stir zucchini in hot oil in large skillet over medium-high heat. Reduce heat to medium. Add shallots and garlic; cook and stir 1 minute. Add tomato; cook and stir 45 seconds. Add basil and cheese. Pour vegetable mixture over penne in large bowl; toss gently to mix.

Nutrients per serving:

Calories	237	Cholesterol	51 mg
Fat	5 g	Sodium	51 mg

Favorite recipe from **National Pasta Association**

Vegetable Stuffed Potatoes

Makes 4 servings

1 cup julienned carrots
1 cup thinly sliced green or red bell peppers
¼ teaspoon Italian seasoning
1 tablespoon FLEISCHMANN'S® Margarine
1 cup julienned zucchini
4 (8-ounce) potatoes, hot baked
2 ounces low-fat Monterey Jack cheese,
   shredded

In large skillet over medium-high heat, cook and stir carrots, peppers and Italian seasoning in margarine until vegetables are tender-crisp. Add zucchini; cook and stir until tender, about 1 minute. Carefully cut lengthwise or pierce tops of potatoes and push ends to open. Spoon vegetable mixture into potatoes evenly; top with cheese. Bake at 375°F for 5 minutes or until cheese melts.

Nutrients per serving:

Calories	255	Cholesterol	10 mg
Fat	6 g	Sodium	142 mg

Glazed Stir-Fry Holiday Vegetables

Makes 6 servings, 3 cups

2 tablespoons sugar
½ teaspoon grated lemon peel
3 tablespoons fresh lemon juice (1 lemon)
1 tablespoon low-sodium soy sauce
2 teaspoons cornstarch
½ cup water
4 teaspoons vegetable oil
3 cups fresh broccoli florets
1 medium red bell pepper, cut into 1-inch pieces
1 cup peeled, julienne-cut jicama
   Lemon zest (slivers of lemon peel)

In small bowl combine sugar, lemon peel, lemon juice, soy sauce and cornstarch. Stir in water; set aside.

Heat oil in large nonstick skillet. Add broccoli and pepper and stir-fry over high heat 2 minutes. Add jicama and stir-fry 1 to 2 minutes or until vegetables are crisp-tender, adding additional oil, if necessary. Pour lemon mixture over vegetables and continue cooking just until glaze thickens. Toss vegetables to coat thoroughly with glaze. Garnish with lemon zest.

Nutrients per serving (½ cup):

Calories	95	Cholesterol	0 mg
Fat	3 g	Sodium	72 mg

Favorite recipe from **The Sugar Association, Inc.**

Sweet and Sour Red Cabbage

Makes 6 servings

1 small head red cabbage (1 pound), shredded
1 medium unpeeled apple, cored and shredded
1 small potato, peeled and shredded
1 small onion, chopped
   Grated peel of ½ SUNKIST® Lemon
   Juice of 1 SUNKIST® Lemon
3 tablespoons firmly packed brown sugar
1 tablespoon red wine vinegar

In large covered nonstick skillet, cook cabbage, apple, potato and onion in 1 cup water over low heat for 15 minutes; stir occasionally. Add remaining ingredients. Cover; cook over low heat an additional 10 minutes, stirring often, until vegetables are tender and mixture thickens slightly.

Nutrients per serving (¾ cup):

Calories	74	Cholesterol	0 mg
Fat	0 g	Sodium	11 mg

Tabbouleh in Tomato Cups

Makes 4 main-dish or 8 side-dish servings

4 large firm, ripe tomatoes (about 8 ounces each)
4 green onions with tops
2 tablespoons olive oil
1 cup bulgur wheat
1 cup water
2 tablespoons lemon juice
1 tablespoon chopped fresh mint leaves *or*
    ½ teaspoon dried mint leaves, crushed
Salt and pepper to taste
Lemon peel and mint leaves for garnish

To prepare tomato cups, remove stems. Cut tomatoes in half crosswise. Carefully loosen pulp from shell with spoon. Scoop pulp and seeds out of tomatoes into medium bowl, leaving shells intact. Invert tomatoes on paper-towel-lined plate; let drain 20 minutes. Meanwhile, chop tomato pulp. Set aside.

Trim off green onions at root ends. Clean onions thoroughly. Thinly slice green onion tops on the diagonal with utility knife; set aside. Thinly slice white parts of onions on the diagonal.

Heat oil in 2-quart saucepan over medium-high heat. Cook and stir white parts of onions in hot oil 1 to 2 minutes until wilted. Add bulgur; cook 3 to 5 minutes until browned.

Tabbouleh in Tomato Cups

America's Choice

Add reserved tomato pulp, water, lemon juice and mint to bulgur mixture. Bring to a boil over high heat; reduce heat to medium-low. Cover; simmer gently 15 to 20 minutes until liquid is absorbed.

Set aside a few sliced green onion tops for garnish; stir remaining green onions into bulgur mixture. Add salt and pepper. Spoon mixture into tomato cups.*

Preheat oven to 400°F. Place filled cups in 13×9-inch baking dish; bake 15 minutes or until heated through. Top with reserved onion tops. Garnish, if desired. Serve immediately.

*Tomato cups may be covered and refrigerated at this point up to 24 hours.

Nutrients per serving:

Calories	231	Cholesterol	0 mg
Fat	8 g	Sodium	27 mg

Beans and Rice Vegetable Medley

Makes 6 servings

1½ teaspoons CRISCO® Vegetable Oil
⅓ cup chopped celery
⅓ cup chopped onion
⅓ cup chopped green bell pepper
¼ cup chopped fresh tomato
1 can (15½ ounces) kidney beans, drained
3½ cups water
1 teaspoon salt
½ to 1 teaspoon black pepper
½ teaspoon dried thyme leaves
1½ cups uncooked brown rice

1. Heat Crisco® Oil in large saucepan on medium heat. Add celery, onion and green pepper. Cook and stir 2 to 3 minutes or until crisp-tender. Stir in tomato. Cook and stir until tomato is softened.

2. Add beans, water, salt, black pepper and thyme. Bring to a boil. Stir in rice. Return to a boil. Reduce heat to low. Cover. Simmer 45 to 55 minutes or until rice is tender and water is absorbed, stirring in additional water as needed.

Nutrients per serving:

Calories	265	Cholesterol	0 mg
Fat	3 g	Sodium	370 mg

Southern Style Succotash

Makes 10 servings

1 tablespoon margarine, melted
1½ teaspoons Worcestershire sauce
1 teaspoon lemon juice
½ teaspoon ground red pepper, divided
3 cups KELLOGG'S® CORN FLAKES® cereal
  Vegetable cooking spray
½ cup chopped onion
⅓ cup chopped green bell pepper
1 clove garlic, chopped
1 can (28 ounces) stewed tomatoes, drained, no
  salt added
1 can (8 ounces) tomato sauce, no salt added
2 tablespoons dried parsley flakes
1 package (1 pound) frozen cut okra, thawed
1 package (10 ounces) frozen whole kernel
  corn, thawed

1. Stir margarine, Worcestershire sauce, lemon juice and ¼ teaspoon red pepper in large skillet over medium heat. Add Kellogg's® Corn Flakes® cereal. Stir gently until cereal becomes lightly browned and crisp. Set aside for topping.

2. In large skillet coated with vegetable cooking spray, cook and stir onion, green pepper and garlic over medium-low heat. Add tomatoes, tomato sauce, parsley and remaining ¼ teaspoon red pepper; stir to combine. Add okra and corn. Stir occasionally until okra is tender. Sprinkle with reserved topping just before serving. Serve hot.

Nutrients per serving:

Calories	110	Cholesterol	0 mg
Fat	2 g	Sodium	120 mg

Microwave Sweet Potato Chips

Makes 4 servings, 2 cups

2 cups sliced sweet potatoes
1 tablespoon brown sugar
2 teaspoons butter

To Microwave: Spread sweet potatoes in single layer in microwave-safe dish. Sprinkle lightly with water. Microwave on HIGH (100% power) 5 minutes. Add brown sugar and butter; toss gently to coat. Spread potatoes out evenly. Microwave 2 to 3 minutes more. Cool slightly before serving.

Nutrients per serving (½ cup):

Calories	59	Cholesterol	5 mg
Fat	2 g	Sodium	21 mg

Favorite recipe from **The Sugar Association, Inc.**

Peas with Cukes 'n' Dill

Peas with Cukes 'n' Dill

Makes 4 side-dish servings

2 pounds fresh peas*
½ medium cucumber, peeled
2 tablespoons butter or margarine
1 teaspoon dried dill weed
  Salt and pepper to taste
  Fresh dill, pineapple sage leaves and edible
    flowers, such as pansies, for garnish

To prepare peas, press each pea pod between thumbs and forefingers to open. Push peas out of each pod into colander with thumb; discard pods. Rinse peas under running water. Drain well; set aside.

Cut cucumber in half lengthwise. Scrape out seeds with spoon and discard. Cut cucumber halves into ¼-inch-thick slices.

Heat butter in medium skillet over medium-high heat until melted and bubbly. Cook and stir peas and cucumber in hot butter 5 minutes or until vegetables are crisp-tender. Stir in dill weed and season with salt and pepper. Transfer to warm serving dish. Garnish, if desired. Serve immediately.

**Or, substitute 1 package (10 ounces) frozen peas, thawed, for fresh peas.*

Nutrients per serving:

Calories	237	Cholesterol	15 mg
Fat	6 g	Sodium	66 mg

Yes, it is possible to have your cake—and eat it too! These light and luscious recipes include moist, tender layer cakes, melt-in-your-mouth pound cakes and rich, creamy cheesecakes. For a fit finale at your next special occasion, Chocolate Cherry Delight Cake is sure to steal the show!

Chocolate Cherry Delight Cake

Makes 12 servings

1 cup sugar
1 cup all-purpose flour
⅓ cup HERSHEY'S Cocoa
¾ teaspoon baking soda
¾ teaspoon baking powder
    Dash salt
½ cup skim milk
¼ cup frozen egg substitute, thawed
¼ cup vegetable oil
1 teaspoon vanilla extract
½ cup boiling water
    Whipped Topping (recipe follows)
1 can (20 ounces) lower calorie cherry pie
    filling, chilled

Heat oven to 350°F. Line bottom of two 9-inch round pans with waxed paper.

In large mixer bowl, combine sugar, flour, cocoa, baking soda, baking powder and salt. Add milk, egg substitute, oil and vanilla; beat on medium speed 2 minutes. Remove from mixer; stir in boiling water (batter will be thin). Pour into prepared pans. Bake 18 to 22 minutes or until wooden toothpick inserted in centers comes out clean. Cool 10 minutes; remove from pans to wire racks. Carefully remove waxed paper. Cool completely.

To assemble dessert, place one cake layer on serving plate. Spread with half of Whipped Topping; top with half of pie filling. Top with second layer. Spread with remaining topping and pie filling. Refrigerate at least 1 hour.

Whipped Topping: In small, deep, narrow-bottom bowl, blend ½ cup cold skim milk, ½ teaspoon vanilla extract and 1 envelope whipped topping mix (to yield 2 cups). Whip at high speed with electric mixer until topping peaks, about 2 minutes. Continue beating 2 minutes longer until topping is light and fluffy.

Nutrients per serving:			
Calories	180	Cholesterol	0 mg
Fat	5 g	Sodium	115 mg

Lemon Poppy Seed Cake

Makes 16 servings

Cake
1 package DUNCAN HINES® Moist Deluxe
    Lemon Supreme Cake Mix
3 egg whites
1¼ cups water
⅓ cup CRISCO® PURITAN® Oil
3 tablespoons poppy seeds

Glaze
1 cup confectioners sugar
3 to 4 teaspoons lemon juice

1. Preheat oven to 350°F. Grease and flour 10-inch Bundt® pan.

2. For Cake, combine cake mix, egg whites, water, oil and poppy seeds in large bowl. Prepare, bake and cool cake following package directions for No Cholesterol recipe.

3. For Glaze, combine sugar and lemon juice in small bowl. Stir until well blended. Drizzle over top of cake.

Nutrients per serving:			
Calories	207	Cholesterol	0 mg
Fat	8 g	Sodium	221 mg

Chocolate Cherry Delight Cake

Danish Orange Loaves

Makes 2 loaves, 12 slices each

Cake
- 1 package DUNCAN HINES® Moist Deluxe Orange Supreme Cake Mix
- 1 package (4-serving size) vanilla instant pudding and pie filling mix
- 4 eggs
- 1 cup dairy sour cream
- ⅓ cup CRISCO® PURITAN® Oil

Frosting
- 2¼ cups confectioners sugar
- 3 tablespoons butter or margarine, melted
- 2 to 3 tablespoons orange juice
- 1 tablespoon grated orange peel

1. Preheat oven to 350°F. Grease and flour two 9×5×3-inch loaf pans.

2. For Cake, combine cake mix, pudding mix, eggs, sour cream and Crisco® Puritan® Oil in large bowl. Beat at medium speed with electric mixer for 3 minutes. Pour batter into pans. Bake at 350°F for 50 to 60 minutes or until wooden toothpick inserted in centers comes out clean. Cool in pans 15 minutes. Loosen loaves from pans. Invert onto cooling racks. Turn right side up. Cool completely.

3. For Frosting, combine confectioners sugar, melted butter and 1 tablespoon orange juice in small bowl. Beat at low speed with electric mixer until blended.

Add remaining juice, 1 teaspoon at a time, until frosting is of spreading consistency. Fold in orange peel. Spread frosting over cooled loaves. Garnish as desired.

Tip: *This recipe may also be baked in a 10-inch Bundt® pan or tube pan for 50 to 60 minutes or until wooden toothpick inserted in center of cake comes out clean.*

Nutrients per serving (1 slice):

Calories	212	Cholesterol	44 mg
Fat	9 g	Sodium	184 mg

Apple-Cinnamon Pecan Cake

Makes 24 servings

- 2 cups all-purpose flour
- 2 teaspoons baking powder
- 1 teaspoon ground cinnamon
- ½ teaspoon ground nutmeg
- ½ cup margarine, softened
- 1 cup granulated sugar
- 2 eggs
- 1 teaspoon vanilla extract
- ⅔ cup *undiluted* CARNATION® Evaporated Lowfat Milk
- 3 cups peeled and finely diced or shredded baking apples (about 2 large)
- ¾ cup (3 ounces) chopped pecans
- 2 tablespoons powdered sugar

Preheat oven to 350°F. In medium bowl, combine flour, baking powder, cinnamon and nutmeg; set aside. In large mixer bowl, cream margarine and granulated sugar; beat in eggs and vanilla. With mixer at low speed, alternately add flour mixture and evaporated lowfat milk, ending with flour mixture. Stir in apples and pecans. Spread batter evenly into lightly greased 13×9-inch baking pan. Bake 40 to 45 minutes or until wooden pick inserted in center comes out clean. Cool 20 minutes. Sift powdered sugar over top. Cool completely before cutting.

Note: *Apples may be shredded by hand or in food processor.*

Nutrients per serving:

Calories	155	Cholesterol	19 mg
Fat	7 g	Sodium	95 mg

Danish Orange Loaf

Rich Chocolate Cake with Raspberry Sauce

Makes 16 servings

2 cups frozen raspberries in syrup, thawed, puréed and strained
2 tablespoons cornstarch
2 cups all-purpose flour
1⅓ cups skim milk
1 cup sugar
⅔ cup FLEISCHMANN'S® Margarine, softened
1 (8-ounce) container EGG BEATERS® 99% Real Egg Product
⅔ cup unsweetened cocoa
1½ teaspoons DAVIS® Baking Powder
1½ teaspoons vanilla extract
½ teaspoon baking soda

In small saucepan, over medium-high heat, cook raspberries and cornstarch, stirring constantly until mixture thickens and begins to boil. Cool; refrigerate.

In large bowl, with electric mixer at low speed, mix flour, milk, sugar, margarine, Egg Beaters®, cocoa, baking powder, vanilla and baking soda just until blended. Beat at high speed for 3 minutes. Spread batter in greased and cocoa-dusted 13×9×2-inch baking pan. Bake at 350°F for 30 to 35 minutes or until wooden toothpick inserted in center comes out clean. Cool in pan 10 minutes. Remove from pan; cool on wire rack. Cut into 16 pieces. Garnish as desired and serve topped with raspberry sauce.

Nutrients per serving:

Calories	232	Cholesterol	0 mg
Fat	8 g	Sodium	161 mg

Strawberry Ice Cream Cake

Makes 12 to 16 servings

1 package DUNCAN HINES® Moist Deluxe Strawberry Supreme Cake Mix

Rum Syrup
⅓ cup boiling water
⅓ cup sugar
⅓ cup cold water
¼ cup dark rum

Filling and Frosting
1 pint strawberry ice cream, softened
1 container (8 ounces) frozen whipped topping, thawed
Fresh strawberries, for garnish

Strawberry Ice Cream Cake

1. Preheat oven to 350°F. Grease and flour two 9-inch round cake pans. Prepare, bake and cool cake following package directions.

2. For Rum Syrup, stir boiling water into sugar in medium bowl. Stir until sugar is dissolved. Add cold water and rum. Cool.

3. Place cake layers on cooling racks in jelly-roll pan. Spoon ½ cup rum syrup evenly over each layer. Freeze 2 hours or until cake layers are firm.

4. For Filling and Frosting, place one cake layer on serving plate. Spread softened ice cream to edges. Place second layer on top of ice cream. Freeze assembled cake until ice cream is firm.

5. Frost sides and top of cake with whipped topping. Garnish with fresh strawberries, if desired. Store in freezer until ready to serve.

Tip: Allow cake to stand at room temperature 10 to 15 minutes before serving. For easiest cutting, use a knife with a thin sharp blade.

Nutrients per serving:

Calories	232	Cholesterol	7 mg
Fat	8 g	Sodium	228 mg

Cherry Angel Roll

Cherry Angel Rolls

Makes 2 cakes, 8 servings each

1 package DUNCAN HINES® Angel Food
    Cake Mix
1 cup chopped maraschino cherries
1 teaspoon reserved maraschino cherry juice
½ cup flaked coconut
1 container (8 ounces) frozen whipped topping,
    thawed
    Confectioners sugar

1. Preheat oven to 350°F. Line two 15½×10½×1-inch jelly-roll pans with aluminum foil.

2. Prepare cake mix following package directions. Divide batter into lined pans. Spread evenly. Cut through batter with knife or spatula to remove large air bubbles. Bake at 350°F for 15 minutes or until set. Invert cakes at once onto clean, lint-free dishtowels dusted with confectioners sugar. Remove foil carefully. Starting at short end, roll up each cake with towel jelly-roll fashion. Cool completely.

3. Drain cherries, reserving 1 teaspoon juice. Fold cherries, coconut and cherry juice into whipped topping. Unroll cakes. Spread half of filling over each cake to edges. Reroll and place seam sides down on serving plate. Dust with confectioners sugar. Refrigerate until ready to serve.

Nutrients per serving:

Calories	211	Cholesterol	0 mg
Fat	6 g	Sodium	113 mg

Pineapple Upside Down Cake

Makes 12 servings

2 cans (8 ounces *each*) pineapple slices in juice,
    undrained
¼ cup raisins
1 cup KELLOGG'S® ALL-BRAN® cereal
¾ cup whole wheat flour
½ cup all-purpose flour
1 teaspoon baking soda
1 teaspoon ground cinnamon
¼ teaspoon salt (optional)
3 tablespoons margarine, softened
¼ cup sugar
4 egg whites
1 cup (8 ounces) low-fat vanilla flavored yogurt
1 teaspoon vanilla extract

Drain pineapple, reserving ¼ cup juice. Arrange pineapple slices in 9-inch round cake pan coated with nonstick cooking spray. Place raisins around and in centers of pineapple slices.

Stir together Kellogg's® All-Bran® cereal, flours, baking soda, cinnamon and salt. Set aside.

In large mixing bowl, beat together margarine and sugar. Add egg whites, yogurt, vanilla and ¼ cup reserved pineapple juice, mixing until blended. Add flour mixture, stirring only until combined. Spread batter over pineapple slices and raisins.

Bake at 350°F about 35 minutes or until wooden toothpick inserted in center comes out clean. Let stand 10 minutes. Turn cake upside down onto serving plate. Remove pan. Cool. Cut into 12 wedges.

Nutrients per serving:

Calories	150	Cholesterol	0 mg
Fat	3 g	Sodium	240 mg

Applesauce Snacking Cake

Makes 48 servings

1¼ cups sweetened applesauce
1 cup NABISCO® 100% Bran
½ cup EGG BEATERS® 99% Real Egg Product
½ cup BRER RABBIT® Light Molasses
1½ cups all-purpose flour
1 teaspoon baking soda
1 teaspoon ground cinnamon
1 cup firmly packed dark brown sugar
½ cup FLEISCHMANN'S® Margarine, softened
½ cup raisins
    Confectioner's sugar (optional)

In medium bowl, mix applesauce, bran, Egg Beaters® and molasses; let stand 5 minutes. In small bowl, blend flour, baking soda and cinnamon; set aside.

In large bowl, with electric mixer at medium speed, beat sugar and margarine until creamy. Beat in bran mixture until smooth. Blend in flour mixture; stir in raisins. Spread batter evenly in ungreased 15×10×1-inch baking pan. Bake at 350°F for 20 to 25 minutes or until wooden toothpick inserted in center comes out clean. Cool in pan on wire rack. Sprinkle with confectioner's sugar if desired; cut into 48 bars.

Nutrients per serving (without confectioner's sugar):

Calories	60	Cholesterol	0 mg
Fat	2 g	Sodium	50 mg

Chocolate Chiffon Cake

Makes 12 servings

  1 bar (4 ounces) sweet baking chocolate
½ cup hot water
  5 eggs, separated
⅔ cup sugar
  1 cup all-purpose flour
  1 teaspoon baking powder
  1 teaspoon vanilla
½ teaspoon salt
  Powdered sugar

Preheat oven to 350°F. Melt chocolate in hot water; set aside. Beat egg whites in large bowl until soft peaks form. Gradually add sugar and beat until stiff and glossy; set aside. Combine melted chocolate mixture, egg yolks, flour, baking powder, vanilla and salt in small bowl; beat 1 minute with electric mixer. Carefully fold chocolate mixture into egg white mixture until blended. Pour into ungreased 10-inch tube pan. Bake 45 to 50 minutes or until top springs back when lightly touched. Invert pan over large funnel or soda bottle; cool completely. Remove cake from pan; sprinkle with powdered sugar.

Nutrients per serving:

Calories	158	Cholesterol	89 mg
Fat	6 g	Sodium	143 mg

Spice Cake with Fresh Peach Sauce

Makes 12 to 16 servings

  1 package DUNCAN HINES® Moist Deluxe
      Spice Cake Mix
Sauce
  6 cups sliced fresh peaches
  1 cup water
⅓ cup sugar
⅛ teaspoon ground cinnamon

1. Preheat oven to 350°F. Grease and flour 10-inch Bundt® or tube pan. Prepare, bake and cool cake following package directions for No Cholesterol recipe. Dust with confectioners sugar, if desired.

2. For Sauce, combine peaches and water in large saucepan. Cook over medium heat 5 minutes. Reduce heat to low. Cover and simmer 10 minutes. Cool. Reserve ½ cup peach slices. Combine remaining peaches with any cooking liquid, sugar and cinnamon in blender or food processor. Process until smooth. Stir in reserved peach slices. To serve, spoon peach sauce over cake slices.

Tip: Fresh peach sauce can be served either warm or chilled.

Nutrients per serving:

Calories	299	Cholesterol	0 mg
Fat	10 g	Sodium	294 mg

Spice Cake with Fresh Peach Sauce

No-Guilt Cheesecake

No-Guilt Cheesecake

Makes 12 servings

4 cups DANNON® Plain Lowfat or Nonfat Yogurt
½ cup graham cracker crumbs
1 tablespoon margarine or butter, melted
1 cup lowfat cottage cheese
3 egg whites
¾ cup sugar
2 tablespoons all-purpose flour
1 tablespoon fresh lemon juice
1 teaspoon vanilla
Sliced fresh fruit
Fresh mint leaves (optional)

Spoon yogurt into large strainer lined with double thickness of cheesecloth or a coffee filter. Place bowl beneath, but not touching strainer to catch liquid. Chill 24 hours. Discard liquid.

Preheat oven to 325°F. In a small bowl combine crumbs and melted margarine. Press evenly into bottom of 7- to 9-inch springform pan; set aside. In food processor or blender combine cottage cheese and egg whites. Process until smooth, scraping down side of container occasionally. Add drained yogurt, sugar, flour, lemon juice and vanilla. Process an additional 30 seconds or until well blended, scraping down side of container occasionally. Pour into crust. Place pan on baking sheet.

Bake 1 hour or until set. Cool to room temperature. Cover; chill several hours or overnight. Serve with fruit. If desired, garnish with mint leaves.

Nutrients per serving:

Calories	140	Cholesterol	5 mg
Fat	3 g	Sodium	179 mg

Snacking Applesauce Cake Squares

Makes 9 servings

⅓ cup butter or margarine, softened
2 eggs
⅔ cup thawed frozen unsweetened apple juice concentrate
½ cup unsweetened applesauce
2 cups all-purpose flour
2 teaspoons baking powder
2 teaspoons ground cinnamon
½ teaspoon baking soda
¼ teaspoon salt
1 large cooking apple, peeled and chopped
Creamy Topping (recipe follows), optional

Preheat oven to 375°F. Grease 8- or 9-inch square baking pan.

Beat butter in large bowl until creamy. Blend in eggs, apple juice concentrate and applesauce. Combine dry ingredients. Gradually add to egg mixture, beating until well blended. Stir in apple. Spread batter evenly into prepared pan.

Bake 20 to 25 minutes or until wooden pick inserted in center comes out clean. Cool on wire rack. Cut into squares; serve warm or at room temperature with Creamy Topping, if desired.

Creamy Topping

½ cup heavy cream
1 teaspoon vanilla extract
¼ teaspoon ground cinnamon

Beat cream in small bowl at high speed of electric mixer until soft peaks form. Beat in vanilla and cinnamon until stiff peaks form.

Nutrients per serving:

Calories	229	Cholesterol	65 mg
Fat	8 g	Sodium	289 mg

Strawberry-Peach Dreamcake

Makes 10 servings

1 envelope KNOX® Unflavored Gelatine
¼ cup cold skim milk
¾ cup skim milk, heated to boiling
10 ounces (about 2 cups) frozen strawberries, thawed
2 tablespoons sugar
1 container (8 ounces) frozen lite whipped topping, thawed
1 can (16 ounces) sliced peaches in natural juice or extra light syrup, drained and chopped
1 (8-inch) angel food cake, cut into 1-inch cubes (about 7 cups)

In blender, sprinkle unflavored gelatine over cold milk; let stand 2 minutes. Add hot milk and process at low speed until gelatine is completely dissolved, about 2 minutes. Add strawberries and sugar; process at high speed until blended. Pour into large bowl; chill, stirring occasionally, until mixture mounds slightly when dropped from spoon, about 20 minutes. Fold in whipped topping, then peaches and cake. Turn into 8-cup bowl, mold or springform pan; chill until firm, about 1½ hours.

Nutrients per serving:

Calories	153	Cholesterol	0 mg
Fat	3 g	Sodium	49 mg

Royal Banana Fruit Shortcake

Makes 8 servings

2 extra-ripe medium DOLE® Bananas, peeled
1 package (18 ounces) yellow cake mix
    Ingredients to prepare cake mix
½ cup DOLE® Sliced Almonds
¾ cup DOLE® Pine-Orange-Guava Juice, divided
1 firm medium DOLE® Banana, peeled
2 cups assorted sliced DOLE® fresh fruit
¼ cup semisweet chocolate chips
½ teaspoon margarine

Place 2 extra-ripe bananas in blender. Blend until smooth. Prepare cake according to package directions, using blended bananas as part of the liquid measured with water.

Spread batter in 2 greased 9-inch round cake pans. Sprinkle tops with almonds. Bake and cool as directed. Use one layer for recipe; freeze second layer for future use.

Pour 3 tablespoons fruit juice onto large cake plate. Place cake on top to absorb juice. Pour another 3 tablespoons juice over cake.

Slice firm banana and combine with other fruits in small bowl. Reserve 1 tablespoon fruit juice for chocolate sauce; pour remaining 5 tablespoons juice over fruit. Arrange fruit and juice mixture over cake.

Royal Banana Fruit Shortcake

Combine chocolate chips, 1 tablespoon reserved fruit juice and margarine in small microwave-safe bowl. Microwave on HIGH (100% power) 10 to 30 seconds or until chocolate chips are soft. Stir until smooth. Drizzle over fruit and cake. Refrigerate 30 minutes.

Prep time: 15 minutes
Bake time: 30 minutes

Nutrients per serving:

Calories	208	Cholesterol	81 mg
Fat	7 g	Sodium	60 mg

Mocha Fudge Marble Delight

Makes 12 servings

Cake
1 package DUNCAN HINES® Moist Deluxe Fudge Marble Cake Mix
1 tablespoon FOLGERS® Coffee Crystals (optional)
1 teaspoon ground cinnamon (optional)
3 egg whites
1¼ cups water
⅓ cup CRISCO® PURITAN® Oil

Frosting
1 teaspoon FOLGERS® Coffee Crystals
¼ teaspoon ground cinnamon
¼ teaspoon hot water
1¼ cups skim milk
1 package (4-serving size) sugar-free chocolate flavor instant pudding and pie filling mix
2 envelopes (1.3 ounces each) whipped topping mix
Chocolate jimmies or decors (optional)

1. Preheat oven to 350°F. Grease and flour two 8- or 9-inch round cake pans.

2. For Cake, empty cake mix into large bowl. Add coffee crystals and cinnamon, if desired. Add egg whites, water and oil. Prepare, bake and cool cake following package directions for No Cholesterol recipe.

3. For Frosting, combine coffee, cinnamon and hot water in custard cup. Place milk in large bowl. Add pudding mix and topping mix. Blend at low speed of electric mixer. Blend in coffee mixture. Beat at high speed 2 to 3 minutes or until stiff, scraping sides and bottom of bowl frequently. Spread between layers, on sides and on top of cake. Sprinkle with chocolate jimmies, if desired.

Nutrients per serving:

Calories	242	Cholesterol	trace
Fat	9 g	Sodium	309 mg

Banana Graham Snacking Cake

Makes 24 servings

1¼ cups all-purpose flour
1 cup NABISCO® Graham Cracker Crumbs
2 teaspoons DAVIS® Baking Powder
1 teaspoon baking soda
⅓ cup FLEISCHMANN'S® Margarine, softened
1¼ cups sugar
¾ cup EGG BEATERS® 99% Real Egg Product
1¼ cups mashed bananas (about 2 large)
⅔ cup plain nonfat yogurt
½ cup walnuts, chopped (optional)
Confectioner's sugar (optional)

In small bowl, combine flour, graham cracker crumbs, baking powder and baking soda; set aside.

In large bowl, with electric mixer at medium speed, beat margarine and sugar until well combined. At low speed, blend in Egg Beaters® and bananas. Add flour mixture alternately with yogurt, mixing until smooth. Stir in walnuts, if desired.

Spoon batter into greased and floured 13×9×2-inch baking pan. Bake at 350°F for 45 minutes or until wooden toothpick inserted in center comes out clean. Cool in pan on wire rack. Dust with confectioner's sugar before serving.

Nutrients per serving (without nuts and confectioner's sugar):

Calories	124	Cholesterol	0 mg
Fat	3 g	Sodium	128 mg

Chocolate Banana Low-Fat Cupcakes

Chocolate Banana Low-Fat Cupcakes

Makes 20 cupcakes

2 cups all-purpose flour
¾ cup sugar, divided
¼ cup HERSHEY'S Cocoa or HERSHEY'S Premium European Style Cocoa
¾ teaspoon baking soda
½ teaspoon baking powder
¼ teaspoon salt
¾ cup (8-ounce container) plain low-fat yogurt (1.5% milkfat)
½ cup mashed ripe banana (about 1 medium)
⅓ cup all-vegetable canola oil
¼ cup skim milk
2 teaspoons vanilla extract
3 egg whites
White Glaze (recipe follows)

Heat oven to 350°F. Line muffin pans with paper or foil-laminated paper baking cups (2½ inches in diameter). In large bowl, stir together flour, ¼ cup sugar, cocoa, baking soda, baking powder and salt; set aside. In small bowl, stir together yogurt, banana, oil, milk and vanilla; set aside. In medium mixer bowl, beat egg whites until soft peaks form. Gradually beat in remaining ½ cup sugar; beat until stiff peaks form. Stir yogurt mixture into flour mixture until dry ingredients are moistened; fold in ⅓ of egg white mixture. Gently fold in remaining egg white mixture. Fill muffin cups ¾ full. Bake 20 to 25 minutes or until wooden toothpick inserted in centers comes out clean. Remove from muffin pans to wire racks; cool completely. Drizzle tops of cupcakes with White Glaze.

White Glaze: In small bowl, combine ½ cup powdered sugar with 3 to 4 teaspoons warm water; stir until smooth and of desired consistency.

Nutrients per serving (1 cupcake):

Calories	140	Cholesterol	0 mg
Fat	4 gm	Sodium	74 mg

Fudge Marble Pound Cake

Fudge Marble Pound Cake

Makes 2 loaves, 18 slices each

1 package DUNCAN HINES® Moist Deluxe
    Fudge Marble Cake Mix
1 package (4-serving size) vanilla instant
    pudding and pie filling mix
4 eggs
1 cup water
⅓ cup CRISCO® PURITAN® Oil

1. Preheat oven to 350°F. Grease and flour two
9×5×3-inch loaf pans.

2. Set aside cocoa packet from Mix. Combine cake
mix, pudding mix, eggs, water and Crisco® Puritan®
Oil in large bowl. Beat at medium speed with electric
mixer for 2 minutes. Measure 1 cup batter; place in
small bowl. Stir in contents of reserved cocoa packet.

3. Spoon half the yellow batter into each loaf pan.
Spoon half the chocolate batter over yellow batter in
each pan. Run knife through batters to marble. Bake
at 350°F for 45 to 50 minutes or until wooden
toothpick inserted in centers comes out clean. Cool in
pans 5 minutes. Loosen cakes from pans. Invert onto
cooling racks. Cool completely. Cut cakes in ½-inch-
thick slices.

Nutrients per serving (1 slice):

Calories	86	Cholesterol	24 mg
Fat	4 g	Sodium	108 mg

Apple Chiffon Cake

Makes 12 servings

Cake
  ⅓ cup CRISCO® PURITAN® Oil
  ¾ cup sugar
  2 eggs
  ¾ cup all-purpose flour
  ½ teaspoon baking powder
  ¼ teaspoon salt
  ¼ teaspoon baking soda
  ¼ teaspoon ground nutmeg
  ¼ teaspoon ground ginger
  1 cup finely chopped peeled apples (about
     2 medium)

Topping
  2 tablespoons sugar
  2 tablespoons finely chopped walnuts
  ½ teaspoon cinnamon

For Cake, heat oven to 350°F. Combine Crisco®
Puritan® Oil and sugar in large bowl at medium
speed of electric mixer. Add eggs. Beat well.

Combine flour, baking powder, salt, baking soda,
nutmeg and ginger. Add to oil mixture. Beat until just
blended. Stir in apples. Spread evenly in ungreased
9×9×2-inch pan.

For Topping, combine sugar, nuts and cinnamon.
Sprinkle over batter.

Bake at 350°F for 25 to 30 minutes or until wooden
toothpick inserted in center comes out clean. Cut into
3×2¼-inch rectangles. Serve warm or at room
temperature.

To Microwave: Prepare Cake and Topping as above.
Spread cake batter in ungreased 11×7-inch microwave-safe
dish. Place in microwave on rack or on glass pie plate
turned upside down. Cover lightly with waxed paper.
Microwave at MEDIUM (50% power) 6 minutes; rotate
dish after 3 minutes. Remove waxed paper. Microwave at
HIGH (100% power) 5 minutes. Rotate dish after
2 minutes. Cut into 3×2¼-inch rectangles. Serve as above.

Nutrients per serving:

Calories	162	Cholesterol	36 mg
Fat	8 g	Sodium	86 mg

Chocolate Cake Fingers

Makes 21 servings

1 cup granulated sugar
1 cup all-purpose flour
⅓ cup HERSHEY₀S Cocoa
¾ teaspoon baking powder
¾ teaspoon baking soda
½ cup skim milk
¼ cup thawed frozen egg substitute
¼ cup canola oil or vegetable oil
1 teaspoon vanilla extract
½ cup boiling water
Powdered sugar
1 teaspoon freshly grated orange peel
1½ cups thawed frozen nondairy whipped topping
42 fresh strawberries or raspberries (optional)

Heat oven to 350°F. Line bottom of 13×9-inch baking pan with waxed paper. In large mixer bowl, stir together granulated sugar, flour, cocoa, baking powder and baking soda. Add milk, egg substitute, oil and vanilla; beat on medium speed of electric mixer 2 minutes. Add water, stirring with spoon until well blended. Pour batter into prepared pan.

Bake 16 to 18 minutes or until wooden toothpick inserted in center comes out clean. Place towel on wire rack; sprinkle with powdered sugar. Invert cake on towel; peel off waxed paper. Turn cake right side up. Cool completely. Cut cake into 42 small rectangles (about 2×1¼ inches). Stir orange peel into whipped topping; spoon dollop on each piece of cake. Garnish with strawberry or raspberry, if desired.

Nutrients per serving:

Calories	80	Cholesterol	0 mg
Fat	3 g	Sodium	35 mg

Della Robbia Cake

Makes 12 servings

Cake
1 package DUNCAN HINES® Angel Food Cake Mix
1½ teaspoons grated lemon peel

Glaze
6 tablespoons sugar
1½ tablespoons cornstarch
1 cup water
1 tablespoon lemon juice
½ teaspoon vanilla extract
Few drops red food coloring
6 cling peach slices
6 medium strawberries, sliced

1. Preheat oven to 375°F.

2. For Cake, prepare cake following package directions adding lemon peel with Cake Flour Mixture (red "B" packet). Bake and cool cake following package directions.

3. For Glaze, combine sugar, cornstarch and water in small saucepan. Cook over medium-high heat until mixture boils and thickens. Remove from heat. Stir in lemon juice, vanilla extract and red food coloring.

4. Alternate peach slices with strawberry slices around top of cooled cake. Pour glaze over fruit and top of cake. Refrigerate leftovers.

Nutrients per serving:

Calories	145	Cholesterol	0 mg
Fat	0 g	Sodium	100 mg

Della Robbia Cake

Individual Strawberry Shortcakes

Makes 10 servings

Strawberry Mixture
  4 cups fresh strawberries, washed, hulled and
    sliced
  2 tablespoons granulated sugar

Shortcake Biscuits
1¾ cups all-purpose flour
  1 tablespoon granulated sugar
  1 tablespoon baking powder
  ½ teaspoon salt (optional)
  ¼ cup CRISCO® Shortening
  ⅔ cup milk

Topping
  1 cup plain nonfat yogurt
  3 tablespoons brown sugar
  ½ teaspoon vanilla

For Strawberry Mixture, combine strawberries and granulated sugar. Cover and refrigerate.

Heat oven to 450°F.

For Shortcake Biscuits, combine flour, granulated sugar, baking powder and salt in bowl. Cut in Crisco® with pastry blender (or 2 knives) until mixture forms coarse crumbs.

Add milk. Stir until dry ingredients are just moistened. Place on floured surface. Knead gently with fingertips 8 to 10 times. Pat or roll into 9-inch circle about ½ inch thick. (Hint: Cover dough with waxed paper. Press and flatten with 9-inch round cake pan until dough is desired thickness.)

Cut with 2½-inch round biscuit cutter. Press dough scraps into ball and flatten again. Cut out a total of 10 biscuits. Place on ungreased baking sheet.

Bake 12 minutes or until tops are golden brown.

For Topping, combine yogurt, brown sugar and vanilla. Stir gently until smooth.

To assemble, split warm or cooled biscuits in half crosswise. Spoon about ¼ cup fruit over bottoms of biscuits. Add tops. Spoon yogurt sauce over tops. Add another spoonful of fruit or top with strawberry fans, if desired.

Nutrients per serving:

Calories	188	Cholesterol	3 mg
Fat	6 g	Sodium	127 mg

Creamy Lemon Cheesecake

Makes 8 servings

Crust
  1 cup graham cracker crumbs
  ¼ cup sugar
  3 tablespoons CRISCO® PURITAN® Oil

Filling
  3 ounces Neufchatel cheese, softened
  2 cups low-fat (1%) cottage cheese
  ½ cup sugar
  2 egg whites
  1 teaspoon freshly grated lemon peel
  3 tablespoons fresh lemon juice
  1 teaspoon vanilla

For Crust, heat oven to 350°F. Combine graham cracker crumbs, sugar, and Crisco® Puritan® Oil in 9-inch pie plate. Mix well with fork. Press firmly against bottom and halfway up side of pie plate.

For Filling, blend neufchatel and cottage cheese in food processor or blender* until completely smooth. Add remaining ingredients. Blend well. Pour mixture into crust.

Bake at 350°F for 30 minutes. Turn oven off; allow cheesecake to remain in oven for 5 minutes. Remove from oven; cool. Refrigerate. Cut into wedges. Garnish with fresh fruit, if desired.

*If blender is used, place sugar, egg whites, lemon peel, lemon juice and vanilla in blender container before adding neufchatel and cottage cheese. Blend until completely smooth, stopping blender and scraping as necessary.

To Microwave: Prepare crust as directed; spoon 2 to 3 tablespoons crust mixture into each of 8 small custard cups. Press firmly against bottoms of cups. Prepare filling as directed; pour about ⅓ cup into each custard cup.

Arrange cups in circle on large microwave-safe platter or directly on floor of microwave oven. Microwave on MEDIUM (50% power) 9 to 10 minutes or until filling begins to set around edges, turning platter or rearranging cups after every 3 minutes.

Let stand on countertop or board 10 minutes. Refrigerate at least 1 hour before serving.

Nutrients per serving:

Calories	256	Cholesterol	11 mg
Fat	10 g	Sodium	378 mg

Individual Strawberry Shortcakes

Raspberry Shortcakes

Makes 8 servings

1½ cups frozen whole raspberries, divided
5 tablespoons sugar, divided
1 cup all-purpose flour
1 teaspoon baking powder
¼ teaspoon baking soda
1 tablespoon margarine
1 egg white
⅓ cup evaporated skim milk
¼ teaspoon almond extract
¾ cup low fat cottage cheese
1 teaspoon lemon juice

Preheat oven to 450°F. Spray baking sheet with nonstick cooking spray.

Toss 1¼ cups raspberries with 2½ tablespoons sugar; set aside in refrigerator. Combine flour, 2 tablespoons sugar, baking powder and baking soda in medium bowl. Cut in margarine with pastry blender or 2 knives; set aside. Beat egg white, milk and almond extract in small bowl; add to flour mixture and mix lightly. Knead slightly on lightly floured board. Roll out to ½-inch thickness. Cut out 8 biscuits with 2½-inch biscuit cutter. Place biscuits on baking sheet. Bake 10 minutes or until lightly browned on top.

Meanwhile, place cottage cheese, remaining 1½ teaspoons sugar and lemon juice in food processor or blender; process until smooth. Fold in remaining ¼ cup raspberries. To serve, split biscuits in half and place each bottom half on individual serving dish. Top each with 2 tablespoons reserved raspberries and 1 tablespoon cheese mixture. Cover with biscuit top. Spoon remaining reserved raspberries and cheese mixture over tops.

Nutrients per serving:			
Calories	166	Cholesterol	1 mg
Fat	2 g	Sodium	190 mg

Favorite recipe from **The Sugar Association, Inc.**

Early American Ginger Cakes

Makes 1 dozen cakes

Cakes
1⅔ cups all-purpose flour
¼ cup sugar
2 tablespoons baking powder
½ teaspoon cinnamon
½ teaspoon ginger
½ teaspoon nutmeg
½ teaspoon salt
½ cup raisins
2 eggs, lightly beaten
¼ cup CRISCO® Vegetable Oil
⅓ cup 2% lowfat milk
½ teaspoon vanilla
½ cup dark molasses

Spiced Sugar Topping* (optional)
2 tablespoons sugar
⅛ teaspoon cinnamon
⅛ teaspoon ginger
⅛ teaspoon nutmeg

1. Heat oven to 375°F. Place paper or foil liners in 12 medium (about 2½-inch) muffin cups.

2. For cakes, combine flour, sugar, baking powder, cinnamon, ginger, nutmeg and salt in medium bowl. Stir in raisins.

3. Combine eggs and Crisco® Oil in small bowl. Mix well. Stir in milk and vanilla. Add molasses. Mix well. Stir into flour mixture. Mix just until moistened. Spoon evenly into muffin cups.

4. For spiced sugar topping, combine sugar, cinnamon, ginger and nutmeg in small bowl. Sprinkle over batter.

5. Bake at 375°F for 16 to 20 minutes or until toothpick inserted in centers comes out clean. Cool.

**Sift confectioners sugar over top of cooled, baked muffins if spiced sugar topping is omitted.*

Nutrients per serving (1 cake):			
Calories	195	Cholesterol	35 mg
Fat	6 g	Sodium	280 mg

Left to right: Raspberry Shortcake, Angel Food Cake with Blueberry Yogurt Sauce

Breathless Peach Cheesecake

Makes 10 servings

1 envelope KNOX® Unflavored Gelatine
¼ cup cold water
1 can (16 ounces) lite peaches, drained and
    juice reserved
1 package (8 ounces) lite cream cheese, softened
¼ cup sugar
2 tablespoons loosely packed mint leaves
    (optional)

In blender, sprinkle unflavored gelatine over cold water; let stand 2 minutes. Meanwhile, in small saucepan, bring reserved juice to a boil. Add hot juice to blender and process at low speed until gelatine is completely dissolved, about 2 minutes. Add remaining ingredients and process at high speed until blended. Pour into 8- or 9-inch pie pan *or* graham cracker crust, if desired. (To prepare crust, combine ¾ cup graham cracker crumbs and 2 tablespoons melted margarine. Press into 8- or 9-inch pie pan.) Chill until firm, about 3 hours. Garnish, if desired, with peach slices and mint leaves.

Nutrients per serving:

| Calories | 146 | Cholesterol | 12 mg |
| Fat | 4 g | Sodium | 213 mg |

Angel Food Cake with Blueberry Yogurt Sauce

Makes 12 servings

½ cup frozen blueberries
    Prepared small round angel food cake
½ cup nonfat vanilla yogurt
3 teaspoons granulated sugar
1 teaspoon lemon juice

Allow blueberries to thaw slightly. Slice angel food cake into 12 pieces. Stir together yogurt, sugar and lemon juice in small bowl. To serve, spoon yogurt mixture and blueberries evenly over cake slices.

Nutrients per serving:

| Calories | 163 | Cholesterol | trace |
| Fat | trace | Sodium | 291 mg |

Favorite recipe from **The Sugar Association, Inc.**

Orange-Almond Angel Food Cake

Orange-Almond Angel Food Cake

Makes 10 servings

1 cup whole natural California Almonds
1 package (14.5 ounces) angel food cake mix,
    plus ingredients to prepare mix
1⅓ cups orange juice
2 tablespoons grated orange peel
    Sorbet (optional)
    Fresh fruit (optional)

Preheat oven to 350°F. Spread almonds in single layer on baking sheet. Toast in oven 12 to 15 minutes until lightly browned, stirring occasionally; cool and chop.

Prepare cake mix according to package directions, substituting orange juice for water called for in package directions. Fold in grated orange peel and ½ cup chopped almonds. Spoon batter into ungreased 10-inch tube pan. Sprinkle with remaining chopped almonds. Bake and cool according to package directions. Serve with sorbet and fresh fruit, if desired.

Nutrients per serving:

| Calories | 271 | Cholesterol | 0 mg |
| Fat | 8 g | Sodium | 181 mg |

Favorite recipe from **Almond Board of California**

Scrumptious Apple Cake

Makes 15 to 20 servings

> 3 egg whites
> 1½ cups sugar
> 1 cup unsweetened applesauce
> 2 cups all-purpose flour
> 2 teaspoons ground cinnamon
> 1 teaspoon baking soda
> ½ teaspoon salt
> 1 teaspoon vanilla extract
> 4 cups tart apples, cored, peeled and thinly sliced (about 5 medium McIntosh or Crispin apples)
> Yogurt Glaze (recipe follows)

Preheat oven 350°F. Beat egg whites until slightly foamy in medium bowl. Stir in sugar and applesauce. Combine flour, cinnamon, baking soda and salt in small bowl. Stir flour mixture and vanilla into applesauce mixture. Spread apples in 13×9-inch baking pan or 9-inch springform pan sprayed with vegetable cooking spray. Spread applesauce mixture over apples.

Bake 35 to 40 minutes until wooden pick inserted in center comes out clean. Cool completely; frost with Yogurt Glaze.

Yogurt Glaze: Combine 1½ cups nonfat plain or vanilla yogurt, 3 tablespoons brown sugar, 1 teaspoon vanilla extract or lemon juice; stir until smooth.

Nutrients per serving:

Calories	170	Cholesterol	1 mg
Fat	trace	Sodium	130 mg

Favorite recipe from **Western New York Apple Growers Association**

Northwoods Buttermilk Cake

Makes 16 servings

> 1 cup whole wheat flour
> 2 cups all-purpose flour
> 2 teaspoons baking soda
> 1 teaspoon ground cinnamon
> ½ teaspoon salt
> ½ teaspoon ground nutmeg
> ½ cup extra light margarine
> 1 cup packed brown sugar
> 1 teaspoon vanilla extract
> 5 egg whites
> ⅔ cup applesauce
> 1 cup buttermilk
> 2 cups well-cooked wild rice

Preheat oven to 350°F. Grease and lightly flour 13×9-inch baking pan.

Combine flours, baking soda, cinnamon, salt and nutmeg in medium bowl; set aside. Beat margarine with electric mixer on medium speed 30 seconds in large bowl; add brown sugar and vanilla. Beat until fluffy. Add egg whites; beat until well blended. Beat in applesauce until well combined. Add flour mixtur and buttermilk alternately to egg mixture, blending well. Stir in wild rice. Spread evenly into prepared pan

Bake 45 to 50 minutes until wooden pick inserted in center comes out clean. (Do not overbake.) Cool completely. Frost with sour cream frosting or top each serving with sweetened whipped cream, if desired.

Nutrients per serving:

Calories	188	Cholesterol	1 mg
Fat	3 g	Sodium	240 mg

Favorite recipe from **Minnesota Cultivated Wild Rice Council**

Calorie Watcher's "Cheesecake"

Makes 4 servings

> 1 envelope unflavored gelatin
> ¼ cup skim milk
> 1 container (16 ounces) low fat cottage cheese with pineapple
> 1 container (8 ounces) vanilla low fat yogurt, divided
> ¼ cup sugar
> ¼ teaspoon salt
> 4 tablespoons graham cracker crumbs
> Strawberries (optional)

Sprinkle gelatin over milk in small saucepan; let stand 1 minute to soften. Cook over low heat 3 to 5 minutes until gelatin is completely dissolved, stirring constantly. Remove from heat; cool slightly.

Place cottage cheese, ½ cup yogurt, sugar and salt in food processor or blender; process until smooth. With motor running, slowly add gelatin mixture through feed tube; process until well combined. Divide 1½ teaspoons cracker crumbs among 4 large dessert or wine glasses. Divide cottage cheese mixture evenly into each glass; sprinkle each with additional 1½ teaspoons cracker crumbs. Cover and refrigerate about 2 hours or until firm. Just before serving, top each "cheesecake" with spoonful of remaining vanilla yogurt. Garnish with strawberries, if desired.

Nutrients per serving:

Calories	250	Cholesterol	7 mg
Fat	2 g	Sodium	700 mg

Favorite recipe from **National Dairy Board**

Individual Cheesecake Delights

Makes 10 servings

10 gingersnaps
½ cup part-skim ricotta cheese
3 ounces light cream cheese (Neufchâtel), softened
⅓ cup sugar
1 egg
1 tablespoon lemon juice
1 teaspoon vanilla extract
¼ cup nonfat vanilla yogurt
¾ cup frozen raspberries *or* 1 ripe nectarine, mashed

Preheat oven to 375°F. Paper-line 10 (2½-inch) muffin cups.

Place 1 gingersnap in each cup. Place cheeses, sugar, egg, lemon juice and vanilla in food processor or blender; process until blended. Pour mixture evenly over gingersnaps.

Bake 15 to 20 minutes until cheesecakes are set. Cool in pan on wire rack; refrigerate until chilled thoroughly. Remove individual cheesecakes from muffin cups and discard paper liners. Place vanilla yogurt and raspberries in food processor or blender; process until smooth. Spread yogurt mixture over cheesecakes.

Nutrients per serving:

Calories	117	Cholesterol	32 mg
Fat	4 g	Sodium	83 mg

Favorite recipe from **The Sugar Association, Inc.**

Today's Slim Blender Cheesecake

Makes 10 to 12 servings

¼ cup graham cracker crumbs
1 cup low fat plain yogurt
4 large eggs, beaten
¾ cup dry milk powder
¾ cup sugar
6 tablespoons all-purpose flour
3 tablespoons lemon juice
1 tablespoon vanilla extract
½ teaspoon salt
3 cups (24 ounces) low fat (1%) Cottage cheese
1 can (20 ounces) crushed pineapple in juice, undrained
Ground cinnamon

Preheat oven to 300°F. Butter 13×9-inch baking pan; dust bottom with cracker crumbs; set aside.

Place yogurt, eggs, milk powder, sugar, flour, lemon juice, vanilla and salt in food processor or blender; process until smooth. Pour into large bowl. Place Cottage cheese and pineapple in food processor or blender; cover and blend until smooth. Add to yogurt mixture. Stir until well blended. Pour into prepared pan. Bake 1 hour and 15 minutes until set. Sprinkle lightly with cinnamon. Cool completely; refrigerate several hours or overnight.

Nutrients per serving:

Calories	199	Cholesterol	75 mg
Fat	3 g	Sodium	394 mg

Favorite recipe from **Wisconsin Milk Marketing Board** © 1994

Butter Recipe Chocolate Snacking Cake

Makes 12 servings, one 13×9-inch cake

1 package (18.5 ounces) DUNCAN HINES® Moist Deluxe Butter Recipe Fudge Cake Mix
6 egg whites
1 cup water
¼ cup CRISCO® Vegetable Oil
12 large marshmallows, cut in half

1. Heat oven to 375°F. Oil and flour 13×9×2-inch pan lightly.

2. Combine cake mix, egg whites, water and ¼ cup Crisco® Oil in large bowl.

3. Beat at low speed of electric mixer until moistened. Beat at medium speed 4 minutes. Pour batter into pan.

4. Bake at 375°F for 28 to 32 minutes or until toothpick inserted in center comes out clean.

5. Place marshmallows, cut sides down, on hot cake to melt.

Nutrients per serving:

Calories	270	Cholesterol	0 mg
Fat	9 g	Sodium	280 mg

Blueberry Angel Food Cake Roll

Blueberry Angel Food Cake Rolls

Makes 2 cakes, 8 servings each

**1 package DUNCAN HINES® Angel Food
  Cake Mix
  Confectioners sugar
1 can (21 ounces) blueberry pie filling
¼ cup confectioners sugar
  Mint leaves, for garnish (optional)**

1. Preheat oven to 350°F. Line two 15½×10½×1-inch jelly-roll pans with aluminum foil.

2. Prepare cake following package directions. Divide into pans. Spread evenly. Cut through batter with knife or spatula to remove large air bubbles. Bake at 350°F for 15 minutes or until set. Invert cakes at once onto clean, lint-free dishtowels dusted with confectioners sugar. Remove foil carefully. Roll up each cake with towel jelly-roll fashion, starting at short end. Cool completely.

3. Unroll cakes. Spread about 1 cup blueberry pie filling to within 1 inch of edges on each cake. Reroll and place seam-side down on serving plate. Dust with ¼ cup confectioners sugar. Garnish with mint leaves, if desired.

Nutrients per serving:

Calories	143	Cholesterol	0 mg
Fat	0 g	Sodium	77 mg

Carrot Pudding Cake with Lemon Sauce

Makes 8 servings

**⅓ cup firmly packed brown sugar
¼ cup liquid vegetable oil margarine
½ cup frozen apple juice concentrate, thawed
3 egg whites, slightly beaten
1 cup QUAKER® Oat Bran hot cereal, uncooked
½ cup all-purpose flour
2 teaspoons baking powder
1 teaspoon ground cinnamon
2 cups shredded carrots (about 4 or 5 medium)
½ cup granulated sugar
4 teaspoons cornstarch
1 cup hot water
1 tablespoon liquid vegetable oil margarine
1 tablespoon lemon juice
½ teaspoon grated lemon peel
1 drop yellow food coloring (optional)**

Heat oven to 325°F. Lightly spray 1½- or 2-quart casserole dish with nonstick cooking spray or oil lightly. In large bowl, combine brown sugar and ¼ cup margarine. Add apple juice concentrate and egg whites, mixing well. Add combined oat bran, flour, baking powder and cinnamon; mix well. Stir in carrots; pour into prepared dish. Bake 45 to 50 minutes or until edges are lightly browned and center is firm. Cool on wire rack about 1 hour. Cut into squares or wedges.

In small saucepan, combine granulated sugar and cornstarch. Gradually add water, mixing until sugar dissolves. Cook over medium heat about 3 minutes, stirring constantly until mixture boils and is thickened and clear. Remove from heat; stir in remaining ingredients. Cool slightly. Spoon 2 tablespoons lemon sauce over each serving.

To Microwave Lemon Sauce: *In 4-cup microwavable measuring cup, combine granulated sugar and cornstarch. Gradually add water, mixing until sugar dissolves. Microwave at HIGH (100% power) 2 to 3 minutes or until mixture boils and is thickened and clear, stirring after every minute. Add remaining ingredients, mixing well. Cool slightly. Serve as directed above.*

Nutrients per serving:

Calories	270	Cholesterol	0 mg
Fat	8 g	Sodium	200 mg

Chocolate Cupcakes

Makes 18 cupcakes

**6 tablespoons light corn oil spread
1 cup sugar
1¼ cups all-purpose flour
⅓ cup HERSHEY'S Cocoa
1 teaspoon baking soda
  Dash salt
1 cup nonfat buttermilk
½ teaspoon vanilla extract
  Powdered sugar**

Heat oven to 350°F. Line muffin pans with paper bake cups (2½ inches in diameter). In large saucepan, melt corn oil spread. Remove from heat; stir in sugar. In small bowl, stir together flour, cocoa, baking soda and salt; add alternately with buttermilk and vanilla to mixture in saucepan. Beat with whisk until well blended. Spoon into bake cups.

Bake 18 to 20 minutes or until wooden toothpick inserted in centers comes out clean. Remove from pans to wire racks; cool completely. Sift powdered sugar over tops.

Nutrients per serving (1 cupcake):

Calories	110	Cholesterol	0 mg
Fat	3 g	Sodium	95 mg

Spicy Pumpkin Torte

Makes 12 servings

Cake
    1 package DUNCAN HINES® Moist Deluxe
        Yellow Cake Mix
    1 teaspoon ground cinnamon
    ½ teaspoon ground nutmeg
    ¼ teaspoon ground cloves

Filling
    1 package (4-serving size) butterscotch flavor
        pudding and pie filling mix
    ½ teaspoon ground cinnamon
    ¼ teaspoon ground ginger
    ⅛ teaspoon ground cloves
    ⅛ teaspoon ground nutmeg
    2 cups skim milk, divided
    ½ cup solid pack pumpkin (not pumpkin pie
        filling)
    1 envelope whipped topping mix
    ½ teaspoon vanilla

Garnish
    2 tablespoons reserved filling

1. Preheat oven to 350°F. Grease and flour two 8- or 9-inch round cake pans.

2. For Cake, combine cake mix, cinnamon, nutmeg and cloves in large bowl. Prepare, bake and cool cake following package directions for No Cholesterol recipe. Refrigerate cooled layers for ease in splitting.

3. For Filling, combine pudding mix, cinnamon, ginger, cloves and nutmeg in large bowl. Stir in 1½ cups skim milk. Cook pudding as directed on package. Add pumpkin. Stir until well blended. Place plastic wrap on surface of pudding. Refrigerate until cool.

4. Prepare whipped topping using remaining ½ cup skim milk and vanilla, following package directions for mixing. Remove 2 tablespoons filling; reserve. Fold whipped topping into remaining filling.

5. To assemble torte, split each cake layer in half horizontally. Spread one-fourth filling mixture on one cake layer. Place second cake layer on top of filling mixture. Repeat with remaining cake layers and filling mixture, ending with last fourth of filling mixture.

6. For Garnish, dot top with reserved filling. Swirl with tip of knife. Refrigerate until ready to serve.

Note: Unused pumpkin can be used to make cookies or muffins.

Nutrients per serving:			
Calories	259	Cholesterol	1 mg
Fat	10 g	Sodium	327 mg

Ginger Cake with Yogurt-Rum Sauce

Makes 12 servings

    2 cups all-purpose flour
    2 teaspoons ground cinnamon
 1¾ teaspoons ground ginger
 1½ teaspoons ground nutmeg
    ¾ teaspoon baking powder
    ¾ teaspoon baking soda
    ½ teaspoon ground cloves
    ⅛ teaspoon salt
    ¾ cup molasses
    2 eggs
    6 tablespoons light olive oil or vegetable oil
    ¼ cup sugar
    ½ cup DANNON® Vanilla Lowfat Yogurt
    ½ cup boiling water
        Yogurt-Rum Sauce (recipe follows)

Preheat oven to 350°F. Spray 8×8-inch baking pan with vegetable cooking spray. In a large bowl combine flour, cinnamon, ginger, nutmeg, baking powder, baking soda, cloves and salt; set aside.

In a medium bowl whisk together molasses, eggs, oil and sugar until well blended. Whisk in yogurt, then boiling water. Pour half the molasses mixture into dry ingredients; stir just until dry ingredients are moistened. Add remaining molasses mixture; stir just until blended. (Batter will be slightly lumpy.) Pour batter into prepared pan.

Bake 45 to 55 minutes or until toothpick inserted into center comes out clean. (Cake surface will crack.) Cool on wire rack at least 30 minutes before serving. Flavor will improve with standing. Serve with Yogurt-Rum Sauce.

Yogurt-Rum Sauce

    ½ cup DANNON® Vanilla Lowfat Yogurt
    4 teaspoons confectioner's sugar
    ¾ teaspoon dark rum

In a small serving bowl combine yogurt, confectioner's sugar and rum; stir well.

Nutrients per serving:			
Calories	280	Cholesterol	45 mg
Fat	8 g	Sodium	117 mg

Star-Spangled Cheesecake

Makes 8 servings

1 KEEBLER® READY-CRUST® Graham
  Cracker Pie Crust
1 egg yolk, beaten

Filling
  1 container (15 ounces) light ricotta cheese
  ½ cup sugar
  ⅓ cup evaporated skim milk
  2 eggs
  2 tablespoons all-purpose flour
  2 teaspoons grated lemon peel
  1 tablespoon lemon juice
  ½ teaspoon vanilla extract
  ¼ teaspoon salt

Sour Cream Topping
  1 cup light sour cream
  2 tablespoons sugar
  1 teaspoon vanilla extract

Fruit Glaze
  ¼ cup red currant jelly
  1 cup fresh raspberries
  1 cup fresh blueberries

Brush egg yolk over pie crust. Bake at 350°F for
5 minutes.

For Filling, while crust is baking, blend ricotta cheese
until smooth in food processor or blender. Add all
remaining filling ingredients; process just until
mixed. Pour into prepared crust; continue to bake
at 350°F for 30 minutes or until center is set.

For Topping, combine sour cream, sugar and vanilla
in small bowl. Spread over cheesecake; continue to
bake at 350°F for 10 minutes. Turn oven off; allow
cheesecake to cool in oven with door ajar for 30
minutes. Remove from oven; cool. Refrigerate at least
3 hours.

For Fruit Glaze, just before serving, melt jelly.
Combine half the jelly with raspberries; arrange
glazed raspberries in single layer over center of
cheesecake. Combine blueberries with remaining
jelly; arrange glazed blueberries in a single layer over
remaining cheesecake to the crust. Refrigerate
15 minutes before cutting.

Nutrients per serving:

Calories	279	Cholesterol	62 mg
Fat	9 g	Sodium	371 mg

Lovely Lemon Cheesecake

Lovely Lemon Cheesecake

Makes 8 servings

1 whole graham cracker, crushed, *or*
  2 tablespoons graham cracker crumbs,
  divided
1 package (4-serving size) JELL-O® Brand
  Sugar Free Lemon Flavor Gelatin
⅔ cup boiling water
1 cup 1% low-fat cottage cheese
1 container (8 ounces) light pasteurized process
  cream cheese product, softened
2 cups thawed COOL WHIP® LITE® Whipped
  Topping
1 cup low-calorie cherry pie filling

Spray 8- or 9-inch springform pan or 9-inch pie plate
lightly with nonstick cooking spray. Sprinkle side with
half the graham cracker crumbs. (If desired, omit
graham cracker crumb garnish; sprinkle bottom of
pan with remaining graham cracker crumbs.)

Completely dissolve gelatin in boiling water in small
bowl. Pour into blender container. Add cheeses; blend
at medium speed, scraping down sides occasionally,
about 2 minutes or until mixture is completely
smooth. Pour into large bowl. Gently stir in whipped
topping. Pour into prepared pan; smooth top.
Sprinkle remaining crumbs around outside edge,
leaving center plain. Chill until set, about 4 hours.

Just before serving, decorate top of cheesecake with
pie filling. Remove sides of pan and cut.

Nutrients per serving:

Calories	160	Cholesterol	15 mg
Fat	7 g	Sodium	330 mg

End your meal on a sweet note and still keep calories and fat in line. Peach, pineapple and pumpkin are just a few of the picture-perfect pies you can indulge in. Kids of all ages will appreciate a cookie jar filled with chocolate chip, molasses or orange sugar cookies, perfect for low-cal snacking anytime.

Fruit Lover's Tart

Makes 1 (9-inch) pie, 8 servings

1¼ cups QUAKER® Oats (quick or old fashioned, uncooked)
⅓ cup firmly packed brown sugar
¼ cup all-purpose flour
2 tablespoons margarine, melted
2 egg whites
1 cup (8 ounces) part-skim ricotta cheese
¼ cup (2 ounces) light cream cheese, softened
2 tablespoons powdered sugar
½ teaspoon grated lemon peel
4½ cups any combination sliced fresh or frozen fruit, thawed, well drained

Heat oven to 350°F. Lightly spray 9-inch pie plate with nonstick cooking spray or oil lightly. Combine oats, brown sugar, flour, margarine and egg whites, mixing until moistened. Press mixture onto bottom and up side of prepared plate. Bake 15 to 18 minutes or until light golden brown. Remove to wire rack; cool completely. Combine cheeses, powdered sugar and lemon peel. Spread onto oat base; top with fruit. Refrigerate 2 hours.

To Microwave: Combine oats, brown sugar, flour, margarine and egg whites, mixing until moistened. Press mixture onto bottom and up side of 9-inch microwavable pie plate. Microwave on HIGH (100% power) 2½ to 3 minutes or until top springs back when lightly touched. Cool completely. Proceed as above.

Nutrients per serving:

Calories	240	Cholesterol	15 mg
Fat	8 g	Sodium	110 mg

Candy-Apple Pie

Makes 8 servings

1¾ cups unsweetened apple juice, divided
⅓ cup cinnamon candies
½ teaspoon vanilla extract
¼ teaspoon red food coloring
4 apples, peeled, cored and sliced (Granny Smith, Rome Beauty or McIntosh)
3 tablespoons cornstarch
1 KEEBLER® READY-CRUST® Graham Cracker Pie Crust
1½ cups thawed frozen light whipped topping
½ teaspoon ground cinnamon

In large saucepan, combine 1½ cups juice, candies, vanilla, food coloring and apples. Bring to a boil. Reduce heat to low and simmer just until apples are tender, about 10 to 15 minutes. Combine remaining ¼ cup juice and cornstarch in small bowl. Stir into apple mixture; continue to cook until mixture boils and thickens. Cook an additional 2 to 3 minutes. Remove from heat; cool to room temperature.

Spoon apple filling into pie crust. Refrigerate several hours or until filling is set. Just before serving, combine whipped topping and cinnamon in small bowl. Top each slice of pie with a dollop of whipped topping mixture.

Nutrients per serving:

Calories	249	Cholesterol	0 mg
Fat	7 g	Sodium	154 mg

Fruit Lover's Tart

Deep-Dish Peach Pie

Makes 1 (8-inch) pie, 8 servings

    Pastry for single crust pie
 1 cup sugar
 2 tablespoons cornstarch
 3 pounds peaches, seeded, pared and sliced
     (about 6 cups)
 2 tablespoons REALEMON® Lemon Juice from
     Concentrate
 1 tablespoon margarine, melted
 ¼ teaspoon almond extract
 2 tablespoons sliced almonds

Preheat oven to 375°F. Remove and reserve
1 tablespoon sugar. In small bowl, combine remaining
sugar and cornstarch. In large bowl, toss peaches
with ReaLemon® brand; add sugar mixture,
margarine and extract. Turn into 8-inch square
baking dish. Roll pastry to 9-inch square; cut slits
near center. Place pastry over filling; turn under
edges, seal and flute. Sprinkle with reserved
1 tablespoon sugar and almonds. Bake 45 to 50
minutes or until golden brown. Cool on wire rack.

Nutrients per serving:

Calories	292	Cholesterol	0 mg
Fat	10 g	Sodium	163 mg

Deep-Dish Peach Pie

Lemon-Poppy Seed Tarts

Makes 6 servings

 1¾ cups skim milk
 1 package (0.9 ounces) sugar-free instant
     vanilla pudding and pie filling
 1 tablespoon poppy seeds
 1½ teaspoons grated lemon peel, divided
 6 KEEBLER® READY-CRUST® Single Serve
     Graham Crusts
 ¾ cup thawed frozen light whipped topping
     Additional grated lemon peel for garnish
     (optional)

In blender container, combine milk, pudding mix,
poppy seeds and 1 teaspoon lemon peel. Cover; blend
on low speed until well mixed and slightly thickened.
Pour evenly into crusts; refrigerate. Just before
serving, combine whipped topping and remaining
½ teaspoon lemon peel in small bowl. Top each tart
with dollop of whipped topping mixture. Sprinkle with
additional grated lemon peel, if desired.

Nutrients per serving:

Calories	141	Cholesterol	2 mg
Fat	6 g	Sodium	193 mg

Lite 'n' Easy Crustless Pumpkin Pie

Makes 1 (10-inch) pie, 10 servings

 2 envelopes unflavored gelatin
 2 tablespoons cold water
 2¼ cups *undiluted* CARNATION® Low Fat
     Evaporated Milk, divided
 1¾ cups (16-ounce can) LIBBY'S® Solid Pack
     Pumpkin
 6 tablespoons packed dark brown sugar
     or low-calorie equivalent
 1 teaspoon pumpkin pie spice
 1 teaspoon vanilla extract

In large bowl, sprinkle gelatin over cold water to
soften; set aside. In small saucepan, heat *1 cup* low
fat evaporated milk just to boiling. Slowly stir hot
milk into gelatin. Mix in *remaining* evaporated milk,
pumpkin, sugar, pumpkin pie spice and vanilla; set
aside. Spray 10-inch glass pie dish with nonstick
cooking spray. Pour pie mixture into dish; refrigerate.

Nutrients per serving:

Calories	97	Cholesterol	2 mg
Fat	trace	Sodium	72 mg

Bistro Pear Tart

Bistro Pear Tart

Makes 1 (9-inch) tart, 10 servings

½ cup sugar
¼ cup cornstarch
2 eggs, slightly beaten
2 cups low fat milk
1 teaspoon grated lemon peel
¼ teaspoon orange extract
   Baked 9-inch tart shell
2 fresh California Bartlett pears, peeled
   and sliced
¼ cup apricot jam, heated

Combine sugar and cornstarch in medium saucepan; whisk in eggs until well blended. Heat milk in small saucepan until hot but not boiling; slowly whisk hot milk into egg mixture. Heat egg mixture until thickened, stirring frequently. Remove from heat; stir in lemon peel and orange extract. Cool completely. Pour into baked tart shell. Arrange sliced pears on top; brush with hot apricot jam.

Nutrients per serving:

Calories	214	Cholesterol	57 mg
Fat	8 g	Sodium	184 mg

Favorite recipe from **California Tree Fruit Agreement**

Iced Coffee and Chocolate Pie

Makes 1 pie, 8 servings

2 envelopes unflavored gelatin
¼ cup cold skim milk
1 cup skim milk, heated to boiling
2 cups vanilla ice milk, softened
⅓ cup sugar
2 tablespoons instant coffee granules
1 teaspoon vanilla extract
1 (6-ounce) KEEBLER® READY-CRUST®
   Chocolate Flavored Pie Crust
   Reduced-calorie whipped topping (optional)
   Chocolate curls (optional)

In blender container, sprinkle gelatin over ¼ cup cold milk; let stand 3 to 4 minutes to soften. Add hot milk; cover and mix on low until gelatin dissolves, about 2 minutes. Add ice milk, sugar, coffee granules and vanilla. Cover and mix until smooth. Pour into pie crust. Refrigerate at least 2 hours. Garnish with whipped topping and chocolate curls, if desired.

Nutrients per serving:

Calories	220	Cholesterol	6 mg
Fat	6 g	Sodium	210 mg

Cranberry Apple Pie with Soft Gingersnap Crust

Makes 1 (8-inch) pie, 8 servings

20 gingersnap cookies
1½ tablespoons margarine, softened
2 McIntosh apples, peeled, cored and quartered
1 cup fresh cranberries
5 tablespoons firmly packed dark brown sugar
¼ teaspoon vanilla extract
¼ teaspoon ground cinnamon
1 teaspoon granulated sugar

Preheat oven to 375°F. Place gingersnaps and margarine in food processor; process until gingersnaps are finely ground. Press gingersnap mixture onto bottom and up side of 8-inch pie plate. Bake 5 to 8 minutes; cool. Chop apples in food processor. Add cranberries, brown sugar, vanilla and cinnamon; pulse just until mixed. Spoon apple-cranberry filling into another 8-inch pie plate or casserole dish. Sprinkle with granulated sugar. Bake 35 minutes or until apples are tender. Spoon filling into gingersnap crust and serve immediately.

Nutrients per serving:

Calories	124	Cholesterol	0 mg
Fat	3 g	Sodium	90 mg

Favorite recipe from **The Sugar Association, Inc.**

Light Lemon Meringue Pie

Makes 1 (9-inch) pie, 8 servings

Crust
1¼ cups all-purpose flour
½ teaspoon salt (optional)
⅓ cup CRISCO® Shortening
¼ cup orange juice

Filling
1 cup sugar
⅓ cup cornstarch
⅛ teaspoon salt (optional)
1½ cups cold water
1 egg yolk, lightly beaten
1 teaspoon finely shredded fresh lemon peel
⅓ cup fresh lemon juice

Meringue
3 egg whites
⅛ teaspoon salt (optional)
¼ cup sugar
½ teaspoon vanilla

For Crust, heat oven to 425°F. Combine flour and salt in bowl. Cut in Crisco® using pastry blender (or 2 knives) until all flour is blended in to form pea-size chunks. Sprinkle orange juice over flour mixture, one tablespoon at a time, tossing lightly with fork until dough forms. (Dough may seem slightly dry and crumbly.) Press into ball.

Press dough ball between hands to form 5- to 6-inch "pancake." Roll between unfloured sheets of waxed paper until one inch larger than upside down pie plate. Peel off top sheet. Flip into 9-inch pie plate. Remove other sheet. Fold edge under and flute. Prick bottom and sides with fork (50 times) to prevent shrinkage.

Bake at 425°F for 10 to 15 minutes or until lightly browned.

For Filling, combine 1 cup sugar, cornstarch and salt in heavy saucepan. Stir in water gradually, blending until smooth. Cook over medium-high heat, stirring constantly until filling comes to boil. Continue to cook, stirring constantly, 5 minutes. Remove from heat.

Stir small amount of hot mixture into egg yolk. Return egg yolk mixture to saucepan. Return saucepan to heat and cook, stirring constantly, 1 minute. Remove from heat. Stir in lemon peel and juice. *Reduce oven temperature to 350°F.*

For Meringue, beat egg whites and salt until frothy. Add ¼ cup sugar gradually, beating well after each addition. Continue beating until stiff, but not dry, peaks form. Fold in vanilla.

Spoon filling into baked pie shell. Spread meringue over filling, sealing meringue to edge of pie shell.

Bake at 350°F for 15 minutes or until golden brown. Cool completely on wire rack. Cut with sharp knife dipped in hot water.

Nutrients per serving:

Calories	289	Cholesterol	27 mg
Fat	9 g	Sodium	24 mg

Zabaglione Tarts with Fresh Berries

Zabaglione Tarts with Fresh Berries

Makes 6 servings

1½ cups skim milk
¼ cup Marsala wine
1 package (0.9 ounces) sugar-free instant vanilla pudding and pie filling
½ cup light frozen whipped topping, thawed
6 KEEBLER® READY-CRUST® Single Serve Graham Crusts
18 fresh strawberries, hulled and halved
Additional thawed frozen light whipped topping

In blender container, combine milk, wine and pudding mix. Cover; blend on low speed until well mixed and slightly thickened. Pour into medium bowl; fold in ½ cup whipped topping. Evenly divide filling among tart shells; arrange strawberries over filling. Just before serving, top each tart with additional whipped topping, if desired.

Nutrients per serving:

Calories	159	Cholesterol	1 mg
Fat	5 g	Sodium	189 mg

Light Custard Cheese Pie

Makes 1 (9-inch) pie, 6 servings

1 (9-inch) graham cracker crumb crust
1 (16-ounce) container BORDEN® Lite-line® or Viva® Cottage Cheese
1 tablespoon REALEMON® Lemon Juice from Concentrate
3 eggs
⅓ cup sugar
⅓ cup BORDEN® Lite-line® or Viva® Protein Fortified Skim Milk
1 teaspoon vanilla extract
1 cup assorted cut-up fresh fruit

Preheat oven to 350°F. In blender container, combine cottage cheese and ReaLemon® brand; blend until smooth. In large mixer bowl, beat eggs and sugar; add cheese mixture, milk and vanilla. Beat until smooth. Pour into crust. Bake 45 minutes or until set. Cool. Chill. Top with fresh fruit and serve. Refrigerate leftovers.

Nutrients per serving:

Calories	288	Cholesterol	113 mg
Fat	10 g	Sodium	452 mg

Luscious Pumpkin Pie

Makes 1 pie, 8 servings

1 teaspoon water
1 egg white
1 (6-ounce) KEEBLER® READY-CRUST® Pie
    Crust, Graham Cracker or Butter Flavored
2 eggs
1½ cups pumpkin pie filling
8 ounces DANNON® Plain Lowfat Yogurt
1 cup evaporated milk
¾ cup sugar
1 teaspoon vanilla extract
1 teaspoon ground cinnamon
¼ teaspoon ground cloves
¼ teaspoon ground ginger
¼ teaspoon ground nutmeg

Preheat oven to 375°F. Beat together water and egg white. Brush inside of pie crust. Place on baking sheet. Bake 3 minutes or until light golden. Cool thoroughly.

In large bowl, lightly beat 2 eggs. Add pumpkin pie filling, yogurt, evaporated milk, sugar, vanilla, cinnamon, cloves, ginger and nutmeg. Stir until thoroughly mixed.

Pour into pie crust. Bake 60 minutes or until set. Cool completely. Serve with whipped cream if desired.

Nutrients per serving:			
Calories	289	Cholesterol	64 mg
Fat	10 g	Sodium	327 mg

Creamy Banana Pie

Makes 8 servings

1 PET-RITZ® All-Vegetable Shortening Deep
    Dish Pie Crust Shell
1 can (12 fluid ounces) PET® Light Evaporated
    Skimmed Milk
1 box (3.4 ounces) French vanilla instant
    pudding and pie filling
½ cup plain nonfat yogurt
2 bananas, thinly sliced

Bake pie crust according to package directions for empty baked crust; cool.

In medium bowl, beat evaporated milk, pudding mix and yogurt until mixture starts to thicken.

Pour half of pudding mixture into cooled crust. Arrange banana slices over pudding mixture; top with remaining pudding mixture. Cover and refrigerate until firm. Garnish with whipped topping, if desired.

Nutrients per serving:			
Calories	129	Cholesterol	2 mg
Fat	2 g	Sodium	245 mg

Easy Pineapple Pie

Makes 6 to 8 servings

1 can (20 ounces) DOLE® Crushed Pineapple
    in Syrup*
1 package (4-serving size) instant lemon
    pudding and pie filling mix
1 cup milk
1 carton (4 ounces) frozen whipped topping,
    thawed
1 teaspoon grated lemon peel
2 tablespoons lemon juice
1 (8- or 9-inch) graham cracker pie crust

Drain pineapple well. Combine pudding mix and milk in medium bowl. Beat 2 to 3 minutes until very thick.

Fold in whipped topping, pineapple, lemon peel and lemon juice. Pour into crust. Cover and refrigerate 4 hours or overnight. Garnish as desired.

Prep time: 5 minutes
Chill time: 4 hours or overnight

*Use pineapple packed in juice, if desired.

Nutrients per serving:			
Calories	251	Cholesterol	2 mg
Fat	10 g	Sodium	321 mg

Easy Pineapple Pie

Cherry Turnovers

Makes 6 turnovers

8 frozen phyllo dough sheets, thawed
¼ cup butter or margarine, melted
6 tablespoons no-sugar-added black cherry
    fruit spread
4½ teaspoons cherry liqueur (optional)
1 egg
1 teaspoon cold water

Preheat oven to 400°F. Lightly brush each phyllo sheet with butter; stack. Cut through all sheets to form six 5-inch squares. Combine fruit spread and cherry liqueur in small bowl. Place 1 tablespoon fruit spread mixture in center of each stack of 8 phyllo squares; brush edges of phyllo with butter. Fold edges over to form triangle; gently press edges together to seal. Place on ungreased cookie sheet. Beat together egg and water; brush over phyllo triangles.

Bake 10 minutes or until golden brown. Cool on wire rack. Serve warm or at room temperature.

Nutrients per serving (1 turnover):			
Calories	206	Cholesterol	56 mg
Fat	9 g	Sodium	201 mg

Slice-of-Summer Tart

Makes 1 (9-inch) tart, 8 servings

Crust
¼ cup light vegetable oil margarine, softened
3 tablespoons packed brown sugar
¼ cup cholesterol-free egg product *or* 2 egg
    whites
¼ teaspoon almond extract
½ cup all-purpose flour
1½ cups Wheat CHEX® brand cereal, crushed to
    ½ cup

Filling
½ cup strawberry-flavored nonfat yogurt
2 to 3 cups fresh fruit, sliced
2 tablespoons honey

Preheat oven to 375°F. In large bowl combine margarine, sugar, egg product and almond extract. Add flour and cereal; mix well. Shape into ball; press

on bottom and sides of ungreased 9-inch tart pan or cake pan with removable bottom.

Bake 12 to 15 minutes or until golden brown. (Pierce crust with knife tip if bubbles form.) Cool completely. Spread yogurt over crust. Arrange fruit over yogurt. Brush honey over fruit, coating well.

Nutrients per serving:			
Calories	159	Cholesterol	trace
Fat	4 g	Sodium	164 mg

Pumpkin Cheesecake Pie

Makes 1 (9-inch) pie, 10 servings

1 envelope KNOX® Unflavored Gelatine
¼ cup cold skim milk
½ cup skim milk, heated to boiling
1 can (16 ounces) pumpkin (about 2 cups)
1 package (8 ounces) lite cream cheese
    (Neufchâtel), softened
¾ cup packed brown sugar
1 teaspoon vanilla extract
1 teaspoon ground cinnamon
½ teaspoon salt
⅛ teaspoon ground cloves
1 cup lite frozen whipped topping, thawed
    Gingersnap Crust (recipe follows), optional

In blender, sprinkle unflavored gelatine over cold milk; let stand 2 minutes. Add hot milk and process at low speed until gelatine is completely dissolved, about 2 minutes. Add pumpkin, cream cheese, brown sugar, vanilla, cinnamon, salt and cloves. Process at high speed until thoroughly blended, scraping sides frequently, about 5 minutes. In large bowl, fold whipped topping into pumpkin mixture. Pour into 9-inch pie pan or Gingersnap Crust. Chill until firm, about 3 hours.

Gingersnap Crust: Combine 1 cup gingersnap cookie crumbs, 1 tablespoon brown sugar and 3 tablespoons melted margarine until blended; press into 9-inch pie pan. Chill.

Nutrients per serving:			
Calories	231	Cholesterol	17 mg
Fat	9 g	Sodium	358 mg

Cherry Turnovers

Pineapple Lime Tartlets

Makes 6 servings

Crust
  6 to 8 graham crackers

Filling
  ¼ cup lime juice
  1 envelope unflavored gelatin
  1 carton (8 ounces) low-fat ricotta cheese
  1¼ cups nonfat plain yogurt, divided
  ½ cup sugar
  1 teaspoon coconut extract
  1 teaspoon grated lime peel

Pineapple Topping
  1 medium DOLE® Fresh Pineapple
  ¾ cup water
  ¼ cup sugar
  1 tablespoon cornstarch
  1 teaspoon grated lime peel

For Crust, arrange crackers in 6 (4½-inch) tart pans with removable bottoms or 1 (9-inch) tart pan with removable bottom. Break crackers to fit.

For Filling, place lime juice in small saucepan. Sprinkle gelatin over juice; let stand 1 minute to soften. Cook over low heat until gelatin is dissolved,

Pineapple Lime Tartlet

stirring frequently; let cool. Process ricotta cheese and ¼ cup yogurt in blender until smooth. Pour into medium bowl. Stir in remaining 1 cup yogurt, sugar, extract and lime peel. Stir in cooled gelatin mixture. Pour into prepared pans; refrigerate at least 2 hours.

For Pineapple Topping, twist crown from pineapple. Cut pineapple in half lengthwise. Refrigerate half for another use. Cut fruit from shell with knife. Cut fruit crosswise into thin slices. Combine water, sugar and cornstarch in large saucepan. Cook, stirring, until sauce boils and thickens. Cool. Add pineapple and lime peel. Arrange over tops of tarts. Garnish as desired.

Prep time: 20 minutes
Cook time: 5 minutes
Chill time: 2 hours

Nutrients per serving:

Calories	271	Cholesterol	13 mg
Fat	5 g	Sodium	184 mg

Easy Dark Cherry Tart

Makes 10 servings

  1¾ cups QUAKER® Oats (quick or old fashioned, uncooked)
  ½ cup all-purpose flour
  ⅓ cup firmly packed brown sugar
  ¼ teaspoon salt (optional)
  ⅓ cup (5⅓ tablespoons) margarine, melted
  2 cans (16 ounces each) pitted dark sweet cherries, undrained
  2 tablespoons granulated sugar
  1 tablespoon cornstarch
  ½ teaspoon almond or vanilla extract

Heat oven to 350°F. Lightly oil 9-inch springform pan or pie plate. Combine oats, flour, brown sugar and salt. Add margarine; mix well. Reserve ⅓ cup for topping; press remaining mixture onto bottom and 1 inch up sides of prepared pan. Bake 15 minutes.

Drain cherries, reserving ⅓ cup liquid. In medium saucepan, combine granulated sugar and cornstarch. Gradually add reserved liquid, stirring until smooth. Add cherries and extract. Bring to a boil, stirring occasionally. Reduce heat; simmer about 1 minute or until thickened and clear, stirring constantly. Pour over baked crust. Sprinkle with reserved oat topping. Bake 15 to 18 minutes or until edges of crust are lightly browned. Store tightly covered in refrigerator.

Nutrients per serving:

Calories	235	Cholesterol	0 mg
Fat	7 g	Sodium	75 mg

Peach-Yogurt Pie with Almond Melba Sauce

Peach-Yogurt Pie with Almond Melba Sauce

Makes 8 servings

2 cups fresh, canned or frozen peach slices, thawed
2 tablespoons granulated sugar
1 tablespoon almond-flavored liqueur
1 quart vanilla-flavored ice milk or frozen yogurt, softened
1 KEEBLER® READY-CRUST® Butter Flavored Pie Crust

Almond Melba Sauce
2 cups fresh or frozen raspberries, thawed
⅓ cup confectioners' sugar
2 tablespoons almond-flavored liqueur
1 tablespoon lemon juice

In blender or food processor, combine peaches, granulated sugar and 1 tablespoon liqueur. (If using fresh peaches, add 1 teaspoon lemon juice.) Cover; blend until smooth. Fold peach purée into softened ice milk or yogurt. Spoon into pie crust and freeze until firm.

For Almond Melba Sauce, place raspberries, confectioners' sugar, 2 tablespoons liqueur and lemon juice in blender or food processor. Cover and process until smooth. Strain to remove seeds. Refrigerate.

To serve, remove pie from freezer and let stand 5 minutes. Top each slice of pie with sauce. Garnish with a dollop of whipped topping and additional peaches and raspberries, if desired.

Nutrients per serving:

Calories	298	Cholesterol	9 mg
Fat	9 g	Sodium	203 mg

Margarita Pie

Margarita Pie

Makes 1 (9-inch) pie, 10 servings

1 envelope KNOX® Unflavored Gelatine
¼ cup cold skim milk
½ cup skim milk, heated to boiling
1 carton (8 ounces) cholesterol free egg substitute
⅔ cup sugar
⅓ cup lime juice
2 to 3 tablespoons tequila
1 teaspoon grated lime peel
1 to 2 drops green food coloring (optional)
1 cup lite frozen whipped topping, thawed
9-inch baked pastry shell

In blender, sprinkle unflavored gelatine over cold milk; let stand 2 minutes. Add hot milk and process at low speed until gelatine is completely dissolved, about 2 minutes. Add egg substitute, sugar, lime juice, tequila, lime peel and food coloring. Process at high speed until thoroughly blended, about 1 minute. Pour into large bowl and chill, stirring occasionally with wire whisk, until mixture mounds slightly when dropped from spoon, about 1 hour. Fold in whipped topping. Pour into pastry shell; chill until firm, about 4 hours. Garnish, if desired, with additional whipped topping and lime slices.

Nutrients per serving:

Calories	184	Cholesterol	0 mg
Fat	7 g	Sodium	155 mg

Apple Cinnamon Tart

Makes 1 (9-inch) tart, 10 servings

1½ cups quick-cooking oats
1 tablespoon plus ½ teaspoon ground cinnamon, divided
¾ cup frozen apple juice concentrate, thawed and divided
2 large apples, peeled if desired, and thinly sliced
1 teaspoon lemon juice
⅓ cup cold water
1 envelope unflavored gelatin
2 cups DANNON® Plain Nonfat or Lowfat Yogurt
¼ cup honey
½ teaspoon almond extract
Fresh mint leaves (optional)

Preheat oven to 350°F. In a small bowl combine oats and 1 tablespoon cinnamon. Toss with ¼ cup apple juice concentrate. Press onto bottom and side of 9-inch pie plate. Bake 5 minutes or until set. Cool on wire rack.

In a medium bowl toss apple slices with lemon juice; arrange on cooled crust in pan and set aside. In a small saucepan combine cold water and remaining ½ cup apple juice concentrate. Sprinkle gelatin over water mixture; let stand 3 minutes to soften. Cook and stir over medium heat until gelatin is completely dissolved; remove from heat. Add yogurt, honey, remaining ½ teaspoon cinnamon and almond extract; blend well. Pour over apples in crust. Chill several hours or overnight. If desired, garnish with mint leaves.

Nutrients per serving:

Calories	170	Cholesterol	trace
Fat	2 g	Sodium	39 mg

Chocolate Silk Pie

Chocolate Silk Pie

Makes 8 servings

1 envelope unflavored gelatin
¼ cup cold water
1 cup DANNON® Plain Nonfat or Lowfat Yogurt
1 cup skim milk
2 teaspoons vanilla
1 package (4-serving size) instant chocolate
    pudding and pie filling mix
⅓ cup sugar
1 packaged graham cracker crumb crust
    (6 ounces)
Reduced-calorie whipped topping

In a small saucepan sprinkle gelatin over water; let stand 3 minutes to soften. Stir over low heat until gelatin is completely dissolved. In food processor or blender combine gelatin mixture and remaining ingredients except crust and topping. Process until well blended. Pour into crust. Cover; chill several hours. Top with whipped topping.

Nutrients per serving:			
Calories	250	Cholesterol	trace
Fat	7 g	Sodium	375 mg

Luscious Lemon Bars

Makes 2 dozen bars

Crust
¼ cup CRISCO® Vegetable Oil
¼ cup granulated sugar
¼ teaspoon salt (optional)
1 cup all-purpose flour
1½ teaspoons skim milk

Filling
1 egg
1 egg white
1 cup granulated sugar
2 teaspoons grated lemon peel
3 tablespoons fresh lemon juice
2 tablespoons all-purpose flour
½ teaspoon baking powder

Drizzle
¾ cup confectioners sugar
1 tablespoon skim milk
½ teaspoon vanilla
¼ teaspoon grated lemon peel

1. Heat oven to 350°F. Oil bottom of 8-inch square pan lightly.

2. For crust, combine ¼ cup Crisco® Oil, granulated sugar and salt (if used) in large bowl. Beat at medium speed of electric mixer until well blended. Add flour and milk. Stir with spoon until well mixed and crumbly. Spoon into pan. Press evenly onto bottom.

3. Bake at 350°F for 15 minutes.

4. For filling, combine egg, egg white, granulated sugar, lemon peel, lemon juice, flour and baking powder in medium bowl. Beat at high speed 3 minutes. Pour over hot baked crust.

5. Bake at 350°F for 25 minutes or until light golden brown. Loosen from edge while still warm. Cool completely.

6. For drizzle, combine confectioners sugar, milk, vanilla and lemon peel in small bowl. Drizzle over top. Allow to stand before cutting into bars.

Nutrients per serving (1 bar):			
Calories	100	Cholesterol	10 mg
Fat	3 g	Sodium	30 mg

Chewy Apple Moons

Makes 1½ dozen cookies

¾ cup thawed frozen unsweetened apple juice
   concentrate
½ cup coarsely chopped dried apples
2 eggs
¼ cup butter or margarine, melted and cooled
1 teaspoon vanilla extract
1¼ cups all-purpose flour
½ teaspoon baking powder
½ teaspoon ground cinnamon
¼ teaspoon salt
⅛ teaspoon ground nutmeg

Preheat oven to 350°F. Combine apple juice
concentrate and apples; let stand 10 minutes. Beat
eggs in medium bowl. Blend in concentrate mixture,
butter and vanilla. Add remaining ingredients; mix
well. Drop tablespoonfuls of dough 2 inches apart
onto greased cookie sheet.

Bake 10 to 12 minutes or until firm and golden
brown. Cool on wire rack. Store in airtight container.

Nutrients per serving (1 cookie):

Calories	89	Cholesterol	31 mg
Fat	3 g	Sodium	80 mg

Pineapple-Raisin Bars

Makes 16 bars

2 eggs
1 cup thawed frozen unsweetened pineapple
   juice concentrate
¼ cup butter or margarine, melted
1 teaspoon vanilla extract
1⅓ cups all-purpose flour
⅔ cup uncooked rolled oats
1 teaspoon baking soda
¼ teaspoon salt
1 teaspoon ground cinnamon
½ teaspoon ground ginger
⅛ teaspoon ground nutmeg
1 can (8 ounces) crushed pineapple in
   unsweetened juice, well drained
¾ cup lightly toasted chopped pecans
½ cup golden raisins

Preheat oven to 350°F. Beat eggs in large bowl.
Blend in pineapple juice concentrate, butter and
vanilla. Add flour, oats, baking soda, salt and spices;
mix well. Stir in pineapple, pecans and raisins.
Spread batter into greased 12×8-inch baking dish.

Bake 18 to 20 minutes or until firm. Cool completely
on wire rack. Cut into bars. Store in airtight container.

Nutrients per serving (1 bar):

Calories	159	Cholesterol	34 mg
Fat	7 g	Sodium	124 mg

Drop Sugar Cookies

Makes 3 dozen cookies

⅓ cup CRISCO® Vegetable Oil
1 cup sugar
1 tablespoon vanilla
1 egg
2½ cups all-purpose flour
¾ teaspoon salt
½ teaspoon baking soda
¼ cup skim milk
   Colored sugar crystals (optional)

1. Heat oven to 400°F. Oil baking sheet lightly.

2. Combine ⅓ cup Crisco® Oil, sugar and vanilla in
large bowl. Add egg. Beat at medium speed of
electric mixer until blended. Stir in flour, salt and
baking soda with spoon until mixture is smooth. Add
milk. Stir until well blended.

3. Drop dough by rounded teaspoonfuls 2 inches
apart onto baking sheet. Flatten with bottom of lightly
oiled glass. Sprinkle with additional granulated sugar
or colored sugar crystals, if desired.

4. Bake at 400°F for 6 to 8 minutes or until just
barely brown around edges. (Avoid overbaking.)
Remove to cooling rack.

Rolled Cookies: *Chill dough one hour or longer. Roll out
on lightly floured surface. Cut into desired shapes. Bake as
above.*

Slice and Bake Cookies: *Shape dough into rolls. Wrap
in plastic wrap or foil. Freeze several hours or overnight.
Slice. Bake as above.*

Nutrients per serving (1 cookie):

Calories	75	Cholesterol	5 mg
Fat	2 g	Sodium	60 mg

Peanut Butter & Banana Cookies

Makes 2 dozen cookies

¼ cup butter or margarine
½ cup mashed ripe bananas (about 2 medium
    bananas)
½ cup no-sugar-added natural peanut butter
1 egg
¼ cup thawed frozen unsweetened apple juice
    concentrate
1 teaspoon vanilla extract
1 cup all-purpose flour
½ teaspoon baking soda
¼ teaspoon salt
½ cup chopped salted peanuts
    Whole peanuts (optional)

Preheat oven to 375°F. Beat butter in large bowl until creamy. Add bananas and peanut butter; beat until smooth. Blend in eggs, apple juice concentrate and vanilla. Beat in flour, baking soda and salt. Stir in chopped peanuts. Drop rounded tablespoonfuls of dough 2 inches apart onto lightly greased cookie sheets; top each with 1 peanut, if desired.

Bake 8 minutes or until set. Cool completely on wire rack. Store in airtight container.

Nutrients per serving (1 cookie):

Calories	100	Cholesterol	14 mg
Fat	6 g	Sodium	84 mg

Wild Rice Applesauce Bars

Makes 48 bars

2 cups well-cooked wild rice
1⅓ cups applesauce
1 cup buttermilk, divided
⅓ cup vegetable shortening
1 cup firmly packed brown sugar
6 egg whites
2 teaspoons vanilla extract
2½ cups all-purpose flour
1 teaspoon baking soda
1 teaspoon salt
1 teaspoon ground cinnamon
1 cup chopped nuts (optional)
    Powdered sugar (optional)

Preheat oven to 350°F. Grease bottom only of 15×10×1-inch baking pan.

Combine wild rice, applesauce and ½ cup buttermilk in medium bowl; mix well. Set aside. Combine shortening, brown sugar, egg whites and vanilla in large bowl; beat with electric mixer on high speed 5 minutes or until smooth and creamy. Add remaining ½ cup buttermilk; beat on low speed until well blended. Add flour, baking soda, salt and cinnamon; beat on low speed until well blended. Stir in wild rice mixture and nuts. Spread in prepared pan.

Bake 20 to 25 minutes until wooden pick inserted in center comes out clean. Sprinkle with powdered sugar. Cool completely. Cut into bars. Store in airtight containers.

Nutrients per serving (1 bar):

Calories	65	Cholesterol	trace
Fat	2 g	Sodium	79 mg

Favorite recipe from **Minnesota Cultivated Wild Rice Council**

Apricot Bars

Makes 1½ dozen bars

2 eggs
1 cup no-sugar-added apricot fruit spread
½ cup butter or margarine, melted
2 teaspoons vanilla extract
1 cup all-purpose flour
⅔ cup uncooked rolled oats
1¼ teaspoons baking powder
¼ teaspoon salt
¾ teaspoon ground cinnamon
¼ teaspoon allspice
⅛ teaspoon mace

Preheat oven to 350°F. Beat eggs in large bowl. Blend in fruit spread, butter and vanilla. Add flour, oats, baking powder, salt and spices; mix well. Spread dough into greased 12×8-inch baking dish. Bake 18 minutes or until golden brown and firm to the touch. Cool completely on wire rack. Cut into bars. Store in airtight container.

Nutrients per serving (1 bar):

Calories	130	Cholesterol	37 mg
Fat	6 g	Sodium	119 mg

Peanut Butter & Banana Cookies

Clockwise from top right: Cocoa Brownie Cookie Bars, Luscious Lemon Bars (page 446), Gingerbread Apple Bars

Gingerbread Apple Bars

Makes 1 dozen bars

1 cup applesauce
½ cup raisins
⅓ cup unsulfured light molasses
1 teaspoon baking soda
2 eggs
¼ cup sugar
¼ cup CRISCO® Vegetable Oil
1½ cups all-purpose flour
1 teaspoon cinnamon
½ teaspoon ginger
¼ teaspoon cloves
⅛ teaspoon salt

1. Heat oven to 350°F. Oil 8-inch square pan lightly.

2. Place applesauce and raisins in small saucepan. Cook and stir on low heat until mixture comes to a boil. Remove from heat. Stir in molasses and baking soda. Cool slightly.

3. Combine eggs and sugar in large bowl. Beat in ¼ cup Crisco® Oil gradually.

4. Combine flour, cinnamon, ginger, cloves and salt in small bowl. Add to egg mixture alternately with applesauce mixture, beginning and ending with flour mixture. Spoon into pan.

5. Bake at 350°F for 30 minutes or until toothpick inserted in center comes out clean. Cool in pan on cooling rack. Cut into bars. Serve warm or at room temperature.

Nutrients per serving (1 bar):

Calories	170	Cholesterol	35 mg
Fat	6 g	Sodium	105 mg

Cocoa Brownie Cookie Bars

Makes 2 dozen bars

4 egg whites
⅓ cup CRISCO® Vegetable Oil
¼ cup nonfat vanilla yogurt
1 teaspoon vanilla
1⅓ cups granulated sugar
½ cup unsweetened cocoa powder
1¼ cups all-purpose flour
¼ teaspoon salt
1 tablespoon confectioners sugar

1. Heat oven to 350°F. Oil bottom of 9-inch square pan lightly.

2. Place egg whites in large bowl. Beat with spoon until slightly frothy. Add ⅓ cup Crisco® Oil, yogurt and vanilla. Mix well. Add granulated sugar and cocoa. Mix well. Add flour and salt. Mix until blended. Pour into pan.

3. Bake at 350°F for 26 to 28 minutes or until done. Cool completely.

4. Sprinkle with confectioners sugar. Cut into bars.

Nutrients per serving (1 bar):

Calories	105	Cholesterol	0 mg
Fat	3 g	Sodium	35 mg

Butterscotch Crispies

Makes 8½ dozen cookies

Nonstick cooking spray
2 cups sifted all-purpose flour
1 teaspoon baking soda
1 teaspoon salt
½ cup margarine, softened
2½ cups firmly packed light brown sugar
2 eggs
2 egg whites
1 teaspoon vanilla extract
2 cups quick-cooking rolled oats
2 cups oven-toasted rice cereal
½ cup chopped walnuts

Preheat oven to 350°F. Spray cookie sheets with nonstick cooking spray. Sift flour, baking soda and salt into medium bowl. Beat margarine and brown sugar in large bowl until light and fluffy. Add eggs and egg whites, 1 at a time, beating well after each addition until fluffy. Stir in vanilla. Add flour mixture, ⅓ at a time; beat until well blended. Stir in oats, cereal and walnuts. Drop by teaspoonfuls 1 inch apart onto prepared cookie sheets.

Bake 10 minutes or until cookies are firm and golden brown. Remove to wire racks; cool completely. Store in airtight containers.

Nutrients per serving (1 cookie):

Calories	50	Cholesterol	4 mg
Fat	1 g	Sodium	30 mg

Favorite recipe from **The Sugar Association, Inc.**

Chocolate Crinkles

Makes 3 dozen cookies

**1 package DUNCAN HINES® Moist Deluxe
    Devil's Food Cake Mix
2 eggs
¼ cup CRISCO® PURITAN® Oil
4 teaspoons milk
½ cup confectioners sugar**

1. Preheat oven to 375°F. Grease cookie sheets.

2. Combine cake mix, eggs, oil and milk in large bowl. Stir until thoroughly blended. Place confectioners sugar in small bowl. Drop rounded teaspoonfuls of dough into confectioners sugar. Roll to coat and form into balls. Place 2 inches apart on cookie sheets.

3. Bake at 375°F for 8 to 9 minutes or until set. Cool 1 minute on cookie sheets. Remove to cooling racks.

Nutrients per serving (1 cookie):

Calories	81	Cholesterol	12 mg
Fat	3 g	Sodium	121 mg

Giant Raisin Bran Cookies

Makes 1½ dozen cookies

**2 cups KELLOGG'S® RAISIN BRAN cereal,
    crushed to 1½ cups
1 cup whole wheat flour
1 cup all-purpose flour
1 teaspoon baking soda
¾ cup margarine, softened
⅔ cup granulated sugar
½ cup firmly packed brown sugar
2 eggs**

Stir together Kellogg's® Raisin Bran cereal, flours and baking soda; set aside.

In large mixing bowl, beat margarine and sugars until light and fluffy. Add eggs; beat well. Stir in cereal mixture; combine thoroughly. Scoop out a scant ¼ cupful of dough for each cookie. Drop onto ungreased cookie sheets, spacing 4 inches apart.

Bake at 350°F about 14 minutes or until lightly browned. Cool on cookie sheets 1 minute. Cool completely on wire racks.

Nutrients per serving (1 cookie):

Calories	190	Cholesterol	24 mg
Fat	9 g	Sodium	183 mg

Apricot-Pecan Tassies

Makes 2 dozen cookies

Crust
**1 cup all-purpose flour
½ cup butter, cut into pieces
6 tablespoons light cream cheese**

Filling
**¾ cup firmly packed light brown sugar
1 egg, lightly beaten
1 tablespoon butter, softened
½ teaspoon vanilla extract
¼ teaspoon salt
⅔ cup diced Dried California Apricot Halves
    (about 4 ounces)
⅓ cup chopped pecans**

For Crust, in food processor, combine flour, ½ cup butter and cream cheese; process until mixture forms a ball. Wrap dough in plastic wrap and refrigerate 15 minutes.

For Filling, combine sugar, egg, 1 tablespoon butter, vanilla and salt in medium bowl; beat until smooth. Stir in apricots and nuts.

Preheat oven to 325°F. Shape dough into 24 (1-inch) balls and place in paper-lined or greased (1½-inch) miniature muffin cups or tart pans. Press dough on bottom and sides of each cup; fill with 1 teaspoon apricot-pecan filling. Bake 25 minutes or until golden and filling sets. Cool slightly and remove from cups. Cooled cookies can be wrapped tightly in plastic and frozen for up to 6 weeks.

Nutrients per serving (1 cookie):

Calories	110	Cholesterol	13 mg
Fat	7 g	Sodium	85 mg

Favorite recipe from **California Apricot Advisory Board**

Chocolate Crinkles

Hermit Cookie Bars

Makes 3 dozen bar cookies

½ cup CRISCO® PURITAN® Oil
¾ cup firmly packed brown sugar
2 eggs
2 tablespoons skim milk
1½ cups all-purpose flour
¾ teaspoon ground cinnamon
½ teaspoon baking soda
½ teaspoon ground nutmeg
¼ teaspoon salt
¼ teaspoon ground cloves
1⅓ cups raisins
½ cup chopped walnuts
2 tablespoons confectioners sugar

Heat oven to 350°F. Oil 13×9×2-inch pan.

Combine Crisco® Puritan® Oil and brown sugar in large bowl. Beat at medium speed of electric mixer. Add eggs, one at a time, beating well after each addition. Mix in milk.

Combine flour, cinnamon, baking soda, nutmeg, salt and cloves. Beat into creamed mixture at low speed until blended. Stir in raisins and nuts. Spread evenly into pan.

Bake at 350°F for 23 to 26 minutes, or until wooden toothpick inserted in center comes out clean. Cool in pan on wire rack. Cut into bars, about 2×1½ inches. Sift confectioners sugar over bars.

Drop Cookie Variation: *Drop batter by level measuring tablespoonfuls 2 inches apart on oiled cookie sheets. Bake at 350°F for 8 to 9 minutes. Remove to cooling rack. Cool. Sift confectioners sugar over cookies.*

An easy make-over: *A light dusting of confectioners sugar is a low-calorie alternative to frosting.*

Nutrients per serving (1 bar):

Calories	96	Cholesterol	12 mg
Fat	4 g	Sodium	33 mg

Peanut Butter Bars

Peanut Butter Bars

Makes 2 dozen bar cookies

1 package DUNCAN HINES® Peanut Butter Cookie Mix
2 egg whites
½ cup chopped peanuts
1 cup confectioners sugar
2 tablespoons water
½ teaspoon vanilla extract

1. Preheat oven to 350°F.

2. Combine cookie mix, contents of peanut butter packet from Mix and egg whites in large bowl. Stir until thoroughly blended. Press in ungreased 13×9×2-inch pan. Sprinkle peanuts over dough. Press lightly.

3. Bake at 350°F for 16 to 18 minutes or until golden brown. Cool completely in pan on wire rack.

4. Combine confectioners sugar, water and vanilla extract in small bowl. Stir until blended. Drizzle glaze over top. Cut into bars.

Nutrients per serving (1 bar):

Calories	65	Cholesterol	0 mg
Fat	7 g	Sodium	104 mg

Macadamia Nut Crunchies

Makes 2 dozen cookies

1 egg, beaten
½ cup mashed ripe bananas (about 2 medium bananas)
⅓ cup butter or margarine, melted
¼ cup no-sugar-added pineapple fruit spread
1 teaspoon vanilla extract
1¼ cups all-purpose flour
⅓ cup unsweetened shredded coconut*
½ teaspoon baking powder
½ teaspoon salt
1 jar (3½ ounces) macadamia nuts, coarsely chopped (about ¾ cup)

Preheat oven to 375°F. Combine egg, bananas, butter, fruit spread and vanilla in medium bowl until well blended. Add flour, coconut, baking powder and salt; mix well. Stir in nuts. Drop tablespoonfuls of dough 2 inches apart onto lightly greased cookie sheets.

Bake 10 to 12 minutes or until lightly browned. Cool completely on wire racks. Store in airtight container.

Unsweetened shredded coconut is available in health food stores.

Nutrients per serving (1 cookie):			
Calories	96	Cholesterol	16 mg
Fat	6 g	Sodium	83 mg

Applesauce-Walnut Cookies

Makes 3 dozen cookies

½ cup margarine, softened
¾ cup sugar
2 egg whites
1 cup unsweetened applesauce
1½ cups all-purpose flour
2 teaspoons baking powder
½ teaspoon baking soda
1 teaspoon ground cinnamon
½ teaspoon ground nutmeg
½ teaspoon ground cloves
¼ teaspoon salt
1½ cups uncooked rolled oats
½ cup diced apples
½ cup raisins
½ cup chopped walnuts

Preheat oven to 375°F. Spray baking sheets with vegetable cooking spray.

Beat margarine and sugar in large bowl with electric mixer until creamy. Beat in egg whites; stir in applesauce. Combine flour, baking powder, baking soda, spices and salt in medium bowl; stir into applesauce mixture. Stir in oats, apples, raisins and walnuts. Drop by level tablespoonfuls 2 inches apart onto prepared baking sheets.

Bake 12 minutes or until edges are lightly browned. Remove to wire racks; completely. Store in airtight container.

Nutrients per serving (1 cookie):			
Calories	93	Cholesterol	0 mg
Fat	4 g	Sodium	31 mg

Favorite recipe from **Western New York Apple Growers Association**

Yogurt Drop Cookies

Makes 36 cookies

1¼ cups all-purpose flour
½ teaspoon baking soda
½ teaspoon grated orange peel
¼ cup shortening
¼ cup margarine or butter
⅔ cup sugar
1 egg
½ cup DANNON® Vanilla Lowfat Yogurt
1 teaspoon vanilla

Preheat oven to 350°F. Grease cookie sheets. In a medium bowl combine flour, baking soda and orange peel; set aside. In a large bowl beat shortening and margarine with electric mixer on medium speed for 30 seconds. Add sugar; beat on medium speed until fluffy. Beat in egg, yogurt and vanilla. Stir in flour mixture. Drop teaspoonfuls of dough, 2 inches apart, onto prepared cookie sheets. Bake 8 minutes or until golden brown. Remove to wire racks to cool.

Nutrients per serving (1 cookie):			
Calories	60	Cholesterol	10 mg
Fat	3 g	Sodium	15 mg

Macadamia Nut Crunchies

Tropical Bar Cookies

Makes 16 cookies

½ cup DOLE® Sliced Almonds, divided
1 cup all-purpose flour
⅓ cup margarine, melted
½ cup sugar, divided
1 can (20 ounces) DOLE® Crushed Pineapple in Syrup, drained
1 package (8 ounces) light cream cheese, softened
1 egg
1 teaspoon vanilla extract
⅓ cup flaked coconut

Preheat oven to 350°F. Chop ¼ cup almonds for crust; mix with flour, margarine and ¼ cup sugar in medium bowl until crumbly. Press onto bottom of 9-inch square pan. Bake 12 minutes.

Beat pineapple, cream cheese, egg, remaining ¼ cup sugar and vanilla in large bowl until blended. Pour over crust. Top with coconut and remaining ¼ cup sliced almonds.

Bake 35 to 40 minutes or until golden brown. Cool on wire rack. Refrigerate at least 2 hours before cutting into bars.

Nutrients per serving (1 bar):			
Calories	199	Cholesterol	28 mg
Fat	10 g	Sodium	111 mg

Tropical Bar Cookies

Double Chocolate Cloud Cookies

Makes about 4 dozen cookies

3 egg whites
⅛ teaspoon cream of tartar
¾ cup sugar
1 teaspoon vanilla extract
2 tablespoons HERSHEY₂S Cocoa or HERSHEY₂S Premium European Style Cocoa
¾ cup HERSHEY₂S Semi-Sweet Chocolate Chips
Chocolate Drizzle Glaze (recipe follows)

Heat oven to 300°F. Place parchment paper on cookie sheets. In large mixer bowl, beat egg whites and cream of tartar until soft peaks form. Gradually add sugar and vanilla, beating until stiff peaks hold their shape, sugar is dissolved and mixture is glossy. Sift cocoa over egg white mixture; gently fold in cocoa just until combined. Fold in chocolate chips. Drop by heaping teaspoonfuls onto prepared cookie sheets. Bake 20 to 25 minutes or just until dry. Carefully peel cookies off paper; cool completely on wire racks. Place waxed paper under wire racks with cookies. Prepare Chocolate Drizzle Glaze; drizzle glaze lightly over cookies. Store, covered, at room temperature.

Chocolate Drizzle Glaze: In top of double boiler over hot, not boiling, water, melt ⅓ cup Hershey₂s Semi-Sweet Chocolate Chips and ½ teaspoon shortening, stirring until smooth. Remove from heat; cool slightly, stirring frequently.

Nutrients per serving (3 cookies):			
Calories	100	Cholesterol	0 mg
Fat	4 g	Sodium	12 mg

Jelly-Filled Dainties

Makes 4 dozen cookies

2 cups all-purpose flour
½ teaspoon salt
2¼ cups KELLOGG'S® CORN FLAKES cereal
1 cup margarine, softened
½ cup firmly packed brown sugar
1 egg
½ teaspoon vanilla extract
1 cup currant, raspberry or strawberry jelly

Stir together flour and salt; set aside. Crush Kellogg's® Corn Flakes cereal into fine crumbs to measure ½ cup; set aside.

In large bowl, blend margarine and sugar. Add egg and vanilla; beat well. Stir in flour mixture.

Shape dough into 1-inch balls. Roll in cereal. Place about 2 inches apart on ungreased cookie sheets. Make an indentation in each cookie using handle of wooden spoon.

Bake at 300°F for 8 to 10 minutes. Remove from oven; press down indentation in each cookie. Return to oven and bake about 10 minutes more or until lightly browned. Cool on cookie sheets 1 minute. Cool completely on wire racks. When cool, fill centers with about 1 teaspoon jelly.

Nutrients per serving (1 cookie):			
Calories	84	Cholesterol	4 mg
Fat	4 g	Sodium	82 mg

Lemon Almond Delights

Makes 3 dozen cookies

1 package DUNCAN HINES® Moist Deluxe
    Lemon Supreme Cake Mix
2 eggs
¼ cup CRISCO® PURITAN® Oil
⅔ cup chopped almonds

1. Preheat oven to 375°F. Grease cookie sheets.

2. Combine cake mix, eggs and oil in large bowl. Stir until thoroughly blended. Stir in chopped almonds. Drop by rounded teaspoonfuls onto cookie sheets.

3. Bake at 375°F for 8 to 9 minutes or until set. Cool 1 minute on cookie sheets. Remove to cooling racks.

Nutrients per serving (1 cookie):			
Calories	90	Cholesterol	12 mg
Fat	4 g	Sodium	97 mg

Cocoa Banana Bars

Cocoa Banana Bars

Makes 9 bar cookies

Bars
⅔ cup QUAKER® Oat Bran hot cereal, uncooked
⅔ cup all-purpose flour
½ cup granulated sugar
⅓ cup unsweetened cocoa
½ cup mashed ripe banana (about 1 large)
¼ cup liquid vegetable oil margarine
3 tablespoons light corn syrup
2 egg whites, lightly beaten
1 teaspoon vanilla
    Strawberry halves (optional)

Glaze
2 teaspoons unsweetened cocoa
2 teaspoons liquid vegetable oil margarine
¼ cup powdered sugar
2 to 2½ teaspoons warm water, divided

For Bars, heat oven to 350°F. Lightly spray 8-inch square baking pan with nonstick cooking spray, or oil lightly. In large bowl, combine oat bran, flour, granulated sugar and ⅓ cup cocoa. Add combined banana, ¼ cup margarine, corn syrup, egg whites and vanilla; mix well. Pour into prepared pan, spreading evenly. Bake 23 to 25 minutes or until center is set. Cool on wire rack. Drizzle glaze over brownies. Top with strawberry halves, if desired. Cut into bars. Store tightly covered.

For Glaze, in small bowl, combine 2 teaspoons cocoa and 2 teaspoons margarine. Stir in powdered sugar and 1 teaspoon water. Gradually add remaining 1 to 1½ teaspoons water to make medium-thick glaze, mixing well.

Nutrients per serving (1 bar):			
Calories	210	Cholesterol	0 mg
Fat	7 g	Sodium	60 mg

Kolacky

Kolacky

Makes 2 dozen pastries

½ cup butter or margarine, softened
3 ounces regular or reduced calorie cream
    cheese, softened
1 teaspoon vanilla extract
1 cup all-purpose flour
⅛ teaspoon salt
6 teaspoons no-sugar-added fruit spread,
    assorted flavors
1 egg
1 teaspoon cold water

Combine butter and cream cheese in large bowl; beat until smooth and creamy. Blend in vanilla. Combine flour and salt; gradually add to butter mixture, mixing until soft dough forms. Divide dough in half; wrap each half in plastic wrap. Refrigerate until firm.

Preheat oven to 375°F. Roll out half the dough on lightly floured pastry cloth or board to ⅛-inch thickness. Cut with top of glass or biscuit cutter into 3-inch rounds. Spoon ½ teaspoon fruit spread onto center of each dough circle. Beat egg with water in small bowl; lightly brush on edges of dough circles. Lift three edges of dough over fruit spread; pinch edges together to seal. Place on ungreased cookie sheets; brush with egg mixture. Repeat with remaining dough and fruit spread.

Bake 12 minutes or until golden brown. Let stand on cookie sheets 1 minute; transfer to wire rack. Cool completely. Store in airtight container.

Nutrients per serving (1 pastry):

Calories	76	Cholesterol	23 mg
Fat	5 g	Sodium	64 mg

Chocolate Crackles

Makes 4 dozen cookies

⅓ cup CRISCO® Vegetable Oil
1½ cups granulated sugar
1½ teaspoons vanilla
1 egg
2 egg whites
1⅔ cups all-purpose flour
½ cup unsweetened cocoa powder
1½ teaspoons baking powder
½ teaspoon salt
½ cup confectioners sugar

1. Heat oven to 350°F.

2. Combine Crisco® Oil, granulated sugar and vanilla in large bowl. Beat at medium speed of electric mixer until blended. Add egg and egg whites. Beat until well blended. Stir in flour, cocoa, baking powder and salt with spoon.

3. Place confectioners sugar in shallow dish or large plastic food storage bag.

4. Shape dough into 1-inch balls. Roll or shake in confectioners sugar until coated. Place about 2 inches apart on ungreased baking sheet.

5. Bake at 350°F for 7 to 8 minutes or until almost no indentation remains when touched lightly. (Do not overbake.) Cool on baking sheet 2 minutes before removing to cooling rack.

Nutrients per serving (1 cookie):

Calories	60	Cholesterol	5 mg
Fat	2 g	Sodium	35 mg

Peach Oatmeal Cookies

Makes 3 dozen cookies

2 eggs
⅔ cup margarine
¾ cup granulated sugar
¾ cup packed brown sugar
1½ teaspoons vanilla extract
1½ cups whole wheat flour
2 teaspoons baking powder
1 teaspoon salt
2½ cups uncooked rolled oats
3 fresh California peaches, diced
    (about 1½ cups)
1 cup raisins

Preheat oven to 350°F. Beat eggs, margarine, sugars and vanilla in large bowl with electric mixer until creamy. Combine flour, baking powder and salt in small bowl. Add flour mixture to egg mixture; beat on low speed 2 to 3 minutes until smooth. Stir in oats, peaches and raisins. Refrigerate until firm.

Drop by tablespoonfuls 2 inches apart onto nonstick baking sheets. Bake 10 to 15 minutes until cookies are golden. Remove to wire racks; cool completely. Store in airtight container.

Nutrients per serving (1 cookie):

Calories	124	Cholesterol	15 mg
Fat	4 g	Sodium	120 mg

Favorite recipe from **California Tree Fruit Agreement**

Cocoa Brownies

Makes 1½ dozen brownies

    4 egg whites
    ½ cup CRISCO® PURITAN® Oil
    1 teaspoon vanilla
    1⅓ cups granulated sugar
    ½ cup unsweetened cocoa
    1¼ cups all-purpose flour
    ¼ teaspoon salt
        Confectioners' sugar (optional)

Heat oven to 350°F. Oil bottom of 9×9-inch pan. Set aside.

Place egg whites in large bowl. Beat with spoon until slightly frothy. Add Crisco® Puritan® Oil and vanilla. Mix thoroughly. Stir in sugar and cocoa. Mix well. Stir in flour and salt until blended. Pour into pan.

Bake at 350°F for 26 to 28 minutes. *Do not overbake.* Cool completely on wire rack before cutting. Sprinkle with confectioners' sugar, if desired.

Nutrients per serving (1 brownie):

Calories	150	Cholesterol	0 mg
Fat	7 g	Sodium	43 mg

Chocolate Chip Cookies

Makes 3 dozen cookies

    2 cups all-purpose flour
    1 teaspoon baking soda
    ½ teaspoon salt
    1 egg
    3 tablespoons water
    1 teaspoon vanilla extract
    1 cup firmly packed brown sugar
    ¼ cup CRISCO® PURITAN® Oil
    ½ cup semi-sweet chocolate chips

Heat oven to 375°F. Oil cookie sheets well.

Combine flour, baking soda and salt. Set aside. Combine egg, water and vanilla. Set aside.

Blend brown sugar and Crisco® Puritan® Oil in large bowl at low speed of electric mixer. Add egg mixture. Beat until smooth. Add flour mixture in three parts at lowest speed. Scrape bowl well after each addition. Stir in chocolate chips.

Drop dough by rounded teaspoonfuls onto cookie sheets. Bake at 375°F for 7 to 8 minutes or until lightly browned. Cool on cookie sheets 1 minute. Remove to wire racks.

Nutrients per serving (1 cookie):

Calories	74	Cholesterol	6 mg
Fat	3 g	Sodium	57 mg

Applesauce Cookies

Makes about 5 dozen cookies

    1 cup all-purpose flour
    1 teaspoon baking powder
    1 teaspoon ground allspice
    ¼ teaspoon salt
    ½ cup margarine, softened
    ½ cup sugar
    2 egg whites
    2 cups rolled oats, uncooked
    1 cup unsweetened applesauce
    ½ cup chopped raisins

Preheat oven to 375°F. Grease cookie sheet. In small bowl, combine flour, baking powder, allspice and salt; set aside. In large bowl, beat margarine and sugar until creamy. Add egg whites; beat well. Beat in flour mixture. Stir in oats, applesauce and raisins, mixing well. Drop by level tablespoonfuls onto prepared cookie sheet. Bake 11 minutes or until edges are lightly browned. Cool on wire rack.

Nutrients per serving (1 cookie):

Calories	45	Cholesterol	0 mg
Fat	2 g	Sodium	34 mg

Favorite recipe from **Western New York Apple Growers Association**

Lemon Cookies

Makes 4 dozen cookies

    ⅔ cup MIRACLE WHIP® Salad Dressing
    1 two-layer yellow cake mix
    2 eggs
    2 teaspoons grated lemon peel
    ⅔ cup ready-to-spread vanilla frosting
    4 teaspoons lemon juice

Preheat oven to 375°F.

Blend salad dressing, cake mix and eggs at low speed with electric mixer until moistened. Add lemon peel. Beat on medium speed 2 minutes. (Dough will be stiff.)

Drop rounded teaspoonfuls of dough, 2 inches apart, onto greased cookie sheets.

Bake 9 to 11 minutes or until lightly browned. (Cookies will still appear soft.) Cool 1 minute; remove from cookie sheets. Cool completely.

Stir together frosting and juice until well blended. Spread on cookies.

Nutrients per serving (1 cookie):

Calories	80	Cholesterol	10 mg
Fat	4 g	Sodium	100 mg

Top to bottom: Cocoa Brownies, Chocolate Chip Cookies

Bottom left to right: Orange Sugar Cookies, Molasses Cookies

Orange Sugar Cookies

Makes 3½ dozen cookies

> 2 cups all-purpose flour
> 1½ teaspoons baking soda
> 1 cup sugar, divided
> ½ cup FLEISCHMANN'S® Margarine, softened
> 2 teaspoons grated orange peel
> 1 teaspoon vanilla extract
> ¼ cup EGG BEATERS® 99% Real Egg Product

In small bowl, combine flour and baking soda; set aside.

In medium bowl, with electric mixer at medium speed, beat ¾ cup sugar, margarine, orange peel and vanilla until creamy. Add Egg Beaters®; beat 1 minute. Gradually stir in flour mixture until blended. Cover; refrigerate dough 1 hour.

Shape dough into 42 (¾-inch) balls; roll in remaining ¼ cup sugar. Place on lightly greased cookie sheets about 2 inches apart. Bake at 375°F for 8 to 10 minutes or until light golden brown. Remove from cookie sheets. Cool on wire racks.

Nutrients per serving (1 cookie):

Calories	60	Cholesterol	0 mg
Fat	2 g	Sodium	49 mg

Molasses Cookies

Makes 4 dozen cookies

> 2 cups all-purpose flour
> 1 cup NABISCO® 100% Bran
> 2 teaspoons baking soda
> 1 cup firmly packed light brown sugar
> ⅔ cup BLUE BONNET® Margarine, softened
> 1 egg
> ⅓ cup BRER RABBIT® Dark Molasses
> ¼ cup granulated sugar
> Water

In small bowl, combine flour, bran and baking soda; set aside.

In large bowl, with electric mixer at medium speed, beat sugar and margarine until creamy. Beat in egg and molasses until smooth. Stir in flour mixture. Cover; refrigerate dough 1 hour.

With greased hands, shape dough into 48 (1¼-inch) balls; roll in granulated sugar. Place on greased and floured cookie sheets about 2 inches apart. Lightly sprinkle dough with water. Bake at 350°F for 10 to 12 minutes or until done. Remove from cookie sheets. Cool on wire racks.

Nutrients per serving (1 cookie):

Calories	73	Cholesterol	4 mg
Fat	3 g	Sodium	72 mg

Mocha Cookies

Makes 40 cookies

> 2½ tablespoons instant coffee
> 1½ tablespoons skim milk
> ⅓ cup firmly packed light brown sugar
> ¼ cup granulated sugar
> ¼ cup margarine, softened
> 1 egg
> ½ teaspoon almond extract
> 2 cups all-purpose flour, sifted
> ¼ cup wheat flakes cereal
> ½ teaspoon ground cinnamon
> ¼ teaspoon baking powder

Preheat oven to 350°F. Spray cookie sheets with nonstick cooking spray. In small cup, dissolve coffee in milk. In large bowl, cream together sugars and margarine. Beat in egg, almond extract and coffee mixture. Stir together flour, cereal, cinnamon and baking powder; beat into sugar mixture gradually. Drop dough by teaspoonfuls, 2 inches apart, onto cookie sheets. Flatten with back of fork. Bake 8 to 10 minutes or until set. Remove from cookie sheets. Cool completely on wire racks.

Nutrients per serving (1 cookie):

Calories	44	Cholesterol	5 mg
Fat	1 g	Sodium	21 mg

Favorite recipe from **The Sugar Association, Inc.**

Fruity Oat Bars

Makes 9 bar cookies

1 package (6 ounces) diced dried mixed fruit
    (about 1⅓ cups)
¾ cup water
¼ teaspoon ground cinnamon
1¼ cups QUAKER® Oats (quick or old fashioned,
    uncooked)
⅓ cup firmly packed brown sugar
¼ cup all-purpose flour
¼ cup margarine, melted

Heat oven to 350°F. In small saucepan, combine
fruit, water and cinnamon. Cook over low heat
10 minutes, stirring constantly, or until almost all
liquid is absorbed. Remove from heat; cover. Set aside.

Combine oats, brown sugar and flour. Add margarine;
mix well until crumbly. Reserve ⅓ cup oat mixture;
press remaining mixture on bottom of 8- or 9-inch
baking pan. Bake 10 to 15 minutes or until golden
brown.

Spread fruit mixture evenly over base; sprinkle with
reserved ⅓ cup oat mixture, patting lightly. Bake
20 minutes or until topping is golden brown. Cool;
cut into bars. Store loosely covered.

Nutrients per serving (1 bar):

Calories	180	Cholesterol	0 mg
Fat	6 g	Sodium	65 mg

Snickerdoodles

Makes 3 dozen cookies

3 tablespoons sugar
1 teaspoon ground cinnamon
1 package DUNCAN HINES® Moist Deluxe
    Yellow Cake Mix
2 eggs
¼ cup CRISCO® PURITAN® Oil

1. Preheat oven to 375°F. Grease cookie sheets.

2. Combine sugar and cinnamon in small bowl. Set
aside.

3. Combine cake mix, eggs and oil in large bowl. Stir
until thoroughly blended. Shape dough into 1-inch
balls. Roll in cinnamon-sugar mixture. Place balls
2 inches apart on cookie sheets. Flatten cookies with
bottom of glass.

4. Bake at 375°F for 8 to 9 minutes or until set. Cool
1 minute on cookie sheets. Remove to cooling racks.

Nutrients per serving (1 cookie):

Calories	80	Cholesterol	12 mg
Fat	3 g	Sodium	97 mg

Chocolate Chip Raspberry Jumbles

Makes 16 bar cookies

1 package DUNCAN HINES® Chocolate Chip
    Cookie Mix
½ cup seedless red raspberry preserves

1. Preheat oven to 350°F.

2. Prepare chocolate chip cookie mix following
package directions. Reserve ½ cup dough.

3. Spread remaining dough into ungreased 9-inch
square pan. Spread preserves over base. Drop
teaspoonfuls of reserved dough randomly over top.
Bake at 350°F for 20 to 25 minutes or until golden
brown. Cool; cut into bars.

Nutrients per serving (1 bar):

Calories	178	Cholesterol	13 mg
Fat	6 g	Sodium	95 mg

Chocolate Chip Raspberry Jumbles

Cappuccino Bon Bons

Cappuccino Bon Bons

Makes 40 bon bons

 1 package DUNCAN HINES® Fudge Brownie
   Mix, Family Size
 2 eggs
 ⅓ cup water
 ⅓ cup CRISCO® PURITAN® Oil
 1½ tablespoons FOLGERS® Instant Coffee
 1 teaspoon ground cinnamon
   Whipped topping
   Ground cinnamon or fresh fruit for garnish

1. Preheat oven to 350°F. Place 1½-inch foil cupcake liners on cookie sheet.

2. Combine brownie mix, eggs, water, oil, instant coffee and 1 teaspoon cinnamon. Stir with spoon until well blended, about 50 strokes. Fill each cupcake liner with 1 measuring tablespoon batter.

3. Bake at 350°F for 12 to 15 minutes or until wooden toothpick inserted in centers comes out clean. Cool completely. Garnish each bon bon with whipped topping and a dash of cinnamon or piece of fruit. Refrigerate until ready to serve.

Tip: To make larger bon bons, use 12 (2½-inch) foil cupcake liners and fill with ¼ cup batter. Bake for 28 to 30 minutes.

Nutrients per serving (1 bon bon):

Calories	87	Cholesterol	11 mg
Fat	4 g	Sodium	53 mg

Banana Cookies

Makes 4 dozen cookies

 2 ripe, medium DOLE® Bananas, peeled
 1½ cups all-purpose flour
 ½ teaspoon baking soda
 ½ teaspoon salt
 ½ teaspoon ground cinnamon
 ¼ teaspoon ground nutmeg
 1½ cups brown sugar, packed
 ¾ cup margarine, softened
 1 egg
 ½ cup light dairy sour cream
 1 teaspoon vanilla extract
 1½ cups rolled oats, uncooked
 1 cup DOLE® Golden Raisins
 ¾ cup DOLE® Chopped Almonds, toasted

Place bananas in blender. Process until puréed; use 1 cup for recipe.

Combine flour, baking soda, salt and spices in small bowl.

Beat brown sugar and margarine in large bowl until light and fluffy. Beat in 1 cup bananas, egg, sour cream and vanilla. Beat in flour mixture until well blended. Stir in oats, raisins and almonds. Cover and refrigerate dough 1 hour to firm.

Drop dough by heaping tablespoons 2 inches apart onto greased cookie sheets.

Bake in 350°F oven 15 to 20 minutes or until cookies are light brown around edges. Cool on wire racks.

Prep time: 20 minutes
Chill time: 60 minutes
Bake time: 20 minutes per batch

Nutrients per serving (1 cookie):

Calories	113	Cholesterol	7 mg
Fat	5 g	Sodium	72 mg

Pineapple Oatmeal Cookies

Makes about 2½ dozen cookies

 1 can (20 ounces) DOLE® Crushed Pineapple
   in Syrup*
 1½ cups firmly packed brown sugar
 1 cup margarine, softened
 1 egg
 3 cups rolled oats, uncooked
 2 cups all-purpose flour
 1 teaspoon baking powder
 1 teaspoon ground cinnamon
 ½ teaspoon salt
 1 cup DOLE® Raisins
 1 cup DOLE® Natural Almonds, toasted,
   chopped

Drain pineapple well; reserve ½ cup syrup.

Beat sugar and margarine in large bowl until light and fluffy. Beat in egg, pineapple and reserved ½ cup syrup. Combine remaining ingredients in medium bowl; blend into pineapple mixture.

Drop dough by 2 heaping tablespoonfuls onto greased cookie sheets. Press lightly with back of spoon.

Bake in 350°F oven 20 to 25 minutes until golden. Cool on wire racks.

Prep time: 15 minutes
Bake time: 25 minutes per batch

*Use pineapple packed in juice, if desired.

Nutrients per serving (1 cookie):

Calories	228	Cholesterol	9 mg
Fat	10 g	Sodium	125 mg

MORE DESSERTS

Discover just how sensational low-calorie desserts can be. Fresh fruit and other healthy ingredients make these scrumptious recipes a dieter's dream come true. Visions of warm-from-the-oven apple crisp, smooth and creamy pudding parfaits and frozen ices and sorbets can become reality today!

Silky Cocoa Creme

Makes 8 servings

1 envelope unflavored gelatin
¼ cup cold water
½ cup sugar
⅓ cup HERSHEY®S Cocoa
¾ cup skim milk
½ cup low-fat part-skim ricotta cheese, at room temperature
1 teaspoon vanilla extract
½ cup thawed frozen non-dairy whipped topping
Fresh strawberries (optional)

In small bowl, sprinkle gelatin over water; allow to stand 2 minutes to soften. In medium saucepan, stir together sugar and cocoa; stir in milk. Cook over medium heat, stirring constantly, until mixture is very hot. Add gelatin mixture, stirring until gelatin is dissolved; pour into medium bowl. Refrigerate until mixture is slightly cold (do not allow to gel). In blender container or food processor blend ricotta cheese and vanilla until smooth; transfer to small bowl. Add whipped topping; stir until combined. Gradually fold ricotta mixture into cocoa mixture; pour into 2-cup mold. Refrigerate until set, about 4 hours. Unmold; serve with strawberries.

Nutrients per serving:

Calories	110	Cholesterol	5 mg
Fat	3 g	Sodium	35 mg

Orange and Raisin Bread Pudding

Makes 6 servings

4 cups ¾-inch raisin bread cubes (about 6 slices)
1 whole egg *plus* 2 egg whites
1½ cups (12-ounce can) *undiluted* CARNATION® Lite Evaporated Skimmed Milk
2 tablespoons honey
1 tablespoon margarine, melted
1 tablespoon grated orange zest
Powdered sugar and orange zest (optional)

Preheat oven to 375°F. Arrange bread cubes in single layer on baking sheet; toast 6 to 8 minutes or until lightly browned. In large bowl, beat egg and egg whites. Add evaporated skimmed milk, honey, margarine and orange zest; beat until blended. Stir in toasted bread cubes; let stand 10 minutes. Spray 1-quart casserole dish with nonstick cooking spray; pour in bread mixture. Set casserole dish in 9-inch square baking pan; fill baking pan with 1 inch hot water.

Bake in 375°F oven 45 to 55 minutes or until puffed and golden brown. Remove casserole from water; cool 5 to 10 minutes. Garnish with powdered sugar and orange zest if desired. Serve warm.

Nutrients per serving:

Calories	172	Cholesterol	39 mg
Fat	4 g	Sodium	220 mg

Silky Cocoa Creme

form sandwich. Repeat with remaining graham crackers and pudding mixture. Press edges of each sandwich into chocolate to coat. Wrap each sandwich with plastic wrap. Freeze until firm, about 6 hours or overnight.

Remove grahamwiches from freezer about 5 mimutes before serving. Let stand at room temperature to soften slightly.

Note: *Store any leftover sandwiches in freezer in plastic bag or airtight container.*

Nutrients per serving (1 sandwich cookie):

Calories	110	Cholesterol		0 mg
Fat	4 g	Sodium		160 mg

Chocolate Pudding Sandwiches

Makes 22 sandwiches

1½ cups cold skim milk
  1 package (4-serving size) JELL-O® Chocolate Flavor Sugar Free Instant Pudding and Pie Filling
3¼ cups (8-ounce container) COOL WHIP® LITE® Whipped Topping, thawed
  1 cup miniature marshmallows
  1 package (9 ounces) chocolate wafer cookies (44 cookies)

Pour milk into large mixing bowl. Add pudding mix. Beat with wire whisk until well blended, 1 to 2 minutes. Gently stir in whipped topping and marshmallows.

For each sandwich, spread about 2 tablespoons pudding mixture onto each of 2 cookies. Lightly press together to form sandwich. Wrap each sandwich with plastic wrap. Repeat with remaining cookies and pudding mixture. Freeze until firm, about 6 hours or overnight.

Remove sandwiches from freezer about 5 minutes before serving. Let stand at room temperature to soften slightly.

Note: *Store any leftover sandwiches in freezer in plastic bag or airtight container.*

Nutrients per serving (1 sandwich cookie):

Calories	100	Cholesterol		0 mg
Fat	3 g	Sodium		170 mg

Left to right: Vanilla Pudding Grahamwiches, Chocolate Pudding Sandwiches

Vanilla Pudding Grahamwiches

Makes 22 sandwiches

1½ cups cold skim milk
  1 package (4-serving size) JELL-O® Vanilla Flavor Sugar Free Instant Pudding and Pie Filling
3¼ cups (8-ounce container) COOL WHIP® LITE® Whipped Topping, thawed
  1 cup miniature marshmallows
22 whole cinnamon graham crackers, broken into 44 squares
  2 squares BAKER'S® Semi-Sweet Chocolate, shaved or grated

Pour milk into large mixing bowl. Add pudding mix. Beat with wire whisk until well blended, 1 to 2 minutes. Gently stir in whipped topping and marshmallows.

For each sandwich, spread about 2 tablespoons pudding mixture onto each of 2 graham cracker squares. Lightly press graham crackers together to

Berried Cantaloupe with Honey Dressing

Makes 4 servings

Honey Dressing (recipe follows)
2 small cantaloupes
2 cups raspberries

Prepare Honey Dressing; cover. Refrigerate. Cut cantaloupes in half; remove seeds. Cover; refrigerate.

When ready to serve, place cantaloupe halves in individual bowls; fill centers with raspberries. Drizzle with dressing.

Honey Dressing
1 cup plain yogurt
2 tablespoons honey
2 teaspoons grated orange peel

Combine all ingredients in small bowl; mix until well blended.

Nutrients per serving:

Calories	156	Cholesterol	4 mg
Fat	2 g	Sodium	54 mg

Apple Cinnamon Dessert

Makes 2 servings

1 cup pared diced apples
2 teaspoons REALEMON® Lemon Juice from Concentrate
1½ tablespoons sugar
⅛ teaspoon ground cinnamon
2 slices BORDEN® Lite-line® American Flavor Process Cheese Product*, cut into small pieces
½ tablespoon low-calorie margarine
2 plain melba rounds, crushed

Preheat oven to 350°F. In small bowl, combine apples, ReaLemon® brand, sugar and cinnamon; mix well. Stir in cheese product pieces. Divide mixture between 2 small baking dishes. Top with margarine; sprinkle with melba crumbs. Bake 12 to 15 minutes or until apples are tender. Refrigerate leftovers.

*"½ the calories"– 8% milkfat product

Nutrients per serving:

Calories	123	Cholesterol	5 mg
Fat	4 g	Sodium	315 mg

Pineapple Shortcake and Banana-Chocolate Sauce

Makes 4 servings

1 medium DOLE® Fresh Pineapple
2 medium DOLE® Oranges, peeled and sectioned
4 slices angel food cake

Banana-Chocolate Sauce
1 extra-ripe small DOLE® Banana
3 tablespoons corn syrup
2 tablespoons unsweetened cocoa
2 teaspoons margarine, melted

Twist crown from pineapple. Cut pineapple in half lengthwise. Refrigerate half for another use, such as fruit salad. Cut fruit from shell with knife. Trim off core and cut fruit into bite-sized chunks. Toss with orange sections.

Arrange cake slices on 4 dessert plates. Mound fruit evenly over cake. Drizzle with Banana-Chocolate Sauce.

For Banana-Chocolate Sauce, place banana in blender; blend until smooth. Add remaining ingredients; blend until smooth.

Prep time: 20 minutes

Nutrients per serving:

Calories	300	Cholesterol	0 mg
Fat	3 g	Sodium	114 mg

Pineapple Shortcake and Banana-Chocolate Sauce

Nectarine-Raspberry Ice

Makes 7½ cups

1 envelope unflavored gelatin
½ cup water
½ cup dry white wine
⅓ cup sugar
1 package (10 ounces) unsweetened frozen
    raspberries, thawed
4 fresh California nectarines, cut into chunks
¼ cup lemon juice
1 teaspoon grated lemon peel

Sprinkle gelatin over water in small saucepan; let stand 1 minute to soften. Stir over medium heat until gelatin is dissolved. Stir in wine and sugar; cook and stir until sugar is dissolved. Remove from heat; set aside. Place raspberries, nectarines, lemon juice and lemon peel in blender; process until smooth. Add wine syrup; blend until combined. Pour into shallow pan and freeze until firm. Soften slightly, then beat smooth with electric mixer. Freeze until ready to serve. Garnish with nectarine slices, if desired.

Nutrients per serving (½ cup):			
Calories	62	Cholesterol	0 mg
Fat	trace	Sodium	1 mg

Favorite recipe from **California Tree Fruit Agreement**

Apple Slices with Citrus-Yogurt Dip

Makes 1¼ cups

2 to 3 Empire apples, cored and sliced
¼ cup lemon juice
1 cup plain low fat yogurt
2 tablespoons honey
1 tablespoon orange juice concentrate
1 teaspoon grated orange peel
½ teaspoon grated lemon peel

Dip apple slices in lemon juice to prevent browning. Combine remaining ingredients in small bowl; stir until well blended. Cover and chill thoroughly. Arrange fresh apple slices on platter; serve with dip.

Nutrients per serving (1 tablespoon dip):			
Calories	26	Cholesterol	trace
Fat	trace	Sodium	9 mg

Favorite recipe from **Western New York Apple Growers Association**

Peach-Lemon Frost

Makes about 5 cups

3 fresh California peaches, quartered
1 cup low fat milk
½ cup lemon juice (about 3 lemons)
2 teaspoons grated lemon peel
3 ice cubes, cracked
½ pint vanilla ice milk

Process peaches in blender or food processor until smooth; measure 2 cups peach purée. Set aside. Rinse out blender. Place reserved peach purée, milk, juice, lemon peel and ice cubes in blender. Process until smooth. With blender running, gradually add ice milk through feed cap until ice milk is incorporated. Pour into glasses; serve immediately.

Nutrients per serving (½ cup):			
Calories	49	Cholesterol	5 mg
Fat	1 g	Sodium	23 mg

Favorite recipe from **California Tree Fruit Agreement**

Fruitful Frozen Yogurt

Makes 5 servings

1 envelope unflavored gelatin
¼ cup cold water
1½ cups fresh fruit purée (any flavor)
1 carton (16 ounces) vanilla yogurt
¼ to ½ cup sugar

Sprinkle gelatin over cold water in small saucepan; let stand 5 minutes to soften. Stir over low heat until gelatin is dissolved. Place fruit purée in large bowl; stir in gelatin mixture and yogurt. Add sugar to taste; mix well. Pour yogurt mixture into 9-inch square pan; freeze until almost firm. Coarsely chop mixture with fork; spoon into chilled bowl. Beat with electric mixer until smooth; freeze until ready to serve.

Note: *Frozen yogurt may also be prepared in ice cream maker according to manufacturer's directions.*

Nutrients per serving (¾ cup):			
Calories	166	Cholesterol	6 mg
Fat	2 g	Sodium	67 mg

Favorite recipe from **Wisconsin Milk Marketing Board © 1994**

Bavarian Rice Cloud with Bittersweet Chocolate Sauce

Makes 10 servings

1 envelope unflavored gelatin
1½ cups skim milk
3 tablespoons sugar
2 cups cooked rice
2 cups thawed frozen light whipped topping
1 tablespoon almond-flavored liqueur
½ teaspoon vanilla extract
Nonstick cooking spray
Bittersweet Chocolate Sauce (recipe follows)
2 tablespoons sliced almonds, toasted

Sprinkle gelatin over milk in small saucepan; let stand 1 minute or until gelatin is softened. Cook over low heat, stirring constantly, until gelatin dissolves. Add sugar and stir until dissolved. Add rice; stir until well blended. Cover and refrigerate until the consistency of unbeaten egg whites. Fold in whipped topping, liqueur, and vanilla. Spoon into 4-cup mold coated with nonstick cooking spray. Cover and refrigerate until firm. To serve, unmold onto serving platter. Spoon Bittersweet Chocolate Sauce over rice dessert. Sprinkle with toasted almonds.

Bittersweet Chocolate Sauce

3 tablespoons unsweetened cocoa powder
3 tablespoons sugar
½ cup low-fat buttermilk
1 tablespoon almond-flavored liqueur

Combine cocoa and sugar in small saucepan. Add buttermilk, mixing well. Place over medium heat, and cook until sugar dissolves. Stir in liqueur; remove from heat.

Tip: *Unmold gelatin desserts onto slightly dampened plate. This will allow you to move the mold and position it on the plate.*

Nutrients per serving:

Calories	146	Cholesterol	1 mg
Fat	3 g	Sodium	211 mg

Favorite recipe from **USA Rice Council**

Bavarian Rice Cloud with Bittersweet Chocolate Sauce

Coconut Grove Mold

Makes 8 servings

1 can (8 ounces) crushed pineapple in unsweetened juice, undrained
Cold water
1 package (4-serving size) JELL-O® Brand Pineapple Flavor Sugar Free Gelatin
1 cup boiling water
1 package (8 ounces) Light PHILADELPHIA BRAND® Neufchatel Cheese, softened
⅓ cup BAKER'S® ANGEL FLAKE® Coconut

Drain pineapple reserving juice. Add enough cold water to juice to measure ¾ cup. Dissolve gelatin in boiling water. Add ¾ cup reserved juice mixture. Beat neufchatel cheese in large mixing bowl at medium speed with electric mixer 1 minute. Gradually add gelatin mixture, mixing until well blended. Chill until thickened but not set; fold in pineapple and coconut. Pour into lightly oiled 4-cup mold; chill until firm. Unmold.

Prep time: 20 minutes plus refrigerating

Nutrients per serving:

Calories	110	Cholesterol	25 mg
Fat	8 g	Sodium	150 mg

Fruit Bread Pudding

Makes 6 servings

4 cups cubed whole wheat bread (about 4 slices)
½ cup diced dried fruit or raisins
1½ cups skim milk
½ cup HEALTHY CHOICE® Cholesterol Free
    Egg Product
¼ cup sugar
1 teaspoon vanilla
¼ teaspoon ground nutmeg

In 1½-quart casserole dish sprayed with nonstick cooking spray, combine bread and fruit. In small bowl, combine milk, egg product, sugar, vanilla and nutmeg. Pour milk mixture over bread. Bake in 350°F oven for 60 minutes or until knife inserted in center comes out clean.

Nutrients per serving:

Calories	160	Cholesterol	5 mg
Fat	1 g	Sodium	190 mg

Berry Good Sundae

Citrus Berry Sherbet

Makes 6 servings

1 envelope unflavored gelatin
    Juice of 3 SUNKIST® Oranges (1 cup)
    Grated peel and juice of 1 SUNKIST® Lemon
¼ cup sugar
1½ cups mashed fresh or thawed frozen
    strawberries or boysenberries (no sugar
    added)
½ cup applesauce

In large saucepan, sprinkle gelatin over orange and lemon juices; allow to stand 2 minutes to soften. Add sugar and lemon peel. Stir over low heat until gelatin and sugar are dissolved. Cool. Stir in strawberries and applesauce. Pour into shallow pan. Freeze until firm, about 4 hours.

Nutrients per serving (½ cup):

Calories	77	Cholesterol	0 mg
Fat	0 g	Sodium	3 mg

Berry Good Sundaes

Makes 4 servings

4 (6-inch) flour tortillas
1½ cups diced peeled nectarines
1½ cups chopped strawberries or raspberries
2 tablespoons sugar
½ teaspoon grated lemon peel
4 scoops (3 ounces *each*) vanilla ice milk
    Fresh mint sprigs

Preheat oven to 350°F. Soften tortillas according to package directions. Press each tortilla down into ungreased 10-ounce custard cup. Bake 10 to 15 minutes or until crisp. Set aside to cool.

Combine nectarines, strawberries, sugar and lemon peel in large bowl; mix gently until well blended. To assemble, remove tortillas from custard cups. Place each tortilla shell on dessert plate and fill with scoop of ice milk. Spoon equal portions of fruit mixture over tops. Garnish with mint sprigs.

Nutrients per serving:

Calories	278	Cholesterol	6 mg
Fat	4 g	Sodium	80 mg

Blueberry Crisp

Makes 8 servings

3 cups cooked brown rice
3 cups fresh blueberries*
¼ cup plus 3 tablespoons firmly packed brown sugar, divided
  Nonstick cooking spray
⅓ cup rice bran
¼ cup whole wheat flour
¼ cup chopped walnuts
1 teaspoon ground cinnamon
3 tablespoons margarine

Combine rice, blueberries, and 3 tablespoons sugar. Coat 8 individual custard cups or 2-quart baking dish with nonstick cooking spray. Place rice mixture in cups or baking dish; set aside. Combine bran, flour, walnuts, remaining ¼ cup sugar, and cinnamon in bowl. Cut in margarine with pastry blender until mixture resembles coarse meal. Sprinkle over rice mixture. Bake at 375°F for 15 to 20 minutes or until thoroughly heated. Serve warm. Garnish as desired.

To Microwave: Prepare as directed using 2-quart microproof baking dish. Cook, uncovered, on HIGH (100% power) 4 to 5 minutes, rotating dish once during cooking time. Let stand 5 minutes. Serve warm.

*Substitute frozen unsweetened blueberries for the fresh blueberries, if desired. Thaw and drain before using. Or, substitute your choice of fresh fruit or combinations of fruit for the blueberries, if desired.

Nutrients per serving:			
Calories	243	Cholesterol	0 mg
Fat	8 g	Sodium	61 mg

Favorite recipe from **USA Rice Council**

Chocolate Berry Trifle

Makes 12 servings

1½ cups cold 2% low-fat milk
1 package (4-serving size) JELL-O® Chocolate Flavor Sugar Free Instant Pudding and Pie Filling
3¼ cups (8-ounce container) COOL WHIP® LITE® Whipped Topping, thawed, divided
¼ cup low-sugar strawberry spread
1 package (10 ounces) ENTENMANN'S® Fat Free Golden Loaf Cake, cut into 12 slices
1 cup raspberries
1 cup sliced strawberries

Pour milk into large mixing bowl. Add pudding mix. Beat with wire whisk until well blended, 1 to 2 minutes. Gently stir in 1 cup whipped topping.

Spread strawberry spread evenly over half the cake slices. Top with remaining cake slices; cut into ½-inch cubes. Place half the cubes in large serving bowl; cover with half the combined fruit. Top with 1 cup whipped topping and pudding. Layer with remaining cake cubes, fruit and whipped topping. Garnish as desired. Refrigerate until ready to serve.

Nutrients per serving:			
Calories	160	Cholesterol	5 mg
Fat	4 g	Sodium	240 mg

Orange Lemon Sorbet

Makes 6 servings

1 cup sugar
1 cup water
1½ cups orange juice
⅓ cup REALEMON® Lemon Juice from Concentrate
2 tablespoons orange-flavored liqueur (optional)
1 teaspoon grated orange rind

In medium saucepan, combine sugar and water. Over medium heat bring to a boil; boil 5 minutes. Chill. Add remaining ingredients to sugar syrup. Pour into 8- or 9-inch square pan; cover and freeze about 1½ hours or until slightly frozen. In large mixer bowl, beat until slushy; return to pan. Cover and freeze 2 hours. In large mixer bowl, beat until smooth; return to pan. Cover and freeze at least 1½ hours before serving. If storing longer, remove from freezer 5 minutes before serving. Return leftovers to freezer.

Nutrients per serving:			
Calories	151	Cholesterol	0 mg
Fat	trace	Sodium	5 mg

Blueberry Crisp

Melon Bubbles

Peach Melba Parfaits

Makes 6 servings

1 (10-ounce) package frozen red raspberries in
  syrup, thawed
¼ cup red currant jelly
1 tablespoon cornstarch
½ of a (½-gallon) carton BORDEN® or
  MEADOW GOLD® Peach Frozen Yogurt
⅔ cup granola or natural cereal

Drain raspberries, reserving ⅔ cup syrup. In small
saucepan, combine reserved syrup, jelly and
cornstarch. Cook and stir until slightly thickened
and glossy. Cool. Stir in raspberries. In 6 parfait or
wine glasses, layer raspberry sauce, frozen yogurt,
raspberry sauce, then granola; repeat. Freeze.
Remove from freezer 5 to 10 minutes before serving.
Garnish as desired. Freeze leftovers.

Nutrients per serving:

| Calories | 268 | Cholesterol | 9 mg |
| Fat | 5 g | Sodium | 75 mg |

Melon Bubbles

Makes 7 (½-cup) servings

1 package (4-serving size) JELL-O® Brand
  Sugar Free Gelatin, any flavor
¾ cup boiling water
½ cup cold water
  Ice cubes
1 cup melon balls (cantaloupe, honeydew or
  watermelon)

Completely dissolve gelatin in boiling water. Combine
cold water and enough ice cubes to measure 1¼
cups. Add to gelatin; stir until slightly thickened.
Remove any unmelted ice. Measure 1⅓ cups gelatin;
add melon. Pour into 7 individual dishes or medium
serving bowl.

Beat remaining gelatin at high speed with electric
mixer until thickened and doubled in volume. Spoon
over gelatin in dishes. Chill until set, about 2 hours.
Garnish as desired.

Nutrients per serving:

| Calories | 14 | Cholesterol | 0 mg |
| Fat | 0 g | Sodium | 50 mg |

Lime Sorbet

Makes 6 servings

4 large limes
1½ cups hot water
6 tablespoons sugar
1 egg white, slightly beaten*
1 drop *each* green and yellow food color
  Mint leaves or citrus leaves, for garnish

Grate peel from 1 lime; set aside. Squeeze juice from
limes to measure ½ cup juice. In 1-quart measure,
combine hot water and sugar; stir to dissolve. In
medium bowl, combine lime juice, lime peel, sugar
mixture, egg white and food colors; blend well. Pour
into shallow pan. Cover and freeze, stirring about
once an hour to break up ice crystals, until firm.
Remove from freezer about 20 minutes before
serving. Garnish with mint leaves or citrus leaves,
if desired.

**Use only clean, uncracked egg.*

Nutrients per serving:

| Calories | 68 | Cholesterol | 0 mg |
| Fat | 0 g | Sodium | 9 mg |

Favorite recipe from **The Sugar Association, Inc.**

Ambrosia Fruit Dessert

Makes 4 servings

1 medium DOLE® Fresh Pineapple
1 medium DOLE® Orange, peeled and sliced
1 red DOLE® Apple, cored and sliced
1 cup seedless DOLE® Grapes

Fruit Glaze
¾ cup DOLE® Pineapple Orange Juice
2 tablespoons orange marmalade
1 tablespoon cornstarch
1 teaspoon rum extract
2 teaspoons grated lime peel

4 teaspoons flaked coconut

Twist crown from pineapple. Cut pineapple in half lengthwise. Refrigerate half for another use, such as fruit salad. Cut fruit from shell with knife. Cut fruit crosswise into thin slices.

Arrange pineapple slices, orange slices, apple slices and grapes evenly on 4 dessert plates. For Fruit Glaze, combine all ingredients except lime peel in saucepan. Cook, stirring, until sauce boils and thickens. Cool. Stir in lime peel. Drizzle Fruit Glaze over arranged fruit. Sprinkle with coconut.

Prep time: 20 minutes

Nutrients per serving:			
Calories	152	Cholesterol	0 mg
Fat	1 g	Sodium	8 mg

Cinnamon Swirl Bread Pudding

Makes 8 servings

8 slices cinnamon swirl or cinnamon raisin bread, cut into cubes
1 envelope KNOX® Unflavored Gelatine
¼ cup cold skim milk
½ cup skim milk, heated to boiling
1 container (8 ounces) 1% milkfat cottage cheese
½ cup cholesterol free egg substitute
½ cup packed brown sugar

In shallow 2-quart casserole, evenly spread bread cubes; set aside.

In blender, sprinkle unflavored gelatine over cold milk; let stand 2 minutes. Add hot milk and process at low speed until gelatine is completely dissolved, about 2 minutes. Add cottage cheese, egg substitute and brown sugar; process at high speed until thoroughly blended. Pour into prepared casserole; toss bread cubes until coated. Chill until firm, about 2 hours.

Nutrients per serving:			
Calories	155	Cholesterol	2 mg
Fat	1 g	Sodium	243 mg

Ambrosia Fruit Dessert

Apricot Mousse

Apricot Mousse

Makes 6 servings

4 cups DANNON® Vanilla Lowfat Yogurt
2 cans (16 to 17 ounces *each*) apricot halves in
    heavy syrup, drained
1 tablespoon sugar
1½ teaspoons orange-flavored liqueur (optional)
1 cup fresh blueberries
4 strawberries
    Mint leaves (optional)

Spoon yogurt into large strainer lined with double thickness of cheesecloth or a coffee filter. Place bowl beneath, but not touching strainer to catch liquid. Cover; chill 24 hours.

Scrape yogurt into a medium bowl. Discard liquid. Place apricots in a food processor or blender. Process until smooth. In a large bowl combine apricot purée, drained yogurt, sugar and liqueur; mix well. Cover; chill at least 30 minutes.

To serve, spoon blueberries into 6 wine glasses or dessert dishes, reserving a few berries for the top. Spoon mousse over berries. Hull strawberries and slice thinly. Top each serving of mousse with a few slices. Sprinkle with remaining blueberries and garnish each with a mint leaf.

Nutrients per serving:

Calories	200	Cholesterol	5 mg
Fat	3 g	Sodium	105 mg

Peach Sorbet

Makes about 1 quart

7 fresh California peaches, quartered
¾ cup sugar
3 tablespoons light corn syrup
1 teaspoon lemon juice

Process peaches in blender or food processor until smooth; measure 3½ cups peach purée. Combine peach purée, sugar, corn syrup and lemon juice in saucepan. Cook over low heat until sugar dissolves. Cool. Prepare in ice cream maker according to manufacturer's directions. Pack into freezer containers. Freeze until firm.

Nutrients per serving (¼ cup):

Calories	69	Cholesterol	0 mg
Fat	trace	Sodium	3 mg

Favorite recipe from **California Tree Fruit Agreement**

Peach-Walnut Praline Sauce

Makes 4 servings

¼ cup packed brown sugar
1½ teaspoons cornstarch
½ cup water
1 tablespoon brandy (optional)
1 teaspoon margarine
½ teaspoon vanilla extract
1 can (16 ounces) sliced peaches in juice, well
    drained
2 tablespoons coarsely chopped walnuts
    Frozen vanilla or peach yogurt *or* angel food
    cake slices

Mix sugar and cornstarch in small saucepan; stir in water. Bring to a boil over medium-high heat. Boil about 1 minute or until thickened, stirring constantly. Reduce heat to low; stir in brandy, margarine and vanilla. Gently stir in peaches and walnuts; simmer 1 to 2 minutes until peaches are warm. Serve over frozen yogurt or angel food cake slices.

Nutrients per serving:

Calories	115	Cholesterol	0 mg
Fat	3 g	Sodium	19 mg

Favorite recipe from **Canned Food Information Council**

Strawberries with Honeyed Yogurt Sauce

Makes 4 servings

1 quart (4 cups) fresh strawberries
1 cup plain low fat yogurt
1 tablespoon orange juice
1 to 2 teaspoons honey
    Ground cinnamon to taste

Rinse and hull strawberries; divide evenly into 4 individual serving dishes. Combine yogurt, orange juice, honey and cinnamon in small bowl until well blended. Spoon sauce over strawberries.

Nutrients per serving:

Calories	91	Cholesterol	3 mg
Fat	1 g	Sodium	41 mg

Favorite recipe from **Perdue® Farms**

Meringue Fruit Cups with Custard Sauce

Makes 8 servings

4 large egg whites, at room temperature
½ teaspoon cream of tartar
  Pinch salt
1 cup sugar
1 can (17 ounces) DEL MONTE® Fruit Cocktail, drained
  Custard Sauce (recipe follows)

Line baking sheet with parchment or waxed paper. With bottom of glass, trace eight 3-inch circles about 2 inches apart on paper. Turn paper over on baking sheet. Beat egg whites until frothy; add cream of tartar and salt. Beat until soft peaks form. Add sugar, 1 tablespoon at a time, and beat until meringue is stiff and shiny, about 10 minutes. Transfer to pastry bag fitted with star tip. Use a little meringue to secure paper to baking sheet.

Pipe 2 tablespoons meringue in center of each circle; spread to edges. Pipe 2 rings, one on top of the other, around edges of circles. Bake in preheated 200°F oven about 1½ hours or until dry but still white. Cool completely. (Meringue may be baked several days ahead and stored in airtight containers.)

Spoon fruit cocktail into meringue cups. Place on individual dessert dishes. Spoon approximately ¼ cup Custard Sauce over each. Garnish with mint leaves, if desired.

Custard Sauce

4 egg yolks,* slightly beaten
¼ cup sugar
  Pinch salt
2 cups milk, scalded
1 teaspoon vanilla extract

In top of double boiler, mix egg yolks, sugar and salt until well blended. Slowly add milk, stirring constantly. Cook over hot water, stirring constantly, until mixture begins to thicken. Remove from heat; stir in vanilla. Refrigerate. Makes about 2½ cups.

Use only clean, uncracked eggs.

Nutrients per serving:
Calories	217	Cholesterol	115 mg
Fat	5 g	Sodium	63 mg

Raspberry Rice aux Amandes

Makes 8 servings

3 cups cooked rice
2 cups skim milk
⅛ teaspoon salt
  Low-calorie sugar substitute to equal
    2 tablespoons sugar
1 teaspoon vanilla extract
¾ cup thawed frozen light whipped topping
3 tablespoons sliced almonds, toasted
1 package (16 ounces) frozen unsweetened raspberries, thawed*

Combine rice, milk, and salt in 2-quart saucepan. Cook over medium heat until thick and creamy, 5 to 8 minutes, stirring frequently. Remove from heat. Cool. Add sugar substitute and vanilla. Fold in whipped topping and almonds. Alternate rice mixture and raspberries in parfait glasses or dessert dishes.

To Microwave: Combine rice, milk, and salt in 1½-quart microproof baking dish. Cover and cook on HIGH (100% power) 3 minutes. Reduce setting to MEDIUM (50% power) and cook 7 minutes, stirring after 3 and 5 minutes. Stir in sugar substitute and vanilla; cool. Fold in whipped topping and almonds. Alternate rice mixture and raspberries in parfait glasses or dessert dishes.

Substitute frozen unsweetened strawberries or other fruit for the raspberries, if desired.

Nutrients per serving:
Calories	180	Cholesterol	2 mg
Fat	3 g	Sodium	369 mg

Favorite recipe from **USA Rice Council**

Meringue Fruit Cup with Custard Sauce

Frozen Chocolate-Cherry Yogurt Cups

Makes 12 servings

¼ cup HERSHEY¦S Cocoa
¼ cup sugar
    Yogurt Cheese (recipe follows)
¼ cup finely chopped maraschino cherries
¼ cup sliced almonds
½ teaspoon vanilla extract
¼ teaspoon almond extract
 1 envelope (1.3 ounces) whipped topping mix
½ cup cold skim milk
12 paper-lined (2½-inch) muffin cups

In medium bowl, stir together cocoa, sugar and Yogurt Cheese until well blended. Stir in cherries, almonds and vanilla and almond extracts. In small deep bowl, combine topping mix and milk; prepare according to package directions. Gradually fold whipped topping into cocoa mixture. Spoon into muffin cups. Cover; freeze until firm. Before serving, allow to stand at room temperature about 5 minutes.

Yogurt Cheese: Line non-metal colander or sieve with large piece of double thickness cheesecloth; place colander over deep bowl. Spoon 2 cups (two 8-ounce containers) vanilla low-fat yogurt (with no gelatin added) into prepared colander; cover. Refrigerate until liquid no longer drains from yogurt, about 24 hours. Remove yogurt from cheesecloth; discard liquid.

Nutrients per serving:

Calories	90	Cholesterol	5 mg
Fat	2 g	Sodium	35 mg

Cranberry Apple Ice

Makes 14 servings, 7 cups

 1 can (12 ounces) frozen apple-cranberry juice concentrate, thawed
1½ cups MOTT'S® Chunky Apple Sauce
 1 bottle (32 ounces) sugar-free lemon-lime flavored carbonated beverage (4 cups)

In 2-quart nonmetal bowl, combine all ingredients; mix well. Cover; freeze until firm. Scoop frozen mixture into 5-ounce drinking cups or spoon into dessert dishes.

Nutrients per serving (½ cup):

Calories	33	Cholesterol	0 mg
Fat	0 g	Sodium	14 mg

Chocolate Peanut Butter Parfaits

Chocolate Peanut Butter Parfaits

Makes 6 servings, 3 cups

2 cups plus 2 tablespoons cold skim milk, divided
2 tablespoons chunky peanut butter
1 cup thawed COOL WHIP® LITE® Whipped Topping
1 package (4-serving size) JELL-O® Chocolate Flavor Sugar Free Instant Pudding and Pie Filling

Add 2 tablespoons milk to peanut butter; stir until well blended. Stir in whipped topping.

Pour the remaining 2 cups milk into medium mixing bowl. Add pudding mix. Beat with wire whisk until well blended, 1 to 2 minutes. Spoon half the pudding mixture into 6 parfait glasses; cover with whipped topping mixture. Top with remaining pudding mixture. Refrigerate until ready to serve.

Nutrients per serving:

Calories	110	Cholesterol	0 mg
Fat	5 g	Sodium	290 mg

Watermelon Ice

Makes 6 servings

4 cups seeded 1-inch watermelon chunks
¼ cup thawed frozen unsweetened pineapple
juice concentrate
2 tablespoons fresh lime juice
Fresh melon balls (optional)
Fresh mint leaves (optional)

Place melon chunks in single layer in plastic freezer bag; freeze about 8 hours or until firm. Place frozen melon in food processor. Let stand 15 minutes to soften slightly. Add pineapple juice and lime juice. Remove plunger from top of food processor to allow air to be incorporated. Process until smooth, scraping down sides of container frequently. Spoon into individual dessert dishes. Serve immediately.* Garnish with melon balls and mint leaves, if desired. Freeze leftovers.

Honeydew Ice: *Substitute honeydew for watermelon and unsweetened pineapple-guava-orange juice concentrate for pineapple juice concentrate. Prepare as directed.*

Cantaloupe Ice: *Substitute cantaloupe for watermelon and unsweetened pineapple-guava-orange juice concentrate for pineapple juice concentrate. Prepare as directed.*

**Ice may be transferred to airtight container and frozen up to 1 month. Let stand at room temperature 10 minutes to soften slightly before serving.*

Nutrients per serving:

Calories	57	Cholesterol	0 mg
Fat	trace	Sodium	3 mg

Nectarine Macedoine with Ice Milk

Makes 4 servings

2 lemons
½ cup orange juice
½ cup sugar
3 fresh California nectarines, cut into wedges
(about 3 cups)
2 cups vanilla ice milk

Squeeze lemons; measure ¼ cup juice. Combine ¼ cup lemon juice, orange juice, squeezed lemon shells and sugar in medium saucepan. Bring to a boil and cook 5 minutes. Remove lemon shells; discard. Place nectarines in bowl. Pour lemon mixture over nectarines. Refrigerate. Spoon evenly into 4 dessert bowls. Top each with ½ cup ice milk.

Nutrients per serving:

Calories	255	Cholesterol	13 mg
Fat	3 g	Sodium	53 mg

Favorite recipe from **California Tree Fruit Agreement**

Lemony Light Vineyard Cups

Makes 6 servings

1 envelope unflavored gelatin
¼ cup cold water
1¼ cups plain low fat yogurt
½ cup orange juice
¼ cup honey
1 tablespoon lemon juice
1 tablespoon grated lemon peel
3 cups seedless or halved, seeded Chilean grapes
Lemon peel strips for garnish (optional)

Sprinkle gelatin over water in small saucepan; let stand 2 minutes to soften. Stir over low heat until gelatin is dissolved. Stir in yogurt, orange juice, honey, lemon juice and grated peel; whisk gently until blended and smooth. Divide grapes evenly among six 6-ounce custard cups or individual dessert dishes. Divide yogurt mixture evenly over grapes in cups. Refrigerate until set. To serve, garnish with lemon peel strips before serving, if desired.

Nutrients per serving:

Calories	145	Cholesterol	3 mg
Fat	1 g	Sodium	40 mg

Favorite recipe from **Chilean Fresh Fruit Association**

Watermelon Ice, Honeydew Ice, Cantaloupe Ice

Orange Terrine with Strawberry Sauce

Orange Terrine with Strawberry Sauce

Makes 12 servings

1 package (3 ounces) ladyfingers, split, divided
2 packages (4-serving size) or 1 package
    (8-serving size) JELL-O® Brand Orange
    Flavor Sugar Free Gelatin
1½ cups boiling water
1 cup orange juice
   Ice cubes
1 tablespoon orange liqueur (optional)
2 teaspoons grated orange peel
3¼ cups (8 ounces) COOL WHIP® LITE®
    Whipped Topping, thawed, divided
1 package (10 ounces) BIRDS EYE®
    Strawberries in Syrup, thawed
1 cup fresh strawberries

Line bottom and sides of 9×5-inch loaf pan with plastic wrap. Stand enough ladyfingers to fit evenly along 2 long sides of pan (cut sides should be facing in).

Dissolve gelatin in boiling water. Combine orange juice and enough ice cubes to measure 1¾ cups. Add to gelatin; stir until slightly thickened. Remove any unmelted ice. Stir in liqueur and orange peel. Gently stir in 2½ cups whipped topping. Spoon gelatin mixture into prepared pan. If necessary, trim ladyfingers to make even with top of gelatin mixture. Arrange remaining ladyfingers evenly on top of mixture. Chill until firm, at least 3 hours.

When ready to serve, place thawed frozen strawberries in blender container; cover. Blend until puréed; strain. Unmold terrine onto serving plate; remove plastic wrap. Decorate with remaining ¾ cup whipped topping and fresh strawberries. Cut into slices. Serve on strawberry purée. Garnish as desired.

Nutrients per serving:			
Calories	100	Cholesterol	25 mg
Fat	3 g	Sodium	60 mg

Apricot Mousse

Makes 4 servings

1 envelope unflavored gelatin
½ cup *undiluted* CARNATION® Lite Evaporated
    Skimmed Milk
2 cups (16-ounce can) apricot halves in juice,
    drained
½ teaspoon vanilla extract
1 egg white*
2 tablespoons granulated sugar

In medium saucepan, sprinkle gelatin over evaporated skimmed milk; let stand for 5 minutes. Cook over low heat, stirring occasionally, until gelatin is dissolved. In blender or food processor, purée enough apricots to measure *1 cup*. Slice any *remaining* apricots for garnish. Stir apricot purée and vanilla into milk mixture. Refrigerate, stirring occasionally, until mixture is thick enough to mound on spoon. In small bowl, beat egg white until soft peaks form. Gradually add sugar. Beat until stiff peaks form and sugar is dissolved. Fold egg mixture into thickened apricot mixture. Spoon into four 4-ounce dessert dishes.

Apricot Almond Mousse: Substitute ¼ teaspoon almond extract for vanilla in recipe.

*Use only clean, uncracked egg.

Nutrients per serving:			
Calories	84	Cholesterol	0 mg
Fat	0 g	Sodium	50 mg

Nilla® Fruit Kabobs with Honey-Lime Sauce

Makes 4 servings

24 NILLA® Wafers
2 cups mixed fresh fruit pieces (pineapple, melon, kiwi, strawberries and banana)
3 tablespoons honey
3 tablespoons lime juice
1 teaspoon cornstarch
¼ teaspoon grated lime peel
⅛ teaspoon ground ginger

On 12 (4-inch) wooden skewers, alternately thread wafers and fruit pieces; refrigerate until serving time. In small saucepan over medium heat, heat honey, lime juice, cornstarch, lime peel and ginger to a boil. Boil for 1 minute, stirring constantly. To serve, place 3 kabobs on each serving plate; drizzle with warm honey-lime sauce. Serve immediately.

Nutrients per serving:

Calories	200	Cholesterol	0 mg
Fat	4 g	Sodium	87 mg

Winter Fruit Tray with Citrus Dip

Makes 6 servings

1 medium DOLE® Fresh Pineapple
1 medium DOLE® Orange, peeled, sliced
1 DOLE® Apple, cored, thinly sliced
1 DOLE® Kiwifruit, peeled, sliced

Citrus Dip
1 carton (8 ounces) nonfat plain yogurt
1 cup light non-dairy whipped topping, thawed
¼ cup powdered sugar
1 teaspoon grated orange peel
1 teaspoon grated lime peel

Twist crown from pineapple. Cut pineapple in half lengthwise. Refrigerate half for another use, such as fruit salad. Cut fruit from shell with knife. Trim off core and cut fruit into bite-size chunks or wedges.

Arrange pineapple chunks, orange slices, apple slices and kiwi slices on platter. Serve with Citrus Dip. Garnish as desired.

For Citrus Dip, combine all ingredients. Spoon into serving bowl. Place on platter with fruit.

Prep time: 20 minutes

Nutrients per serving:

Calories	137	Cholesterol	1 mg
Fat	4 g	Sodium	33 mg

Filled Chocolate Meringues

Makes 2 dozen meringues

2 egg whites, at room temperature
¼ teaspoon cream of tartar
   Dash salt
½ cup sugar
½ teaspoon vanilla extract
2 tablespoons HERSHEY'S Cocoa
   Chocolate-Cheese Filling (recipe follows)
   Raspberries
   Mint leaves

Heat oven to 275°F. Place parchment paper on cookie sheets. In small mixer bowl, beat egg whites with cream of tartar and salt until soft peaks form. Beat in sugar, 1 tablespoon at a time, until stiff, glossy peaks form. Fold in vanilla. Sift cocoa over top of egg white mixture; gently fold in cocoa until combined. Drop by tablespoonfuls onto parchment paper. With back of small spoon, make indentation in center of each mound. Bake 45 minutes or until meringue turns a light cream color and feels dry to the touch. Carefully peel meringues off parchment paper; cool completely on wire racks. To serve, spoon or pipe about 2 teaspoons Chocolate-Cheese Filling into center of each meringue. Garnish each with a raspberry and a mint leaf.

Chocolate-Cheese Filling: In blender container or food processor, combine 1 cup part-skim ricotta cheese, 2 tablespoons Hershey's Cocoa, 1 tablespoon sugar and ½ teaspoon vanilla extract; blend until smooth. Cover; refrigerate.

Nutrients per serving (1 filled meringue):

Calories	40	Cholesterol	5 mg
Fat	1 g	Sodium	25 mg

Filled Chocolate Meringues

Rice Pudding

Rice Pudding

Makes 6 servings

3 cups 2% low-fat milk
1 large stick cinnamon
1 cup uncooked long-grain rice
2 cups water
½ teaspoon salt
Peel of an orange or lemon
¾ cup sugar
¼ cup raisins
2 tablespoons dark rum

Heat milk and cinnamon in small saucepan over medium heat until milk is infused with flavor of cinnamon, about 15 minutes. Combine rice, water, and salt in 2- to 3-quart saucepan. Bring to a boil; stir once or twice. Place orange peel on top of rice. Reduce heat to low; cover and simmer 15 minutes or until rice is tender and liquid is absorbed. Remove and discard orange peel. Strain milk and stir into cooked rice. Add sugar and bring to a boil. Reduce heat to low; simmer 20 minutes or until thickened, stirring often. Add raisins and rum; bring to a boil. Reduce heat to low and simmer 10 minutes. Serve hot. Garnish as desired. To reheat, add a little milk to restore creamy texture.

Nutrients per serving:

Calories	297	Cholesterol	10 mg
Fat	3 g	Sodium	259 mg

Favorite recipe from **USA Rice Council**

Cherry Almond Supreme

Makes 6 servings, about 3 cups

1 can (8 ounces) pitted dark sweet cherries in light syrup, undrained
1 package (4-serving size) JELL-O® Brand Cherry Flavor Sugar Free Gelatin
¾ cup boiling water
Ice cubes
2 tablespoons chopped toasted almonds
1 cup thawed COOL WHIP® LITE® Whipped Topping

Drain cherries, reserving syrup. If necessary, add enough water to reserved syrup to measure ½ cup. Cut cherries into quarters. Completely dissolve gelatin in boiling water. Combine measured syrup and enough ice to measure 1¼ cups. Add to gelatin; stir until slightly thickened. Remove any unmelted ice. Chill until thickened. Measure 1¼ cups gelatin; stir in half the cherries and half the nuts. Set aside.

Gently stir whipped topping into remaining gelatin. Add remaining cherries and nuts; spoon into 6 dessert glasses. Chill until set but not firm, about 15 minutes. Top with clear gelatin mixture. Chill until set, about 1 hour.

Nutrients per serving:

Calories	70	Cholesterol	0 mg
Fat	3 g	Sodium	65 mg

Baked Apple Crumble

Makes 8 servings

Apple Layer
6 cups sliced, peeled Golden Delicious or Rome Beauty apples (about 2 pounds or 6 medium)
2 tablespoons orange or other fruit juice
¾ cup firmly packed light brown sugar
½ cup all-purpose flour
½ teaspoon ground cinnamon
3 tablespoons CRISCO® Oil or CRISCO® PURITAN® Oil

Topping (optional)
½ cup vanilla low-fat yogurt, divided

For Apple Layer, heat oven to 375°F. Oil 2-quart casserole or baking dish. Arrange apples evenly in dish. Drizzle with orange juice. Combine sugar, flour and cinnamon. Mix in Crisco® Oil until crumbly. Spoon over apples. Bake at 375°F for 35 minutes or until apples are tender. Cool slightly. Serve warm.

For Topping, spoon 1 tablespoon vanilla yogurt over each serving.

Nutrients per serving:

Calories	210	Cholesterol	0 mg
Fat	6 g	Sodium	10 mg

Poached Dried Fruit Compote

Makes 6 servings

**8 ounces mixed dried fruit, such as apricots,
   pears, apples and prunes**
1½ cups water
½ cup white Riesling or Rhine wine*
2 cinnamon sticks
4 whole cloves

Combine all ingredients in medium saucepan. Bring
to a boil over high heat. Reduce heat to low; simmer,
uncovered, 12 to 15 minutes or until fruit is tender.
Cool. Discard cinnamon sticks and cloves. Serve
warm, at room temperature or chilled in individual
dessert bowls. Garnish with additional cinnamon
sticks, if desired.

**You may substitute white grape juice for wine.*

Nutrients per serving:

Calories	106	Cholesterol	0 mg
Fat	trace	Sodium	8 mg

Nectarine Crème Fraîche

Makes 4 servings

2 fresh California nectarines, sliced
1 cup plain low fat yogurt
2 to 3 drops almond extract
1 teaspoon honey or sugar
1 envelope unflavored gelatin
2 tablespoons water

Place nectarines, yogurt and almond extract in
blender; blend until smooth. Blend in honey. Combine
gelatin and water in small saucepan; let stand
1 minute to soften. Stir over low heat until gelatin
dissolves. Add gelatin mixture to blender. Blend
10 seconds. Refrigerate until thickened. Spoon into
stemmed glasses and refrigerate until set. Garnish
with additional nectarine slices and mint sprigs, if
desired.

Nutrients per serving:

Calories	79	Cholesterol	3 mg
Fat	1 g	Sodium	42 mg

Favorite recipe from **California Tree Fruit Agreement**

Creamy Rice Bavarian with Raspberries

Makes 12 servings

½ cup uncooked long grain rice
2 cups cold water, divided
2 envelopes KNOX® Unflavored Gelatine
½ cup cholesterol free egg substitute
½ cup sugar
1½ cups skim milk
1 teaspoon vanilla extract
⅛ teaspoon ground nutmeg
**2 cups (12 ounces) frozen whipped topping,
   thawed**
Raspberry Sauce (recipe follows)

In medium saucepan, combine rice with 1½ cups
water; bring to a boil. Reduce heat and simmer,
covered, 30 minutes or until very tender; cool.

In small saucepan, sprinkle unflavored gelatine over
remaining ½ cup water; let stand 1 minute. Stir over
low heat until gelatine is completely dissolved, about
3 minutes.

In blender or food processor, process egg substitute
and sugar until sugar is dissolved, about 2 minutes.
While processing, through feed cap, gradually add
milk and gelatine mixture; process until blended.
Pour into large bowl; stir in vanilla and nutmeg. Chill
until mixture mounds slightly when dropped from
spoon, about 5 minutes. Fold in cooled rice, then
whipped topping. Pour into 6½-cup mold or bowl;
chill until firm, about 3 hours.

Unmold and serve with Raspberry Sauce. Garnish, if
desired, with fresh raspberries and strawberries.

Raspberry Sauce: In small bowl, combine
1 package (12 ounces) frozen unsweetened
raspberries, thawed, puréed and sieved to remove
seeds, ⅓ cup black currant liqueur and
3 tablespoons sugar; chill. Makes 1½ cups sauce.

Nutrients per serving:

Calories	217	Cholesterol	1 mg
Fat	8 g	Sodium	38 mg

Poached Dried Fruit Compote

Raspberry Yogurt Parfaits

Makes 8 servings

¾ cup water
¾ cup UNCLE BEN'S® Rice In An Instant
2 cartons (8 ounces *each*) raspberry low-fat
   yogurt
2 cups fresh raspberries

In small saucepan, bring water to a boil. Stir in rice. Cover; remove from heat and set aside for 5 minutes or until all liquid is absorbed. Cool to room temperature. Stir in yogurt; refrigerate at least 30 minutes. Just before serving, layer rice mixture and berries in parfait glasses or dessert dishes.

Note: For variety, mix and match your favorite fresh fruit with your favorite fruit-flavored yogurt.

Nutrients per serving:			
Calories	100	Cholesterol	2 mg
Fat	trace	Sodium	35 mg

Frozen Banana Dessert Cups

Makes 8 to 12 servings

2 extra-ripe, medium DOLE® Bananas, peeled
1 cup DOLE® Fresh Strawberries
1 can (8 ounces) DOLE® Crushed Pineapple in
   Juice, drained
2 tablespoons honey
   Dash ground nutmeg
1 cup frozen whipped topping, thawed
¼ cup DOLE® Chopped Almonds
1 cup DOLE® Pure & Light Mountain Cherry
   Juice
1 tablespoon cornstarch
1 tablespoon sugar
   Sliced DOLE® fresh fruit for garnish

Frozen Banana Dessert Cup

Place bananas, strawberries, pineapple, honey and nutmeg in blender container. Process until smooth. Pour into large bowl. Fold in whipped topping and almonds. Line 12 (2½-inch) muffin cups with foil liners. Fill with banana mixture. Cover and freeze until firm. Blend cherry juice, cornstarch and sugar in small saucepan. Cook, stirring, until sauce boils and thickens. Cool.

To serve, spoon cherry sauce onto each serving plate. Remove foil liners from dessert cups. Invert on top of sauce. Arrange fresh fruit around each dessert cup. Garnish as desired.

Nutrients per serving:			
Calories	99	Cholesterol	0 mg
Fat	3 g	Sodium	3 mg

Lite Chocolate Mint Parfaits

Makes 7 servings

⅔ cup sugar
¼ cup HERSHEY'S Cocoa
3 tablespoons cornstarch
   Dash salt
2½ cups cold skim milk, divided
1 tablespoon margarine-type vegetable oil
   spread
1½ teaspoons vanilla extract, divided
1 envelope (1.3 ounces) whipped topping mix
¼ teaspoon mint extract
3 to 4 drops red food color

In medium saucepan, combine sugar, cocoa, cornstarch and salt; gradually stir in 2 cups skim milk. Cook over medium heat, stirring constantly, until mixture boils; boil and stir 1 minute. Remove from heat; blend in vegetable oil spread and 1 teaspoon vanilla. Pour into medium bowl. Press plastic wrap onto surface of pudding; refrigerate.

In small bowl, combine topping mix, remaining ½ cup cold skim milk and remaining ½ teaspoon vanilla; prepare according to package directions. Fold ½ cup whipped topping into pudding. Blend mint extract and red food color into remaining topping. Alternately spoon chocolate pudding and mint whipped topping into parfait glasses. Refrigerate.

Nutrients per serving:			
Calories	160	Cholesterol	0 mg
Fat	2 g	Sodium	95 mg

Crème Caramel

Makes 6 servings

¾ cup sugar, divided
2 cups 2% low-fat milk
1 carton (8 ounces) HEALTHY CHOICE®
    Cholesterol Free Egg Product
½ teaspoon vanilla extract

Place ½ cup sugar in small heavy saucepan. Cook over low heat until sugar melts and turns golden brown. Pour immediately into 6 custard cups. Cool. In medium bowl, combine milk, egg product, remaining ¼ cup sugar and vanilla. Stir until sugar dissolves. Pour into custard cups. Place cups in baking pan; fill pan with 1 inch hot water. Bake in 350°F oven for 50 minutes or until custard is just set in center. Refrigerate. To serve, run knife around edges of cups and unmold onto serving plate.

Nutrients per serving:

Calories	160	Cholesterol	5 mg
Fat	2 g	Sodium	100 mg

Strawberry Ice

Makes 6 servings

1 cup sugar
½ cup water
3 tablespoons REALEMON® Lemon Juice from
    Concentrate
1 quart (about 1½ pounds) fresh strawberries,
    cleaned and hulled
    Red food coloring (optional)

In blender container, combine sugar, water and ReaLemon® brand; mix well. Gradually add strawberries; blend until smooth, adding food coloring, if desired. Pour into 8-inch square pan; cover and freeze about 1½ hours. In medium mixer bowl, beat until slushy. Cover and return to freezer. Place in refrigerator 1 hour before serving to soften. Freeze leftovers.

Nutrients per serving:

Calories	162	Cholesterol	0 mg
Fat	0 g	Sodium	3 mg

Black Forest Parfait

Black Forest Parfaits

Makes 12 servings

2 cups cold 2% low-fat milk, divided
4 ounces neufchatel cheese
1 package (4-serving size) JELL-O® Chocolate
    Flavor Sugar Free Instant Pudding and Pie
    Filling
1 package (15 ounces) ENTENMANN'S® Fat
    Free Chocolate Loaf, cubed
1 can (20 ounces) reduced-calorie cherry pie
    filling
1 square BAKER'S® Semi-Sweet Chocolate,
    grated

Pour ½ cup milk into blender container. Add neufchatel cheese; cover. Blend until smooth. Add remaining 1½ cups milk and pudding mix; cover. Blend until smooth.

Divide cake cubes evenly among 12 individual dishes. Reserve a few cherries for garnish if desired; spoon remaining cherry pie filling over cake cubes. Top with pudding mixture. Refrigerate until ready to serve. Garnish with reserved cherries and chocolate.

Nutrients per serving:

Calories	190	Cholesterol	10 mg
Fat	4 g	Sodium	340 mg

Pinwheel Cake and Cream

Makes 12 servings

2 cups cold skim milk
1 package (4-serving size) JELL-O® Vanilla
    Flavor Sugar Free Instant Pudding and Pie
    Filling
1 cup thawed COOL WHIP® LITE® Whipped
    Topping
1 small peach, peeled, chopped
1 teaspoon grated orange peel
1 package (10 ounces) ENTENMANN'S® Fat
    Free Golden Loaf, cut into slices
2 cups cut-up summer fruits (peaches,
    nectarines, berries, seedless grapes)

Pour milk into medium mixing bowl. Add pudding
mix. Beat with wire whisk until well blended, 1 to 2
minutes. Gently stir in whipped topping, peach and
peel. Arrange cake slices on serving plate. Spoon
pudding mixture evenly over cake; top with fruits.
Serve immediately or cover and refrigerate until ready
to serve.

Nutrients per serving:

Calories	120	Cholesterol	0 mg
Fat	1 g	Sodium	230 mg

Crispy Baked Apple Slices

Makes 6 servings

2½ pounds (5 to 6 large) Golden Delicious or
    Rome Beauty apples, peeled and sliced
    (about 5 cups)
 2 tablespoons apple juice
½ cup all-purpose flour
½ cup firmly packed light brown sugar
½ teaspoon ground cinnamon
¼ cup BUTTER FLAVOR CRISCO®

Preheat oven to 375°F. Grease 2-quart ovenproof
dish. Arrange apples evenly in dish. Pour apple juice
over apples. In medium bowl, combine flour, sugar
and cinnamon. Cut in Butter Flavor Crisco® until
crumbly. Spoon evenly over apples.

Bake at 375°F for 35 minutes or until apples are
tender. Cool slightly. Serve warm. Top with vanilla
yogurt, if desired.

Nutrients per serving:

Calories	289	Cholesterol	0 mg
Fat	9 g	Sodium	10 mg

Ambrosia Fruit Custard

Makes 4 servings

1 package (4-serving size) sugar-free instant
    vanilla pudding
  Ingredients for pudding
1 teaspoon grated DOLE® Lemon peel
1 tablespoon DOLE® Lemon juice
½ teaspoon coconut or almond extract
1 can (8 ounces) DOLE® Pineapple Tidbits,
    drained
1 cup assorted sliced fresh fruit
¼ cup mini marshmallows *or* flaked coconut

Prepare pudding in medium bowl according to
package directions. Stir in lemon peel, lemon juice
and extract. Reserve ¼ cup pudding for topping.

Spoon remaining pudding equally into 4 dessert
bowls. Combine remaining ingredients in small bowl.
Spoon over top of pudding in dessert bowls. Drizzle
with reserved pudding.

Prep time: 15 minutes

Nutrients per serving:

Calories	139	Cholesterol	0 mg
Fat	2 g	Sodium	203 mg

Banana-Kiwi Pudding

Makes 4 servings

1⅓ cups cooked rice
1⅓ cups skim milk
  1 teaspoon vanilla extract
    Low-calorie sugar substitute to equal
      2 tablespoons sugar
  1 ripe banana
¼ cup whipping cream, whipped
  2 kiwifruit, sliced, for garnish

Cook rice and milk in 2-quart saucepan over medium
heat until thick and creamy, 5 to 8 minutes, stirring
frequently. Remove from heat; cool. Stir in vanilla and
sugar substitute. Just before serving, mash banana;
fold banana and whipped cream into pudding.
Garnish with kiwifruit slices.

Nutrients per serving:

Calories	197	Cholesterol	12 mg
Fat	4 g	Sodium	306 mg

Favorite recipe from **USA Rice Council**

Pear Fans with Creamy Custard Sauce

Apple-Honeydew Ice

Makes 10 servings, 5 cups

2 cups sugar-free lemon-lime flavored
    carbonated beverage
1 cup MOTT'S® Regular Apple Sauce
1 small honeydew melon, seeded, rind removed,
    cut into chunks
⅛ teaspoon ground ginger
2 to 3 drops green food color (optional)

In food processor or blender, combine all ingredients;
process until smooth. Pour into 8- or 9-inch nonmetal
square pan. Cover; freeze until firm. Scoop frozen
mixture into dessert dishes.

Nutrients per serving (½ cup):

Calories	37	Cholesterol	0 mg
Fat	0 g	Sodium	14 mg

Pear Fans with Creamy Custard Sauce

Makes 8 servings

8 canned pear halves in juice, drained
    Creamy Custard Sauce (recipe follows)
8 raspberries (optional)
8 mint leaves (optional)

Cut pear halves into thin slices with sharp knife,
cutting up to, but not through, stem ends. Holding
stem end in place, gently fan out slices from stem.
Place on dessert plates. Spoon about ⅓ cup Creamy
Custard Sauce around pears. Place raspberry and
mint leaf at stem end of each pear, if desired.

Creamy Custard Sauce

3 cups cold 2% lowfat milk
1 package (4-serving size) JELL-O® Vanilla
    Flavor Sugar Free Instant Pudding and Pie
    Filling
¼ teaspoon ground cinnamon (optional)

Pour milk into large mixing bowl. Add pudding mix
and cinnamon. Beat with wire whisk until well
blended, 1 to 2 minutes; cover. Refrigerate until ready
to use.

Nutrients per serving:

Calories	160	Cholesterol	20 mg
Fat	4 g	Sodium	420 mg

Rhubarb Crisp

Makes 4 to 6 servings

6 cups chopped fresh rhubarb
½ cup firmly packed brown sugar
⅓ cup all-purpose flour
⅓ cup rolled oats, uncooked
½ teaspoon ground cinnamon
3 tablespoons margarine or butter
    Whipped topping or ice milk (optional)

Preheat oven to 350°F. Place rhubarb in 8-inch
square baking dish. Combine brown sugar, flour, oats
and cinnamon in medium bowl; cut in margarine with
pastry blender until mixture resembles coarse
crumbs. Sprinkle crumb mixture over rhubarb. Bake
30 minutes, or until lightly browned. Serve hot or
cold with whipped topping or ice milk, if desired.
Garnish as desired.

Nutrients per serving:

Calories	187	Cholesterol	0 mg
Fat	6 g	Sodium	77 mg

Frozen Orange Cream

Makes 8 servings

1 package (4-serving size) JELL-O® Brand
  Orange Flavor Sugar Free Gelatin
¾ cup boiling water
2 cups skim milk
1 can (6 ounces) frozen apple juice concentrate,
  thawed
1 cup thawed COOL WHIP® LITE® Whipped
  Topping
1 can (11 ounces) mandarin orange segments,
  well drained

Completely dissolve gelatin in boiling water. Stir in milk and apple juice concentrate. (Mixture will appear curdled but will be smooth when frozen.) Pour into 13×9-inch metal pan. Freeze until about 1 inch of icy crystals forms around edges, about 1 hour. Spoon mixture into chilled bowl; beat with electric mixer until smooth. Gently stir in whipped topping. Spoon a scant ⅔ cup mixture into each of 8 custard cups. Freeze about 6 hours or overnight.

To serve, reserve 8 orange segments for garnish. Process remaining oranges in blender until smooth. Remove custard cups from freezer; let stand 15 minutes. Run knife around edges of cups; invert onto dessert plates and unmold. Garnish each dessert with about 1 tablespoon puréed oranges, 1 reserved orange segment and a mint leaf, if desired. Store leftover desserts in freezer.

Nutrients per serving:

Calories	100	Cholesterol	0 mg
Fat	1 g	Sodium	75 mg

All-American Pineapple & Fruit Trifle

Makes 8 to 10 servings

1 DOLE® Fresh Pineapple
1 cup frozen sliced peaches, thawed
1 cup frozen strawberries, thawed and sliced
1 cup frozen raspberries, thawed
1 angel food cake (10 inches in diameter)
1 package (4-serving size) instant sugar-free
  vanilla pudding mix
⅓ cup cream sherry
½ cup thawed frozen whipped topping

Twist crown from pineapple. Cut pineapple in half lengthwise. Refrigerate half for another use, such as fruit salad. Cut fruit from shell with knife. Cut fruit into thin wedges. Reserve 3 wedges for garnish; combine remaining pineapple wedges with peaches, strawberries and raspberries.

Cut cake in half. Freeze half for another use. Tear remaining cake half into chunks.

Prepare pudding according to package directions.

In 2-quart glass bowl, layer half of each: cake, sherry, fruit mixture and pudding. Repeat layers once. Cover; refrigerate 1 hour or overnight.

Just before serving, garnish with whipped topping, reserved pineapple wedges and mint leaves.

Prep time: 20 minutes
Chill time: 1 hour

Nutrients per serving:

Calories	173	Cholesterol	4 mg
Fat	2 g	Sodium	129 mg

All-American Pineapple & Fruit Trifle

Crunchy Apple Crisp

Makes 4 servings

4 cups peeled, sliced apples*
¼ cup water or apple juice
4 teaspoons firmly packed brown sugar
2 teaspoons lemon juice
¾ teaspoon ground cinnamon
½ cup QUAKER® Oats (quick or old fashioned, uncooked)
2 tablespoons chopped almonds
1 tablespoon firmly packed brown sugar
1 tablespoon margarine, melted

Heat oven to 375°F. Combine apples, water, 4 teaspoons brown sugar, lemon juice and cinnamon; toss lightly to coat apples. Place apple mixture in 8-inch square baking dish.

Combine remaining ingredients; mix well. Sprinkle over apples. Bake about 30 minutes or until apples are tender and topping is lightly browned. Serve warm or chilled.

Or substitute one 20-ounce can unsweetened sliced apples, drained, or two 16-ounce cans "lite" sliced peaches, drained, reserving ¼ cup peach juice to replace apple juice. Prepare as directed above; decrease baking time to 20 to 22 minutes. Serve as above.

Nutrients per serving:			
Calories	185	Cholesterol	0 mg
Fat	6 g	Sodium	37 mg

Chocolate Banana Pops

Makes 10 pops

2 cups cold skim milk
1 package (4-serving size) JELL-O® Chocolate Flavor Sugar Free Instant Pudding and Pie Filling
1 cup thawed COOL WHIP® LITE® Whipped Topping
½ cup mashed banana

Pour milk into medium mixing bowl. Add pudding mix. Beat with wire whisk until well blended, 1 to 2 minutes. Gently stir in whipped topping and banana.

Spoon about ⅓ cup pudding mixture into each of ten (5-ounce) paper cups. Insert wooden stick or plastic spoon into each for handle. Freeze until firm, about 5 hours. To serve, press firmly on bottom of cup to release pop.

Nutrients per serving:			
Calories	60	Cholesterol	0 mg
Fat	1 g	Sodium	160 mg

Baked Caramel Rice Custard

Makes 8 servings

3 cups skim milk
½ cup uncooked CREAM OF RICE® Hot Cereal
¾ cup EGG BEATERS® 99% Real Egg Product
1 cup sugar, divided
1 teaspoon vanilla extract
Prepared whipped topping (optional)

In large saucepan, over medium heat, heat milk just to a boil; sprinkle in cereal. Cook for 1 minute, stirring constantly. Slowly add egg product, ⅓ cup sugar and vanilla, stirring constantly. Cook over low heat for 4 to 5 minutes until mixture begins to thicken.

In small saucepan, over medium-high heat, heat remaining ⅔ cup sugar until melted and golden brown. Quickly pour melted sugar into 1½-quart baking dish, tilting to coat dish; pour in milk mixture. Place baking dish in large shallow pan filled to a 1-inch depth with hot water. Bake at 325°F for 60 to 70 minutes or until knife inserted in center comes out clean. Cool at least 15 minutes; unmold onto serving plate. Serve warm or cold with whipped topping if desired. Garnish as desired.

Nutrients per serving:			
Calories	178	Cholesterol	2 mg
Fat	trace	Sodium	78 mg

Orange-Apple Ice

Makes 12 servings, 6 cups

1 jar (23 ounces) MOTT'S® Natural or Regular Apple Sauce
⅓ cup orange marmalade
3 egg whites, beaten stiff*

In medium bowl, combine apple sauce and marmalade; mix well. Carefully fold in beaten egg whites. Pour into 8- or 9-inch square pan. Cover; freeze until firm. Scoop frozen mixture into dessert dishes or orange shells.

Tip: To make orange shells, use sharp knife to make sawtooth cut around middle of fruit, cutting inside to center only. Twist, pull apart and remove inside portion, scraping shells clean with spoon.

**Use only clean, uncracked eggs.*

Nutrients per serving (½ cup):			
Calories	51	Cholesterol	0 mg
Fat	0 g	Sodium	15 mg

Crunchy Apple Crisp

Florida Grapefruit Mousse

Makes 6 servings

5 tablespoons thawed frozen Florida grapefruit juice concentrate, divided
1 teaspoon unflavored gelatin
1 tablespoon granulated sugar
2 Florida grapefruit
¾ cup evaporated whole or skim milk, chilled
3 tablespoons powdered sugar

Combine 2 tablespoons juice concentrate and gelatin in small saucepan, stirring until gelatin softens. Add granulated sugar and 2 tablespoons juice concentrate. Heat over medium heat 3 to 5 minutes until gelatin dissolves, stirring constantly. Remove from heat; cool.

Meanwhile, peel grapefruit and remove white pith. Section grapefruit, removing membrane that separates fruit segments. Cut fruit segments into bite-sized pieces; set aside. Beat evaporated milk in medium bowl with electric mixer until frothy. Add remaining 1 tablespoon juice concentrate; beat until mixture becomes stiff. Add powdered sugar; beat 10 seconds more until combined. Fold in cooled gelatin mixture until blended. Fold in reserved grapefruit; spoon into parfait glasses. Serve immediately or refrigerate.

Nutrients per serving (with evaporated whole milk):			
Calories	111	Cholesterol	9 mg
Fat	3 g	Sodium	35 mg

Nutrients per serving (with evaporated skim milk):			
Calories	93	Cholesterol	1 mg
Fat	0 g	Sodium	38 mg

Favorite recipe from **Florida Department of Citrus**

Peach Yogurt Freeze with Raspberry Swirl

Makes 10 to 12 servings, about 1½ quarts

1 can (16 ounces) California cling peach halves in juice or extra light syrup
½ cup liquid egg substitute
½ cup sugar
1 cup light cream
1 carton (8 ounces) peach low fat yogurt
2 tablespoons light corn syrup
1 carton (8 ounces) raspberry low fat yogurt

Drain peaches, reserving liquid for another use. Place peaches in food processor or blender; process until smooth. Beat egg substitute in large bowl with electric mixer until light yellow and thick. Gradually add sugar, mixing well. Blend in cream, peach purée, peach yogurt and corn syrup. To freeze, pour peach

mixture into ice cream maker. Freeze according to manufacturer's directions. Place frozen mixture in airtight container, alternating with raspberry yogurt. Run knife through several times to make swirls. Cover; freeze until firm. Let soften slightly in refrigerator before serving.

Freezer Method: Turn peach mixture into 8-inch square pan and freeze solid, covering with plastic wrap when partially frozen. Cut frozen mixture into small chunks. Place in chilled bowl. Beat with electric mixer on low speed until smooth, then beat on high speed until light and fluffy.

Nutrients per serving:			
Calories	164	Cholesterol	24 mg
Fat	7 g	Sodium	52 mg

Favorite recipe from **California Cling Peach Advisory Board**

Banana Lemon Yogurt Pops

Makes 6 servings

2 egg whites
2 tablespoons sugar
1 ripe banana, peeled and sliced
2 cartons (8 ounces *each*) lemon-flavored yogurt
6 (5-ounce) paper cups
6 wooden sticks

Beat egg whites in medium bowl with electric mixer on high speed until soft peaks form. Gradually add sugar, beating until stiff peaks form. Place banana and yogurt in blender or food processor; process until smooth. Fold yogurt mixture into egg white mixture. Divide mixture evenly among paper cups; insert wooden sticks. Freeze pops until frozen. To serve, peel away paper from pops.

Nutrients per serving:			
Calories	120	Cholesterol	3 mg
Fat	1 g	Sodium	61 mg

Favorite recipe from **The Sugar Association, Inc.**

Fresh Nectarine Ovenbake

Makes 6 servings

- 2 tablespoons margarine
- 3 eggs
- ¾ cup low fat milk
- ¾ cup all-purpose flour
- 6 fresh California nectarines, sliced (about 4 cups)
- 1 tablespoon packed brown sugar
- ¾ cup plain low fat yogurt
- 2 tablespoons low calorie maple syrup

Preheat oven to 450°F. Place margarine in 10- or 12-inch skillet with ovenproof handle. Place in oven to heat margarine. Meanwhile, beat eggs in medium bowl with wire whisk until light and lemon-colored; beat in milk. Gradually stir in flour; beat until smooth. Remove skillet from oven. Pour egg batter into skillet. Bake 15 minutes. *Reduce oven temperature to 350°F.* Bake 10 minutes more until pancake is puffed and browned. Meanwhile, toss nectarines with brown sugar in serving bowl; set aside. In small bowl, mix yogurt with syrup. Serve hot ovenbake topped with nectarines and yogurt mixture.

Nutrients per serving:

Calories	245	Cholesterol	136 mg
Fat	8 g	Sodium	110 mg

Favorite recipe from **California Tree Fruit Agreement**

Toasted Almond and Fig Ice Cream

Makes 6 servings

- ⅓ cup whole California Almonds
- 2 tablespoons Marsala
- 8 dried figs, sliced (about ½ cup)
- 1½ cups low fat milk
- 3 egg yolks
- ¾ cup sugar
- 1 cup low fat yogurt

Preheat oven to 350°F. Spread almonds in single layer on baking sheet. Toast in oven 5 to 8 minutes until browned, stirring occasionally. Coarsely chop almonds; set aside.

Sprinkle Marsala over figs in small bowl. Cover and marinate 2 hours. Bring milk to a boil in heavy medium saucepan. Whisk together egg yolks and sugar in medium bowl until light and lemon-colored.

Whisk in hot milk. Return egg yolk mixture to saucepan. Cook over low heat until mixture coats back of spoon, stirring constantly. *(Do not boil.)* Remove from heat; strain into medium bowl and cool. Whisk in yogurt. Pour custard mixture into ice cream maker and freeze according to manufacturer's directions. When ice cream is almost firm, stir in reserved figs and almonds. Continue to churn until ice cream is firm. Serve immediately; freeze leftovers.

Nutrients per serving:

Calories	298	Cholesterol	113 mg
Fat	9 g	Sodium	65 mg

Favorite recipe from **Almond Board of California**

Peanut Butter & Banana Booster

Makes 4 servings

- 1 envelope KNOX® Unflavored Gelatine
- ½ cup cold skim milk
- 1 cup skim milk, heated to boiling
- 1 small banana, cut into thirds
- ⅓ cup sugar
- ¼ cup creamy peanut butter
- ½ teaspoon vanilla extract
- 1 cup ice cubes (about 6 to 8)

In blender, sprinkle unflavored gelatine over cold milk; let stand 2 minutes. Add hot milk and process at low speed until gelatine is completely dissolved, about 2 minutes. Add banana, sugar, peanut butter and vanilla; process at high speed until blended. While processing, through feed cap, add ice cubes, 1 at a time; process at high speed until ice is melted. Serve immediately.

Nutrients per serving (1 cup):

Calories	220	Cholesterol	2 mg
Fat	9 g	Sodium	125 mg

Strawberry-Banana Granité

Strawberry-Banana Granité

Makes 5 servings

2 ripe medium bananas, peeled and sliced
   (about 2 cups)
2 cups unsweetened frozen strawberries (do not
   thaw)
¼ cup no-sugar-added strawberry pourable
   fruit*
   Whole fresh strawberries (optional)
   Fresh mint leaves (optional)

Place banana slices in plastic bag; freeze until firm.
Place frozen banana slices and frozen strawberries in
food processor. Let stand 10 minutes for fruit to
soften slightly. Add pourable fruit. Remove plunger
from top of food processor to allow air to be
incorporated. Process until smooth, scraping down
sides of container frequently. Serve immediately.**
Garnish with fresh strawberries and mint leaves, if
desired. Freeze leftovers.

*You may substitute 3 tablespoons no-sugar-added
strawberry fruit spread combined with 1 tablespoon warm
water for pourable fruit.*

**Granité may be transferred to airtight container and
frozen up to 1 month. Let stand at room temperature
10 minutes to soften slightly before serving.*

Nutrients per serving:

Calories	77	Cholesterol	0 mg
Fat	trace	Sodium	8 mg

Hot Butter Rum Sauce

Makes 1⅔ cups

1 cup sugar
2 tablespoons cornstarch
⅛ teaspoon salt
¾ cup water
¼ cup dark rum
2 tablespoons butter

Combine sugar, cornstarch and salt in medium
saucepan. Stir in water. Heat over medium heat until
mixture comes to a boil. Boil 1 minute or until
thickened. Remove from heat. Stir in rum and butter
until butter is melted.

Nutrients per serving (2 tablespoons sauce):

Calories	85	Cholesterol	5 mg
Fat	2 g	Sodium	39 mg

Favorite recipe from **Wisconsin Milk Marketing Board** © 1994

Meringue-Filled Pears

Makes 4 to 6 servings

1 can (29 ounces) Bartlett pear halves
2 tablespoons packed brown sugar
1 teaspoon grated lemon peel
½ teaspoon ground nutmeg
2 egg whites
   Dash salt
2 tablespoons granulated sugar
2 tablespoons slivered almonds (optional)

Preheat oven to 325°F. Drain pears, reserving ⅓ cup
liquid. Place pears, cut sides up, in 8-inch square
baking pan. Pour reserved pear liquid into pan.
Combine brown sugar, lemon peel and nutmeg in
small bowl; mix well. Sprinkle mixture evenly over
pears. Beat egg whites and salt in medium bowl with
electric mixer until soft peaks form. Gradually add
granulated sugar and beat until stiff peaks form.
Spoon egg white mixture evenly over pear halves;
sprinkle with almonds, if desired.

Bake 15 to 20 minutes until thoroughly heated and
golden brown on top. Serve warm.

Nutrients per serving:

Calories	118	Cholesterol	0 mg
Fat	trace	Sodium	45 mg

Favorite recipe from **Pacific Coast Canned Pear Service**

California Plum Sorbet

Makes 6 servings

12 fresh California plums, sliced
3 tablespoons sugar
1 cup orange juice
1 tablespoon grated orange peel

Place all ingredients in food processor or blender;
blend until smooth. Pour into loaf pan; freeze about
4 hours. About 30 minutes before serving, process
again until smooth. Return to freezer until ready to
serve.

Note: *Sorbet may also be prepared in ice cream maker
according to manufacturer's directions.*

Nutrients per serving:

Calories	164	Cholesterol	0 mg
Fat	1 g	Sodium	trace

Favorite recipe from **California Tree Fruit Agreement**

Plums and Bavarian Cream

Plums and Bavarian Cream

Makes 6 servings

9 fresh California plums, sliced and divided
3 egg whites
⅓ cup sugar
¼ cup plain low fat yogurt

Process 4 plums in blender or food processor until smooth; measure 1 cup plum purée and set aside. Beat egg whites and sugar in large bowl with electric mixer until stiff peaks form. Fold in reserved plum purée and yogurt. Place remaining plums in serving bowl. Spoon plum mixture on top. Garnish with mint and additional plum slices, if desired.

Nutrients per serving:

Calories	106	Cholesterol	trace
Fat	trace	Sodium	32 mg

Favorite recipe from **California Tree Fruit Agreement**

Satin Chocolate Mousse

Makes 4 servings

1 teaspoon KNOX® Unflavored Gelatine
¼ cup cold skim milk
½ cup skim milk, heated to boiling
¼ cup semi-sweet chocolate chips
1 container (8 ounces) 1% milkfat cottage cheese
¼ cup sugar
1 teaspoon vanilla extract

In blender, sprinkle unflavored gelatine over cold milk; let stand 2 minutes. Add hot milk and process at low speed until gelatine is completely dissolved, about 2 minutes. Add chocolate and process at high speed until completely melted, about 1 minute. Add remaining ingredients and process at high speed until blended. Pour into medium serving bowl or individual cups; chill until set, about 2 hours.

Variation: Before serving, whisk mousse until smooth and serve as a dip with fresh fruit and cubed angel food or pound cake!

Nutrients per serving:

Calories	167	Cholesterol	3 mg
Fat	4 g	Sodium	255 mg

Nectarine Meringue Crowns

Makes 6 servings

2 egg whites
⅛ teaspoon *each* cream of tartar and ground nutmeg
⅔ cup sugar
1 can (6 ounces) frozen cranberry juice concentrate, thawed
½ cup water
1½ tablespoons cornstarch
5 fresh California nectarines, sliced (about 3 cups)

Preheat oven to 250°F. Place egg whites in medium bowl; add cream of tartar and nutmeg. Beat with electric mixer until foamy. Gradually add sugar, beating constantly until stiff and glossy. Divide egg mixture into 6 equal mounds on baking sheet. With back of spoon, shape into round tarts. Bake 1 hour. Cool. Pour concentrate into saucepan. Stir in water and cornstarch. Cook until sauce is thickened and clear, stirring constantly. Cool. Fill each meringue tart with ½ cup nectarine slices. Spoon sauce over fruit.

Nutrients per serving:

Calories	168	Cholesterol	trace
Fat	trace	Sodium	7 mg

Favorite recipe from **California Tree Fruit Agreement**

Fruit Trifle

Makes 8 servings

- ½ cup jellied cranberry sauce
- 3 tablespoons water
- 1 package (4-serving size) instant vanilla pudding mix
- 1 cup milk
- 1 cup DANNON® Vanilla or Lemon Lowfat Yogurt
- 1 package (3 ounces) ladyfingers (about 12), split
- 1½ cups fresh peach slices or frozen unsweetened peach slices, thawed, well drained and divided
- 1½ to 2 cups fresh strawberry halves, orange sections or grape halves, divided

In a small saucepan heat cranberry sauce and water until cranberry sauce is melted. Use wire whisk to beat until smooth. Cool. Prepare pudding mix according to package directions, using milk and yogurt in place of milk called for on package.

In a 1½-quart soufflé dish or straight-sided serving bowl arrange enough of the ladyfingers to cover bottom and sides of dish. Combine 1 cup peaches and 1 cup strawberries. Spoon half of fruit mixture over ladyfingers in dish. Spread half of pudding mixture over fruit. Top with half of cranberry mixture. Arrange remaining ladyfingers on top. Repeat fruit and pudding layers. Spoon remaining cranberry mixture in center. Cover; chill at least 4 hours.

To serve, arrange remaining peaches and strawberries on top. Serve immediately.

Nutrients per serving:

Calories	180	Cholesterol	45 mg
Fat	2 g	Sodium	127 mg

Fresh Pineapple "Sundaes"

Makes 8 servings

- 1 DOLE® Fresh Pineapple
- 1 cup low fat milk
- ¼ cup instant vanilla pudding mix
- 6 tablespoons chopped nuts, toasted
- 3 tablespoons shredded coconut, toasted

Twist crown from pineapple. Cut pineapple lengthwise into quarters. Cut fruit from shell and core. Cut pineapple into chunks. Divide among eight 1-cup soufflé or dessert bowls.

Place milk and pudding mix in blender; process 40 seconds until well blended. Transfer to large bowl; refrigerate 10 minutes. Spoon evenly over pineapple. Sprinkle with nuts and coconut. Serve immediately.

Prep time: 20 minutes
Chill time: 10 minutes

Nutrients per serving:

Calories	114	Cholesterol	1 mg
Fat	5 g	Sodium	45 mg

Fresh Pineapple "Sundaes"

Quick "Baked" Apples

Makes 4 servings

4 cooking apples*
2 tablespoons chopped raisins
2 tablespoons chopped dates
2 tablespoons chopped walnuts or pecans
1 tablespoon butter or margarine, melted
1 teaspoon cornstarch
¾ teaspoon ground cinnamon
¾ cup thawed frozen unsweetened apple juice
    concentrate
    Sour cream or crème fraîche (optional)

To Microwave: Remove peel from top and halfway down sides of each apple, starting at stem end. With apple corer or sharp knife, remove core to within ¼ inch of apple bottom, leaving bottom stem intact. Repeat with remaining apples. Place apples in 9-inch microwave-safe pie plate or shallow baking dish. Combine raisins, dates, walnuts and butter in small bowl; spoon evenly into centers of apples. Combine cornstarch and cinnamon in separate small bowl. Blend in apple juice concentrate; drizzle over apples. Microwave, uncovered, on HIGH (100% power) 10 to 12 minutes or until apples are tender when pierced with sharp knife, rotating dish after 6 minutes. Let stand 5 to 10 minutes before serving. Spoon juices from dish over apples. Serve warm or at room temperature with sour cream, if desired.

**Use Jonathan, McIntosh or Rome Beauty apples.*

Note: For 2 servings, cut all ingredients in half. Peel, core and fill apples as directed. Place in 9-inch microwave-safe pie plate or shallow baking dish. Microwave on HIGH (100% power) 5 to 8 minutes or until tender when pierced with sharp knife, rotating dish after 4 minutes. Continue as directed.

Nutrients per serving:

Calories	251	Cholesterol	8 mg
Fat	6 g	Sodium	44 mg

Sparkling Pear Fruit Cup

Makes 6 to 8 servings

2 U.S.A. Bartlett green pears, cored and cubed
1 U.S.A. Bartlett red pear or Red Delicious
    apple, cored and cubed
1 can (11 ounces) mandarin oranges, drained
½ cup fresh or frozen blueberries
½ cup *each* pink Chablis wine* and orange juice

Combine pears, oranges and blueberries in serving bowl. Combine wine and orange juice in small bowl; stir well. Pour over fruit; toss gently. Refrigerate 30 minutes before serving.

**Ginger ale may be substituted for pink Chablis.*

Nutrients per serving:

Calories	67	Cholesterol	0 mg
Fat	trace	Sodium	10 mg

Favorite recipe from **Oregon Washington California Pear Bureau**

Steamed Pears with Raspberry Yogurt Sauce

Makes 4 servings

2 large fresh California Bartlett pears, pared,
    halved and cored
    Lemon juice
1 package (12 ounces) frozen unsweetened
    raspberries, thawed
1 teaspoon sugar
¼ cup plain low fat yogurt
    Orange peel strips for garnish (optional)
    Fresh mint leaves for garnish (optional)

Rub pears with lemon juice to prevent browning. Place steamer rack in large saucepan or Dutch oven. Add enough water to cover bottom of pan (water should not touch rack). Place pear halves, cut sides down, on steamer rack; cover. Heat over medium heat until water boils. Reduce heat to low; steam pears 4 to 5 minutes until tender when pierced with knife tip. Cool to room temperature; refrigerate until cold.

Meanwhile, place raspberries in blender or food processor; blend until smooth. Press through sieve to remove seeds. Stir sugar into yogurt. Place yogurt in pastry bag fitted with fine tip or in clean plastic squeeze-type mustard or ketchup bottle. Pour about ¼ cup raspberry purée onto each of 4 dessert plates. Pipe yogurt in spiral design on sauce. Draw knife from center of plate to edge, spoke-fashion, to create web design. Place each chilled pear half, cut side down, in center of sauce on individual plates. Garnish with orange peel and mint leaves, if desired.

Nutrients per serving:

Calories	148	Cholesterol	trace
Fat	trace	Sodium	11 mg

Favorite recipe from **California Tree Fruit Agreement**

Quick "Baked" Apples

Apple Walnut Bread Pudding

Makes 8 servings

- 4 slices firm-textured white bread
- 2 teaspoons margarine, melted
- 2 medium apples, chopped
- ¼ cup chopped walnuts
- 2 cups cold 2% low-fat milk
- ½ cup thawed frozen egg substitute
- 1 teaspoon vanilla
- 1 package (4-serving size) JELL-O® Vanilla Flavor Sugar Free Pudding and Pie Filling
- 1 teaspoon ground cinnamon, divided

Heat oven to 350°F.

Lightly brush bread with margarine; cut into ½-inch cubes. Place on cookie sheet. Bake 10 minutes or until lightly toasted. Place cubes in shallow 1½-quart baking dish. Add apples and walnuts; toss lightly.

Pour milk, egg substitute and vanilla into large mixing bowl. Beat with wire whisk until well blended. Add pudding mix and ½ teaspoon cinnamon; whisk until well blended. Pour over bread mixture; sprinkle with remaining cinnamon. Bake 30 minutes. Remove from oven; let stand 10 minutes before serving.

Nutrients per serving:

Calories	130	Cholesterol	5 mg
Fat	5 g	Sodium	190 mg

Apple Walnut Bread Pudding

Delicious Apple Compote

Makes 6 servings

- 2 Red or Golden Delicious apples
- 2 cups seeded 1-inch watermelon chunks
- 1 cup grapes, seeded if necessary
- 1 orange, peeled and separated into segments
- 1 banana, peeled and sliced into 1-inch chunks
- 2 cups chilled ginger ale
- 2 tablespoons lime juice

Core apples; cut into bite-sized pieces. Place apples, watermelon, grapes, orange and banana in large bowl; toss well. Combine ginger ale and lime juice in small cup; pour over fruit. Toss and serve immediately.

Nutrients per serving:

Calories	104	Cholesterol	0 mg
Fat	1 g	Sodium	2 mg

Favorite recipe from **Washington Apple Commission**

Baked Bananas

Makes 8 servings

- 3 tablespoons CRISCO® Shortening
- 2 teaspoons grated lemon peel
- 2 teaspoons lemon juice
- 6 firm ripe bananas
- ½ cup firmly packed dark brown sugar

Preheat oven to 350°F. Place Crisco® in shallow 3-quart baking dish. Set in oven for 3 to 5 minutes or until Crisco® is melted. Remove from oven; stir in lemon peel and lemon juice. Peel bananas; cut in half crosswise and then lengthwise. Place in baking dish, turning to coat with Crisco® mixture. Sprinkle brown sugar over bananas.

Bake at 350°F for 20 to 25 minutes or until brown sugar is melted and bananas are tender. Serve hot.

Nutrients per serving:

Calories	171	Cholesterol	0 mg
Fat	5 g	Sodium	7 mg

Milk Chocolate Fondue

Makes 1¾ cups

1 package (12 ounces) milk chocolate chips
1 can (5 fluid ounces) PET® Light Skimmed
    Evaporated Milk
2 tablespoons Grand Marnier or kirsch
    (optional)
½ teaspoon vanilla extract
    Angel food cake cubes, fresh fruit or pretzels,
    for dipping

In fondue pot or medium saucepan, combine chocolate chips and evaporated milk. Cook over low heat until chocolate is melted, stirring occasionally.

Stir in liqueur and vanilla. Serve with angel food cake cubes, fresh fruit or pretzels.

Nutrients per serving (2 tablespoons fondue with ¹⁄₁₂th of an angel food cake):

Calories	264	Cholesterol	5 mg
Fat	8 g	Sodium	162 mg

Frozen Apple Sauce 'n' Fruit Cup

Chilled Lemonade Dessert

Makes 8 servings

1½ cups cold water
1 (3-ounce) package JELL-O® Brand Lemon
    Flavor Sugar Free Gelatin Dessert
1 (8-ounce) package Light PHILADELPHIA
    BRAND® Neufchatel Cheese, softened
⅓ cup frozen lemonade concentrate, thawed
1 teaspoon grated lemon peel
2 cups thawed COOL WHIP® Non-Dairy
    Whipped Topping

Bring water to a boil. Gradually add to gelatin in small bowl; stir until dissolved. Beat neufchatel cheese, lemonade concentrate and peel in large mixing bowl at medium speed with electric mixer until well blended. Stir in gelatin; chill until thickened but not set. Fold in whipped topping; pour into lightly oiled 6-cup mold. Chill until firm. Unmold. Garnish as desired.

Variation: Substitute 8 individual ½-cup molds for 6-cup mold.

Nutrients per serving:

Calories	160	Cholesterol	25 mg
Fat	10 g	Sodium	150 mg

Frozen Apple Sauce 'n' Fruit Cup

Makes 7 servings, 3½ cups

1 can (11 ounces) mandarin orange segments,
    drained
1 package (10 ounces) frozen strawberries,
    thawed
1 cup MOTT'S® Chunky or Regular Apple
    Sauce
1 cup seedless grapes (optional)
2 tablespoons orange juice concentrate

In medium bowl, combine all ingredients. Spoon fruit mixture into individual dishes or paper cups. Freeze until firm. Remove from freezer about 30 minutes before serving. Garnish if desired.

Nutrients per serving (½ cup):

Calories	107	Cholesterol	0 mg
Fat	0 g	Sodium	5 mg

Coconut-Date-Nut Quick Bread

Coconut-Date-Nut Quick Bread

Makes 12 servings

2 cups all-purpose flour
2 teaspoons baking powder
½ teaspoon baking soda
½ teaspoon salt
2 eggs
¾ cup thawed frozen unsweetened apple juice concentrate
¼ cup butter or margarine, melted
¼ cup milk
2 teaspoons vanilla extract
1 cup chopped pitted dates
½ cup chopped walnuts or pecans
⅓ cup unsweetened shredded coconut*
Cream cheese (optional)

Preheat oven to 350°F. Grease 9×5-inch loaf pan.

Combine flour, baking powder, baking soda and salt in medium bowl; set aside. Beat eggs in separate medium bowl with electric mixer. Blend in apple juice concentrate, butter, milk and vanilla. Add to flour mixture; mix just until moistened. Stir in dates, walnuts and coconut. Spread in prepared pan.

Bake 45 minutes or until wooden pick inserted in center comes out clean. Cool 10 minutes in pan on wire rack. Remove from pan; cool completely on wire rack. Slice; serve at room temperature or toast slices and spread with cream cheese, if desired.

Unsweetened shredded coconut is available in health food stores.

Nutrients per serving:

Calories	242	Cholesterol	46 mg
Fat	9 g	Sodium	255 mg

Strawberries 'n' Cream Fool

Makes about 10 servings

1 envelope KNOX® Unflavored Gelatine
¼ cup cold water
10 ounces (about 2 cups) frozen strawberries, thawed
¼ cup frozen orange juice concentrate, partially thawed and undiluted
¼ cup sugar
1 container (8 ounces) lite frozen whipped topping, thawed

In small saucepan, sprinkle unflavored gelatine over cold water; let stand 1 minute. Stir over low heat until gelatine is completely dissolved, about 3 minutes.

In blender, process strawberries, orange juice concentrate and sugar until smooth. While processing, through feed cap, gradually add gelatine mixture and process until blended. In large bowl, fold whipped topping into 1 cup strawberry mixture; turn into 6-cup serving bowl. Gently fold in remaining strawberry mixture, just until marbled. Chill until set, about 2 hours.

Nutrients per serving (½ cup):

Calories	87	Cholesterol	0 mg
Fat	3 g	Sodium	1 mg

Ricotta Cheese Dessert Pancakes

Makes about 6 servings, 18 pancakes

⅓ cup part-skim ricotta cheese
¼ cup milk
1 egg
2 tablespoons thawed frozen unsweetened apple juice concentrate
1 tablespoon butter or margarine, melted
¾ teaspoon vanilla extract
½ cup all-purpose flour
½ teaspoon baking powder
⅛ teaspoon ground nutmeg
1 cup *plus* 2 tablespoons no-sugar-added pourable fruit,* any flavor (optional)

Preheat lightly oiled griddle or skillet over medium heat. Place ricotta cheese in food processor; cover and process until smooth. Add milk, egg, apple juice concentrate, butter and vanilla; process until blended. Add flour, baking powder and nutmeg; pulse just until dry ingredients are moistened. Drop heaping tablespoonfuls of batter 4 inches apart onto prepared griddle. Cook 1 to 2 minutes until bubbles appear on surface; turn over with flat spatula. Continue cooking about 30 seconds or until lightly browned. Serve warm with pourable fruit.

¾ cup no-sugar-added fruit spread combined with 6 tablespoons warm water may be substituted.

Nutrients per serving (3 pancakes):

Calories	212	Cholesterol	46 mg
Fat	4 g	Sodium	126 mg

Peaches & Cinnamon Rice Pudding

Makes 4 servings

1 cup water
⅓ cup uncooked regular long-grain rice
    (not converted)
1 tablespoon butter or margarine
⅛ teaspoon salt
1 can (16 ounces) sliced peaches in unsweetened
    juice, undrained
½ cup milk, divided
2 teaspoons cornstarch
½ teaspoon ground cinnamon
¼ cup no-sugar-added peach fruit spread
½ cup heavy cream (optional)
1 tablespoon no-sugar-added peach fruit spread
    (optional)
    Fresh peach slices (optional)
    Cinnamon sticks (optional)

Combine water, rice, butter and salt in medium saucepan. Bring to a boil over high heat. Reduce heat to low. Cover; simmer about 25 minutes or until rice is tender. Remove from heat. Drain canned peaches, reserving ½ cup juice; set peaches aside. Add reserved juice and ¼ cup milk to rice; set aside. Combine cornstarch and cinnamon in small bowl; mix well. Gradually add remaining ¼ cup milk, stirring until smooth. Add to rice mixture; return to heat. Bring to a boil over medium-high heat, stirring constantly. Reduce heat to low. Simmer, stirring frequently, about 2 minutes or until thickened. Remove from heat; stir in ¼ cup fruit spread. Cool to room temperature, stirring occasionally.

Chop drained peaches; stir into pudding. Serve at room temperature or chilled. If desired, beat cream and 1 tablespoon fruit spread until soft peaks form. Serve with pudding. Garnish with fresh peach slices and cinnamon sticks, if desired.

Nutrients per serving:

Calories	197	Cholesterol	12 mg
Fat	4 g	Sodium	119 mg

No-Bake Fruit Crisp

Makes 6 servings

2 cans (16 ounces *each*) California chunky
    mixed fruit in juice or extra light syrup
1 cup cinnamon granola cereal
¼ cup toasted sliced almonds
2 tablespoons margarine
2 tablespoons packed brown sugar
1 teaspoon ground cinnamon
½ cup vanilla nonfat yogurt
¼ teaspoon ground nutmeg

Drain fruit, reserving liquid for another use; set aside fruit. Combine granola and almonds in small bowl. Melt margarine in small saucepan over medium heat. Blend in brown sugar and cinnamon; simmer about 2 minutes or until sugar is dissolved, stirring constantly. Pour over granola mixture; toss to coat. Cool. Combine yogurt and nutmeg in small bowl. To serve, spoon about ½ cup chunky mixed fruit onto each serving plate. Top with yogurt mixture and sprinkle with granola mixture.

Nutrients per serving:

Calories	223	Cholesterol	0 mg
Fat	7 g	Sodium	107 mg

Favorite recipe from **California Cling Peach Advisory Board**

Gingersnap Sandwiches

Makes 15 sandwiches

1 McIntosh apple, peeled and cored
½ cup low fat cottage cheese
2 tablespoons sugar
30 gingersnaps

Shred apple in food processor or by hand with grater. Place cottage cheese in food processor or blender; blend until smooth. Add apple and sugar; blend until combined. Spread apple filling onto flat sides of 15 gingersnaps; top each with another gingersnap to make a sandwich.

Nutrients per serving (1 sandwich):

Calories	57	Cholesterol	trace
Fat	1 g	Sodium	78 mg

Favorite recipe from **The Sugar Association, Inc.**

Peaches & Cinnamon Rice Pudding

California Apricot-Cherry Cornmeal Cobbler

Makes 8 servings

2 cups sliced fresh California apricots (about
  1 pound)
⅓ cup sugar
2 cups pitted fresh California cherries (about
  8 ounces)
1 cup *plus* 1 tablespoon all-purpose flour,
  divided
½ cup yellow cornmeal
5½ teaspoons sugar, divided
2 teaspoons baking powder
¼ teaspoon salt
5 tablespoons unsalted butter
½ teaspoon grated orange peel
¾ cup low fat milk

Preheat oven to 375°F. Combine apricots and
⅓ cup sugar in small bowl. Combine cherries
and 1 tablespoon flour in separate small bowl; set
aside. Combine remaining 1 cup flour, cornmeal,
4½ teaspoons sugar, baking powder and salt in large
bowl. Cut in butter with pastry blender or 2 knives
until mixture resembles coarse crumbs; stir in orange
peel. Stir in milk just until flour mixture is moistened.
Place reserved apricot mixture and cherry mixture in
1½ quart baking dish; top with batter. Sprinkle with
remaining 1 teaspoon sugar. Bake 25 to 30 minutes
until golden brown. Let cool slightly and serve.

Nutrients per serving:

Calories	247	Cholesterol	21 mg
Fat	9 g	Sodium	83 mg

Favorite recipe from **California Apricot Advisory Board**

Raspberry-Coulis Dessert Sauce

Makes 1 cup

2 cups (1 pint) fresh or thawed frozen
  unsweetened raspberries
½ cup no-sugar-added seedless raspberry fruit
  spread
1½ tablespoons orange-flavored liqueur
  (optional)

Place raspberries in blender or food processor; cover
and blend until smooth. Strain into small bowl using
double thickness of cheesecloth; discard seeds. Add
fruit spread and liqueur to raspberry purée; mix well.
Store in refrigerator up to 1 week. Serve over fresh
fruit or cake slices.

Nutrients per serving (1 tablespoon sauce):

Calories	29	Cholesterol	0 mg
Fat	trace	Sodium	0 mg

California Apricot-Cherry Cornmeal Cobbler

Peach Ice Cream

Makes 7 cups

7 fresh California peaches, quartered
2 cups low fat milk
1 envelope unflavored gelatin
1 cup plain low fat yogurt
½ cup sugar
1 tablespoon vanilla extract

Chop enough peaches to measure 1 cup. Place remaining peaches in blender or food processor; blend until smooth. Measure 2½ cups peach purée; set aside. Combine milk and gelatin in medium saucepan; let stand 1 minute to soften. Stir over medium heat until gelatin dissolves; remove from heat. Add chopped peaches, reserved peach purée, yogurt, sugar and vanilla extract to gelatin mixture; mix well. Pour mixture into ice cream maker; prepare according to manufacturer's directions. Pack into freezer containers. Freeze until firm.

Nutrients per serving (½ cup):			
Calories	85	Cholesterol	4 mg
Fat	1 g	Sodium	30 mg

Favorite recipe from **California Tree Fruit Agreement**

Grapefruit Sorbet with Candied Zest

Makes 8 servings, about 1 quart

3 to 4 large Florida grapefruit*
2 cups sugar
1 cup water
2 tablespoons lime juice
Fresh mint leaves for garnish

Grate enough grapefruit rind to make ½ cup zest; set aside. Juice grapefruit to make 2 cups juice. Strain juice to remove any seeds, reserving pulp. Add pulp to juice; set aside. Place sugar, water and zest in 1-quart saucepan; stir well. Bring to a boil over medium-high heat. Remove from heat; remove ¾ of zest with slotted spoon. Place zest in airtight container and refrigerate until sorbet is ready to serve. Let grapefruit syrup cool.

Combine cooled sugar mixture, reserved grapefruit juice and lime juice; cover and refrigerate until cold. Place mixture in ice cream maker and freeze according to manufacturer's directions. Transfer sorbet to 1-quart plastic container. Cover with plastic wrap *and* plastic lid to prevent ice crystals from forming. Freeze until ready to serve. Let stand 10 minutes to soften before serving. Garnish each serving with reserved candied zest and mint leaves.

You may substitute 2 cups 100% pure Florida grapefruit juice plus 1 grapefruit.

Nutrients per serving (½ cup):			
Calories	205	Cholesterol	0 mg
Fat	0 g	Sodium	1 mg

Favorite recipe from **Florida Department of Citrus**

Spicy Pear Squares

Makes about 3 dozen squares

½ cup butter or margarine
¾ cup granulated sugar
2 eggs
¾ cup all-purpose flour
1 teaspoon *each* baking powder and ground cinnamon
½ teaspoon *each* baking soda, salt and ground nutmeg
¼ teaspoon ground cloves
1 can (16 ounces) Bartlett pears, well drained and chopped
¾ cup quick-cooking rolled oats
½ cup *each* raisins and coarsely chopped walnuts
Powdered sugar

Preheat oven to 375°F. Grease 13×9-inch baking pan. Beat butter and sugar in large bowl with electric mixer until creamy. Beat in eggs, 1 at a time, mixing thoroughly after each addition. Combine flour, baking powder, cinnamon, baking soda, salt, nutmeg and cloves in small bowl. Mix well. Add to butter mixture; mix well. Stir in pears, oats, raisins and walnuts. Spread into prepared pan.

Bake 20 to 30 minutes until wooden pick inserted near center comes out clean. Sprinkle lightly with powdered sugar. Cut into squares; serve warm.

Nutrients per serving (1 square):			
Calories	83	Cholesterol	22 mg
Fat	4 g	Sodium	78 mg

Favorite recipe from **Pacific Coast Canned Pear Service**

Gingered Peach Sauce

Gingered Peach Sauce

Makes about 1 cup

1 can (16 ounces) sliced peaches in unsweetened
  juice, drained
1½ teaspoons minced fresh ginger
2 tablespoons almond-flavored liqueur
  (optional)

Place peaches in food processor; cover and process
until smooth, scraping down sides of container once.
Add ginger and liqueur, if desired; process until
smooth. Serve with fresh fruit.

Nutrients per serving (1 tablespoon):			
Calories	13	Cholesterol	0 mg
Fat	0 g	Sodium	1 mg

Almond-Pumpkin Chiffon Pudding

Makes 8 servings

½ cup chopped California Almonds
1 envelope unflavored gelatin
1 cup low fat milk
1 cup canned pumpkin
½ teaspoon pumpkin pie spice
1 container (8 ounces) plain low fat yogurt
3 egg whites
  Dash salt
⅔ cup packed brown sugar

Preheat oven to 350°F. Spread almonds in single
layer on baking sheet. Toast in oven 5 to 8 minutes
until browned, stirring occasionally.

Sprinkle gelatin over milk in small saucepan; let
stand 5 minutes to soften. Stir over low heat until milk
is hot and gelatin dissolves; remove from heat. Stir in
pumpkin and spice; transfer to large bowl. Cool to
room temperature; stir in yogurt. Chill until mixture
begins to thicken. Beat egg whites and salt in medium
bowl with electric mixer until soft peaks form.
Gradually beat in brown sugar, beating until stiff
peaks form; fold into pumpkin mixture. Sprinkle
1 tablespoon almonds over bottom of oiled 6-cup
mold. Fold remaining almonds into pumpkin mixture.
Spoon mixture into mold. Chill until firm. Unmold to
serve.

Nutrients per serving:			
Calories	169	Cholesterol	4 mg
Fat	5 g	Sodium	98 mg

Favorite recipe from **Almond Board of California**

Microwave Streusel Pears

Makes 6 servings

3 tablespoons granulated sugar
1 tablespoon fresh lemon juice
6 cups firm pear slices (about 6 medium pears)
1 cup quick-cooking rolled oats
⅓ cup firmly packed brown sugar
2 tablespoons all-purpose flour
½ teaspoon ground cinnamon
¼ teaspoon ground nutmeg
4 tablespoons margarine

To Microwave: Stir together granulated sugar and lemon
juice in large bowl; add pears and toss well. Lightly coat
8-inch square microwave-safe baking pan with nonstick
cooking spray; place pears in prepared pan. Combine oats,
brown sugar, flour, cinnamon and nutmeg in medium bowl.
Cut in margarine with pastry blender or 2 knives until
mixture is crumbly. Sprinkle over pears. Microwave,
uncovered, on HIGH (100% power) 7 to 9 minutes until
pears are fork-tender, rotating dish once during cooking.
Serve warm.

Nutrients per serving:			
Calories	295	Cholesterol	0 mg
Fat	9 g	Sodium	236 mg

Favorite recipe from **The Sugar Association, Inc.**

Fresh Peach Buttermilk Sherbet

Makes about 5 cups sherbet

3 fresh California peaches, sliced
1 cup sugar
1 egg*
4½ teaspoons lemon juice
¾ teaspoon grated lemon peel
1½ teaspoons vanilla extract
  Dash salt
2 cups buttermilk

Place peaches, sugar, egg, lemon juice, lemon peel,
vanilla and salt in blender or food processor; process
until smooth. Blend in buttermilk. Pour peach mixture
into ice cream maker; prepare according to
manufacturer's directions. Pack into freezer
containers. Freeze until firm.

**Use only clean, uncracked egg.*

Nutrients per serving (½ cup):			
Calories	121	Cholesterol	28 mg
Fat	1 g	Sodium	58 mg

Favorite recipe from **California Tree Fruit Agreement**

CALORIE, FAT & CHOLESTEROL COUNTER

Your diet affects a lot more than just your waistline. Food choices and eating habits influence not only the shape of your body but your overall health as well.

To help you choose low-cholesterol, low-fat foods from the vast array of products at your local supermarket, we have included this counter. The counter provides values for hundreds of common foods, identified by brand and/or generic name, as well as almost 200 items from fast-food menus. The data comes from the United States Department of Agriculture, manufacturers and processors, and directly from food labels.

Separate columns list the calorie (CAL.) and cholesterol (CHOL.) content of each item. Fat is broken down to show amounts of total fat (FAT) and saturated fat (SAT. FAT). Fats are shown in grams (g); cholesterol is indicated in milligrams (mg). Percentage of calories from total fat and saturated fat is also included. These percentage figures provide a useful guide to fat content because the percentage of fat in a given item doesn't change, regardless of the portion size. For example, between 76 and 81 percent of the calories in peanut butter come from fat, regardless of whether you eat a spoonful or the entire jar.

With a simple formula, you can calculate the fat percentages for foods not included on our list. Since every gram of fat provides your body with 9 calories, simply multiply the grams of fat (or saturated fat) by 9, and divide the result by the total number of calories. Multiply your answer by 100. This gives the percentage of total calories that come from fat (or saturated fat). For example, one raw egg contains 6 grams of fat and has 80 calories. Using the formula, multiply 6 by 9 to get 54; divide 54 by 80 to get 0.675, and multiply 0.675 by 100 to get 67.5 percent (which is then rounded off to 68 percent). Thus, 68 percent of the calories in one raw egg come from fat.

Foods in the counter are grouped into common categories, such as "Beverages" and "Poultry," and are arranged in alphabetical order. After a brief description of each item, a specific portion size is given. The values in each column pertain to the portion size listed. Some food items have "na" or "tr" listed in one of the columns. The "na" means that the content was not available to us at the time of printing. The "tr" means that the food item contains only trace amounts of the substance. When trace amounts are shown for fat or saturated fat, it then becomes impossible to calculate the exact percentage of calories from fat or saturated fat. In this instance, "na" (not available) is also used. However, as a practical matter, if only trace amounts of these elements are present, the percentage of calories they provide is generally quite low, usually less than ten percent.

The symbol "<" means "less than," so "<1" indicates the presence of less than one unit of whatever is being measured (less than one percent, less than one gram). Fractional amounts have been rounded off. Finally, while every effort has been made to ensure that the values listed are as accurate as possible, they are subject to change as food processors modify ingredients and methods of preparation.

Be sure to take note of the Low-Fat Alternatives chart at the end of the counter. This at-a-glance guide provides a number of low-fat alternatives to high-fat foods.

Baked Goods

FOOD/PORTION SIZE	CAL.	FAT		SAT. FAT		CHOL.
		Total (g)	As % of Cal.	Total (g)	As % of Cal.	(mg)
CAKE						
Angel Food Cake Mix, Duncan Hines, 1/12 of cake	140	0	0	0	0	0
Chocolate Loaf, Fat & Cholesterol Free, Entenmann's, 1 oz. slice	70	0	0	0	0	0
Coffeecake, Butter Streusel, Sara Lee, 1/8 of cake (1.4 oz.)	160	7	39	na	na	na
Cupcakes Lights, Hostess, 1 cupcake, 1½ oz.	130	2	14	0	0	0
Devil's Food Cake Mix, Moist Deluxe, Duncan Hines, 1/12 of cake, regular recipe	280	15	48	4	13	65
Same as above, no-cholesterol recipe	270	14	47	2	7	0
Fudge Marble Supreme Cake Mix, Moist Deluxe, Duncan Hines, 1/12 of cake, regular recipe	260	11	38	3	10	65
Same as above, no-cholesterol recipe	250	10	36	2	7	0
Gingerbread Cake & Cookie Mix, Betty Crocker, 1/9 of cake (1.6 oz.), regular recipe	220	7	29	2	8	30
Same as above, no-cholesterol recipe	210	6	26	0	0	0
Golden Loaf, Fat & Cholesterol Free, Entenmann's, 1 oz. slice	70	0	0	0	0	0
Lemon Supreme Cake Mix, Moist Deluxe, Duncan Hines, 1/12 of cake, regular recipe	260	11	38	3	10	65
Same as above, no-cholesterol recipe	250	10	36	2	7	0
Orange Supreme Cake Mix, Duncan Hines, 1/12 of cake, regular recipe	260	11	38	3	10	65
Same as above, no-cholesterol recipe	250	10	36	2	7	0
Pound Cake, All-Butter, Sara Lee, 1 oz. slice	130	7	48	0	0	na
Pound Cake, Free & Light, Sara Lee, 1 oz. slice	70	0	0	0	0	0
Spice Cake Mix, Moist Deluxe, Duncan Hines, 1/12 of cake, regular recipe	260	11	38	3	10	65
Same as above, no-cholesterol recipe	250	10	36	2	7	0
Strawberry Supreme Cake Mix, Moist Deluxe, Duncan Hines, 1/12 of cake, regular recipe	260	11	38	3	10	65
Same as above, no-cholesterol recipe	250	10	36	2	7	0
Twinkies Lights, Hostess, 1 cake, 1½ oz.	130	2	14	0	0	0
White Cake Mix, Lovin' Lites, Pillsbury (using egg whites), 1/12 of cake	170	2	11	<1	na	0

FOOD/PORTION SIZE	CAL.	FAT		SAT. FAT		CHOL. (mg)
		Total (g)	As % of Cal.	Total (g)	As % of Cal.	
White Cake Mix, Moist Deluxe, Duncan Hines, regular recipe, 1⁄12 of cake	270	12	40	3	11	65
Same as above, no-cholesterol recipe	250	10	36	2	7	0
Yellow Cake Mix, Moist Deluxe, Duncan Hines, 1⁄12 of cake, regular recipe	260	11	38	3	10	65
Same as above, no-cholesterol recipe	250	10	36	2	7	0
COOKIES						
Chocolate Chip, Chips Ahoy, Nabisco, 1 cookie	50	2	36	tr	<1	0
Chocolate chip, refrigerated dough, 1 cookie	56	3	48	1	16	6
Chocolate Chip Mix, Duncan Hines, 1 cookie	65	3	42	2	28	8
Fig Newtons, Nabisco, 1 cookie	60	1	15	tr	<1	0
Nilla Wafers, Nabisco, 3 cookies	60	2	3	tr	tr	5
Oatmeal Raisin, Fat & Cholesterol Free, Entenmann's, 2 cookies	80	0	0	0	0	0
Oreos, Nabisco, 1 cookie	50	2	36	tr	<1	<2
Peanut Butter Mix, Duncan Hines, 1 cookie	70	4	51	1	13	8
Sandwich (chocolate or vanilla), 1 cookie	49	2	37	1	18	0
Shortbread, commercial, 1 small cookie	39	2	46	1	23	7
Sugar, refrigerated dough, 1 cookie	59	3	46	1	15	7
Teddy Grahams Bearwiches, Nabisco, 4 cookies	70	3	39	tr	<1	0
PASTRY						
Coffeecake, Easy Mix, Aunt Jemima, ⅛ of cake	170	5	26	na	na	na
Danish, fruit, 4¼-in. round, 1 pastry	235	13	50	4	15	56
Danish, plain, 1 oz.	110	6	49	2	16	24
Danish, plain, 4¼-in. round, 1 pastry	220	12	49	4	16	49
Toaster, 1 pastry	210	6	26	2	9	0
PIE						
(All pies include crust made with enriched flour and vegetable shortening.)						
Apple, ⅙ of 9-in. pie	405	18	40	5	11	0
Apple, Homestyle, Sara Lee, ⅙ of pie	433	20	42	na	na	0
Blueberry, ⅙ of 9-in. pie	380	17	40	4	9	0
Cherry, ⅙ of 9-in. pie	410	18	40	5	11	0

FOOD/PORTION SIZE	CAL.	FAT		SAT. FAT		CHOL.
		Total (g)	As % of Cal.	Total (g)	As % of Cal.	(mg)
Custard, ⅙ of 9-in. pie	330	17	46	6	16	169
Lemon meringue, ⅙ of 9-in. pie	355	14	35	4	10	143
Peach, ⅙ of 9-in. pie	405	17	38	4	9	0
Pecan, ⅙ of 9-in. pie	575	32	50	5	8	95
Piecrust, Butter Flavor, Keebler, 1 shell, 6 oz.	880	40	41	8	8	0
Piecrust, Chocolate Flavor, Keebler, 1 shell, 6 oz.	960	40	38	8	8	0
Piecrust, Graham Cracker, Keebler, 1 shell, 6 oz.	960	48	45	8	8	0
Piecrust, Graham Cracker, single serve, Keebler, 1 shell	100	5	45	1	9	0
Piecrust, mix, 9-in., 2-crust pie	1485	93	56	23	14	0
Piecrust, Pet Ritz, 1 shell	720	48	60	12	15	0
Piecrust, Pet Ritz, Deep Dish, all vegetable shortening, 1 shell	780	54	62	12	14	0
Pumpkin, ⅙ of 9-in. pie	320	17	48	6	17	109

MISCELLANEOUS

FOOD/PORTION SIZE	CAL.	FAT		SAT. FAT		CHOL.
Brownies, Fudge, Light, Betty Crocker, 1/24 of package as prepared	100	1	9	na	na	0
Brownies, Fudge Brownie Mix, Duncan Hines, 1 brownie	130	5	35	na	na	0
Doughnuts, cake, plain, 1 doughnut	210	12	51	3	13	20
Doughnuts, yeast, glazed, 1 doughnut	192	13	61	5	23	29
Pizza Crust, All Ready, Pillsbury, ⅛ of crust	90	1	10	0	0	0

Baking Products & Condiments

FOOD/PORTION SIZE	CAL.	FAT		SAT. FAT		CHOL.
		Total (g)	As % of Cal.	Total (g)	As % of Cal.	(mg)
Bacos, 2 tsp.	25	1	36	na	na	0
Baking Powder, Davis, 1 tsp.	8	0	0	0	0	0
Baking soda for home use, 1 tsp.	5	0	0	0	0	0
Barbecue Sauce, Kraft, 1 tbsp.	23	tr	na	tr	na	0
Barbecue Sauce, Original, Open Pit, 1 tbsp.	25	0	0	0	0	0
Barley, pearled, light, uncooked, 1 cup	700	2	3	<1	tr	0
Bulgur, uncooked, 1 cup	600	3	5	1	2	0
Butterscotch Topping, Artificially Flavored, Kraft, 1 tbsp.	60	1	15	0	0	0

FOOD/PORTION SIZE	CAL.	FAT Total (g)	FAT As % of Cal.	SAT. FAT Total (g)	SAT. FAT As % of Cal.	CHOL. (mg)
Cajun Magic Seasoning, K-Paul Enterprises, 1 tsp.	20	0	0	0	0	0
Caramel Topping, Kraft, 1 tbsp.	60	0	0	0	0	0
Catsup, 1 tbsp.	15	tr	na	tr	na	0
Catsup, Weight Watchers, 1 tbsp.	12	0	0	0	0	0
Celery seed, 1 tsp.	10	1	90	tr	na	0
Chili powder, 1 tsp.	10	tr	na	<1	na	0
Chili Sauce, Bennet's, 1 tbsp.	16	0	0	0	0	0
Chili Sauce, Heinz, 1 tbsp.	16	0	0	0	0	0
Chocolate, Semi-Sweet, Baker's, 1 oz.	140	15	96	na	na	0
Chocolate, Unsweetened Chocolate Baking Bar, Baker's, 1 oz.	140	15	96	na	na	0
Chocolate Caramel Topping, Kraft, 1 tbsp.	60	0	0	0	0	0
Chocolate Chips, Mini, Hershey's, ¼ cup	220	12	49	7	29	10
Chocolate Chips, Real, Semi-Sweet, Baker's, ¼ cup	200	12	54	7	32	0
Chocolate Chips, Semi-Sweet, Hershey's, ¼ cup	220	12	49	7	29	8
Chocolate Flavored Chips, Semi-Sweet, Baker's, ¼ cup	200	9	41	7	29	0
Chocolate Topping, Kraft, 1 tbsp.	50	0	0	0	0	0
Cinnamon, 1 tsp.	5	tr	na	tr	na	0
Cocktail Sauce, Sauceworks, 1 tbsp.	14	0	0	0	0	0
Cocoa Powder, Hershey's, ¼ cup	91	3	30	2	20	0
Coconut, Angel Flake, Baker's (bag), ⅓ cup	115	8	63	8	63	0
Coconut, Premium Shred, Baker's, ⅓ cup	140	9	58	9	58	0
Cornmeal, degermed, enriched, dry, 1 cup	500	2	4	<1	na	0
Cornmeal, whole-ground, unbolted, dry, 1 cup	435	5	10	<1	na	0
Curry powder, 1 tsp.	5	tr	na	na	na	0
Flour, buckwheat, light, sifted, 1 cup	340	1	3	<1	na	0
Flour, cake/pastry, enriched, sifted, spooned, 1 cup	350	1	3	<1	na	0
Flour, self-rising, enriched, unsifted, spooned, 1 cup	440	1	2	<1	na	0
Flour, wheat, all-purpose, sifted, spooned, 1 cup	420	1	2	<1	na	0
Flour, wheat, all-purpose, unsifted, spooned, 1 cup	455	1	2	<1	na	0
Flour, whole-wheat from hard wheats, stirred, 1 cup	400	2	5	<1	na	0
Frosting, Chocolate-flavored, Creamy Deluxe, Betty Crocker, 1/12 of tub	160	7	39	2	11	0
Frosting, Chocolate Fudge, Lovin' Lites, Pillsbury, 1/12 of can (1⅓ oz.)	120	2	15	tr	na	0

FOOD/PORTION SIZE	CAL.	FAT Total (g)	FAT As % of Cal.	SAT. FAT Total (g)	SAT. FAT As % of Cal.	CHOL. (mg)
Frosting, Cream Cheese, Duncan Hines, 1 tbsp.	60	3	45	1	15	0
Garlic powder, 1 tsp.	10	tr	na	tr	na	0
Garlic powder with parsley, Lawry's, 1 tsp.	12	tr	na	0	0	0
Honey, strained or extracted, 1 tbsp.	65	0	0	0	0	0
Horseradish, Cream Style, Prepared, Kraft, 1 tbsp.	12	1	75	0	0	0
Horseradish, Prepared, Kraft, 1 tbsp.	10	0	0	0	0	0
Horseradish Sauce, Kraft, 1 tbsp.	50	5	90	1	18	5
Hot Fudge Topping, Kraft, 1 tbsp.	70	3	39	1	13	0
Hot Fudge Topping, Light, J.M. Smucker, 1 tbsp.	35	tr	na	0	0	na
Jam, Strawberry, Smucker's, 1 tbsp.	54	0	0	0	0	na
Jams and preserves, 1 tbsp.	55	tr	na	0	0	0
Jellies, 1 tbsp.	50	tr	na	tr	na	0
Marshmallow Creme, Kraft, 1 oz.	90	0	0	0	0	0
Mayonnaise, 1 tbsp.	100	11	99	2	18	8
Mayonnaise, Cholesterol Free, Hellman's, 1 tbsp.	50	5	90	1	18	0
Mayonnaise, Hellmann's, 1 tbsp.	100	11	99	2	18	7
Mayonnaise, Light, Reduced Calorie, Kraft, 1 tbsp.	50	5	90	1	18	5
Mayonnaise, Light Reduced Calorie, Hellman's, 1 tbsp.	50	5	90	1	18	5
Mayonnaise, Nonfat, Kraft Free, 1 tbsp.	12	0	0	0	0	0
Mayonnaise, Real, Kraft, 1 tbsp.	100	12	100	2	18	5
Molasses, Light, Brer Rabbit, 1 tbsp.	56	0	0	0	0	0
Mustard, Dijon, Grey Poupon, 1 tbsp.	20	1	45	0	0	0
Mustard, Creamy Spread, French's, 1 tbsp.	8	tr	tr	0	0	0
Mustard, Horseradish, Kraft, 1 tbsp.	14	1	64	0	0	0
Mustard, prepared yellow, 1 tbsp.	15	tr	na	tr	na	0
Mustard, Pure Prepared, Kraft, 1 tbsp.	11	1	82	0	0	0
Onion powder, 1 tsp.	5	tr	na	tr	na	0
Oregano, 1 tsp.	5	tr	na	tr	na	0
Paprika, 1 tsp.	6	tr	na	tr	na	0
Parsley Patch Italian Seasoning, McCormick, 1 tsp.	8	0	0	0	0	0
Pepper, ground, black, 1 tsp.	5	tr	na	tr	na	0
Picante Sauce, Medium, Pace, 2 tbsp.	3	tr	na	na	na	na
Pineapple Topping, Kraft, 1 tbsp.	50	0	0	0	0	0
Preserves, Apricot, Kraft, 1 tbsp.	54	0	0	0	0	0
Relish, sweet, finely chopped, 1 tbsp.	20	tr	na	tr	na	0

FOOD/PORTION SIZE	CAL.	FAT		SAT. FAT		CHOL.
		Total (g)	As % of Cal.	Total (g)	As % of Cal.	(mg)
Salad Dressing, Free Nonfat, Miracle Whip, 1 tbsp.	20	0	0	0	0	0
Salad Dressing, Light, Miracle Whip, 1 tbsp.	45	4	80	1	20	5
Salad Dressing, Miracle Whip, 1 tbsp.	70	7	90	1	13	5
Salsa, Thick & Chunky, Mild, Ortega, 1 tbsp.	4	0	0	0	0	0
Salt, 1 tsp.	0	0	0	0	0	0
Sandwich Spread, Kraft, 1 tbsp.	50	5	90	1	18	5
Seasoning Blend, Mrs. Dash, 1 tsp.	12	0	0	0	0	0
Seasoning Mixture, Original Recipe for Chicken, Shake 'N Bake, ¼ pouch	80	tr	na	tr	na	0
Soy sauce, ready to serve, 1 tbsp.	11	0	0	0	0	0
Steak Sauce, A1, 1 tbsp.	14	0	0	0	0	0
Strawberry Topping, Kraft, 1 tbsp.	50	0	0	0	0	0
Sugar, brown, packed, 1 cup	820	0	0	0	0	0
Sugar, powdered, sifted, spooned into cup, 1 cup	385	0	0	0	0	0
Sugar, white granulated, 1 cup	770	0	0	0	0	0
Sweet 'n Sour Sauce, Sauceworks, 1 tbsp.	25	0	0	0	0	0
Syrup, chocolate-flavored syrup or topping, fudge type, 2 tbsp.	125	5	36	3	22	0
Syrup, chocolate-flavored syrup or topping, thin type, 2 tbsp.	85	tr	na	<1	na	0
Syrup, molasses, cane, blackstrap, 2 tbsp.	85	0	0	0	0	0
Syrup, Regular, Log Cabin, 1 oz. (about 2 tbsp.)	100	tr	na	tr	na	0
Syrup, table (corn & maple), 2 tbsp.	122	0	0	0	0	0
Tabasco Sauce, ¼ tsp.	0	0	0	0	0	0
Tartar sauce, 1 tbsp.	75	8	96	1	12	4
Tartar Sauce, Fat Free, Cholesterol Free, Nonfat, Kraft, 1 tbsp.	16	0	0	0	0	0
Tartar Sauce, Hellmann's, 1 tbsp.	70	8	100	1	13	5
Tartar Sauce, Natural Lemon Herb Flavor, Sauceworks, 1 tbsp.	70	8	100	1	13	5
Tartar Sauce, Sauceworks, 1 tbsp.	50	5	90	1	18	5
Vinegar, Apple Cider, Heinz, 2 tbsp.	4	0	0	0	0	0
Vinegar, Cider, Heinz, 2 tbsp.	4	0	0	0	0	0
Vinegar, Gourmet Wine, Heinz, 2 tbsp.	8	0	0	0	0	0
Vinegar, Wine, Red or White, Heinz, 2 tbsp.	4	0	0	0	0	0
Worcestershire Sauce, Heinz, 1 tbsp.	12	0	0	0	0	0
Yeast, baker's dry active, 1 package	20	tr	na	tr	na	0
Yeast, brewer's dry, 1 tbsp.	25	tr	na	tr	na	0

Beverages

FOOD/PORTION SIZE	CAL.	FAT		SAT. FAT		CHOL. (mg)
		Total (g)	As % of Cal.	Total (g)	As % of Cal.	
ALCOHOL						
Beer, light, 12 fl. oz.	95	0	0	0	0	0
Beer, regular, 12 fl. oz.	150	0	0	0	0	0
Gin, rum, vodka, whiskey, 80-proof, 1½ fl. oz.	97	0	0	0	0	0
Gin, rum, vodka, whiskey, 90-proof, 1½ fl. oz.	110	0	0	0	0	0
Wine, table, red, 3½ fl. oz.	74	0	0	0	0	0
Wine, table, white, 3½ fl. oz.	70	0	0	0	0	0
COFFEE						
Brewed, 6 fl. oz.	tr	tr	na	tr	na	0
Café Francais, General Foods International Coffees, 6 fl. oz.	50	3	54	0	0	0
Café Francais, General Foods Sugar Free International Coffees, 6 fl. oz.	35	2	51	0	0	0
Coffee Flavor Instant Hot Beverage, Postum, 6 fl. oz.	12	0	0	0	0	0
Instant, Folger's, 1 tbsp.	8	0	0	0	0	0
JUICE						
Apple, bottled or canned, 1 cup	115	tr	na	tr	na	0
Apple, Pure 100%, Kraft, 8 fl. oz.	107	0	0	0	0	0
Apple/Cranberry Fruit Blends, Del Monte, approx. 8 fl. oz.	140	0	0	0	0	0
Cherry, Pure & Light, Dole, 1 cup	120	0	0	0	0	0
Cranberry Juice Cocktail, Ocean Spray, 8 fl. oz.	144	0	0	0	0	0
Grape, canned or bottled, 1 cup	155	tr	na	<1	na	0
Grape, frozen concentrate, sweetened, diluted, 1 cup	125	tr	na	<1	na	0
Grapefruit, canned, sweetened, 1 cup	115	tr	na	tr	na	0
Grapefruit, canned, unsweetened, 1 cup	95	tr	na	tr	na	0
Grapefruit, frozen concentrate, unsweetened, diluted, 1 cup	100	tr	na	tr	na	0
Grapefruit, raw, 1 cup	95	tr	na	tr	na	0
Lemon, canned or bottled, unsweetened, 1 cup	50	1	18	<1	2	0
Lemon, raw, 1 cup	60	tr	na	tr	na	0
Lemon, ReaLemon Juice from Concentrate, Borden, 1 cup	48	0	0	0	0	0

FOOD/PORTION SIZE	CAL.	FAT Total (g)	FAT As % of Cal.	SAT. FAT Total (g)	SAT. FAT As % of Cal.	CHOL. (mg)
Lime, canned or bottled, unsweetened, 1 cup	50	1	18	<1	2	0
Lime, raw, 1 cup	65	tr	na	tr	na	0
Orange, canned, unsweetened, 1 cup	105	tr	na	tr	na	0
Orange, chilled, 1 cup	110	1	8	<1	tr	0
Orange, frozen concentrate, diluted, 1 cup	110	tr	na	tr	na	0
Orange, Minute Maid, 100% pure orange juice from concentrate, 6 fl.oz.	90	0	0	0	0	0
Orange, raw, 1 cup	110	tr	na	<1	<1	0
Orange and grapefruit, canned, 1 cup	105	tr	na	tr	na	0
Peach, Pure & Light, Dole, 8 fl. oz.	120	0	0	0	0	0
Pineapple, Canned, Dole, 8 fl. oz.	133	0	0	0	0	0
Pineapple, unsweetened, canned, 1 cup	140	tr	na	tr	na	0
Pineapple-Orange, Dole, 8 fl. oz.	120	0	0	0	0	0
Pineapple-Orange Fruit Blends, Del Monte, approx. 8 fl. oz.	140	0	0	0	0	0
Pineapple-Orange-Guava, Dole, 8 fl. oz.	133	<1	0	0	0	0
Pineapple-Passion-Banana, Dole, 1 cup	133	0	0	0	0	0
Prune, canned or bottled, 1 cup	180	tr	na	tr	na	0
Raspberry, Pure & Light, Dole, 8 fl. oz.	133	0	0	0	0	0
Tomato, canned, 1 cup	40	tr	na	tr	na	0
Vegetable Juice, V-8, 8 fl. oz.	47	0	0	0	0	0

MILK

FOOD/PORTION SIZE	CAL.	FAT Total (g)	FAT As % of Cal.	SAT. FAT Total (g)	SAT. FAT As % of Cal.	CHOL. (mg)
Buttermilk, 1 cup	100	2	18	1	9	9
Canned, condensed, sweetened, 1 cup	980	27	25	17	16	104
Canned, evaporated, skim, 1 cup	200	1	5	<1	1	9
Canned, evaporated, whole, 1 cup	340	19	50	12	32	74
Chocolate, low fat (1%), 1 cup	160	3	17	2	11	7
Chocolate, low fat (2%), 1 cup	180	5	25	3	15	17
Chocolate Malt Flavor, Ovaltine Classic, ¾ oz.	80	0	0	0	0	0
Cocoa Mix, Milk Chocolate, Carnation, 1 envelope	110	1	8	tr	<1	1
Cocoa Mix, Rich Chocolate, Carnation, 1 envelope	110	1	8	1	8	1
Cocoa Mix, Rich Chocolate with Marshmallows, Carnation, 1 envelope	110	1	8	1	8	2
Dried, nonfat, instant, 1 cup	245	tr	na	<1	1	12
Dried, nonfat, instant, 1 envelope (3⅕ oz.) (makes 1 quart liquid milk)	325	1	3	<1	1	17
Eggnog, commercial, 1 cup	340	19	50	11	29	149
Evaporated Filled Milk, Milnot, 2 tbsp.	37	2	49	tr	<1	na
Evaporated Milk, Carnation, 2 tbsp.	43	3	63	na	na	na

FOOD/PORTION SIZE	CAL.	FAT Total (g)	FAT As % of Cal.	SAT. FAT Total (g)	SAT. FAT As % of Cal.	CHOL. (mg)
Evaporated Milk, Pet, 2 tbsp.	43	3	63	2	42	9
Evaporated Skim Milk, Light, Pet, 2 tbsp.	25	0	0	0	0	3
Evaporated Skim Milk, Lite, Carnation, 2 tbsp.	25	0	0	0	0	3
Fudge Drink, Chocolate, Slender, 10 fl. oz.	220	4	16	na	na	4
Low fat (2%), milk solids added, 1 cup	125	5	36	3	22	18
Low fat (2%), no milk solids, 1 cup	120	5	38	3	23	18
Malt Drink, Chocolate, Slender, 10 fl. oz.	220	4	16	na	na	4
Malted, chocolate, powder, ¾ oz.	84	1	11	<1	5	1
Malted, chocolate, powder, prepared with 8 oz. whole milk	235	9	34	6	23	34
Malted, natural, powder, prepared with 8 oz. whole milk	235	10	38	6	23	37
Malt Flavor, Ovaltine Classic, ¾ oz. dry	80	tr	na	tr	na	0
Nonfat (skim), milk solids added, 1 cup	90	1	10	<1	4	5
Nonfat (skim), no milk solids, 1 cup	86	tr	na	<1	3	4
Quik, Chocolate, Nestlé, ¾ oz. (2 ½ tsp.)	90	1	10	0	0	0
Shake Mix, Alba 77 Fit n' Frosty, all flavors, 1 envelope	70	0	0	0	0	3
Skim Milk, Fortified, Lite-line or Viva, Borden, 1 cup	100	1	9	tr	<1	5
Whole (3.3% fat), 1 cup	150	8	48	5	30	33
Whole, Borden, 1 cup	150	8	48	na	na	na

SOFT DRINKS, CARBONATED

FOOD/PORTION SIZE	CAL.	FAT Total (g)	FAT As % of Cal.	SAT. FAT Total (g)	SAT. FAT As % of Cal.	CHOL. (mg)
7-Up, Diet, 6 fl. oz.	2	0	0	0	0	na
7-Up, Diet Cherry, 6 fl.oz.	2	0	0	0	0	na
Club soda, 6 fl. oz.	0	0	0	0	0	0
Coca-Cola Classic, 6 fl. oz.	72	0	0	0	0	0
Diet Coke, 6 fl. oz.	0	0	0	0	0	na
Diet Coke, Caffeine Free, 6 fl.oz.	0	0	0	0	0	na
Diet Pepsi, Caffeine Free, 6 fl. oz.	0	0	0	0	0	na
Diet-Rite, Black Cherry, 6 fl. oz.	2	0	0	0	0	na
Diet-Rite, Cola, 6 fl. oz.	2	0	0	0	0	na
Diet-Rite, Pink Grapefruit, 6 fl. oz.	2	0	0	0	0	na
Diet-Rite, Red Raspberry, 6 fl. oz.	2	0	0	0	0	na
Dr. Pepper, Diet, 6 fl. oz.	2	0	0	0	0	na
Fresca, 6 fl. oz.	2	0	0	0	0	na
Ginger Ale, Canada Dry, Diet, 6 fl. oz.	2	0	0	0	0	na
Grape, carbonated, 6 fl. oz.	90	0	0	0	0	0
Orange, carbonated, 6 fl. oz.	90	0	0	0	0	0

FOOD/PORTION SIZE	CAL.	FAT Total (g)	FAT As % of Cal.	SAT. FAT Total (g)	SAT. FAT As % of Cal.	CHOL. (mg)
Pepsi-Cola, Diet, 6 fl. oz.	0	0	0	0	0	na
Root beer, 6 fl. oz.	83	0	0	0	0	0
Root Beer, Dad's, Diet, 6 fl. oz.	2	0	0	0	0	na
SOFT DRINKS, NONCARBONATED						
Country Time Drink Mix, Sugar Sweetened, Lemonade/Pink Lemonade, 8 fl. oz.	80	0	0	0	0	0
Country Time Drink Mix, Sugar Sweetened, Lemon-Lime, 8 fl. oz.	80	0	0	0	0	0
Country Time Sugar Free Drink Mix, Lemonade/Pink Lemonade, 8 fl. oz.	4	0	0	0	0	0
Country Time Sugar Free Drink Mix, Lemon-Lime, 8 fl. oz.	4	0	0	0	0	0
Crystal Light Sugar Free Drink Mix, all flavors, 8 fl. oz.	4	0	0	0	0	0
Grape drink, noncarbonated, canned, 6 fl. oz.	100	0	0	0	0	0
Hi-C Cherry Drink, 6 fl. oz.	100	0	0	0	0	0
Hi-C Citrus Cooler Drink, 6 fl. oz.	100	0	0	0	0	0
Hi-C Double Fruit Cooler Drink, 6 fl. oz.	90	0	0	0	0	0
Hi-C Fruit Punch Drink, 6 fl. oz.	100	0	0	0	0	0
Hi-C Hula Punch Drink, 6 fl. oz.	80	0	0	0	0	0
Kool-Aid Koolers Juice Drink, all flavors, approx. 8 fl. oz.	130	0	0	0	0	0
Kool-Aid Soft Drink Mix, Sugar-Sweetened, all flavors, 8 fl. oz.	80	0	0	0	0	0
Kool-Aid Soft Drink Mix, Unsweetened, all flavors, 8 fl. oz.	2	0	0	0	0	0
Kool-Aid Soft Drink Mix, Unsweetened, all flavors, with sugar added, 8 fl. oz.	100	0	0	0	0	0
Kool-Aid Sugar-Free Soft Drink Mix, all flavors, 8 fl. oz.	4	0	0	0	0	0
Lemonade concentrate, frozen, diluted, 6 fl. oz.	80	tr	na	tr	na	0
Lemon Lime, Gatorade, 8 fl. oz.	50	0	0	0	0	na
Limeade concentrate, frozen, diluted, 6 fl. oz.	75	tr	na	tr	na	0
Ocean Spray, Cran-Apple Drink, 6 fl. oz.	130	0	0	0	0	na
Ocean Spray, Cran-Grape Drink, 6 fl. oz.	130	0	0	0	0	na
Ocean Spray, Cran-Raspberry Drink, 6 fl. oz.	110	0	0	0	0	na
Pineapple-grapefruit juice drink, 6 fl. oz.	90	tr	<1	0	0	0
Wyler's Punch Mix, Sweetened, all flavors, 8 fl. oz.	90	0	0	0	0	na
Wyler's Punch Mix, Unsweetened, all flavors, 8 fl. oz.	2	0	0	0	0	na

FOOD/PORTION SIZE	CAL.	FAT Total (g)	FAT As % of Cal.	SAT. FAT Total (g)	SAT. FAT As % of Cal.	CHOL. (mg)
TEA						
Berry, Crystal Light Fruit-Tea Sugar Free Drink Mix, 8 fl. oz.	4	0	0	0	0	0
Brewed, Lipton, 8 fl. oz.	3	tr	<1	0	0	0
Citrus, Crystal Light Fruit-Tea Sugar Free Drink Mix, 8 fl. oz.	4	0	0	0	0	0
Iced Tea, Crystal Light Sugar Free Drink Mix, 8 fl. oz.	4	0	0	0	0	0
Instant, powder, sweetened, 8 fl. oz.	85	tr	na	tr	na	0
Instant, powder, unsweetened, 8 fl.oz.	tr	tr	na	tr	na	0
Natural Brew, Crystal Light Fruit-Tea Sugar Free Drink Mix, 8 fl. oz.	4	0	0	0	0	0
Tropical Fruit, Crystal Light Fruit-Tea Sugar Free Drink Mix, 8 fl. oz.	4	0	0	0	0	0

Breads & Cereals

FOOD/PORTION SIZE	CAL.	FAT Total (g)	FAT As % of Cal.	SAT. FAT Total (g)	SAT. FAT As % of Cal.	CHOL. (mg)
BISCUITS						
Baking powder, home recipe, 1 biscuit	100	5	45	1	9	tr
Baking powder, refrigerated dough, 1 biscuit	65	2	28	1	14	1
BREAD						
Boston brown, canned, 3¼ × ½-in. slice	95	1	9	<1	3	3
Cracked-wheat, 1 slice	65	1	14	<1	3	0
Crumbs, enriched, dry, grated, 1 cup	390	5	12	2	5	5
French, enriched, 5 × 2½ × 1-in. slice	100	1	9	<1	3	0
Frozen Bread Dough, Honey Wheat, Rhodes, 1 slice, approx. 28 g (1 oz.)	69	1	13	tr	<1	0
Frozen Bread Dough, Texas White Roll, Rhodes, 2 oz.	150	4	24	1	6	0
Frozen Bread Dough, Texas Whole Wheat, Rhodes, 2 oz.	129	1	7	tr	<1	0
Italian, enriched, 4½ × 3¼ × ¾-in. slice	85	tr	na	tr	na	0
Oat, Hearty Slices Crunchy Oat Bread, Pepperidge Farm, 1 slice	95	2	19	1	5	0
Oat, Oat Bran Bread, Roman Meal, 1 slice	70	tr	<1	na	na	0
Pita, enriched, white, 6-in. diameter, 1 pita	165	1	5	<1	<1	0
Pumpernickel, ⅔ rye, ⅓ wheat, 1 slice	80	1	11	<1	2	0

FOOD/PORTION SIZE	CAL.	FAT		SAT. FAT		CHOL.
		Total (g)	As % of Cal.	Total (g)	As % of Cal.	(mg)
Raisin, enriched, 1 slice	65	1	14	<1	3	0
Rye, ⅔ wheat, ⅓ rye, 4¾ × 3¾ × 7/16-in. slice	65	1	14	<1	3	0
Vienna, enriched, 4¾ × 4 × ½-in. slice	70	1	13	<1	3	0
Wheat, Soft, Brownberry, 1 slice	70	1	13	tr	<1	0
Wheat, Stoneground 100% Wheat, Wonder, 1 slice	70	1	13	na	na	0
White, Country White Hearty Slices, Pepperidge Farm, 1 slice	95	1	9	1	5	0
White, enriched, soft crumbs, 1 cup	120	2	15	<1	5	0
White, Home Pride Buttertop, 1 slice	70	1	13	tr	<1	1
White, Wonder, 1 slice	70	1	13	tr	<1	0
Whole-wheat, 16-slice loaf, 1 slice	70	1	13	<1	5	0
CEREALS, COLD						
40% Bran Flakes, Post, 1 oz. (⅔ cup)	90	tr	<1	tr	<1	0
100% Bran, Nabisco, 1 oz. (⅓ cup)	70	1	8	tr	<1	0
100% Natural, Oats & Honey, Quaker, 1 oz. (¼ cup)	130	6	40	4	27	0
All-Bran, Kellogg's, 1 oz. (⅓ cup)	70	1	13	tr	<1	0
Alpha-Bits, Post, 1 oz.	110	1	8	tr	<1	0
Apple Jacks, Kellogg's, 1 oz.	110	0	0	0	0	0
Bran Flakes, Kellogg's, 1 oz. (¾ cup)	90	0	0	0	0	0
Bran Flakes, Post, 1 oz.	90	0	0	0	0	0
Cap'n Crunch, Quaker, 1 oz. (¾ cup)	120	3	23	2	15	0
Cap'n Crunch Peanut Butter, Quaker, 1 oz.	127	3	21	2	14	na
Cheerios, General Mills, 1 oz. (1¼ cups)	110	2	16	tr	<1	0
Cheerios, Honey-Nut, General Mills, 1 oz. (¾ cup)	110	1	8	tr	<1	0
Cocoa Krispies, Kellogg's, 1 oz.	110	0	0	0	0	0
Cocoa Pebbles, Post, 1 oz.	110	1	8	1	8	0
Cocoa Puffs, General Mills, 1 oz.	110	1	8	tr	<1	0
Common Sense Oat Bran, Kellogg's, 1 oz.	100	1	9	tr	<1	0
Complete Bran Flakes, Kellogg's, 1 oz.	90	0	0	0	0	0
Corn Chex, Ralston, 1 oz.	110	0	0	0	0	0
Corn Flakes, Kellogg's, 1 oz. (1¼ cups)	100	0	0	0	0	0
Corn Flakes, Post Toasties, 1 oz. (1¼ cups)	110	tr	<1	tr	<1	0
Corn Flakes, Total, 1 oz. (1 cup)	110	1	8	tr	<1	0
Cracklin' Oat Bran, Kellogg's, 1 oz.	110	4	33	tr	<1	0
Froot Loops, Kellogg's, 1 oz. (1 cup)	110	1	8	tr	<1	0
Frosted Mini-Wheats, Kellogg's, 1 oz.	100	0	0	0	0	0

FOOD/PORTION SIZE	CAL.	FAT		SAT. FAT		CHOL. (mg)
		Total (g)	As % of Cal.	Total (g)	As % of Cal.	
Fruit & Fibre—Dates, Raisins, Walnuts, Post, 1 oz.	90	1	10	tr	<1	0
Fruit & Fibre—Harvest Medley, Post, 1 oz.	92	1	10	tr	<1	0
Fruit & Fibre—Mountain Trail, Post, 1 oz.	90	1	10	tr	<1	0
Fruit & Fibre—Tropical Fruit, Post, 1 oz.	90	1	10	tr	<1	0
Fruity Pebbles, Post, 1 oz.	113	1	8	1	8	0
Golden Grahams, General Mills, 1 oz. (¾ cup)	110	1	8	tr	<1	0
Granola, Nature Valley, 1 oz. (⅓ cup)	125	5	36	3	22	tr
Granola with Almonds, Sun Country, 1 oz.	130	5	35	1	7	0
Granola with Raisins, Hearty, C.W. Post, 1 oz.	125	4	29	3	32	0
Granola with Raisins, Sun Country, 1 oz.	125	5	36	1	7	0
Grape-Nuts, Post, 1 oz.	110	0	0	0	0	0
Grape-Nuts Flakes, Post, 1 oz.	105	1	9	tr	<1	0
Honeycomb, Post, 1 oz.	110	0	0	0	0	0
Just Right with Fiber Nuggets, Kellogg's, 1 oz.	100	1	9	tr	<1	0
Just Right with Fruit & Nuts, Kellogg's, 1 oz.	140	1	8	tr	<1	0
Kix, General Mills, 1 oz.	110	0	0	0	0	0
Life, Quaker Oats, 1 oz.	111	2	16	tr	<1	na
Life, Cinnamon, Quaker Oats, 1 oz.	101	2	18	tr	<1	0
Lucky Charms, General Mills, 1 oz. (1 cup)	110	1	8	tr	<1	0
Mueslix Five Grain, Kellogg's, 1 oz.	96	1	9	tr	<1	0
Natural Raisin Bran, Post, 1 oz.	87	0	0	0	0	0
Nutri Grain Almonds & Raisins, Kellogg's, 1 oz.	100	2	18	0	0	0
Nutri Grain Biscuits, Kellogg's, 1 oz.	90	0	0	0	0	0
Nutri Grain Wheat, Kellogg's, 1 oz.	100	0	0	0	0	0
Nutri Grain Wheat & Raisins, Kellogg's, 1 oz.	130	0	0	0	0	0
Oat Bran, Quaker, 1 oz.	110	2	16	tr	<1	0
Product 19, Kellogg's, 1 oz. (¾ cup)	110	tr	<1	0	0	0
Puffed Rice, Quaker Oats, ½ oz.	54	tr	<1	tr	<1	0
Puffed Wheat, Quaker Oats, ½ oz.	54	tr	<1	tr	<1	0
Raisin Bran, Kellogg's, 1 oz. (¾ cup)	120	1	8	tr	<1	0
Raisin Bran, Post, 1 oz. (½ cup)	85	1	11	0	0	0
Rice Chex, Ralston, 1 oz.	110	1	11	0	0	0
Rice Krispies, Kellogg's, 1 oz. (1 cup)	110	0	0	0	0	0
Shredded Wheat, Nabisco, 1 biscuit, ⅚ oz.	80	<1	na	tr	<1	0
Shredded Wheat, Spoon Size, Nabisco, 1 oz.	90	<1	na	tr	<1	0
Special K, Kellogg's, 1 oz. (1⅓ cups)	110	tr	<1	0	0	tr
Sugar Frosted Flakes, Kellogg's, 1 oz. (¾ cup)	110	tr	<1	0	0	0
Super Golden Crisp, Post, 1 oz.	110	0	0	0	0	0
Trix, General Mills, 1 oz. (1 cup)	110	1	8	tr	<1	0

FOOD/PORTION SIZE	CAL.	FAT Total (g)	FAT As % of Cal.	SAT. FAT Total (g)	SAT. FAT As % of Cal.	CHOL. (mg)
Wheat Chex, Ralston Purina, 1 oz.	100	0	0	0	0	0
Wheat Germ, Honey Crunch, Kretschmer, 1 oz.	105	3	26	tr	<1	0
Wheaties, General Mills, 1 oz. (1 cup)	100	tr	<1	tr	<1	0

CEREALS, HOT

FOOD/PORTION SIZE	CAL.	Total (g)	As % of Cal.	Total (g)	As % of Cal.	CHOL. (mg)
Corn grits, regular/quick, enriched, 1 cup	145	tr	na	tr	na	0
Cream of Rice, 1 oz.	100	0	0	na	na	0
Cream of Wheat, Mix 'n Eat, plain, 1 packet	100	tr	<1	0	0	0
Cream of Wheat, regular/quick/instant, 1 cup	149	tr	<1	0	0	0
Malt-O-Meal, Chocolate, 1 oz.	100	0	0	0	0	na
Oat Bran, Quaker Oats, 1 oz.	92	2	20	na	na	0
Oats, Instant, Apple Cinnamon, Quaker Oats, 1¼ oz.	134	2	13	1	7	0
Oats, Instant, Bananas & Cream, Quaker Oats, 1¼ oz.	160	2	11	1	6	0
Oats, Instant, Blueberries & Cream, Quaker Oats, 1¼ oz.	130	2	14	tr	<1	0
Oats, Instant, Cinnamon Spice, Quaker Oats, 1⅔ oz.	160	2	11	tr	<1	0
Oats, Instant, Maple & Brown Sugar, Quaker Oats, 1½ oz.	163	2	11	tr	<1	0
Oats, Instant, Peaches & Cream, Quaker Oats, 1¼ oz.	136	2	13	tr	<1	0
Oats, Instant, Raisin Date Walnut, Quaker Oats, 1⅓ oz.	130	2	14	tr	<1	0
Oats, Instant, Raisin Spice, Quaker Oats, 1½ oz.	159	2	11	tr	<1	0
Oats, Instant, Regular, Quaker Oats, dry, 1 oz.	109	2	17	tr	<1	0
Oats, Instant, Strawberries & Cream, Quaker Oats, 1¼ oz.	136	2	13	tr	<1	0
Oats, Quick or Old Fashioned, Quaker Oats, dry, 1 oz.	100	2	17	tr	<1	0
Wheateena, 1 oz.	100	1	9	na	na	na
Whole Wheat Hot Natural, Quaker Oats, 1 oz.	92	1	10	tr	<1	0

CRACKERS

FOOD/PORTION SIZE	CAL.	Total (g)	As % of Cal.	Total (g)	As % of Cal.	CHOL. (mg)
Cheese, plain, 1-in. square, 10 crackers	50	3	54	<1	16	6
Cheese, sandwich/peanut butter, 1 sandwich	40	2	45	<1	9	1
Graham, Nabisco, 1 sheet	60	1	15	<1	na	0
Graham, plain, 2½-in. square, 2 crackers	60	1	15	<1	6	0

FOOD/PORTION SIZE	CAL.	FAT		SAT. FAT		CHOL. (mg)
		Total (g)	As % of Cal.	Total (g)	As % of Cal.	
Oat Bran, Sunshine, 8 crackers (½ oz.)	80	4	45	1	11	0
Ritz, Nabisco, ½ oz. (4 crackers)	70	4	51	<1	na	0
Rye-Bran Crispbread, Kavli, 1 slice	30	0	0	0	0	0
Rye wafers, whole-grain, 2 wafers	55	1	16	<1	5	0
Rykrisp, (Natural), ½ cracker	40	0	0	0	0	0
Saltines, 4 crackers	50	1	18	<1	9	4
Snack-type, standard, 1 round cracker	15	1	60	<1	12	0
Town House, Low Sodium, Keebler, 4 crackers	70	4	51	3	39	0
Wheat, thin, 4 crackers	35	1	26	<1	13	0
Wheat Thins, Original, Nabisco, 8 crackers (½ oz.)	70	3	39	na	na	0
Whole Wheat Wafers, Triscuit, Nabisco, ½ oz. (3 wafers)	60	2	30	na	na	0
MUFFINS						
Apple Streusel, Breakfast, Hostess, 1 muffin	100	1	9	tr	<1	0
Banana Nut, Frozen, Healthy Choice, 1 muffin	180	6	30	tr	<1	0
Blueberry, Bakery Style Muffin Mix, Duncan Hines, 1 muffin	180	5	25	na	na	na
Blueberry, Frozen, Healthy Choice, 1 muffin	190	4	19	tr	<1	0
Blueberry, mix, 1 muffin	140	5	32	1	6	45
Blueberry, Wild, Light, Betty Crocker, regular recipe, 1 muffin	70	tr	na	na	na	20
Same as above, no-cholesterol recipe	70	tr	na	na	na	0
Bran, mix, 1 muffin	140	4	26	1	6	28
Bran, with Raisins, Pepperidge Farm, 1 muffin (2 oz.)	170	6	32	1	5	0
Cinnamon Swirl, Bakery Style Muffin Mix, Duncan Hines, 1 muffin	200	7	32	na	na	na
English, plain, enriched, 1 muffin	140	1	6	<1	2	0
English, Thomas', 1 muffin, 57 g (2 oz.)	130	1	7	na	na	0
ROLLS						
Dinner, enriched commercial, 1 roll	85	2	21	<1	5	tr
Frankfurter/hamburger, enriched commercial, 1 roll	115	2	16	<1	4	tr
Hard, enriched commercial, 1 roll	155	2	12	<1	2	tr
Hoagie/submarine, enriched commercial, 1 roll	400	8	18	2	5	tr

FOOD/PORTION SIZE	CAL.	FAT Total (g)	FAT As % of Cal.	SAT. FAT Total (g)	SAT. FAT As % of Cal.	CHOL. (mg)
MISCELLANEOUS						
Bagel, plain/water, enriched, 1 bagel	200	2	9	<1	1	0
Bagels, Egg, Lender's, 1 bagel (2 oz.)	150	1	6	na	na	0
Bagels, Plain, Lender's, 1 bagel (2 oz.)	150	1	6	na	na	0
Bran, unprocessed, Quaker Oats, ¼ oz.	21	tr	<1	tr	<1	0
Breadsticks, Pillsbury, 1 stick	100	2	18	tr	na	0
Croissant, with enriched flour, 1 croissant	235	12	46	4	15	13
Melba toast, plain, 1 piece	20	tr	na	<1	5	0
Pancake & Waffle Mix, Extra Light, Hungry Jack, regular recipe, three 4-in. pancakes	190	6	28	1	47	55
Same as above, no-cholesterol recipe	170	4	21	<1	<1	0
Pancakes & Waffle Mix, Original, Aunt Jemima, regular recipe, 3 to 4 pancakes	190	6	28	na	na	65
Same as above, no-cholesterol recipe	170	3	16	na	na	0
Stuffing, Herb Seasoned, Pepperidge Farm, 1 oz.	110	1	8	na	na	na
Stuffing Mix, Chicken Flavored, Stove Top One Step, 1 oz.	120	3	23	na	na	0
Stuffing Mix, Croutettes, Kellogg's, 1 oz.	93	3	29	na	na	0
Stuffing mix, moist, prepared from mix, 1 cup	420	26	56	5	11	67
Taco Shell, Ortega, 1 shell	70	3	39	0	0	0
Tortillas, corn, 1 tortilla	65	1	14	<1	1	0
Tortilla, Corn, Azteca, 1 tortilla	45	0	0	0	0	0
Tortillas, Flour, Azteca, 7-inch, 1 tortilla	80	2	23	0	0	0
Waffles, Home Style, Aunt Jemima, frozen, 1 waffle (1¼ oz.)	90	3	30	na	na	na
Wheat Bran, Kretschmer, 1 oz.	57	2	32	na	na	0

Candy

FOOD/PORTION SIZE	CAL.	FAT Total (g)	FAT As % of Cal.	SAT. FAT Total (g)	SAT. FAT As % of Cal.	CHOL. (mg)
Almond Joy, 1 bar (1.76 oz.)	250	14	50	na	na	na
Baby Ruth, 1 bar (2.1 oz.)	290	14	43	8	25	0
Butterfinger Bar, 1 bar (2.1 oz.)	280	12	39	5	16	0
Butter Mints, Kraft, 1 mint	8	0	0	0	0	0
Caramels, Kraft, 1 caramel	30	1	30	0	0	0
Chocolate, sweet dark, 1 oz.	152	10	59	6	36	0
Chocolate Fudgies, Kraft, 1 fudgie	35	1	26	0	0	0

FOOD/PORTION SIZE	CAL.	FAT Total (g)	As % of Cal.	SAT. FAT Total (g)	As % of Cal.	CHOL. (mg)
Crunch, Nestlé, 1.4 oz.	200	10	45	na	na	na
Fudge, chocolate, plain, 1 oz.	117	3	23	2	15	1
Gum drops, 1 oz.	100	tr	na	tr	na	0
Hard candy, 1 oz.	110	0	0	0	0	0
Jelly beans, 1 oz.	105	tr	na	tr	na	0
Jet-Puffed Marshmallows, Kraft, 1 marshmallow	25	0	0	0	0	0
Kisses, Hershey's, 9 pieces	220	13	53	8	33	10
Kit-Kat, 1³⁄₂₅ oz.	172	9	47	6	31	8
M & M's Peanut Chocolate Candies, 1 oz.	150	7	42	na	na	na
M & M's Plain Chocolate Candies, 1 oz.	140	6	39	na	na	na
Milk chocolate, plain, 1 oz.	147	9	55	5	31	6
Milk chocolate, with almonds, 1 oz.	152	9	53	5	30	5
Milk chocolate, with peanuts, 1 oz.	154	10	58	4	23	5
Milk chocolate, with rice cereal, 1 oz.	140	7	45	4	26	6
Milk Chocolate Bar, Hershey's, 1 bar	250	12	43	7	25	12
Milky Way Bar, 1 bar (2.15 oz.)	280	11	35	na	na	na
Miniature Marshmallows, Kraft, 10 marshmallows	18	0	0	0	0	0
Mr. Goodbar, Hershey's, 1.65 oz.	240	15	56	na	na	na
Party Mints, Kraft, 1 mint	8	0	0	0	0	0
Peanut Brittle, Kraft, 1 oz.	130	5	35	1	7	0
Peanut Butter Cups, Reese's, 2 cups	280	17	55	6	19	8
Snickers, 1 bar (2.7 oz.)	280	13	42	na	na	na
Special Dark, Hershey's, 1.75 oz.	280	16	51	9	29	4

Cheese

FOOD/PORTION SIZE	CAL.	FAT Total (g)	As % of Cal.	SAT. FAT Total (g)	As % of Cal.	CHOL. (mg)
American, Pasteurized Process Cheese Slices, Deluxe, Kraft, 1 oz.	110	9	74	5	41	25
American, Sharp, Pasteurized Process Slices, Old English, Kraft, 1 oz.	110	9	74	5	41	30
American Flavor, Imitation Pasteurized Process Cheese Food, Golden Image, 1 oz.	90	6	60	2	20	5
American Flavored, Singles Pasteurized Process Cheese Product, Light n' Lively, 1 oz.	70	4	51	3	39	13

FOOD/PORTION SIZE	CAL.	FAT		SAT. FAT		CHOL.
		Total (g)	As % of Cal.	Total (g)	As % of Cal.	(mg)
American Flavor Process Cheese, Low Sodium, Weight Watchers, 1 slice	35	1	26	1	26	5
American Process Cheese, Borden Lite-line, 1 oz.	50	2	36	1	18	5
American Singles Pasteurized Process Cheese Food, Kraft, 1 oz.	90	7	70	4	40	25
Blue, 1 oz.	100	8	72	6	54	21
Blue, Natural, Kraft, 1 oz.	100	9	81	5	45	30
Brick, Natural, Kraft, 1 oz.	110	9	74	5	41	30
Camembert, 1 wedge (⅓ of 4-oz. container)	115	9	70	6	47	27
Cheddar, Extra Sharp, Cold Pack Cheese Food, Cracker Barrel, 1 oz.	90	7	70	4	40	20
Cheddar, Free 'n Lean, Alpine Lace, 1 oz.	35	0	0	0	0	5
Cheddar, Light Naturals Reduced Fat, Kraft, 1 oz.	80	5	56	3	34	20
Cheddar, Mild, Imitation, Golden Image, 1 oz.	110	9	74	2	16	5
Cheddar, Natural, Kraft, 1 oz.	110	9	74	5	41	30
Cheddar, Port Wine, Cheese Log with Almonds, Cracker Barrel, 1 oz.	90	6	60	3	30	15
Cheddar, Port Wine, Cold Pack Cheese Food, Cracker Barrel, 1 oz.	100	7	63	4	36	20
Cheddar, Preferred Light, Fancy Supreme Shredded, Sargento, 1 oz.	90	5	50	3	30	15
Cheddar, Reduced Fat, Dorman's Light, 1 oz.	80	5	56	3	34	20
Cheddar, Sharp, Cheese Ball with Almonds, Cracker Barrel, 1 oz.	100	7	63	3	27	20
Cheddar, Sharp, Cold Pack Cheese Food, Cracker Barrel, 1 oz.	100	7	63	4	36	20
Cheddar, Sharp, Process Cheese, Borden Lite-line, 1 oz.	50	2	36	1	18	5
Cheddar, shredded, 1 cup	455	34	67	23	45	120
Cheddar, Smokey, Cheese Log with Almonds, Cracker Barrel, 1 oz.	90	6	60	3	30	15
Cheddar Flavored, Sharp, Singles Pasteurized Process Cheese Product, Light n' Lively, 1 oz.	70	4	51	2	26	15
Cheese Food, Cold Pack with Real Bacon, Cracker Barrel, 1 oz.	90	7	70	4	40	20
Cheese Food, Pasteurized Process Sharp Singles, Kraft, 1 oz.	100	8	72	5	45	25
Cheese Spread, Hot Mexican, Pasteurized Process, Velveeta, 1 oz.	80	6	68	3	34	20
Cheese Spread, Mild Mexican, Pasteurized Process, Velveeta, 1 oz.	80	6	68	3	34	20
Cheese Spread, Pasteurized Process, Velveeta, 1 oz.	80	6	68	4	45	20

FOOD/PORTION SIZE	CAL.	FAT Total (g)	FAT As % of Cal.	SAT. FAT Total (g)	SAT. FAT As % of Cal.	CHOL. (mg)
Cheese Spread, Slices, Pasteurized Process, Velveeta, 1 oz.	90	6	60	4	40	20
Cheez Whiz, Mild Mexican, Pasteurized Process Cheese Spread, 1 oz.	80	6	68	4	45	20
Cheez Whiz, Pasteurized Process Cheese Spread, 1 oz.	80	6	68	3	34	20
Cheez Whiz with Jalapeño Pepper, Pasteurized Process Cheese Spread, 1 oz.	80	6	68	4	45	20
Colby, Imitation, Golden Image, 1 oz.	110	9	74	2	16	5
Cottage, creamed, Borden, 1 cup	240	10	38	na	na	na
Cottage, creamed, large curd, 1 cup	235	10	38	6	23	34
Cottage, creamed, small curd, 1 cup	215	9	35	6	25	31
Cottage, Lite n' Lively, 1 cup	160	2	11	2	11	10
Cottage, low fat (2%), 1 cup	205	4	18	3	13	19
Cottage, Lowfat, Lite-line or Viva, Borden, 1 cup	90	1	10	tr	na	5
Cottage, uncreamed, dry curd, 1 cup	125	1	7	<1	3	10
Cream Cheese, Philadelphia Brand, 1 oz.	100	10	90	6	54	30
Cream Cheese, Whipped, with Chives, Philadelphia Brand, 1 oz.	90	8	80	5	50	30
Cream Cheese, Whipped, with Onions, Philadelphia Brand, 1 oz.	90	8	80	5	50	25
Cream Cheese, Whipped, with Smoked Salmon, Philadelphia Brand, 1 oz.	90	8	80	5	50	30
Cream Cheese Product, Pasteurized Process, Light, Philadelphia Brand, 1 oz.	60	5	75	3	45	10
Cream Cheese with Chives, Soft, Philadelphia Brand, 1 oz.	90	9	90	5	50	30
Cream Cheese with Chives & Onion, Soft, Philadelphia Brand, 1 oz.	100	9	81	5	45	30
Cream Cheese with Herbs & Garlic, Soft, Philadelphia Brand, 1 oz.	100	9	81	5	45	25
Cream Cheese with Olives & Pimento, Soft, Philadelphia Brand, 1 oz.	90	8	80	5	50	25
Cream Cheese with Pimentos, Philadelphia Brand, 1 oz.	90	9	90	5	50	30
Cream Cheese with Pineapple, Soft, Philadelphia Brand, 1 oz.	90	8	80	5	50	25
Cream Cheese with Smoked Salmon, Soft, Philadelphia Brand, 1 oz.	90	9	90	5	50	25
Cream Cheese with Strawberries, Soft, Philadelphia Brand, 1 oz.	90	8	80	5	50	20
Edam, Natural, Kraft, 1 oz.	90	7	70	4	40	20
Feta, 1 oz.	75	6	72	4	48	25
Feta, Churny Athenos, 1 oz.	75	7	84	4	48	25

FOOD/PORTION SIZE	CAL.	FAT Total (g)	FAT As % of Cal.	SAT. FAT Total (g)	SAT. FAT As % of Cal.	CHOL. (mg)
Gouda, Natural, Kraft, 1 oz.	110	9	74	5	41	30
Hickory Smoke Flavor Pasteurized Process Cheese Spread, Squeez-A-Snak, 1 oz.	80	7	79	4	45	20
Jalapeño Pasteurized Process Cheese Spread, Kraft, 1 oz.	80	6	68	4	45	20
Jalapeño Pepper Spread, Kraft, 1 oz.	70	5	64	3	39	15
Jalapeño Singles Pasteurized Process Cheese Food, Kraft, 1 oz.	90	7	70	4	40	25
Limburger, Natural, Little Gem Size, Mohawk Valley, 1 oz.	90	8	80	5	50	25
Limburger Pasteurized Process Cheese Spread, Mohawk Valley, 1 oz.	70	6	77	3	39	20
Monterey Jack, Natural, Kraft, 1 oz.	110	9	74	5	41	30
Monterey Jack Singles Pasteurized Process Cheese Food, Kraft, 1 oz.	90	7	70	4	40	25
Monti-Jack-Lo, Alpine Lace, 1 oz.	80	5	56	3	34	15
Mozzarella, Low Moisture, Casino, 1 oz.	90	7	70	4	40	25
Mozzarella, made with part-skim milk, 1 oz.	72	5	63	3	38	16
Mozzarella, made with whole milk, 1 oz.	80	6	68	4	45	22
Mozzarella, Part-Skim, Low Moisture, Kraft, 1 oz.	80	5	56	3	34	15
Mozzarella, Preferred Light Fancy Supreme Shredded, Sargento, 1 oz.	60	3	45	na	na	10
Mozzarella, Preferred Light Sliced, Sargento, 1 oz.	60	3	45	2	30	10
Mozzarella, Truly Lite, Frigo, 1 oz.	60	2	30	na	na	8
Mozzarella String with Jalapeño Pepper, Part-Skim, Low Moisture, Kraft, 1 oz.	80	5	56	3	34	20
Muenster, 1 oz.	104	8	69	4	35	27
Munster, Lo-Chol Cheese Alternative, Dorman's, 1 oz.	100	7	63	1	9	5
Neufchatel Light, Philadelphia Brand, 1 oz.	80	7	79	4	45	25
Olives & Pimento Spread, Kraft, 1 oz.	60	5	75	3	45	15
Parmesan, Grated, 1 tbsp.	25	2	72	1	36	4
Parmesan, Grated, Kraft, 1 oz.	130	9	62	5	35	30
Parmesan, Natural, Kraft, 1 oz.	100	7	63	4	36	20
Parmesan, Preferred Light Grated Gourmet, Sargento, 1 tbsp.	25	2	72	tr	na	4
Pimento Cheese Spread, Pasteurized Process, Velveeta, 1 oz.	80	6	68	3	34	20
Pimento Pasteurized Process Cheese Slices, Deluxe, Kraft, 1 oz.	100	8	72	5	45	25
Pimento Singles Pasteurized Process Cheese Food, Kraft, 1 oz.	90	7	70	4	40	25

FOOD/PORTION SIZE	CAL.	FAT		SAT. FAT		CHOL.
		Total (g)	As % of Cal.	Total (g)	As % of Cal.	(mg)
Pimento Spread, Kraft, 1 oz.	70	5	64	3	39	15
Provolone, 1 oz.	100	8	72	5	45	20
Ricotta, made with part-skim milk, 1 cup	340	19	50	12	32	76
Ricotta, made with whole milk, 1 cup	430	30	63	20	42	126
Ricotta, Natural Nonfat, Polly-O Free, 1 oz.	25	0	0	0	0	0
Ricotta, Reduced Fat, Polly-O Lite, 1 oz.	35	2	51	1	26	5
Romano, Grated, Kraft, 1 oz.	130	9	62	6	42	30
Romano, Natural, Casino, 1 oz.	100	7	63	4	36	20
Sandwich Slices with Vegetable Oil, Lunch Wagon, 1 oz.	90	7	70	2	20	5
Swiss, 1 oz.	105	8	69	5	43	26
Swiss, Light, No Salt, Dorman's, 1 oz.	90	5	50	3	30	15
Swiss, Natural, Kraft, 1 oz.	110	8	65	5	41	25
Swiss, Preferred Light, Sargento, 1 oz.	90	5	50	3	30	15
Swiss Flavor Process Cheese, Lite-line, Borden, 1 oz.	50	2	36	1	18	10
Swiss Pasteurized Process Cheese Slices, Deluxe, 1 oz.	90	7	70	4	40	25
Swiss Singles Pasteurized Process Cheese Food, Kraft, 1 oz.	90	7	70	4	40	25

Cream & Creamers

FOOD/PORTION SIZE	CAL.	FAT		SAT. FAT		CHOL.
		Total (g)	As % of Cal.	Total (g)	As % of Cal.	(mg)
Coffee Rich, ½ oz.	20	2	90	tr	na	0
Cool Whip Extra Creamy Dairy Recipe Whipped Topping, Birds Eye, 1 tbsp.	14	1	64	1	64	0
Cool Whip Lite Whipped Topping, Birds Eye, 1 tbsp.	8	tr	na	na	na	0
Cool Whip Non-Dairy Whipped Topping, Birds Eye, 1 tbsp.	12	1	75	tr	na	0
Cream, sour, 1 tbsp.	25	3	100	2	72	5
Cream, Sour, Land O Lakes, 1 tbsp.	30	3	90	2	60	5
Cream, Sour, Light, Land O Lakes, 1 tbsp.	20	1	45	1	45	3
Cream, Sour, Light n' Lively Free, Kraft, 1 tbsp.	10	0	0	0	0	0
Cream, Sour Half and Half, Breakstone's Light Choice, 1 tbsp.	20	1	45	1	45	5
Cream, sweet, half-and-half, 1 tbsp.	20	2	90	2	90	6
Cream, sweet, light/coffee/table, 1 tbsp.	30	3	90	2	60	10

FOOD/PORTION SIZE	CAL.	FAT		SAT. FAT		CHOL.
		Total (g)	As % of Cal.	Total (g)	As % of Cal.	(mg)
Cream, sweet, whipping, unwhipped, heavy, 1 cup	832	84	91	55	59	336
Cream, sweet, whipping, unwhipped, heavy, 1 tbsp.	52	6	100	3	52	21
Cream, sweet, whipping, unwhipped, light, 1 cup	700	69	89	46	59	272
Cream, sweet, whipping, unwhipped, light, 1 tbsp.	44	5	100	3	61	17
Creamer, sweet, imitation, liquid, 1 tbsp.	20	1	45	1	45	0
Creamer, Sweet, Powdered, Cremora Lite, 1 tsp.	8	tr	na	0	0	0
Cream Topping, Real, Kraft, 1 tbsp.	8	tr	56	tr	56	3
Whipped topping, cream, pressurized, 1 tbsp.	10	1	90	<1	36	2
Whipped Topping, Kraft, 1 tbsp.	9	tr	77	tr	77	0
Whipped topping, sweet, imitation, frozen, 1 tbsp.	15	1	60	1	60	0
Whipped topping, sweet, imitation, pressurized, 1 tbsp.	10	1	90	<1	72	2
Whipped topping, sweet, powdered, prepared with whole milk, 1 tbsp.	10	1	90	<1	72	tr
Whipped Topping Mix, Dream Whip, prepared with water, 1 tbsp.	5	0	0	0	0	0
Whipped Topping Mix, Reduced Calorie, D-Zerta, prepared, 1 tbsp.	8	1	100	tr	na	0

Eggs

FOOD/PORTION SIZE	CAL.	FAT		SAT. FAT		CHOL.
		Total (g)	As % of Cal.	Total (g)	As % of Cal.	(mg)
Cholesterol Free Egg Product, Healthy Choice, ¼ cup	30	<1	na	na	na	0
Egg Beaters, Fleischmann's, ¼ cup	25	0	0	0	0	0
Egg Substitute, Scramblers, ¼ cup	60	3	45	tr	na	0
Large, fried in butter, 1 egg	95	7	76	3	33	278
Large, hard-cooked, 1 egg	80	6	68	2	23	213
Large, poached, 1 egg	80	6	68	2	23	213
Large, raw, white only, 1 white	15	0	0	0	0	0
Large, raw, whole, 1 egg	80	6	68	2	23	213
Large, raw, yolk only, 1 yolk	65	6	83	2	28	213
Scrambled, with milk, cooked in margarine, 1 egg	100	7	63	2	18	215

Fast Foods

FOOD/PORTION SIZE	CAL.	FAT Total (g)	FAT As % of Cal.	SAT. FAT Total (g)	SAT. FAT As % of Cal.	CHOL. (mg)
ARBY'S						
Dressing, Blue Cheese, 2 oz.	295	31	95	6	18	50
Dressing, Buttermilk Ranch, 2 oz.	349	40	100	6	15	6
Dressing, Honey French, 2 oz.	322	27	75	4	11	0
Dressing, Light Italian, 2 oz.	23	1	39	tr	na	0
Dressing, Weight Watchers Creamy French, 1 oz.	48	3	56	1	19	0
Dressing, Weight Watchers Creamy Italian, 1 oz.	29	3	93	1	31	0
Light Roast Beef Deluxe Sandwich	294	10	31	4	12	42
Light Roast Chicken Deluxe Sandwich	263	6	21	2	7	39
Light Roast Turkey Deluxe Sandwich	260	5	17	2	7	30
Salad, Chef	205	10	44	4	18	126
Salad, Garden	109	5	41	3	25	12
Salad, Roast Chicken	184	7	34	3	15	36
Salad, Side	25	tr	na	0	0	0
BURGER KING						
Bacon Double Cheeseburger	507	30	53	14	25	108
Cheeseburger	318	15	42	7	20	50
Chicken BK Broiler Sandwich	267	8	27	2	7	45
Chunky Chicken Salad	142	4	25	1	6	49
Croissan'wich with Bacon	353	23	59	8	20	230
Croissan'wich with Ham	351	22	56	7	18	236
Croissan'wich with Sausage	534	40	67	14	24	258
French Fries, lightly salted, medium	372	20	48	5	12	0
French Toast Sticks, 1 order	538	32	54	8	13	52
Hamburger	272	11	36	4	13	37
Ocean Catch Fish Fillet	479	33	62	8	15	45
Onion Rings, 1 order	339	19	50	5	13	0
Pie, Apple	311	14	41	4	12	4
Salad, Chef	178	9	46	4	20	103
Whopper	614	36	53	12	18	91
Whopper with Cheese	706	44	56	16	20	116
DAIRY QUEEN						
Banana Split	510	11	19	8	14	30
Fish Fillet sandwich	370	16	39	3	7	45

FOOD/PORTION SIZE	CAL.	FAT Total (g)	FAT As % of Cal.	SAT. FAT Total (g)	SAT. FAT As % of Cal.	CHOL. (mg)
Fish Fillet with Cheese sandwich	420	21	45	6	13	60
Grilled Chicken Fillet sandwich	300	8	24	2	6	50
Hamburger, Single	310	13	38	6	17	45
"Heath" "Blizzard," small	560	23	37	11	18	40
Malt, Regular Vanilla	610	14	21	8	12	45
Parfait, Peanut Buster	710	32	41	10	13	30
Shake, Regular Chocolate	540	14	23	8	13	45
Sundae, Regular Chocolate	300	7	21	5	15	20
DOMINO'S						
Pizza, Cheese, 2 slices	376	10	24	6	14	19
Pizza, Deluxe, 2 slices	498	20	36	9	16	40
Pizza, Double Cheese/Pepperoni, 2 slices	545	25	44	13	21	48
Pizza, Ham, 2 slices	417	11	24	6	13	26
Pizza, Pepperoni, 2 slices	460	18	35	8	16	28
Pizza, Sausage/Mushroom, 2 slices	430	16	33	8	17	28
Pizza, Veggie, 2 slices	498	19	34	10	18	36
DUNKIN' DONUTS						
Apple Filled Cinnamon	190	9	43	2	9	0
Boston Kreme	240	11	41	2	8	0
Chocolate Frosted Yeast Ring	200	10	45	2	9	0
Glazed Yeast Ring	200	9	41	2	9	0
Honey Dipped Cruller	260	11	38	2	7	0
Jelly Filled	220	9	37	2	8	0
Plain Cake Ring	262	18	62	4	14	0
Powdered Cake Ring	270	16	53	3	10	0
KENTUCKY FRIED CHICKEN						
Buttermilk Biscuit, 2.3 oz.	235	12	46	3	11	1
Coleslaw, 3.2 oz.	114	6	47	1	8	4
Corn-On-the-Cob, 2.6 oz.	90	2	20	1	10	tr
Extra Tasty Crispy, center breast, 3.9 oz.	344	21	55	5	13	80
Extra Tasty Crispy, drumstick, 2.4 oz.	205	14	61	3	13	72
Extra Tasty Crispy, wing, 2 oz.	231	17	66	4	16	63
French Fries, 2.7 oz.	244	12	44	3	11	2
Hot & Spicy, center breast, 4.3 oz.	382	25	59	6	14	84
Hot & Spicy, drumstick, 2.5 oz.	207	14	61	3	13	75
Hot & Spicy, wing, 2.2 oz.	244	18	66	4	15	65

FOOD/PORTION SIZE	CAL.	FAT		SAT. FAT		CHOL.
		Total (g)	As % of Cal.	Total (g)	As % of Cal.	(mg)
Hot Wings, six wings, 4.8 oz.	471	33	63	8	15	150
Kentucky Nuggets, six, 3.4 oz.	284	18	57	4	13	66
Mashed Potatoes & Gravy, 3.5 oz.	71	2	25	0	0	tr
Sauce, Barbeque, 1 oz.	35	1	26	0	0	tr
Sauce, Sweet 'N Sour, 1 oz.	58	1	16	0	0	tr
Skinfree Crispy, center breast, 4 oz.	296	16	49	3	9	59
Skinfree Crispy, thigh, 3 oz.	256	17	60	4	14	68
LONG JOHN SILVER'S						
Baked Chicken, Light Herb	130	4	28	na	na	65
Baked Fish, Lemon Crumb, 3 pieces	150	1	6	na	na	110
Baked Fish, Lemon Crumb, 2 pieces, Rice, and Small Salad (w/o dressing)	320	4	11	na	na	75
Baked Shrimp, Scampi Sauce	120	5	38	na	na	205
Cole Slaw	140	6	39	na	na	15
Rice Pilaf	210	2	9	na	na	0
Salad, Small (w/o dressing)	8	0	0	0	0	0
McDONALD'S						
Big Mac	500	26	47	9	16	100
Biscuit with Bacon, Egg, and Cheese	440	26	53	8	16	240
Biscuit with Sausage	420	28	60	8	17	44
Biscuit with Sausage and Egg	505	33	59	10	18	260
Cheeseburger	305	13	38	5	15	50
Chicken McNuggets (6 pieces)	270	15	50	<4	12	55
Cone, Low Fat Frozen Yogurt, Vanilla	105	1	9	<1	4	3
Cookies, Chocolaty Chip, 1 box	330	15	41	4	11	4
Cookies, McDonaldland, 1 box	290	9	28	1	3	0
Danish, Apple	390	17	39	4	9	25
Danish, Cinnamon Raisin	440	21	43	5	10	34
Danish, Iced Cheese	390	21	48	6	14	47
Danish, Raspberry	410	16	35	3	7	26
Dressing, Lite Vinaigrette, 1 oz.	24	1	38	<1	8	0
Dressing, Ranch, 1 oz.	110	10	82	2	16	10
Egg McMuffin	280	11	35	4	13	235
Eggs, Scrambled, 2 eggs	140	10	64	3	19	425
Filet-O-Fish sandwich	370	18	44	4	10	50
French Fries, small	220	12	49	<3	10	9
Hamburger	255	9	32	3	11	37
Hashbrowns	130	7	48	1	7	0

FOOD/PORTION SIZE	CAL.	FAT		SAT. FAT		CHOL.
		Total (g)	As % of Cal.	Total (g)	As % of Cal.	(mg)
Hotcakes with 2 pats margarine and 1½ oz. syrup	440	12	25	2	4	8
McLean Deluxe	320	10	28	4	11	60
Milk Shake, Chocolate Low Fat	320	<2	5	<1	2	10
Milk Shake, Strawberry Low Fat	320	<2	4	<1	2	10
Milk Shake, Vanilla Low Fat	290	<2	4	<1	2	10
Pie, Apple	260	15	52	4	14	6
Quarter Pounder	410	20	44	8	18	85
Quarter Pounder with Cheese	510	28	49	11	19	115
Salad, Chef	170	9	48	4	21	111
Salad, Chicken, Chunky	150	4	24	1	6	78
Salad, Garden	50	2	36	<1	11	65
Sauce, Barbecue, 1 serving	50	<1	9	<1	2	0
Sauce, Hot Mustard, 1 serving	70	4	51	<1	6	5
Sauce, Sweet-n-Sour, 1 serving	60	<1	3	0	0	0
Sausage	160	15	84	5	28	43
Sausage McMuffin	345	20	52	7	18	57
Sausage McMuffin with Egg	430	25	52	8	17	270
Sundae, Hot Caramel Low Fat Frozen Yogurt	270	3	10	<2	5	13
Sundae, Hot Fudge Low Fat Frozen Yogurt	240	3	11	2	8	6
Sundae, Strawberry Low Fat Frozen Yogurt	210	1	4	<1	2	5
PIZZA HUT						
Hand-Tossed, Cheese, 2 slices medium (15-inch), 7.9 oz.	518	20	35	14	24	55
Hand-Tossed, Supreme, 2 slices medium (15-inch), 8.5 oz.	540	26	43	14	23	55
Pan, Super Supreme, 2 slices medium (15-inch), 9.2 oz.	563	26	42	12	19	55
Pan, with cheese, 2 slices medium (15-inch), 7.3 oz.	492	18	33	9	16	34
Personal Pan, Pepperoni, whole (5-inch), 9.1 oz.	675	29	39	12	16	53
Personal Pan, Supreme, whole (5-inch), 9.4 oz.	647	28	39	11	15	49
Thin 'n Crispy, Pepperoni, 2 slices medium (15-inch), 5.2 oz.	413	20	44	11	24	46
Thin 'n Crispy, Supreme, 2 slices medium (15-inch), 7.1 oz.	459	22	43	11	22	42

FOOD/PORTION SIZE	CAL.	FAT Total (g)	FAT As % of Cal.	SAT. FAT Total (g)	SAT. FAT As % of Cal.	CHOL. (mg)
SUBWAY						
BMT Salad, small	369	30	73	10	24	66
BMT Sub, Italian Roll, 6-inch	491	28	51	10	18	66
Club Salad, small	225	13	52	3	12	42
Club Sub, Italian Roll, 6-inch	346	11	29	4	10	42
Cold Cut Combo Salad, small	305	26	77	6	18	83
Cold Cut Combo Sub, Italian Roll, 6-inch	427	20	42	6	13	83
Ham & Cheese Salad, small	200	12	54	3	14	36
Ham & Cheese Sub, Italian Roll, 6-inch	322	9	25	3	8	36
Meatball Sub, Italian Roll, 6-inch	459	22	43	8	16	44
Roast Beef Salad, small	222	10	41	4	16	38
Roast Beef Sub, Italian Roll, 6-inch	345	12	31	4	10	38
Seafood & Crab Salad, small	371	30	73	5	12	28
Seafood & Crab Sub, Italian Roll, 6-inch	493	28	51	5	9	28
Steak & Cheese Sub, Italian Roll, 6-inch	383	16	38	6	14	41
Tuna Salad, small	430	38	80	6	13	43
Tuna Sub, Italian Roll, 6-inch	551	36	59	7	11	43
Turkey Breast Salad, small	201	11	49	3	13	33
Turkey Breast Sub, Italian Roll, 6-inch	322	10	28	3	8	33
Veggies & Cheese Sub, Italian Roll, 6-inch	268	9	30	3	10	9
TACO BELL						
Burrito, Bean	447	14	28	4	8	9
Burrito, Beef	493	21	38	8	15	57
Burrito, Chicken	334	12	32	4	11	52
Burrito, Combo	407	16	35	5	11	33
Burrito Supreme	503	22	39	8	14	33
Cinnamon Twists	171	8	42	3	16	0
Meximelt, Beef	266	15	51	8	27	38
Meximelt, Chicken	257	15	53	7	25	48
Nachos	346	18	47	6	16	9
Nachos Bellgrande	649	35	49	12	17	36
Pintos & Cheese	190	9	43	4	19	16
Pizza, Mexican	575	37	58	11	17	52
Salad, Taco	905	61	61	19	19	80
Salad, Taco, w/o shell	484	31	58	14	26	80
Salsa	18	0	0	0	0	0
Sauce, Hot Taco, 1 packet	3	0	0	0	0	0
Sauce, Taco, 1 packet	2	0	0	0	0	0
Taco	183	11	54	5	25	32
Taco Bellgrande	335	23	62	11	30	56

FOOD/PORTION SIZE	CAL.	FAT Total (g)	FAT As % of Cal.	SAT. FAT Total (g)	SAT. FAT As % of Cal.	CHOL. (mg)
Taco, Soft	225	12	48	5	20	32
Taco, Soft, Chicken	213	10	42	4	17	52
Taco, Soft, Steak	218	11	45	5	21	30
WENDY'S						
Big Classic Sandwich, with Kaiser Bun	570	33	52	6	9	90
Chicken Nuggets, Crispy, 6 pieces	280	20	64	5	16	50
Chicken Sandwich	430	19	40	3	6	60
Chili, Regular, 9 oz.	220	7	29	3	12	45
Cookie, Chocolate Chip, 1 cookie	275	13	43	4	13	15
Fish Fillet Sandwich	460	25	49	5	10	55
Fries, small (3⅕ oz.)	240	12	45	3	11	0
Frosty Dairy Dessert, small	400	14	32	5	11	50
Grilled Chicken Sandwich	340	13	34	3	8	60
Hamburger, Kid's Meal, with White Bun	260	9	31	3	10	35
Hamburger, Single, Plain, ¼-lb.	340	15	40	6	16	65
Nuggets Sauce, Barbeque, 1 packet	50	<1	na	tr	na	0
Nuggets Sauce, Honey, 1 packet	45	<1	na	tr	na	0
Nuggets Sauce, Sweet & Sour, 1 packet	45	<1	na	tr	na	0
Nuggets Sauce, Sweet Mustard, 1 packet	50	1	18	<1	na	0
Potato, Hot Stuffed Baked, Bacon & Cheese	520	18	31	5	9	20
Potato, Hot Stuffed Baked, Broccoli & Cheese	400	16	36	3	7	tr
Potato, Hot Stuffed Baked, Cheese	420	15	32	4	9	10
Potato, Hot Stuffed Baked, Chili & Cheese	500	18	32	4	7	25
Potato, Hot Stuffed Baked, Plain	270	<1	na	tr	na	0
Potato, Hot Stuffed Baked, Sour Cream & Chives	500	23	41	9	16	25
Salad, Chef (take-out)	180	9	45	na	na	120
Salad, Garden (take-out)	102	5	44	na	na	0
Salad, Taco	660	37	50	na	na	35
Swiss Deluxe Sandwich, Jr.	360	18	45	3.3	8	40

Fats & Oils

FOOD/PORTION SIZE	CAL.	FAT Total (g)	FAT As % of Cal.	SAT. FAT Total (g)	SAT. FAT As % of Cal.	CHOL. (mg)
Butter, approx. 1 tbsp.	100	11	99	7	63	31
Butter, Land O Lakes, 1 tbsp.	100	11	99	7	63	30

FOOD/PORTION SIZE	CAL.	FAT Total (g)	FAT As % of Cal.	SAT. FAT Total (g)	SAT. FAT As % of Cal.	CHOL. (mg)
Butter, Whipped, Land O Lakes, 1 tbsp.	60	7	100	4	60	20
Butter Buds, ½ teaspoon	4	0	0	0	0	0
Lard, 1 tbsp.	115	13	100	5	39	12
Margarine, Blue Bonnet, 1 tbsp.	100	11	99	2	18	0
Margarine, Extra Light, Promise, 1 tbsp.	50	6	98	<1	na	0
Margarine, imitation, soft, 1 tbsp.	50	5	90	1	18	0
Margarine, Light, Parkay, stick, 1 tbsp.	70	7	90	1	13	0
Margarine, Parkay, 1 tbsp.	100	11	99	2	18	0
Margarine, regular, hard, 1 tbsp. (⅛ stick)	100	11	99	2	18	0
Margarine, regular, hard, approx. 1 tsp.	35	4	100	1	26	0
Margarine, regular, soft, 1 tbsp.	100	11	99	2	18	0
Margarine, Soft, Parkay, 1 tbsp.	100	11	99	2	18	0
Margarine, Soft, Parkay Corn Oil, 1 tbsp.	100	11	99	2	18	0
Margarine, Soft Diet, Parkay Reduced Calorie, 1 tbsp.	50	6	100	1	18	0
Margarine, spread, hard, 1 tbsp. (⅛ stick)	75	9	100	2	24	0
Margarine, spread, hard, approx. 1 tsp.	25	3	100	1	36	0
Margarine, Squeezable, Shedd's Spread Country Crock, 1 tbsp.	80	9	100	1	11	0
Margarine, Squeeze Parkay, 1 tbsp.	90	10	100	2	20	0
Margarine, Stick, Corn, Mazola, 1 tbsp.	100	11	99	2	18	0
Margarine, Stick, Corn Oil, Fleischmann's, 1 tbsp.	100	11	99	2	18	0
Margarine, Stick, Corn Oil, Mazola, 1 tbsp.	100	11	99	2	18	0
Margarine, Stick, Soy Oil, Chiffon, 1 tbsp.	100	11	99	2	18	0
Margarine, Stick, Soy Oil, Weight Watchers Reduced-Calorie, 1 tbsp.	60	7	100	1	15	0
Margarine, Stick, Sunflower Oil, Promise, 1 tbsp.	90	10	100	2	20	0
Margarine, Tub, Soy Oil, Chiffon, 1 tbsp.	90	10	100	1	10	0
Margarine, Tub, Soy Oil, Weight Watchers Reduced-Calorie Light Spread, 1 tbsp.	50	6	100	1	18	0
Margarine, Tub, Sunflower Oil, Promise, 1 tbsp.	90	10	100	2	20	0
Oil, Canola, Crisco Puritan, 1 tbsp.	120	13	98	1	18	0
Oil, Corn, Mazola, 1 tbsp.	120	14	100	2	15	0
Oil, Olive, Bertolli, 1 tbsp.	120	14	100	2	15	0
Oil, Olive, Filippo Berio, 1 tbsp.	120	14	100	2	15	0
Oil, peanut, 1 tbsp.	125	14	100	2	14	0
Oil, Peanut, Hollywood, 1 tbsp.	120	14	100	4	30	0
Oil, Safflower, Hollywood, 1 tbsp.	120	14	100	1	8	0
Oil, Soybean, Crisco, 1 tbsp.	120	13	98	2	15	0
Oil, soybean-cottonseed blend, hydrogenated, 1 tbsp.	125	14	100	3	22	0

FOOD/PORTION SIZE	CAL.	FAT Total (g)	FAT As % of Cal.	SAT. FAT Total (g)	SAT. FAT As % of Cal.	CHOL. (mg)
Oil, sunflower, 1 tbsp.	125	14	100	1	7	0
Oil, Sunflower, Sunlite, 1 tbsp.	120	14	100	1	7	0
Oil, Vegetable, Crisco, 1 tbsp.	120	14	100	1	7	0
Shortening, Vegetable, Crisco, 1 tbsp.	110	12	98	3	25	0
Shortening, Vegetable, Crisco Butter Flavor, 1 tbsp.	110	12	98	3	25	0
Spray, Cooking (Vegetable Oil), Pam, 2½-second spray	14	2	100	tr	na	0
Spray, No-Stick (Vegetable), Mazola, 2½-second spray	6	1	100	tr	na	0
Spread, 50% Fat, Parkay, 1 tbsp.	60	7	100	1	15	0
Spread, Parkay (50% vegetable oil), 1 tbsp.	60	7	100	1	15	0
Spread, Stick, Touch of Butter, Kraft, 1 tbsp.	90	10	90	2	20	0
Spread, Tub, (Vegetable), Shedd's, 1 tbsp.	70	7	90	1	13	0

Fish & Shellfish

FOOD/PORTION SIZE	CAL.	FAT Total (g)	FAT As % of Cal.	SAT. FAT Total (g)	SAT. FAT As % of Cal.	CHOL. (mg)
Catfish, breaded, fried, 3 oz.	194	11	52	na	na	69
Catfish, skinless, baked w/o fat, 3 oz.	120	5	38	1	8	60
Clams, Canned, Liquid and Solids, Doxsee, ½ cup	59	tr	na	0	0	38
Clams, raw, meat only, 3 oz.	65	1	14	<1	4	43
Cod, fillets (frozen), Booth, 4 oz.	90	1	10	na	na	na
Cod, skinless, broiled w/o fat, 3 oz.	90	1	10	0	0	50
Crabmeat, canned, 1 cup	135	3	20	<1	3	135
Fish sticks (frozen), reheated, 4 × ½-in. stick	70	3	39	1	13	26
Flounder, baked, with lemon juice, w/o added fat, 3 oz.	80	1	11	<1	4	59
Haddock, breaded, fried, 3 oz.	175	9	46	2	10	75
Haddock, skinless, baked w/o fat, 3 oz.	90	1	10	0	0	60
Halibut, broiled, with butter, with lemon juice, 3 oz.	140	6	39	3	19	62
Herring, pickled, 3 oz.	190	13	62	4	19	85
Lobster, boiled, 3 oz.	100	1	9	0	0	100
Mackerel, skinless, broiled w/o fat, 3 oz.	190	12	57	3	14	60
Orange roughy, broiled, 3 oz.	130	7	48	0	0	20
Oysters, breaded, fried, 1 oyster	90	5	50	1	10	35
Oysters, raw, meat only, 1 cup	160	4	23	1	6	120

FOOD/PORTION SIZE	CAL.	FAT		SAT. FAT		CHOL.
		Total (g)	As % of Cal.	Total (g)	As % of Cal.	(mg)
Perch, ocean, breaded, fried, 1 fillet	185	11	54	3	15	66
Perch, Ocean, Natural Fillets (frozen), Taste O'Sea, 4 oz.	100	3	27	na	na	na
Pollock, skinless, broiled w/o fat, 3 oz.	100	1	9	0	0	80
Salmon, Pink, Bumble Bee, 3½ oz.	138	6	39	2	13	40
Salmon, Pink (in spring water), Chicken of the Sea, 3½ oz.	105	4	30	na	na	na
Salmon, red, baked, 3 oz.	140	5	32	1	6	60
Salmon, smoked, 3 oz.	150	8	48	3	18	51
Sardines, canned in oil, drained, 3 oz.	175	11	57	2	10	121
Sardines (in olive oil), King Oscar, 3¾ oz.	460	16	31	3	6	na
Scallops, breaded (frozen), reheated, 6 scallops	195	10	46	3	14	70
Scallops, broiled, 3 oz. (5.7 large or 14 small)	150	1	6	0	0	60
Shrimp, boiled, 3 oz.	110	2	16	0	0	160
Shrimp, canned, drained solids, 3 oz.	103	1	9	tr	na	148
Shrimp, French fried, 3 oz. (7 medium)	189	9	43	2	10	137
Snapper, cooked by dry heat, 3 oz.	109	2	17	na	na	40
Sole, baked, with lemon juice, w/o added fat, 3 oz.	90	1	10	tr	na	49
Surimi seafood, crab flavored, chunk style, ½ cup	84	tr	na	tr	na	25
Trout, Rainbow, skinless, broiled w/o fat, 3 oz.	130	4	28	1	7	60
Tuna, Albacore (in water), Bumble Bee, 2 oz.	70	1	13	tr	na	24
Tuna, Chunk Light (in spring water), StarKist, ½ cup	77	1	12	tr	na	26
Tuna, Chunk Light (in vegetable oil), Bumble Bee, 2 oz.	160	12	68	2	11	24
Tuna, Chunk Light (in water), Bumble Bee, 2 oz.	70	1	13	1	13	27

Frozen Appetizers & Entrées

FOOD/PORTION SIZE	CAL.	FAT		SAT. FAT		CHOL.
		Total (g)	As % of Cal.	Total (g)	As % of Cal.	(mg)
APPETIZERS						
Chicken Nuggets, Weight Watchers, approx. 6 oz.	270	12	40	4	13	50
Ravioli, Baked Cheese, Weight Watchers, 9 oz.	290	12	37	5	16	85

FOOD/PORTION SIZE	CAL.	FAT Total (g)	FAT As % of Cal.	SAT. FAT Total (g)	SAT. FAT As % of Cal.	CHOL. (mg)
MEAT ENTRÉES						
Beef Pot Pie, Swanson, 7 oz.	370	19	46	na	na	na
Lasagna with Meat Sauce, Weight Watchers, 11 oz.	330	11	30	5	14	60
Pizza, Cheese Party, Totino's, 5 oz. (½ pizza)	290	10	31	3	9	15
Pizza, Sausage, Pepperoni, & Mushroom, Stouffer's French Bread Deluxe, 1 piece, about 6 oz.	420	19	41	na	na	na
Pizza, Sausage French Bread, Lean Cuisine, 6 oz.	350	11	28	3	8	40
Pizza, Vegetable, Tombstone Light, ⅕ pizza (4⅓ oz.)	200	7	32	na	na	10
Salisbury Steak, Hungry Man, Swanson, 16¼ oz.	630	32	46	na	na	na
Salisbury Steak, Lean Cuisine, 9½ oz.	240	7	26	2	8	45
Salisbury Steak Dinner, Healthy Choice, 11½ oz.	300	7	21	3	9	50
Sirloin Beef with Barbecue Sauce Dinner, Healthy Choice, 11 oz.	300	6	18	3	9	50
Spaghetti, Lean Cuisine, 11½ oz.	270	6	20	2	7	30
Szechwan Beef with Noodles, Lean Cuisine, 8⅝ oz.	259	9	31	3	10	83
MISCELLANEOUS						
Macaroni & Cheese, Lean Cuisine, 9 oz.	290	9	28	4	12	30
Pasta Classic, Healthy Choice, 12½ oz.	310	3	9	tr	na	35
POULTRY ENTRÉES						
Breast of Chicken Marsala, Lean Cuisine, 8⅛ oz.	190	5	24	2	9	65
Chicken, Broccoli & Cheddar Turnovers, Quaker Ovenstuffs, 4¾ oz.	350	16	41	na	na	na
Chicken, Fried, Plump & Juicy, Swanson, 3¼ oz.	270	16	53	na	na	na
Chicken a la King, Weight Watchers, 9 oz.	220	8	33	2	8	55
Chicken Burritos, Weight Watchers, 7⅗ oz.	310	13	38	4	12	60
Chicken Cacciatore, Lean Cuisine, 10⅞ oz.	280	10	32	2	6	45
Chicken Dijon Dinner, Healthy Choice, 11 oz.	260	3	10	1	3	45
Chicken Fettucini, Weight Watchers, 8¼ oz.	280	9	29	3	10	40
Chicken Parmigiana Dinner, Healthy Choice, 11½ oz.	270	3	10	2	7	50

FOOD/PORTION SIZE	CAL.	FAT Total (g)	FAT As % of Cal.	SAT. FAT Total (g)	SAT. FAT As % of Cal.	CHOL. (mg)
Mesquite Chicken Dinner, Healthy Choice, 10½ oz.	340	1	3	tr	na	45
Pot Pie, Chicken, Swanson, 7 oz.	390	23	53	na	na	na
SEAFOOD ENTRÉES						
Filet of Fish Divan, Lean Cuisine, 12⅜ oz.	270	9	30	2	7	90
Fish Dijon, Light Entrée, Mrs. Paul's, 8¾ oz.	200	5	23	na	na	60
Fish Fillet Au Gratin, Booth, 9½ oz.	280	8	26	na	na	72
Fish Fillet Florentine, Booth, 9½ oz.	260	8	28	na	na	82
Fish Florentine, Light Entrée, Mrs. Paul's, 8 oz.	220	8	33	na	na	95
Fish Mornay, Light Entrée, Mrs. Paul's, 9 oz.	230	10	39	na	na	80
Seafood Linguini, Weight Watchers, 9 oz.	210	7	30	1	4	5
Shrimp Primavera with Fettuccine, Booth, 10 oz.	200	3	14	na	na	0
Shrimp with Lobster Sauce, Fresh & Lite, La Choy, 10 oz.	210	7	30	na	na	na
Tuna Lasagna, Lean Cuisine, 9¾ oz.	280	10	32	4	13	25

Frozen Desserts

FOOD/PORTION SIZE	CAL.	FAT Total (g)	FAT As % of Cal.	SAT. FAT Total (g)	SAT. FAT As % of Cal.	CHOL. (mg)
DAIRY						
Frozen Dairy Dessert, Strawberry, Healthy Choice, ½ cup	110	1	8	1	8	5
Frozen Dessert, Nonfat, Chocolate Flavor, Sealtest Free, ½ cup	110	0	0	na	na	0
Frozen Yogurt, Peach, Borden, ½ cup	100	2	18	na	na	na
Frozen Yogurt, Peach, Sealtest, ½ cup	100	0	0	na	na	0
Ice Cream, Butter Pecan, Breyers, ½ cup	150	8	48	7	42	na
Ice Cream, Chocolate, Breyers, ½ cup	160	8	45	5	28	na
Ice Cream, Chocolate, Sealtest, ½ cup	140	7	45	na	na	na
Ice Cream, Peach, Natural, Breyers, ½ cup	140	12	77	4	26	na
Ice Cream, Strawberry, Natural, Breyers, ½ cup	130	6	42	4	28	na
Ice Cream, Vanilla, Natural, Breyers, ½ cup	180	12	60	5	25	na
Ice Cream, Vanilla, Sealtest, ½ cup	140	7	45	5	32	na

FOOD/PORTION SIZE	CAL.	FAT Total (g)	FAT As % of Cal.	SAT. FAT Total (g)	SAT. FAT As % of Cal.	CHOL. (mg)
Ice Cream, Vanilla/Chocolate/ Strawberry, Sealtest, ½ cup	140	6	39	na	na	na
Ice Milk, Chocolate, Weight Watchers, ½ cup	110	3	25	1	8	10
Ice Milk, Neapolitan, Weight Watchers, ½ cup	110	3	25	1	8	10
Ice milk, vanilla, soft serve, ½ cup	113	3	20	2	12	7
Ice Milk, Vanilla, Weight Watchers, ½ cup	100	3	27	1	9	10
Sherbet, ½ cup	135	2	13	1	7	7
Sherbet, Orange, Borden, ½ cup	120	1	8	na	na	na
Sherbet, Raspberry Real Fruit, Dean Foods, ½ cup	110	1	7	na	na	na
SPECIALTY BARS						
Fruit Bars, all flavors, Jell-O, 1 bar	45	0	0	0	0	0
Fruit n' Juice Bars, Pineapple, Dole, 1 bar	70	1	13	na	na	na
Gelatin Pops, all flavors, Jell-O, 1 bar	35	0	0	0	0	0
Popsicle, 3-fl.-oz. size, 1 popsicle	70	0	0	0	0	0
Pudding Pops, Chocolate, Jell-O, 1 bar	80	2	23	2	23	0
Pudding Pops, Chocolate- Caramel Swirl, Jell-O, 1 bar	80	2	23	2	23	0
Pudding Pops, Chocolate-Covered Chocolate, Jell-O, 1 bar	130	7	48	5	35	0
Pudding Pops, Chocolate-Covered Vanilla, Jell-O, 1 bar	130	7	48	5	35	0
Pudding Pops, Vanilla, Jell-O, 1 bar	70	2	26	2	26	0
Pudding Pops, Vanilla with Chocolate Chips, Jell-O, 1 bar	80	3	34	2	23	0
Pudding Snacks, Chocolate, Jell-O, 4 oz.	160	5	28	2	11	0
Pudding Snacks, Chocolate, Jello-O Free, 4 oz.	100	0	0	0	0	0
Vanilla Ice Cream, Dark Chocolate Coating, Eskimo Pie, 1 bar (3 fl. oz.)	180	12	60	na	na	na

Fruit

FOOD/PORTION SIZE	CAL.	FAT Total (g)	FAT As % of Cal.	SAT. FAT Total (g)	SAT. FAT As % of Cal.	CHOL. (mg)
Apples, dried, sulfured, 10 rings	155	tr	na	tr	na	0
Apples, raw, unpeeled, 3¼-in. diameter, 1 apple	125	1	7	<1	<1	0
Apple Sauce, Natural, Mott's, 1 cup	100	0	0	0	0	0

FOOD/PORTION SIZE	CAL.	FAT Total (g)	FAT As % of Cal.	SAT. FAT Total (g)	SAT. FAT As % of Cal.	CHOL. (mg)
Apple Sauce, Canned, Regular or Chunky, Mott's, 1 cup	114	0	0	0	0	0
Applesauce, canned, sweetened, 1 cup	195	tr	na	<1	<1	0
Applesauce, canned, unsweetened, 1 cup	105	tr	na	tr	na	0
Apricots, canned, heavy syrup pack, 3 halves	70	tr	na	tr	na	0
Apricots, canned, juice pack, 3 halves	40	tr	na	tr	na	0
Apricots, dried, cooked, unsweetened, 1 cup	210	tr	na	tr	na	0
Apricots, dried, uncooked, 1 cup	310	1	3	tr	na	0
Apricots, raw, 3 apricots	50	tr	na	tr	na	0
Avocados, raw, whole, California, 1 avocado	305	28	83	5	15	0
Avocados, raw, whole, Florida, 1 avocado	340	23	61	5	13	0
Bananas, raw, 1 banana	105	1	9	<1	2	0
Blackberries, raw, 1 cup	75	1	12	<1	2	0
Blueberries, frozen, sweetened, 10 oz.	230	tr	na	tr	na	0
Blueberries, raw, 1 cup	80	1	11	tr	<1	0
Cantaloupe, raw, ½ melon	95	1	9	<1	<1	0
Cherries, sour, red, pitted, canned water pack, 1 cup	90	tr	<1	<1	1	0
Cherries, sweet, raw, 10 cherries	50	1	18	<1	2	0
Cranberry sauce, sweetened, canned, strained, 1 cup	420	tr	na	tr	na	0
Dates, chopped, ½ cup	245	<1	2	<1	<1	0
Dates, whole, w/o pits, 10 dates	230	tr	na	<1	<1	0
Figs, dried, 10 figs	475	2	4	<1	<1	0
Fruit, Mixed, in Syrup, Birds Eye Quick Thaw Pouch, 5 oz.	120	0	0	na	na	0
Fruit, Mixed, Libby's Chunky, Lite, ½ cup	50	0	0	na	na	na
Fruit Cocktail, Del Monte, ½ cup	80	0	0	na	na	na
Fruit Cocktail, Del Monte Lite, ½ cup	50	0	0	na	na	na
Fruit Cocktail, Libby's Lite, ½ cup	50	0	0	na	na	na
Grapefruit, canned, with syrup, 1 cup	150	tr	na	tr	na	0
Grapefruit, raw, ½ grapefruit	40	tr	na	tr	na	0
Grapes, Thompson seedless, 10 grapes	35	tr	na	<1	3	0
Grapes, Tokay/Emperor, seeded, 10 grapes	40	tr	na	<1	2	0
Honeydew melon, raw, ¹⁄₁₀ melon	45	tr	na	tr	na	0
Kiwifruit, raw, w/o skin, 1 kiwifruit	45	tr	na	tr	na	0
Lemons, raw, 1 lemon	15	tr	na	tr	na	0
Mandarin Orange Segments, Dole, ½ cup	70	<1	<1	0	0	0
Mangos, raw, 1 mango	135	1	7	<1	<1	0
Nectarines, raw, 1 nectarine	65	1	14	<1	1	0
Olives, canned, green, 4 medium or 3 extra large	15	2	100	<1	12	0

FOOD/PORTION SIZE	CAL.	FAT Total (g)	FAT As % of Cal.	SAT. FAT Total (g)	SAT. FAT As % of Cal.	CHOL. (mg)
Olives, ripe, mission, pitted, 3 small or 2 large	15	2	100	<1	18	0
Oranges, raw, whole, w/o peel and seeds, 1 orange	60	tr	na	tr	na	0
Papayas, raw, ½-in. cubes, 1 cup	65	tr	na	<1	1	0
Peaches, canned, heavy syrup, 1 cup	190	tr	na	tr	na	0
Peaches, canned, juice pack, 1 cup	110	tr	na	tr	na	0
Peaches, dried, uncooked, 1 cup	380	1	2	<1	<1	0
Peaches, frozen, sliced, sweetened, 1 cup	235	tr	na	tr	na	0
Peaches, raw, whole, 2½-in. diameter, 1 peach	35	tr	na	tr	na	0
Peaches, Sliced, Lite, Libby's, 1 cup	100	0	0	na	na	na
Pears, Bartlett, raw with skin, 1 pear	100	1	9	tr	na	0
Pears, Bosc, raw with skin, 1 pear	85	1	11	tr	na	0
Pears, canned, heavy syrup, 1 cup	190	tr	na	tr	na	0
Pears, canned, juice pack, 1 cup	125	tr	na	tr	na	0
Pears, D'Anjou, raw with skin, 1 pear	120	1	8	tr	na	0
Pears, Halves, Lite, Libby's, ½ cup	60	0	0	na	na	na
Pineapple, Canned, Heavy Syrup Dole, (all cuts), ½ cup	91	0	0	0	0	0
Pineapple, canned, heavy syrup, sliced, 1 slice	45	tr	na	tr	na	0
Pineapple, Canned, Juice Pack Dole, (all cuts), ½ cup	70	0	0	0	0	0
Pineapple, canned, juice pack slices, 1 slice	35	tr	na	tr	na	0
Pineapple, raw, diced, ½ cup	38	tr	12	tr	na	0
Plums, canned, purple, juice pack, 3 plums	55	tr	na	tr	na	0
Plums, raw, 1½-in. diameter, 1 plum	15	Total	na	Total	na	0
Plums, raw, 2⅛-in. diameter, 1 plum	35	tr	na	tr	na	0
Prunes, dried, cooked, unsweetened, 1 cup	225	tr	na	tr	na	0
Prunes, dried, uncooked, 4 extra large or 5 large	115	tr	na	tr	na	0
Raisins, seedless, ½-oz. packet, 1 packet	40	tr	na	tr	na	0
Raisins, seedless, 1 cup	435	1	12	<1	<1	0
Raspberries, frozen, sweetened, 1 cup	255	tr	na	tr	na	0
Raspberries, in Lite Syrup, Birds Eye Quick Thaw Pouch, 5 oz.	100	1	9	na	na	0
Raspberries, raw, 1 cup	60	1	15	tr	na	0
Rhubarb, cooked, added sugar, 1 cup	280	tr	na	tr	na	0
Strawberries, frozen, sweetened, sliced, 1 cup	245	tr	<1	tr	<1	0
Strawberries, Halved, in Lite Syrup, Birds Eye Quick Thaw Pouch, 5 oz.	90	0	0	0	0	0

FOOD/PORTION SIZE	CAL.	FAT Total (g)	FAT As % of Cal.	SAT. FAT Total (g)	SAT. FAT As % of Cal.	CHOL. (mg)
Strawberries, Halved, in Syrup, Birds Eye Quick Thaw Pouch, 5 oz.	120	tr	<1	tr	<1	0
Strawberries, raw, whole, 1 cup	45	1	20	tr	na	0
Tangerines, raw, 2⅜-in. diameter, 1 tangerine	35	tr	na	tr	na	0
Watermelon, raw, 4×8-in. wedge, 1 piece	155	2	12	<1	2	0
Watermelon, raw, diced, 1 cup	50	1	18	<1	2	0

Gelatin, Pudding & Pie Filling

FOOD/PORTION SIZE	CAL.	FAT Total (g)	FAT As % of Cal.	SAT. FAT Total (g)	SAT. FAT As % of Cal.	CHOL. (mg)
All flavors, Gelatin, Jell-O, ½ cup (average)	80	0	0	0	0	0
All flavors, Gelatin, Low Calorie, D-Zerta, ½ cup (average)	8	0	0	0	0	0
All flavors, Gelatin, Sugar Free, Jell-O, ½ cup (average)	8	0	0	0	0	0
Banana, Pudding & Pie Filling, Instant, Sugar Free Jell-O, with 2% milk, ½ cup	80	2	23	1	11	10
Banana Cream, Pudding & Pie Filling, Instant, Jell-O, with whole milk, ½ cup	160	4	23	3	17	15
Banana Cream, Pudding & Pie Filling, Jell-O, with whole milk, ⅙ pie (excluding crust)	100	3	27	2	18	10
Butter Pecan, Pudding & Pie Filling, Instant, Jell-O, with whole milk, ½ cup	170	5	26	3	16	15
Butterscotch, Pudding, Reduced Calorie, D-Zerta, with skim milk, ½ cup	70	0	0	0	0	0
Butterscotch, Pudding & Pie Filling, Instant, Jell-O, with whole milk, ½ cup	160	4	23	3	17	15
Butterscotch, Pudding & Pie Filling, Instant, Sugar Free, Jell-O, with 2% milk, ½ cup	90	2	20	1	10	10
Butterscotch, Pudding & Pie Filling, Jell-O, with whole milk, ½ cup	170	4	21	3	16	15
Chocolate, pudding, canned, 5-oz. can	205	11	48	9	40	1
Chocolate, Pudding, Reduced Calorie, D-Zerta, with skim milk, ½ cup	70	tr	na	tr	na	2
Chocolate, Pudding & Pie Filling, Instant, Jell-O, with whole milk, ½ cup	180	4	20	3	15	15
Chocolate, Pudding & Pie Filling, Instant, Sugar Free, Jell-O, with 2% milk, ½ cup	90	3	30	2	20	10
Chocolate, Pudding & Pie Filling, Jell-O, with whole milk, ½ cup	160	4	23	2	11	15

FOOD/PORTION SIZE	CAL.	FAT Total (g)	FAT As % of Cal.	SAT. FAT Total (g)	SAT. FAT As % of Cal.	CHOL. (mg)
Chocolate, Pudding & Pie Filling, Sugar Free, Jell-O, with 2% milk, ½ cup	90	3	30	2	20	10
Chocolate, Rich & Luscious Mousse, Jell-O, with whole milk, ½ cup	150	6	36	4	24	9
Chocolate Fudge, Pudding & Pie Filling, Instant, Jell-O, with whole milk, ½ cup	180	5	25	3	15	15
Chocolate Fudge, Pudding & Pie Filling, Instant, Sugar Free, Jell-O, with 2% milk, ½ cup	100	3	27	2	18	10
Chocolate Fudge, Pudding & Pie Filling, Jell-O, with whole milk, ½ cup	160	4	23	2	11	15
Chocolate Fudge, Rich & Luscious Mousse, Jell-O, with whole milk, ½ cup	140	6	39	4	26	10
Coconut Cream, Pudding & Pie Filling, Instant Jell-O, with whole milk, ½ cup	180	6	30	4	20	15
Coconut Cream, Pudding & Pie Filling, Jell-O, with whole milk, ⅙ pie (excluding crust)	110	4	33	2	16	10
Custard, baked, 1 cup	305	13	38	7	21	278
Custard, Golden Egg, Mix, Jell-O Americana, with whole milk, ½ cup	160	5	28	3	17	80
Lemon, Pudding & Pie Filling, Instant, Jell-O, with whole milk, ½ cup	170	4	21	3	16	15
Lemon, Pudding & Pie Filling, Jell-O, with whole milk, ⅙ pie (excluding crust)	170	2	11	na	na	90
Milk Chocolate, Pudding & Pie Filling, Instant, Jell-O, with whole milk, ½ cup	180	5	25	3	15	17
Milk Chocolate, Pudding & Pie Filling, Jell-O, with whole milk, ½ cup	160	4	23	2	11	17
Pineapple Cream, Pudding & Pie Filling, Instant, Jell-O, with whole milk, ½ cup	160	4	23	2	11	17
Pistachio, Pudding & Pie Filling, Instant, Jell-O, with whole milk, ½ cup	170	5	26	3	16	17
Pistachio, Pudding & Pie Filling, Instant, Sugar Free, Jell-O, with 2% milk, ½ cup	100	3	27	2	3	10
Rice Pudding, Jell-O Americana, with whole milk, ½ cup	170	4	21	2	11	17
Tapioca, pudding, prepared with whole milk, ½ cup	145	4	25	2	12	17
Vanilla, French, Pudding & Pie Filling, Instant, Jell-O, with whole milk, ½ cup	160	4	23	2	11	17
Vanilla, French, Pudding & Pie Filling, Jell-O, with whole milk, ½ cup	170	4	21	3	16	17

FOOD/PORTION SIZE	CAL.	FAT Total (g)	FAT As % of Cal.	SAT. FAT Total (g)	SAT. FAT As % of Cal.	CHOL. (mg)
Vanilla, pudding, canned, 5-oz. can	220	10	41	10	41	1
Vanilla, Pudding, Reduced Calorie, D-Zerta, with skim milk, ½ cup	70	0	0	0	0	0
Vanilla, pudding, regular (cooked) dry mix, made with whole milk, ½ cup	145	4	25	2	12	15
Vanilla, Pudding & Pie Filling, Instant, Jell-O, with whole milk, ½ cup	170	4	21	3	16	17
Vanilla, Pudding & Pie Filling, Instant, Sugar Free, Jell-O, with 2% milk, ½ cup	90	2	20	1	10	9
Vanilla, Pudding & Pie Filling, Jell-O, with whole milk, ½ cup	160	4	23	3	17	17
Vanilla, Pudding & Pie Filling, Sugar Free, Jell-O, with 2% milk, ½ cup	80	2	23	0	0	10
Vanilla, Tapioca, Pudding, Jell-O Americana, with whole milk, ½ cup	160	4	23	3	17	17

Gravies & Sauces

FOOD/PORTION SIZE	CAL.	FAT Total (g)	FAT As % of Cal.	SAT. FAT Total (g)	SAT. FAT As % of Cal.	CHOL. (mg)
GRAVIES						
Beef, canned, 1 cup	125	5	36	3	22	7
Beef, Franco-American, 2 oz.	35	2	51	na	na	na
Brown, from dry mix, 1 cup	80	2	23	1	11	2
Brown, with onions, Heinz, HomeStyle, 2 oz.	25	1	36	na	na	na
Chicken, canned, 1 cup	190	14	66	4	19	5
Chicken, Franco-American, 2 oz.	45	4	80	na	na	na
Chicken, from dry mix, 1 cup	85	2	21	<1	5	tr
Turkey, Canned, Heinz HomeStyle, 2 oz.	25	1	36	0	0	0
SAUCES						
Barbecue sauce, *see* BAKING PRODUCTS & CONDIMENTS						
Cheese, from dry mix, prepared with milk, 2 tbsp.	38	2	47	1	24	7
Hollandaise, prepared with water, 2 tbsp.	30	3	90	2	60	7
Picante Sauce, Old El Paso, 2 tbsp.	12	0	0	0	0	0
Picante Sauce, Pace, 2 tbsp.	9	0	0	0	0	0

FOOD/PORTION SIZE	CAL.	FAT Total (g)	FAT As % of Cal.	SAT. FAT Total (g)	SAT. FAT As % of Cal.	CHOL. (mg)
Soy sauce, *see* BAKING PRODUCTS & CONDIMENTS						
Spaghetti, Chunky Garden Style, with Mushrooms and Green Peppers, Ragu, 4 oz.	70	3	39	na	na	0
Spaghetti, Extra Chunky, Garden Tomato with Mushrooms, Prego, 4 oz.	100	6	54	tr	na	52
Spaghetti, Extra Chunky, Mushroom and Tomato, Prego, 4 oz.	110	5	41	na	na	na
Spaghetti, Extra Chunky, Tomato and Onion, Prego, 4 oz.	140	6	39	na	na	na
Spaghetti, Plain, Prego, 4 oz.	140	5	32	1	6	0
Spaghetti, Ragu, 4 oz.	80	3	34	tr	na	0
Spaghetti, Thick & Hearty, Ragu, 4 oz.	140	5	32	tr	na	0
Spaghetti, with Meat, Homestyle, Ragu, 4 oz.	70	2	26	tr	na	2
Spaghetti, with Meat, Prego, 4 oz.	150	6	36	2	12	4
Spaghetti, with Meat, Ragu, 4 oz.	80	3	34	tr	na	2
Spaghetti, with Mushrooms, Prego, 4 oz.	140	5	32	1	6	0
Spaghetti, with Mushrooms, Ragu, 4 oz.	80	4	45	tr	na	0
Spaghetti, with Mushrooms, Thick & Hearty, Ragu, 4 oz.	140	5	32	tr	na	0
White, prepared with milk, 2 tbsp.	30	2	49	1	23	5

Legumes & Nuts

FOOD/PORTION SIZE	CAL.	FAT Total (g)	FAT As % of Cal.	SAT. FAT Total (g)	SAT. FAT As % of Cal.	CHOL. (mg)
BEANS						
Black, dry, cooked, drained, 1 cup	225	1	4	tr	<1	0
Chickpeas, dry, cooked, drained, 1 cup	270	4	13	tr	<1	0
Great Northern, dry, cooked, drained, 1 cup	210	1	4	tr	<1	0
Lentils, dry, cooked, 1 cup	215	1	4	tr	<1	0
Lima, dry, cooked, drained, 1 cup	216	1	4	tr	<1	0
Lima, immature seeds, frozen, cooked, drained: thick-seeded types (Fordhooks), 1 cup	170	1	5	tr	<1	0
Lima, immature seeds, frozen, cooked, drained: thin-seeded types (baby limas), 1 cup	188	1	5	tr	<1	0
Peas (Navy), dry, cooked, drained, 1 cup	258	1	3	tr	<1	0
Pinto, dry, cooked, drained, 1 cup	234	1	4	tr	<1	0

FOOD/PORTION SIZE	CAL.	FAT		SAT. FAT		CHOL.
		Total (g)	As % of Cal.	Total (g)	As % of Cal.	(mg)
Pork and Beans, Van Camp's, 1 cup	227	1	5	na	na	0
Red kidney, canned, 1 cup	216	1	4	tr	<1	0
Refried, canned, 1 cup	268	3	10	1	3	15
Refried, Vegetarian, Old El Paso, 1 cup	140	2	13	na	na	0
Snap, canned, drained, solids (cut), 1 cup	25	tr	na	tr	na	0
Snap, cooked, drained, from frozen (cut), 1 cup	35	tr	na	tr	na	0
Snap, cooked, drained, from raw (cut and French style), 1 cup	45	tr	na	<1	2	0
Sprouts, (mung), raw, 1 cup	30	tr	na	tr	na	0
Tahini, 1 tbsp.	95	7	66	1	9	0
Vegetarian Beans in Tomato Sauce, Heinz, 1 cup	250	2	7	na	na	0
White, with sliced frankfurters, canned, 1 cup	365	18	44	7	17	30
NUTS						
Almonds, shelled, whole, 1 oz.	165	15	82	1	5	0
Almonds, shelled, sliced, 1 oz.	170	13	69	1	5	0
Almonds, Sliced, Blue Diamond, 1 oz.	150	13	78	1	6	0
Almonds, Whole, Blue Diamond, 1 oz.	150	13	78	1	6	0
Brazil, shelled, whole, 1 oz.	185	19	92	4	19	0
Cashews, salted, dry roasted, 1 cup	869	65	67	14	14	0
Cashews, salted, roasted in oil, 1 cup	869	67	69	14	14	0
Chestnuts, European, roasted, shelled, 1 cup	350	3	8	tr	<1	0
Coconut, raw, piece, 45 g (1.6 oz.)	160	15	84	13	73	0
Filberts (hazelnuts), chopped, 1 cup	955	84	79	7	7	0
Macadamia, salted, roasted in oil, 1 cup	1088	103	85	16	13	0
Mixed, with peanuts, salted, dry roasted, 1 oz.	170	13	69	2	11	0
Mixed, with peanuts, salted, roasted in oil, 1 oz.	175	14	72	2	10	0
Peanut Butter, 2 tbsp.	190	16	76	2	9	0
Peanut Butter, Creamy, Skippy, 2 tbsp.	190	17	81	3	14	0
Peanut Butter, Extra Crunchy, Jif, 2 tbsp.	180	16	80	na	na	0
Peanuts, Dry Roasted, Planter's, 1 oz.	160	14	79	2	11	0
Peanuts, salted, roasted in oil, 1 cup	869	64	66	9	9	0
Pecans, halves, 1 cup	760	68	81	6	7	0
Pistachios, dried, shelled, 1 oz.	165	13	71	2	11	0
Walnuts, black, chopped, 1 cup	760	62	73	4	5	0

FOOD/PORTION SIZE	CAL.	FAT		SAT. FAT		CHOL.
		Total (g)	As % of Cal.	Total (g)	As % of Cal.	(mg)
Walnuts, English or Persian, pieces/chips, 1 cup	770	66	77	6	7	0
PEAS						
Black-eyed, dry, cooked, 1 cup	190	1	5	<1	1	0
Split, dry, cooked, 1 cup	230	1	4	<1	<1	0
SEEDS						
Pumpkin/squash kernels, dry, hulled, 1 oz.	155	13	75	2	12	0
Sesame, dry, hulled, 1 tbsp.	45	4	80	<1	12	0
Sunflower, dry, hulled, 1 oz.	160	14	79	<2	8	0
SOY PRODUCTS						
Miso, 1 cup	568	14	22	2	3	0
Soybeans, dry, cooked, drained, 1 cup	298	13	39	2	6	0
Tofu, firm, 2 oz.	82	5	55	tr	na	0

Meat

FOOD/PORTION SIZE	CAL.	FAT		SAT. FAT		CHOL.
		Total (g)	As % of Cal.	Total (g)	As % of Cal.	(mg)
BEEF						
Chipped, dried, 2½ oz.	118	3	23	1	8	50
Chuck blade, lean only, braised/simmered/ pot roasted, approx. 2¼ oz.	168	9	48	4	21	66
Corned, canned, 3 oz.	213	16	68	5	21	83
Corned, lean, Carl Buddig, 1 oz.	40	2	45	na	na	na
Ground, Extra Lean, Healthy Choice, 3 oz.	98	3	28	2	7	55
Ground, patty, lean, broiled, 3 oz.	230	16	63	6	27	74
Ground, patty, regular, broiled, 3 oz.	245	18	66	7	26	76
Heart, lean, braised, 3 oz.	150	5	30	2	12	164
Liver, fried, 3 oz.	185	7	34	3	15	410
Roast, eye of round, lean only, oven cooked, approx. 2½ oz.	135	5	33	2	13	52
Roast, rib, lean only, oven cooked, approx. 2¼ oz.	150	9	54	4	24	49
Roast, tip, lean only, oven cooked, approx. 2½ oz.	135	5	33	2	13	52

FOOD/PORTION SIZE	CAL.	FAT Total (g)	FAT As % of Cal.	SAT. FAT Total (g)	SAT. FAT As % of Cal.	CHOL. (mg)
Round, bottom, lean only, braised/simmered/ pot roasted, 2⅖ oz.	175	8	41	3	15	75
Steak, cubed, lean only, broiled, 2½ oz.	170	9	48	4	21	66
Steak, sirloin, lean only, broiled, 2½ oz.	150	6	36	3	18	64
FRANKS & SAUSAGES						
Frankfurter, Chicken, Health Valley, 1 frank	145	12	74	4	25	27
Franks, Beef, Oscar Mayer, 1 frank	144	14	88	6	38	28
Franks, Eckrich, 1 frank	190	17	81	na	na	na
Franks, Healthy Choice, 1 frank	50	1	18	<1	na	15
Franks, Jumbo Beef, Eckrich, 1 frank	190	17	81	na	na	na
Franks, Lite, Eckrich, 1 frank	120	10	75	na	na	25
Sausage, beef and pork, frankfurters, cooked, 1 frank	183	16	79	6	30	29
Sausage, pork, brown/serve, browned, 1 link	50	5	90	2	36	9
Sausage, pork, links, 1 link (1 oz.)	50	4	72	2	36	11
Sausage, Pork, Regular, Jimmy Dean, 1 patty (1⅕ oz.)	140	13	84	na	na	na
Turkey Breakfast Sausage, Louis Rich, 1 oz.	54	4	67	2	33	22
Turkey Smoked Sausage, Louis Rich, 1 oz.	43	2	50	.6	13	18
Wieners, Oscar Mayer, 1 link	144	13	81	5	31	27
GAME						
Buffalo, roasted, 3 oz.	111	2	16	<1	na	52
Venison, roasted, 3 oz.	134	3	20	1	7	95
LAMB						
Chops, shoulder, lean only, braised, approx. 1¾ oz.	135	7	47	3	20	44
Leg, lean only, roasted, approx. 2⅔ oz.	140	6	39	3	19	65
Loin, chop, lean only, broiled, approx. 2⅓ oz.	182	10	49	4	20	60
Rib, lean only, roasted, 2 oz.	130	7	48	4	28	50
LUNCHEON MEATS						
Bologna, Beef, Oscar Mayer, 28 g (1 oz.)	90	8	80	4	40	20
Bologna, Lite, Oscar Mayer, 28 g (1 oz.)	70	6	77	na	na	15
Bologna, Oscar Mayer, 15 g (½ oz.)	50	4	72	2	36	9
Braunschweiger sausage, 2 oz.	205	18	79	7	31	88
Chicken, roll, light, 2 oz.	90	4	40	1	10	28

FOOD/PORTION SIZE	CAL.	FAT Total (g)	FAT As % of Cal.	SAT. FAT Total (g)	SAT. FAT As % of Cal.	CHOL. (mg)
Ham, chopped, 8-slice (6-oz.) pack, 2 slices	98	7	64	3	28	23
Ham, Cooked, Eckrich Lite, 1 oz.	25	1	36	na	na	15
Ham, extra lean, cooked, 2 slices (2 oz.)	75	3	36	1	12	27
Ham, regular, cooked, 2 slices (2 oz.)	105	6	51	2	17	32
Pork, canned lunch meat, spiced/unspiced, 2 slices, 42 g (1½ oz.)	140	13	84	5	32	26
Salami sausage, cooked, 2 oz.	141	11	70	5	32	37
Salami sausage, dry, 12-slice (4-oz.) pack, 2 slices	84	6	64	2	21	16
Sandwich spread, pork/beef, 1 tbsp.	35	3	77	<1	23	6
Turkey, breast meat, loaf, 8-slice (6-oz.) pack, 2 slices	45	1	20	<1	4	17
Turkey, Oscar Mayer, ¾ oz.	22	1	41	tr	na	8
Turkey, Salami, 1 slice, 28 grams	54	4	67	1	17	20
Turkey, thigh meat, ham cured, 2 oz.	75	3	36	1	12	32
Turkey Bologna, Louis Rich Turkey Cold Cuts, 28 g (1 oz.)	61	5	74	2	30	22
Turkey Breast, Healthy Choice, 2 oz.	60	1	15	na	na	25
Turkey Breast, Light, Eckrich, 1 oz.	30	1	30	0	0	10
Turkey Breast, Oven Roasted, Deli Thin Louis Rich, 22 grams	24	1	38	tr	tr	8
Turkey Breast, Oven Roasted, Eckrich Lite, 1 oz.	30	1	31	na	na	10
Turkey Ham, Louis Rich Turkey Cold Cuts, 21 g (¾ oz.)	25	1	36	0	0	14
Turkey Ham, Smoked, Louis Rich Turkey Cold Cuts, 28 g (1 oz.)	34	1	26	1	26	19
Turkey Pastrami, Louis Rich Turkey Cold Cuts, 23 g (⅘ oz.)	24	1	38	0	0	14
Vienna sausage, 7 per 4-oz. can, 1 sausage, 16 g (approx. ½ oz.)	45	4	80	2	40	8

PORK

FOOD/PORTION SIZE	CAL.	FAT Total (g)	FAT As % of Cal.	SAT. FAT Total (g)	SAT. FAT As % of Cal.	CHOL. (mg)
Bacon, Canadian, cured, cooked, 2 slices	86	4	42	1	10	27
Bacon, Low Salt, Armour, 2 slices	76	8	95	2	24	12
Bacon, regular, cured, cooked, 3 medium slices	108	9	75	3	25	16
Chop, loin, fresh, lean only, broiled, 2½ oz.	163	7	39	3	17	69
Chop, loin, fresh, lean only, pan fried, approx. 2½ oz.	181	10	50	4	20	73
Ham, Baked, Oscar Mayer, 21 g (¾ oz.)	21	1	43	tr	na	11
Ham, Boiled, Oscar Mayer, 21 g (¾ oz.)	26	1	35	tr	na	12
Ham, Breakfast Slice, Oscar Mayer, 1 slice	50	2	36	tr	na	20

FOOD/PORTION SIZE	CAL.	FAT Total (g)	FAT As % of Cal.	SAT. FAT Total (g)	SAT. FAT As % of Cal.	CHOL. (mg)
Ham, canned, roasted, 3 oz.	140	7	45	2	13	35
Ham, leg, fresh, lean only, roasted, 2½ oz.	156	8	46	3	17	67
Ham, light cure, lean only, roasted, approx. 2½ oz.	107	4	34	1	8	38
Ham, Lower Salt, Light, Eckrich, 1 oz.	25	1	36	0	0	15
Ham, Low Salt, Armour, 1 oz.	40	3	68	1	23	15
Rib, fresh, lean only, roasted, 2½ oz.	173	8	42	3	16	56
Shoulder cut, fresh, lean only, braised, 2⅖ oz.	169	8	43	3	16	78
Tenderloin, roasted, lean, 3 oz.	139	4	26	1	6	67
Turkey Bacon, Louis Rich, 1 slice	32	2	56	tr	na	10
VEAL						
Cubed, lean only, braised, 3½ oz.	188	4	19	1	5	145
Cutlet, leg, lean only, braised, 3½ oz.	203	6	27	2	9	135
Rib, lean only, roasted, 3½ oz.	177	7	36	2	10	115

Packaged Entrées

FOOD/PORTION SIZE	CAL.	FAT Total (g)	FAT As % of Cal.	SAT. FAT Total (g)	SAT. FAT As % of Cal.	CHOL. (mg)
Beef Noodle, Hamburger Helper, prepared with meat, 1 cup	320	15	42	7	20	79
Beef Stew, Dinty Moore, 10 oz.	270	13	43	na	na	na
Cheeseburger Macaroni, Hamburger Helper, prepared with meat, 1 cup	370	19	46	na	na	na
Chicken, Sweet & Sour, La Choy, ¾ cup	230	2	8	tr	<1	103
Chili con carne with beans, canned, 1 cup	286	13	41	6	19	43
Chow Mein, Beef, La Choy, ¾ cup	60	1	15	tr	na	25
Chow Mein, Chicken, La Choy, ¾ cup	80	3	34	na	na	na
Egg Noodle and Cheese Dinner, Kraft, ¾ cup	340	17	45	4	11	50
Egg Noodle with Chicken Dinner, Kraft, ¾ cup	240	9	34	2	8	45
Lasagna, Hamburger Helper, prepared with meat, 1 cup	340	14	37	na	na	na
Macaroni and Cheese Deluxe Dinner, Kraft, ¾ cup	260	8	28	4	14	20
Macaroni and Cheese Dinner, Original, Kraft, ¾ cup	290	13	40	na	na	na
Shells and Cheese Dinner, Velveeta, ½ cup	210	8	34	4	17	20

FOOD/PORTION SIZE	CAL.	FAT		SAT. FAT		CHOL.
		Total (g)	As % of Cal.	Total (g)	As % of Cal.	(mg)
Spaghetti, Mild American Style Dinner, Kraft, 1 cup	300	7	21	2	6	0
Spaghetti Dinner, Tangy Italian Style, Kraft, 1 cup	310	48	23	2	6	5
Spaghetti in tomato sauce with cheese, canned, 1 cup	190	2	9	<1	2	3
Spaghetti with Meat Sauce, Top Shelf 2-Minute Entrée, Hormel, 10 oz.	260	6	21	na	na	20
Spaghetti with Meat Sauce Dinner, Kraft, 1 cup	360	14	35	4	10	15

Pasta

FOOD/PORTION SIZE	CAL.	FAT		SAT. FAT		CHOL.
		Total (g)	As % of Cal.	Total (g)	As % of Cal.	(mg)
Egg Noodles, Creamette, 2 oz.	210	3	13	na	na	55
Egg Noodles Substitute, Cholesterol Free, No Yolks, 2 oz. dry	200	1	5	na	na	0
Linguine, Fresh, Di Giorno, Cholesterol Free, 3 oz.	250	3	11	na	na	0
Macaroni, enriched, cooked, firm, hot, 1 cup	190	1	5	<1	<1	0
Macaroni, enriched, cooked, tender, cold, 1 cup	115	tr	na	<1	<1	0
Macaroni, enriched, cooked, tender, hot, 1 cup	155	1	6	<1	<1	0
Macaroni and cheese dishes, *see* PACKAGED ENTRÉES						
Noodle Roni Fettucini, prepared with margarine and 2% milk, ½ cup	291	17	53	5	15	28
Noodle Roni Parmesano, prepared with margarine and 2% milk, ½ cup	250	14	50	4	14	21
Noodle Roni Romanoff, prepared with margarine and 2% milk, ½ cup	213	8	34	3	13	25
Noodle Roni Stroganoff, prepared with margarine and 2% milk, ½ cup	290	11	34	4	12	47
Noodles, chow mein, canned, 1 cup	220	11	45	2	8	5
Noodles, Creamette, all types except egg, 2 oz.	210	1	4	na	na	0
Noodles, egg, enriched, cooked, 1 cup	200	2	9	1	5	50
Spaghetti, enriched, cooked, firm, hot, 1 cup	190	1	5	<1	<1	0
Spaghetti, enriched, cooked, tender, hot, 1 cup	155	1	6	0	0	0

FOOD/PORTION SIZE	CAL.	FAT Total (g)	FAT As % of Cal.	SAT. FAT Total (g)	SAT. FAT As % of Cal.	CHOL. (mg)
Spaghetti with sauce/meat, *see* PACKAGED ENTRÉES						

Poultry

FOOD/PORTION SIZE	CAL.	FAT Total (g)	FAT As % of Cal.	SAT. FAT Total (g)	SAT. FAT As % of Cal.	CHOL. (mg)
Chicken, boneless, canned, 5 oz.	235	11	42	3	11	88
Chicken, boneless, skinless, Perdue, Fit 'n Easy, Oven Stuffer Roaster Breast, 1 oz.	30	<1	<1	<1	<1	17
Chicken, boneless, skinless, Perdue, Fit 'n Easy, Pick of the Chick, 1 oz.	30	<1	<1	<1	<1	17
Chicken, breast, flesh only, roasted, 3 oz.	140	3	19	<1	6	73
Chicken, broiler-fryer, breast, w/o skin, roasted, 3½ oz.	165	4	22	1	5	85
Chicken, drumstick, roasted, approx. 1.6 oz.	75	2	24	<1	8	26
Chicken, light and dark meat, flesh only, stewed, 1 cup	332	17	46	1	3	117
Chicken, liver, cooked, 1 liver	30	1	30	<1	12	120
Chicken, white and dark meat, w/o skin, roasted, 3½ oz.	190	7	33	2	9	89
Cold cuts, chicken or turkey, *see* LUNCHEON MEATS *in* MEAT section						
Duck, flesh only, roasted, ½ duck, approx. 7¾ oz.	445	24	49	11	22	197
Frankfurters, chicken, *see* FRANKS & SAUSAGES in MEAT section						
Turkey, dark meat only, w/o skin, roasted, 3½ oz.	187	7	34	2	10	85
Turkey, flesh only, 1 light and 2 dark slices, 85 g (3 oz.)	145	4	25	1	6	65
Turkey, flesh only, light and dark meat, chopped or diced, roasted, 1 cup, 140 g (5 oz.)	240	7	26	2	8	106
Turkey, flesh only, light meat, roasted, 2 pieces, 85 g (3 oz.)	135	3	20	1	7	59
Turkey, frozen, boneless, light and dark meat, seasoned, chunked, roasted, 3 oz.	130	5	35	2	14	45

FOOD/PORTION SIZE	CAL.	FAT Total (g)	As % of Cal.	SAT. FAT Total (g)	As % of Cal.	CHOL. (mg)
Turkey, Ground, Lean, Louis Rich, cooked, 1 oz.	52	2	35	1	17	25
Turkey, Ground, Louis Rich, cooked, 1 oz.	60	4	60	1	15	25
Turkey, patties, breaded, battered, fried, 1 patty	180	12	60	3	15	40
Turkey, smoked, 1 slice, 28 grams	32	1	28	.4	11	12
Turkey, white meat only, w/o skin, roasted, 3½ oz.	157	3	17	1	6	69
Turkey and gravy, frozen, 5 oz. pkg.	95	3	28	1	9	18
Turkey Breast Steaks, Louis Rich, 1 oz.	39	tr	tr	.2	5	18

Rice

FOOD/PORTION SIZE	CAL.	FAT Total (g)	As % of Cal.	SAT. FAT Total (g)	As % of Cal.	CHOL. (mg)
Beef Flavor, Rice-A-Roni, prepared with margarine, ½ cup	170	5	26	1	5	0
Boil-in-Bag, Uncle Ben's, about ½ cup cooked	80	<1	<1	na	na	na
Brown, cooked, hot, ½ cup	115	tr	4	<1	1	0
Brown & Wild, Mushroom Recipe, Uncle Ben's, ½ cup cooked	130	1	7	na	na	na
Chicken Flavor, Rice-A-Roni, prepared with margarine, ½ cup	171	5	26	1	5	tr
Chicken Vegetable, Rice-A-Roni, prepared with margarine, ½ cup	139	3	19	1	6	0
Extra-Long-Grain, Riceland, ½ cup cooked	100	0	0	0	0	na
Fast Cook, Uncle Ben's, about ⅔ cup cooked	110	<1	<1	na	na	na
Herb Rice Au Gratin, Country Inn, Uncle Ben's, prepared with margarine, ½ cup	170	5	26	2	11	11
Instant, ready-to-serve, cooked, hot, ½ cup	90	0	0	0	0	0
Long Grain, Natural, Converted, Uncle Ben's, ⅔ cup cooked	120	0	0	0	0	na
Long Grain & Wild, Minute Rice, ½ cup cooked	120	0	0	0	0	0
Long Grain & Wild, Original Recipe, Uncle Ben's, about ½ cup cooked	100	<1	<9	na	na	na
Long Grain & Wild, Rice-A-Roni, prepared with margarine, ½ cup	137	3	20	1	7	0
Minute Rice, w/o salt or butter, ⅔ cup cooked	120	0	0	na	na	0

FOOD/PORTION SIZE	CAL.	FAT Total (g)	FAT As % of Cal.	SAT. FAT Total (g)	SAT. FAT As % of Cal.	CHOL. (mg)
Parboiled, cooked, hot, ½ cup	93	tr	na	tr	na	0
Parboiled, raw, ½ cup	343	tr	1	<1	<1	0
Savory Broccoli Au Gratin, Rice-A-Roni, prepared with margarine, ½ cup	178	10	51	3	15	4
Savory Rice Pilaf, Rice-A-Roni, prepared with margarine, ½ cup	186	5	24	1	5	tr
White, enriched, cooked, hot, ½ cup	113	tr	na	<1	<1	0

Salad Dressings

FOOD/PORTION SIZE	CAL.	FAT Total (g)	FAT As % of Cal.	SAT. FAT Total (g)	SAT. FAT As % of Cal.	CHOL. (mg)
Bacon, Creamy, Reduced Calorie, Kraft, 1 tbsp.	30	2	60	0	0	0
Bacon & Tomato, Kraft, 1 tbsp.	70	7	90	1	13	0
Blue Cheese, Chunky, Healthy Sensation!, 1 tbsp.	20	0	0	na	na	0
Blue Cheese, Chunky, Kraft, 1 tbsp.	60	6	90	1	15	5
Blue Cheese, Chunky, Reduced Calorie, Kraft, 1 tbsp.	30	2	60	1	30	5
Blue Cheese, Lite, Less Oil, Wish-Bone, 1 tbsp.	40	4	90	tr	na	0
Blue Cheese and Herb, Good Seasons, prepared with oil and vinegar, 1 tbsp.	70	8	100	na	na	0
Buttermilk, Creamy, Kraft, 1 tbsp.	80	8	90	1	11	5
Buttermilk, Creamy, Reduced Calorie, Kraft, 1 tbsp.	30	3	90	0	0	5
Buttermilk, Farm Style, Good Seasons, with whole milk and mayonnaise, 1 tbsp.	58	6	93	na	na	0
Caesar, Weight Watchers, 1 tbsp.	4	0	0	0	0	na
Cheese Garlic, Good Seasons, with vinegar and oil, 1 tbsp.	7	8	100	na	na	0
Cheese Italian, Good Seasons, with vinegar and oil, 1 tbsp.	70	8	100	na	na	0
Coleslaw, Kraft, 1 tbsp.	70	6	77	1	13	10
Cucumber, Creamy, Kraft, 1 tbsp.	70	8	100	1	13	0
Cucumber, Creamy, Reduced Calorie, Kraft, 1 tbsp.	25	2	72	0	0	0
French, Catalina Brand, Kraft, 1 tbsp.	60	5	75	1	15	0
French, Kraft, 1 tbsp.	60	6	90	1	15	0

FOOD/PORTION SIZE	CAL.	FAT		SAT. FAT		CHOL.
		Total (g)	As % of Cal.	Total (g)	As % of Cal.	(mg)
French, Lite, Less Oil, Wish-Bone, 1 tbsp.	30	2	60	0	0	0
French, No Oil, Pritikin, 1 tbsp.	10	0	0	0	0	0
French, Reduced Calorie, Kraft, 1 tbsp.	20	1	45	0	0	0
French, Sweet 'n Spicy Lite, Wish-Bone, 1 tbsp.	16	0	0	0	0	0
French, Weight Watchers, 1 tbsp.	10	0	0	0	0	na
Garlic, Creamy, Kraft, 1 tbsp.	50	5	90	1	18	0
Garlic and Herbs, Good Seasons, with oil and vinegar, 1 tbsp.	70	8	100	na	na	0
Golden Caesar, Kraft, 1 tbsp.	70	7	90	1	13	0
Herb, Classic, Good Seasons, with vinegar and oil, 1 tbsp.	70	8	100	na	na	0
Honey Dijon, Healthy Sensation!, 1 tbsp.	25	0	0	na	na	0
Italian, Creamy, Lite, Less Oil, Wish-Bone, 1 tbsp.	6	0	0	0	0	0
Italian, Creamy, Reduced Calorie, Kraft, 1 tbsp.	25	2	72	0	0	0
Italian, Good Seasons, with oil and vinegar, 1 tbsp.	71	8	100	na	na	0
Italian, Healthy Sensation!, 1 tbsp.	6	0	0	na	na	0
Italian, Lite, Good Seasons, with oil and vinegar, 1 tbsp.	26	3	100	na	na	0
Italian, Lite, Wish-Bone, 1 tbsp.	6	1	100	0	0	0
Italian, Mild, Good Seasons, with oil and vinegar, 1 tbsp.	73	8	99	na	na	0
Italian, No Oil, Good Seasons, with vinegar and water, 1 tbsp.	7	0	0	na	na	0
Italian, No Oil, Pritikin, 1 tbsp.	10	0	0	0	0	0
Italian, Oil-Free, Kraft, 1 tbsp.	4	0	0	0	0	0
Italian, Olive Oil Classics, Wishbone, 1 tbsp.	33	3	82	.4	11	0
Italian, Weight Watchers, 1 tbsp.	6	0	0	0	0	na
Italian, Wishbone, 1 tbsp.	45	5	100	1	20	0
Italian, Zesty, Good Seasons, with oil and vinegar, 1 tbsp.	71	8	100	na	na	0
Italian, Zesty, Kraft, 1 tbsp.	50	5	90	1	18	0
Italian, Zesty, Reduced Calorie, Kraft, 1 tbsp.	20	2	90	0	0	0
Lemon Herb, Good Seasons, with oil and vinegar, 1 tbsp.	70	8	100	na	na	0
Miracle Whip, Free Nonfat, 1 tbsp.	5	0	0	0	0	0
Miracle Whip Light Reduced Calorie Salad Dressing with No Cholesterol, 1 tbsp.	45	4	80	1	20	0
Miracle Whip Salad Dressing, 1 tbsp.	70	7	90	1	13	5
Oil & Vinegar, Kraft, 1 tbsp.	70	8	100	1	13	0
Ranch, Original, Hidden Valley Ranch, 1 tbsp.	80	8	90	na	na	10

FOOD/PORTION SIZE	CAL.	FAT Total (g)	As % of Cal.	SAT. FAT Total (g)	As % of Cal.	CHOL. (mg)
Ranch, Original, Take Heart, Hidden Valley Ranch, 1 tbsp.	20	1	45	na	na	0
Reduced Calorie, Catalina Brand, Kraft, 1 tbsp.	18	1	50	0	0	0
Red Wine, Vinegar and Oil, Kraft, 1 tbsp.	60	4	60	1	15	0
Russian, Reduced Calorie, Kraft, 1 tbsp.	30	1	30	0	0	0
Thousand Island, Kraft, 1 tbsp.	60	5	75	1	15	5
Thousand Island, Lite, Less Oil, Wish-Bone, 1 tbsp.	40	0	0	na	na	0
Thousand Island, Reduced Calorie, Kraft, 1 tbsp.	20	2	90	0	0	0
Thousand Island & Bacon, Kraft, 1 tbsp.	60	6	90	1	10	0
Tomato Vinaigrette, Weight Watchers, 1 tbsp.	8	0	0	0	0	na

Snacks

FOOD/PORTION SIZE	CAL.	FAT Total (g)	As % of Cal.	SAT. FAT Total (g)	As % of Cal.	CHOL. (mg)
CORN CHIPS						
Bugles, 1 oz.	150	8	48	7	42	0
Doritos, Cool Ranch, 1 oz.	144	7	44	2	13	0
Doritos, Nacho Cheese, 1 oz.	143	7	44	2	13	0
Fritos Corn Chips, 1 oz.	154	9	53	3	18	0
Tortilla Chips, Restaurant Style, Tostitos, 1 oz.	140	7	45	na	na	0
Tostitos, Traditional, 1 oz.	145	8	50	1	6	0
DIPS						
Avocado (guacamole), Kraft, 2 tbsp.	50	4	72	2	36	0
Bacon & Horseradish, Kraft, 2 tbsp.	60	5	75	3	45	0
Blue Cheese, Kraft Premium, 2 tbsp.	50	4	72	2	36	10
Clam, Kraft, 2 tbsp.	60	4	60	1	15	10
Cucumber, Creamy, Kraft Premium, 2 tbsp.	50	4	72	3	54	10
French Onion, Kraft, 2 tbsp.	60	4	60	2	30	0
Green Onion, Kraft, 2 tbsp.	60	4	60	2	30	0
Jalapeño Pepper, Kraft, 2 tbsp.	50	4	72	2	36	0
Nacho Cheese, Kraft Premium, 2 tbsp.	55	4	65	2	33	10
Onion, Creamy, Kraft Premium, 2 tbsp.	45	4	80	2	40	10

FOOD/PORTION SIZE	CAL.	FAT Total (g)	FAT As % of Cal.	SAT. FAT Total (g)	SAT. FAT As % of Cal.	CHOL. (mg)
FRUIT SNACKS						
Fruit Roll-Ups, Cherry, ½ oz.	50	1	18	0	0	0
Fruit Roll-Ups, Grape, ½ oz.	50	1	18	0	0	0
Fruit Roll-Ups, Watermelon, ½ oz.	60	1	15	tr	na	0
Fruit Wrinkles, Orange, Betty Crocker, 1 pouch	100	2	18	tr	na	0
Fruit Wrinkles, Strawberry, Betty Crocker, 1 pouch	100	2	18	tr	na	0
Fun Fruits, Fantastic Fruit Punch, Sunkist, 1 oz.	100	1	9	na	na	na
Fun Fruits, Grape, Sunkist, 1 oz.	100	1	9	na	na	na
GRANOLA						
Apple, Chewy Granola Bar, Quaker Oats, 1 oz.	120	3	23	tr	na	tr
Chocolate Chip, Chewy Granola Bar, Quaker Oats, 1 oz.	130	5	35	tr	na	tr
Chocolate Covered Caramel Nut Dipps, Quaker Oats, 1 bar	140	6	39	3	19	4
Chocolate Covered Chocolate Chip Dipps, Quaker Oats, 1 bar	138	7	46	4	26	4
Chocolate Covered Peanut Butter Dipps, Quaker Oats, 1 bar	141	7	45	4	26	3
Chocolate Graham & Marshmallow, Chewy Granola Bar, Quaker Oats, 1 oz.	126	4	29	2	14	tr
Nut & Raisin, Chunky, Chewy Granola Bar, Quaker Oats, 1 oz.	133	6	41	2	14	tr
Oats n' Honey, Granola Bar, Nature Valley, 1 bar	120	5	38	2	15	0
Peanut Butter Chocolate Chip, Chewy Granola Bar, Quaker Oats, 1 oz.	131	5	34	2	14	tr
POPCORN						
Air-popped, unsalted, 1 cup	30	tr	na	tr	na	0
Microwave, Butter, Orville Redenbacher, 1 cup	28	2	49	tr	na	0
Microwave, Natural, Orville Redenbacher, 1 cup	28	2	57	1	8	0
Popped in vegetable oil, salted, 1 cup	55	3	49	<1	8	0
Sugar syrup coated, 1 cup	135	1	6	<1	<1	0
POTATO CHIPS						
Lays, 1 oz.	152	9	53	2	12	0

FOOD/PORTION SIZE	CAL.	FAT		SAT. FAT		CHOL. (mg)
		Total (g)	As % of Cal.	Total (g)	As % of Cal.	
Lays, Bar-B-Que, 1 oz.	149	9	54	2	12	0
O'Grady's, 1 oz.	150	9	54	2	12	0
O'Grady's, Au Gratin, 1 oz.	147	8	49	2	12	1
Pringles, 1 oz.	170	13	69	2	11	0
Pringles, Sour Cream n' Onion, 1 oz.	170	13	69	2	11	0
Pringles Light, Ranch, 1 oz.	150	8	48	2	12	0
Ruffles, 1 oz.	151	10	60	2	12	0
Ruffles, Cajun Spice, 1 oz.	154	10	58	2	12	0
Ruffles, Sour Cream & Onion, 1 oz.	150	9	54	2	12	1
PRETZELS						
Enriched flour, 2¼-in. sticks, 10 pretzels	10	tr	na	tr	na	0
Enriched flour, twisted, dutch, 1 pretzel	65	1	14	<1	1	0
Enriched flour, twisted, thin, 10 pretzels	240	2	8	<1	1	0
Mister Salty, Sticks, 1 oz.	110	1	18	tr	na	0
Mister Salty, Twists, 1 oz.	110	2	16	tr	na	0
Pretzel Chips, Mr. Phipps, ½ oz. (8 chips)	60	1	15	na	na	0
Rold Gold, Thin, 1 oz.	110	1	8	na	na	0

Soups

FOOD/PORTION SIZE	CAL.	FAT		SAT. FAT		CHOL. (mg)
		Total (g)	As % of Cal.	Total (g)	As % of Cal.	
Asparagus, Cream of, Campbell's, 4 oz. condensed, 8 oz. as prepared	80	4	45	na	na	<5
Bean with bacon, canned, condensed, prepared with water, 1 cup	173	6	31	2	10	3
Beef broth bouillon consommé, canned, condensed, prepared with water, 1 cup	29	0	0	0	0	0
Beef noodle, canned, condensed, prepared with water, 1 cup	85	3	32	1	11	5
Bouillon (beef or chicken), Wylers, 1 tsp.	6	0	0	0	0	0
Chicken, broth, College Inn, 7 oz.	35	3	77	1	26	5
Chicken, cream of, canned, condensed, prepared with milk, 1 cup	190	11	52	5	24	27
Chicken, cream of, canned, condensed, prepared with water, 1 cup	115	7	55	2	16	10
Chicken noodle, canned, condensed, prepared with water, 1 cup	75	2	24	<1	8	7

FOOD/PORTION SIZE	CAL.	FAT		SAT. FAT		CHOL.
		Total (g)	As % of Cal.	Total (g)	As % of Cal.	(mg)
Chicken noodle, dehydrated, prepared with water, 6 oz.	40	1	23	<1	5	3
Chicken Noodle, Hearty, Campbell's Healthy Request, 8 oz.	80	2	23	na	na	25
Chicken Noodle, Old Fashioned, Healthy Choice, 7½ oz.	90	3	30	1	na	20
Chicken Noodle, Progresso, 9.5 oz.	120	4	30	na	na	40
Chicken rice, canned, condensed, prepared with water, 1 cup	60	2	30	<1	8	7
Clam chowder, Manhattan, canned, condensed, prepared with water, 1 cup	80	2	23	<1	5	2
Clam chowder, New England, canned, condensed, prepared with milk, 1 cup	163	6	33	3	17	22
Minestrone, canned, condensed, prepared with water, 1 cup	80	3	34	<1	7	2
Minestrone, Progresso, 9½ oz.	130	4	28	na	na	0
Mushroom, cream of, canned, condensed, prepared with milk, 1 cup	203	13	58	5	22	20
Mushroom, cream of, canned, condensed, prepared with water, 1 cup	129	9	63	3	21	2
Mushroom, Cream of, Healthy Request, Campbell's, 4 oz. condensed, 8 oz. as prepared	60	2	30	na	na	<5
Noodle Soup Mix with Real Chicken Broth, Lipton, 8 oz.	70	2	26	na	na	na
Onion, dehydrated, prepared with water, 1 packet	20	tr	na	<1	5	0
Onion-Mushroom Recipe Soup Mix, Lipton, 8 oz.	40	<1	<1	na	na	na
Onion Soup Recipe Mix, Lipton, 8 oz.	20	0	0	na	na	na
Pea, green, canned, condensed, prepared with water, 1 cup	164	3	16	1	5	0
Tomato, canned, condensed, prepared with milk, 1 cup	160	6	34	3	17	17
Tomato, canned, condensed, prepared with water, 1 cup	85	2	21	<1	4	9
Tomato vegetable, dehydrated, prepared with water, 6 oz.	40	1	23	<1	7	0
Turkey Noodle, Campbell's, 4 oz. condensed, 8 oz. as prepared	70	2	26	na	na	15
Vegetable, Vegetarian, Campbell's, 4 oz. condensed, 8 oz. as prepared	80	2	23	na	na	0
Vegetable beef, canned, condensed, prepared with water, 1 cup	80	2	23	<1	10	5

Vegetables

FOOD/PORTION SIZE	CAL.	FAT Total (g)	FAT As % of Cal.	SAT. FAT Total (g)	SAT. FAT As % of Cal.	CHOL. (mg)
ALFALFA						
Seeds, sprouted, raw, 1 cup	10	tr	na	tr	na	0
ARTICHOKES						
Globe or French, cooked, drained, 1 artichoke	53	tr	na	tr	na	0
Jerusalem, red, sliced, 1 cup	114	tr	na	0	0	0
ASPARAGUS						
Canned, spears, 4 spears	10	tr	na	tr	na	0
Cuts & tips, cooked, drained, from raw, 1 cup	45	1	20	<1	2	0
Cuts & tips, from frozen, 1 cup	50	1	18	<1	4	0
Spears, cooked, drained, from raw, 4 spears	15	tr	na	tr	na	0
Spears, from frozen, 4 spears	15	tr	na	<1	6	0
BAMBOO SHOOTS						
Canned, drained, 1 cup	25	1	36	<1	4	0
BEANS						
Baby Lima, Birds Eye Regular Vegetables, approx. 3⅓ oz.	98	0	0	0	0	0
Fordhook Lima, Birds Eye Regular Vegetables, approx. 3⅓ oz.	94	0	0	0	0	0
Green, Blue Lake, Del Monte, ½ cup	20	0	0	0	0	0
Green, Cut, Birds Eye Regular Vegetables, 3 oz.	23	0	0	0	0	0
Green, French Cut, Birds Eye Deluxe, 3 oz.	25	0	0	0	0	0
Green, Whole, Birds Eye Deluxe Vegetables, 3 oz.	25	0	0	0	0	0
Sprouts (mung), cooked, drained, 1 cup	25	tr	na	tr	na	0
BEETS						
Canned, drained, solids, diced or sliced, 1 cup	55	tr	na	tr	na	0
Cooked, drained, diced or sliced, 1 cup	55	tr	na	tr	na	0
Cooked, drained, whole, 2 beets	30	tr	na	tr	na	0
Greens, leaves and stems, cooked, drained, 1 cup	40	tr	na	tr	na	0

FOOD/PORTION SIZE	CAL.	FAT		SAT. FAT		CHOL.
		Total (g)	As % of Cal.	Total (g)	As % of Cal.	(mg)
BROCCOLI						
Cooked, drained, from frozen, 1 piece (4½-5 in. long)	10	tr	tr	tr	tr	0
Cooked, drained, from frozen, chopped, 1 cup	50	tr	tr	tr	tr	0
Raw, 1 spear	40	1	23	<1	2	0
Spears, cooked, drained, from raw, 1 cup (½-in. pieces)	45	tr	tr	<1	2	0
BRUSSELS SPROUTS						
Cooked, drained, from frozen, 1 cup	65	1	14	<1	1	0
Cooked, drained, from raw, 1 cup	60	1	15	<1	3	0
CABBAGE						
Chinese pak-choi, cooked, drained, 1 cup	20	tr	na	tr	na	0
Chinese pe-tsai, raw, 1-in. pieces, 1 cup	10	tr	na	tr	na	0
Common varieties, cooked, drained, 1 cup	30	tr	na	tr	na	0
Red, raw, coarsely shredded or sliced, 1 cup	20	tr	na	tr	na	0
Savoy, raw, coarsely shredded or sliced, 1 cup	20	tr	na	tr	na	0
CARROTS						
Canned, sliced, drained, solids, 1 cup	35	tr	na	<1	3	0
Cooked, sliced, drained, from frozen, 1 cup	55	tr	na	tr	na	0
Cooked, sliced, drained, from raw, 1 cup	70	tr	na	<1	1	0
Raw, w/o crowns or tips, scraped, grated, 1 cup	45	tr	na	tr	na	0
CAULIFLOWER						
Cooked, drained, from frozen (flowerets), 1 cup	35	tr	na	<1	3	0
Cooked, drained, from raw (flowerets), 1 cup	30	tr	na	tr	na	0
CELERY						
Pascal type, raw, large outer stalk, 1 stalk	5	tr	na	tr	na	0
Pascal type, raw, pieces, diced, 1 cup	20	tr	na	tr	na	0

FOOD/PORTION SIZE	CAL.	FAT		SAT. FAT		CHOL.
		Total (g)	As % of Cal.	Total (g)	As % of Cal.	(mg)
COLLARDS						
Cooked, drained, from frozen (chopped), 1 cup	60	1	15	<1	2	0
Cooked, drained, from raw (leaves w/o stems), 1 cup	25	tr	<1	<1	5	0
CORN						
Sweet, canned, cream style, 1 cup	185	1	5	<1	1	0
Sweet, cooked, drained, from frozen, 1 ear (3½ in.)	60	tr	na	<1	2	0
Sweet, cooked, drained, from raw, 1 ear (5 × 1¾ in.)	85	1	11	<1	2	0
Sweet, cooked, drained, kernels, 1 cup	135	tr	na	tr	na	0
Sweet, vacuum packed, whole kernel, 1 cup	165	1	5	<1	1	0
CUCUMBER						
Peeled slices, ⅛ in. thick (large 2⅛-in. diameter, small 1¾ in. diameter), 6 large or 8 small	5	tr	na	tr	na	0
EGGPLANT						
Cooked, steamed, 1 cup	25	tr	na	tr	na	0
ENDIVE						
Curly (including escarole), raw, small pieces, 1 cup	10	tr	na	tr	na	0
GARLIC						
Clove, 1 medium	4	tr	na	0	0	0
GREENS						
Dandelion, cooked, drained, 1 cup	34	1	26	<1	3	0
Mustard, w/o stems and midribs, cooked, drained, 1 cup	20	tr	na	tr	na	0
Turnip, cooked, drained, from frozen (chopped), 1 cup	50	1	19	<1	4	0
Turnip, cooked, drained, from raw (leaves & stems), 1 cup	30	tr	na	<1	3	0

FOOD/PORTION SIZE	CAL.	FAT Total (g)	FAT As % of Cal.	SAT. FAT Total (g)	SAT. FAT As % of Cal.	CHOL. (mg)
KALE						
Cooked, drained, from frozen, chopped, 1 cup	40	1	23	<1	2	0
Cooked, drained, from raw, chopped, 1 cup	40	1	21	<1	2	0
KOHLRABI						
Thickened bulblike stem, cooked, drained, diced, 1 cup	50	tr	na	tr	na	0
LETTUCE						
Butterhead, as Boston types, raw, leaves, 1 outer or 2 inner leaves	tr	tr	na	tr	na	0
Crisphead, as iceberg, raw, ¼ of head, 1 wedge	20	tr	na	tr	na	0
Crisphead, as iceberg, raw, pieces, chopped, shredded, 1 cup	5	tr	na	tr	na	0
Looseleaf (bunching varieties including romaine or cos), chopped or shredded, 1 cup	10	tr	na	tr	na	0
MIXED VEGETABLES						
Baby Carrots, Peas, Pearl Onions, Birds Eye Deluxe Vegetables, 3⅓ oz.	50	0	0	0	0	0
Bavarian Style Vegetables, Birds Eye International Recipe, 3⅓ oz.	109	6	50	1	8	14
Broccoli, Baby Carrots, Water Chestnuts, Birds Eye Farm Fresh Mix, 3⅕ oz.	28	0	0	0	0	0
Broccoli, Carrots, Pasta, Birds Eye Combination Vegetables, 3⅓ oz.	89	4	40	tr	na	0
Broccoli, Cauliflower, Carrots, Birds Eye Farm Fresh Mix, 3⅕ oz.	20	0	0	0	0	0
Broccoli, Corn, Red Pepper, Birds Eye Farm Fresh Mix, 3⅕ oz.	40	0	0	0	0	0
Broccoli, Green Beans, Pearl Onions, Red Peppers, Birds Eye Farm Fresh Mix, 3⅕ oz.	20	0	0	0	0	0
Broccoli, Red Peppers, Bamboo Shoots, and Straw Mushrooms, Birds Eye Farm Fresh Mix, 3⅕ oz.	20	0	0	0	0	0
Brussels Sprouts, Cauliflower, Carrots, Birds Eye Farm Fresh Mix, 3⅕ oz.	24	0	0	0	0	0
Cauliflower, Baby Carrots, Snow Pea Pods, Birds Eye Farm Fresh Mix, 3⅕ oz.	24	0	0	0	0	0
Chinese Style, Birds Eye International Recipe, 3⅓ oz.	79	5	57	tr	na	0

FOOD/PORTION SIZE	CAL.	FAT		SAT. FAT		CHOL. (mg)
		Total (g)	As % of Cal.	Total (g)	As % of Cal.	
Chinese Style, Birds Eye Stir-Fry Vegetables, prepared with soybean oil, 3⅓ oz.	107	8	67	1	8	tr
Chow Mein Style, Birds Eye International Recipe, 3⅓ oz.	89	3	30	1	10	tr
Corn, Green Beans, Pasta, Birds Eye Combination Vegetables, 3⅓ oz.	109	5	41	1	8	1
Green Beans, French, Toasted Almond, Birds Eye Combination Vegetables, prepared with margarine, 3 oz.	93	5	48	tr	na	0
Green Peas, Pearl Onions, Birds Eye Combination Vegetables, prepared with margarine, 3⅓ oz.	98	3	28	tr	na	0
Italian Style, Birds Eye International Recipe, 3⅓ oz.	109	6	50	1	8	0
Japanese Style, Birds Eye International Recipe, 3⅓ oz.	99	5	45	1	9	tr
Japanese Style, Birds Eye Stir-Fry Vegetables, prepared with soybean oil, 3⅓ oz.	120	8	60	1	8	0
Mandarin Style, Birds Eye International Recipe, 3⅓ oz.	89	4	40	tr	na	tr
New England Style Vegetables, Birds Eye International Recipe, 3⅓ oz.	129	7	49	1	78	tr
Pasta Primavera Style, Birds Eye International Recipe, prepared with 2% milk, 3⅓ oz.	103	4	35	1	9	5
Rice, Green Peas, Mushrooms, Birds Eye Combination Vegetables, prepared with margarine, 2⅓ oz.	72	0	0	0	0	0
San Francisco Style, Birds Eye International Recipe, 3⅓ oz.	99	5	45	tr	na	tr
Spinach, Creamed, Birds Eye Combination Vegetables, 3 oz.	60	4	60	tr	na	0
MIXED VEGETABLES WITH SAUCE						
Broccoli, Cauliflower, Carrots, Cheese Sauce, Birds Eye Cheese Sauce Combination Vegetables, 5 oz.	100	4	36	1	9	5
Broccoli, Cauliflower, Creamy Italian Cheese Sauce, Birds Eye Cheese Sauce Combination Vegetables, 4½ oz.	90	6	60	3	30	14
Green Peas, Potatoes, Cream Sauce, Birds Eye Combination Vegetables, prepared with 2% milk and margarine, 2⅗ oz.	99	5	45	1	9	3

FOOD/PORTION SIZE	CAL.	FAT Total (g)	FAT As % of Cal.	SAT. FAT Total (g)	SAT. FAT As % of Cal.	CHOL. (mg)
Mixed Vegetables with Onion Sauce, Birds Eye Combination Vegetables, prepared with margarine, 2⅗ oz.	44	2	41	tr	na	0
Peas, Pearl Onions, Cheese Sauce, Birds Eye Cheese Sauce Combination Vegetables, prepared with margarine, 5 oz.	140	4	26	1	6	5
MUSHROOMS						
Canned, drained, solids, 1 cup	35	tr	na	<1	3	0
Cooked, drained, 1 cup	40	1	23	<1	2	0
Raw, sliced or chopped, 1 cup	20	tr	na	tr	na	0
OKRA						
Pods, 3×⅝ in., cooked, 8 pods	27	tr	na	tr	na	0
ONIONS						
Cooked (whole or sliced), drained, 1 cup	60	tr	na	<1	2	0
Raw, chopped, 1 cup	55	tr	na	<1	2	0
Raw, sliced, 1 cup	40	tr	na	<1	2	0
Rings, breaded par-fried, frozen, prepared, 2 rings	80	5	56	2	23	0
Spring, raw, bulb (⅜-in. diameter) and white portion of top, 6 onions	10	tr	na	tr	na	0
PARSLEY						
Raw, 10 sprigs	5	tr	na	tr	na	0
PARSNIPS						
Cooked, (diced or 2-in. lengths), drained, 1 cup	125	tr	na	<1	<1	0
PEAS						
Black-eyed, immature seeds, cooked, drained, from frozen, 1 cup	225	1	4	<1	1	0
Black-eyed, immature seeds, cooked, drained, from raw, 1 cup	180	1	5	<1	2	0
Green, canned, drained, solids, 1 cup	115	1	8	<1	1	0
Green, frozen, cooked, drained, 1 cup	125	tr	na	<1	1	0

FOOD/PORTION SIZE	CAL.	FAT		SAT. FAT		CHOL. (mg)
		Total (g)	As % of Cal.	Total (g)	As % of Cal.	
Pods, edible, cooked, drained, 1 cup	65	tr	na	<1	1	0
PEPPERS						
Hot chili, raw, 1 pepper	20	tr	na	tr	na	0
Sweet (about 5 per lb., whole), stem and seeds removed, raw, 1 pepper	20	tr	na	tr	na	0
Sweet (about 5 per lb., whole), stem and seeds removed, cooked, drained, 1 pepper	15	tr	na	tr	na	0
PICKLES						
Bread and Butter Sticks, Vlasic, 2 sticks	18	0	0	0	0	0
Cucumber, dill, medium whole, 1 pickle (3¾-in. long, 1¼-in. diameter)	5	tr	na	tr	na	0
Cucumber, Dill, Whole, Claussen, 1 oz.	4	<1	<1	na	na	0
Cucumber, fresh-pack slices, 2 slices (1½-in. diameter, ¼-in. thick)	10	tr	na	tr	na	0
Cucumber, sweet gherkin, small, 1 pickle (whole, about 2½-in. long, ¾-in. diameter)	20	tr	na	tr	na	0
POTATOES						
Baked (about 2 per lb. raw), flesh only, 1 potato	145	tr	na	tr	na	0
Baked (about 2 per lb. raw), with skin, 1 potato	220	tr	na	<1	<1	0
Boiled (about 3 per lb. raw), peeled after boiling, 1 potato	120	tr	na	tr	na	0
Boiled (about 3 per lb. raw), peeled before boiling, 1 potato	115	tr	na	tr	na	0
Canned, Whole New, Del Monte, ½ cup	45	0	0	0	0	0
French-Fried, Microwave Crinkle-Cut, Ore-Ida, 3 oz.	163	7	39	na	na	0
French fried, strip (2 to 3½ in. long), fried in vegetable oil, 10 strips	160	8	45	3	17	0
French fried, strip (2 to 3½ in. long), oven heated, 10 strips	110	4	33	2	16	0
Sweet, candied, 2½ × 2-in. piece, 1 piece	145	3	19	1	6	8
Sweet, canned, solid packed, mashed, 1 cup	260	1	3	<1	<1	0
Sweet, cooked (baked in skin), 1 potato	115	tr	na	tr	na	0
Sweet, cooked (boiled w/o skin), 1 potato	160	tr	na	<1	<1	0
Sweet, vacuum pack, 2¾ × 1-in. piece	35	tr	na	tr	na	0
Twice-Baked, Ore-Ida, 5 oz.	200	8	36	na	na	0

FOOD/PORTION SIZE	CAL.	FAT		SAT. FAT		CHOL.
		Total (g)	As % of Cal.	Total (g)	As % of Cal.	(mg)
Wedges, Frozen Homestyle, OreIda, 3 oz.	110	3	35	tr	na	0
PUMPKIN						
Canned, 1 cup	85	1	11	<1	4	0
Cooked, from raw, mashed, 1 cup	50	tr	na	<1	2	0
Solid Pack, Libby's, 1 cup	80	1	11	0	0	0
RADISHES						
Raw, stem ends and rootlets cut off, 4 radishes	5	tr	na	tr	na	0
SPINACH						
Cooked, drained, from frozen (leaf), 1 cup	55	tr	na	<1	2	0
Cooked, drained, from raw, 1 cup	40	tr	na	<1	2	0
Raw, chopped, 1 cup	10	tr	na	tr	na	0
SQUASH						
Summer (all varieties), cooked, sliced, drained, 1 cup	35	1	26	<1	3	0
TOMATOES						
Chili Style Chunky Tomatoes, Del Monte, ½ cup	30	<1	<1	na	na	na
Italian Style Pear-Shaped, Contadina, ½ cup	25	<1	<1	na	na	na
Juice, canned, 1 cup	40	tr	na	tr	na	0
Pasta Ready, Contadina, ½ cup	50	2	36	tr	na	0
Paste, canned, 1 cup	220	2	8	<1	1	0
Paste, Contadina, 2 oz.	50	<1	<1	na	na	na
Purée, canned, 1 cup	105	tr	na	tr	na	0
Raw, 2⅗-in. diameter (3 per 12-oz. pkg.), 1 tomato	25	tr	na	tr	na	0
Sauce, Canned, Contadina, ½ cup	30	1	30	0	0	0
Stewed, Canned, Contadina, ½ cup	35	1	26	0	0	0
Stewed, Canned, Italian Style, Del Monte, ½ cup	30	0	0	0	0	0
Stewed, Canned, Original Style, Del Monte, ½ cup	35	0	0	0	0	0
Vegetable Juice, V-8, 6 fl. oz.	35	0	0	0	0	0
Whole Peeled, Contadina, ½ cup	25	<1	<1	na	na	na

FOOD/PORTION SIZE	CAL.	FAT Total (g)	FAT As % of Cal.	SAT. FAT Total (g)	SAT. FAT As % of Cal.	CHOL. (mg)
VEGETABLES WITH SAUCE						
Broccoli with Cheese Sauce, Birds Eye Cheese Sauce Combination Vegetables, 5 oz.	120	6	45	2	15	5
Broccoli with Creamy Italian Cheese Sauce, Birds Eye Cheese Sauce Combination Vegetables, 4½ oz.	90	6	60	3	30	15
Brussels Sprouts with Cheese Sauce, Birds Eye Cheese Sauce Combination Vegetables, 4½ oz.	120	6	45	2	15	5
Cauliflower with Cheese Sauce, Birds Eye Cheese Sauce Combination Vegetables, 5 oz.	110	6	49	2	16	5

Yogurt

FOOD/PORTION SIZE	CAL.	FAT Total (g)	FAT As % of Cal.	SAT. FAT Total (g)	SAT. FAT As % of Cal.	CHOL. (mg)
Blueberry, Dannon, 8 oz.	259	3	10	2	7	11
Blueberry, Dannon Fresh Flavors, 8 oz.	216	4	17	2	8	0
Blueberry, Dannon Light, 8 oz.	100	0	0	0	0	5
Blueberry, Lite n' Lively, 5 oz.	150	1	6	na	na	10
Blueberry, Yoplait, 6 oz.	190	3	14	2	9	11
Cherry, Yoplait 150, 6 oz.	150	0	0	0	0	5
Lemon, Dannon, 8 oz.	200	3	14	na	na	15
Plain, Dannon, 8 oz.	140	4	26	na	na	na
Raspberry, Yoplait Fat Free, 6 oz.	160	0	0	0	0	5
Strawberry, Dannon Fresh Flavors, 8 oz.	216	4	17	2	8	11
Strawberry, Light, Yoplait, 6 oz.	80	0	0	0	0	<5
Strawberry, Lite n' Lively, 5 oz.	150	2	12	na	na	10
Strawberry, Weight Watchers Ultimate 90, 8 oz.	90	0	0	0	0	5
Strawberry, Yoplait 150, 6 oz.	150	0	0	0	0	5
Vanilla, Dannon, 8 oz.	200	3	14	na	na	15

Low-Fat Alternatives

Substituting lower-fat foods for high-fat fare is an easy, practical way to get started on the road to a healthier diet. Instead of giving up your favorite foods, simply make a few trade-offs and watch how quickly the fat and calories you save add up.

INSTEAD OF:	SUBSTITUTE:	TO SAVE: FAT (grams)	TO SAVE: CAL.
BEVERAGES			
1 cup whole milk	1 cup 2% milk	3	30
1 cup 2% milk	1 cup skim milk	4	20
8 ounce chocolate milkshake	8 ounces 1% chocolate milk	3	108
BREADS			
1 croissant	1 bagel	11	85
1 cake doughnut	1 blueberry muffin	6	30
1 blueberry muffin	1 English muffin	4	50
½ cup granola cereal	½ cup whole-grain wheat flakes	7	65
CONDIMENTS & SAUCES			
2 tablespoons hot fudge sauce	2 tablespoons chocolate syrup	4	32
1 tablespoon mayonnaise	1 tablespoon light, reduced calorie mayonnaise	6	50
1 tablespoon light, reduced calorie mayonnaise	1 tablespoon mustard	4	35
1 tablespoon tartar sauce	1 tablespoon fat-free tartar sauce	8	59
1 tablespoon margarine	1 tablespoon light margarine	4	30
1 tablespoon light margarine	1 tablespoon preserves	7	15
1 tablespoon Italian salad dressing	1 tablespoon light Italian salad dressing	4	44
DAIRY			
1 ounce cream cheese	1 ounce Neufchâtel cheese	3	20
1 tablespoon whipped heavy cream	1 tablespoon frozen non-dairy whipped topping	4	40
1 ounce Cheddar cheese	1 ounce part-skim mozzarella cheese	4	30
1 ounce Swiss cheese	1 ounce light Swiss cheese	3	20

INSTEAD OF:	SUBSTITUTE:	TO SAVE:	
		FAT (grams)	CAL.
½ cup sour cream	¼ cup light sour cream	8	40
½ cup light sour cream	¼ cup plain yogurt	3	45
½ cup peach ice cream	½ cup orange sherbet	10	15
½ cup orange sherbet	½ cup peach frozen yogurt	2	35
8 ounces blueberry yogurt	8 ounces light blueberry yogurt	3	159
2 large eggs	½ cup egg substitute	12	110
MEAT			
3 strips bacon	1 slice Canadian bacon	7	66
1 bacon cheeseburger	1 plain hamburger	16	219
1 all-beef frankfurter	1 chicken frankfurter	5	45
3 ounces broiled lean ground beef	3 ounces cooked lean ground turkey	10	74
3 ounces lean pork chop, broiled	3 ounces roasted pork tenderloin	4	57
2 ounces Braunschweiger sausage	2 ounces light bologna	6	65
3½ ounces chicken, light meat only, with skin, fried	3½ ounces chicken, light meat only, with skin, stewed	2	45
3½ ounces chicken, light meat only, with skin, stewed	3½ ounces chicken, light meat only, without skin, roasted	7	38
SNACKS & DESSERTS			
1 ounce potato chips	1 ounce pretzels	9	37
3 ounces french fries	1 medium baked potato	14	54
2 cups popcorn popped in vegetable oil	2 cups air-popped popcorn	5	50
1 ounce plain milk chocolate	1 ounce caramels	6	34
1 ounce caramels	1 ounce jelly beans	3	8
1 slice spice cake	1 slice angel food cake	11	120
2 chocolate chip cookies	2 graham crackers	3	40
½ cup instant chocolate pudding, prepared with whole milk	½ cup sugar-free instant chocolate pudding, prepared with 2% milk	3	90

Acknowledgments

The publishers would like to thank the companies and organizations listed below for the use of their recipes in this book.

Almond Board of California
American Celery Council
American Lamb Council
Armour Swift-Eckrich
Best Foods, a Division of CPC International Inc.
Black-Eyed Pea Jamboree—Athens, Texas
Blue Diamond Growers
Borden Kitchens, Borden, Inc.
British Columbia Farmed Salmon Institute
California Apricot Advisory Board
California Cling Peach Advisory Board
California Tree Fruit Agreement
Canned Food Information Council
Checkerboard Kitchens, Ralston Purina Company
Chilean Fresh Fruit Association
Christopher Ranch of Gilroy
Claussen Pickle Company
Clear Springs Trout Company
ConAgra Frozen Foods
The Creamette Company
The Dannon Company, Inc.
Del Monte Foods
Dole Food Company, Inc.
Filippo Berio Olive Oil
Florida Department of Citrus
Florida Tomato Committee
Heinz U.S.A.
Hershey Chocolate U.S.A.
Keebler Company
Kellogg Company
Kraft General Foods, Inc.
Land O'Lakes, Inc.
Lawry's® Foods, Inc.
Thomas J. Lipton Co.

Louis Rich Company
McIlhenny Company
Minnesota Cultivated Wild Rice Council
Mott's U.S.A., A division of Cadbury Beverages Inc.
Nabisco Foods Group
National Broiler Council
National Dairy Board
National Fisheries Institute
National Live Stock and Meat Board
National Pasta Association
National Pork Producers Council
National Turkey Federation
Nestlé Food Company
Norseland Foods, Inc.
North Dakota Barley Council
Oregon Washington California Pear Bureau
Pace Foods, Inc.
Pacific Coast Canned Pear Service
Perdue Farms
Pet Incorporated
Pollio Dairy Products
The Procter & Gamble Company
The Quaker Oats Company
Reckitt & Colman Inc.
Sargento Cheese Company, Inc.
StarKist Seafood Company
The Sugar Association, Inc.
Sunkist Growers, Inc.
Surimi Seafood Education Center
Uncle Ben's Rice
USA Rice Council
Washington Apple Commission
Western New York Apple Growers Association, Inc.
Wisconsin Milk Marketing Board

Photo Credits

The publishers would like to thank the companies and organizations listed below for the use of their photographs in this book.

Almond Board of California
American Celery Council
American Lamb Council
Armour Swift-Eckrich
Best Foods, a Division of CPC International Inc.
British Columbia Farmed Salmon Institute
Borden Kitchens, Borden, Inc.
California Apricot Advisory Board
California Tree Fruit Agreement
Clear Springs Trout Company
Chilean Fresh Fruit Association
The Creamette Company
The Dannon Company, Inc.
Del Monte Foods
Dole Food Company, Inc.
Filippo Berio Olive Oil
Heinz U.S.A.
Keebler Company
Kellogg Company
Kraft General Foods, Inc.
Land O'Lakes, Inc.
Thomas J. Lipton Co.

Louis Rich Company
Mott's U.S.A., A division of Cadbury Beverages Inc.
Nabisco Foods Group
National Live Stock and Meat Board
National Pasta Association
National Pork Producers Council
National Turkey Federation
Nestlé Food Company
Pace Foods, Inc.
Perdue Farms
The Procter & Gamble Company
The Quaker Oats Company
Reckitt & Colman Inc.
Sargento Cheese Company, Inc.
StarKist Seafood Company
The Sugar Association, Inc.
Surimi Seafood Education Center
Uncle Ben's Rice
USA Rice Council
Western New York Apple Growers Association, Inc.
Wisconsin Milk Marketing Board

INDEX

METRIC CONVERSION CHART

VOLUME MEASUREMENTS (dry)

$\frac{1}{8}$ teaspoon = 0.5 mL
$\frac{1}{4}$ teaspoon = 1 mL
$\frac{1}{2}$ teaspoon = 2 mL
$\frac{3}{4}$ teaspoon = 4 mL
1 teaspoon = 5 mL
1 tablespoon = 15 mL
2 tablespoons = 30 mL
$\frac{1}{4}$ cup = 60 mL
$\frac{1}{3}$ cup = 75 mL
$\frac{1}{2}$ cup = 125 mL
$\frac{2}{3}$ cup = 150 mL
$\frac{3}{4}$ cup = 175 mL
1 cup = 250 mL
2 cups = 1 pint = 500 mL
3 cups = 750 mL
4 cups = 1 quart = 1 L

VOLUME MEASUREMENTS (fluid)

1 fluid ounce (2 tablespoons) = 30 mL
4 fluid ounces ($\frac{1}{2}$ cup) = 125 mL
8 fluid ounces (1 cup) = 250 mL
12 fluid ounces (1$\frac{1}{2}$ cups) = 375 mL
16 fluid ounces (2 cups) = 500 mL

WEIGHTS (mass)

$\frac{1}{2}$ ounce = 15 g
1 ounce = 30 g
3 ounces = 90 g
4 ounces = 120 g
8 ounces = 225 g
10 ounces = 285 g
12 ounces = 360 g
16 ounces = 1 pound = 450 g

DIMENSIONS

$\frac{1}{16}$ inch = 2 mm
$\frac{1}{8}$ inch = 3 mm
$\frac{1}{4}$ inch = 6 mm
$\frac{1}{2}$ inch = 1.5 cm
$\frac{3}{4}$ inch = 2 cm
1 inch = 2.5 cm

OVEN TEMPERATURES

250°F = 120°C
275°F = 140°C
300°F = 150°C
325°F = 160°C
350°F = 180°C
375°F = 190°C
400°F = 200°C
425°F = 220°C
450°F = 230°C

BAKING PAN SIZES

Utensil	Size in Inches/Quarts	Metric Volume	Size in Centimeters
Baking or Cake Pan (square or rectangular)	8 × 8 × 2	2 L	20 × 20 × 5
	9 × 9 × 2	2.5 L	22 × 22 × 5
	12 × 8 × 2	3 L	30 × 20 × 5
	13 × 9 × 2	3.5 L	33 × 23 × 5
Loaf Pan	8 × 4 × 3	1.5 L	20 × 10 × 7
	9 × 5 × 3	2 L	23 × 13 × 7
Round Layer Cake Pan	8 × 1½	1.2 L	20 × 4
	9 × 1½	1.5 L	23 × 4
Pie Plate	8 × 1¼	750 mL	20 × 3
	9 × 1¼	1 L	23 × 3
Baking Dish or Casserole	1 quart	1 L	—
	1½ quart	1.5 L	—
	2 quart	2 L	—